CONTENTS

iii

Contents

iv

Delphi Database Development

TED BLUE • JOHN KASTER • GREG LIEF • LOREN SCOTT

M&T BOOKS

M&T Books

A Division of MIS:Press, Inc.
A Subsidiary of Henry Holt and Company, Inc.
115 West 18th Street
New York, New York 10011

Copyright © 1996, by M&T Books.

Printed in the United States of America

Library of Congress Cataloging-in-Publication Data

Delphi database development / Ted Blue ... [et al.].
   p.   cm.
  ISBN 1-55851-469-4
  1. Database design. 2. Delphi (Computer file) I. Blue, Ted.
QA76.9.D26D45   1996
005.75'6—dc20
                                                       96-10942
                                                           CIP

10 9 8 7 6 5 4 3 2 1

Associate Publisher: *Paul Farrell*
Managing Editor: *Cary Sullivan*
Editor: *Judy Brief*
Copy Edit Manager: *Shari Chappell*
Production Editor: *Anne Incao*
Technical Editor: *Cecilia Smith*
Copy Editor: *Sara Black*

CHAPTER 5: BDE FUNCTION REFERENCE 457

v

Contents

vi

Contents

x

Contents

Contents

INTRODUCTION

Thank you for your interest in *Delphi Database Development!* A short summary of the contents of our book follows. Whether you've already purchased the book and want to know what to expect, or if you're just browsing in the computer-related section of your bookstore, please take a moment to read on.

ABOUT THIS BOOK

Although the first release of Borland's Delphi was released fairly recently (February 1995), already there have been many books on the subject of application development with this product. Oddly enough, even though one of Delphi's major strengths is in its power to easily develop professional database applications, none of these already published books deals specifically with this topic.

There are several possible reasons for this phenomenon:

- Perhaps the authors of these other books have primarily a Pascal language background rather than a database application development background.
- Perhaps other authors found the database-specific documentation provided by Borland to be too sparse to go into much effort on their own to get "down and dirty" with the Borland Database Engine (BDE) or other advanced functionality provided in the database APIs and components.

Fortunately for you, gentle reader (and unfortunately for us, your humble authors!), we had to figure out for ourselves exactly how the BDE, its associated components, and its APIs work. All four of us authors have many years of experience developing database applications with a variety of languages, and quickly found that even the robust development environment Delphi provides was not sufficient for our needs. Before we decided to do this book, we had unearthed the bulk of the information you will find in these pages, because we needed it ourselves.

Somewhere along the line, we realized that this book would be a tremendous asset to Delphi developers, particularly because we constantly wished for it ourselves. This book is an ambitious undertaking, with many hours of research, trial, and error behind the scenes of every page. Because there are many entry-level and general-purpose Delphi books already in print, this book discusses neither the basics of Delphi programming nor the Object Pascal language. Having said that, we are still confident that you will find many valuable and powerful techniques in our sample source code that you can use in your own database application development.

If you are looking for 1001 ways to draw ellipses and circles on a form, you've come to the wrong book! If you are looking for a comprehensive reference on controlling every aspect of database development in Delphi, you need look no further. *Delphi Database Development* concentrates specifically on the information required to assist professional Delphi developers in creating robust database applications.

ORGANIZATION OF THIS BOOK

This book is designed to be used as a reference rather than as a tutorial. Therefore, you do not need to read it sequentially from start to finish in order to benefit from its contents. Instead, we have organized it in chapters divided by major database-related topics. The items within each chapter are listed alphabetically. If you are not exactly sure of the name of the item you need, categorical cross-references allow you to locate what you are looking for not by what it is *called*, but by what it *does*.

Every property, method, and event from every visual and nonvisual database-related component is completely documented and clearly explained with short, practical examples of each. The accompanying CD-ROM contains additional, complete Delphi applications, including source code, that demonstrate how to put all this information to work in real-world applications.

This book is divided into the following distinct sections:

Database Reference—Database classes and data-aware controls

BDE Reference—Borland Database Engine functions listed in alphabetical order

Appendices—Cross-references, SQL reference, and additional information

Each chapter in the Database Reference section starts with an overview of the components discussed in that chapter, followed by an alphabetically ordered, detailed reference listing of those component classes, including information about their properties, methods, and events. This allows you to get a quick review of the entire group of components at a glance, as well as detailed information at the most basic level.

The BDE Reference section discusses each of the BDE functions in alphabetical order, using a similar format (an overview, followed by a reference).

The Appendices section includes a categorical cross-reference to all of the classes, components and functions listed in this book, as well as a class hierarchy chart.

Source code examples are used where appropriate to illustrate how a given component, class, or function might be used in a typical application. Note that the code examples are sometimes just code fragments and, as such, will not normally include preliminary setup code, error-handling code, or other extraneous code that does not directly pertain to the component, class, or function being illustrated.

The CD-ROM included with this book contains complete examples of a number of database applications, in order to fully illustrate how the various components, classes, and functions work together to get a particular job done. Also included on the CD-ROM are useful shareware and public domain programs, some of which are geared toward database application development in Delphi. In addition, you'll find issues of *Delphi Informant* and *Delphi Aquarium*.

Component and Class Listings

Reference material for components and classes is organized in a top-down approach wherever possible, with the summary and overview information listed first, for convenience. Subsequent sections are progressively more detailed as needed to fully describe the component, class, or function. Where a component has a property that is itself a component or class, a cross-reference to that component or class is used to avoid repetitive data.

A typical reference section for a component or class would look like the following:

CLASS NAME	
Unit:	<Unit where component class resides>
Parent class:	<Class from which this component inherits >
Child classes:	<Classes that inherit from this component>
Description:	<Description of component>
See also:	<further references>

This listing may be followed by one or more tables or figures that pertain to the component, as well as source code examples where appropriate. Note that for components, the class name for the component is used, rather than the component name. Since the class name is usually the same as the component name, except that it is preceded by a 'T', you would need to look for the class form of the name rather than the component name itself (e.g., TTable instead of Table). This avoids confusion where component names also represent other database objects (i.e., Table, DataSet, Report).

Function and Procedure Listings

Functions and procedures are listed in alphabetical order in the BDE Reference section. A typical function or procedure listing would look like the following:

FUNCTION OR PROCEDURE NAME	
Unit:	<Unit where function or procedure resides>
Prototype:	Function (Type: ParameterName, ...): ReturnType; Procedure (Type: ParameterName, ...);
See also:	<Cross-references>
Description:	<Description>
See also:	<further references>

The Prototype is formatted according to standard Object Pascal conventions (see Syntactic Conventions). Cross-references may include other functions or procedures that are related to the listed routine, and may also include references to classes and components as appropriate. The listing may also be followed by one or more source code examples that illustrate usage for that routine.

4

PRINTING CONVENTIONS

This book uses different typographical and syntactic conventions to distinguish the various components of the reference sections. These conventions are described in this section.

Typographic Conventions

Table I.1 describes the various font and text conventions used in this book:

TABLE I.1 TYPOGRAPHIC CONVENTIONS

CONVENTION	DESCRIPTION	EXAMPLE
UPPERCASE	Field, table, database, and index names. Also used for SQL keywords, and file and directory names.	The LNAME index refers to the LAST.NAME field in the CUSTOMER table
ProperCase	Names of Object Pascal objects, classes, properties, methods, functions, procedures and variables. Also used for type names.	Place a TDataSource component on your form, and set its DataSet property to the name the name of an existing TTable object.

lowercase	Object Pascal keywords.	`var`
		`  MyString: String;`
		`  x: Integer;`
		`    MyTable: TTable;`
		`    begin`
		`    ...`
		`    end;`

italic	New terms, emphasized words. In source code listings, comments are italicized.	`{ this is a source code comment }`

bold	Object Pascal reserved words or compiler options.	`for x := 1 to 100 do`
		`begin`
		`  x := x + 1;`
		`end;`

monospaced	Source code listings and text as it appears on the screen. Also used for any text that you must type in.	`while not CustTable.EOF do`
		`begin`
		`  CustTable.Next;`
		`end;`

Syntactic Conventions

This book uses certain syntactic conventions to distinguish the various parts of source code and other language-related statements. This section describes those conventions.

Table I.2 lists the different symbols that are used in the syntax of this book:

TABLE I.2 SYNTACTIC SYMBOLS

SYMBOL	DESCRIPTION
[]	Square brackets are used to enclosed optional items in syntax diagrams or to denote sets or arrays in source code listings.
<>	Angle brackets are used to indicate token names in syntax diagrams.
...	An ellipsis is used to indicate a repeatable item.

SYNTAX DIAGRAMS

Syntax diagrams are a shorthand way to describe the correct syntax for a given statement or expression. They are most commonly used to describe function and procedure prototypes in the reference listings. This book uses the same formatting standard commonly found in Object Pascal texts.

PROCEDURE PROTOTYPES

The format for procedure prototype declarations follows:

```
<Proc>[(<ParamList>:<ParamType> [,<ParamList>:<ParamType> ... ])];
```

<Proc>	Name of the procedure
<ParamList>	Comma-separated list of parameter names
<ParamType>	Data type for <ParamList>

FUNCTION PROTOTYPES

The format for function prototype declarations follows:

```
<Func>[(<ParamList>:<ParamType> [,<ParamList>:<ParamType> ... ])]: <RetType>;
```

<Func>	Name of the function
<ParamList>	Comma-separated list of parameter names
<ParamType>	Data type for <ParamList>
<RetType>	Return type for the function

VARIABLE NAMING: HUNGARIAN NOTATION

A variable-naming convention that indicates the type of the variable is also used in the source code in this book. This naming convention uses proper-cased names, with leading lowercase letters indicating the type, and an uppercase letter as the beginning of the variable name. This convention is called Hungarian Notation after its creator, Charles Simonyi.

PREFIX	EXAMPLE	DATA TYPE
a	aNums[1] := 1;	Arrays
b	bTest := nOne > nTwo;	Logical (boolean) values
c	cCR := #13;	Single-byte character values
d	dNow := Date	TDateTime values
i	iNum := 0;	Integer or ShortInt values
l	lVal := 2;	LongInt values
o	oTable := TTable.Create(nil);	Objects
r	rVal := 123.456;	Real numbers
rec	recDate.Year := 1996;	Records
s	sProd := 'Delphi';	Character string

We hope that you will find these documentation standards efficient and helpful and that they will increase your comprehension of the materials in this book.

If you are specifically coming from an Xbase background, the appendix "Xbase to Delphi Command/Function Equivalents" is sure to save you many hours of hunting through the Delphi documentation.

CHAPTER I

Overview of Database Development in Delphi

Introduction

Delphi is based on the Object Pascal language, which is not designed specifically for database application development. However, the database application components provided with Delphi compensate quite nicely for the genericity of the Pascal language. In fact, by simply dropping a few data access component icons on your application forms, it is possible to actually create fully functional, albeit simple, database applications *without writing a single line of code*!

This chapter offers an introduction to the various database development tools included with Delphi.

Delphi's Database Architecture

In Delphi, database applications are created by combining various visual and nonvisual components on forms. These components are connected together through their DataSource or DataSet properties. All data control components in Delphi are designed to be *data-aware*; i.e., they display and update data contained in a table.

The DataSource component dictates the origin of the data to be accessed. The DataSet component is a collection of data determined by a TTable, TQuery, or TStoredProc component. TTable is used for Paradox and dBASE tables and includes every row in the data set. TQuery is used to make a selection of records from a table, usually from Structured Query Language (SQL) statements. These DataSources and DataSets can be passed directly to the Borland Database Engine (BDE) for operations not directly supported by their containing components.

There is more functionality available in the BDE than in the Delphi data component level. However, the BDE is the low-level interface, so it should be used only when necessary. The components are *wrappers* that make calling the BDE functions more convenient, and the BDE provides all the actual database services supported by Delphi. Support for SQL databases, Paradox and dBASE files, and ODBC connectivity is all provided by the Borland Database Engine.

DATABASES AND TABLES

Many Xbase developers commonly refer to a **.DBF** file as a database. In the truest sense of the word, this is not completely accurate. A dBASE **.DBF** file is a table, not a database. Likewise, a Paradox **.DB** file is a table.

A *database* comprises one or more tables. Each *table* contains a series of records. Each *record* has a fixed length and structure. A record is made up of one or more *fields,* which may each contain data of various types (CHARACTER, NUMERIC, LOGICAL, DATE, MEMO, etc.). If you are familiar with SQL, *tuples* are the same thing as records, and *row* is the common SQL term for records. *Columns* are synonymous with fields.

N O T E

For specific information on the exact file structures of some popular database file formats, see Appendix F (File Structures).

The basic structure of a table is shown in the Figure 1.1.

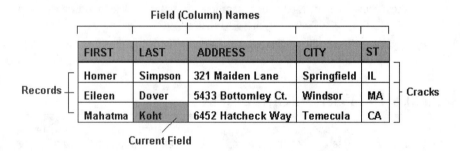

FIGURE 1.1 BASIC TABLE STRUCTURE.

DELPHI'S DATABASE DEVELOPMENT TOOLS

The Borland Database Engine consists of a set of DLL functions that can be called from any programming language capable of calling Windows DLL functions. It is the heart of database application development in Delphi. However, there are many other tools included that work with it to make the Delphi developer's job as simple as possible.

Table 1.1 contains a brief listing of the primary database development tools included with Delphi.

TABLE 1.1 PRIMARY DATABASE DEVELOPMENT TOOLS

TOOL	PURPOSE
Borland Database Engine	Provides access to data contained in file-based Paradox and dBASE tables and from local InterBase server databases.
BDE configuration utility	Creates and manages database connection aliases used by the BDE, adds new ODBC driver connections, and configures system defaults.
Data access components	Non visual components that provide access to databases, tables, stored procedures, and custom component editors.
Data control components	Visual components that provide user interface to database tables. These include browse grids, edit boxes, combo boxes, list boxes, and so on.
Database Desktop (DBD)	Utility for browsing, creating, indexing, and querying Paradox and dBASE tables and SQL databases.
InterBase SQL Link	Native driver that connects a Delphi application to the Local InterBase Server.
Local InterBase Server	Allows developers to build and test Delphi applications on a single-user multi-instance desktop SQL server, then upsize them to a production database, such as Oracle, Sybase, Informix, or InterBase on a remote server.
ReportSmith	Complete report creation, viewing, and printing facility.
SQL drivers	Both SQL Links and ReportSmith provide direct drivers that connect Delphi database applications to remote SQL and ODBC-compliant database servers, such as Oracle, Sybase, Informix, and InterBase.
Visual Query Builder	Creates SQL statements by visually manipulating tables and columns.

BORLAND DATABASE ENGINE

The BDE included with Delphi is the same engine that powers Borland's dBASE and Paradox products. The BDE is comprised of a set of DLL API function calls that manage all the low-level handling of the data and indices within your Delphi application. Since the BDE is built into Delphi, you can create database applications without knowing anything about it.

Most database operations in Delphi can be handled through the setting of properties or calling of methods. However, Delphi power-users may find a need to go directly to the BDE's API function calls to accomplish tasks that cannot be done through pure Delphi VCL calls.

The documentation for the BDE API functions (Dbi*) is not included with Delphi's Desktop edition. It is included at no charge as part of the Delphi Client/Server edition. It may also be ordered at an additional charge for Delphi Desktop owners. Unfortunately, this printed documentation and the Windows help file that it includes were designed for use by C programmers, not Delphi programmers, and have very few examples. Hopefully, this will be addressed in future releases.

Fortunately for you, gentle reader, *this* book includes complete documentation of these functions for use by Delphi programmers. (After all, that's part of the reason you bought it, right?)

THE BDE CONFIGURATION UTILITY

The Borland Database Engine configuration utility enables you to configure BDE aliases and change the settings reflecting your specific environment in the BDE configuration file, **IDAPI.CFG**.

BDE aliases can be used in place of an explicit drive and path as the AliasName property of the TDatabase component and as the DatabaseName property of the TTable and TQuery components.

To run the BDE configuration utility, double-click the **BDE configuration utility** icon in the Delphi program group, or by simply run **DBECFG.EXE** from the Windows Program Manager.

The Drivers page of the BDE Configuration Utility, as it appears in Windows 95, is shown Figure 1.2.

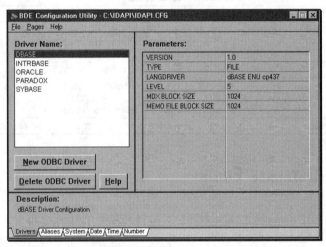

FIGURE 1.2 THE DRIVERS PAGE.

DATA ACCESS COMPONENTS

The Data Access Component palette (shown in Figure 1.3) is a set of nonvisual components that connect your Delphi application to the data through the BDE. They connect to the visual data controls, such as the grid control, and provide connections required for reporting and querying.

FIGURE 1.3 DATA ACCESS COMPONENT PALETTE.

Delphi includes the following data access components:

Icon	Component	Description
![icon]	TDataSource	Provides an interface between one or more Data Control components on your form and a TTable or TQuery component.
![icon]	TTable	Provides an interface between one or more TDataSource components and the BDE.
![icon]	TQuery	Provides an SQL interface between one or more TDataSource components and the BDE.
![icon]	TStoredProc	Provides and interface to stored procedures on a server database.
![icon]	TDatabase	Provides an interface directly to a database or BDE alias.
![icon]	TSession	Provides global control over database connections for an application (*New in Delphi 2.0*).
![icon]	TBatchMove	Provides a mechanism for moving entire tables and databases.
![icon]	TUpdateSQL	Provides access to a TQuery component associated with a specified SQL statement (*New in Delphi 2.0*).
![icon]	TReport	Provides an interface to the ReportSmith run-time engine.

11

DATA CONTROL COMPONENTS

The Data Controls page of the Component palette (shown in Figure 1.4) provides the visual controls used to display and edit data from a database. These components include a browse grid, data edit boxes, list boxes, combo boxes, check boxes, radio groups, navigator buttons, and more.

FIGURE 1.4 DATA CONTROLS PAGE OF THE COMPONENT PALETTE.

Delphi includes the following data control components:

Icon	Component	Description
	TDBGrid	Provides a data-aware browse grid-style display of data in a database table or query.
	TDBNavigator	Provides a pre-built set of data-aware buttons to control navigation, inserts, deletes, posting and canceling of edits, and data refreshes.
	TDBText	Provides a data-aware Label-type display of field data, without allowing the user to modify the field's contents.
	TDBEdit	Provides a data-aware Edit-type control for display and/or modification of non-memo field data.
	TDBMemo	Provides a data-aware Memo-type control for display and/or modification of memo field data.
	TDBImage	Provides a data-aware display of graphic images stored in a BLOB (Binary Large OBject) field.
	TDBListBox	Provides a data-aware list box that stores the selected list item in the designated field.
	TDBComboBox	Provides a data-aware list box that stores the selected list item in the designated field.
	TDBCheckBox	Provides a data-aware check box for displaying and/or modification of a logical field value.
	TDBRadioGroup	Provides a data-aware group of radio buttons for display and/or modification of mutually exclusive values for a field.
	TDBLookupListBox	Provides a data-aware list box that retrieves its list values from a lookup table for display (*New in Delphi 2.0*).
	TDBLookupComboBox	Provides a data-aware combo box that retrieves its list values from a lookup table for display (*New in Delphi 2.0*).
	TDBCtrlGrid	Provides customized display of data in panels (*New in Delphi 2.0*).

DATABASE DESKTOP

The Database Desktop is a stand-alone utility that provides a quick and easy way to create, modify, query, index, and copy database tables, including Paradox, dBASE, and SQL tables. You do not have to own Paradox or dBASE to use the DBD with desktop files in these formats.

The DBD can copy data and data dictionary information from one format to another. For example, you can copy a Paradox table to an existing database on a remote SQL server.

In the Figure 1.5, the Database Desktop is browsing a Paradox table under Windows 95.

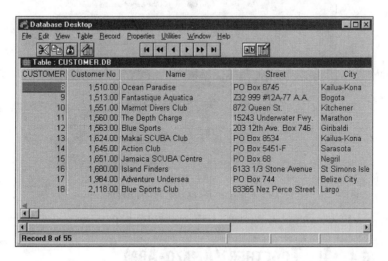

FIGURE 1.5 THE DATABASE DESKTOP.

To start Database Desktop from within Delphi's IDE, select **Database Desktop** from the Tools menu. The Database Desktop can also be run outside of Delphi's IDE by double-clicking the **Database Desktop** icon in the Delphi program group or by simply running **DBD.EXE** from the Windows Program Manager.

DATABASE FORM EXPERT

The Database Form Expert is an amazing tool, in both its power and its ease of use. Given an existing table to work from, the Database Form Expert can automate many of the tasks necessary for creating data-entry or tabular forms standard in almost every Windows database application. It can generate simple or master/detail forms using TTable or TQuery components. The Database Form Expert automates such form-building tasks as:

- Placing database components on a form.
- Connecting TDataSet components (for example, TTable and TQuery) to a database.
- Connecting TDataSource components to interactive data control components and TTable or TQuery data access objects.
- Writing SQL statements for TQuery objects.
- Defining a tab order for components.

The best way to learn about the Database Form Expert is to start with an existing dBase or Paradox table, fire it up, and follow the prompts. It's amazingly simple to follow from there.

14

The opening screen of the Database Form Expert is shown below:

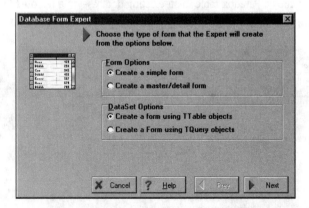

FIGURE 1.6 THE DATABASE FORM EXPERT.

To open the Database Form Expert, select **Database Form Expert** from Delphi's Help menu.

PUTTING IT ALL TOGETHER (AMAZO-APP)

In this section, we'll combine TTable, TDataSource, TDBGrid, and TDBNavigator components to create a simple single-form, single-table application called Amazo-App (shown in Figure 1.7). In its basic form, Amazo-App could require no code at all. However, to also provide a demonstration of accessing table data directly, without data-aware controls like TDBGrid, we'll add two other features to Amazo-App. These will be a Tlabel control that displays a dynamic record position value, and a Tbutton control that, when clicked, swaps the contents of the first two fields for the entire table.

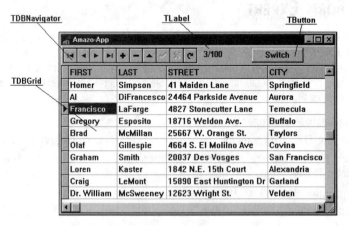

FIGURE 1.7 AMAZO-APP—A SINGLE FORM, SINGLE-TABLE APPLICATION.

Step 1—Know Your Data

Before we create Amazo-App, we need to have an existing table of data to work with. This example uses a dBase table called **TEST.DBF** that is located in the **C:\DATA** directory, which contains 100 records of the following structure:

NAME	TYPE	LEN	DEC
FIRST	C	20	
LAST	C	20	
STREET	C	30	
CITY	C	30	
STATE	C	2	
ZIP	C	10	
HIREDATE	D	8	
MARRIED	L	1	
AGE	N	2	0
SALARY	N	6	0
NOTES	C	70	

NOTE

A **TEST.DBF** of this structure is located in the **\DATA** directory of the included CD-ROM.

Step 2—Create a New Project

To begin creating the application itself, select **New Project** from Delphi's File menu. From the Object Inspector window, change the Caption property of Form1 to **Amazo-App**.

Step 3—Add the Data Access Components

From the component palette's Data Access page, click and drop one **TTable** and one **TDataSource** component icon onto the form.

On the form, click on the **TTable** icon to select it. By default, this object will be called **Table1**. In the Object Inspector window, set the following properties for the Table1 object:

DatabaseName: **C:\DATA**

TableName: **TEST**

TableType: **ttDBase**

NOTE

The **C:\DATA** directory could be set up as a database alias through the BDE configuration utility. However, to keep things simple for now, we'll just enter the drive and path directly.

Now, click on the **TDataSource** icon to select it and set the following properties for it in the Object Inspector window. (*From this point on, when we say 'set a property,' assume it is to be set in the Object Inspector window. This saves _us_ a lot of redundant typing and saves _you_ a lot of redundant reading.*):

DataSet: **Table1**

This tells TDataSource that it will be getting its data from Table1. This TDataSource object will, by default, be named **DataSource1**. It will relay information between Table1 and your visual data-aware controls.

Step 4—Add the Data-Aware Components

Actually, before we add the data-aware components, we need to add a panel to the form, just for aesthetic purposes. From the Standard page of the component palette, click and drop a **TPanel** component onto the form. Blank out the Caption property, and then set the Align property to **alTop**. This locks it to the top of the form.

Now we are ready to grab some data-aware components. First, from the Data Controls page, select the **TDBNavigator** component and drop it onto the panel we just added. Click and drag it to the left side of the panel so it looks just about like Figure 1.7. Then just set the DataSource property to **DataSource1**. This points to the TDataSource component we previously placed on the form.

Now, also from the **Data Controls** page of the Component palette, select a **TDBGrid** control and drop it on the form, below the panel. Then set the following properties:

Align: **alClient**

DataSource: **DataSource1**

Select the **TTable** component (**Table1**) by clicking on it. Now set its Active property to True. You should immediately see live data from **C:\DATA\TEST.DBF** in the browse window. This is a basic, no code required, Delphi database application that supports adding, deleting, editing, and navigating through records.

Next we will write code to do some hands-on data access.

Step 5—Add the New Features

FEATURE #1:

The first additional feature we will add to Amazo-App is a TLabel component used as a record position indicator, just to the right of the TDBNavigator buttons. This will show the current record number as we move through the table with the navigator buttons.

From the component palette's Standard page, select a **TLabel** component and position it just to the right of the **TDBNavigator** buttons on the panel. You can either blank out the label's Caption property or leave it alone. This is not critical because Amazo-App will be changing it anyway at start-up.

While the TTable RecordCount property tells us the number of records in the table, TTable offers no way of getting the physical record number for the current cursor position in the table. For this, we must create our own Recno function using calls to the BDE's API functions.

Besides writing the Recno function itself, we must remember to add the new function prototype for Recno to the top of our unit. To do this, add the following line of code just above the start of the `private` declarations section:

```
function TForm1.Recno( oTable: TTable ): Longint;
```

Lastly, because our Recno function makes calls to certain Dbi* functions (the BDE's API function names all begin with Dbi), we must also add dbitypes, dbiprocs, and dbierrs to the uses section of this unit.

The complete Delphi source for the Recno() function used by Amazo-App is shown below.

```
{Retrieves physical record number a la xBase. Under Delphi 1, requires
 DBITYPES, DBIPROCS, and DBIERRS in the uses clause of the unit. Under
 Delphi 2, use the BDE unit instead. Function takes one argument
 of type TTable (e.g., Table1).}
function TForm1.Recno( oTable: TTable ): Longint;
var
  rError: DBIResult;
  rRecProp: RECprops;
  szErrMsg: DBIMSG;
begin
  Result := 0;
  try
    oTable.UpdateCursorPos;
    rError := DbiGetRecord( oTable.Handle, dbiNOLOCK, nil, @rRecProp );
    if rError = DBIERR_NONE then
      Result := rRecProp.iPhyRecNum
    else
      case rError of
        DBIERR_BOF: Result := 1;
        DBIERR_EOF: Result := oTable.RecordCount + 1;
      else
        begin
          DbiGetErrorString( rError, szErrMsg );
          ShowMessage( StrPas( szErrMsg ));
        end;
      end;
  except
    on E: EDBEngineError do ShowMessage( E.Message );
  end;
end;
```

To dynamically update the record position, display each time a navigator button is clicked or the grid is scrolled, we only need to add the following bit of code to the `OnDataChange` event of the TDataSource component:

```
Label1.Caption := IntToStr( Recno( Table1 )) + '/' +
                  IntToStr( Table1.RecordCount );
```

FEATURE #2

The second additional feature also demonstrates an operation requiring hand-coding. This will be a **Switch** button, that, when clicked, will perform the virtually useless (yet educational) task of skipping through the entire table, from top to bottom, swapping the contents of the FIRST name field with those in the LAST name field.

To add this feature, select a **TButton** component from the Component palette's Standard page and drop it on the panel to the right of the record position label we just added. Size and position the button so it resembles the button shown in Figure 1.7. Set the button's Caption property to **Switch**.

From the Object Inspector window, select the **Events** page and double-click the **OnClick** event to open the source window. Add the following code to the TButton's OnClick event:

```
procedure TForm1.Button1Click(Sender: TObject);
var
   sFirst, sLast: String;
begin
   with Table1 do
   begin
     {Disable screen updates until finished to eliminate screen flicker}
     DisableControls;
     {Make sure we start from the top of the table}
     First;
     {Process all records until End Of File (EOF) }
     while not EOF do
     begin
       {Retrieve and Save the current FIRST and LAST values}
       sFirst := FieldByName( 'FIRST' ).AsString;
       sLast := FieldByName( 'LAST' ).AsString;
       {Put record in Edit mode and Swap them }
       Edit;
       FieldByName( 'FIRST' ).AsString := sLast;
       FieldByName( 'LAST' ).AsString := sFirst;
       {Move to next record}
       Next; { Post not necessary because Next implicitly posts changes}
     end;
     {Reset record pointer to top}
     First;
     {Update screen display}
     EnableControls;
   end;
end;
```

Step 6—All Done

That's it! All that's left is to press **F9** and run the program. Click the **Switch** button and watch the data in the FIRST and LAST name fields swap back and forth.

SUMMARY

If you are just starting out with Delphi, this short introduction should have given you a taste of just how simple it can be to create professional-quality database applications in Delphi.

19

In the next two chapters, we'll dive deeper into Delphi's tool box of components. These are the building blocks that will allow you to perform Delphi's magic.

CHAPTER 2

The Data Access Components

OVERVIEW

There are two pages on the Component Palette that pertain to databases. The Data Access page contains several nonvisual components that are used to establish connections to databases and queries. (See Figure 2.1.) The Data Controls page contains several data-aware controls that are used in conjunction with the Data Access components to display data on your forms. This chapter will discuss the Data Access components. The Data Control Components will be discussed in the next chapter.

FIGURE 2.1 THE DATA ACCESS PAGE.

The Data Access components are summarized in Table 2.1 (in the order that they appear on the component palette):

TABLE 2.1 THE DATA CONTROL COMPONENTS

Icon	Component	Description
	TDataSource	Provides an interface between one or more Data Control components on your form and a TTable or TQuery component.
	TTable	Provides an interface between one or more TDataSource components and the BDE.
	TQuery	Provides an SQL interface between one or more TDataSource components and the BDE.
	TStoredProc	Provides and interface to stored procedures on a server database.
	TDatabase	Provides an interface directly to a database or BDE alias.

continued

TABLE 2.1 CONTINUED

Icon	Component	Description
	TSession	Provides global control over database connections for an application (*New in Delphi 2.0*).
	TBatchMove	Provides a mechanism for moving entire tables and databases.
	TUpdateSQL	Provides access to a TQuery component associated with a specified SQL statement (*New in Delphi 2.0*).
	TReport	Provides an interface to the ReportSmith run-time engine.

DELPHI'S DATABASE ARCHITECTURE

A bit of background may be helpful at this point. Delphi's database architecture is designed in such a way as to provide the maximum amount of flexibility when working with databases. Although the individual data access components may at first seem to be disparate, they are designed to integrate together in various ways to accomplish even the most demanding database management tasks.

Data can be stored in any format that is recognized by the Borland Database Engine. A typical database connection layout would have a table component connected to a specific table through the BDE, and a DataSource component connected to the table component by setting DataSource.DataSet property to point to the Table object. All the data-aware controls for a given form could then be connected directly to the DataSource object via each control's DataSource property. For example, the following code fragment would establish such a connection:

```
{ Connect the table object to the BDE alias or data directory }
Table1.DatabaseName := 'C:\DATA';

{ Connect the table object to a specific table }
Table1.TableName := 'CONTACTS.DBF';

{ Open the table }
Table1.Open;

{ Connect the DataSource object to the Table object}
DataSource1.DataSet := Table1;

{ Connect any data-aware controls to the DataSource object }
DBGrid1.DataSource := DataSource1;
DBEdit1.DataSource := DataSource1;
...
```

For additional information about working with database components, see the *Database Application Developers Guide* that is included with your Delphi package.

DATA ACCESS COMPONENTS REFERENCE

All the nonvisual components that are involved with data access are documented in this section, in the order that they appear on the Delphi 1.0 Component Palette, with the exception of the abstract components TDataSet and TDBDataSet, which are documented first: TDataSet and TDBDataSet incorporate much of the functionality of the TTable, TQuery, and TStoredProc components (collectively known as the DataSet components), and documenting them in this way avoids having to repeat properties, methods, and events that are common to all the data set components.

Each component is followed by tables that summarize the properties, events and methods for that component, which are in turn followed by a more detailed alphabetical listing for each of the properties, events and methods for that component.

TDataSet Component

Unit

DB

Inherits from

TComponent

Description

TDataset is an abstract class that defines much of the functionality for its immediate descendant TDBDataSet, and ultimately the data set components TTable, TQuery and TStoredProc. The following tables summarize the properties (Table 2.2), methods (Table 2.3), and events (Table 2.4) defined by the TDataset component:

TABLE 2.2 TDATASET PROPERTIES

PROPERTY	DATA TYPE	RUN-TIME ONLY	READ-ONLY	DESCRIPTION
Active	Boolean	No	No	True if DataSet is open, False if not.
AutoCalcFields	Boolean	No	No	Determines if OnCalcFields is activated when the DataSet is edited.
BOF	Boolean	Yes	Yes	True when DataSet is known to be at the first record.
CanModify	Boolean	Yes	Yes	Specifies whether the DataSet can be modified.
DataSource	TDataSource	Yes	No	For a TQuery, specifies a DataSet to search for values for unbound SQL parameters.
EOF	Boolean	Yes	Yes	True if DataSet is known to be at its last row.
FieldCount	Integer	Yes	Yes	Contains the number of fields in the DataSet.

continued

TABLE 2.2 CONTINUED

FieldDefs	TFieldDefs	Yes	No	Contains information about each TFieldDef in the DataSet.
Fields	TField	Yes	No	Contains the TField objects associated with this DataSet
Handle	hDBICur	Yes	Yes	Provides a handle to the DataSet for use with BDE API functions.
Locale	Pointer	Yes	Yes	Specifies the BDE language driver used for this DataSet.
Modified	Boolean	Yes	Yes	Specifies whether a field in the current record has changed since the last update.
RecordCount	Longint	Yes	Yes	Specifies the number of records in the DataSet.
State	TDataSetState	Yes	Yes	Specifies the current state of the DataSet.

TABLE 2.3 TDATASET METHODS

METHOD	DESCRIPTION
Append	Adds a new, empty record to the end of the DataSet.
AppendRecord	Adds a new record to the end of the DataSet initialized to a specified set of values.
Cancel	Cancels a pending Edit, Append, or Insert operation.
CheckBrowseMode	Verifies that the DataSet is in dsBrowse mode.
ClearFields	Sets all fields in the current record to NULL or empty.
Close	Closes the DataSet.
CursorPosChanged	Notifies the BDE that a change has been made to the cursor position by a direct call to the BDE.
Delete	Deletes the current record.
DisableControls	Temporarily disconnects the DataSet from any DataSource components. Use EnableControls to restore connection.
Edit	Places the DataSet in dsEdit mode.
EnableControls	Restores connection from the DataSet to DataSource components after a call to DisableControls.
FieldByName	Retrieves the TField object associated with a specified field name.
FindField	Returns the TField object associated with a specified field name, or NIL if field is not in DataSet.
First	Moves cursor to first record in the active range for the DataSet.
FreeBookmark	Deallocates memory for a TBookmark object.
GetBookmark	Creates a TBookmark object that points to the current record in the DataSet.
GetFieldNames	Initializes a TStrings object with a list of the names of the fields in the DataSet.
GotoBookmark	Moves the cursor to the record associated with a specified TBookmark.
Insert	Inserts a new, empty record at the current position in the DataSet.

InsertRecord	Inserts a new record at the current position of the DataSet initialized to a specified set of values.
Last	Moves the cursor to the last record in the active range for the DataSet.
MoveBy	Moves the cursor by a specified number of records.
Next	Moves the cursor to the next record in the DataSet.
Open	Opens the DataSet.
Post	Writes the current record to the DataSet.
Prior	Moves the cursor to the previous record.
Refresh	Rereads all records from the DataSet.
SetFields	Assigns specified values to the fields in a DataSet.
UpdateCursorPos	Sets the BDE cursor to the position of the DataSet's cursor.
UpdateRecord	Causes DataSource to update fields in the DataSet with values in the data-aware controls.

TABLE 2.4 TDATASET EVENTS

EVENT	DESCRIPTION
AfterCancel	Activated after a call to the Cancel method.
AfterClose	Activated after a call to the Close method.
AfterDelete	Activated after a call to the Delete method.
AfterEdit	Activated after a call to the Edit method.
AfterInsert	Activated after a call to the Insert method.
AfterOpen	Activated after a call to the Open method.
AfterPost	Activated after a call to the Post method.
BeforeCancel	Activated before a call to the Cancel method.
BeforeClose	Activated before a call to the Close method.
BeforeDelete	Activated before a call to the Delete method.
BeforeEdit	Activated before a call to the Edit method.
BeforeInsert	Activated before a call to the Insert method.
BeforeOpen	Activated before a call to the Open method.
BeforePost	Activated before a call to the Post method.
OnCalcFields	Activated when a record is read from the database and when a field is modified if the AutoCalcFields flag is True.
OnNewRecord	Activated when a new record is added to the DataSet.

Note: All TDataset events are of type TDatasetNotifyEvent.

See Also

TQuery, TStoredProc, TTable

TDataSet.Active Property

Declaration

```
{ DB.PAS }
property Active: Boolean read GetActive write SetActive
    default False;
```

Description

True if DataSet is open, False if it is not.

Example

```
{ This example sets Active to True }
Table1.Open;
```

```
{ This example closes the database }
Table1.Active := False;
```

Notes

Active is set to True automatically when the data set is opened and to False when it is closed. Assigning a value to Active will cause the database to open or close as appropriate, as shown in the preceding example.

See Also

TDataset.Close, TDataset.Open

TDataSet.AfterCancel Event

Declaration

```
{ DB.PAS }
property AfterCancel: TDataSetNotifyEvent read FAfterCancel
    write FAfterCancel;

TDataSetNotifyEvent = procedure(DataSet: TDataSet) of object;
```

Description

Activated after a call to the Cancel method.

Example

```
{ Display a message that the operation was canceled }
procedure TForm1.Table1AfterCancel(DataSet: TDataset);
begin
    ShowMessage('Operation canceled.');
end;
```

Notes

The OnCancel event is not activated if the DataSet is not in Edit state or there are no pending changes.

See Also

TDataset.BeforeCancel, TDataset.Cancel

TDataSet.AfterClose Event

Declaration

```
{ DB.PAS }
property AfterClose: TDataSetNotifyEvent read FAfterClose
    write FAfterClose;

TDataSetNotifyEvent = procedure(DataSet: TDataSet) of object;
```

Description

Activated after a call to the Close method, or when the Active property is set to False.

Example

```
{ Close any lookup tables that were opened in the BeforeOpen event handler }
procedure TForm1.CustomerTableAfterClose(DataSet: TDataset);
begin
    { OrdersTable was used to look up data for each Customer record }
    OrdersTable.Close;
end;
```

Notes

The AfterClose event handler is a good place to close any lookup tables needed by the main table, as shown in the preceding example.

See Also

TDataset.BeforeClose, TDataset.Close

TDataSet.AfterDelete Event

Declaration

```
{ DB.PAS }
property AfterDelete: TDataSetNotifyEvent read FAfterDelete
    write FAfterDelete;
TDataSetNotifyEvent = procedure(DataSet: TDataSet) of object;
```

Description

Activated after a call to the Delete method.

Example

```
{ Display a message after record is deleted }
procedure TForm1.Table1AfterDelete(DataSet: TDataset);
begin
    ShowMessage('Record deleted. Get over it.');
end;
```

Notes

The AfterDelete event is activated only after the record has been deleted and the cursor moved to the subsequent record.

See Also

TDataset.BeforeDelete, TDataset.Delete

TDataSet.AfterEdit Event

Declaration

```
{ DB.PAS }
property AfterEdit: TDataSetNotifyEvent read FAfterEdit
    write FAfterEdit;
TDataSetNotifyEvent = procedure(DataSet: TDataSet) of object;
```

Description

Activated after a call to the Edit method.

Example

```
{ Display a message when editing begins }
procedure TForm1.Table1AfterEdit(DataSet: TDataset);
begin
    ShowMessage('Entering edit mode...');
end;
```

Notes

The AfterEdit event is activated after a call to Edit (or, if AutoEdit is True, after the user types into an associated data-aware control) but before changes are made to the record.

See Also
TDataset.BeforeEdit, TDataset.Edit

TDATASET.AFTERINSERT EVENT

Declaration

```
{ DB.PAS }
property AfterInsert: TDataSetNotifyEvent read FAfterInsert
    write FAfterInsert;
TDataSetNotifyEvent = procedure(DataSet: TDataSet) of object;
```

Description
Activated after a call to the Insert or Append methods.

Example

```
{ Display a message showing that the data set is in Insert mode }
procedure TForm1.Table1AfterInsert(DataSet: TDataset);
begin
    ShowMessage('Insert operation started...');
end;
```

Notes
The AfterInsert method is activated before a new record is added to the DataSet.

See Also
TDataset.Append, TDataset.Insert, TDataset.BeforeAppend, TDataset.BeforeInsert

TDATASET.AFTEROPEN EVENT

Declaration

```
{ DB.PAS }
property AfterOpen: TDataSetNotifyEvent read FAfterOpen
    write FAfterOpen;

TDataSetNotifyEvent = procedure(DataSet: TDataSet) of object;
```

Description
Activated after a call to the Open method or when setting the Active property to True.

Example

```
{ Show a message to user when table opens }
procedure TForm1.Table1AfterOpen(DataSet: TDataset);
begin
   ShowMessage('Table1 is now open for business');
end;
```

Notes

Attempts to Close a table within this procedure are ignored.

See Also

TDataset.BeforeOpen, TDataset.Open

TDATASET.AFTERPOST EVENT

Declaration

```
{ DB.PAS }
property AfterPost: TDataSetNotifyEvent read FAfterPost
     write FAfterPost;

TDataSetNotifyEvent = procedure(DataSet: TDataSet) of object;
```

Description

Activated after a call to the Post method.

Example

```
{ Display message after post is complete }
procedure TForm1.Table1AfterPost(DataSet: TDataset);
begin
   ShowMessage('Record posted.');
end;
```

Notes

The cursor may not be positioned on the newly posted record if a range is in effect and the key value for the posted record is not within that range.

See Also

TDataset.BeforePost, TDataset.Post

TDATASET.APPEND METHOD

Declaration

```
{ DB.PAS }
procedure Append;
```

Description

Adds a new, empty record to the end of the DataSet.

Example

```
{ Add a new, empty record to the end of the data set }
Table1.Append;
Table1CUSTNAME.Value := 'New Customer';
Table1.Post;
```

Notes

Append moves the cursor to the end of file prior to initializing the record edit buffers with empty values. The record is not physically added to the data set until the Post method is called.

See Also

TDataset.AppendRecord, TDataset.BeforeInsert, TDataset.Insert

TDataSet.AppendRecord Method

Declaration

```
{ DB.PAS }
procedure AppendRecord(const Values: Array of const);
```

Description

Adds a new record to the end of the data set initialized to a specified set of values. Each element of Values corresponds to the field in the data set at that position in the Fields array. If Values contains less then the total number of fields, the remaining fields are left unassigned (NULL). The data types of the individual elements of Values must be assignment compatible with the field either directly or through the use of the field's assignment properties (AsString, AsBoolean, etc.).

Example

```
{ Pre-initialize a record prior to editing }
Table1.AppendRecord(['Mouse', 'Mickey', 1001, True]);

{ edit record... }

Table1.Post;
```

Notes

AppendRecord moves the cursor to the end of file prior to initializing the record edit buffers with the specified values. The record is not physically added to the DataSet until the Post method is called.

See Also

TDataset.Append, TDataset.Insert

TDataSet.AutoCalcFields Property

Declaration

```
{ DB.PAS }
property AutoCalcFields: Boolean read FAutoCalcFields
    write FAutoCalcFields default True;
```

Description

Determines if OnCalcFields is activated when the DataSet is edited.

Example

```
{ Prevent OnCalcFields from being called on edit }
Table1.AutoCalcFields := False;
```

Notes

OnCalcFields is called whenever the application retrieves a record from the data set, regardless of the setting of AutoCalcFields. If AutoCalcFields is True, do not attempt to modify a non-calculated field within the OnCalcFields event handler, as it could lead to recursion.

See Also

TDataset.OnCalcFields

TDataSet.BeforeCancel Event

Declaration

```
{ DB.PAS }
property BeforeCancel: TDataSetNotifyEvent read FBeforeCancel
    write FBeforeCancel;

TDataSetNotifyEvent = procedure(DataSet: TDataSet) of object;
```

Description

Activated before a call to the Cancel method.

Example

```
{ Canceling a cancel operation using BeforeCancel }
procedure TForm1.Table1BeforeCancel(DataSet: TDataset);
```

```
var
   op: String;
begin
   if Dataset.State = dsInsert then
      op := 'Add'
   else
      op := ''Edit';
   { If user cancels the cancel, raise a silent exception }
   if MessageDlg('Cancel ' + op + ' operation?',
               mtConfirmation, [mbYes, mbNo], 0) <> mrYes then
      SysUtils.Abort;
end;
```

Notes

Raising an exception within the BeforeCancel aborts the cancel operation, as shown in the preceding example.

See Also

TDataset.AfterCancel, TDataset.Cancel

TDataSet.BeforeClose Event

Declaration

```
{ DB.PAS }
property BeforeClose: TDataSetNotifyEvent read FBeforeClose
   write FBeforeClose;

TDataSetNotifyEvent = procedure(DataSet: TDataSet) of object;
```

Description

Activated before the DataSet is closed with a call to the Close method or by setting the Active property to False.

Example

```
{ Post any pending changes prior to closing }
procedure TForm1.Table1BeforeClose(DataSet: TDataset);
begin
   if (Dataset.State in [dsEdit,dsInsert]) and
      (MessageDlg('Post pending changes?', mtConfirmation,
         [mbYes,mbNo], 0) = mrYes) then
      Dataset.Post;
end;
```

Notes

Raising an exception within the BeforeClose event will cancel the close operation.

See Also

TDataset.AfterClose, TDataset.Close

TDATASET.BEFOREDELETE EVENT

Declaration

```
{ DB.PAS }
property BeforeDelete: TDataSetNotifyEvent read FBeforeDelete
    write FBeforeDelete;

TDataSetNotifyEvent = procedure(DataSet: TDataSet) of object;
```

Description

Activated before a call to the Delete method.

Example

```
{ Confirm deletes using BeforeDelete event handler }
procedure TForm1.Table1BeforeDelete(DataSet: TDataset);
begin
   if MessageDlg('Delete this record?', mtConfirmation,
         mbYesNoCancel, 0) <> mrYes then
      SysUtils.Abort;
end;
```

Notes

Raising an exception within the BeforeDelete event handler will cancel the delete operation, as shown in the preceding example.

See Also

TDataset.AfterDelete, TDataset.Delete

TDATASET.BEFOREEDIT EVENT

Declaration

```
{ DB.PAS }
property BeforeEdit: TDataSetNotifyEvent read FBeforeEdit
    write FBeforeEdit;

TDataSetNotifyEvent = procedure(DataSet: TDataSet) of object;
```

Description

Activated before a call to the Edit method.

Example

```
{ Confirm editing using the BeforeEdit event handler }
procedure TForm1.Table1BeforeEdit(DataSet: TDataset);
begin
    if MessageDlg('Edit this record?', mtConfirmation,
         mbYesNoCancel, 0) <> mrYes then
      SysUtils.Abort;
end;
```

Notes

Raising an exception within the BeforeEdit event handler will cause the edit operation to abort, as shown in the preceding example.

See Also

TDataset.AfterEdit, TDataset.Edit

TDATASET.BEFOREINSERT EVENT

Declaration

```
{ DB.PAS }
property BeforeInsert: TDataSetNotifyEvent read FBeforeInsert
    write FBeforeInsert;

TDataSetNotifyEvent = procedure(DataSet: TDataSet) of object;
```

Description

Activated before a call to the Insert method.

Example

```
{ Confirm record add using the BeforeInsert event handler }
procedure TForm1.Table1BeforeInsert(DataSet: TDataset);
begin
    if MessageDlg('Add a new record?', mtConfirmation,
         mbYesNoCancel, 0) <> mrYes then
      SysUtils.Abort;
end;
```

Notes

Raising an exception within the BeforeInsert event handler will cancel the Insert operation, as shown in the preceding example.

See Also

TDataset.AfterAppend, TDataset.AfterInsert, TDataset.Append, TDataset.Insert

TDATASET.BEFOREOPEN EVENT

Declaration

```
{ DB.PAS }
property BeforeOpen: TDataSetNotifyEvent read FBeforeOpen
     write FBeforeOpen;

TDataSetNotifyEvent = procedure(DataSet: TDataSet) of object;
```

Description

Activated before a call to the Open method.

Example

```
{Ensure that any look-up tables required by Table1 are open }
procedure TForm1.Table1BeforeOpen(DataSet: TDataset);
begin
   Table2.Open;
   Table3.Open;
end;
```

Notes

Raising an exception within the BeforeOpen event handler will cancel the Open operation.

See Also

TDataset.AfterOpen, TDataset.Open

TDATASET.BEFOREPOST EVENT

Declaration

```
{ DB.PAS }
property BeforePost: TDataSetNotifyEvent read FBeforePost
     write FBeforePost;

TDataSetNotifyEvent = procedure(DataSet: TDataSet) of object;
```

Description

Activated before a call to the Post method, after the UpdateRecord method has been called to store changes in the data-aware controls to the record.

Example

```
{ Perform record-level validation using the BeforePost handler }
procedure TForm1.PaymentTableBeforePost(DataSet: TDataset);
begin
   if (PaymentTablePAYDATE.Value > Date) or
      (PaymentTablePAYAMOUNT.Value <= 0) then
   begin
      ShowMessage('Invalid entry');
      SysUtils.Abort;
   end;
end;
```

Notes

Raising an exception within the BeforePost event handler will cancel the Post operation.

See Also

TDataset.AfterPost, TDataset.Post

TDataSet.BOF Property

Declaration

```
{ DB.PAS }
property BOF: Boolean read FBOF;
```

Description

Run-time only, read-only. True when data set is known to be at the first record.

Example

```
{ Process records in reverse order }
Table1.Last;
while not Table1.BOF do
begin
   Listbox1.Add(FloatToStr(Table1RECEIVABLE.Value));
   Table1.Prior;
end;
```

Notes

The BOF property will indicate true only when it is known that the cursor is on the first record in the data set. This occurs only when the table is first opened, or after a call to First, or when a call to Prior fails. The "first" record will vary depending on whether a range is in effect and what index is currently active.

See Also

TDataset.EOF

TDATASET.CANCEL METHOD

Declaration

```
{ DB.PAS }
procedure Cancel;
```

Description

Cancels a pending Edit, Append, or Insert operation and returns data set to Browse state. Any pending changes to the record are discarded.

Example

```
{ Typical use of the Cancel method }
Table1.Edit;
if EditForm.ShowModal = mrOK then
   Table1.Post
else
   Table1.Cancel;
```

Notes

No exception will be generated if the data set is not in Edit or Insert mode.

See Also

TDataset.Append, TDataset.Edit, TDataset.Insert

TDATASET.CANMODIFY PROPERTY

Declaration

```
{ DB.PAS }
property CanModify: Boolean read FCanModify;
```

Description

Run-time only, read-only. Specifies whether the data set can be modified.

Example

```
{ Attempt to edit only if data set is modifiable }
if Table1.CanModify then
begin
   Table1.Edit;
   Table1DUEDATE.Value := Date;
   Table1.Post;
end
else
   ShowMessage('Table is not modifiable!');
```

Notes

Setting the ReadOnly property to True will set the CanModify property to False. Setting the ReadOnly property to False will set the CanModify property to True only if the table can be modified. Other factors such as security and data access privileges may affect whether a table can be modified or not.

See Also

TDataset.Active, TDataset.ReadOnly

TDataSet.CheckBrowseMode Method

Declaration

```
{ DB.PAS }
procedure CheckBrowseMode;
```

Description

Verifies that the data set is in dsBrowse mode, is open, and has no pending changes.

Example

```
{ Force the data set into Browse state }
Table1.CheckBrowseMode;
```

Notes

The CheckBrowseMode method will call Post if the data set is currently in dsEdit, dsInsert, or dsSetKey mode to post any pending changes prior to setting the data set to dsBrowse mode. If the data set is not open, an exception will be generated.

See Also

TDataset.State

TDataSet.ClearFields Method

Declaration

```
{ DB.PAS }
procedure ClearFields;
```

Description

Sets all fields in the current record to NULL or empty.

Example

```
{ Clear the current record }
Table1.Edit;
Table1.ClearFields;
Table1.Post;
```

Notes

An exception will be generated if the data set is not in Edit mode when ClearFields is called.

See Also

TDataset.Edit

TDataSet.Close Method

Declaration

```
{ DB.PAS }
procedure Close;
```

Description

Closes the data set.

Example

```
{ Close a query }
Query1.Close;
```

Notes

Closing the data set cancels all pending changes. Use the BeforePost event handler to post any pending changes to the data set prior to closing.

See Also

TDataset.Active, TDataset.Open

TDataSet.CursorPosChanged Method

Declaration

```
{ DB.PAS }
procedure CursorPosChanged;
```

Description

Notifies the BDE that a change has been made to the cursor position by a direct call to the BDE.

Example

```
{ Move to a specified record }
DbiSetToRecordNo(Table1.Handle, 1234);
```

```
{ Notify BDE that cursor position has changed }
Table1.CursorPosChanged;
```

Notes

The CursorPosChanged method is necessary only if you have made direct calls to the BDE using a data set's Handle property.

See Also

BDE Function Reference, TDataset.UpdateCursorPos

TDataSet.DataSource Property

Applies to

TQuery component

Declaration

```
{ DB.PAS }
property DataSource: TDataSource read GetDataSource;
```

Description

Run-time only. For a TQuery, specifies a data set from which to retrieve values for unbound SQL parameters.

Example

See TQuery.DataSource for an example of using the DataSource property.

Notes

The name of the parameter must match a field name in the master table.

See Also

TQuery.DataSource, TQuery.SQL

TDataSet.Delete Method

Applies to

TQuery and TTable component

Declaration

```
{ DB.PAS }
procedure Delete;
```

Description

Deletes the current record.

Example

```
{ Delete the current record }
Table1.Delete;
```

Notes

After the record is successfully deleted, the cursor is moved to the next record, or to the previous record if at the last record in the data set.

See Also

TDataset.AfterDelete, TDataset.BeforeDelete

TDataSet.DisableControls Method

Declaration

```
{ DB.PAS }
procedure DisableControls;
```

Description

Temporarily disconnects the data set from any DataSource components. Use EnableControls to restore connection.

Example

```
{ Disable data-aware controls while searching for a lookup value
var
   bm: TBookmark;
   Total: Double;
begin
   Total := 0;
   bm := Table1.GetBookmark
   Table1.DisableControls;
   Table1.First;
   while not Table1.EOF do
   begin
      Total := Total + Table1PAYAMT.Value;
      Table1.Next;
   end;
   Table1.GotoBookmark(bm);
   Table1.FreeBookmark(bm);
   Table1.EnableControls;
end;
```

Notes

Calls to DisableControls and EnableControls can be nested, but only the last (outer) call to EnableControls will actually re-enable the controls.

See Also

TDataset.EnableControls

TDataSet.Edit Method

Applies to

TQuery and TTable components

Declaration

```
{ DB.PAS }
procedure Edit;
```

Description

Places the data set in dsEdit mode.

Example

```
{ Edit a value in the current record }
if Table1.CanModify then
begin
    Table1.Edit;
    Table1PARTNUM.Value := '1234-A';
    Table1.Post;
end;
```

Notes

An exception will be raised if the table is not modifiable when the Edit method is called.

See Also

TDataset.AfterEdit, TDataset.BeforeEdit, TDataset.Post

TDATASET.ENABLECONTROLS METHOD

Declaration

```
{ DB.PAS }
procedure EnableControls;
```

Description

Restores connection from the data set to DataSource components after a call to DisableControls.

Example

```
{ Tthis example shows how nesting is handled - this call is the outer level
  call to DisableControls }
Table1.DisableControls;

{ Fetch next ID number using NextIDNum function defined below... }
NextID := NextIDNum;

{ Add record to system using next ID number }
Table1.Insert;
Table1.IDNUM.Value := NextID;

{ Controls are enabled only after this call... }
Table1.EnableControls;

...

function NextIDNum: Longint;
begin
```

```
{ This call is nested - 2nd level }
Table1.DisableControls;

{ Do something useful }
Table1.Last;
Result := Table1IDNUM.Value + 1;

{ Controls are still disabled after this call... }
Table1.EnableControls;
end;
```

Notes

Calls to DisableControls and EnableControls should be paired due to nesting behavior.

See Also

TDataset.DisableControls

TDATASET.EOF PROPERTY

Declaration

```
{ DB.PAS }
property EOF: Boolean read FEOF;
```

Description

Run-time only, read-only. True if data set is known to be at its last row.

Example

```
{ Loop until end of file is reached }
Table1.First;
while not Table1.EOF do
begin
   ...
   Table1.Next;
end;
```

Notes

The EOF property is True only if the data set is known to be at the end of the set of records. This occurs only when the data set is empty, the Last method is called, or a call to Next fails.

See Also

TDataset.BOF

TDataSet.FieldByName Method

Declaration

```
{ DB.PAS }
function FieldByName(const FieldName: String): TField;
```

Description

Retrieves the TField object associated with a specified field name.

Example

```
{ Retrieve the TField object associated with the FIRST_NAME field }
Field := Table1.FieldByName('FIRST_NAME');
```

Notes

The field that is returned may have been created at Design-time, using the Fields Editor, or dynamically at run-time by Delphi. See the TField Component Reference chapter for additional information.

See Also

TDataset.FieldCount, TDataset.FieldDefs, TDataset.FindField, TField Component Reference

TDataSet.FieldCount Property

Applies to

TQuery, TTable, and TStoredProc components. Also applies to TDBGrid and TDBLookupList components.

Declaration

```
{ DB.PAS }
property FieldCount: Integer read GetFieldCount;
```

Description

Run-time only, read-only. Contains the number of fields in the data set.

Example

```
{ Count the number of string fields in the data set }
StringFieldCount := 0;
for x := 1 to Table1.FieldCount - 1 do
   if Table1.Fields[x].DataType = ftString then
      Inc(StringFieldCount);
```

Notes

The number of fields specified in FieldCount may not be the same as the number of fields in the actual database, as you can create or remove field definitions using the Fields Editor at design-time.

See Also

TDataset.FieldByName, TDataset.FieldDefs, TDataset.FindField

TDataSet.FieldDefs Property

Declaration

```
{ DB.PAS }
property FieldDefs: TFieldDefs read FFieldDefs write SetFieldDefs;
```

Description

Run-time only. Contains information about each TFieldDef in the data set.

Example

```
{ List field information for a table without opening it }
Table1.FieldDefs.Update;
with Table1 do
   for x := 1 to (FieldDefs.Count - 1) do
          Listbox1.Add('Name: ' + IntToStr(FieldDefs[x].Name) +
              ' Position: ' + IntToStr(FieldDefs[x].FieldNo) +
              ' Size: ' + IntToStr(FieldDefs[x].Size));
```

Notes

The TFieldDefs list is automatically created for each data set that is opened.

See Also

'TFieldDef' in DELPHI.HLP, TDataset.Fields, TField

TDataSet.Fields Property

Declaration

```
{ DB.PAS }
property Fields[Index: Integer]: TField read GetField write SetField;
```

Description

Run-time only. Contains the TField objects associated with this data set.

Example

```
{ See if any fields contain NULL values }
for x := 0 to Table1.FieldCount - 1 do
   if Fields[x].IsNull then
      ShowMessage('Field ' + Field[x].DisplayName + ' is NULL!');
```

Notes

See the TField Component Reference chapter for a complete description of TField objects.

See Also

TDataset.FieldDefs, TField

TDATASET.FINDFIELD METHOD

Declaration

```
{ DB.PAS }
function FindField(const FieldName: String): TField;
```

Description

Returns the TField object associated with a specified field name or NIL if field is not in data set.

Example

```
{ See if the field WHATZIT is in the data set }
Field := Table1.FindField('WHATZIT');
if Field = nil then
   ShowMessage('WHATZIT is not in this data set!');
```

Notes

The FindField method differs from FieldByName in that FindField returns a NIL if the field is not in the data set where FieldByName generates an exception.

See Also

TDataset.FieldByName

TDATASET.FIRST METHOD

Declaration

```
{ DB.PAS }
procedure First;
```

Description

Moves cursor to first record in the active range for the data set.

Example

```
{ Find the first record in the active range for the data set }
Table1.First;
```

Notes

The "first" record may differ depending on whether an index is active and whether a range or filter is in effect.

See Also

TDataset.Last, TDataset.MoveBy, TDataset.Next, TDataset.Prior

TDataSet.FreeBookmark Method

Declaration

```
{ DB.PAS }
procedure FreeBookmark(Bookmark: TBookmark);
```

Description

Deallocates memory for a TBookmark object.

Example

```
{ Allocate, utilize, and then free a bookmark }
var
    BookMark: TBookMark;
begin
    BookMark := Query1.GetBookmark;
    try
        Table1.MoveBy(123);
        ...
        Table1.GotoBookmark(Bookmark);
    finally
        FreeBookmark(BookMark);
    end;
end;
```

Notes

Bookmarks are not freed automatically; they must be freed with the FreeBookmark method.

See Also

TDataset.GetBookmark, TDataset.GotoBookmark

TDATASET.GETBOOKMARK METHOD

Declaration

```
{ DB.PAS }
function GetBookmark: TBookmark;
```

Description

Creates a TBookmark object that points to the current record in the data set.

Example

```
{ Allocate memory for a bookmark }
var
   BookMark: TBookMark;
begin
   BookMark := Table1.GetBookmark;
   try
      Table1.First;
      ...
      Table1.GotoBookmark(Bookmark);
   finally
      FreeBookmark(Bookmark);
   end;
end;
```

Notes

Creating a bookmark allocates memory that must be freed using FreeBookmark. Code that uses GetBookmark should use a resource protection block as shown in the preceding example to ensure that the memory allocated for a TBookmark object is freed properly.

See Also

TDataset.FreeBookmark, TDataset.GotoBookmark

TDATASET.GETFIELDNAMES METHOD

Declaration

```
{ DB.PAS }
procedure GetFieldNames(List: TStrings);
```

Description

Initializes a TStrings object with a list of the names of the fields in the data set.

Example

```
{ List all fields in the current data set }
Query1.GetFieldNames(Listbox1.Items);
```

Notes

The TStrings object specified in List is cleared before the field names are added to it.

See Also

TDataset.FieldDefs, TDataset.Fields

TDATASET.GOTOBOOKMARK METHOD

Declaration

```
{ DB.PAS }
procedure GotoBookmark(Bookmark: TBookmark);
```

Description

Moves the cursor to the record associated with a specified TBookmark.

Example

```
{ Search routine with optional return }
var
   Bookmark: TBookmark;
begin
   Bookmark := Table1.GetBookmark;
   try
      Table1.SetKey;
      Table1COMPANY.Value := 'WAHOO LIMITED';
      if not Table1.GotoKey then
      Table1.GotoBookmark(Bookmark);
   finally
      FreeBookmark(Bookmark);
      end;
end;
```

Notes

An exception is raised if the record referred to by the specified bookmark is not in the data set.

See Also

TDataset.FreeBookmark, TDataset.GetBookmark

TDATASET.HANDLE PROPERTY

Declaration

```
{ DB.PAS }
property Handle: hDBICur read FHandle;
```

Description

Run-time only, read-only. Provides a handle to the data set for use with BDE API functions.

Example

```
{ This example shows how to display the relative position of the current
  record in the data set for a Paradox table }
procedure TForm1.DataSource1DataChange(Sender: TObject;
     Field: TField);
var
   RecProp: RecProps;
   SeqNo: Longint;
   Percent: Byte;
begin
   { This insures that the underlying record is the same as that pointed to
     on the data-aware controls }
   Table1.UpdateCursorPos;

   { If at end of file, the Sequence Number is invalid }
   if Table1.EOF then
     Percent := 100;
   else
   begin
      { Fetch the Record Properties structure }
      DbiGetRecord(Table1.Handle, dbiNOLOCK, nil, @RecProp);

      { Retrieve the Sequence Number from RecProp }
      SeqNo := RecProp.iSeqNum;

      { Calculate the relative position within the data set }
      Percent := round((SeqNo / Table1.RecordCount) * 100);
   end;

      { display the position }
   Label1.Caption := IntToStr(Percent) + '%';
end;
```

Notes

The Handle property is normally used only when calling the BDE functions directly. See the BDE Function Reference for more information.

See Also

TSession.Handle, BDE Function Reference

TDataSet.Insert Method

Applies to

Tquery and Ttable components

Declaration

```
{ DB.PAS }
procedure Insert;
```

Description

Inserts a new, empty record at the current position in the data set.

Example

```
{ Insert a record at the current position }
Table1.Insert;
Table1ACCT_NUM.Value := 112233;
Table1.Post;
```

Notes

The Insert method adds a record at the current position. Once posted, the record may move to another position within the data set based on the value of a key field.

See Also

TDataset.AfterInsert, TDataset.Append, TDataset.BeforeInsert, TDataset.InsertRecord, TDataset.Post

TDataSet.InsertRecord Method

Applies to

TQuery and TTable components

Declaration

```
{ DB.PAS }
procedure InsertRecord(const Values: Array of const);
```

Description

Inserts a new record at the current position of the data set initialized to a specified set of values. Each element of Values corresponds to the field in the data set at that position in the Fields array. If Values contains less then the total number of fields, the remaining fields are left unassigned (NULL). The data types of the individual elements of Values must be assignment compatible with the field either directly or through the use of the field's assignment properties (AsString, AsBoolean, etc.).

Example

```
{ Insert a preinitialized record at the current position }
Table1.InsertRecord(['Duck', 'Donald', False, 1, 123.45]);
{ edit initial values here }
...
Table1.Post;
```

Notes

InsertRecord does not move the cursor prior to initializing the record edit buffers with the specified values. The record is not physically added to the data set until the Post method is called.

See Also

TDataset.Insert

TDataSet.Last Method

Declaration

```
{ DB.PAS }
procedure Last;
```

Description

Moves the cursor to the last record in the active range for the data set.

Example

```
{ Move to the last record in the data set }
Table1.Last;
```

Notes

The "last" record may vary depending on whether an index is active or whether a range is in effect for the data set.

See Also

TDataset.First, TDataset.Next, TDataset.MoveBy, TDataset.Prior

TDataSet.Locale Property

Declaration

```
{ DB.PAS }
property Locale: TLocale read FLocale;
```

Description

Run-time only, read-only. Specifies the BDE language driver used for this data set.

Example

```
{ Retrieve the current language driver }
LangDriver := Table1.Locale;
```

Notes

The Locale property is normally used only in direct calls to the BDE. See the BDE Function Reference for more information.

See Also

BDE Function Reference, TDataset.DriverName

TDataSet.Modified Property

Declaration

```
{ DB.PAS }
property Modified: Boolean read FModified;
```

Description

Run-time only, read-only. Specifies whether a field in the current record has changed since the last update.

Example

```
{ Determine if the current record has been modified }
if (Table1.State in [dsEdit,dsInsert]) and Table1.Modified then
   Table1.Post;
```

Notes

The Modified property is automatically set to False when the Cancel or Post methods are called.

See Also

TDataset.Cancel, TDataset.Post, TDataset.UpdateRecord

TDataSet.MoveBy Method

Declaration

```
{ DB.PAS }
procedure MoveBy(Distance: Integer);
```

Description

Moves the cursor by a specified number of records. If Distance is positive, the cursor is moved forward; if negative, backward; if zero, the cursor is not moved.

Example

```
{ Sample one out of every ten records }
Table1.First;
CancelCount := 0;
while not Table1.EOF do
begin
    if Table1CANCELLED.Value = True then
        inc(CancelCount)
    else
        Table1.MoveBy(10);
end;
```

Notes

If the data set is in Edit or Insert mode, an implicit Post will be done prior to moving the cursor.

See Also

TDataset.First, TDataset.Last, TDataset.Next, TDataset.Prior

TDataSet.Next Method

Declaration

```
{ DB.PAS }
procedure Next;
```

Description

Moves the cursor to the next record in the data set.

Example

```
{ Iterate through all of the records in the data set }
Table1.First;
while not Table1.EOF do
   Table1.Next;
```

Notes

An implicit Post is done prior to moving the cursor if the data set is in Edit or Insert mode when Next is called.

See Also

TDataset.First, TDataset.Last, TDataset.MoveBy, TDataset.Prior

TDataSet.OnCalcFields Event

Declaration

```
{ DB.PAS }
property OnCalcFields: TDataSetNotifyEvent read FOnCalcFields
     write FOnCalcFields;

TDataSetNotifyEvent = procedure(DataSet: TDataSet) of object;
```

Description

Activated when a record is read from the database and when a field is modified (if the AutoCalcFields flag is True). When the OnCalcFields event is activated, the data set is placed into CalcFields state, in which no noncalculated field modifications are allowed. The data set is returned to its previous state after the procedure assigned to the OnCalcFields event handler returns.

Example

```
{ Initialize a calculated field from a lookup table }
procedure TForm1.OrdersTableCalcFields(DataSet: TDataset);
begin
   { Look up the part record in the Parts table }
   PartsTable.SetKey;
   PartsTablePARTNUM.Value := OrdersTablePARTNUM.Value;
   PartsTable.GotoKey;

   { Stored the part description in the calculated field }
   OrdersTablePARTDESC.Value := PartsTableDESC.Value;
end;
```

58

Notes

Do not attempt to update the data set (with a Post operation, for example) within the OnCalcFields event handler, as it could lead to recursion if the AutoCalcFields property is True. Also, calculated fields cannot be modified outside of the OnCalcFields event handler.

See Also

TDataset.AutoCalcFields

TDataSet.OnNewRecord Event

Declaration

```
{ DB.PAS }
property OnNewRecord: TDataSetNotifyEvent read FOnNewRecord
    write FOnNewRecord;

TDataSetNotifyEvent = procedure(DataSet: TDataSet) of object;
```

Description

Activated when a new record is added to the data set, between the BeforeInsert and AfterInsert events. Within an OnNewRecord event handler, field values may be initialized without setting the Modified value to True.

Example

```
{ Initialize field values for a new record using OnNewRecord }
procedure TForm1.Table1NewRecord(DataSet: TDataset);
begin
   { Setting these fields does NOT cause Modified to be True! }
   Table1CITY.Value := 'San Diego';
    Table1STATE.Value := 'CA';
end;
```

Notes

Changes made to the record after the OnNewRecord event handler executes will cause Modified to be True.

See Also

TDataset.AfterInsert, TDataset.BeforeInsert, TDataset.Modified

TDataSet.Open Method

Declaration

```
{ DB.PAS }
procedure Open;
```

Description

Opens the data set.

Example

```
{ One way to open a data set }
Table1.Open;

{ Here is another... }
Table1.Active := True;
```

Notes

Opening a data set with Open has the same effect as setting the Active property to True.

See Also

TDataset.Active, TDataset.Close

TDATASET.POST METHOD

Declaration

```
{ DB.PAS }
procedure Post;
```

Description

Writes the current record to the data set.

Example

```
{ Post the record if any changes are pending }
if (Table1.State in [dsEdit,dsInsert]) and Table1.Modified then
   Table1.Post;
```

Notes

Calling Post when the data set is not in Edit or Insert mode will raise an exception.

See Also

TDataset.Append, TDataset.Edit, TDataset.Insert

TDATASET.PRIOR METHOD

Declaration

```
{ DB.PAS }
procedure Prior;
```

Description

Moves the cursor to the previous record.

Example

```
{ Move to the previous record }
Table1.Prior;

{ Here's another way... }
Table1.MoveBy(-1);
```

Notes

If the data set is on the first record in the active range, the BOF property is set to True and the cursor is not moved.

See Also

TDataset.First, TDataset.Last, TDataset.MoveBy, TDataset.Next

TDataSet.RecordCount Property

Declaration

```
{ DB.PAS }
property RecordCount: Longint read GetRecordCount;
```

Description

Run-time only, read-only. Specifies the number of records in the data set. The RecordCount value may vary from the number of records in the currently active range. dBase tables, for example, always return the total number of records in the data file, regardless of any range settings that may be in effect.

Example

```
{ Determine the total number of records in the data set }
if Query1.RecordCount > 1000000000 then
   ShowMessage('Over a billion served!!');
```

Notes

The number of records returned may include deleted records, depending on the table type.

See Also

TDataset.SetRange

TDataSet.Refresh Method

Declaration

```
{ DB.PAS }
procedure Refresh;
```

Description

Rereads all records from the data set.

Example

```
{ Insure the query is up to date }
Query1.Refresh;
```

Notes

The Refresh method is also called from the Refresh button on the TDBNavigator.

See Also

TDataset.UpdateRecord

TDataSet.SetFields Method

Declaration

```
{ DB.PAS }
procedure SetFields(const Values: array of const);
```

Description

Assigns specified values to the fields in a data set based on the physical order of the fields. Each element of Values corresponds to the field in that position in the data set. If the number of fields exceeds the number of elements in Values, the remaining fields are unchanged. To leave a given field unchanged, use the NULL keyword, or use the NIL keyword to set the field to its default value.

Example

```
{ Write an entire record at once for a record with fields in the order
  FIRSTNAME, LASTNAME, ADDRESS1, ADDRESS2, CITY, STATE, ZIP, PHONE, EMAIL.
  Note the use of the nil and NULL keywords for unused fields. }
CustTable.Edit;
CustTable.SetFields(['Doe','John','1234 Main Street', NULL,
    'Anytown','AZ','12345','555-1234',nil]);
CustTable.Post;
```

Notes

An exception will be generated if the data set is not in Edit mode prior to calling SetFields.

See Also

TDataset.Fields

TDataSet.State Property

Declaration

```
{ DB.PAS }
property State: TDataSetState read FState;

TDataSetState = (dsInactive, dsBrowse, dsEdit, dsInsert,
    dsSetKey, dsCalcFields);
```

Description

Specifies the current state of the DataSet. A DataSet is always in one of several states, depending on what action is being performed on the DataSet at a given moment. The possible values for TDataSetState are shown in Table 2.5.

TABLE 2.5 TDATASETSTATE CONSTANTS

TDATASETSTATE CONSTANT	DESCRIPTION
dsBrowse	Normal idle state when data set is open.
dsCalcFields	The OnCalcFields event handler is activated.
dsEdit	The data set is in Edit mode, where records may be modified.
dsInactive	The data set is closed.
dsInsert	The data set is in Insert mode, where a new record may be added.
dsSetKey	The data set is in Search mode.

When in a specific mode, calling certain methods will change the DataSet state as appropriate. Calling the Insert method, for example, puts the DataSet into Insert mode. From Insert mode, a successful Post operation will return the data set to Browse mode, and so on. The CalcField state is entered whenever the values for calculated fields need to be recalculated (i.e., when in the OnCalcFields event handler). Figure 2.2 illustrates how this interaction takes place.

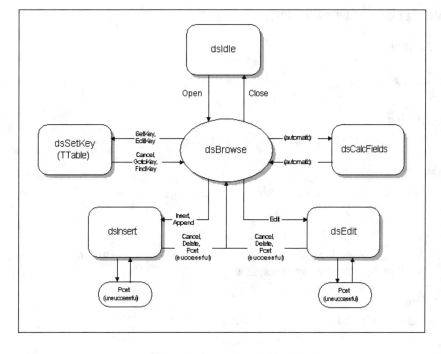

FIGURE 2.2 DATASET STATES.

Example

```
{ Post a record only when in Edit or Insert mode, as an exception will be
  generated if the data set is in any other mode when Post is called }
if Table1.State in [dsEdit,dsInsert] then
   Table1.Post;
```

Notes

The State diagram is also shown in **DELPHI.HLP**.

See Also

TDataset.Append, TDataset.Edit, TDataset.EditKey, TDataset.Insert, TDataset.SetKey

TDataSet.UpdateCursorPos Method

Declaration

```
{ DB.PAS }
procedure UpdateCursorPos;
```

Description

Sets the BDE cursor to the position of the data set's cursor.

Example

```
{ Synchronize the BDE cursor with the data set's cursor }
Query1.UpdateCursorPos;
```

Notes

The UpdateCursorPos method is useful if you make direct calls to the BDE functions. See the BDE Function Reference for more information.

See Also

TDataset.CursorPosChanged

TDataSet.UpdateRecord Method

Declaration

```
{ DB.PAS }
procedure UpdateRecord;
```

Description

Causes DataSource to update fields in the data set with values in the data-aware controls.

Example

```
{ Ensure field values are the same as those in all data-aware controls
  attached (through DataSources) to the data set }
Table1.UpdateRecord;
```

Notes

Calling UpdateRecord does not Post the data to the data set, it simply notifies each DataSource attached to the data set to update the data set with the values currently in the data-aware controls attached to those DataSource components.

See Also

TDataset.Refresh

TDBDataset Component

Unit

DB

Inherits from

TDataset

Description

TDBDataset is an abstract class that inherits all the functionality of the TDataSet class and defines several additional properties designed to interface with databases. These properties are common to all the data set components (TTable, TQuery, and TStoredProc). Table 2.6 summarizes those properties:

TABLE 2.6 TDBDATASET PROPERTIES

PROPERTY	DATA TYPE	RUN-TIME ONLY	READ-ONLY	DESCRIPTION
Database	TDatabase	Yes	Yes	Specifies the database component that the DataSet is attached to.
DatabaseName	TFilename	No	No	Specifies the name of the database that the DataSet is attached to.
DBHandle	hDBIDb	Yes	Yes	Provides a handle to the database for use with BDE API function calls.
DBLocale	Pointer	Yes	Yes	Specifies the language driver used by the BDE.

See Also

TDataset, TQuery, TTable, TStoredProc

TDBDATASET.DATABASE PROPERTY

Applies to

TTable and TQuery components

Declaration

```
{ DB.PAS }
property Database: TDatabase read FDatabase;
```

Description

Run-time only, read-only. Specifies the database component to which the DataSet is attached.

Example

```
{ Assign a database component to a data set }
Query1.Database := Database1;
```

Notes

If a TDatabase component is not created at design-time, a temporary database component will be created for the application at run-time.

See Also

TDBDataset.DatabaseName

TDBDataSet.DatabaseName Property

Declaration

```
{ DB.PAS }
property DatabaseName: TFileName read FDatabaseName
    write SetDatabaseName;
```

Description

Specifies the name of the database to which the DataSet is attached. The DatabaseName property can contain any of the following values:

- A valid BDE alias
- A valid directory path that contains the database files
- A directory path and file name for a Local InterBase Server database
- An application-specific alias defined by a TDatabase component

Example

```
{ Assign a new database name to a table at run-time }
Table1.Close;
Table1.DatabaseName := 'C:\DATA';
Table1.Open;
```

Notes

An exception is generated if the DataSet is active when an attempt is made to assign a value to the DatabaseName property.

See Also

TDBDataset.Database

TDBDataSet.DBHandle Property

Declaration

```
{ DB.PAS }
property DBHandle: hDBIDb read GetDBHandle;
```

Description

Run-time only, read-only. Provides a handle to the database for use with BDE API function calls.

Example

```
{ Close a database }
DbiCloseDatabase(Database1.Handle);
```

Notes

The DBHandle property is normally used only when calling the BDE functions directly. See the BDE Function Reference for more information.

See Also

TDataset.Handle, BDE Function Reference

TDBDataSet.DBLocale Property

Applies to

TTable, TQuery, and TStoredProc components

Declaration

```
{ DB.PAS }
property DBLocale: TLocale read GetDBLocale;
```

Description

Run-time only, read-only. Specifies the language driver used by the BDE.

Notes

The DBLocale property is normally used only when calling the BDE functions directly. See the BDE Function Reference for more information.

See Also

BDE Function Reference

TDataSource Component

Unit

DB

Inherits from

TComponent

Description

The DataSource component establishes a connection between one or more Data Control (data-aware) components and either a TTable or TQuery component. Data Control components connect to a DataSource through their DataSource properties, and a DataSource connects to a Table or Query through its DataSet property. A simple example of this connection is shown in Figure 2.3.

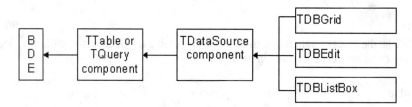

FIGURE 2.3 TYPICAL DATA ACCESS CONNECTIONS.

The following tables summarize the properties (Table 2.7), methods (Table 2.8), and events (Table 2.9) defined by the TDataSource component.

TABLE 2.7 TDATASOURCE PROPERTIES

PROPERTY	DATA TYPE	RUN-TIME ONLY	READ-ONLY	DESCRIPTION
AutoEdit	Boolean	No	No	Determines if the DataSet is automatically placed in dsEdit mode when a user types values in a data-aware control.
DataSet	TDataset	No	No	Specifies the DataSet (TTable or TQuery) from which the TDataSource retrieves its data.
Enabled	Boolean	No	No	Specifies whether data-aware controls are updated when the record in the DataSet is changed.
State	TDatasetState	Yes	Yes	Specifies the state of the DataSet.

TABLE 2.8 T<small>DATA</small>S<small>OURCE</small> M<small>ETHODS</small>

METHOD	DESCRIPTION
Edit	Calls the DataSet's Edit method.

TABLE 2.9 T<small>DATA</small>S<small>OURCE</small> E<small>VENTS</small>

EVENT	DATA TYPE	DESCRIPTION
OnDataChange	TDataChangeEvent	Activated when State is no longer in dsInactive mode.
OnStateChange	TNotifyEvent	Activated when the State property changes.
OnUpdateData	TNotifyEvent	Activated when the current record is about to be updated.

See Also

TQuery, TTable

TDATASOURCE.AUTOEDIT PROPERTY

Declaration

```
{ DB.PAS }
property AutoEdit: Boolean read FAutoEdit write FAutoEdit
    default True;
```

Description

Determines if the data set is automatically placed into Edit mode when a user types values into a data-aware control.

Example

```
{ If not in AutoEdit mode, the data-aware controls will not be editable
  unless an explicit call to Edit is made }
if DataSource1.AutoEdit = False then
    DataSource1.Dataset.Edit;
```

Notes

Data-aware controls are not editable if AutoEdit is False until an explicit call to Edit is made, as shown in the preceding example.

See Also

TDataset.Edit

TDataSource.DataSet Property

Declaration

```
{ DB.PAS }
property DataSet: TDataSet read FDataSet write SetDataSet;
```

Description

Specifies the data set (TTable or TQuery) that the TDataSource uses to retrieve its data.

Example

```
{ Set the DataSource to a table on the main form from within the sub-form's
  OnCreate event handler }
procedure TForm1.FormCreate(Sender: TObject);
begin
   DataSource1.DataSet := MainForm.CustTable;
end;
```

Notes

The DataSet property can be reset at run-time to switch data-aware controls between multiple DataSets or to connect to a DataSet that is on another form, as shown in the preceding example.

See Also

TTable, TQuery, TStoredProc

TDataSource.Edit Method

Declaration

```
{ DB.PAS }
procedure Edit;
```

Description

Calls the data set's Edit method if AutoEdit is True and State is dsBrowse.

Example

```
{ For this setup... }
DataSource1.Dataset := Table1;

{ This works... }
DataSource1.Edit;

{ ... and so does this }
Table1.Edit;
```

Notes

If the DataSet property is not assigned when Edit is called, an exception is generated.

See Also

TDataSet.Edit

TDATASOURCE.ENABLED PROPERTY

Declaration

```
{ DB.PAS }
property Enabled: Boolean read FEnabled write SetEnabled
    default True;
```

Description

Specifies whether data-aware controls are updated when the record in the data set is changed.

Example

```
{ Prevent the data-aware controls from being updated }
DataSource1.Enabled := False;

{ Locate a record... }
Table1.First;
while Table1CUSTID.Value <> 123 and not Table1.EOF do
   Table1.Next;

{ Enable the data-aware controls again }
DataSource1.Enabled := True;
```

Notes

Setting the Enabled property to False clears any data currently in the data-aware controls. Use DisableControls and EnableControls to perform the same operation while retaining any text currently in the data-aware controls.

See Also

TDataSet.EnableControls, TDataSet.DisableControls

TDATASOURCE.ONDATACHANGE EVENT

Declaration

```
{ DB.PAS }
property OnDataChange: TDataChangeEvent read FOnDataChange
    write FOnDataChange;
```

```
TDataChangeEvent = procedure(Sender: TObject; Field: TField)
    of object;
```

Description

Activated when State is no longer in dsInactive mode or when a data-aware control notifies the DataSource that something has changed. Notification occurs, and the OnDataChange event is activated, when the following items have changed due to field modifications or record pointer movement:

- A Field component (i.e., TStringField, TFloatField, etc.)
- The current record in this DataSet
- The database component for this DataSet
- Contents of any data-aware controls
- Layout (e.g., columns moved in a DBGrid component)

Example

```
{ Do-nothing event handler that indicates a change has occurred }
procedure TForm1.DataSource1DataChange(Sender: TObject;
    Field: TField);
begin
  if Field <> nil then
     ShowMessage('Something has changed for field ' +
     Field.DisplayName)
  else
     ShowMessage('Something has changed all fields');
end;
```

Notes

The Field parameter will contain the field that was involved in the change for single-field operations, otherwise it will contain NIL.

See Also

TDataSource.OnStateChange, TDataSource.State

TDATASOURCE.ONSTATECHANGE EVENT

Declaration

```
{ DB.PAS }
property OnStateChange: TNotifyEvent read FOnStateChange
    write FOnStateChange;

TNotifyEvent = procedure(Sender: TObject) of object;
```

Description

Activated when the State property changes (e.g., from dsBrowse to dsInsert).

Example

```
{ Enable and disable buttons based on State changes }
procedure TForm1.DataSource1StateChange(Sender: TObject);
begin
   OkButton.Enabled := (DataSource1.State in [dsEdit,dsInsert]);
   CancelButton.Enabled := (DataSource1.State in [dsEdit, dsInsert]);
   EditButton.Enabled := (DataSource1.State = dsBrowse);
   ...
end;
```

Notes

It is important to check the value of DataSet prior to performing operations that involve the DataSet, as the OnStateChange event can occur even for NIL DataSets.

See Also

TDataSource.OnDataChange, TDataSource.State

TDataSource.OnUpdateData Event

Declaration

```
{ DB.PAS }
property OnUpdateData: TNotifyEvent read FOnUpdateData
     write FOnUpdateData;

TNotifyEvent = procedure(Sender: TObject) of object;
```

Description

Activated on a call to Post or UpdateRecords when the current record is about to be updated.

Example

```
{ Keep track of the number of modifications made for this session }
const
   ModCount: Longint = 0;

...

procedure TForm1.DataSource1UpdateData(Sender: TObject);
begin
   Inc(ModCount);
end;
```

Notes

The OnUpdateData event notifies all data-aware controls to give them the opportunity to update their associated fields.

See Also

TDataset.BeforePost, TDataSource.OnDataChange

TDATASOURCE.STATE PROPERTY

Declaration

```
{ DB.PAS }
property State: TDataSetState read FState;
```

Description

Run-time only, read-only. Specifies the state of the data set. The TDataSource.State property reflects the values of the State property for the current data set, with the exception that if Enabled is False or the DataSet property has not been assigned a value, State will be dsInactive. See TDataSet.State for a complete description of the State property.

Example

```
{ Set a button based on the DataSource (Dataset) state }
if DataSource1.Enabled and DataSource1.DataSet <> nil then
   CancelButton.Enabled := DataSource1.State in [dsEdit,dsInsert];
```

Notes

The State property can be queried either at the DataSource or the DataSet (Table, Query, or StoredProc) component in most cases.

See Also

TDataSource.OnStateChange

TTABLE COMPONENT

Unit

DBTABLES

Inherits from

TDBDataset

Description

The TTable component establishes a connection between a TDataSource and a database engine (either the BDE or an SQL server). TTable defines the interface to a table in a database, including which fields are available (via the TDBDataSet.Fields property) and how the table is accessed.

TTable inherits much of its functionality directly from TDBDataSet (and ultimately from TDataSet) and defines additional properties and methods designed specifically to manage tables. The following tables summarize the properties (Table 2.10) and methods (Table 2.11) defined by the TTable component.

TABLE 2.10 TTABLE PROPERTIES

PROPERTY	DATA TYPE	RUN-TIME ONLY	READ-ONLY	DESCRIPTION
Exclusive	Boolean	No	No	Specifies whether to open the table exclusively.
IndexDefs	TIndexDefs	Yes	Yes	Contains information about all the indexes in the table.
IndexFieldCount	Integer	Yes	Yes	Contains the number of actual fields referenced by the current index.
IndexFieldNames	String	No	No	Specifies which fields to use as an index for the table.
IndexFields	TField	Yes	Yes	Contains information about each of the fields used in the current index for the table.
IndexName	String	No	No	Specifies the name of the current (active) index.
KeyExclusive	Boolean	Yes	No	Specifies whether to exclude matching records from a range or search operation.
KeyFieldCount	Integer	Yes	No	Limits the number of key fields to use for search operations using the current index.
MasterFields	String	No	No	Specifies the field(s) used to link a detail and master table in a master-detail relationship.
MasterSource	TDataSource	No	No	Specifies the master table's DataSource for a detail table in a master-detail relationship.
ReadOnly	Boolean	No	No	Specifies whether a table is opened for read operations only.
TableName	TFileName	No	No	Specifies the table that TTable component is attached to.
TableType	TTableType	No	No	Specifies the type of Table (Default, ASCII, dBase, or Paradox).
UpdateMode	TUpdateMode	No	No	Determines how records will be located when performing updates.

TABLE 2.11 TTABLE METHODS

METHOD	DESCRIPTION
AddIndex	Creates a new index for the table.
ApplyRange	Applies a range specified by SetRangeStart and SetRangeEnd.
BatchMove	Performs a batch operation using Table as the Destination.
CancelRange	Cancels a range set by ApplyRange.
Create	Creates a new instance of a TTable object.
CreateTable	Creates a new table.
DeleteIndex	Deletes a specified index.
DeleteTable	Deletes a specified table.
EditKey	Allows modification of search buffers without clearing them first.
EditRangeEnd	Allows modification of range ending value without clearing it first.
EditRangeStart	Allows modification of range starting value without clearing it first.
EmptyTable	Deletes all records in TableName.
FindKey	Performs an exact field-order search using the current Index.
FindNearest	Performs an inexact field-order search using the current Index.
GetIndexNames	Stores the names of the indexes for TableName in a specified TStrings object.
GotoCurrent	Synchronizes the cursor positions of two tables in the same database.
GotoKey	Performs an exact indexed search using the current values of the search buffers.
GotoNearest	Performs an inexact indexed search using the current values of the search buffers.
SetKey	Allows modification of search buffers after clearing them.
SetRange	Applies a specified range filter.
SetRangeEnd	Sets the starting value for a range filter.
SetRangeStart	Sets the ending value for a range filter.

See Also

TDatabase, TDataSet, TDBDataSet, TQuery, TStoredProc

TTABLE.ADDINDEX METHOD

Declaration

```
{ DBTABLES.PAS }
procedure AddIndex(const Name, Fields: String;
    Options: TIndexOptions);

TIndexOptions = set of (ixPrimary, ixUnique, ixDescending,
    ixCaseInsensitive, ixExpression);
```

Description

Creates a new index for the table. Name is the index (or tag) name, Fields is a semicolon separated list of fields to include in the index, and Options is a set of TIndexOptions values for creation of the index. The possible values for the constants in TIndexOptions are listed in Table 2.12.

TABLE 2.12 TINDEXOPTION CONSTANTS

TINDEXOPTION CONSTANT	DESCRIPTION
ixPrimary	Creates a primary index (Paradox).
IxUnique	Creates an index where only unique values are stored for the key field.
IxDescending	Creates an index in descending order
ixCaseInsensitive	Creates a case-insensitive index (not valid for dBase tables).
IxExpression	Creates a dBase expression index.

Example

```
{ Create a simple index }
Table1.AddIndex('LASTNAME', 'LASTNAME;FIRSTNAME', []);

{ Creates a primary index for a Paradox table }
Table1.AddIndex('CUSTID', 'CUSTID', [ixPrimary, ixUnique]);

{ Create a descending index }
Table1.AddIndex('BALANCE', 'BALANCE', [ixDescending]);

{ Create an index that is unique, case-insensitive, and descending }
Table1.AddIndex('ACCTNUM', 'ACCTNUM',
    [ixUnique, ixCaseInsensitive, ixDescending]);

{ Create a dBase expression index }
Table1.AddIndex('NAME','upper(LAST_NAME + FIRST_NAME)',
    [ixExpression]);
```

Notes

Creating an index for a dBASE table with the ixCaseInsensitive option will generate an exception. An exception will also be generated if the table is not opened exclusively when the AddIndex method is called.

The declaration for the TIndexOptions type in the Delphi documentation differs from the actual declaration in the VCL source code. The ixExpression TIndexOption constant is not documented in Delphi, and the ixNonMaintained constant does not appear in the declaration.

Expression indexes have certain limitations within Delphi. For example, the list of indexes that is displayed in a TTable's IndexFieldNames property does not include indexes that are created as expression indexes, and not all table operations (FindKey and SetKey) recognize expression indexes.

See Also

TTable.DeleteIndex, TTable.IndexDefs, TTable.IndexName

TTABLE.APPLYRANGE METHOD

Declaration

```
{ DBTABLES.PAS }
procedure ApplyRange;
```

Description

Applies a range specified by SetRangeStart and SetRangeEnd.

Example

```
{ Set a range of records limited to the state of California }
Table1.IndexName := 'STATE';

{ Set starting value for the range }
Table1.SetRangeStart;
Table1STATE.Value := 'CA';

{ Set the ending value for the range }
Table1.SetRangeEnd;
Table1STATE.Value := 'CA';

{ Finally, apply the settings to establish the range }
Table1.ApplyRange;
```

Notes

A range is effective only if the active index is on the key field used in the range.

See Also

TTable.CancelRange, TTable.KeyExclusive, TTable.SetRange, TTable.SetRangeEnd, TTable.SetRangeStart

TTABLE.BATCHMOVE METHOD

Declaration

```
{ DBTABLES.PAS }
function BatchMove(ASource: TDataSet; AMode: TBatchMode): Longint;

TBatchMode = (batAppend, batUpdate, batAppendUpdate,
     batDelete, batCopy);
```

Description

Performs a batch operation using Table as the Destination. The ASource parameter is the data set that contains the source records for the batch operation. The possible values for the AMode parameter are listed in Table 2.30.

Example

```
{ This example appends the contents of TempTable into SalesTable }
SalesTable.BatchMove(TempTable, batAppend);
```

Notes

See the TBatchMove component listing for a complete description of batch move operations.

See Also

TBatchMove

TTABLE.CANCELRANGE METHOD

Declaration

```
{ DBTABLES.PAS }
procedure CancelRange;
```

Description

Cancels a range set by ApplyRange or SetRange.

Example

```
{ Cancel the current range to view all records in table }
Table1.CancelRange;
```

Notes

No exception is generated if no range is currently in effect when the CancelRange method is called.

See Also

TTable.ApplyRange, TTable.EditRange, TTable.SetRange

TTABLE.CREATE METHOD

Declaration

```
{ DBTABLES.PAS }
constructor Create(AOwner: TComponent); override;
```

Description

Creates a new instance of a TTable object at run-time.

Example

```
{ Create a new TTable object at run-time to open an existing table }
Table1 := TTable.Create(Self);
Table1.DatabaseName := 'DBDEMOS';
Table1.TableName := 'BIOLIFE.DB';
Table1.Open;
```

Notes

The parameter Self in the preceding example would normally refer to the form that will own the newly created TTable object. An exception will be generated if you attempt to open the table before assigning valid values to the DatabaseName and TableName properties.

See Also

TTable.CreateTable

TTABLE.CREATETABLE METHOD

Declaration

```
{ DBTABLES.PAS }
procedure CreateTable;
```

Description

Creates a new table.

Example

```
{ Restructure an existing table }
Table1.DatabaseName := 'C:\DATA';
Table1.TableName := 'TEMP';
Table1.TableType := ttDBase;

{ Field definitions must be set }
with Table1.FieldDefs do
begin
   Clear;
   Add('Field1', ftInteger, 0);
   Add('Field2', ftString, 10);
end;

{ Index definitions, if any, must be set }
with Table1.IndexDefs do
```

```
begin
   Clear;
   Add('Field1', 'Field1', [ixUnique]);
end;
```

```
{ Create the newly specified table }
Table1.CreateTable;
```

Notes

Creating a table overwrites any tables of the same name in the specified database. For numeric values, passing any value other than zero for the field length will generate an exception. Note that there is also no way, via the CreateTable method, to specify the decimal value for a numeric field. See ISQL's CREATETABLE command or Appendix F of this book (File Formats) for table creation routines that support specifying decimal precision.

See Also

TTable.DeleteTable, TTable.Create

TTABLE.DELETEINDEX METHOD

Declaration

```
{ DBTABLES.PAS }
procedure DeleteIndex(const Name: String);
```

Description

Deletes a specified index.

Example

```
{ Remove a temporary index }
Table1.Exclusive := True;
Table1.Open;
if Table1.Active then
   Table1.DeleteIndex('TMPINDEX');
```

Notes

Table must be opened exclusively or an exception will be generated when the call to DeleteIndex is made.

See Also

TTable.AddIndex

TTABLE.DELETETABLE METHOD

Declaration

```
{ DBTABLES.PAS }
procedure DeleteTable;
```

Description

Deletes a specified table.

Example

```
{ Delete a temporary table }
Table1.Close;
Table1.DeleteTable;
```

Notes

The table must be closed prior to calling the DeleteTable method, or an exception will be generated.

See Also

TTable.CreateTable

TTABLE.EDITKEY METHOD

Declaration

```
{ DBTABLES.PAS }
procedure EditKey;
```

Description

Allows modification of search buffers without clearing them first.

Example

```
{ Perform a SetKey operation }
Table1.SetKey;
Table1FIRSTNAME.Value := 'Donald';
Table1LASTNAME.Value := 'Duck';
Table1ADDRESS.Value := 'DisneyLand';
Table1.GotoKey;

{ Perform the same search using a different value for one of the search
  parameters }
Table1.EditKey;
Table1FIRSTNAME.Value := 'Daisy';
Table1.GotoKey;
```

Notes

The search buffers remain intact until another call to SetKey is made or until they are explicitly cleared or changed using EditKey or until the table is closed.

See Also

TTable.SetKey

TTABLE.EDITRANGEEND METHOD

Declaration

```
{ DBTABLES.PAS }
procedure EditRangeEnd;
```

Description

Allows modification of range ending value without clearing it first.

Example

```
{ Set a range from start of file to 'CA' }
Table1.SetRangeEnd;
Table1STATE.Value := 'CA';
Table1.ApplyRange;

{ Edit the ending range based on user input }
Table1.EditRangeEnd;
Table1STATE.Value := Edit1.Text;
Table1.ApplyRange;
```

Notes

The range settings remain in effect until another call to SetRange is made or until they are explicitly cleared or changed using EditRange or until the table is closed.

See Also

TTable.ApplyRange, TTable.EditRange, TTable.EditRangeStart, TTable.SetRange

TTABLE.EDITRANGESTART METHOD

Declaration

```
{ DBTABLES.PAS }
procedure EditRangeStart;
```

Description

Allows modification of range starting value without clearing it first.

Example

```
{ Set a range from 'CA' to end of file }
Table1.SetRangeStart;
Table1STATE.Value := 'CA';
Table1.ApplyRange;

{ Edit the ending range based on user input }
Table1.EditRangeStart;
Table1STATE.Value := Edit1.Text;
Table1.ApplyRange;
```

Notes

The range settings remain in effect until another call to SetRange is made or until they are explicitly cleared or changed using EditRange or until the table is closed.

See Also

TTable.ApplyRange, TTable.EditRange, TTable.EditRangeEnd, TTable.SetRange

TTABLE.EMPTYTABLE METHOD

Declaration

```
{ DBTABLES.PAS }
procedure EmptyTable;
```

Description

Deletes all records in TableName

Example

```
{ ZAP all records from a table }
Table1.Exclusive := True;
Table1.Open;
if Table1.Active then
   Table1.EmptyTable;
```

Notes

Table must be opened exclusively, or an exception will be generated when the EmptyTable method is called.

See Also

TTable.Exclusive

TTABLE.EXCLUSIVE PROPERTY

Declaration

```
{ DBTABLES.PAS }
property Exclusive: Boolean read FExclusive write SetExclusive
    default False;
```

Description

Specifies whether to open the table exclusively.

Example

```
{ Open the table exclusively }
Table1.Close;
Table1.Exclusive := True;
Table1.Open;
```

Notes

The table must be closed prior to setting the Exclusive property or an exception will be generated.

See Also

TTable.Active

TTABLE.FINDKEY METHOD

Declaration

```
{ DBTABLES.PAS }
function FindKey(const KeyValues: Array of const): Boolean;
```

Description

Performs an exact field-order search using the current Index. The KeyValues array must contain a value of the correct data type for the corresponding field in that position in the data set. If the number of elements in KeyValues is less than the number of fields in the data set, the remaining fields are assumed to be NULL.

Example

```
{ Perform an exact search }
Table1.IndexName := 'LASTNAME';
if Table1.FindKey(['SMITH','JOHN',]) then
   { do something with the found record }
else
   ShowMessage('Record not found!');
```

Notes

The FindKey method will return True if the search value was found or False if not. Paradox and dBase tables must be indexed on the key field(s). SQL tables can use any column names specified in the IndexNames property.

See Also

TTable.FindNearest, TTable.GotoKey, TTable.GotoNearest, TTable.SetKey

TTable.FindNearest Method

Declaration

```
{ DBTABLES.PAS }
procedure FindNearest(const KeyValues: Array of const);
```

Description

Performs an inexact field-order search using the current Index.

Example

```
{ Perform an inexact search }
Table1.IndexName := 'LASTNAME';
if Table1.FindNearest(['SMITH','JOHN',]) then
   { do something with the found record }
else
   ShowMessage('Record not found! Will this one do?');
```

Notes

Paradox and dBASE tables must be indexed on the key field(s). SQL tables can use any column names specified in the IndexNames property.

See Also

TTable.FindKey, TTable.GotoKey, TTable.GotoNearest, TTable.SetKey

TTable.GetIndexNames Method

Declaration

```
{ DBTABLES.PAS }
procedure GetIndexNames(List: TStrings);
```

Description

Stores the names of the indexes for TableName in a specified TStrings object.

Example

```
{ Initialize a listbox with the names of the indexes for this table }
Table1.GetIndexNames(Listbox1.Items);
```

Notes

The list of names returned by GetIndexNames is the same drop-down list shown in the Object Inspector for the IndexName property.

See Also

TTable.IndexName

TTABLE.GOTOCURRENT METHOD

Declaration

```
{ DBTABLES.PAS }
procedure GotoCurrent(Table: TTable);
```

Description

Synchronizes the cursor positions of two tables in the same database.

Example

```
{ Move the cursor for Table1 to the same position as Table2 }
Table1.GotoCurrent(Table2);
```

Notes

Both tables must be in the same database, or an exception will be generated.

See Also

TTable.DatabaseName, TTable.TableName

TTABLE.GOTOKEY METHOD

Declaration

```
{ DBTABLES.PAS }
function GotoKey: Boolean;
```

Description

Performs an exact indexed search using the current values of the search buffers.

Example

```
{ Set up the search using SetKey }
Table1.SetKey;
Table1ZIPCODE.Value := '90001';

{ Perform the search - if the exact value is not found, the cursor is
  positioned at EOF }
Table1.GotoKey;
```

Notes

The GotoKey method requires that the search buffers be initialized to the search values prior to calling it. If the field search values are not those of the active index, the search will fail. The GotoKey method returns True if the record is found, False if not.

See Also

TTable.FindKey, TTable.FindNearest, TTable.GotoNearest, TTable.SetKey

TTABLE.GotoNearest Method

Declaration

```
{ DBTABLES.PAS }
procedure GotoNearest;
```

Description

Performs an inexact indexed search using the current values of the search buffers.

Example

```
{ Set up the search using SetKey }
Table1.SetKey;
Table1ZIPCODE.Value := '90001';

{ Perform the search - if an exact match is not found, the cursor is
  positioned at the next record in sequence }
Table1.GotoNearest;
```

Notes

The GotoNearest method requires that the search buffers be initialized to the search values prior to calling it. If the field search values are not those of the active index, the search will fail.

See Also

TTable.FindKey, TTable.FindNearest, TTable.GotoKey, TTable.SetKey

TTable.IndexDefs Property

Declaration

```
{ DBTABLES.PAS }
property IndexDefs: TIndexDefs read FIndexDefs;
```

Description

Run-time only, read-only. Contains information about all of the indexes in the table. The TIndexDefs component has the properties and methods shown in Table 2.13. Each element of the TIndexDefs object is a TIndexDef object, which contains information about a single index in the table. A list of the TIndexDef properties and methods is shown in Table 2.14.

TABLE 2.13 TINDEXDEFS PROPERTIES AND METHODS

INDEXDEF PROPERTY OR METHOD	DESCRIPTION
Add method	Creates a new TIndexDef object and adds it to the Items property.
Assign method	Clears the Items property; then creates a new set of TIndexDef objects in Items.
Clear method	Frees all the items in the Items property.
Count property	Specifies the number of entries in the Items property.
Create method	Creates a new TIndexDefs object for a specified table.
FindIndexForFields method	Locates the TIndexDef object associated with a specified field.
IndexOf method	Returns the position of a specified TIndexDef object in Items.
Items property	Contains a list of TIndexDef objects, one per index.
Update method	Refreshes the Items list with current index information.

TABLE 2.14 TINDEXDEF PROPERTIES AND METHODS

TINDEXDEF PROPERTIES AND METHODS	DESCRIPTION
Create method	Creates a new TIndexDef object.
Expression property	Contains a dBase index expression.
Fields property	A string that contains a list of semicolon-separated field names for the index.
Name property	Name of the index.
Options property	Set of values of type TIndexOptions.

Example

```
{ Refresh index information }
Table1.IndexDefs.Update;
{ Locate the IndexDef object associated with the FIRSTNAME field }
FirstNameIndexDef :=
    Table1.IndexDefs.FindIndexForFields('FIRSTNAME');
```

Notes

In order to ensure that the IndexDefs property contains accurate values, be sure to call its Update method prior to using it as the state of the indexes may differ.

See Also

TTable.GetIndexNames, TTable.IndexName

TTABLE.INDEXFIELDCOUNT PROPERTY

Declaration

```
{ DBTABLES.PAS }
property IndexFieldCount: Integer read GetIndexFieldCount;
```

Description

Run-time only, read-only. Contains the number of actual fields referenced by the current index.

Example

```
{ Display the number of fields referenced by this index }
ShowMessage('There are ' + IntToStr(Table1.IndexFieldCount) +
    ' fields referenced by the current index');
```

Notes

The value of IndexFieldCount is zero if the table is not open and one for a primary index.

See Also

TTable.IndexFieldNames, TTable.IndexFields

TTABLE.INDEXFIELDNAMES PROPERTY

Declaration

```
{ DBTABLES.PAS }
property IndexFieldNames: String read GetIndexFieldNames
    write SetIndexFieldNames;
```

Description

Specifies which fields to use as an index for the table. Multiple field names must be separated by semicolons. The physical position of the fields in the table can be specified by number if desired, rather than by name. For SQL tables, the field names map to existing table columns. For dBASE and Paradox tables, the values in IndexFieldNames will be mapped to existing indexes.

Example

```
{ Set IndexFieldNames to search the LASTNAME and FIRSTNAME fields }
Table1.IndexFieldNames := 'LASTNAME;FIRSTNAME';
```

Notes

If the specified field names cannot be mapped to existing SQL columns or dBASE/Paradox indexes, an exception is generated. The IndexFieldNames and IndexName properties are mutually exclusive—setting one will automatically clear the other.

See Also

TTable.IndexFieldCount, TTable.IndexFields

TTABLE.INDEXFIELDS PROPERTY

Declaration

```
{ DBTABLES.PAS }
property IndexFields[Index: Integer]: TField read GetIndexField
    write SetIndexField;
```

Description

Run-time only, read-only. Contains information about each of the fields used in the current index for the table.

Example

```
{ Another method for returning a list of field names for an index }
for x := 0 to Table1.IndexFieldCount - 1 do
   FieldNameStr := FieldNameStr + Table1.IndexFields[x].FieldName;
```

Notes

Information contained in IndexFields is not valid if the table is not open.

See Also

TTable.IndexFieldCount, TTable.IndexFieldNames

TTABLE.INDEXNAME PROPERTY

Declaration

```
{ DBTABLES.PAS }
property IndexName: string read GetIndexName write SetIndexName;
```

Description

Specifies the name of the current (active) index.

Example

```
{ Switch indexes at run-time }
var
    CurrIndex: String;
begin
    CurrIndex := Table1.IndexName;
    Table1.IndexName := 'ACCTNUM';
    Table1.FindKey([12345]);
    { do something useful }
    ...
    Table1.IndexName := CurrIndex;
end;
```

Notes

The IndexName and IndexFieldNames properties are mutually exclusive. Setting one will automatically clear the other.

See Also

TTable.DatabaseName, TTable.TableName

TTABLE.KEYEXCLUSIVE PROPERTY

Declaration

```
{ DBTABLES.PAS }
property KeyExclusive: Boolean read GetKeyExclusive
    write SetKeyExclusive;
```

Description

Run-time only. Specifies whether to exclude matching records from a range or search operation. For ranges, when KeyExclusive is True, the records are included using the formula StartRange <= Value >= EndRange, and when KeyExclusive is False, using the formula StartRange < Value > EndRange. For search operations, when KeyExclusive is True, the cursor will be placed on the next record in sequence after the matching record, if found, and when KeyExclusive is False, the cursor will remain on the matching record, if found.

Example

```
{ Exclude the range boundaries }
Table1.KeyExclusive := True;
```

```
{ This range will exclude the any matching records in the range }
Table1.SetRange(['CA'],['NY']);

{ Set back to False for searching }
Table1.KeyExclusive := False;

{ Search will move cursor to matched record }
Table1.FindKey(['NV']);
```

Notes

The default value of KeyExclusive is True.

See Also

TTable.FindKey, TTable.GotoKey, TTable.KeyFieldCount, TTable.SetRange

TTABLE.KEYFIELDCOUNT PROPERTY

Declaration

```
{ DBTABLES.PAS }
property KeyFieldCount: Integer read GetKeyFieldCount
    write SetKeyFieldCount;
```

Description

Run-time only. Limits the number of key fields to use for search operations using the current index.

Example

```
{ The current index references three fields }
Table1.IndexFieldNames := 'CITY;STATE;ZIP';

{ Let's limit that to two }
Table1.KeyFieldCount := 2;

{ This search will use only CITY and STATE }
Table1.FindKey(['San Diego','CA','92121']);
```

Notes

Values for KeyFieldCount greater than one are meaningful only if the current index references more than one field.

See Also

TTable.IndexFieldNames, TTable.IndexFields

TTable.MasterFields Property

Applies to

TTable component

Declaration

```
{ DBTABLES.PAS }
property MasterFields: String read GetMasterFields
    write SetMasterFields;
```

Description

Specifies the field(s) used to link a detail and master table in a master-detail relationship. Multiple fields must be separated with semicolons. Once established, a one-to-many relationship exists between the master table (indicated by the MasterSource property) and the detail table (the current table). When the cursor is moved in the master table, the detail table is restricted to records that match the key field in the master table, as if an active range had been set to that value.

Example

```
{ Set the MasterFields property at run-time }
Table2.MasterFields := 'ORDERNO;ITEMNO';
```

Notes

At design-time, you can use the Field Link Designer to set the MasterFields property after setting the MasterSource property. The MasterFields property is used in conjunction with the MasterSource property. The active index must be for the field specified in the MasterFields property.

See Also

Field Link Designer in **DELPHI.HLP**, TTable.MasterSource

TTable.MasterSource Property

Declaration

```
{ DBTABLES.PAS }
property MasterSource: TDataSource read GetDataSource
    write SetDataSource;
```

Description

Specifies the master table's DataSource for a detail table in a master-detail relationship.

Example

```
{ This example sets a one-to-many relationship between Customer and Orders }
OrdersTable.DataSource := OrdersSource;
CustTable.MasterSource := OrdersSource;
CustTable.MasterFields := 'ORDERNO;ITEMNO';
```

Notes

The MasterSource property is used in conjunction with the MasterFields property.

See Also

TTable.MasterFields

TTABLE.READONLY PROPERTY

Declaration

```
{ DBTABLES.PAS }
property ReadOnly: Boolean read FReadOnly write SetReadOnly
    default False;
```

Description

Specifies whether a table is opened for read operations only.

Example

```
{ Set the table for read-only operations }
Table1.Close;
Table1.ReadOnly := True;
Table1.Open;
```

Notes

An exception will be raised if the table is open when the ReadOnly property is assigned.

See Also

TTable.Exclusive

TTABLE.SETKEY METHOD

Declaration

```
{ DBTABLES.PAS }
procedure SetKey;
```

Description

Allows modification of search buffers after clearing them. SetKey puts the data set into SetKey state, in which values can be assigned to the search buffers that correspond to each field. A subsequent call to a search method (FindKey, GotoKey, etc.) uses those values for the search operation.

Example

```
{ Set up to search for an address }
Table1.SetKey;
Table1ADDRESS.AsString := '8888 Melrose Place';
Table1CITY.AsString := 'Hollywood';
Table1STATE.AsString := 'CA';
Table1.GotoKey;
```

Notes

The values entered into the search buffers remain there until another call to SetKey clears the values, or the values are modified after a call to EditKey.

See Also

TTable.EditKey, TTable.FindKey, TTable.GotoKey

TTABLE.SETRANGE METHOD

Declaration

```
{ DBTABLES.PAS }
procedure SetRange(const StartValues, EndValues: Array of const);
```

Description

Applies a specified range filter. The StartValues parameter contains a list of field values to search for the first value in the range, and the EndValues parameter contains a list of field values to search for the ending value in the range. Each of the parameters contains values that correspond to the position of the index field in the data set and can contain more than one value.

Example

```
{ Show only records in the range 1000 to 2000 }
Table1.SetRange([1000],[2000] );
```

Notes

For dBASE and Paradox fields, indexes must exist for any fields referenced by position. For SQL databases, any field specified in the IndexFieldNames property may be used.

See Also

TTable.ApplyRange, TTable.KeyExclusive, TTable.SetRangeEnd, TTable.SetRangeStart

TTABLE.SETRANGEEND METHOD

Declaration

```
{ DBTABLES.PAS }
procedure SetRangeEnd;
```

Description

Sets the ending value for a range filter.

Example

```
{ Set the range of record from the beginning of the file to 2000 inclusive }
Table1.KeyExclusive := False;
Table1.SetRangeEnd;
Table1CUSTID.Value := 2000;
Table1.ApplyRange;
```

Notes

Range is not active until a call to ApplyRange is made.

See Also

TTable.ApplyRange, TTable.SetRange, TTable.SetRangeStart

TTABLE.SETRANGESTART METHOD

Declaration

```
{ DBTABLES.PAS }
procedure SetRangeStart;
```

Description

Sets the ending value for a range filter.

Example

```
{ Set the range of records from 2000 to the end of the file }
Table1.KeyExclusive := False;
Table1.SetRangeStart;
Table1CUSTID.Value := 2000;
Table1.ApplyRange;
```

Notes

Range is not active until a call to ApplyRange is made.

See Also

TTable.ApplyRange, TTable.SetRange, TTable.SetRangeEnd

TTABLE.TABLENAME PROPERTY

Declaration

```
{ DBTABLES.PAS }
property TableName: TFileName read FTableName write SetTableName;
```

Description

Specifies the name of the table used by the Ttable component.

Example

```
{ Set the table name }
Table1.DatabaseName := 'DBDEMOS';
Table1.TableName := 'CLIENT';
```

Notes

The table must exist in the database specified by the DatabaseName property.

See Also

TTable.DatabaseName

TTABLE.TABLETYPE PROPERTY

Declaration

```
{ DBTABLES.PAS }
property TableType: TTableType read FTableType
    write SetTableType default ttDefault;

TTableType = (ttDefault, ttParadox, ttDBase, ttASCII);
```

Description

Specifies the type of Table (Default, ASCII, dBASE or Paradox).

Example

```
{ Set the table type for Paradox files }
Table1.TableType := ttParadox;
```

Notes

The ttDefault table type will attempt to auto-detect the table type based on the filename extension of the selected table.

See Also

TTable.IsSQLBased

TTABLE.UPDATEMODE PROPERTY

Declaration

```
{ DBTABLES.PAS }
property UpdateMode;
```

Description

Determines how records will be located when performing updates. When a record is posted, the record to update is located using the original values from the record. The UpdateMode property determines how this search is performed. The possible values for UpdateMode are listed in Table 2.15 from the most restrictive mode to the least restrictive.

TABLE 2.15 UPDATEMODE CONSTANTS FOR TTABLE

UPDATEMODE CONSTANT	DESCRIPTION
WhereAll	Every column is used to find the record to update.
WhereChanged	Only key columns and columns that have changed are used to find the record to update.
WhereKeyOnly	Only key columns are used to find the record to update.

Example

```
{ Set to the most restrictive level of checking }
Table1.UpdateMode := WhereAll;
```

Notes

An exception is generated if a record matching the original values cannot be located, based on the UpdateMode.

See Also

TQuery.RequestLive

TQUERY COMPONENT

Unit

DBTABLES

Inherits from

TDBDataset

Description

The TQuery component establishes an SQL connection between a DataSource and either the BDE or an SQL server. TQuery allows your application to issue SQL statements to the connected database engine (either the BDE or an SQL server). The resulting data are then routed to the DataSource for interfacing with data-aware controls.

TQuery can return both editable and read-only result sets. Executing an SQL statement against a table accessed by TQuery is a matter of storing the SQL statement in the SQL property (a TStrings object) and using the Open or ExecSQL methods to run the query. TQuery also supports parameterized queries through the use of the Params property.

TQuery inherits much of its functionality from TDBDataset (and ultimately TDataset). TQuery also defines additional properties and methods to facilitate handling of SQL operations. The following tables summarize the properties (Table 2.16) and methods (Table 2.17) defined by the TQuery component.

TABLE 2.16 TQUERY PROPERTIES

PROPERTY	DATA TYPE	RUN-TIME ONLY	READ-ONLY	DESCRIPTION
DataSource	TDataSource	No	No	Specifies a data set to search for values for unbound SQL parameters.
Local	Boolean	Yes	Yes	Specifies whether the data set is attached to a local (Paradox, dBASE) or nonlocal (SQL server) table.
ParamCount	Word	Yes	Yes	Specifies the number of parameters contained in the Params array.
Params	TParams	No	Yes	Zero-based array of parameters derived from the contents of the SQL property.
Prepared	Boolean	Yes	No	Specifies whether the Prepare method has been called.
RequestLive	Boolean	No	No	If True and the SQL syntax permits it, specifies that a live result set is returned.
SQL	TStrings	No	No	Stores the SQL query statement.
StmtHandle	hDBIStmt	Yes	Yes	Provides a handle to the result of the last query for use with BDE API function calls.
Text	PChar	Yes	Yes	Contains the actual text of the SQL statement as sent to the BDE.

UniDirectional	Boolean	No	No	Specifies whether to return a unidirectional result set.
UpdateMode	TUpdateMode	No	No	Determines how records will be located when performing updates.

TABLE 2.17 TQUERY METHODS

METHOD	DESCRIPTION
ExecSQL	Executes an SQL statement that does not return a result set (INSERT, UPDATE, DELETE, etc.).
ParamByName	Returns a TParam object by the specified name.
Prepare	Sends a parameterized query to the database engine for parsing and optimization.
UnPrepare	Sets the Prepared property to false to ensure that the query will be Prepared again when sent to the server.

See Also

TDataset, TDBDataset, TStoredProc, TTable

TQUERY.DATASOURCE PROPERTY

Applies to

TQuery component

Declaration

```
{ DBTABLES.PAS }
property DataSource: TDataSource read GetDataSource
    write SetDataSource;
```

Description

Run-time only. Specifies a data set from which to retrieve values for unbound SQL parameters. The DataSource property allows a query to be used as the detail table in a master-detail relationship, in much the same way as a two tables would be linked using the MasterSource and MasterFields properties. The DataSource property can be used to supply parameter information directly from the master table for an existing SQL query in the detail query.

In the following example, when the cursor moves in the master table, the EmployeeQuery.SQL statement will be executed using the CompanyTable value from the CUSTID field, which will in turn restrict the records in the query to only those that match the same CUSTID value as is in the master table record.

Example

```
{ Establish an SQL-based Master-Detail relationship - first, set the SQL
  statement in the Query component with a parameter for the key }
EmployeeQuery.SQL.Add('SELECT * FROM COMPANY WHERE CUSTNO = :CustNo');
```

```
{ The datasource connections should look like this }
EmployeeSource.Dataset := EmployeeQuery;
CompanySource.Dataset := CompanyTable;

{ Set the query to point to the master table's datasource }
EmployeeQuery.DataSource := CompanySource;

{ Set up two grids to display the data }
DBGrid1.DataSource := CompanySource;
DBGrid2.DataSource := EmployeeSource;
```

Notes

The name of the parameter must match a field name in the master DataSet.

See Also

TDataset.DataSource, TQuery.Params, TQuery.SQL

TQuery.ExecSQL Method

Declaration

```
{ DBTABLES.PAS }
procedure ExecSQL;
```

Description

Executes an SQL statement that does not return a result set (i.e., INSERT, UPDATE, DELETE, or any DDL statement).

Example

```
{ Specify, then run an SQL statement }
Query1.Close;
Query1.SQL.Clear;
Query1.SQL.Add('DELETE * FROM CUSTOMER WHERE ACCTNUM = 1000');
Query1.ExecSQL;
```

Notes

If the statement returns a result set (e.g., SELECT), use Open instead.

See Also

TQuery.Params, TQuery.SQL

TQuery.Local Property

Declaration

```
{ DBTABLES.PAS }
property Local: Boolean read FLocal;
```

Description

Run-time only, read-only. Specifies whether the data set is attached to a local (Paradox, dBASE) or nonlocal (SQL server) table.

Example

```
{ Display only local table data }
DataSource1.Enabled := Table1.Local;
```

Notes

It is sometimes useful to know whether a table is local or not due to the differences in the way that certain operations are performed on SQL tables rather than local tables.

See Also

TDataSet.DriverName

TQuery.ParamByName Method

Declaration

```
{ DBTABLES.PAS }
function ParamByName(const Value: String): TParam;
```

Description

Returns a TParam object by the specified name.

Example

```
{ Set a value for a specified parameter }
Query1.ParamByName('CUSTNO').AsInteger := 54321;
```

Notes

Using ParamByName is safer than relying on the position of the parameter within the Params list, which could be easily changed.

See Also

TQuery.Params

TQUERY.PARAMCOUNT PROPERTY

Declaration

```
{ DBTABLES.PAS }
property ParamCount: Word read GetParamsCount;
```

Description

Run-time only, read-only. Specifies the number of parameters contained in the Params array.

Example

```
{ Iterate through all available parameters }
for x := 1 to Query1.ParamCount - 1 do
  Listbox1.Add(Query1.Params[x].Name);
```

Notes

The ParamCount property is automatically maintained as parameters are added or removed from the SQL statement.

See Also

TQuery.Params

TQUERY.PARAMS PROPERTY

Declaration

```
{ DBTABLES.PAS }
property Params: TParams read FParams write SetParamsList;
```

Description

Read-only. Zero-based array of parameters derived from the contents of the SQL property.

Example

```
{ Assign parameters in sequence }
Params[0].AsString := 'Smith';          { First column: FIRSTNAME }
Params[1].AsInteger := 33;              { Second column: AGE }
...
```

Notes

Accessing parameters based on their ordinal position in the Params array is not as safe as using the ParamByName method to retrieve the specified TParam object to work with.

See Also

TQuery.ParamCount, TQuery.ParamByName

TQuery.Prepare Method

Declaration

```
{ DBTABLES.PAS }
procedure Prepare;
```

Description

Sends a parameterized query to the database engine for parsing and optimization. Calling the Prepare method is not required, but it can substantially improve performance, depending on the server configuration, for dynamic queries that will run multiple times.

Prepare is called automatically when you use the Parameters Editor to set the parameters at design-time. When finished with the query, the UnPrepare method should be called to release any database resources used by Prepare.

Example

```
{ Prepare a query }
Query1.Close;
Query1.SQL.Clear;
Query1.SQL.Add('SELECT * FROM CUSTOMER WHERE CITY = "San Diego"');
Query1.Prepare;
Query1.Open;
```

Notes

An exception will be generated if you do not Close the query prior to calling Prepare.

See Also

TQuery.Prepared, TQuery.UnPrepare

TQuery.Prepared Property

Declaration

```
{ DBTABLES.PAS }
property Prepared: Boolean read FPrepared write SetPrepare;
```

Description

Run-time only. Specifies whether the Prepare method has been called.

Example

```
{ If not done, do it }
if not Query1.Prepared then
begin
   Query1.Close;
   Query1.Prepare;
end;
```

Notes

The Prepared property can be set to True at design-time to prevent a query from being automatically Prepared, or to False to force a call to Prepare.

See Also

TQuery.Prepare, TQuery.UnPrepare

TQUERY.REQUESTLIVE PROPERTY

Declaration

```
{ DBTABLES.PAS }
property RequestLive: Boolean read FRequestLive
    write FRequestLive default False;
```

Description

If True and the SQL syntax permits it, specifies that a live result set is returned. In general, the syntax requirements for returning a live result set are as follows:

- For local (Paradox, dBASE) tables, the query must involve a single table. In addition, the query must not use any of the following:
  - Aggregate functions (e.g., SUM, AVG)
  - An ORDER BY clause
  - Calculated fields in SELECT
  - A WHERE clause that consists solely of column names compared to scalar constants (LIKE and other comparison operators, combined with AND and OR are allowed)
  - For server tables where the query is using pass-through SQL, the query is valid if it involves a single table and does not use the aggregate functions.

Example

```
{ Request a live result set }
Query1.RequestLive := True;
```

Notes

Certain SQL servers may impose additional requirements in order to return a live result set. If RequestLive is True but the SQL statement does not permit a live result set, the result set is returned as read-only.

See Also

TQuery.UniDirectional

TQUERY.SQL PROPERTY

Declaration

```
{ DBTABLES.PAS }
property SQL: TStrings read FSQL write SetQuery;
```

Description

Stores the SQL query statement as a list of strings.

Example

```
{ Create an SQL statement for a query, the hard way... }
Query1.SQL.Clear;
Query1.SQL.Add('SELECT');
Query1.SQL.Add(' *');
Query1.SQL.Add(' FROM');
Query1.SQL.Add(' VENDORS');
Query1.SQL.Add(' WHERE');
Query1.SQL.Add(' STATE');
Query1.SQL.Add(' =');
Query1.SQL.Add(' "CA"');
Query1.SQL.Add(' ORDER');
Query1.SQL.Add(' BY');
Query1.SQL.Add(' CITY');
```

Notes

Multiple statements in an SQL property are not allowed unless such batch statement processing is supported by the server.

See Also

TQuery.Params

TQUERY.STMTHANDLE PROPERTY

Declaration

```
{ DBTABLES.PAS }
property StmtHandle: hDBIStmt read FStmtHandle;
```

Description

Run-time only, read-only. Provides a handle to the result of the last query for use with Borland Database Engine API function calls.

Example

```
{ Set 'RequestLive' property for the query's result set }
DbiSetProp(DBIObj(Query1.StmtHandle), stmtLIVENESS, Longint(wantLIVE));
```

Notes

The StmtHandle property is normally used only when making calls directly to the BDE functions. See the BDE Function Reference for more information.

See Also

BDE Function Reference

TQUERY.TEXT PROPERTY

Declaration

```
{ DBTABLES.PAS }
property Text: PChar read FText;
```

Description

Run-time only, read-only. Contains the actual text of the SQL statement as sent to the BDE (that is, with parameter information merged).

Example

```
{ Text is a PChar type that can be retrieved from the query }
var
    QueryText: PChar;
```

```
begin
   QueryText := Query1.Text;
   { process QueryText here... }
end;
```

Notes

It may be useful to inspect the Text statement to determine whether the results of your SQL statement are being passed to the server as expected.

See Also

TQuery.SQL

TQUERY.UNIDIRECTIONAL PROPERTY

Declaration

```
{ DBTABLES.PAS }
property UniDirectional: Boolean read FUniDirectional
     write FUniDirectional default False;
```

Description

Specifies whether to return a unidirectional result set, that is, one that can be browsed only in the forward direction.

Example

```
{ Request a unidirectional result set for this query }
Query1.UniDirectional := True;
```

Notes

A unidirectional result set requires less memory, as the records do not have to be cached.

See Also

TQuery.RequestLive

TQUERY.UNPREPARE METHOD

Declaration

```
{ DBTABLES.PAS }
procedure UnPrepare;
```

Description

Sets the Prepared property to false to ensure that the query will be Prepared again when sent to the server.

Example

```
{ UnPrepare in order to prepare for the next query execution }
Query1.UnPrepare;
```

Notes

Calling the UnPrepare method sets the Prepared property to False. Since a Prepare statement consumes some database resources, it is a good idea to call UnPrepare after you are finished using the query.

See Also

TQuery.Prepare, TQuery.Prepared

TQUERY.UPDATEMODE PROPERTY

Declaration

```
{ DBTABLES.PAS }
property UpdateMode;
```

Description

Determines how records will be located when performing updates. When a record is posted, the record to update is located using the original values from the record. The UpdateMode property determines how this search is performed. The possible values for UpdateMode are listed in Table 2.18 from the most restrictive mode to the least restrictive.

TABLE 2.18 UPDATEMODE CONSTANTS

UPDATEMODE CONSTANT	DESCRIPTION
WhereAll	Every column is used to find the record to update.
WhereChanged	Only key columns and columns that have changed are used to find the record to update.
WhereKeyOnly	Only key columns are used to find the record to update.

Example

```
{ Set updates to least restrictive, only if no other users will be updating
  records }
Query1.UpdateMode := WhereKeyOnly;
```

Notes

The UpdateMode property applies only to live result sets.

See Also

TQuery.SQL

TStoredProc Component

Unit

DBTABLES

Inherits from

TDBDataset

Description

The TStoredProc component enables execution of a server stored procedure. The general steps for this process follow:

1. Set the DatabaseName property.
2. Set any input parameters with the Params property or the Parameters Editor.
3. Prepare the stored procedure using the Prepare method or the Parameters Editor.
4. Execute the stored procedure using the ExecProc method.
5. The output parameters will be stored in Params.

TStoredProc inherits much of its functionality from TDBDataset (and ultimately TDataset) and defines additional properties and methods to facilitate the handling of stored procedures. The following tables summarize the properties (Table 2.19) and methods (Table 2.20) defined by the TStoredProc component.

TABLE 2.19 TSTOREDPROC PROPERTIES

PROPERTY	DATA TYPE	RUN-TIME ONLY	READ-ONLY	DESCRIPTION
Overload	Word	No	No	Specifies numerically which overloaded procedure to run on an Oracle server.
ParamBindMode	TParamBindMode	No	No	Specifies whether the Params parameters will be matched to the stored procedure parameters by name or number.
ParamCount	Word	Yes	Yes	Contains the number of parameters defined in the Params property.
Params	TParams	No	No	Array of input and output parameters to be used with the stored procedure.

continued

TABLE 2.19 CONTINUED

PROPERTY	DATA TYPE	RUN-TIME ONLY	READ-ONLY	DESCRIPTION
Prepared	Boolean	Yes	No	Specifies whether the stored procedure has been sent to the server for parsing and optimization.
StmtHandle	hDBIStmt	Yes	Yes	Provides a handle to the last query result for use with BDE API function calls.
StoredProcName	String	No	No	Specifies the name of the stored procedure.

TABLE 2.20 TStoredProc Methods

METHOD	DESCRIPTION
CopyParams	Copies parameter information from one stored procedure to another.
DescriptionsAvailable	Determines whether stored procedure parameter information is available from the server.
ExecProc	Executes the stored procedure.
GetResults	Fetches the output parameters on a Sybase server.
ParamByName	Returns a TParam object specified by name.
Prepare	Sends the stored procedure to the server for parsing and optimization.
UnPrepare	Sets the Prepared flag to False to ensure that the stored procedure will be Prepared when sent to the server.

See Also

TDatabase, TDataset, TDBDataset

TStoredProc.CopyParams Method

Declaration

```
{ DBTABLES.PAS }
procedure CopyParams(Value: TParams);
```

Description

Copies parameter information from a stored procedure to the Value parameter.

Example

```
{ This example saves and restores the current parameters for a stored
  procedure }
var
   OrigParams: TParams;
```

```
begin
   OrigParams := TParams.Create;

   { Save the current parameters for later restoration }
   StoredProc1.CopyParams(Parameters);

   { Modify the parameters here... }
   StoredProc1.Params.Clear;
   ...

   { Perform the operation with the modified parameters }
   StoredProc1.ExecProc;

   { Restore original parameters }
   StoredProc1.Params := Parameters;
   OrigParams.Free;
end;
```

Notes

The CopyParams can be used to copy parameters from one stored procedure to another.

See Also

TStoredProc.Params

TStoredProc.DescriptionsAvailable Method

Declaration

```
{ DBTABLES.PAS }
function DescriptionsAvailable: Boolean;
```

Description

Determines whether stored procedure parameter information is available from the server.

Example

```
{ Determine whether parameter information is available from the server }
if not StoredProc1.DescriptionsAvailable then
   ShowMessage('Parameter information unavailable');
```

Notes

Various servers may require additional information to retrieve the parameter details.

See Also

TStoredProc.Params

TStoredProc.ExecProc Method

Declaration

```
{ DBTABLES.PAS }
procedure ExecProc;
```

Description

Executes the stored procedure.

Example

```
{ Execute the stored procedure using the ExecProc method }
StoredProc1.ExecProc;
```

Notes

Assumes the stored procedure has been property initialized.

See Also

TStoredProc.GetResults

TStoredProc.GetResults Method

Declaration

```
{ DBTABLES.PAS }
procedure GetResults;
```

Description

Fetches the output parameters on a Sybase-stored procedure that returns a result set.

Example

```
{ Fetch the output parameters }
StoredProc1.Open;
...

{ This must be called before attempting to retrieve any parameter information }
StoredProc1.GetResults;

{ Query output parameters }
ShowMessage('Output parameter is ', StoredProc1.ParamByName('Total'));
```

Notes

Applies only to Sybase servers.

See Also

TStoredProc.ExecProc

TStoredProc.Overload Property

Declaration

```
{ DBTABLES.PAS }
property Overload: Word read FOverload write SetOverload default 0;
```

Description

Specifies numerically which overloaded procedure to run on an Oracle server.

Example

```
{ Let's run, oh, the third overloaded procedure... }
StoredProc1.Overload := 3;
StoredProc1.ExecProc;
```

Notes

The default value of zero indicates that there will be no overloading. This property applies only to Oracle servers.

See Also

TStoredProc.Params, TStoredProc.StoredProcName

TStoredProc.ParamBindMode Property

Declaration

```
{ DBTABLES.PAS }
property ParamBindMode: TParamBindMode read FBindMode
    write FBindMode default pbByName;

TParamBindMode = (pbByName, pbByNumber);
```

Description

Specifies whether the Params parameters will be matched to the stored procedure parameters by name or by number.

Example

```
{ Live dangerously, reference parameters by number... }
StoredProc1.ParamBindMode := pbByNumber;
```

Notes

Referencing parameters by number is not as safe as by name, as the relative positions of the individual parameters may be changed.

See Also

TStoredProc.Params

TStoredProc.ParamByName Method

Declaration

```
{ DBTABLES.PAS }
function ParamByName(const Value: String): TParam;
```

Description

Returns a TParam object specified by name.

Example

```
{ Adjust a parameter value }
StoredProc1.ParamByName('Year').AsInteger := 1989;
```

Notes

Referencing a parameter by name is safer than by number, as the relative positions of the parameters may be changed.

See Also

TStoredProc.Params

TStoredProc.ParamCount Property

Declaration

```
{ DBTABLES.PAS }
property ParamCount: Word read GetParamsCount;
```

Description

Contains the number of parameters defined in the Params property.

Example

```
{ List all of the parameters in the Params property }
for x := 1 to StoredProc1.ParamCount - 1 do
   Listbox1.Items.Add(StoredProc1.Params[x].Name + '=' +
      StoredProc1.Params[x].AsString);
```

Notes

The ParamCount property is automatically maintained as you add and remove parameters from the Params property.

See Also

TStoredProc.Params

TSTOREDPROC.PARAMS PROPERTY

Declaration

```
{ DBTABLES.PAS }
property Params: TParams read FParams write SetParamsList;
```

Description

Array of input and output parameters to be used with the stored procedure.

Example

```
{ Create input parameters }
StoredProc1.Params.CreateParam(ftString, 'State',
    ptInput).AsString := 'CA';
StoredProc1.Params.CreateParam(ftInteger,'Rank',
    ptInput).AsInteger := 1;

{ Create output parameters }
StoredProc1.Params.CreateParam(ftInteger, 'Rainfall', ptOutput);
StoredProc1.Open;
```

Notes

The Params array allows access to the TParam objects that it stores. See TParam in **DELPHI.HLP** for additional information.

See Also

TParam in **DELPHI.HLP**, TStoredProc.ParamByName, TStoredProc.ParamCount

TStoredProc.Prepare Method

Declaration

```
{ DBTABLES.PAS }
procedure Prepare;
```

Description

Sends the stored procedure to the server for parsing and optimization.

Example

```
{ Prepare this stored procedure }
if not StoredProc1.Prepared then
    StoredProc1.Prepare;
```

Notes

Prepare sets the Prepared flag to True.

See Also

TStoredProc.Prepared, TStoredProc.UnPrepare

TStoredProc.Prepared Property

Declaration

```
{ DBTABLES.PAS }
property Prepared: Boolean read FPrepared write SetPrepare;
```

Description

Specifies whether the stored procedure has been sent to the server for parsing and optimization.

Example

```
{ Determine whether the stored procedure has been prepared or not }
if not StoredProc1.Prepared then
    { handle it };
```

Notes

The Prepared property is automatically set to True when the Prepare method is called and to False when the UnPrepare method is called.

See Also

TStoredProc.Prepare, TStoredProc.UnPrepare

TStoredProc.StmtHandle Property

Declaration

```
{ DBTABLES.PAS }
property StmtHandle: hDBIStmt read FStmtHandle;
```

Description

Provides a handle to the last query result for use with BDE API function calls.

Example

```
{ Set type of result set table to Paradox for a stored procedure }
DbiSetProp(DBIObj((StoredProc1.StmtHandle), stmtANSTYPE,
Longint(szPARADOX));
```

Notes

The StmtHandle property is normally used only when calling the BDE functions directly. See the BDE Function Reference for more information.

See Also

BDE Function Reference

TStoredProc.StoredProcName Property

Declaration

```
{ DBTABLES.PAS }
property StoredProcName: String read GetProcName write SetProcName;
```

Description

Specifies the name of the stored procedure.

Example

```
{ Determine the name of the stored procedure }
Edit1.Text := StoredProc1.StoredProcName;
```

Notes

An Oracle server allows multiple procedures with the same name. See TStoredProc.Overload for more information.

See Also

TStoredProc.Overload

TStoredProc.UnPrepare Method

Declaration

```
{ DBTABLES.PAS }
procedure UnPrepare;
```

Description

Sets the Prepared flag to False to ensure that the stored procedure will be Prepared when sent to the server.

Example

```
{ Ensure valid preparation }
StoredProc1.UnPrepare;
```

Notes

Calling the UnPrepare method notifies the server to release any resources allocated to the stored procedure.

See Also

TStoredProc.Prepare, TStoredProc.Prepared

TDatabase Component

Unit

DB

Inherits from

TComponent

Description

The TDatabase component establishes a connection to a database. If no TDatabase component is explicitly created for a database that you use in your application, Delphi will create a temporary TDatabase component for that database automatically at run-time.

Creating a TDatabase component in your application gives you a great deal of control over the management of the specified database. For example, you can establish a persistent connection to the database, customize logins, control transactions, and create local BDE aliases. It also provides a single point for access to all the data sets that are in use and a single point for modifying the alias name if necessary.

The following tables summarize the properties (Table 2.21), methods (Table 2.22), and events (Table 2.23) for the TDatabase component.

TABLE 2.21 TDATABASE PROPERTIES

PROPERTY	DATA TYPE	RUN-TIME ONLY	READ-ONLY	DESCRIPTION
AliasName	TSymbolString	No	No	Name of an existing BDE alias.
Connected	Boolean	No	No	Indicates whether a database connection has been established.
DatabaseName	TFilename	No	No	Defines a local, application-specific alias.
DatasetCount	Integer	Yes	Yes	Contains the number of data set components currently attached to the database.
Datasets	TDBDataset	Yes	Yes	Contains a set of pointers to the data set components currently attached to the database.
DriverName	TSymbolString	No	No	Contains a BDE driver name.
Handle	hDBIDb	Yes	Yes	Provides a database handle to be used with BDE API function calls.
IsSQLBased	Boolean	Yes	Yes	True if DriverName is other than STANDARD.
KeepConnection	Boolean	No	No	Specifies whether an application remains connected to the database even when no tables are open.
Locale	Pointer	Yes	Yes	Specifies the BDE language driver used for the database.
LoginPrompt	Boolean	No	No	Specifies whether the standard login dialog box is displayed when the application attempts to connect to the database.
Params	TStrings	No	No	Specifies the parameters required to open an SQL server database.

continued

TABLE 2.21 CONTINUED

PROPERTY	DATA TYPE	RUN-TIME ONLY	READ-ONLY	DESCRIPTION
Temporary	Boolean	Yes	No	True if the TDatabase component was created dynamically at run-time by Delphi, rather than at design-time.
TransIsolation	TTransIsolation	No	No	Specifies the transaction isolation level used by an SQL server.

TABLE 2.22 TDATABASE METHODS

METHOD	DESCRIPTION
Close	Closes the TDatabase and all associated data set components.
CloseDatasets	Closes the data sets associated to TDatabase without closing the database.
Commit	Commits the current transactions.
Open	Connects the TDatabase to the database engine (SQL server or BDE).
Rollback	Cancels and reverts pending transactions.
StartTransaction	Starts a new transaction.

TABLE 2.23 TDATABASE EVENTS

EVENT	DATA TYPE	DESCRIPTION
OnLogin	TLoginEvent	Activated on connection to a database when the LoginPrompt property is True.

See Also

TDataset, TQuery, TTable

TDATABASE.ALIASNAME PROPERTY

Declaration

```
{ DB.PAS }
property AliasName: TSymbolStr read GetAliasName write SetAliasName;
```

Description

Name of an existing BDE alias or (for local tables) a directory where the data files reside. AliasName and DriverName are mutually exclusive—setting one will clear the other, since both properties specify a driver type.

Example

```
{ Set the alias to an existing BDE alias }
Database1.AliasName := 'DBDEMOS';
```

Notes

If the Connected property is True when an attempt is made to modify AliasName, an exception will be generated.

See Also

Aliases in **DELPHI.HLP**, TDatabase.DriverName

TDATABASE.CLOSE METHOD

Declaration

```
{ DB.PAS }
procedure Close;
```

Description

Closes the TDatabase and all associated data set components.

Example

```
{ If not the top dog, shut em down... }
if SecurityLevel < TopMost then
   Database1.Close;
```

Notes

Issuing a Close command has the same effect as setting the Connected property to False.

See Also

TDatabase.Close, TDatabase.CloseDatasets, TDatabase.Connected

TDATABASE.CLOSEDATASETS METHOD

Declaration

```
{ DB.PAS }
procedure CloseDatasets;
```

Description

Closes the DataSets associated to TDatabase without closing the database.

Example

```
{ Close all data sets but leave the Database connected }
Database1.CloseDatasets;
```

Notes

The CloseDataSets command may be useful to prepare for batch operations.

See Also

TDatabase.Close, TDatabase.Open

TDATABASE.COMMIT METHOD

Declaration

```
{ DB.PAS }
procedure Commit;
```

Description

Commits the current transactions.

Example

```
{ Commit the currently pending transaction }
Database1.StartTransaction;
...
Database1.Commit;
```

Notes

If no transaction is active, an exception will be generated. Calling Commit on a Paradox or dBASE table is not allowed and will raise an exception.

See Also

TDatabase.StartTransaction, TDatabase.Rollback

TDATABASE.CONNECTED PROPERTY

Declaration

```
{ DB.PAS }
property Connected: Boolean read GetConnected write SetConnected
    default False;
```

Description

Indicates whether a database connection has been established.

Example

```
{ Determine whether a connection to the database exists }
if Database1.Connected then
   { perform processing here };
```

Notes

It is possible to keep the connection to a database open even when all its tables are closed, using the KeepConnection property.

See Also

TDatabase.KeepConnection

TDATABASE.DATABASENAME PROPERTY

Declaration

```
{ DB.PAS }
property DatabaseName: TFileName read FDatabaseName
    write SetDatabaseName;
```

Description

Defines a local, application-specific alias.

Example

```
{ Database component is attached to an existing BDE alias }
Database1.AliasName := 'DBDEMOS';

{ Create an application-specific alias }
Database1.DatabaseName := 'DEMO';

{ Attach a table component to this database component }
Table1.DatabaseName := 'DEMO';

{ Table1 can now access all tables in DBDEMOS alias }
Table1.TableName := 'CUSTOMER';
```

Notes

An exception will be raised if an attempt is made to set this property when Connected is True.

See Also

TDatabase.Connected

TDATABASE.DATASETCOUNT PROPERTY

Declaration

```
{ DB.PAS }
property DatasetCount: Integer read GetDatasetCount;
```

Description

Run-time only, read-only. Contains the number of data set components currently attached to the database.

Example

```
{ Refresh all open tables }
for x := 0 to (Database1.DatasetCount - 1) do
    Database1.DataSets[x].Refresh;
```

Notes

The DatasetCount property is useful for performing operations on all open tables using the DataSets list, as shown in the preceding example.

See Also

TDatabase.Datasets

TDATABASE.DATASETS PROPERTY

Declaration

```
{ DB.PAS }
property Datasets[Index: Integer]: TDBDataset read GetDataset;
```

Description

Contains a set of pointers to the data set components currently attached to the database.

Example

```
{ This example displays the State for each open table }
InactiveCount := 0;
```

```
BrowseCount := 0;
EditCount := 0;
InsertCount := 0;
SetKeyCount := 0;
CalcFieldsCount := 0;

{ For each open table }
for x := 1 to (Database1.DatasetCount - 1) do
begin
    { Tally the State }
    case Database1.Datasets[x].State of
        dsInactive: Inc(InactiveCount);
        dsBrowse: Inc(BrowseCount);
        dsEdit: Inc(EditCount);
        dsInsert: Inc(InsertCount);
        dsSetKey: Inc(SetKeyCount);
        dsCalcFields: Inc(CalcFieldsCount);
    end;
end;

{ Display the results in a listbox }
Listbox1.Items.Add('Inactive mode: ' + IntToStr(InactiveCount));
Listbox1.Items.Add('Browse mode: ' + IntToStr(BrowseCount));
Listbox1.Items.Add('Edit mode: ' + IntToStr(EditCount));
Listbox1.Items.Add('Insert mode: ' + IntToStr(InsertCount));
Listbox1.Items.Add('SetKey mode: ' + IntToStr(SetKeyCount));
Listbox1.Items.Add('CalcFields mode: ' + IntToStr(CalcFieldsCount));
```

Notes

The DataSets property lists only active tables. If a table is closed, it is automatically removed from the list.

See Also

TDatabase.DatasetCount

TDATABASE.DRIVERNAME PROPERTY

Declaration

```
{ DB.PAS }
property DriverName: TSymbolStr read GetDriverName
    write SetDriverName;
```

Description

Contains a BDE driver name. DriverName and AliasName are mutually exclusive—clearing one will set the other, as both properties specify a driver type.

Example

```
{ Reset Database at run-time to connect to a local table }
Database1.Connected := False;
Database1.AliasName := 'DBDEMOS';
Database1.DriverName := 'STANDARD';
Database1.Connected := True;
```

Notes

An exception will be raised if an attempt is made to assign the value of DriverName when the Connected property is True.

See Also

TDatabase.AliasName, TDatabase.Connected

TDATABASE.HANDLE PROPERTY

Declaration

```
{ DB.PAS }
property Handle: hDBIDb read FHandle;
```

Description

Run-time only, read-only. Provides a database handle to be used with BDE API function calls.

Example

```
{ Fetch the handle for the current database }
hDB := Database1.Handle;
```

Notes

Handle is not valid if the Connected property is False.

See Also

BDE Function Reference

TDATABASE.IsSQLBASED PROPERTY

Declaration

```
{ DB.PAS }
property IsSQLBased: Boolean read GetIsSQLBased;
```

Description

Run-time only, read-only. True if DriverName is other than STANDARD.

Example

```
{ Execute a stored procedure only for SQL based tables }
if Database.IsSQLBase then
   StoredProc1.ExecProc;
```

Notes

IsSQLBased will always be False for Paradox, dBASE, and ASCII tables.

See Also

TDatabase.DriverName

TDATABASE.KEEPCONNECTION PROPERTY

Declaration

```
{ DB.PAS }
property KeepConnection: Boolean read FKeepConnection
    write SetKeepConnection default True;
```

Description

Specifies whether an application remains connected to the database even when no tables are open.

Example

```
{ Override the default setting }
Database1.KeepConnection := False;
```

Notes

The default setting for KeepConnection is True.

See Also

TDatabase.Connected

TDATABASE.LOCALE PROPERTY

Declaration

```
{ DB.PAS }
property Locale: TLocale read FLocale;
```

Description

Run-time only, read-only. Specifies the BDE language driver used for the database.

Notes

Normally used only with BDE function calls. Actual conversion are done using AnsiToNative and NativeToAnsi functions.

See Also

BDE Function Reference, AnsiToNative and NativeToAnsi in **DELPHI.HLP**

TDATABASE.LOGINPROMPT PROPERTY

Declaration

```
{ DB.PAS }
property LoginPrompt: Boolean read FLoginPrompt
    write FLoginPrompt default True;
```

Description

Specifies whether the standard login dialog box is displayed when the application attempts to connect to the database. The Login dialog box is also displayed in design-time when you attempt to connect to a server database.

Example

```
{ Suppress the display of the login dialog box }
Database1.LoginPrompt := False;
Database1.Params.Add('USER NAME=JOHNDOE');
Database1.Params.Add('PASSWORD=SECRET');
```

Notes

In order to log into a database without using the Login dialog box, your application must supply the login information (user id, password, etc.) via the Params property or through the OnLogin event handler. The preceding method is not very secure—see OnLogin for an alternative method of logging into a database without the Login dialog box. Note that different servers may require additional login information.

See Also

TDatabase.OnLogin, TDatabase.Params

TDATABASE.ONLOGIN EVENT

Declaration

```
{ DB.PAS }
property OnLogin: TLoginEvent read FOnLogin write FOnLogin;
```

Description

Activated on connection to a database when the LoginPrompt property is True.

Example

```
{ This example resets the user name and password }
procedure TForm1.Database1Login(Database: TDatabase;
  LoginParams: TStrings);
begin
  { Reset the login parameters for this user }
  Database.Params.Values['USER NAME'] := 'MICKEYMOUSE';
  Database.Params.Values['PASSWORD'] := 'DISNEY';
end;
```

Notes

This method is more secure than simply setting the USER NAME and PASSWORD in the Params property. Note that different servers may require additional login information.

See Also

TDatabase.LoginPrompt, TDatabase.Params

TDATABASE.OPEN METHOD

Declaration

```
{ DB.PAS }
procedure Open;
```

Description

Connects the TDatabase to the database engine (SQL server or BDE).

Example

```
{ Connect to the database }
Database1.Open;
```

Notes

Calling Open sets the Connected property to True if the connection was successful.

See Also

TDatabase.Close, TDatabase.Connected

TDATABASE.PARAMS PROPERTY

Declaration

```
{ DB.PAS }
property Params: TStrings read FParams write SetParams;
```

Description

Specifies the parameters required to open an SQL server database.

Example

```
{ Set parameters for login }
Database1.Params.Add('USER NAME=JDOE');
Database1.Params.Add('PASSWORD=NobodyKnows');
```

Notes

Different server databases may require additional login information.

See Also

TDatabase.LoginPrompt, TDatabase.OnLogin

TDATABASE.ROLLBACK METHOD

Declaration

```
{ DB.PAS }
procedure Rollback;
```

Description

Cancels and reverts pending transactions on an SQL server.

Example

```
{ Cancel an aborted transaction by rolling back the changes }
try
    { Start a multirecord transaction }
```

```
    Database1.StartTransaction;

    { Delete all records for this customer }
    Table1.SetKey;
    Table1CUSTID.Value := 1001;
    Table1.GotoKey;
    while Table1CUSTID.Value = 1001 do
        Table1.Delete;

    { Commit the changes }
    Database1.Commit;
except
    Database1.Rollback;
end;
```

Notes

Calling RollBack on a Paradox or dBase table is not allowed, and will raise an exception.

See Also

TDatabase.Commit, TDatabase.StartTransaction

TDATABASE.STARTTRANSACTION METHOD

Declaration

```
{ DB.PAS }
procedure StartTransaction;
```

Description

Starts a new transaction.

Example

```
{ Start a transaction }
Database1.StartTransaction;
try
    { perform multirecord updates here }
    ...
    Database1.Commit;
except
    Database1.Rollback;
end;
```

Notes

An exception will be raised if Connected is False. Calling StartTransaction on a Paradox or dBASE table is not allowed and will raise an exception.

See Also

TDatabase.Rollback, TDatabase.StartTransaction

TDATABASE.TEMPORARY PROPERTY

Declaration

```
{ DB.PAS }
property Temporary: Boolean read FTemporary write FTemporary;
```

Description

Run-time only. True if the TDatabase component was created dynamically at run-time by Delphi, rather than at design-time.

Example

```
{ Preserve the dynamically created Database object }
Table1.Database.Temporary := False;
...
Table1.Database.Free;
```

Notes

Setting Temporary for a dynamically created Database to False will preserve the temporary database until you call Free to destroy it. Setting Temporary to True will cause the Database to be freed automatically when the last data set attached to it is closed.

See Also

TDBDataset.Database

TDATABASE.TRANSISOLATION PROPERTY

Declaration

```
{ DB.PAS }
property TransIsolation: TTransIsolation read FTransIsolation
    write FTransIsolation default tiReadCommitted;

TTransIsolation = (tiDirtyRead, tiReadCommitted, tiRepeatableRead);
```

Description

Specifies the transaction isolation level used by an SQL server as shown in Table 2.24.

TABLE 2.24 TRANSACTION ISOLATION LEVELS

TRANSACTION ISOLATION LEVEL (LOWEST TO HIGHEST)	DESCRIPTION
tiDirtyRead	Specifies that the transaction can read changes to the database that have been made by other transactions that are uncommitted.
TiReadCommitted	Specifies that the transaction can only read changes to the database made by other transactions that have been committed.
TiRepeatableRead	Specifies that the transaction cannot read changes to previously read data by other transactions, ensuring that any records that have been read will not change if read again.

Example

```
{ Set the transaction isolation level to ignore records that have changed but
  have already been read }
Database1.TransIsolation := tiRepeatableRead;
```

Notes

Transaction isolation levels determine how multiple transactions that are reading the same data interact with each other. Actual server support for the various isolations levels may be implemented differently on various servers. Note that any ODBC drivers used must also support the specified isolation level.

See Also

Transactions in **DELPHI.HLP**, TDatabase.Commit, TDatabase.Rollback, TDatabase.StartTransaction

TSession Component

Unit

DB

Inherits from

TComponent

Description

The TSession component establishes a connection from the BDE to all of the databases (TDatabase components) in your application. A global variable of type TSession called Session is automatically created for you each time your application runs. This allows you global control over all of the databases in your application.

The following tables summarize the properties (Table 2.25), methods (Table 2.26), and events (Table 2.27) for the TSession component

TABLE 2.25 TSESSION PROPERTIES

PROPERTY	DATA TYPE	RUN-TIME ONLY	READ-ONLY	DESCRIPTION
Active[1]	Boolean	No	No	Determines whether the session is currently active.
DatabaseCount	Integer	Yes	Yes	Contains the current number of TDatabase components attached to he Session variable.
Databases	TDatabase.Indexed Property	Yes	Yes	Contains a list of all of the active TDatabase components currently attached to the Session variable.
Handle	HDBISES	Yes	Yes	Contains a handle to the session.
KeepConnections	Boolean	Yes	No	Determines whether automatically created TDatabase components remain connected even if none of their tables are open. Defaults to True.
Locale	TLocale	Yes	Yes	Contains the language driver used with the Session variable.
NetFileDir	String	Yes	No	Specifies the directory that contains the **PDOXUSRS.NET** network control file.
PrivateDir	String	Yes	No	Specifies the directory for storage of temporary files.
SessionName[2]	String	No	No	Specifies the name of the current session.

TABLE 2.26 TSESSION METHODS

METHOD	DESCRIPTION
AddPassword	Adds a new password to the current session.
Close[3]	Deactivates the current session.
CloseDatabase	Closes a specified TDatabase component.
DropConnections	Disconnects all inactive databases.
FindDatabase	Searches the Databases property for a database name.
GetAliasNames	Initializes a stringlist with the names of all defined BDE aliases but not application-specific aliases.
GetAliasParams	Initializes a stringlist with the parameters associated with a specified BDE alias name.
GetDatabaseNames	Initializes a stringlist with the names of all defined BDE aliases including application-specific aliases.
GetDriverNames	Initializes a stringlist with the names of all currently installed BDE drivers.

[1] Delphi 2.0 only

[2] Delphi 2.0 only

[3] Delphi 2.0 only

GetDriverParams	Initializes a stringlist with the default parameters for a specified driver name.
GetPassword	Invokes any OnPassword event or displays the default password dialog box.
GetTableNames	Initializes a stringlist with the names of all of the tables in a specified database, or only those matching a specified wildcard pattern.
GetStoredProcNames	Initializes a stringlist with the names of all stored procedures defined for a specified SQL database.
Open[4]	Activates the current session.
OpenDatabase	Locates or creates a specified TDatabase component and opens it.
RemoveAllPasswords	Discards all previously entered password information.
RemovePassword	Removes a specified password from the current set of authorizations.

TABLE 2.27 TSESSION EVENTS

EVENT	DATA TYPE	DESCRIPTION
OnPassword	TPasswordEvent	Executed whenever a Paradox table is opened when the application does not have sufficient access rights to open that table.
OnStartup[5]	TNotifyEvent	Executes whenever a session is activated.

Notes

In Delphi 1.0, you cannot and should not explicitly create or destroy a TSession component—one is created for you automatically when your application runs. In Delphi 2.0, a TSession component has been added to the Component Palette. The TSession component allows you to explicitly create and modify one or more TSession components at design-time, which then overrides the virtual component that would have been automatically created at run-time.

See Also

TDatabase

TSESSION.ACTIVE PROPERTY

Declaration

```
{ DB.PAS }
property Active: Boolean read GetActive write SetActive default False;
```

Description

Deactivates the current session. This has the effect of closing all database connections for the specified session, which in turn closes all active data sets.

---

[4] Delphi 2.0 only

[5] Delphi 2.0 only

Example

```
{ Activate a session }
Session1.Active := True;
```

Notes

Delphi 2.0 only. Setting the Active property to True has the same effect as calling the Open method, and setting it to False has the same effect as calling the Close method. An exception is generated if no valid SessionName has been specified when Active is set to True.

See Also

TSession.Open, TSession.Close

TSESSION.ADDPASSWORD METHOD

Declaration

```
{ DB.PAS }
procedure AddPassword(const Password: String);
```

Description

Adds a new password to the current session.

Example

```
{ Add a password for this session }
Session.AddPassword('TopSecret');
```

Notes

For use with Paradox tables only. If a Paradox table requires a password, the user will be prompted to enter that password unless the Session variable contains a valid password for that table.

See Also

TSession.GetPassword, TSession.OnPassword

TSESSION.CLOSE METHOD

Declaration

```
{ DB.PAS }
procedure Close;
```

Description

Deactivates the current session, disconnects any database connections and closes all tables associated with this session.

Example

```
{ Total database shutdown! }
Session1.Close;
```

Notes

Delphi 2.0 only. Calling Close has the same effect as setting the Active property to False.

See Also

TSession.Active, TSession.Open

TSession.CloseDatabase ethod

Declaration

```
{ DB.PAS }
procedure CloseDatabase(Database: TDatabase);
```

Description

Closes a specified database component and decrement the DatabaseCount property.

Example

```
{ Open and work with a database, safely closing it after }
Database1 := Session.OpenDatabase('DBDEMOS');
try
   { Perform database operations }
finally
   { Ensure that the database is closed even on exception }
   CloseDatabase(Database1);
end;
```

Notes

Closing a database component would normally be handled automatically when the last table associated with a database component is closed, unless the KeepConnections property is True. The CloseDatabase method should always be used within a **try..finally** block to ensure proper handling of database connections. Note that the Delphi 1.0 documentation shows passing a string with the database name to CloseDatabase. This is incorrect, it should take a parameter of type TDatabase.

See Also

TSession.OpenDatabase, TSession.KeepConnections

TSession.DatabaseCount Property

Declaration

```
{ DB.PAS }
property DatabaseCount: Integer read GetDatabaseCount;
```

Description

Read-only, run-time only. Contains a count of the TDatabase components currently associated with the session.

Example

```
{ Indicate how many databases are currently active }
Edit1.Text := IntToStr(Session.DatabaseCount);
```

Notes

DatabaseCount is automatically adjusted as databases are opened and closed (with OpenDatabase and CloseDatabase, for example).

See Also

TSession.CloseDatabase, TSession.Databases, TSession.OpenDatabase

TSession.Databases Property

Declaration

```
{ DB.PAS }
property Databases[Index: Integer]: TDatabase read GetDatabase;
```

Description

Run-time only, read-only. Contains a list of all currenly active TDatabase components associated with the session.

Example

```
{ Commit changes to all tables in all databases using BDE function }
with Session do
for nDatabase := 0 to (DatabaseCount - 1) do
   for nDataSet := 0 to (Databases[nDatabase].DataSetCount - 1) do

      DbiSaveChanges(Databases[nDatabase].Datasets[nDataSet].Handle);
```

Notes

The Databases property is an indexed property that can be accessed as if it were an array, using a numeric index starting at zero.

See Also

TSession.DatabaseCount

TSession.DropConnections Method

Declaration

```
{ DB.PAS }
procedure DropConnections;
```

Description

Disconnects all inactive database connections.

Example

```
{ Drop all inactive connections for this session }
Session.DropConnections;
```

Notes

Virtual (automatically created) TDatabase components keep their connections to a server open by default even when not in use to avoid having to log onto the server each time a data set is opened. The DropConnections method closes any of those database components that are currently inactive. It does not close currently active databases.

See Also

TDatabase.Temporary, TSession.KeepConnections

TSession.FindDatabase Method

Applies to

TSession component

Declaration

```
{ DB.PAS }
function FindDatabase(const DatabaseName: String): TDatabase;
```

Description

Locates and returns a specific TDatabase component by name.

Example

```
{ Find and close a specific database }
Database := Session.FindDatabase('DBDEMOS');
if Database <> nil then
   Database.Close;
```

Notes

If a database name that does not exist is specified, FindDatabase returns NIL.

See Also

TSession.DatabaseName, TSession.Databases

TSession.GetAliasNames Method

Declaration

```
{ DB.PAS }
procedure GetAliasNames(List: TStrings);
```

Description

Initializes a StringList with a list of BDE aliases, excluding application-specific aliases.

Example

```
{ Retrieve a list of BDE alias names }
var
   AliasNamesList: TStringList;
begin
   AliasNamesList := TStringList.Create;
   try
   Session.GetAliasNames(AliasNamesList);
   ListBox1.Items := AliasNamesList;
   finally
      AliasNamesList.Free;
   end;
end;
```

Notes

The List parameter is cleared prior to filling it with alias names.

See Also

TSession.GetAliasParams, TSession.GetDatabaseNames

TSession.GetAliasParams Method

Declaration

```
{ DB.PAS }
procedure GetAliasParams(const AliasName: String; List: TStrings);
```

Example

```
{ Retrieve a list of parameters for a specified alias }
var
   AliasParamsList: TStringList;
begin
   AliasParamsList := TStringList.Create;
   try
   Session.GetAliasParams('DBDEMOS',AliasParamsList);
   ListBox1.Items := AliasParamsList;
   finally
      AliasParamsList.Free;
   end;
end;
```

Notes

The List parameter is cleared prior to adding any alias parameters to it.

See Also

TSession.GetAliasNames

TSession.GetDatabaseNames Method

Declaration

```
{ DB.PAS }
procedure GetDatabaseNames(List: TStrings);
```

Description

Initializes a StringList with the names of all defined BDE alias names, including any application-specific aliases.

Example

```
{ Retrieve a list of BDE alias names and local aliases }
var
    AliasNamesList: TStringList;
begin
    AliasNamesList := TStringList.Create;
    try
    Session.GetAliasNames(AliasNamesList);
    ListBox1.Items := AliasNamesList;
    finally
        AliasNamesList.Free;
    end;

end;
```

Notes

The List parameter is cleared prior to adding any alias names to it.

See Also

TSession.GetAliasNames

TSESSION.GETDRIVERNAMES METHOD

Declaration

```
{ DB.PAS }
procedure GetDriverNames(List: TStrings);
```

Description

Initializes a StringList with the names of all drivers currently installed in the BDE.

Example

```
{ Retrieve a list of BDE driver names }
var
    DriverNamesList: TStringList;
begin
    DriverNamesList := TStringList.Create;
    try
    Session.GetDriverNames(DriverNamesList);
    ListBox1.Items := DriverNamesList;
    finally
        DriverNamesList.Free;
    end;
end;
```

Notes

Both Paradox and dBASE databases are included under the 'STANDARD' driver name. The List parameter is cleared prior to adding any database names to it.

See Also

TSession.GetAliasNames, TSession.GetDatabaseNames, TSession.GetDriverParams

TSESSION.GETDRIVERPARAMS METHOD

Declaration

```
{ DB.PAS }
procedure GetDriverParams(const DriverName: String; List: TStrings);
```

Description

Initializes a StringList with the default parameters for a specified BDE driver.

Example

```
{ Retrieve a list of parameters for a given BDE driver }
var
   DriverParamsList: TStringList;
begin
    DriverParamsList := TStringList.Create;
    try
    Session.GetDriverParams('STANDARD');
    Edit1.Text := DriverParamsList[0]; { PATH }
    finally
       DriverParamsList.Free;
    end;
end;
```

Notes

The List parameter is cleared prior to adding any items to it. The 'STANDARD' driver will have only one parameter of the form 'PATH='. The parameter list returned for SQL tables will have varying parameters, depending on the SQL server.

See Also

TSession.GetAliasNames, TSession.GetDriverNames

TSESSION.GETPASSWORD METHOD

Declaration

```
{ DB.PAS }
function GetPassword: Boolean;
```

Description

Invokes any procedure assigned to the OnPassword event handler. If no event handler is specified for the OnPassword event, the default password dialog box is displayed.

Example

```
{ Invoke password handling using the default password dialog box}
if Session.GetPassword then
   { allow access... }
else
   Halt;
```

Notes

If the default password dialog box is displayed, it returns True if the user chooses the OK button; otherwise, it returns False.

See Also

TSession.AddPassword, TSession.OnPassword

TSESSION.GETTABLENAMES METHOD

Declaration

```
{ DB.PAS }
procedure GetTableNames(const DatabaseName, Pattern: String;
     Extensions, SystemTables: Boolean; List: TStrings);
```

Description

Initializes a StringList with the names of all tables in the specified database that match Pattern. If Extensions is True for non-SQL databases, includes table file name extensions. If SystemTables is True, includes system table information for SQL databases.

Example

```
{ Retrieve a list of all tables that start with 'C' }
var
   TableList: TStringList;
begin
   TableList := TStringList.Create;
   try
   Session.GetTableNames('DBDEMOS', 'C*', True, False, TableList);
   ListBox1.Items := TableList;
   finally
      TableList.Free;
```

```
    end;
end;
```

Notes

The example shown in the Delphi 1.0 help file incorrectly shows passing only four parameters to the GetTableNames method—the Pattern parameter is missing. The List parameter is cleared prior to adding any table names to it.

See Also

TSession.GetAliasNames, TSession.GetDriverNames

TSESSION.GETSTOREDPROCNAMES METHOD

Declaration

```
{ DB.PAS }
procedure GetStoredProcNames(const DatabaseName: string;
List: TStrings);
```

Description

Initializes a StringList with the names of all stored procedures defined for a specified SQL database.

Example

```
{ Retrieve a list of all tables that start with 'C' }
var
   StoredProcList: TStringList;
begin
   StoredProcList := TStringList.Create;
   try
   Session.GetStoredProcNames('DBDEMOS', StoredProcList);
   ListBox1.Items := StoredProcList;
   finally
      StoredProcList.Free;
   end;
end;
```

Notes

The List parameter is cleared prior to adding any stored procedure names to it. This method is not valid for desktop (Paradox and dBASE) databases.

See Also

TSession.GetAliasNames, TSession.GetDriverNames, TSession.GetTableNames

TSESSION.HANDLE PROPERTY

Declaration

```
{ DB.PAS }
property Handle: HDBISES read GetHandle;
```

Description

Run-time only, read-only. Supplies a handle to the current session for use with BDE function calls.

Example

```
{ This example closes the current session  }
retval := DbiCloseSession(Session1.Handle);
if retval = DBI_ERRNONE then
  ShowMessage('Session is closed')
else if retval = DBI_ERRINVALIDSESHANDLE then
    ShowMessage('Session handle is invalid');
```

Notes

Normally used only when making calls directly to the Borland Database Engine API.

See Also

BDE Function Reference

TSESSION.KEEPCONNECTIONS PROPERTY

Declaration

```
{ DB.PAS }
property KeepConnections: Boolean read FKeepConnections
    write FKeepConnections default True;
```

Description

Run-time only in Delphi 1.0. Specifies whether automatically created TDatabase components will remain connected when all their data sets are closed. If KeepConnections is True, the application will maintain connections for all database components until the application terminates or until the DropConnections method is called. If False, the application will disconnect from a database when all that database's data sets are closed.

Example

```
{ Override the default value to ensure automatic database disconnection
  when all data sets for a database are closed }
Session.KeepConnections := False;
```

Notes

The value of the KeepConnections property determines the initial value for the KeepConnection property for automatically created TDatabase components. This property has no effect on connections for explicitly created TDatabase components.

See Also

TDatabase.KeepConnection, TSession.DropConnections

TSession.Locale Property

Public

Declaration

```
{ DB.PAS }
property Locale: TLocale read FLocale;
```

Description

Run-time only, read-only. Identifies the language driver used with the session component.

Example

```
{ Retrieve language driver for this session }
LangDriver := Session.Locale;
```

Notes

The Locale property is normally used only when calling the BDE API functions directly.

See Also

BDE Function Reference

TSession.NetFileDir Property

Declaration

```
{ DB.PAS }
property NetFileDir: String read GetNetFileDir write SetNetFileDir;
```

Description

Run-time only in Delphi 1.0. The NetFileDir property specifies the directory that contains the **PDOXUSRS.NET** network control file, which enables multiple users to share the same Paradox tables across a network.

Example

```
{ Ensure that all users of this application are using the same network
  control file - assumes read/write/create access rights }
Session.NetFileDir := 'F:\PUBLIC\APPS';
```

Notes

Assigning a value to the NetFileDir overrides the Net Dir setting for the Paradox driver as specified in the BDE configuration utility. All users that need to share the same Paradox database must specify the same directory and must have read, write, and create access rights to that directory.

See Also

TSession.PrivateDir

TSession.OnPassword Event

Declaration

```
{ DB.PAS }
property OnPassword: TPasswordEvent read FOnPassword
    write FOnPassword;

TPasswordEvent = procedure(Sender: TObject;
    var Continue: Boolean) of Object;
```

Description

Run-time only in Delphi 1.0. The OnPassword event is executed whenever a Paradox table is opened without sufficient access rights. The Sender parameter contains the Session object. The Continue parameter determines whether another attempt to access the database will be allowed. The procedure assigned to the OnPassword event handler should add any available passwords to the Session and set Continue to True, or should set Continue to False if no additional passwords are available.

Example

```
{ This example shows how to establish a simple password handler }
procedure TForm1.FormCreate(Sender: TObject);
begin
    { Assign a procedure to handle passwords }
    Session.OnPassword := GetPassword;
    Table1.Open;
end;

{ Password handler - parameter list must match TPasswordEvent }
procedure GetPassword(Sender: TObject; var Continue: Boolean);
const
    Tries: Byte = 0;
```

```
var
    PasswordDlg: TPasswordDlg;
begin
    PasswordDlg := TPasswordDlg.Create(Form1);
    try
        if (Tries < 3) and (PasswordDlg.ShowModal = mrOK) then
        begin
            (Sender as TSession).AddPassword(PasswordDlg.Password.Text);
            Continue := True;
            inc(Tries);
        end else
        begin
            Tries := 0;
            Continue := False;
        end;
    finally
        PasswordDlg.Free;
    end;
end;
```

Notes

If no procedure is assigned to the OnPassword event handler, the default password dialog box will be displayed to allow the user to enter a new password. If using the default password dialog box, entering an invalid password will generate an exception. The procedure assigned to OnPassword cannot be a method of an object (e.g., Form1.GetPassword), it must be a stand-alone procedure.

See Also

TSession.AddPassword, TSession.GetPassword

TSession.OnStartup Event

Declaration

```
{ DB.PAS }
property OnStartup: TNotifyEvent read FOnStartup write FOnStartup;

{ CLASSES.PAS }
TNotifyEvent = procedure(Sender: TObject) of object;
```

Description

Example

```
{ Example of using the OnStartup event }
procedure TForm1.FormCreate(Sender: TObject);
begin
    { Assign a procedure to be called at startup }
```

```
    Session.OnStartup := StartupMsg;
end;

    { Event handler parameter list must match TNotifyEvent }
procedure StartupMsg(Sender: TObject);
begin
    ShowMessage('Session ' + Session.SessionName + ' is started');
end;
```

Notes

Delphi 2.0 only. The procedure assigned to the OnStartup event cannot be a method of an object; it must be a standalone procedure.

See Also

TSession.Active, TSession.Open

TSession.Open Method

Declaration

```
{ DB.PAS }
procedure Open;
```

Description

Activates the current session and attempts to connect to all its databases.

Example

```
{ Open a session - Delphi 2.0 only }
if not Session1.Open then exit;
```

Notes

Delphi 2.0 only. Calling the Open method has the same effect as assigning True to the Active property.

See Also

TSession.Active, TSession.Close, TSession.OnStartup

TSession.OpenDatabase Method

Declaration

```
{ DB.PAS }
function OpenDatabase(const DatabaseName: String): TDatabase;
```

Description

Opens and returns a TDatabase component of a specified name. If no such database exists, a new TDatabase component is created, opened, and returned.

Example

```
{ Open and work with a database, safely closing it after }
Database1 := Session.OpenDatabase('DBDEMOS');
try
   { Perform database operations... }
finally
   { Ensure that the database is closed even on exception }
   CloseDatabase(Database1);
end;
```

Notes

This method increments the DatabaseCount property on successful opening of a database. The OpenDatabase method should always be used in conjunction with a try. Finally, block to ensure proper handling of database connections. The Delphi 1.0 documentation shows passing a string with the database name to CloseDatabase in its example. This is incorrect, it should take a parameter of type TDatabase.

See Also

TSession.CloseDatabase

TSESSION.PRIVATEDIR PROPERTY

Declaration

```
{ DB.PAS }
property PrivateDir: String read GetPrivateDir write SetPrivateDir;
```

Description

Run-time only in Delphi 1.0. Specifies the directory where temporary files, such as those used to process local SQL statements, are stored.

Example

```
{ Set the private directory at run-time based on user input }
Session.PrivateDir := Edit1.Text;
```

Notes

This property should be set only when one instance of your application will be running at one time, to avoid interference between the temporary files of multiple instances of your application.

See Also

TSession.NetFileDir

TSESSION.REMOVEALLPASSWORDS METHOD

Declaration

```
{ DB.PAS }
procedure RemoveAllPasswords;
```

Description

Discards all previously entered password information. Subsequent attempts to access the database will require new password information prior to opening the affected table.

Example

```
{ Discard all current password information }
Session.RemoveAllPasswords;
```

Notes

This method affects Paradox databases only.

See Also

TSession.AddPassword, TSession.GetPassword, TSession.RemovePassword

TSESSION.REMOVEPASSWORD METHOD

Declaration

```
{ DB.PAS }
procedure RemovePassword(const Password: String);
```

Description

Removes a specified password from the list of passwords.

Example

```
{ Remove a temporary password }
Session.RemovePassword('TEMPORARY');
```

Notes

This method applies only to Paradox databases.

See Also

TSession.AddPassword, TSession.GetPassword, TSession.RemovePasswords

TSession.SessionName Property

Declaration

```
{ DB.PAS }
property SessionName: string read FSessionName write SetSessionName;
```

Description

Specifies the name of a particular session

Example

```
{ Retrieve the current session name }
ThisSession := Session1.SessionName;
```

Notes

Delphi 2.0 only. Note that SessionName is distinct from the component's name, which is stored in the Name property. Each SessionName must be unique within an application.

See Also

TSession.Active

TBatchMove Component

Unit

DBTABLES

Inherits from

TComponent

Description

TBatchMove is designed to facilitate operations that involve groups of records or entire tables. To perform most common operations, such as Append, Update, Copy and Delete, you would normally perform the following steps:

1. Set the Source and Destination properties to the desired data sets.
2. Set the Mode to the operation desired.
3. Run the batch operation using the Execute method.

The tables that follow list the properties (Table 2.28) and methods (Table 2.29) for the TBatchMove component.

TABLE 2.28 TBATCHMOVE PROPERTIES

PROPERTY	DATA TYPE	RUN-TIME ONLY	READ-ONLY	DESCRIPTION
AbortOnKeyViol	Boolean	No	No	Specifies whether an integrity violation aborts the batch operation.
AbortOnProblem	Boolean	No	No	Specifies whether a data size problem aborts the batch operation.
ChangedCount	Longint	Yes	Yes	Contains the number of records that were changed in the batch operation.
ChangedTableName	TFilename	No	No	Specifies the local table to which to copy records that were changed during the batch operation.
Destination	TTable	No	No	Specifies the destination table for the batch operation.
KeyViolCount	Longint	Yes	Yes	Contains the number of records that violated integrity constraints.
KeyViolTableName	TFilename	No	Yes	Specifies the name of a local table to contain all the records that violate integrity constraints.
Mappings	TStrings	No	No	A list of fields in Destination that correspond to fields in Source.
Mode	TBatchMode	No	No	Specifies the mode (Append, Update, Copy, Delete) for the batch operation.
MovedCount	Longint	Yes	Yes	Contains the total number of records processed by the batch operation (including those with integrity and data size problems).
ProblemCount	Longint	Yes	Yes	Contains the number of records that had data size problems.
ProblemTableName	TFilename	No	No	Specifies a table to store records that could not be processed due to data size problems.
RecordCount	Longint	No	No	Controls the number of records that will be moved during the batch operation.
Source	TDataset	No	No	Specifies the TTable or TQuery object that is the source of data for the batch operation.
Transliterate	Boolean	No	No	Specifies whether data will be translated from Source to Destination's character set.

TABLE 2.29 TBATCHMOVE METHODS

METHOD	DESCRIPTION
Execute	Executes the batch operation.

See Also

TDataset, TQuery, TTable

TBatchMove.AbortOnKeyViol Property

Applies to

TBatchMove component

Declaration

```
{ DBTABLES.PAS }
property AbortOnKeyViol: Boolean read FAbortOnKeyViol
    write FAbortOnKeyViol default True;
```

Description

Specifies whether an integrity violation aborts the batch operation. If AbortOnKeyViol is True, the Execute method terminates the operation as soon as a key violation is detected. If False, the records that would cause the violations are stored in the table specified by KeyViolTableName.

Example

```
{ Specify that key violations do not abort the procedure }
BatchMove1.AbortOnKeyViol := False;

{ Store key violation records in a table }
BatchMove1.KeyViolTableName := 'VIOLATE';
```

Notes

If no table is specified in the KeyViolTableName property and AbortOnKeyViol is False, records that violate key constraints will be discarded.

See Also

TBatchMove.AbortOnProblem, TBatchMove.ChangedCount, TBatchMove.ChangedTableName, TBatchMove.KeyViolCount, TBatchMove.KeyViolTableName

TBatchMove.AbortOnProblem Property

Declaration

```
{ DBTABLES.PAS }
property AbortOnProblem: Boolean read FAbortOnProblem
    write FAbortOnProblem default True;
```

Description

Specifies whether a data size problem aborts the batch operation. If AbortOnProblem is False and any of a source record's data would be lost when moved to the destination table, that record would be stored in the table specified in the ProblemTableName property.

Example

```
{ Specify that records with data width problems do not abort }
BatchMove1.AbortOnProblem := False;

{ Store the overlength records in a temporary table }
BatchMove1.ProblemTableName := 'PROBLEM';
```

Notes

If AbortOnProblem is False and no table name is specified in the ProblemTableName property, no source records will be stored, and data may be lost in the transfer.

See Also

TBatchMove.AbortOnKeyViol, TBatchMove.ChangedCount, TBatchMove.ChangedTableName, TBatchMove.ProblemCount, TBatchMove.ProblemTableName

TBatchMove.ChangedCount Property

Declaration

```
{ DBTABLES.PAS }
property ChangedCount: Longint read FChangedCount;
```

Description

Run-time only, read-only. Contains the number of records that were modified in some manner during the batch operation, due to conversions, data width problems, etc.

Example

```
{ Determine the percent of records that were changed during the batch
  operation }
PercentChanged := BatchMove1.ChangedCount / BatchMove1.MovedCount) * 100;
```

Notes

The ChangedCount value is valid even if no table is specified in the ChangedTableName property.

See Also

TBatchMove.AbortOnKeyViol, TBatchMove.AbortOnProblem, TBatchMove.ChangedTableName

TBatchMove.ChangedTableName Property

Declaration

```
{ DBTABLES.PAS }
property ChangedTableName: TFileName read FChangedTableName
     write FChangedTableName;
```

Description

Specifies a local table which to copy records that were changed during the batch operation.

Example

```
{ Create a table to store original form of any changed records }
BatchMove1.ChangedTableName := 'CHANGED';
```

Notes

If no table name is specified for ChangedTableName and ChangedCount is greater than zero, some data may have been lost during the transfer. The table specified by ChangedTableName will be created as a local (Paradox or dBASE) table.

See Also

TBatchMove.AbortOnKeyViol, TBatchMove.AbortOnProblem, TBatchMove.ChangedCount

TBatchMove.Destination Property

Declaration

```
{ DBTABLES.PAS }
property Destination: TTable read FDestination write FDestination;
```

Description

Specifies the destination table for the batch operation

Example

```
{ Specify the destination table for the batch operation }
BatchMove1.Destination := Table2;
```

Notes

This property is required for a typical batch operation. Note that the value for Destination must be a TTable object, unlike Source, which can specify either a TTable or TQuery object. The destination table may or may not need to exist, depending on the Mode used.

See Also

TBatchMove.Source

TBatchMove.Execute Method

Declaration

```
{ DBTABLES.PAS }
procedure Execute;
```

Description

Executes the batch operation

Example

```
{ Assign the source table - must already exist }
BatchMove1.Source := Table1;

{ Assign the destination table - will be created }
BatchMove1.Destination := Table2;

{ Set the batch operation mode }
BatchMove1.Mode := batCopy;

{ Execute the operation }
BatchMove1.Execute;
```

Notes

Destination table will be overwritten if it already exists

See Also

TBatchMove.Destination, TBatchMove.Mode, TBatchMove.Source

TBatchMove.KeyViolCount Property

Declaration

```
{ DBTABLES.PAS }
property KeyViolCount: Longint read FKeyViolCount;
```

Description

Run-time only, read-only. Contains the number of records that violated integrity (key) constraints during the batch operation.

Example

```
{ Calculate the percentage of key violations in this batch }
PercentKeyViol :=
    (BatchMove1.KeyViolCount / BatchMove1.MovedCount) * 100;
```

Notes

Meaningful only when AbortOnKeyViol is False, as there will always be only one record in the table specified by KeyViolTable if AbortOnKeyViol is True—the batch process will be terminated on the first encounter of a key violation.

See Also

TBatchMove.AbortOnKeyViol, TBatchMove.AbortOnProblem, TBatchMove.ChangedCount, TBatchMove.ChangedTableName, TBatchMove.KeyViolTableName

TBATCHMOVE.KEYVIOLTABLENAME PROPERTY

Declaration

```
{ DBTABLES.PAS }
property KeyViolTableName: TFileName read FKeyViolTableName
    write FKeyViolTableName;
```

Description

Specifies the name of a local table to contain all the records that violate integrity constraints.

Example

```
{ Specify a table to create for storing any records that violate key
  constraints }
BatchMove1.KeyViolTableName := 'VIOLATE';
```

Notes

The table specified by KeyViolTableName will be created as a local (Paradox) table. If a table of that name already exists, it will be overwritten.

See Also

TBatchMove.AbortOnKeyViol, TBatchMove.AbortOnProblem, TBatchMove.ChangedCount, TBatchMove.ChangedTableName, TBatchMove.KeyViolCount

TBATCHMOVE.MAPPINGS PROPERTY

Declaration

```
{ DBTABLES.PAS }
property Mappings: TStrings read FMappings write SetMappings;
```

Description

A list of fields in Destination that correspond to fields in Source for the batch operation. By default, fields are mapped based on their physical positions within the Source and Destination tables. Use the Mappings property to override those defaults if the structure of the Source and Destination tables differ. A mapping is formatted as DestinationField = SourceField or simply FieldName if the name of the field is identical in both tables, with one mapping per line.

Example

```
{ Create a map between Source and Destination field names }
BatchMove1.Mappings.Add('LastName = Last');
BatchMove1.Mappings.Add('FirstName = First');
BatchMove1.Mappings.Add('AcctNo = Account');
BatchMove1.Mappings.Add('City = Address3');
BatchMove1.Mappings.Add('Zip = ZipCode');
```

Notes

If the data type or length of the field in Destination differs from that in Source, the data will be copied on a best fit basis, truncating and performing simple conversions where possible. If a field name that is not mapped exists in Destination, its value will be NULL.

See Also

TBatchMove.Destination, TBatchMove.Source

TBATCHMOVE.MODE PROPERTY

Declaration

```
{ DBTABLES.PAS }
property Mode: TBatchMode read FMode write FMode default batAppend;

TBatchMode = (batAppend, batUpdate, batAppendUpdate, batDelete, batCopy);
```

Description

Specifies the mode (Append, Update, Append/Update, Copy or Delete) for the batch operation, as listed in Table 2.30.

TABLE 2.30 TBATCHMODE CONSTANTS

TBATCHMODE CONSTANT	DESCRIPTION	NOTES
batAppend	Copies all records from Source to Destination.	Destination must not contain any records with the same key as any of the records in Source.
batUpdate	Updates all records in Destination to match those in Source.	Destination must contain a record with the same key value for each record in Source.
batAppendUpdate	Appends any records to Destination that do not already exist in Source; updates all records in Destination that match those in Source	Records are considered "same" if they have the same key values in Source and Destination.
batDelete	Deletes all records in Destination that match those in Source.	Each record in Source must have a record in Destination with the same key value.
batCopy	Creates a new copy of Source as Destination.	Destination will be overwritten if it already exists.

Example

```
{ Specify an Append operation if the Destination table exists }
if FileExists(BatchMove1.Destination) then
   BatchMove1.Mode := batAppend
else
   BatchMove1.Mode := batCopy;
```

Notes

The table specified by Destination in batCopy mode will be created as a local (Paradox or dBASE) table.

See Also

TBatchMove.Destination, TBatchMove.Execute, TBatchMove.Source

TBATCHMOVE.MOVEDCOUNT PROPERTY

Declaration

```
{ DBTABLES.PAS }
property MovedCount: Longint read FMovedCount;
```

Description

Run-time only, read-only. Specifies the number of records that were actually processed by the Execute method.

Example

```
{ Display the number of records moved by the batch operation }
BatchMove1.Execute;
ShowMessage(IntToStr(BatchMove1.MovedCount) +
    ' records were transferred');
```

Notes

Run-time only, read-only. The value of MovedCount includes any records that had size or integrity problems but not those that violated key constraints.

See Also

TBatchMove.Execute

TBatchMove.ProblemCount Property

Declaration

```
{ DBTABLES.PAS }
property ProblemCount: Longint read FProblemCount;
```

Description

Run-time only, read-only. Contains the number of records that, because of data size problems, could not be moved to Destination.

Example

```
{ Display number of records that had data size problems }
BatchMove1.Execute;
ShowMessage(IntToStr(BatchMove1.ProblemCount) +
    ' source records too large');
```

Notes

Meaningful only if AbortOnProblem is False.

See Also

TBatchMove.AbortOnKeyViol, TBatchMove.AbortOnProblem, TBatchMove.ChangedCount, TBatchMove.ChangedTableName, TBatchMove.ProblemTableName

TBATCHMOVE.PROBLEMTABLENAME PROPERTY

Declaration

```
{ DBTABLES.PAS }
property ProblemTableName: TFileName read FProblemTableName
    write FProblemTableName;
```

Description

Specifies a table to store records that could not be processed due to data size problems.

Example

```
{ Store all oversize records in a temporary table }
BatchMove1.ProblemTableName := 'PROBLEM';
```

Notes

Table is created as a local (Paradox or dBASE) table. If a table exists of the same name, it will be overwritten.

See Also

TBatchMove.AbortOnKeyViol, TBatchMove.AbortOnProblem, TBatchMove.ChangedCount, TBatchMove.ChangedTableName, TBatchMove.ProblemCount

TBATCHMOVE.RECORDCOUNT PROPERTY

Declaration

```
{ DBTABLES.PAS }
property RecordCount: Longint read FRecordCount
    write FRecordCount default 0;
```

Description

Limits the number of records that will be moved during the batch operation.

Example

```
{ Limit the batch operation to the first 1000 records }
BatchMove1.RecordCount := 1000;
```

Notes

A value of zero will allow all records to be moved in the batch operation.

See Also

TBatchMove.Source

TBatchMove.Source Property

Declaration

```
{ DBTABLES.PAS }
property Source: TDataSet read FSource write FSource;
```

Description

Specifies the TTable or TQuery object that is the source of data for the batch operation.

Example

```
{ Set the source data set }
BatchMove1.Source := SourceTable;
```

Notes

Although the Source can be a TTable or TQuery object, the Destination must be a TTable object.

See Also

TBatchMove.Destination

TBatchMove.Transliterate Property

Declaration

```
{ DBTABLES.PAS }
property Transliterate: Boolean read FTransliterate
    write FTransliterate default True;
```

Description

Specifies whether data will be translated from Source to Destination's character set during the batch move operation.

Example

```
{ Suppress transliteration during batch move }
BatchMove1.Transliterate := False;
```

Notes

Translation is done via the AnsiToNative and NativeToAnsi functions using DBLocale.

See Also

AnsiToNative and NativeToAnsi in DELPHI.HLP, TBatchMove.DBLocale, TBatchMove.Destination, TBatchMove.Source

TReport Component

Unit

REPORT

Inherits from

TComponent

Description

TReport establishes an interface to the ReportSmith run-time engine and enables printing of a report that has been designed in ReportSmith. The following tables summarize the properties (Table 2.31) and methods (Table 2.32) defined by the TReport component.

TABLE 2.31 TREPORT PROPERTIES

PROPERTY	DATA TYPE	RUN-TIME ONLY	READ-ONLY	DESCRIPTION
AutoUnload	Boolean	No	No	Determines whether the run-time engine for ReportSmith unloads itself from memory after running a report.
EndPage	Word	No	No	Specifies the last page of the report to print.
InitialValues	TStrings	No	No	Contains a list of report variables used to run the report.
MaxRecords	Word	No	No	Specifies the maximum number of records to print for the report.
Preview	Boolean	No	No	Specifies whether the report will be displayed in a preview window prior to printing.
PrintCopies	Word	No	No	Specifies the number of copies of the report to print.
ReportDir	String	No	No	Specifies the directory that the report file is contained in.
ReportHandle	Word	Yes	Yes	Provides a handle to ReportSmith.
ReportName	String	No	No	Specifies the name of the report file.

continued

TABLE 2.31 CONTINUED

PROPERTY	DATA TYPE	RUN-TIME ONLY	READ-ONLY	DESCRIPTION
StartPage	Word	No	No	Specifies which page of the report to start printing.
VersionMajor	Integer	Yes	Yes	Contains the major version number for ReportSmith.
VersionMinor	Integer	Yes	Yes	Contains the minor version number for ReportSmith.

TABLE 2.32 TREPORT METHODS

METHOD	DESCRIPTION
CloseApplication	Sends a DDE message to ReportSmith run-time to stop execution.
CloseReport	Sends a DDE message to ReportSmith run-time to stop printing the report.
Connect	Connects the report to a database.
Print	Sends a DDE message to ReportSmith run-time to print the report.
RecalcReport	Sends a DDE message to ReportSmith to recalculate and rerun the report.
Run	Loads ReportSmith run-time and runs the report.
RunMacro	Sends a DDE message to ReportSmith run-time to run a specified ReportBasic macro.
SetVariable	Sends a DDE string message to ReportSmith run-time to change the value of a specified report variable.
SetVariableLines	Sends a DDE TStrings message to ReportSmith run-time to change the value of a specified report variable.

TREPORT.AUTOUNLOAD PROPERTY

Applies to

TReport component

Declaration

```
{ REPORT.PAS }
property AutoUnload: Boolean read FAutoUnload
    write FAutoUnload default False;
```

Description

Determines whether the Run-time engine for ReportSmith unloads itself from memory after running a report.

Example

```
{ Leave the report engine loaded for this batch of reports }
Report1.AutoUnload := False;
```

```
Report2.AutoUnload := False;

{ Set the last report to unload the engine }
Report3.AutoUnload := True;

{ Run the first report, loads the engine }
Report1.Run;

{ Run the second report, engine already loaded }
Report2.Run;

{ Run the last report, engine already loaded, unloads when done }
Report3.Run;
```

Notes

It may be useful to keep the report engine loaded in order to print multiple reports, rather than to reload the engine each time.

See Also

TReport.CloseApplication

TREPORT.CLOSEAPPLICATION METHOD

Declaration

```
{ REPORT.PAS }
function CloseApplication(ShowDialogs: Boolean): Boolean;
```

Description

Sends a DDE message to ReportSmith Run-time to stop execution.

Example

```
{ Send a message to ReportSmith to shut down }
Report1.CloseApplication;
```

Notes

CloseApplication returns True only if ReportSmith was able to receive the DDE message.

See Also

TReport.AutoUnload

TREPORT.CLOSEREPORT METHOD

Declaration

```
{ REPORT.PAS }
function CloseReport(ShowDialogs: Boolean): Boolean;
```

Description

Sends a DDE message to ReportSmith run-time to stop printing the report.

Example

```
{ Send a DDE message to ReportSmith to stop printing this report }
Report1.CloseReport;
```

Notes

CloseReport returns True only if ReportSmith was able to receive the DDE message.

See Also

TReport.CloseApplication

TReport.Connect Method

Declaration

```
{ REPORT.PAS }
function Connect(ServerType: Word; const ServerName, UserName,
     Password, DatabaseName: String): Boolean;
```

Description

Connects the report to a database. The ServerName, UserName, Password, and DatabaseName parameters are self-explanatory. The ServerType parameter can be any of the values shown in Table 2.33.

TABLE 2.33 SERVERTYPE VALUES FOR TREPORT.CONNECT METHOD

SERVERTYPE VALUE	SERVER
0	Named Connection
1	Reserved
2	dBASE
3	Excel
4	Paradox
5	ASCII
6	SQL Server
7	Oracle
8	DB2
10	Sybase
11	BTrieve
12	Gupta

13	Ingres
16	TeraData
17	DB2/Gupta
19	Unify
40	dBASE (via ODBC)
41	Excel (via ODBC)
42	Paradox (via ODBC)
48	BTrieve (via ODBC)
55	Generic ODBC driver
61	Paradox (via IDAPI)
62	dBASE (via IDAPI)
67	InterBase (via IDAPI)

Example

```
{ This shows a connection to an InterBase server }
Report1.Connect(67, "ISERVER", "JDOE", "SECRET", "SALESDB");

{ This shows a connection to a local database }
Report1.Connect(2);
```

Notes

For Paradox and dBASE databases, the ServerName, UserName, Password and DatabaseName parameters should be set to empty strings. If a particular parameter is not valid for your server, use a null string for that parameter.

See Also

TReport.Run

TREPORT.ENDPAGE PROPERTY

Declaration

```
{ REPORT.PAS }
property EndPage: Word read FEndPage write FEndPage default 9999;
```

Description

Specifies the last page of the report to print.

Example

```
{ Set the last page to 100 }
Report1.EndPage;
```

Notes

The default value of 9999 allows all pages to print.

See Also

TReport.StartPage

TReport.InitialValues Property

Declaration

```
{ REPORT.PAS }
property InitialValues: TStrings read GetInitialValues
    write SetInitialValues;
```

Description

Contains a list of report variables used to run the report.

Example

```
{ Add two report variables }
Report1.InitialValues.Add('@Variable1=<100>');
Report1.InitialValues.Add('@Variable2=<text>');
Report1.Run;
```

Notes

Specifying values in the InitialValues property can bypass the dialog box prompts that request those values when a report is run.

See Also

TReport.SetVariable, TReport.SetVariableLines

TReport.MaxRecords Property

Declaration

```
{ REPORT.PAS }
property MaxRecords: Word read FMaxRecords write FMaxRecords
    default 0;
```

Description

Specifies the maximum number of records to print for the report.

Example

```
{ Limit the report to the first 100 records }
Report1.MaxRecords := 100;
```

Notes

Setting the MaxRecords property is useful for generating sample reports.

See Also

TReport.Run

TREPORT.PREVIEW PROPERTY

Declaration

```
{ REPORT.PAS }
property Preview: Boolean read FPreview write FPreview default False;
```

Description

Specifies whether the report will be displayed in a preview window prior to printing.

Example

```
{ Display the report in a preview window }
Report1.PrintPreview := True;
```

Notes

The report can be printed from the preview window.

See Also

TReport.Print

TREPORT.PRINT METHOD

Declaration

```
{ REPORT.PAS }
function Print: Boolean;
```

Description

Sends a DDE message to ReportSmith run-time to print the report.

Example

```
{ Request printing }
if Report1.Print then
    { Report is printing... }
else
    { ReportSmith was unable to receive the Print request };
```

Notes

The Print method differs from Run in that the report engine is assumed to be loaded.

See Also

TReport.PrintCopies

TREPORT.PRINTCOPIES PROPERTY

Declaration

```
{ REPORT.PAS }
property PrintCopies: Word read FNumCopies write FNumCopies
    default 1;
```

Description

Specifies the number of copies of the report to print.

Example

```
{ Set the number of copies to 3 }
Report1.PrintCopies := 3;
```

Notes

The default value for PrintCopies is 1.

See Also

TReport.Print

TREPORT.RECALCREPORT METHOD

Declaration

```
{ REPORT.PAS }
function RecalcReport: Boolean;
```

Description

Sends a DDE message to ReportSmith to recalculate and rerun the report.

Example

```
{ Modify a report variable, then request recalculation }
Report1.SetVariable('Company', 'ACME');
if Report1.RecalcReport then
   { report is recalculated and run }
else
   { ReportSmith could not receive the Recalc request };
```

Notes

RecalcReport return False if ReportSmith was unable to receive the DDE message to recalculate the report.

See Also

TReport.Run

TREPORT.REPORTDIR PROPERTY

Declaration

```
{ REPORT.PAS }
property ReportDir: String read GetReportDir write SetReportDir;
```

Description

Specifies the directory where ReportSmith stores and finds reports.

Example

```
{ Allow user to set the ReportDir property }
Report1.ReportDir := Edit1.Text;
```

Notes

If the ReportDir property contains a valid directory entry, the path need not be specified in the ReportName property.

See Also

TReport.ReportName

TREPORT.REPORTHANDLE PROPERTY

Declaration

```
{ REPORT.PAS }
property ReportHandle: hWND read FReportHandle;
```

Description

Run-time only, read-only. Provides a handle to ReportSmith.

Example

```
{ This example uses ReportHandle to retrieve the window placement for
  ReportSmith and reset it to display in the top left corner of the screen }
var
   WindowPlacement: PWindowPlacement;
begin
   GetWindowPlacement(Report1.ReportHandle, WindowPlacement);
   WinPlacement^.rcNormalPosition.Top := 0;
   WinPlacement^.rcNormalPosition.Left := 0;
   SetWindowPlacement(Report1.ReportHandle, WindowPlacement);
end;
```

Notes

The ReportHandle property returns a handle for use with the Windows API functions. See **WINAPI.HLP** for additional information.

See Also

Windows API Reference (**WINAPI.HLP**)

TREPORT.REPORTNAME PROPERTY

Declaration

```
{ REPORT.PAS }
property ReportName: String read GetReportName write SetReportName;
```

Description

Specifies the name of the report file.

Example

```
{ Specify a fully qualified report name... }
Report1.ReportName := 'C:\APPS\REPORTS\SALES\QRT4\SUMMARY.RPT';

{ ...or just the report name if the path is stored in ReportDir }
Report1.ReportName := 'SUMMARY.RPT';
```

Notes

If the correct path is already specified in the ReportDir property, enter just the report name.

See Also

TReport.ReportDir

TREPORT.RUN METHOD

Declaration

```
{ REPORT.PAS }
procedure Run;
```

Description

Loads ReportSmith run-time and runs the report

Example

```
{ Load ReportSmith and run the report specified in the ReportName property }
Report1.Run;
```

Notes

Compare this to the Print command, which assumes that ReportSmith is already loaded.

See Also

TReport.Print

TREPORT.RUNMACRO METHOD

Declaration

```
{ REPORT.PAS }
function RunMacro(Macro: PChar): Boolean;
```

Description

Sends a DDE message to ReportSmith run-time to run a specified ReportBasic macro.

Example

```
{ Run the SUBTOTAL macro }
Report1.RunMacro('SUBTOTAL.MAC');
```

Notes

The RunMacro method returns False if ReportSmith is unable to receive the DDE message.

See Also

TReport.SetVariable, TReport.SetVariableLines

TReport.SetVariable Method

Declaration

```
{ REPORT.PAS }
function SetVariable(const Name, Value: String): Boolean;
```

Description

Sends a DDE string message to ReportSmith run-time to change the value of a specified report variable.

Example

```
{ Send ReportSmith a request to reset a variable }
if Report1.SetVariable('City','Cucamonga') then
   { ReportSmith received the request }
else
   { ReportSmith was unable to receive the request };
```

Notes

The SetVariable method returns False if ReportSmith is unable to accept the DDE message.

See Also

TReport.SetVariableLines

TReport.SetVariableLines Method

Declaration

```
{ REPORT.PAS }
function SetVariableLines(const Name: String;
    Value: TStrings): Boolean;
```

Description

Sends a DDE TStrings message to ReportSmith run-time to change the value of a specified report variable, using the values stored in the Value parameter.

Example

```
{ Send a message to reset a variable to the values in a TStrings object }
var
   Value: TStrings;
begin
   Value := TStrings.Create;
   Value.Add('1234 Main Street');
   Value.Add('Anytown, USA');
   Report1.SetVariableLines('Address', Value);
   Value.Free;
end;
```

Notes

The SetVariableLines method returns False if ReportSmith is unable to receive the DDE message.

See Also

TReport.SetVariable

TREPORT.STARTPAGE PROPERTY

Declaration

```
{ REPORT.PAS }
property StartPage: Word read FStartPage write FStartPage default 1;
```

Description

Specifies which page of the report to start printing.

Example

```
{ Allow user to specify starting page }
Report1.StartPage := StrToInt(Edit1.Text);
```

Notes

The default value for StartPage is 1.

See Also

TReport.EndPage

TREPORT.VERSIONMAJOR PROPERTY

Declaration

```
{ REPORT.PAS }
property VersionMajor: Integer read FVersionMajor;
```

Description

Run-time only, read-only. Contains the major version number (left of the decimal) for ReportSmith.

Example

```
{ Inspect the major version number }
if Report1.VersionMajor > 2 then
   ShowMessage('Did somebody upgrade my copy of ReportSmith?');
```

Notes

The minor version number is stored in the VersionMinor property.

See Also

TReport.VersionMinor

TREPORT.VERSIONMINOR PROPERTY

Declaration

```
{ REPORT.PAS }
property VersionMinor: Integer read FVersionMinor;
```

Description

Run-time only, read-only. Contains the minor version number (to the right of the decimal) for ReportSmith.

Example

```
{ Find the full version number for this copy of ReportSmith }
Version := Report1.VersionMajor + Report1.VersionMinor;
if Version < 2.5 then
   ShowMessage('Did someone restore last year's tape backup?');
```

Notes

The major version number is stored in the VersionMajor property.

See Also

TReport.VersionMajor

CHAPTER 3

Visual Data Controls

OVERVIEW

Delphi provides a robust set of data-aware visual controls that can be used to display and/or edit data from a table. By default, all these are accessible on the Data Controls page of the Component Palette.

In this chapter, we will thoroughly examine the properties, methods, and events associated with each of these controls. Also, although many of the properties can be set at design-time with the Object Inspector, there will be situations where you will need to manipulate these controls at run-time. To facilitate this, we will also present numerous source code examples to give you ideas for more flexibility when working with these controls.

FIGURE 3.1 THE DATA CONTROLS PAGE.

The Data Controls components are summarized in the following table (in the order that they appear on the component palette):

DATA CONTROL COMPONENTS

ICON	COMPONENT	DESCRIPTION
	TDBGrid	Provides a data-aware browse grid-style display of data in a database table or query.
	TDBNavigator	Provides a pre-built set of data-aware buttons to control navigation, inserts, deletes, posting and canceling of edits, and data refreshes.
	TDBText	Provides a data-aware Label-type display of field data, without allowing the user to modify the field's contents.
	TDBEdit	Provides a data-aware Edit-type control for display and/or modification of non-memo field data.

continued

Icon	Component	Description
	TDBMemo	Provides a data-aware Memo-type control for display and/or modification of memo field data.
	TDBImage	Provides a data-aware display of graphic images stored in a BLOB (Binary Large OBject) field.
	TDBListBox	Provides a data-aware list box that stores the selected list item in the designated field.
	TDBComboBox	Provides a data-aware list box that stores the selected list item in the designated field.
	TDBCheckBox	Provides a data-aware check box for displaying and/or modification of a logical field value.
	TDBRadioGroup	Provides a data-aware group of radio buttons for display and/or modification of mutually exclusive values for a field.
	TDBLookupListBox	Provides a data-aware list box that retrieves its list values from a lookup table for display (*New in Delphi 2.0*).
	TDBLookupComboBox	Provides a data-aware combo box that retrieves its list values from a lookup table for display (*New in Delphi 2.0*).
	TDBCtrlGrid	Provides customized display of data in panels (*New in Delphi 2.0*).

COMMON ATTRIBUTES

In an attempt to eliminate severe redundancy, the following three tables list the properties (Table 3.1), methods (Table 3.2), and events (Table 3.3) common to all visual data controls. Immediately following these tables is an alphabetical listing of all these attributes. Except where noted, you can safely assume that all the visual data controls documented later in this chapter have these attributes.

TABLE 3.1 COMMON PROPERTIES

Property	Data Type	Run-Time Only	Read-Only	Description
Align	TAlign	Yes	No	Determines alignment of control within its container/parent.
Color	TColor	No	No	Color in which to display the control (see ParentColor property).
ComponentIndex	Integer	Yes	Yes	Zero-based position of the control in its owner's Components property list.

Ctl3D	Boolean	No	No	Determines whether control will be displayed as three- (T) or two- (F) dimensional (see ParentCtl3D)
Cursor	TCursor	No	No	Image that appears when mouse cursor passes over this control
DataField	String	No	No	Name of field to which control is linked
DataSource	TDataSource	No	No	DataSet to which the control is linked
DragCursor	TCursor	No	No	Image that appears when mouse is being dragged over the control
DragMode	TDragMode	No	No	Determines whether or not control can be dragged automatically by user
Enabled	Boolean	No	No	Determines whether data in control should be updated when record pointer changes
Field	TField	Yes	Yes	Field to which the control is linked
Font	TFont	No	No	Font used to display control's text (see ParentFont property)
Handle	THandle (HWnd)	Yes	Yes	Handle to control (useful for Windows API function calls)
Height	Integer	No	No	Vertical size of control (in pixels)
HelpContext	THelpContext	No	No	Unique number for calling context-specific help relevant to this control
Hint	String	No	No	Text to be displayed when user moves cursor over the control (see ShowHint and ParentShowHint)
Left	Integer	No	No	Horizontal coordinate of control's left edge (in pixels) relative to its Owner
Name	String	No	No	Name assigned to control
Owner	TComponent	Yes	Yes	Form that owns the control
Parent	TWinControl	Yes	No	Parent of control
ParentColor	Boolean	No	No	Determines whether control uses its own Color property or that of Parent
ParentCtl3D	Boolean	No	No	Determines whether control uses its own Ctl3D property or that of Parent
ParentFont	Boolean	No	No	Determines whether control uses its own Font property or that of Parent
ParentShowHint	Boolean	No	No	Determines whether control uses its ShowHint property or that of Parent
PopupMenu	TPopupMenu	No	No	Pop-up menu that appears when user right-clicks within this control
Readonly	Boolean	No	No	Determines whether user can change data in the field linked to this control
ShowHint	Boolean	No	No	Determines whether Hint should be displayed if mouse cursor rests briefly upon control (see ParentShowHint)
Showing	Boolean	Yes	Yes	Indicates whether control is currently visible on-screen

continued

TABLE 3.1 CONTINUED

PROPERTY	DATA TYPE	RUN-TIME ONLY	READ-ONLY	DESCRIPTION
TabOrder	TTabOrder	No	No	Position of control in its Parent's tab order (for Tab key navigation).
TabStop	Boolean	No	No	Determines whether user can press Tab to access the control.
Tag	Longint	No	No	User-definable ID for control.
Top	Integer	No	No	Top left corner of control relative to its Owner (in pixels).
Visible	Boolean	No	No	Determines whether control should be displayed on-screen.
Width	Integer	No	No	Horizontal size of control (in pixels).

TABLE 3.2 COMMON METHODS

METHOD	DESCRIPTION
BeginDrag	Starts the dragging of the control.
BringToFront	Puts control in front of all other windowed components in its parent form or panel.
CanFocus	Indicates whether control can receive focus.
ClientToScreen	Translates a point from client area coordinates to global screen coordinates.
Create	Allocates memory to create the control.
Destroy	Destroys the control and releases its memory.
Dragging	Indicates whether control is being dragged.
EndDrag	Ends the dragging of control.
Focused	Determines whether control has focus.
Free	Destroys the control and releases its memory.
GetTextBuf	Retrieves text associated with control.
GetTextLen	Retrieves length of text associated with control.
Hide	Hides control by setting Visible property to False.
Invalidate	Forces control to be repainted.
Refresh	Calls Invalidate and Update methods.
Repaint	Same as Refresh method but does not erase what already appears on-screen.
ScaleBy	Scales control to a specified percentage of its former size.
ScreenToClient	Translates a point from global screen coordinates to client area coordinates.
ScrollBy	Scrolls the contents of the control.
SendToBack	Puts control behind all other windowed components in its parent.
SetBounds	Sets boundaries for control.
SetFocus	Activates the control by giving it input focus.
SetTextBuf	Sets the text associated with control.
Show	Displays control by setting Visible property to True.
Update	Processes any pending paint messages for control.

TABLE 3.3 COMMON EVENTS

EVENT	DATA TYPE	DESCRIPTION
OnClick	TNotifyEvent	Occurs when user clicks upon the control.
OnDragDrop	TDragDropEvent	Occurs when user drops the control.
OnDragOver	TDragOverEvent	Occurs when user drags an object over the control.
OnEndDrag	TEndDragEvent	Occurs when user stops dragging the control.
OnEnter	TNotifyEvent	Occurs when control becomes active.
OnExit	TNotifyEvent	Occurs when control loses input focus.
OnKeyDown	TKeyEvent	Occurs when user presses a key with control active.
OnKeyPress	TKeyPressEvent	Occurs when user presses a character key.
OnKeyUp	TKeyEvent	Occurs when user releases a key with control active.

ALIGN PROPERTY

Declaration

```
{ CONTROLS.PAS }
property Align: TAlign read FAlign write SetAlign default alNone;

{ CONTROLS.PAS }
TAlign = (alNone, alTop, alBottom, alLeft, alRight, alClient);
```

Description

Run-time only. The Align property determines how the control will be aligned within its parent form. It is an enumerated type (TAlign) that can be set to one of the values shown in Table 3.4.

TABLE 3.4 ALIGN VALUES

VALUE	DESCRIPTION
alNone	Control remains where you place it within the form (default).
alTop	Control moves to top of form and resizes horizontally to fill the width of the form.
alBottom	Control moves to bottom of form and resizes horizontally to fill the width of the form.
alLeft	Control moves to left side of form and resizes vertically to fill the height of the form.
alRight	Control moves to right side of form and resizes vertically to fill the height of the form.
alClient	Control resizes to fill entire unoccupied client area of form.

Example

```
{ Example 1: Force a grid to occupy entire form }
DBGrid1.Align := alClient;

{ Example 2: Lock a navigator to the top of a form }
DBNavigator1.Align := alTop;
```

BEGINDRAG METHOD

Declaration

```
{ CONTROLS.PAS }
procedure BeginDrag(Immediate: Boolean);
```

Description

The BeginDrag method is used for dragging the control. If the parameter passed to this method is True, the mouse cursor changes in accordance with the DragCursor property, and the drag operation begins immediately. If the parameter is False, the mouse pointer does not change, and the drag operation does not begin until the user moves the mouse at least five pixels. This is useful in that it allows a control to accept mouse clicks without automatically beginning a drag operation.

You need to call BeginDrag only if the control's DragMode property is set to dmManual.

See Also

DragCursor property, DragMode property, EndDrag method

BRINGTOFRONT METHOD

Declaration

```
{ CONTROLS.PAS }
procedure BringToFront;
```

Description

The BringToFront method puts the control in front of all other windowed components on its parent. This is particularly useful when you have overlapped components.

Example

```
{ This statement could be put in the OnEnter event handler for the control
  to ensure that they are completely visible }
ControlName.BringToFront;
```

See Also

SendToBack method

CANFOCUS METHOD

Declaration

```
{ CONTROLS.PAS }
function CanFocus : Boolean;
```

Description

The CanFocus method indicates whether the control can receive input focus. It returns True if both the control and its parent(s) have their Visible and Enabled properties set to True.

See Also

Enabled property, Parent property, Visible property

CLIENTTOSCREEN METHOD

Declaration

```
{ CONTROLS.PAS }
function ClientToScreen(const Point: TPoint): TPoint;
```

Description

The ClientToScreen method translates a point within the control from client area coordinates to global screen coordinates.

Example

```
var
    p : TPoint;
begin
    p := ControlName.ClientToScreen(Point(0,0));
    MessageDlg('Relative screen position is X: ' + IntToStr(p.x) +
               ' Y: ' + IntToStr(p.y), mtInformation, [mbOK], 0);
end;
```

See Also

ScreenToClient method

COLOR PROPERTY

Declaration

```
{ CONTROLS.PAS }
property Color: TColor read FColor write SetColor
    stored IsColorStored default clWindow;
```

Description

The Color property dictates the color in which the control will be displayed. If the ParentColor property is set to True, then changing the Color property of the control's parent will also automatically change the Color property of the control.

When you assign a value to the control's Color property, its ParentColor property will automatically be set to False.

Table 3.5 lists the stock color values.

TABLE 3.5 COLOR VALUES (CONSTANT)

VALUE	DESCRIPTION
clBlack	Black
clMaroon	Maroon
clGreen	Green
clOlive	Olive green
clNavy	Navy blue
clPurple	Purple
clTeal	Teal
clGray	Gray
clSilver	Silver
clRed	Red
clLime	Lime green
clBlue	Blue
clFuchsia	Fuchsia
clAqua	Aqua
clWhite	White

However, rather than hard-coding colors, you may wish to use the values shown in Table 3.6, which map to the user's environment and thus allow more personalization.

TABLE 3.6 COLOR VALUES (ENVIRONMENTAL)

VALUE	DESCRIPTION
clBackground	Color of Windows background
clActiveCaption	Color of title bar in the active (focused) window
clInactiveCaption	Color of title bar in inactive windows
clMenu	Background color for menus
clWindow *(default)*	Background color for windows
clWindowFrame	Color for window frames
clMenuText	Color of text on menus
clWindowText	Color of text in windows
clCaptionText	Color of text in active window's title bar
clActiveBorder	Color of border in active window
clInactiveBorder	Color of border in inactive windows
clAppWorkSpace	Color of application workspace
clHighlight	Background color for selected text
clHighlightText	Color of selected text

clBtnFace	Color of button faces
clBtnShadow	Color of button shadows
clGrayText	Color of dimmed text
clBtnText	Color of text on buttons
clInactiveCaptionText	Color of text on title bars of inactive windows
clBtnHighlight	Color of button highlighting

Notes

If you require a greater degree of control over the color settings, you can specify hexadecimal constants rather than the values listed in Table 3.6. These constants should be 4 bytes in length. The lower 3 bytes represent the RGB color levels for blue, green, and red. For example, the value $00FF0000 represents full-intensity blue, the value $0000FF00 is full-intensity green, and $000000FF is full-intensity red.

The highest-order byte dictates which palette to use. if the value is zero ($00), the closest color found in the system palette will be used. If the value is one ($01), the color will be obtained from the currently realized palette (as set by the Windows API RealizePalette function). If the value is two ($02), the color will be obtained from the logical palette for the current device context (as set by the Windows API SelectPalette function).

Example

```
{ Two different ways to change color to purple: the first is great for
  readability, and the second is great for bitheads }
ControlName.Color := clPurple;
ControlName.Color := $00FF00FF;
```

See Also

ParentColor property

COMPONENTINDEX PROPERTY

Declaration

```
{ CLASSES.PAS }
property ComponentIndex: Integer read GetComponentIndex
  write SetComponentIndex;
```

Description

Run-time and read-only. The ComponentIndex property denotes the position of the control within its owner's Components property list. This list is zero-based (i.e., the first component in the list will have a value of 0).

Ctl3D Property

Declaration

```
{ CONTROLS.PAS }
property Ctl3D: Boolean read FCtl3D write SetCtl3D
    stored IsCtl3DStored;
```

Description

The Ctl3D property dictates whether the control will be displayed as three-dimensional (sculpted) or two-dimensional (flat). By default, Ctl3D will be set to True. However, if the ParentCtl3D property is True, the Ctl3D property of the control's Parent will be used instead.

Notes

The **CTL3DV2.DLL** dynamic-link library must be available in order to display a 3-D control.

See Also

ParentCtl3D property

Cursor Property

Declaration

```
{ CONTROLS.PAS }
property Cursor: TCursor read FCursor write SetCursor
    default crDefault;
```

Description

The Cursor property dictates which image will be displayed when the mouse cursor passes over the control. Table 3.7 lists the available stock values for this property.

TABLE 3.7 CURSOR VALUES

CONSTANT	VALUE
crDefault	0
crNone	−1
crArrow	−2
crCross	−3
crIBeam	−4
crSize	−5
crSizeNESW	−6
crSizeNS	−7

crSizeNWSE	−8
crSizeWE	−9
crUpArrow	−10
crHourGlass	−11
crDrag	−12
crNoDrop	−13
crHSplit	−14
crVSplit	−15
crMultiDrag	−16
crSQLWait	−17

Example

```
{ Use cross cursor }
ControlName.Cursor := crCross;
```

See Also

DragCursor property

DataField Property

Declaration

```
{ DBCTRLS.PAS }
property DataField: String read GetDataField write SetDataField;
```

Description

The DataField property contains the name of the field to which the control should be linked. The field should be accessible through a data source that would be specified in the DataSource property.

Notes

The discussions of the Create method elsewhere in this chapter each contain comprehensive examples of how to create these controls dynamically. Please refer to those examples for an illustration of how to set the DataField property.

Also note that certain controls are not field-specific (e.g., TDBGrid, TDBNavigator). These controls will not have a DataField property because it would make no sense for them to do so.

See Also

DataSource property, Field property

DataSource Property

Declaration

```
{ DBCTRLS.PAS }
property DataSource: TDataSource read GetDataSource
    write SetDataSource;
```

Description

The DataSource property contains the data source to which the control should be linked. This data source should in turn be linked to a TTable or TQuery object.

Example

The discussions of the Create method elsewhere in this chapter each contain comprehensive examples of how to create these controls dynamically. Please refer to those examples for an illustration of how to set the DataSource property.

See Also

DataField property

Destroy Method

Declaration

```
{ DBCTRLS.PAS }
destructor Destroy; override;
```

Description

The Destroy method destroys the control and releases the memory previously allocated to it. It is unlikely that you will need to call this method directly. If you have given the control an owner, you do not need to call Destroy explicitly to get rid of it. If you have not given the control an owner, you should call the Free method rather than Destroy.

See Also

Free method

DragCursor Property

Declaration

```
{ CONTROLS.PAS }
property DragCursor: TCursor read FDragCursor write FDragCursor
    default crDrag;
```

Description

The DragCursor property indicates which mouse cursor image will be displayed if the user commences a drag operation from the control. The default value is crDrag. Refer to the Cursor property discussion for a complete list of available values.

Example

```
{ Use I-beam cursor when dragging this control }
ControlName.DragCursor := crIBeam;
```

See Also

Cursor property

DRAGGING METHOD

Declaration

```
{ CONTROLS.PAS }
function Dragging: Boolean;
```

Description

The Dragging method returns True if the control is being dragged, or False if it is not.

See Also

DragMode property

DRAGMODE PROPERTY

Declaration

```
{ CONTROLS.PAS }
property DragMode: TDragMode read FDragMode write FDragMode
   default dmManual;

TDragMode = (dmManual, dmAutomatic);
```

Description

The DragMode property dictates whether the user can automatically drag the control by left-clicking upon it. If this is set to dmManual (which is the default value), the control cannot be dragged until you programmatically call its BeginDrag method.

Example

```
if MessageDlg('Allow drag and drop', mtInformation,
              [mbYes, mbNo], 0) = mrYes then
   ControlName.DragMode := dmAutomatic
else
   ControlName.DragMode := dmManual;
```

See Also

BeginDrag method, DragCursor property, EndDrag method

ENABLED PROPERTY

Declaration

```
{ CONTROLS.PAS }
property Enabled: Boolean read FEnabled write SetEnabled
   default True;
```

Description

The Enabled property dictates whether the data in the control should be updated when the record in its corresponding DataSource is changed. If Enabled is set to its default value of True, the control will be updated. Otherwise, the control will be cleared, and it will not be updated as the user moves through the dataset.

This can also be accomplished by using the DisableControls and EnableControls methods, which are available to TTable and TQuery objects.

Example

```
{ Temporarily disable updates }
ControlName.Enabled := False;
for x := 1 to 5 do
   ControlName.DataSource.DataSet.Next;
{ re-enable updates }
ControlName.Enabled := True;
```

See Also

DataSource property

ENDDRAG METHOD

Declaration

```
{ CONTROLS.PAS }
procedure EndDrag(Drop: Boolean);
```

Description

The EndDrag method terminates the drag operation. The Drop parameter determines whether or not the control will actually be dropped (True = yes, False = no).

See Also

BeginDrag method, DragMode property

Focused Method

Declaration

```
{ CONTROLS.PAS }
function Focused: Boolean;
```

Description

The Focused method indicates whether or not the control is currently active. If Focused returns True, then the control does indeed have input focus.

Notes

Another way to determine the control which has input focus is to check a TForm's ActiveControl property.

See Also

Enabled property

Font Property

Declaration

```
{ CONTROLS.PAS }
property Font: TFont read FFont write SetFont stored IsFontStored;
```

Description

The Font property dictates how the control's text will be displayed. If not specified, this will default to the font used by the form that owns the control.

Examples

```
{ Embolden caption if check box is checked }
if DBCheckBox1.Checked then
   DBCheckBox1.Font.Style := DBCheckBox1.Font.Style + [fsBold]
else
```

```
        DBCheckBox1.Font.Style := DBCheckBox1.Font.Style - [fsBold];
```

{ Set an OnChange event handler so that we can continuously check for the
* presence of a substring within an edit control }*
```
procedure TForm1.DBEdit1Change(Sender: TObject);
begin
    if Pos('DELPHI', UpperCase(DBEdit1.Text)) > 0 then
        DBEdit1.Font.Style := DBEdit1.Font.Style + [fsItalic]
    else
        DBEdit1.Font.Style := DBEdit1.Font.Style - [fsItalic];
end;
```

See Also

Caption property, ParentFont property

FREE METHOD

Declaration

```
procedure Free;
```

Description

The Free method destroys the control and releases the memory previously allocated to it. You would need to call Free only if you have created the control on-the-fly without giving it an owner.

Example

```
var
    cb : TDBCheckBox;
{ click on button1 to create an owner-less check box on-the-fly }
procedure TForm1.Button1Click(Sender: TObject);
begin
    cb := TDBCheckBox.Create(Self);
    cb.Parent      := Form1;
    cb.Top         := 10;
    cb.Left        := 30;
    cb.Caption     := 'Active?';
    cb.DataSource := Customer; {NOTE: this assumes that Customer data
                                 source was created at design time}
    cb.DataField   := 'Active';
end;
{ Click on button2 to remove previously created check box }
procedure TForm1.Button2Click(Sender: TObject);
begin
    cb.Free;
end;
```

GETTEXTBUF METHOD

Declaration

```
{ CONTROLS.PAS }
function GetTextBuf(Buffer: PChar; BufSize: Integer): Integer;
```

Description

The GetTextBuf method copies the text associated with the control (generally either its Caption or Text property) into a null-terminated string (Buffer). The BufSize parameter limits the number of characters to be copied. GetTextBuf returns the number of characters copied.

Notes

GetTextBuf is primarily for manipulating strings that are longer than 255 characters (i.e., PChars). If the text associated with the control is that of its Caption property, then it is overkill to use GetTextBuf because all Captions are limited to 255 characters.

Example

```
{ Copy all text from one DBMemo to another }
var
    buffer : PChar;
    bytes  : Integer;
begin
    bytes := DBMemo1.GetTextLen;
    if bytes > 0 then
    begin
        Inc(bytes);                {to accommodate null terminator}
        GetMem(buffer, bytes);     {allocate memory for PChar }
        DBMemo1.GetTextBuf(buffer, bytes);
        DBMemo2.Text := StrPas(buffer);
        FreeMem(buffer, bytes);    {Free memory allocated to PChar }
    end;
end;
```

See Also

GetTextLen method, SetTextBuf method

GETTEXTLEN METHOD

Declaration

```
{ CONTROLS.PAS }
function GetTextLen: Integer;
```

Description

The GetTextLen method returns the number of characters contained in the text associated with the control.

Notes

GetTextLen is primarily for testing strings that are longer than 255 characters.

See Also

Caption property, GetTextBuf method, SetTextBuf method

HANDLE PROPERTY

Declaration

```
{ CONTROLS.PAS }
property Handle: HWnd read GetHandle;
```

Description

The Handle property is used only if you should need to pass the control's handle to a Windows API function. Although you should rarely need to do this, there are some useful exceptions. These examples will be presented throughout this chapter within the context of specific controls.

Notes

Run-time and read-only

HEIGHT PROPERTY

Declaration

```
{ CONTROLS.PAS }
property Height: Integer read FHeight write SetHeight;
```

Description

The Height property contains the vertical size of the control in pixels.

Example

```
{ set control height to fit the height of its font }
ControlName.Height := - (ControlName.Font.Height);
```

See Also

SetBounds method, Width property

HELPCONTEXT PROPERTY

Declaration

```
{ CONTROLS.PAS }
property HelpContext: THelpContext read FHelpContext
    write FHelpContext default 0;
```

Description

The HelpContext property contains a unique number used to identify a topic in the application's help file that is relevant to the control. By default, this will contain the value zero (0), which means that no context-specific help is available for this control.

Example

```
{ Attach MYAPP.HLP to this application }
Application.HelpFile := 'MYAPP.HLP';
{ Attach help topic #1000 in that file to this control }
ControlName.HelpContext := 1000;
```

See Also

TApplication.HelpFile property, TApplication.OnHelp method

HIDE METHOD

Declaration

```
{ CONTROLS.PAS }
procedure Hide;
```

Description

The Hide method renders the control invisible by setting its Visible property to False.

See Also

Show method, Showing property, Visible property

HINT PROPERTY

Declaration

```
{ CONTROLS.PAS }
property Hint: String read GetHint write SetHint;
```

Description

The Hint property contains text to be displayed when the OnHint event occurs for the control. This generally occurs when the user rests the mouse cursor upon the control for longer than a certain period of time (which you can specify by setting the Application.HintPause property).

By default, this text will be displayed in a small box just beneath the control. In order to display this hint, the ShowHint properties for both the check box and the application must have been set to True. (The Application.ShowHint is set to True by default.)

You may also specify two hints by separating them with a pipe character (|). The text preceding the pipe character will be displayed next to the control when the user momentarily rests the mouse cursor upon it. The text following the pipe character will be displayed according to the logic in the Application.ShowHint event handler. The following example demonstrates this. The word Active? will appear next to the control, and Customer active status will appear in the Panel1 component whenever the mouse cursor passes over the control.

Example

```
{ Procedure declaration, appears in interface section }
procedure ShowHint(Sender: TObject);

Application.ShowHint := True;   { This is the default value }
Application.OnHint := ShowHint;
CONtrolName.Hint := 'Active? | Customer active status';
ControlName.ShowHint := True;

procedure TForm1.ShowHint(Sender: TObject);
begin
    Panel1.Caption := Application.Hint;
end;
```

See Also

ParentShowHint property, ShowHint property, TApplication.ShowHint property, TApplication.OnHint property

INVALIDATE METHOD

Declaration

```
{ CONTROLS.PAS }
procedure Invalidate; virtual;
```

Description

The Invalidate method forces the control to be redrawn as soon as possible. It is unlikely that you will need to use this method.

See Also

Refresh method, Repaint method

LEFT PROPERTY

Declaration

```
{ CONTROLS.PAS }
property Left: Integer read FLeft write SetLeft;
```

Description

The Left property contains the horizontal position of the control (in pixels) relative to the form that owns it. This will be set at design-time dependent upon where you place the control, but you are always free to change it at run-time.

See Also

SetBounds method, Top property

NAME PROPERTY

Declaration

```
{ CLASSES.PAS }
property Name: TComponentName read GetName write SetName
    stored False;
```

Description

The Name property identifies the control, thus allowing you to write code to access it at run-time. Unless you like deliberately causing yourself maintenance grief, we highly recommend that you set the value of this property only at design-time.

ONDRAGDROP EVENT

Declaration

```
{ CONTROLS.PAS }
property OnDragDrop: TDragDropEvent read FOnDragDrop
    write FOnDragDrop;
TDragDropEvent = procedure(Sender, Source: TObject;
    X, Y: Integer) of object;
```

Description

The OnDragDrop event occurs when an object is dropped onto the control. You should write an OnDragDrop event handler to specify what you want to happen when the user drops an object. Four parameters are passed to your OnDragDrop event handler: Sender (the control); Source (the object being dropped); X and Y (mouse cursor coordinates).

Example

Specific examples will be provided throughout this chapter within the context of certain controls.

See Also

DragCursor property, DragMode property, OnDragOver event

OnDragOver Event

Declaration

```
{ CONTROLS.PAS }
property OnDragOver: TDragOverEvent read FOnDragOver
   write FOnDragOver;

TDragOverEvent = procedure(Sender, Source: TObject; X, Y: Integer;
    State: TDragState; var Accept: Boolean) of object;

TDragState = (dsDragEnter, dsDragLeave, dsDragMove);
```

Description

The OnDragOver event occurs when an object is dragged over the control. You should write an OnDragOver event handler to determine whether the control is able to accept the object. The parameters passed to your OnDragOver event handler are Sender (the control), Source (the object being dragged), X and Y (mouse cursor coordinates); State (the status of the object being dragged in relation to the control); and Accept, which should be set to a boolean value (True indicates that the control can accept the object, and False means that it cannot).

Example

Specific examples will be provided throughout this chapter within the context of certain controls.

See Also

DragCursor property, OnDragDrop event

ONENDDRAG EVENT

Declaration

```
{ CONTROLS.PAS }
property OnEndDrag: TEndDragEvent read FOnEndDrag write FOnEndDrag;

TEndDragEvent = procedure(Sender, Target: TObject;
   X, Y: Integer) of object;
```

Description

The OnEndDrag event occurs whenever the user stops dragging the control. The drag operation ends either by dropping the control or by releasing the mouse button. You can write an OnEndDrag event handler to implement special processing to occur when the drag operation stops. The parameters passed to your OnEndDrag event handler will be: Sender (the control), Target (the object upon which you are dropping the control), X and Y (mouse cursor coordinates). If the drag operation is canceled, then Target will have the value of NIL, which can be tested as shown in the following example.

Example

```
{ When finished dragging a control, disable it if we have actually dropped
  it upon something }
procedure TForm1.ControlNameEndDrag(Sender, Target: TObject;
  X, Y: Integer);
begin
  if Target <> nil then
      (Sender as TControl).Enabled := False;
end;
```

See Also

BeginDrag method, DragCursor property, DragMode property

ONENTER EVENT

Declaration

```
{ CONTROLS.PAS }
property OnEnter: TNotifyEvent read FOnEnter write FOnEnter;

{ CLASSES.PAS }
TNotifyEvent = procedure(Sender: TObject) of object;
```

Description

The OnEnter event occurs when the user gives the control focus. It can be used for special processing, such as changing color as shown in the following example.

204

Examples

```
{ Example 1: Change color of a control to indicate that it is active }
var
    OldColor : TColor;

{ Make control blue upon entry and save its current color }
procedure TForm1.ControlNameEnter(Sender: TObject);
begin
    with Sender as TDBEdit do begin
        OldColor := Color;
        Color := clBlue;
    end;
end;

{ Reset original color upon exit }
procedure TForm1.ControlNameExit(Sender: TObject);
begin
    (Sender as TDBEdit).Color := OldColor;
end;

{ Example 2: Amorphous navigator. Let's assume that your form has
  master/detail tables and a DBNavigator attached to the master
  data source. The grid is attached to the detail data source. this
  logic will cause the DBNavigator to effectively control the grid
  when you make the grid active. Try it! }
procedure TForm1.DBGrid1Enter(Sender: TObject);
begin
    DBNavigator.DataSource := DetailDataSource;
end;

procedure TForm1.DBGrid1Exit(Sender: TObject);
begin
    DBNavigator.DataSource := MasterDataSource;
end;

{ Example 3: Display both scroll bars on a memo, but only while the memo
  has input focus }
procedure TForm1.DBMemo1Enter(Sender: TObject);
begin
    DBMemo1.ScrollBars := ssBoth;
end;

procedure TForm1.DBMemo1Exit(Sender: TObject);
begin
    DBMemo1.ScrollBars := ssNone;
end;
```

See Also

OnExit event

ONEXIT EVENT

Declaration

```
{ CONTROLS.PAS }
property OnExit: TNotifyEvent read FOnExit write FOnExit;
```

```
{ CLASSES.PAS }
TNotifyEvent = procedure(Sender: TObject) of object;
```

Description

The OnExit event occurs when the control loses focus (i.e., the user moves to a different control).

Example

See the example provided with the OnEnter discussion.

See Also

OnEnter event

ONKEYDOWN EVENT

Declaration

```
{ CONTROLS.PAS }
property OnKeyDown: TKeyEvent read FOnKeyDown write FOnKeyDown;
```

```
TKeyEvent = procedure(Sender: TObject; var Key: Word;
    Shift: TShiftState) of object;
```

```
{ CLASSES.PAS }
TShiftState = set of (ssShift, ssAlt, ssCtrl,
    ssLeft, ssRight, ssMiddle, ssDouble);
```

Description

The OnKeyDown event occurs when a user presses a key while the control has focus. You can write an OnKeyDown event handler to handle special keypresses, including function keys or keypresses combined with the **Shift, Alt,** and/or **Ctrl** keys. Parameters passed to your OnKeyDown event handler are Key (the numeric code associated with the keypress) and Shift (status of special keys, such as **Shift, Alt,** and **Ctrl,** and of mouse buttons).

Notes

A complete list of numeric codes associated with these keypresses can be found by searching for the topic "Virtual Key Codes" in the Delphi on-line help file. Alternatively, you can identify a key by its ASCII value (assuming, of course, that it has an ASCII value).

Table 3.8 lists the possible TShiftState values.

TABLE 3.8 TSHIFTSTATE VALUES

VALUE	DESCRIPTION
ssShift	The **Shift** key is held down.
ssAlt	The **Alt** key is held down.
ssCtrl	The **Ctrl** key is held down.
ssLeft	The left mouse button is held down.
ssRight	The right mouse button is held down.
ssMiddle	The middle mouse button is held down.
ssDouble	Both the left and right mouse buttons are being held down.

Example

Specific examples will be provided throughout this chapter within the context of certain controls.

See Also

OnKeyPress event, OnKeyUp event, OnMouseDown event

ONKEYPRESS EVENT

Declaration

```
{ CONTROLS.PAS }
property OnKeyPress: TKeyPressEvent read FOnKeyPress
    write FOnKeyPress;

TKeyPressEvent = procedure(Sender: TObject; var Key: Char) of object;
```

Description

The OnKeyPress event occurs when a user presses a key that has a corresponding ASCII value while the control has focus. The Key parameter passed to your OnKeyPress event handler is the character that was pressed.

Notes

If you need to trap special (non-ASCII) keys, you should use the OnKeyDown event.

Example

Specific examples will be provided throughout this chapter within the context of certain controls.

See Also

OnKeyDown event

ONKEYUP EVENT

Declaration

```
{ CONTROLS.PAS }
property OnKeyUp: TKeyEvent read FOnKeyUp write FOnKeyUp;

TKeyEvent = procedure(Sender: TObject; var Key: Word;
    Shift: TShiftState) of object;

{ CLASSES.PAS }
TShiftState = set of (ssShift, ssAlt, ssCtrl,
    ssLeft, ssRight, ssMiddle, ssDouble);
```

Description

The OnKeyUp event occurs when a user releases a key while the control has focus. OnKeyUp handles special keypresses, including function keys or keypresses combined with the **Shift, Alt,** and/or **Ctrl** keys. Parameters passed to your OnKeyUp event handler are Key (the numeric code associated with the keypress) and Shift (status of special keys, such as **Shift, Alt,** and **Ctrl,** and of mouse buttons).

Notes

A complete list of numeric codes associated with these keypresses can be found by searching for the topic "Virtual Key Codes" in the Delphi on-line help file. Alternatively, you can identify a key by its ASCII value (if it has an ASCII value).

See the OnKeyDown discussion for a list of TShiftState values.

See Also

OnKeyDown event

OWNER PROPERTY

Declaration

```
{ CLASSES.PAS }
property Owner: TComponent read FOwner;
```

Description

The Owner property is the component that owns the control (i.e., the form upon which the control resides).

Notes

Run-time and read-only

See Also

Parent property

PARENT PROPERTY

Declaration

```
{ CONTROLS.PAS }
property Parent: TWinControl read FParent write SetParent;
```

Description

Run-time only. The Parent property holds a reference to the windowed control that is the parent of the control. *This must be specified if you are creating a visual control programmatically at run-time.*

See Also

Owner property

PARENTCOLOR PROPERTY

Declaration

```
{ CONTROLS.PAS }
property ParentColor: Boolean read FParentColor write
SetParentColor
   default True;
```

Description

The ParentColor property determines where the control will look for its color information. If this is set to its default value of True, the control will be drawn in the color specified by its parent's Color property. If ParentColor is set to False, the control will be drawn based upon its own Color property.

Notes

Changing a control's Color property implicitly sets the ParentColor property to False.

Example

```
{ Display a check box in red if it is checked }
if DBCheckBox1.Checked = True then
    { The next statement implicitly sets ParentColor to False }
    DBCheckBox1.Color := clRed;
else
    { Revert back to parent's color }
    DBCheckBox1.ParentColor := True;
```

See Also

Color property, Parent property

PARENTCTL3D PROPERTY

Declaration

```
{ CONTROLS.PAS }
property ParentCtl3D: Boolean read FParentCtl3D
        write SetParentCtl3D default True;
```

Description

The ParentCtl3D property helps determine whether the control will be displayed as three- or two-dimensional. If ParentCtl3D is set to its default value of True, the Ctl3D property of the control's parent will be used. If ParentCtl3D is set to False, the control's dimensionality will be dictated by its own Ctl3D property.

Notes

Changing a control's Ctl3D property implicitly sets the ParentCtl3D property to False.

See Also

Ctl3D property, Parent property

PARENTFONT PROPERTY

Declaration

```
{ CONTROLS.PAS }
property ParentFont: Boolean read FParentFont write SetParentFont default
    True;
```

Description

The ParentFont property dictates where the control looks to determine the font in which its text will be displayed. If ParentFont is set to its default value of True, any text associated with the control will be displayed in the font attached to its parent. Otherwise, the control's own Font property will be used to display its text.

Notes

Changing the control's Font property implicitly sets the ParentFont property to False.

Example

```
{ Change font of a check box if it is checked }
if DBCheckBox1.Checked then begin
   { These statements implicitly set ParentFont to False }
   DBCheckBox1.Font.Name  := 'Times New Roman';
   DBCheckBox1.Font.Size  := 12;
end
else
   DBCheckBox1.ParentFont := True;
```

See Also

Font property, Parent property

PARENTSHOWHINT PROPERTY

Declaration

```
{ CONTROLS.PAS }
property ParentShowHint: Boolean read FParentShowHint
   write SetParentShowHint default True;
```

Description

The ParentShowHint property dictates where the control looks to determine whether or not the text in its Hint property should be displayed. If ParentShowHint is set to its default value of True, the control's hint will be displayed if its parent's ShowHint property is set to True. If ParentShowHint is set to False, the control's hint will be displayed only if its own ShowHint property is set to True.

Notes

Changing a control's ShowHint property implicitly sets the ParentShowHint property to False.

Example

```
{ Enable hints at the form level and thus for the control too }
Form1.ShowHint := True;
ControlName.ParentShowHint := True;
```

See Also

Hint property, ShowHint property

POPUPMENU PROPERTY

Declaration

```
{ CONTROLS.PAS }
property PopupMenu: TPopupMenu read FPopupMenu write FPopupMenu;
```

Description

The PopupMenu property contains the pop-up menu, if any, that is attached to the control. If this is defined, it will appear either: (a) when the user clicks the right mouse button within the control (assuming that the pop-up menu's AutoPopup property is set to True) or (b) when the pop-up menu's Popup method is executed.

Notes

Another possibility is to call the PopupMenu.Popup method within the OnEnter event handler for your control. This would force the pop-up menu to appear immediately whenever the user tabbed to (or clicked upon) the control. This could be useful in terms of prevalidation; on the other hand, it could perhaps drive the user insane.

Example

```
{ This logic creates a cut/copy/paste pop-up menu at run-time, and attaches
  it to an edit box.  If you have already created the pop-up menu at
  design-time, remove that part of the code. }

procedure TForm1.FormCreate(Sender: TObject);
var
   pm : TPopupMenu;
   mi : TMenuItem;
begin
   { create PopupMenu object }
   pm := TPopupMenu.Create(Application);
   { create "Cut" MenuItem object }
   mi := TMenuItem.Create(pm);
```

```
    mi.Caption := 'Cu&t';
    mi.OnClick := EditCut;
    pm.Items.Add(mi);   { attach to pop-up menu }
    { create "Copy" MenuItem object }
    mi := TMenuItem.Create(pm);
    mi.Caption := '&Copy';
    mi.OnClick := EditCopy;
    pm.Items.Add(mi);   { attach to pop-up menu }
    { create "Paste" MenuItem object }
    mi := TMenuItem.Create(pm);
    mi.Caption := '&Paste';
    mi.OnClick := EditPaste;
    pm.Items.Add(mi);   { attach to pop-up menu }
    { attach pop-up menu to the edit box }
    DBEdit1.PopupMenu := pm;
end;

procedure TForm1.EditCopy(Sender : TObject);
begin
    DBEdit1.CopyToClipboard;
end;

procedure TForm1.EditCut(Sender : TObject);
begin
    DBEdit1.CutToClipboard;
end;

procedure TForm1.EditPaste(Sender : TObject);
begin
    DBEdit1.PasteFromClipboard;
end;
```

READONLY PROPERTY

Declaration

```
{ DBCTRLS.PAS }
property ReadOnly: Boolean read GetReadOnly write SetReadOnly
    default False;
```

Description

The ReadOnly property determines whether or not the user's changes to the control will affect the field linked to it. If ReadOnly is set to its default value of False, the user can change the value of the field by changing the control (provided that the dataset is in edit mode). If ReadOnly is set to True, the user will not be able to modify the value of the field linked to the control.

Example

```
{ Allow user to edit field attached to this control only if their security
  level is greater than 50 }
CОntrolName.ReadOnly := (iSecurity < 51);
```

See Also

Enabled property

REFRESH METHOD

Declaration

```
{ CONTROLS.PAS }
procedure Refresh;
```

Description

The Refresh method erases, then repaints, the control. It calls the Repaint, Invalidate, and Update methods.

See Also

Repaint method, Invalidate method, Update method

REPAINT METHOD

Declaration

```
{ CONTROLS.PAS }
procedure Repaint; virtual;
```

Description

The Repaint method redraws the control without erasing what is already on-screen.

See Also

Refresh method

SCALEBY METHOD

Declaration

```
{ CONTROLS.PAS }
procedure ScaleBy(M, D: Integer);
```

Description

The ScaleBy method allows you to adjust the size of the control by a specified percentage. The M and D parameters refer to the multiplier and divisor, respectively.

Example

```
{ Make a control one third of its original size }
ControlName.ScaleBy(1, 3);
```

See Also

Height property, Width property

SCREENTOCLIENT METHOD

Declaration

```
{ CONTROLS.PAS }
function ScreenToClient(const Point: TPoint): TPoint;
```

Description

The ScreenToClient method translates a point on the screen from global screen coordinates to client area coordinates relative to the control.

See Also

ClientToScreen method

SCROLLBY METHOD

Declaration

```
{ CONTROLS.PAS }
procedure ScrollBy(DeltaX, DeltaY: Integer);
```

Description

The ScrollBy method scrolls the contents of a control.

SENDTOBACK METHOD

Declaration

```
{ CONTROLS.PAS }
procedure SendToBack;
```

Description

The SendToBack method puts the control behind all other windowed components on the same form. The control will automatically lose input focus if it has it when you call this method. As with BringToFront, this is particularly useful when you have overlapped components.

See Also

BringToFront method

SetBounds Method

Declaration

```
{ CONTROLS.PAS }
procedure SetBounds(ALeft, ATop, AWidth, AHeight: Integer); virtual;
```

Description

The SetBounds method allows you to set the boundary properties for any control at one fell swoop. The parameters ALeft, ATop, AWidth, and AHeight will set the Left, Top, Width, and Height properties, respectively. If you are planning to change more than one of these properties, use SetBounds so that the control will only need to be repainted once.

Example

```
{ Position the control at coordinate 10, 100 relative to the top left
  corner of its parent form.  Set its Width to 50 pixels and its Height
  to 20 pixels }
ControlName.SetBounds(10, 100, 50, 20);
```

See Also

Height property, Left property, Top property, Width property

SetFocus Method

Declaration

```
{ CONTROLS.PAS }
procedure SetFocus; virtual;
```

Description

The SetFocus method activates the control by giving it input focus. This can be used to override the user's default tabbing order.

Notes

This will trigger an OnEnter event.

See Also

Enabled property

SetTextBuf Method

Declaration

```
{ CONTROLS.PAS }
procedure SetTextBuf(Buffer: PChar);
```

Description

The SetTextBuf method assigns the contents of a null-terminated string (Buffer) to the text associated with the control (either its Caption or Text property).

Notes

As with the GetTextBuf method, SetTextBuf is primarily for manipulating strings that are longer than 255 characters (i.e., PChars). If the text associated with a control is in its Caption property (which is limited to 255 characters), you should instead assign that property directly.

See Also

Caption property, GetTextBuf method, GetTextLen method

Show Method

Declaration

```
{ CONTROLS.PAS }
procedure Show;
```

Description

The Show method sets the control's Visible property to True, thus causing it to be displayed.

See Also

Hide method

ShowHint Property

Declaration

```
{ CONTROLS.PAS }
property ShowHint: Boolean read FShowHint write SetShowHint
    stored IsShowHintStored;
```

Description

The ShowHint property helps determine whether or not the control should display its Hint text when the mouse cursor rests momentarily upon it. If ShowHint is set to True, the hint will be displayed. If ShowHint is set to its default value of False, the hint will not be displayed (unless the ParentShowHint property is set to True and the ShowHint property of the control's parent is also set to True).

Notes

Changing a control's ShowHint property will implicitly set its ParentShowHint property to False.

Example

See the example provided for the Hint property.

See Also

Hint property, Parent property

SHOWING PROPERTY

Declaration

```
{ CONTROLS.PAS }
property Showing: Boolean read FShowing;
```

Description

Run-time and read-only. The Showing property indicates whether the control is currently visible upon the screen. If the control's Visible property, and that of its parent(s), are all set to True, Showing will be True as well.

See Also

Visible property

TABORDER PROPERTY

Declaration

```
{ CONTROLS.PAS }
property TabOrder: TTabOrder read GetTabOrder write SetTabOrder default -1;

{ CONTROLS.PAS }
TTabOrder = -1..32767;
```

Description

The TabOrder property indicates the position of the control in its parent's tabbing order. It is relevant only when the TabStop property is set to True.

The initial value of TabOrder will be based upon the order in which you add the control to the form, but you are always free to change it after the fact. The TabOrder property is unique for each control on a form. If you change the TabOrder for the control, the TabOrder property for the other components on the form will automatically be renumbered accordingly.

The TabOrder value should be between zero (0) and the total number of components on the form.

Example

```
{ Make a control last in tabbing order }
ControlName.TabOrder := ControlName.Owner.ComponentCount;
```

See Also

TabStop property

TabStop Property

Declaration

```
{ CONTROLS.PAS }
property TabStop: Boolean read FTabStop write SetTabStop;
```

Description

The TabStop property dictates whether or not the user will be able to move to the control with the Tab key. If TabStop is set to its default value of True, the user will be able to Tab to the control. If TabStop is set to False, the user will only be able to activate the control by clicking upon it.

See Also

TabOrder property

Tag Property

Declaration

```
{ CLASSES.PAS }
property Tag: Longint read FTag write FTag default 0;
```

Description

The Tag property can be used to store an integer value with the control, which you can then use as additional identification. By default, Tag is not used by Delphi.

TOP PROPERTY

Declaration

```
{ CONTROLS.PAS }
property Top: Integer read FTop write SetTop;
```

Description

The Top property contains the vertical position of the top left corner of the control (in pixels) relative to the form that owns it. Ordinarily, this will be set at design-time based upon where you place the control, but you are always free to change it at run-time.

See Also

Left property, SetBounds method

UPDATE METHOD

Declaration

```
{ CONTROLS.PAS }
procedure Update; virtual;
```

Description

The Update method causes any pending paint messages (i.e., Invalidate) for the control to be processed.

See Also

Invalidate method, Repaint method

VISIBLE PROPERTY

Declaration

```
{ CONTROLS.PAS }
property Visible: Boolean read FVisible write SetVisible
   default True;
```

Description

The Visible property dictates whether or not the control will appear on-screen. If set to its default value of True, the control will be seen; otherwise, it will be hidden from view. The Show method sets this property to True.

See Also

Show method, Showing property

WIDTH PROPERTY

Declaration

```
{ CONTROLS.PAS }
property Width: Integer read FWidth write SetWidth;
```

Description

The Width property contains the horizontal size of the control in pixels.

See Also

Left property, SetBounds method

TDBCheckBox

Unit

DBCtrls

Inherits from

TCustomCheckBox

Description

The TDBCheckBox component is most commonly linked to a boolean field in a data set to retrieve and/or update the value of that field. However, through the use of its ValueChecked and ValueUnchecked properties, TDBCheckBox can also be linked to character fields if the situation warrants.

The following tables summarize the properties (Table 3.9), methods (Table 3.10), and events (Table 3.11) for TDBCheckBox.

TABLE 3.9 TDBCHECKBOX PROPERTIES

PROPERTY	DATA TYPE	RUN-TIME ONLY	READ-ONLY	DESCRIPTION
Alignment	TAlignment	No	No	Determines whether caption text is displayed to left or right of check box.
AllowGrayed	Boolean	No	No	Determines whether check box can have two (F) or three (T) states.
Caption	String	No	No	Text displayed beside the check box.
Checked	Boolean	No	No	Determines whether check box is selected (T) or unselected (F).
Field	TField	Yes	Yes	Field to which the check box is linked.
Handle	THandle (HWnd)	Yes	Yes	Handle to check box (for Windows API function calls).
State	TCheckBoxState	Yes	No	Determines current state of check box.
ValueChecked	String	No	No	Custom value(s) which determine(s) whether check box should be checked.
ValueUnchecked	String	No	No	Custom value(s) which determine(s) whether check box should be unchecked.

TABLE 3.10 TDBCHECKBOX METHODS

METHOD	DESCRIPTION
Create	Allocates memory to create the check box.

TABLE 3.11 TDBCHECKBOX EVENTS

EVENT	DATA TYPE	DESCRIPTION
OnClick	TNotifyEvent	Occurs when user clicks upon the check box.
OnDragDrop	TDragDropEvent	Occurs when user drops the check box.
OnDragOver	TDragOverEvent	Occurs when user drags an object over the check box.
OnEndDrag	TEndDragEvent	Occurs when user stops dragging the check box.
OnEnter	TNotifyEvent	Occurs when check box becomes active.
OnExit	TNotifyEvent	Occurs when check box loses input focus.
OnKeyDown	TKeyEvent	Occurs when user presses a key with check box active.
OnKeyPress	TKeyPressEvent	Occurs when user presses a character key.
OnKeyUp	TKeyEvent	Occurs when user releases a key with check box active.
OnMouseDown	TMouseEvent	Occurs when user presses mouse button with mouse pointer over the check box.
OnMouseMove	TMouseMoveEvent	Occurs when user moves mouse button if mouse pointer is over the check box.
OnMouseUp	TMouseEvent	Occurs when user releases mouse button with mouse pointer over the check box.

TDBCHECKBOX.ALIGNMENT PROPERTY

Declaration

```
{ DBCTRLS.PAS }
property Alignment: TLeftRight read FAlignment write SetAlignment
    default taRightJustify;

{ CLASSES.PAS }
TAlignment = (taLeftJustify, taRightJustify);
```

Description

If the check box is two-dimensional (i.e., the Ctl3D property is set to False), the Alignment property determines where the caption text will be displayed. By default, the caption will be displayed to the right of the check box.

Table 3.12 shows the two possible values for Alignment.

TABLE 3.12 TDBCHECKBOX.ALIGNMENT VALUES

VALUE	DESCRIPTION
taLeftJustify	Caption text appears to the left of the check box.
taRightJustify	Caption text appears to the right of the check box (default).

Example

```
{ Display caption to left of check box }
DBCheckBox1.Ctl3D := False;      { Required! }
DBCheckBox1.Alignment := taLeftJustify;
```

See Also

Caption property

TDBCHECKBOX.ALLOWGRAYED PROPERTY

Declaration

```
{ STDCTRLS.PAS }
property AllowGrayed: Boolean read FAllowGrayed write FAllowGrayed
    default False;
```

Description

The AllowGrayed property determines whether the check box can have two or three possible states. If AllowGrayed is True, the user can check, gray, or uncheck the check box. If AllowGrayed is False, the user can only check or uncheck the check box. By default, AllowGrayed is False.

Example

```
{ Allow the user to gray the check box }
DBCheckBox1.AllowGrayed := True;
```

See Also

Checked property, State property

TDBCheckBox.Caption Property

Declaration

```
{ CONTROLS.PAS }
property Caption: TCaption read GetText write SetText;
```

Description

The Caption property is a string containing text to be displayed next to the check box. If the check box is three-dimensional, the Caption text will always be displayed to the right of the check box. If the check box is two-dimensional, the position of the Caption text will be dictated by the value of Alignment property.

You may designate an accelerator key by preceding one of the characters within the Caption with an ampersand (&).

Example

```
{ Change the caption and set its accelerator to 'A' }
DBCheckBox1.Caption := '&Active?';
```

See Also

Alignment property, Font property

TDBCheckBox.Checked Property

Declaration

```
{ STDCTRLS.PAS }
property Checked: Boolean read GetChecked write SetChecked
   stored False;
```

Description

The Checked property determines whether or not the check box is selected. If this property contains True, a check mark will appear in the check box. If Checked contains False, the check box will either be unchecked or grayed, depending upon the value of the AllowGrayed property.

Example

```
{ Manually uncheck the check box }
DBCheckBox1.Checked := False;
```

See Also

AllowGrayed property, State property

TDBCheckBox.Create Method

Declaration

```
{ DBCTRLS.PAS }
constructor Create(AOwner: TComponent); override;
```

Description

As you may expect, the Create method creates a check box. You would call this method only if you needed to create a check box manually at run-time. If you give the check box an owner, the check box will automatically be destroyed when its owner is destroyed.

Note: If you create a check box manually with this method, you must specify its Parent property in order for the check box to be displayed on-screen.

Notes

If you do not want the check box to have an owner, pass Self as the parameter to the Create method. For a demonstration of this logic, refer to the example accompanying the discussion of the TDBCheckBox.Free method.

Example

```
{ Create check box on-the-fly and link it to the Active field in the
  Customer table, which is located in C:\DATA dir. This also creates the
  TTable and TDataSource objects on-the-fly. If you have created them at
  design-time, then you can eliminate those sections of this code. }
var
    cb : TDBCheckBox;
    t : TTable;
    d : TDataSource;
begin
    { Create TTable object to access Customer table }
    t := TTable.Create(Application);
    t.DatabaseName := 'c:\data';
    t.TableName := 'customer.dbf';
    t.Open;
    { Create TDataSource object to link to Customer table }
    d := TDataSource.Create(Application);
```

```
    d.DataSet := t;
    { now create check box }
    cb := TDBCheckBox.Create(Form1);
    cb.Parent     := Form1;   { very important! }
    cb.Top        := 10;
    cb.Left       := 30;
    cb.Alignment  := taLeftJustify;
    cb.Caption    := 'Active?';
    cb.DataSource := d;  { link to DataSource created above }
    cb.DataField  := 'Active';
    cb.Hint       := 'Is the customer active?';
    cb.ShowHint   := True;
end;
```

See Also

Free method

TDBCHECKBOX.FIELD PROPERTY

Declaration

```
{ DBCTRLS.PAS }
property Field: TField read GetField;
```

Description

Run-time and read-only. The Field property contains the field to which the DBCheckBox is linked. This can be used if you want to manipulate the field directly.

Example

```
{ Set value of field linked to check box to True }
if not (DBCheckBox1.DataSource.State in [dsEdit, dsInsert]) then
   DBCheckBox1.DataSource.DataSet.Edit;
DBCheckBox1.Field.AsBoolean := True;
DBCheckBox1.DataSource.DataSet.Post;
```

See Also

DataField property, DataSource property, TField chapter

TDBCHECKBOX.ONCLICK EVENT

Declaration

```
{ CONTROLS.PAS }
property OnClick: TNotifyEvent read FOnClick write FOnClick;
```

```
{ CLASSES.PAS }
TNotifyEvent = procedure(Sender: TObject) of object;
```

Description

The OnClick event takes place when any of the following things happen:

- The user clicks upon the check box.
- The user presses **Spacebar** when the check box has focus.
- The user presses the accelerator key associated with the check box.
- The check box's Checked property is changed.

Example

```
{ Synchronize check box #2 to check box #1 }
procedure TForm1.DBCheckBox1Click(Sender: TObject);
begin
    DBCheckBox2.Checked := DBCheckBox1.Checked;
end;
```

See Also

Checked property, State property

TDBCheckBox.OnDragDrop Event

Declaration

```
{ CONTROLS.PAS }
property OnDragDrop: TDragDropEvent read FOnDragDrop
    write FOnDragDrop;

TDragDropEvent = procedure(Sender, Source: TObject;
    X, Y: Integer) of object;
```

Description

The OnDragDrop event occurs when an object is dropped onto the check box. You should write an OnDragDrop event handler to specify what you want to happen when the user drops an object. Four parameters are passed to your OnDragDrop event handler: Sender (the check box); Source (the object being dropped); X and Y (mouse cursor coordinates).

Example

```
{ Change status of check box #1 to that of the check box being dropped
  upon it }
procedure TForm1.DBCheckBox1DragDrop(Sender, Source: TObject;
    X, Y: Integer);
begin
```

```
    if Source is TDBCheckBox then
        DBCheckBox1.Checked := (Source as TDBCheckBox).Checked;
end;
```

See Also

DragCursor property, DragMode property, OnDragOver event

TDBCheckBox.OnDragOver Event

Declaration

```
{ CONTROLS.PAS }
property OnDragOver: TDragOverEvent read FOnDragOver
    write FOnDragOver;

TDragOverEvent = procedure(Sender, Source: TObject; X, Y: Integer;
    State: TDragState; var Accept: Boolean) of object;

TDragState = (dsDragEnter, dsDragLeave, dsDragMove);
```

Description

The OnDragOver event occurs when an object is dragged over the check box. You should write an OnDragOver event handler to determine whether the check box is able to accept the object. The parameters passed to your OnDragOver event handler are Sender (the check box), Source (the object being dragged), X and Y (mouse cursor coordinates); State (the status of the object being dragged in relation to the check box); and Accept, which should be set to a boolean value (True indicates that the check box can accept the object, and False means that it cannot).

Example

```
{ Configure check box to only accept other DBCheckBoxes }
procedure TForm1.DBCheckBox1DragOver(Sender, Source: TObject;
    X, Y: Integer; State: TDragState; var Accept: Boolean);
begin
    Accept := (Source is TDBCheckBox);
end;
```

See Also

DragCursor property, OnDragDrop event

TDBCheckBox.OnEndDrag Event

Declaration

```
{ CONTROLS.PAS }
property OnEndDrag: TEndDragEvent read FOnEndDrag write FOnEndDrag;
```

```
TEndDragEvent = procedure(Sender, Target: TObject;
   X, Y: Integer) of object;
```

Description

The OnEndDrag event occurs whenever the user stops dragging the check box. The drag operation ends either by dropping the check box or by releasing the mouse button. You can write an OnEndDrag event handler to implement special processing to occur when the drag operation stops. The parameters passed to your OnEndDrag event handler will be Sender (the check box), Target (the object upon which you are dropping the check box), and X and Y (mouse cursor coordinates). If the drag operation is canceled, then Target will have the value of NIL, which can be tested as shown in the following example.

Example

```
{ When finished dragging check box, disable it if we have actually dropped
   it upon something }
procedure TForm1.DBCheckBox1EndDrag(Sender, Target: TObject;
   X, Y: Integer);
begin
   if Target <> nil then
      (Sender as TDBCheckBox).Enabled := False;
end;
```

See Also

BeginDrag method, DragCursor property, DragMode property

TDBCheckBox.OnKeyDown Event

Declaration

```
{ CONTROLS.PAS }
property OnKeyDown: TKeyEvent read FOnKeyDown write FOnKeyDown;

TKeyEvent = procedure(Sender: TObject; var Key: Word;
   Shift: TShiftState) of object;

{ CLASSES.PAS }
TShiftState = set of (ssShift, ssAlt, ssCtrl,
   ssLeft, ssRight, ssMiddle, ssDouble);
```

Description

The OnKeyDown event occurs when a user presses a key while the check box has focus. You can write an OnKeyDown event handler to handle special keypresses, including function keys or keypresses combined with the **Shift, Alt,** and/or **Ctrl** keys. Parameters passed to your OnKeyDown event handler are Key (the numeric code associated with the keypress) and Shift (status of special keys, such as **Shift, Alt, Ctrl,** and mouse buttons).

Notes

A complete list of numeric codes associated with these keypresses can be found by searching for the topic "Virtual Key Codes" in the Delphi on-line help file. Alternatively, you can identify a key by its ASCII value (assuming, of course, that it has an ASCII value).

Example

```
{ Allow the user to move the check box by holding down ALT and pressing
  one of the arrow keys }
procedure TForm1.DBCheckBox1KeyDown(Sender: TObject; var Key: Word;
    Shift: TShiftState);
begin
   if Shift = [ssAlt] then
      case Key of
         VK_UP    : DBCheckBox1.Top := DBCheckBox1.Top - 1;
         VK_DOWN  : DBCheckBox1.Top := DBCheckBox1.Top + 1;
         VK_LEFT  : DBCheckBox1.Left := DBCheckBox1.Left - 1;
         VK_RIGHT : DBCheckBox1.Left := DBCheckBox1.Left + 1;
      end;
end;
```

See Also

OnKeyPress event, OnKeyUp event, OnMouseDown event

TDBCheckBox.OnKeyPress Event

Declaration

```
{ CONTROLS.PAS }
property OnKeyPress: TKeyPressEvent read FOnKeyPress
    write FOnKeyPress;

TKeyPressEvent = procedure(Sender: TObject; var Key: Char) of object;
```

Description

The OnKeyPress event occurs when a user presses a key that has a corresponding ASCII value while the check box has focus. The Key parameter passed to your OnKeyPress event handler is the character that was pressed.

Notes

If you need to trap special (non-ASCII) keys, you should use the OnKeyDown event.

Example

```
{ Allow the user to move the check box by pressing [U]p, [D]own, [L]eft,
  or [R]ight }
```

```
procedure TForm1.DBCheckBox1KeyPress(Sender: TObject; var Key: Char);
begin
    case Key of
        'U', 'u': DBCheckBox1.Top := DBCheckBox1.Top - 1;
        'D', 'd': DBCheckBox1.Top := DBCheckBox1.Top + 1;
        'L', 'l': DBCheckBox1.Left := DBCheckBox1.Left - 1;
        'R', 'r': DBCheckBox1.Left := DBCheckBox1.Left + 1;
    end;
end;
```

See Also

OnKeyDown event

TDBCHECKBOX.ONKEYUP EVENT

Declaration

```
{ CONTROLS.PAS }
property OnKeyUp: TKeyEvent read FOnKeyUp write FOnKeyUp;

TKeyEvent = procedure(Sender: TObject; var Key: Word;
    Shift: TShiftState) of object;

{ CLASSES.PAS }
TShiftState = set of (ssShift, ssAlt, ssCtrl,
    ssLeft, ssRight, ssMiddle, ssDouble);
```

Description

The OnKeyUp event occurs when a user releases a key while the check box has focus. OnKeyUp handles special keypresses, including function keys or keypresses combined with the **Shift, Alt,** and/or **Ctrl** keys. Parameters passed to your OnKeyUp event handler are Key (the numeric code associated with the keypress) and Shift (status of special keys, such as **Shift, Alt, Ctrl,** and mouse buttons).

Notes

A complete list of numeric codes associated with these keypresses can be found by searching for the topic "Virtual Key Codes" in the Delphi on-line help file. Alternatively, you can identify a key by its ASCII value (if it has an ASCII value).

See the OnKeyDown discussion for a list of TShiftState values.

See Also

OnKeyDown event

TDBCheckBox.OnMouseDown Event

Declaration

```
{ CONTROLS.PAS }
property OnMouseDown: TMouseEvent read FOnMouseDown
    write FOnMouseDown;

TMouseEvent = procedure(Sender: TObject; Button: TMouseButton;
    Shift: TShiftState; X, Y: Integer) of object;

TMouseButton = (mbLeft, mbRight, mbMiddle);

{ CLASSES.PAS }
TShiftState = set of (ssShift, ssAlt, ssCtrl,
    ssLeft, ssRight, ssMiddle, ssDouble);
```

Description

The OnMouseDown event occurs when the user presses a mouse button while the mouse cursor is over the check box. The following parameters are passed to your OnMouseDown event handler: Button (identifies which mouse button was pressed), Shift (status of special keys and mouse buttons), and X and Y (screen coordinates of mouse cursor).

See Also

OnKeyDown event, OnMouseUp event

TDBCheckBox.OnMouseMove Event

Declaration

```
{ CONTROLS.PAS }
property OnMouseMove: TMouseMoveEvent read FOnMouseMove
    write FOnMouseMove;

TMouseMoveEvent = procedure(Sender: TObject; Shift: TShiftState;
    X, Y: Integer) of object;

{ CLASSES.PAS }
TShiftState = set of (ssShift, ssAlt, ssCtrl,
    ssLeft, ssRight, ssMiddle, ssDouble);
```

Description

The OnMouseMove event occurs when the user moves the mouse while the mouse cursor is over the check box. The following parameters are passed to your OnMouseMove event handler: Shift (status of special keys and mouse buttons) and X and Y (screen coordinates of mouse cursor).

See Also

OnKeyDown event, OnMouseDown event, OnMouseUp event

TDBCheckBox.OnMouseUp Event

Declaration

```
{ CONTROLS.PAS }
property OnMouseUp: TMouseEvent read FOnMouseUp write FOnMouseUp;

TMouseEvent = procedure(Sender: TObject; Button: TMouseButton;
    Shift: TShiftState; X, Y: Integer) of object;

TMouseButton = (mbLeft, mbRight, mbMiddle);

{ CLASSES.PAS }
TShiftState = set of (ssShift, ssAlt, ssCtrl,
    ssLeft, ssRight, ssMiddle, ssDouble);
```

Description

The OnMouseUp event occurs when the user releases a mouse button while the mouse cursor is over the check box. The following parameters will be passed to your OnMouseUp event handler: Button (identifies which mouse button was pressed), Shift (status of special keys and mouse buttons), and X and Y (screen coordinates of mouse cursor).

See Also

OnKeyDown event, OnMouseDown event

TDBCheckBox.State Property

Declaration

```
{ STDCTRLS.PAS }
property State: TCheckBoxState read FState write SetState
    default cbUnchecked;

{ STDCTRLS.PAS }
TCheckBoxState = (cbUnchecked, cbChecked, cbGrayed);
```

Description

The State property indicates whether the check box is checked, unchecked, or grayed. The three possible values are cbUnchecked, cbChecked, and cbGrayed, all of which are self-explanatory. By default, the check box will be unchecked.

Example

```
{ Set check box to grayed }
DBCheckBox1.State := cbGrayed;
```

See Also

AllowGrayed property, Checked property

TDBCheckBox.ValueChecked Property

Declaration

```
{ DBCTRLS.PAS }
property ValueChecked: String read GetValueCheck write SetValueCheck;
```

Description

The ValueChecked property allows you to connect character-type fields to TDBCheckboxes. If the value in the field matches one of the strings in ValueChecked, the check box will be checked. By default, ValueChecked will contain the string 'True'. However, you can change this to anything that you prefer, including a semicolon-delimited list of items. (See the following example.)

If you check the check box, the string in ValueChecked will be stored in the field. If you are using a list of items, the first of these will be stored in the field.

The ValueChecked property has no relevance when the check box is connected to a logical field.

Example

```
{ Connect check box to a character field indicating marital status. If field
  contains 'M' for married, turn on the check }
DBCheckBox1.ValueChecked := 'M';
DBCheckBox1.ValueUnchecked := 'S;D;W';
```

See Also

ValueUnchecked property

TDBCheckBox.ValueUnchecked Property

Declaration

```
{ DBCTRLS.PAS }
property ValueUnchecked: string read GetValueUncheck
      write SetValueUncheck;
```

Description

In conjunction with the ValueChecked property, ValueUnchecked allows you to connect character-type fields to TDBCheckboxes. If the value in the field matches one of the strings in ValueUnchecked, the check box will be unchecked.

234

By default, ValueUnchecked will contain the string 'False'. You can change this to one or more different values. As with ValueChecked, multiple items should be semicolon-delimited.

If you uncheck the check box, the string in ValueUnchecked will be stored in the field. If you are using a list of items, the first of these will be stored in the field.

The ValueUnchecked property has no relevance when the check box is connected to a logical field.

See Also

ValueChecked property

TDBComboBox

Unit

DBCtrls

Inherits from

TCustomComboBox

Description

The TDBComboBox component allows the user to change the value of a field either by typing a value or making a selection from a list of choices.

The following three tables summarize the properties (Table 3.13), methods (Table 3.14), and events (Table 3.15) for TDBComboBox.

TABLE 3.13 TDBComboBox Properties

Property	Data Type	Run-Time Only	Read-Only	Description
BoundsRect	TRect	Yes	No	The bounding rectangle of the combo box with respect to its parent
DropDownCount	Integer	No	No	Number of items to be displayed in the drop-down list
Field	TField	Yes	Yes	Field to which the combo box is linked
Handle	THandle (HWnd)	Yes	Yes	Handle to combo box (for Windows API function calls)
ItemHeight	Integer	No	No	Height (in pixels) of a single item in the drop-down list (applies to fixed owner-draw combo boxes only)

ItemIndex	Integer	Yes	No	Ordinal position of currently selected item in the drop-down list.
Items	TStrings	No	No	The items that appear in the drop-down list for selection.
SelLength	Integer	Yes	No	Length (in characters) of selected text in combo box's edit control.
SelStart	Integer	Yes	No	Starting position of selected text in combo box's edit control (zero-based).
SelText	String	Yes	No	The selected text, if any, in the combo box's edit control.
Sorted	Boolean	Yes	No	Determines whether Items should be automatically sorted in ascending alphabetical order.
Style	TComboBoxStyle	No	No	Determines how combo box will display its items (see following details).
Text	String	Yes	No	Text visible in combo box's edit control.

TABLE 3.14 TDBComboBox Methods

METHOD	DESCRIPTION
Clear	Deletes all items and text from combo box.
Create	Allocates memory to create the combo box.
SelectAll	Selects entire text in the combo box's edit control.

TABLE 3.15 TDBComboBox Events

EVENT	DATA TYPE	DESCRIPTION
OnChange	TNotifyEvent	Occurs when user selects an item in the drop-down list.
OnClick	TNotifyEvent	Occurs when user single-clicks upon the combo box.
OnDblClick	TNotifyEvent	Occurs when user double-clicks upon the combo box.
OnDragDrop	TDragDropEvent	Occurs when user drops the combo box.
OnDragOver	TDragOverEvent	Occurs when user drags an object over the combo box.
OnDrawItem	TDrawItemEvent	Occurs whenever an item in the drop-down list has to be redisplayed (gives developer full control over display).
OnEndDrag	TEndDragEvent	Occurs when user stops dragging the combo box.
OnKeyDown	TKeyEvent	Occurs when user presses a key with combo box active.
OnKeyPress	TKeyPressEvent	Occurs when user presses a character key.
OnKeyUp	TKeyEvent	Occurs when user releases a key with combo box active.
OnMeasureItem	TMeasureItemEvent	Occurs whenever an item in the drop-down list of a variable style combo box has to be redisplayed (see Style property).

TDBComboBox.Clear Method

Declaration

```
{ STDCTRLS.PAS }
procedure Clear;
```

Description

The Clear method effectively zaps the combo box by removing all text from its edit control and all options from its drop-down list (i.e., clearing its Items properties). It is most useful when you want to fill the drop-down list with completely different items.

See Also

Items property, Text property

TDBComboBox.Create Method

Declaration

```
{ DBCTRLS.PAS }
constructor Create(AOwner: TComponent); override;
```

Description

The Create method can be used to create a combo box manually at run-time. If you give the combo box an owner, the combo box will automatically be destroyed when its owner is destroyed.

Note: If you create a combo box manually with this method, you must specify its Parent property in order for the combo box to be displayed on-screen.

Notes

If you do not want the combo box to have an owner, pass Self as the parameter to the Create method. (See the example accompanying the discussion of the TDBCheckBox.Free method.)

Example

```
{ Create combo box on-the-fly and link it to the Name field in the Articles
  table, which is located in C:\AQUARIUM\ARTICLES. }
var
    cb : TDBComboBox;
    t  : TTable;
    d  : TDataSource;
begin
    { create TTable object to access Articles
```

```
   t := TTable.Create(Application);
   t.DatabaseName := 'c:\aquarium\articles';
   t.TableName := 'articles.dbf';
   t.Open;
   { create TDataSource object to link to Articles table }
   d := TDataSource.Create(Application);
   d.DataSet := t;
   { now create the combo box }
   cb := TDBComboBox.Create(Form1);
   cb.Parent     := Form1;  { Very important! }
   cb.Top        := 50;
   cb.Left       := 10;
   cb.DataSource := d;  { Link to DataSource created above }
   cb.DataField  := 'Name';
   { Fill drop-down list with possible choices }
   cb.Items.Add('Ted Blue');
   cb.Items.Add('John Kaster');
   cb.Items.Add('Greg Lief');
   cb.Items.Add('Loren Scott');
end;
```

See Also

Free method

TDBComboBox.DropDownCount Property

Declaration

```
{ STDCTRLS.PAS }
property DropDownCount: Integer read FDropDownCount
   write FDropDownCount default 8;
```

Description

The DropDownCount property dictates how many items should be visible in the drop-down list. By default, this is set to either 8 or the maximum number of items in the drop-down list, whichever is higher.

Example

```
{ Show ten items at a time in the drop-down list }
DBComboBox1.DropDownCount := 10;
```

See Also

Items property

TDBCOMBOBOX.FIELD PROPERTY

Declaration

```
{ DBCTRLS.PAS }
property Field: TField read GetField;
```

Description

Run-time and read-only. The Field property contains the field to which the DBComboBox is linked. This can be used to manipulate the field directly.

Example

```
{ Set value of field to the first string in the Items property }
if not (DBComboBox1.DataSource.State in [dsEdit, dsInsert]) then
   DBComboBox1.DataSource.DataSet.Edit;
DBComboBox1.Field.AsString := DBComboBox1.Items[0];
DBComboBox1.DataSource.DataSet.Post;
```

See Also

DataField property, DataSource property, TField chapter

TDBCOMBOBOX.HANDLE PROPERTY

Declaration

```
{ CONTROLS.PAS }
property Handle: HWnd read GetHandle;
```

Description

Run-time and read-only. The Handle property is useful should you need to pass the combo box's handle to a Windows API function.

Example

```
{ Force drop-down list to be visible }
SendMessage(DBComboBox1.Handle, cb_ShowDropDown, 1, 0);
{ Force drop-down list to be hidden }
SendMessage(DBComboBox1.Handle, cb_ShowDropDown, 0, 0);
```

TDBCOMBOBOX.ITEMHEIGHT PROPERTY

Declaration

```
{ STDCTRLS.PAS }
property ItemHeight: Integer read GetItemHeight write SetItemHeight;
```

Description

The ItemHeight property contains the height (in pixels) of an item in the combo box's drop-down list. It applies only when the combo box's Style property is csOwnerDrawFixed.

Example

```
{ Set height for each item to 10 pixels }
DBComboBox1.Style := csOwnerDrawFixed
DBComboBox1.ItemHeight := 10;
```

See Also

Font property, Style property

TDBCOMBOBOX.ITEMINDEX PROPERTY

Declaration

```
{ STDCTRLS.PAS }
property ItemIndex: Integer read GetItemIndex
   write SetItemIndex;
```

Description

Run-time only. The ItemIndex property contains the ordinal position of the currently selected item in the drop-down list. Changing this value will also change the text shown in the edit area (i.e., the Text property).

Example

```
{ Select the second item in the drop-down list, which will also change the
  Text property }
DBComboBox1.ItemIndex := 2;
```

See Also

Items property, Text property

TDBCOMBOBOX.ITEMS PROPERTY

Declaration

```
{ STDCTRLS.PAS }
property Items: TStrings read FItems write SetItems;
```

Description

The Items property contains the strings that will be displayed in the drop-down list. You can manipulate them by using the Add, Exchange, Delete, Insert, and Move methods.

Example

```
{ Example #1: Refill the combo box from a look-up table }
DBComboBox1.Clear;
Table1.DisableControls;
Table1.First;
while not Table1.EOF do
    begin
        DBComboBox1.Items.Add( Table1.FieldByName('NAME').AsString );
        Table1.Next;
    end;
Table1.EnableControls;

{ Example #2: Refill the combo box from a memo }
DBComboBox1.Items := Memo1.Lines;
```

See Also

ItemHeight property, ItemIndex property, Selected property

TDBComboBox.OnChange Event

Declaration

```
{ STDCTRLS.PAS }
property OnChange: TNotifyEvent read FOnChange write FOnChange;

{ CLASSES.PAS }
TNotifyEvent = procedure(Sender: TObject) of object;
```

Description

The OnChange event occurs whenever the user types into the combo box's edit area or selects an item from its drop down list.

Example

```
{ Update the contents of an edit control with the current value of the
  combo box }
procedure TForm1.DBComboBox1Change(Sender: TObject);
begin
        Edit1.Text := DBComboBox1.Text;
end;
```

See Also

Items property, Text property

TDBComboBox.OnClick Event

Declaration

```
{ CONTROLS.PAS }
property OnClick: TNotifyEvent read FOnClick write FOnClick;

{ CLASSES.PAS }
TNotifyEvent = procedure(Sender: TObject) of object;
```

Description

The OnClick event occurs when the user selects an item from the drop-down list.

Example

See example provided with TDBComboBox.OnChange event discussion.

See Also

Items property, OnChange event, OnDblClick event

TDBComboBox.OnDblClick Event

Declaration

```
{ CONTROLS.PAS }
property OnDblClick: TNotifyEvent read FOnDblClick write FOnDblClick;

{ CLASSES.PAS }
TNotifyEvent = procedure(Sender: TObject) of object;
```

Description

The OnDblClick event occurs whenever the user double-clicks upon the combo box.

Example

See example provided with TDBComboBox.OnChange method discussion.

See Also

OnChange event, OnClick event

TDBComboBox.OnDragDrop Event

Declaration

```
{ CONTROLS.PAS }
property OnDragDrop: TDragDropEvent read FOnDragDrop
   write FOnDragDrop;

TDragDropEvent = procedure(Sender, Source: TObject;
   X, Y: Integer) of object;
```

Description

The OnDragDrop event occurs when an object is dropped onto the combo box. You should write an OnDragDrop event handler to specify what you want to happen when the user drops an object. Four parameters are passed to your OnDragDrop event handler: Sender (the combo box), Source (the object being dropped), and X and Y (mouse cursor coordinates).

Example

```
{ Allow user to drop an edit control onto the combo box }
procedure TForm1.DBComboBox1DragDrop(Sender, Source: TObject;
   X, Y: Integer);
begin
    if Source is TEdit then
        DBComboBox1.Items.Add( (Source as TEdit).Text );
end;
```

See Also

DragCursor property, DragMode property, OnDragOver method

TDBComboBox.OnDragOver Event

Declaration

```
{ CONTROLS.PAS }
property OnDragOver: TDragOverEvent read FOnDragOver
   write FOnDragOver;

TDragOverEvent = procedure(Sender, Source: TObject; X, Y: Integer;
   State: TDragState; var Accept: Boolean) of object;
TDragState = (dsDragEnter, dsDragLeave, dsDragMove);
```

Description

The OnDragOver event occurs when an object is dragged over the combo box. By writing an OnDragOver event handler, you can determine when the combo box can accept the object. The parameters passed to your OnDragOver event handler are Sender (the combo box), Source (the object being dragged), X and Y (mouse cursor coordinates), State (the status of the object being dragged in relation to the combo box), and Accept, which should be set to a boolean value (True means the combo box can accept the object, and False means that it cannot).

Example

```
{ Configure combo box to accept edit controls only }
procedure TForm1.DBComboBox1DragOver(Sender, Source: TObject;
   X, Y: Integer; State: TDragState; var Accept: Boolean);
begin
   Accept := (Source is TEdit);
end;
```

See Also

DragCursor property, OnDragDrop event

TDBComboBox.OnDrawItem Event

Declaration

```
{ STDCTRLS.PAS }
property OnDrawItem: TDrawItemEvent read FOnDrawItem
   write FOnDrawItem;

TDrawItemEvent = procedure(Control: TWinControl; Index: Integer;
   Rect: TRect; State: TOwnerDrawState) of object;

TOwnerDrawState = set of (odSelected, odGrayed, odDisabled,
   odChecked, odFocused);
```

Description

The OnDrawItem event applies only if you have specified the combo box style as owner-draw. In this case, you should write an OnDrawItem event handler to draw the combo box items, be it in the edit area or the drop-down list. The parameters passed to your OnDrawItem event handler are Control (the combo box), Index (the position within the Items property of the item being drawn), TRect (a rectangle in which to draw the item), and State (the status of the item being drawn). Table 3.16 lists the possible state values.

TABLE 3.16 TOwnerDrawState Values

Value	Description
odSelected	The item is currently selected
odGrayed	Not applicable for combo boxes
odDisabled	The combo box is disabled
odChecked	Not applicable for combo boxes
odFocused	The item currently has focus

Notes

Drawing in your OnDrawItem event handler should take place on the canvas. You have control over the canvas' Font, Pen, and Brush properties and can draw graphics including bit maps, lines, rectangles, and so on. See the "TCanvas" topic in the Delphi on-line help for more information about the possibilities.

Example

```
{ If item matches current value of linked field, draw it in red }
procedure TForm1.DBComboBox1DrawItem(Control: TWinControl; Index:
    Integer; Rect: TRect; State: TOwnerDrawState);
begin
   DBComboBox1.Canvas.FillRect(Rect);
   if DBComboBox1.Items[Index] = DBComboBox1.Field.AsString then
      DBComboBox1.Canvas.Font.Color := clRed;
   DBComboBox1.Canvas.TextOut(Rect.Left, Rect.Top,
                              DBComboBox1.Items[Index])
end;
```

See Also

TCanvas object

TDBComboBox.OnEndDrag Event

Declaration

```
{ CONTROLS.PAS }
property OnEndDrag: TEndDragEvent read FOnEndDrag write FOnEndDrag;

TEndDragEvent = procedure(Sender, Target: TObject;
   X, Y: Integer) of object;
```

Description

The OnEndDrag event occurs whenever the user stops dragging the combo box. The drag operation ends either by dropping the combo box or by releasing the mouse button. Write an OnEndDrag event handler if you need to implement special processing to occur when the drag operation stops. The parameters passed to your OnEndDrag event handler will be Sender (the combo box), Target (the object upon which you are dropping the combo box), and X and Y (mouse cursor coordinates). If the drag operation is canceled, then Target will have the value of NIL, which can be tested as shown in the following example.

Example

```
{ if combo box was dropped on an edit control, change its text }
procedure TForm1.DBComboBox1EndDrag(Sender, Target: TObject;
   X, Y: Integer);
```

```
begin
   if Target is TEdit then
       (Target as TEdit).Text := DBComboBox1.Text;
end;
```

See Also

BeginDrag method, DragCursor property, DragMode property

TDBCOMBOBOX.ONKEYDOWN EVENT

Declaration

```
{ CONTROLS.PAS }
property OnKeyDown: TKeyEvent read FOnKeyDown write FOnKeyDown;

TKeyEvent = procedure(Sender: TObject; var Key: Word;
   Shift: TShiftState) of object;

{ CLASSES.PAS }
TShiftState = set of (ssShift, ssAlt, ssCtrl,
   ssLeft, ssRight, ssMiddle, ssDouble);
```

Description

The OnKeyDown event occurs when a user presses a key while the combo box has focus.
You can write an OnKeyDown event handler to handle special keypresses, including function
keys or keypresses combined with the **Shift**, **Alt**, and/or **Ctrl** keys. Parameters passed to your
OnKeyDown event handler are Key (the numeric code associated with the keypress) and Shift
(status of special keys, such as **Shift, Alt, Ctrl,** and mouse buttons).

Notes

A complete list of numeric codes associated with these keypresses can be found by searching for
the topic "Virtual Key Codes" in the Delphi on-line help file. Alternatively. you can identify a key
by its ASCII value if it has one.

Example

```
{ Allow the user to insert new items in the drop-down list by pressing Ins,
  and delete the currently selected item in the list by pressing Del }
procedure TForm1.DBComboBox1KeyDown(Sender: TObject; var Key: Word;
  Shift: TShiftState);
begin
   case Key of
      vk_Insert: DBComboBox1.Items.Add('new item');
      vk_Delete: DBComboBox1.Items.Delete(DBComboBox1.ItemIndex);
   end;
end;
```

See Also

OnKeyPress event, OnKeyUp event, OnMouseDown event

TDBComboBox.OnKeyPress Event

Declaration

```
{ CONTROLS.PAS }
property OnKeyPress: TKeyPressEvent read FOnKeyPress
   write FOnKeyPress;

TKeyPressEvent = procedure(Sender: TObject; var Key: Char) of object;
```

Description

The OnKeyPress event occurs when a user presses a key that has a corresponding ASCII value while the combo box has focus. You can write an OnKeyPress event handler to attach special processing to certain keys. The Key parameter passed to your OnKeyPress event handler is the character that was pressed.

Notes

If you need to trap special (non-ASCII) keys, you should use the OnKeyDown event.

Example

```
{ Rudimentary incremental search }
{ Declare this in the protected section of your form }
SearchString : String;

procedure TForm1.ListBox1KeyPress(Sender: TObject; var Key: Char);
var
   x : Integer;
   temp : String;
   iLength : Integer;
begin
    if (Key = #8) and (Length(SearchString) > 1) then
       temp := Copy(temp, 1, Length(temp) - 1)
    else if (Key <> #8) then
       temp := SearchString + Key;
    else
       temp := '';
    if Length(temp) > 0 then begin
       x := 0;
       iLength := Length(temp);
       while (x < ListBox1.Items.Count) and
          (temp <> Copy(ListBox1.Items[x], 1, iLength)) do
          Inc(x);
       if x < ListBox1.Items.Count then begin
          SearchString := temp;
```

```
        ListBox1.ItemIndex := x;
        ListBox1.Refresh;
    end;
  end;
end;
```

See Also

OnKeyDown event

TDBComboBox.OnMeasureItem Event

Declaration

```
{ STDCTRLS.PAS }
property OnMeasureItem: TMeasureItemEvent read FOnMeasureItem
   write FOnMeasureItem;

TMeasureItemEvent = procedure(Control: TWinControl; Index: Integer;
   var Height: Integer) of object;
```

Description

The OnMeasureItem event occurs just prior to redisplaying an item in a combo box whose style is set to csOwnerDrawVariable. You can write an OnMeasureItem event handler that specifies the height to use for displaying the item. Your OnMeasureItem event handler receives the following three parameters: Control (the combo box), Index (the ordinal position of the item in the combo box's Items property), and Height (item's height in pixels). Height is passed by reference, so the assumption is that you will change its value within your event handler.

Notes

The OnDrawItem event takes place immediately after the OnMeasureItem event.

Example

```
{ This example is used for a combo box that has bit maps associated with each
  of its strings.  Adjusts height of each item based upon bit map height }
procedure TForm1.DBComboBox1MeasureItem(Control: TWinControl;
   Index: Integer; var Height: Integer);
var
   Bitmap: TBitmap;
begin
   with Control as TDBComboBox do
   begin
      Bitmap := TBitmap(Items.Objects[Index]);
      if Bitmap <> nil then
         if Bitmap.Height > Height then
            Height := Bitmap.Height;
   end;
end;
```

See Also

OnDrawItem event, Style property

TDBComboBox.SelectAll Method

Declaration

```
{ STDCTRLS.PAS }
procedure SelectAll;
```

Description

The SelectAll method is self-explanatory, it selects (highlights) all the text in the combo box's edit area.

See Also

Text property

TDBComboBox.SelLength Property

Declaration

```
{ STDCTRLS.PAS }
property SelLength: Integer read GetSelLength write SetSelLength;
```

Description

The SelLength returns the length, in characters, of the currently selected portion of the combo box's edit area. If it contains zero, then no text is selected.

Example

```
{ Programmatically highlight first five characters of text }
DBComboBox1.SelStart := 0;
DBComboBox1.SelLength := 5;
```

See Also

SelStart property, SelText property

TDBComboBox.SelStart Property

Declaration

```
{ STDCTRLS.PAS }
property SelStart: Integer read GetSelStart write SetSelStart;
```

Description

The SelStart returns the starting position of the currently selected text, if any, in the combo box's edit area.

Example

```
{ Programmatically move the cursor to the end of the text }
DBComboBox1.SelStart := Length(DBComboBox1.Text);
```

See Also

SelLength property, SelText property

TDBComboBox.SelText Property

Declaration

```
{ STDCTRLS.PAS }
property SelText: string read GetSelText write SetSelText;
```

Description

The SelText returns the currently selected text, if any, in the combo box's edit area.

See Also

SelLength property, SelText property

TDBComboBox.Sorted Property

Declaration

```
{ STDCTRLS.PAS }
property Sorted: Boolean read FSorted write SetSorted default False;
```

Description

The Sorted property dictates whether the items in the drop-down list should be shown in ascending alphabetical order. If set to its default value of False, the items will shown in natural (unsorted) order.

Example

```
{ Allow the user to dictate sorted order with the following OnClick event
  handler, which is attached to a check box }
procedure TForm1.CheckBox1Click(Sender: TObject);
begin
   DBComboBox1.sorted := CheckBox1.Checked;
end;
```

See Also

Items property

TDBCOMBOBOX.STYLE PROPERTY

Declaration

```
{ STDCTRLS.PAS }
property Style: TComboBoxStyle read FStyle write SetStyle
    default csDropDown;

TComboBoxStyle = (csDropDown, csSimple, csDropDownList,
                  csOwnerDrawFixed, csOwnerDrawVariable);
```

Description

The Style property determines how the items in the drop-down list should be displayed. It can be used to prevent the user from typing into the text area (i.e., csDropDownList). The two owner-draw styles can be used to draw graphics (e.g., bit maps).

Table 3.17 shows the possible values for the Style property.

TABLE 3.17 TComboBoxStyle Values

VALUE (* = DEFAULT)	DESCRIPTION
csDropDown*	Items are strings, each with the same height. Text area will display the contents of the linked field. The user can change the value of the field either by typing into text area or making a selection from the drop-down list.
csSimple	Items are strings. No drop-down list. Text area will display the contents of the linked field. The user can change the value of the field either by typing into text area or pressing the up/down areas to select from items.
csDropDownList	Items are strings, each with the same height. Text area is read-only and will display the contents of the linked field. The user can change the value of the field only by making a selection from the drop-down list.
csOwnerDrawFixed	Drop-down list contains strings or graphics, each item having the height specified by the ItemHeight property. Text area is read-only and will be blank unless current field contents match one of the items in the drop-down list. The user can change the value of the field only by selecting one of the strings from the drop-down list. Drawing must be handled by writing an OnDrawItem event handler.
csOwnerDrawVariable	Items may be strings or graphics, each of which may have a different height. Text area is read-only and will be blank unless current field contents match one of the items in the drop-down list. The user can change the value of the field only by selecting one of the strings from the drop-down list. Height for each item should be determined by writing an OnMeasureItem handler. Drawing should be handled by writing an OnDrawItem event handler.

Example

See example provided with discussion of TDBComboBox.OnMeasureItem event.

See Also

ItemHeight property, Items property, OnDrawItem event, OnMeasureItem event

TDBComboBox.Text Property

Declaration

```
{ CONTROLS.PAS }
property Text: TCaption read GetText write SetText;

TCaption = String[255];
```

Description

The Text property contains the text currently displayed in the combo box's edit area.

Notes

Run-time and read-only

See Also

SelLength property, SelStart property, SelText property

TDBCtrlGrid (New in Delphi 2.0)

Unit

DBCGrids

Inherits from

TWinControl

Description

The TDBCtrlGrid component is similar to TDBGrid in that it allows you to view multiple records at once. However, TDBCtrlGrid is far more versatile because it permits you to create a free-form layout for each record (rather than restricting you to a single row as does TDBGrid). You can use multiple controls to represent each record.

CAVEAT: The initial release of Delphi 2.0 only supports the following data-aware controls within a TDBCtrlGrid: TDBCheckBox, TDBComboBox, TDBEdit, TDBLookupComboBox, and DBText. Memo/image support is conspicuous by its absence.

The following tables summarize the properties (Table 3.18), methods (Table 3.19), and events (Table 3.20) for TDBCtrlGrid.

TABLE 3.18 TDBCTRLGRID PROPERTIES

PROPERTY	DATA TYPE	RUN-TIME ONLY	READ-ONLY	DESCRIPTION
AllowDelete	Boolean	No	No	Determines whether user can delete records in grid.
AllowInsert	Boolean	No	No	Determines whether user can add records in grid.
Canvas	TCanvas	Yes	Yes	Provides access to drawing surface for grid.
ColCount	Integer	No	No	Number of columns in grid.
EditMode	Boolean	Yes	No	Keeps track of whether grid is currently in edit mode.
Orientation	TDBCtrlGrid-Orientation	No	No	Determines orientation of grid.
PanelBorder	TDBCtrlGrid-Border	No	No	Determines border (if any) of panels within grid.
PanelCount	Integer	Yes	Yes	Number of panels currently visible on screen
PanelHeight	Integer	No	No	Height (in pixels) of each panel
PanelIndex	Integer	Yes	No	Number of currently selected panel
PanelWidth	Integer	No	No	Width (in pixels) of each panel
RowCount	Integer	No	No	Number of rows within grid
ShowFocus	Boolean	Yes	No	Determines whether to draw rectangle around selected panel.

TABLE 3.19 TDBCTRLGRID METHODS

METHOD	DESCRIPTION
Create	Allocates memory to create the grid.
DoKey	Key handling logic for the grid, which you can replace or supplement.
GetTabOrderList	Generates a list of controls in the grid, sequenced by tab order.

TABLE 3.20 TDBCTRLGRID EVENTS

EVENT	DATA TYPE	DESCRIPTION
OnClick	TNotifyEvent	Occurs when user clicks upon the grid.
OnDblClick	TNotifyEvent	Occurs when user double-clicks upon the grid.
OnMouseDown	TMouseEvent	Occurs when user presses mouse button with mouse pointer over the grid.

OnMouseMove	TMouseMoveEvent	Occurs when user moves mouse button if mouse pointer is over the grid.
OnMouseUp	TMouseEvent	Occurs when user releases mouse button with mouse pointer over the grid.
OnPaintPanel	TPaintPanelEvent	Occurs whenever a panel in the grid is redrawn.
OnStartDrag	TStartDragEvent	Occurs when user begins a drag-and-drop operation with the grid.

TDBCtrlGrid.AllowDelete Property

Declaration

```
{ DBCGRIDS.PAS }
property AllowDelete: Boolean read FAllowDelete write FAllowDelete
        default True;
```

Description

The AllowDelete property dictates whether or not the user should be allowed to delete records from the grid. By default, this will be set to True.

See Also

AllowInsert property

TDBCtrlGrid.AllowInsert Property

Declaration

```
{ DBCGRIDS.PAS }
property AllowInsert : Boolean read FAllowInsert
        write FAllowInsert default True;
```

Description

The AllowInsert property dictates whether or not the user should be allowed to insert records in the grid. By default, this will be set to True.

See Also

AllowDelete property

TDBCtrlGrid.Canvas Property

Declaration

```
{ DBCGRIDS.PAS }
property Canvas: TCanvas read FCanvas;
```

Description

Run-time and read-only. The Canvas property gives you access to a drawing surface within the grid. Although the Canvas itself is read-only, you can change its Brush, Font, and Pen properties to customize drawing for the grid.

See Also

OnPaintPanel event

TDBCTRLGRID.COLCOUNT PROPERTY

Declaration

```
{ DBCGRIDS.PAS }
property ColCount: Integer read FColCount write SetColCount;
```

Description

The ColCount property dictates how many columns will be in the grid. When the grid is initially created, this will be set to 1, although you are free to change it either at design-time or run-time.

See Also

PanelHeight property, PanelWidth property, RowCount property

TDBCTRLGRID.CREATE METHOD

Declaration

```
{ DBCGRIDS.PAS }
constructor Create(AOwner: TComponent); override;
```

Description

The Create method can be used to create a grid manually at run-time. If you give the grid an owner, the grid will go to the bit bucket at the same time as its owner.

Note: If you create a grid manually with this method, you must specify its Parent property in order for the grid to be displayed on-screen.

Notes

If you do not want the grid to have an owner, pass Self as the parameter to the Create method. For an example of this logic, see the TDBCheckBox.Free method.

Example

```
{ Create a grid on-the-fly and link it to the articles table, which is
  located in C:\BIOLIFE.DB. This also creates the TTable and TDataSource
```

```
objects on-the-fly. If you have created them at design-time, then eliminate
that part of the code }
procedure TForm1.FormCreate(Sender: TObject);
var
   g : TDBCtrlGrid;
   t : TTable;
   d : TDataSource;
   e : TDBEdit;
   e2: TDBEdit;
begin
   { Create TTable object to access Articles table }
   t := TTable.Create(Application);
   t.DatabaseName := 'c:';
   t.TableName := 'biolife.db';
   t.Open;
   { Create TDataSource object to link to Articles table }
   d := TDataSource.Create(Application);
   d.DataSet := t;
   { Now create the grid }
   g := TDBCtrlGrid.Create(self);
   g.Parent       := self;   { Very important! }
   g.ColCount     := 2;
   g.RowCount     := 5;
   g.PanelHeight  := 120;
   g.PanelWidth   := 150;
   g.Orientation  := goHorizontal;
   g.DataSource   := d;   { Link to DataSource created above }
   { Now create and add two edit controls to the grid }
   e := TDBEdit.Create(g);
   e.Parent       := g;
   e.Left         := 10;
   e.Top          := 10;
   e.DataField    := 'Category';
   e.DataSource   := g.DataSource;
   e2             := TDBEdit.Create(g);
   e2.Parent      := g;
   e2.Left        := 10;
   e2.Top         := 30;
   e2.DataField   := 'Common_Name';
   e2.DataSource  := g.DataSource;
end;
```

See Also

Free method

TDBCTRLGRID.DOKEY METHOD

Declaration

```
{ DBCGRIDS.PAS }
property DoKey : TDBCtrlGridKey;
```

```
TDBCtrlGridKey = (gkNull, gkEditMode, gkPriorTab, gkNextTab,
                  gkLeft, gkRight, gkUp, gkDown, gkScrollUp,
                  gkScrollDown, gkPageUp, gkPageDown, gkHome,
                  gkEnd, gkInsert, gkAppend, gkDelete, gkCancel);
```

256

Description

The DoKey method event occurs whenever the user presses a key within the grid. You can also call it directly to simulate a keypress, as shown in the following example.

Example

```
{ Simulate PageDown }
DBCtrlGrid1.DoKey( gkPageDown );
```

See Also

OnKeyPress event

TDBCtrlGrid.EditMode Property

Declaration

```
{ DBCGRIDS.PAS }
property EditMode: Boolean read GetEditMode write SetEditMode;
```

Description

Run-time only. The EditMode property tracks whether or not the grid is currently in edit mode. Although it is scoped as public and, therefore available to your code, there does not seem to be good reason to manipulate it directly.

TDBCtrlGrid.GetTabOrderList Method

Declaration

```
{ DBCGRIDS.PAS }
property GetTabOrderList (List: TList);
```

Description

This method builds a list of the controls contained within the grid. The controls are sequenced by their tab order. This relies upon the FindNextControl method. This would be useful in the event that you had to change the tabbling order of those controls programmatically.

TDBCtrlGrid.GetTabOrderList Method

Declaration

```
{ DBCGRIDS.PAS }
property GetTabOrderList(List: TList);
```

Description

This method builds a list of the controls contained within the grid. The controls are sequenced by their tab order. This relies upon the FindNextControl method. This would be useful in the event that you had to change the tabbing order of those controls programmatically.

TDBCtrlGrid.OnClick Event

Declaration

```
{ CONTROLS.PAS }
property OnClick: TNotifyEvent read FOnClick write FOnClick;
```

```
{ CLASSES.PAS }
TNotifyEvent = procedure(Sender: TObject) of object;
```

Description

The OnClick event occurs whenever the user clicks upon a panel within the grid.

See Also

OnDblClick event

TDBCtrlGrid.OnDblClick Event

Declaration

```
{ CONTROLS.PAS }
property OnDblClick: TNotifyEvent read FOnDblClick write FOnDblClick;
```

```
{ CLASSES.PAS }
TNotifyEvent = procedure(Sender: TObject) of object;
```

Description

The OnDblClick event occurs whenever the user double-clicks upon a panel within the grid.

Example

```
{ Bring up a form view of record currently highlighted in grid and allow
  user to edit }
procedure TForm1.DBCtrlGrid1DblClick(Sender: TObject);
var
   f : TFormView;
begin
   f := TFormView.Create(self);
   f.DataSource1.DataSet := DBCtrlGrid1.DataSource.DataSet;
   f.DataSource1.DataSet.Edit;
   if f.Showmodal = mrOK then
      f.DataSource1.DataSet.Post
   else
      f.DataSource1.DataSet.Cancel;
   f.Release;
end;
```

TDBCtrlGrid.OnPaintPanel Event

Declaration

```
{ DBCTRLS.PAS }
property OnPaintPanel: TPaintPanelEvent read FOnPaintPanel write
FOnPaintPanel

TPaintPanelEvent = procedure(DBCtrlGrid: TDBCtrlGrid; Index: Integer)
                   of objects;
```

Description

The OnPaintPanel event occurs whenever a panel within the grid is redrawn. This takes place just before the controls within the panel are displayed. This event accepts two parameters: *DBCtrlGrid* (the grid which is currently being displayed); and *Index* (the panel which is being repainted).

See Also

Canvas property

TDBCtrlGrid.OnStartDrag Event

Declaration

```
{ CONTROLS.PAS }
property OnStartDrag: TStartDragEvent read FOnStartDrag
         write FOnStartDrag;

{ CONTROLS.PAS }
TStartDragEvent = procedure(Sender: TObject;
     var DragObject: TDragObject) of object;
```

Description

The OnStartDrag event occurs whenever the user commences a drag-and-drop operation with the grid.

See Also

DragMode property

TDBCTRLGRID.ORIENTATION PROPERTY

Declaration

```
{ DBCGRIDS.PAS }
property Orientation: TDBCtrlGridOrientation read FOrientation
        write SetOrientation default goVertical;

TDBCtrlGridOrientation = (goVertical, goHorizontal);
```

Description

The Orientation property determines whether the grid will be displayed and navigable horizontally or vertically. The default orientation is vertical. This can be useful when you have to fit the grid into a small screen area.

TDBCTRLGRID.PANELBORDER PROPERTY

Declaration

```
{ DBCGRIDS.PAS }
property PanelBorder: TDBCtrlGridBorder read FPanelBorder
        write SetPanelBorder default gbRaised;

TDBCtrlGridBorder = (gbNone, gbRaised);
```

Description

The PanelBorder property dictates whether or not the panels within the grid should have a border. If set to its default value of gbRaised, the panels will have a raised border. Set this to gbNone if you would prefer the panels not to have a border.

TDBCTRLGRID.PANELHEIGHT PROPERTY

Declaration

```
{ DBCGRIDS.PAS }
property PanelHeight: Integer read FPanelHeight
        write SetPanelHeight;
```

Description

The PanelHeight property determines the height of each panel within the grid. When the grid is initially created, this will be set to 72 pixels.

Example

See the example provided with the TDBCtrlGrid.Create discussion.

See Also

PanelWidth property

TDBCTRLGRID.PANELINDEX PROPERTY

Declaration

```
{ DBCGRIDS.PAS }
property PanelIndex: Integer read FPanelIndex write SetPanelIndex;
```

Description

Run-time only. The PanelIndex property indicates which panel is currently selected within the grid.

TDBCTRLGRID.PANELWIDTH PROPERTY

Declaration

```
{ DBCGRIDS.PAS }
property PanelWidth: Integer read FPanelWidth
        write SetPanelWidth;
```

Description

The PanelWidth property determines the width of each panel within the grid. When the grid is initially created, this will be set to 200 pixels.

Example

See the example provided with the TDBCtrlGrid.Create discussion.

See Also

PanelHeight property

TDBCTRLGRID.ROWCOUNT PROPERTY

Declaration

```
{ DBCGRIDS.PAS }
property RowCount: Integer read FRowCount write SetRowCount;
```

Description

The RowCount property dictates how many rows will be in the grid. When the grid is initially created, this will be set to 3, although you are free to change it either at design-time or run-time.

See Also

ColCount property, PanelHeight property, PanelWidth property

TDBCTRLGRID.SHOWFOCUS PROPERTY

Declaration

```
{ DBCGRIDS.PAS }
property ShowFocus: Boolean read FShowFocus write FShowFocus
        default True;
```

Description

The ShowFocus property dictates whether or not to draw a dotted rectangle around the currently selected panel. By default, this will be activated. If you want to disable this, you must do so in code, because this property is not available at design-time.

Example

```
{ Turn off the rectangle, let users fend for themselves }
DBCtrlGrid1.ShowFocus := False;
```

TDBEdit

Unit

DBCtrls

Inherits from

TCustomMaskEdit

Description

The TDBEdit component displays the value of a field in an edit control. The user can change the value of the field by typing into the edit control.

The following tables summarize the properties (Table 3.21), methods (Table 3.22), and events (Table 3.23) for TDBEdit.

TABLE 3.21 TDBEDIT PROPERTIES

PROPERTY	DATA TYPE	RUN-TIME ONLY	READ-ONLY	DESCRIPTION
AutoSelect	Boolean	Yes	No	Determines whether to select text automatically when edit box gains focus
AutoSize	Boolean	No	No	Determines whether to resize edit box automatically when its font changes (applies only if edit box has a border)
BorderStyle	TBorderStyle	No	No	Dictates whether or not edit box will have a border
CharCase	TEditCharCase	No	No	Determines case of text in edit box
EditText	String	Yes	Yes	Text seen in edit box (same as Text property unless EditMask is in effect)
Field	TField	Yes	Yes	Field to which the edit box is linked
Handle	THandle (HWnd)	Yes	Yes	Handle to edit box (for Windows API function calls)
IsMasked	Boolean	No	No	Indicates whether an EditMask is in effect
MaxLength	Integer	No	No	Maximum number of characters that can be entered into the edit box
Modified	Boolean	Yes	No	Indicates whether text in edit box has been modified
PasswordChar	Char	No	No	Character to use for hidden (password) data entry in edit box
SelLength	Integer	Yes	No	Length (in characters) of selected text in edit box's edit control
SelStart	Integer	Yes	No	Starting position of selected text in edit box's edit control (zero-based)
SelText	String	Yes	No	The selected text, if any, in the edit box's edit control
ShowHint	Boolean	No	No	Determines whether Hint should be displayed if mouse cursor rests briefly upon edit box (see ParentShowHint)
Text	String	No	No	Text displayed in edit box's edit control

TABLE 3.22 TDBEDIT METHODS

METHOD	DESCRIPTION
Clear	Deletes all text in edit box.
ClearSelection	Deletes all selected text in edit box.
CopyToClipboard	Copies selected text in edit box to the clipboard.
Create	Allocates memory to create the edit box.
CutToClipboard	Deletes selected text in edit box and copies it to the clipboard.
GetSelTextBuf	Retrieves edit box's selected text (for strings longer than 255 characters).
PasteFromClipboard	Copies text in clipboard into edit box at current cursor position.
SelectAll	Selects entire text in the edit box.
SetSelTextBuf	Sets the edit box's highlighted text (for strings longer than 255 characters).
ValidateEdit	Ensures that all required characters have been entered in edit box.

TABLE 3.23 TDBEDIT EVENTS

EVENT	DATA TYPE	DESCRIPTION
OnChange	TNotifyEvent	Occurs when the text in the edit box is changed.
OnClick	TNotifyEvent	Occurs when user single-clicks upon the edit box.
OnDblClick	TNotifyEvent	Occurs when user double-clicks upon the edit box.
OnDragDrop	TDragDropEvent	Occurs when user drops the edit box.
OnDragOver	TDragOverEvent	Occurs when user drags an object over the edit box.
OnEndDrag	TEndDragEvent	Occurs when user stops dragging the edit box.
OnKeyDown	TKeyEvent	Occurs when user presses a key while in edit box.
OnKeyPress	TKeyPressEvent	Occurs when user presses a character key in edit box.
OnKeyUp	TKeyEvent	Occurs when user releases a key with edit box active.
OnMouseDown	TMouseEvent	Occurs when user presses mouse button with mouse pointer over the edit box.
OnMouseMove	TMouseMoveEvent	Occurs when user moves mouse button if mouse pointer is over the edit box.
OnMouseUp	TMouseEvent	Occurs when user releases mouse button with mouse pointer over the edit box.

TDBEDIT.AUTOSELECT PROPERTY

Declaration

```
{ STDCTRLS.PAS }
property AutoSelect: Boolean read FAutoSelect write FAutoSelect
  default True;
```

Description

The AutoSelect property determines whether or not the text in the edit box will automatically be selected as the edit box is activated. If set to its default value of True, the text will be selected.

See Also

SelText property, Text property

TDBEDIT.AUTOSIZE PROPERTY

Declaration

```
{ STDCTRLS.PAS }
property AutoSize: Boolean read FAutoSize write SetAutoSize
    default True;
```

Description

Assuming that the edit box has a border, setting the AutoSize property to True will cause its height to be adjusted to accommodate any changes to the font. If AutoSize is set to False, the edit box will not automatically adjust to accommodate font changes, which will in turn look somewhat strange.

See Also

BorderStyle property, Font property, Height property

TDBEDIT.BORDERSTYLE PROPERTY

Declaration

```
{ STDCTRLS.PAS }
property BorderStyle: TBorderStyle read FBorderStyle
    write SetBorderStyle default bsSingle;

TBorderStyle = (bsSingle, bsNone);
```

Description

The BorderStyle property dictates whether or not the edit box should have a border. If set to its default value of bsSingle, the edit box will have a border. Set this to bsNone if you do not want the edit box to have a border.

If BorderStyle is set to bsSingle and the AutoSize property is set to True, the height of the edit box will automatically be resized if its font changes.

See Also

AutoSize property, Font property

TDBEDIT.CHARCASE PROPERTY

Declaration

```
{ STDCTRLS.PAS }
property CharCase: TEditCharCase read FCharCase write SetCharCase
   default ecNormal;

{ STDCTRLS.PAS }
TEditCharCase = (ecNormal, ecUpperCase, ecLowerCase);
```

Description

The CharCase property dictates how the text in the edit box will be displayed. This is useful to force uppercase data entry to preclude the need for case conversion (e.g., password checks, searches). Table 3.24 lists the possible values of this property.

TABLE 3.24 TDBEDIT.CHARCASE VALUES

VALUE	DESCRIPTION
ecNormal	Text is displayed unchanged (default)
ecUpperCase	Text is displayed entirely in uppercase
ecLowerCase	Text is displayed entirely in lowercase

Example

```
{ Allow user to toggle between upper- and lowercase via a check box }
if CheckBox1.Checked then
   DBEdit1.CharCase := ecUpperCase
else
   DBEdit1.CharCase := ecLowerCase;
```

See Also

Text property

TDBEDIT.CLEAR METHOD

Declaration

```
{ STDCTRLS.PAS }
procedure Clear;
```

Description

The Clear method deletes all text from the edit box.

See Also

Text property

TDBEDIT.CLEARSELECTION METHOD

Declaration

```
{ STDCTRLS.PAS }
procedure ClearSelection;
```

Description

The ClearSelection method is similar to the Clear method, except that it deletes only the selected text from the edit box.

Notes

As of this writing, the ClearSelection method did not appear to have any effect upon TDBEdit boxes, regardless of whether or not the edit box had input focus when the method was called.

See Also

Clear method, SelLength property, SelStart property, SelText property

TDBEDIT.COPYTOCLIPBOARD METHOD

Declaration

```
{ STDCTRLS.PAS }
procedure CopyToClipboard;
```

Description

The CopyToClipboard method copies the edit box's selected text (if any) to the clipboard.

See Also

CutToClipboard method, PasteFromClipboard method, SelText property

TDBEDIT.CREATE METHOD

Declaration

```
{ DBCTRLS.PAS }
constructor Create(AOwner: TComponent); override;
```

Description

The Create method can be used to create an edit box manually at run-time. If you give the edit box an owner, the edit box will automatically be destroyed when its owner is destroyed.

Note: If you create an edit box manually with this method, you must specify its Parent property in order for the edit box to be displayed on-screen.

Notes

If you do not want the edit box to have an owner, pass Self as the parameter to the Create method. (See the example accompanying the discussion of the TDBCheckBox.Free method.)

Example

```
{ Create edit box on-the-fly and link it to the Title field in the Articles
  table, which is located in C:\AQUARIUM\ARTICLES. This also creates the
  TTable and TDataSource objects on-the-fly. If you have created them at
  design-time, then you can eliminate those sections of code }
var
    eb : TDBEdit;
    t : TTable;
    d : TDataSource;
begin
  { create TTable object to access Articles table }
  t := TTable.Create(Application);
  t.DatabaseName := 'c:\aquarium\articles';
  t.TableName := 'articles.dbf';
  t.Open;
  { Create TDataSource object to link to Articles table }
  d := TDataSource.Create(Application);
  d.DataSet := t;
  { now create the edit box }
  eb := TDBEdit.Create(Form1);
  eb.Parent := Form1;    { Very important! }
  eb.SetBounds(10,10,120,24);
  eb.CharCase := ecUpperCase;
  eb.DataSource := d;   { Link to DataSource created above }
  eb.DataField := 'Title';
  eb.Hint := 'The title of the article';
  eb.ShowHint := True;
end;
```

See Also

Free method

TDBEDIT.CUTTOCLIPBOARD METHOD

Declaration

```
{ STDCTRLS.PAS }
procedure CutToClipboard;
```

Description

The CutToClipboard method deletes the edit box's selected text (if any) and copies it to the clipboard.

Example

See the example provided with the TDBEdit.OnKeyDown event discussion.

See Also

CopyToClipboard method, PasteFromClipboard method, SelText property

TDBEDIT.EDITTEXT PROPERTY

Declaration

```
{ MASK.PAS }
property EditText: String read GetEditText write SetEditText;
```

Description

Run-time only. The EditText property contains the text currently displayed in the edit box. Its contents will match the Text property unless the field linked to the edit box has an active EditMask.

See Also

TField object, IsMasked property, Text property

TDBEDIT.FIELD PROPERTY

Declaration

```
{ DBCTRLS.PAS }
property Field: TField read GetField;
```

Description

The Field property contains the field to which the edit box is linked. This can be used to manipulate the field directly.

Notes

Run-time and read-only

Example

```
{ Set value of linked field to the text in the edit box }
if not (DBEdit1.DataSource.State in [dsEdit, dsInsert]) then
   DBEdit1.DataSource.DataSet.Edit;
```

```
DBEdit1.Field.AsString := DBEdit1.Text;
DBEdit1.DataSource.DataSet.Post;
```

See Also

DataField property, DataSource property, TField chapter

TDBEdit.GetSelTextBuf Method

Declaration

```
{ STDCTRLS.PAS }
function GetSelTextBuf(Buffer: PChar; BufSize: Integer): Integer;
```

Description

The GetSelTextBuf method copies the edit box's selected text (if any) into a null-terminated string (Buffer). The BufSize parameter limits the number of characters to be copied. This method returns the number of characters copied.

Notes

GetSelTextBuf is for manipulating strings that are longer than 255 characters. Most TDBEdit boxes will not be this long, so, therefore, it is unlikely that you will need to use this method.

Example

See example provided with the TDBMemo.GetSelTextBuf method.

See Also

GetTextBuf method, GetTextLen method, SetSelTextBuf method, Text property

TDBEdit.Handle Property

Declaration

```
{ CONTROLS.PAS }
property Handle: HWnd read GetHandle;
```

Description

Run-time and read-only. The Handle property is useful should you need to pass the edit box's handle to a Windows API function.

Example

```
{ Undo most recent change to edit box }
SendMessage(DBEdit1.Handle, EM_UNDO, 0, 0);
```

TDBEdit.IsMasked Property

Declaration

```
{ MASK.PAS }
property IsMasked: Boolean read GetMasked;
```

Description

The IsMasked property indicates whether the edit box has a mask or not. If the field linked to the edit box has an active EditMask, then IsMasked will be True. Otherwise, IsMasked will be False.

Notes

Read-only

Example

```
{ Set edit mask for date fields }
if (not DBEdit1.IsMasked) and (DBEdit1.Field is TDateField) then
   DBEdit1.Field.EditMask := '##/##/##';
```

See Also

EditText property, TField object

TDBEdit.MaxLength Property

Declaration

```
{ STDCTRLS.PAS }
property MaxLength: Integer read FMaxLength write SetMaxLength
   default 0;
```

Description

The MaxLength property can be used to limit the number of characters entered into the edit box. By default, this value is zero (0), which means that there is no limit. When you link the edit box to a character field, MaxLength will automatically be set to match the length of that field.

TDBEdit.Modified Property

Declaration

```
{ STDCTRLS.PAS }
property Modified: Boolean read GetModified write SetModified;
```

Description

The Modified property indicates whether the user has changed the text in the edit box. If Modified contains the value True, then the text has indeed been altered. This can be used, for example, to verify that the user wants to cancel the current edit operation.

Example

```
{ If user has modified the text, request confirmation before allowing them
  to cancel the edit operation }
if (DBEdit1.Modified) and (MessageDlg('Are you sure?',
        mtConfirmation, [mbOk,mbCancel], 0) = mrOk) then
  Cancel;
```

TDBEDIT.ONCHANGE EVENT

Declaration

```
{ STDCTRLS.PAS }
property OnChange: TNotifyEvent read FOnChange write FOnChange;

{ CLASSES.PAS }
TNotifyEvent = procedure(Sender: TObject) of object;
```

Description

The OnChange event occurs whenever the user changes the text in the edit box.

Example

```
{ Perform an incremental search in another table whenever text in edit
  box changes }
procedure TForm1.DBEdit1Change(Sender: TObject);
begin
  Table2.FindNearest([DBEdit1.Text]);
end;
```

See Also

Text property

TDBEDIT.ONCLICK EVENT

Declaration

```
{ CONTROLS.PAS }
property OnClick: TNotifyEvent read FOnClick write FOnClick;

{ CLASSES.PAS }
TNotifyEvent = procedure(Sender: TObject) of object;
```

Description

The OnClick event occurs when the user single-clicks within the edit box.

See Also

OnChange event, OnDblClick event

TDBEDIT.ONDBLCLICK EVENT

Declaration

```
{ CONTROLS.PAS }
property OnDblClick: TNotifyEvent read FOnDblClick write FOnDblClick;

{ CLASSES.PAS }
TNotifyEvent = procedure(Sender: TObject) of object;
```

Description

The OnDblClick event occurs whenever the user double-clicks within the edit box.

See Also

OnChange event, OnClick event

TDBEDIT.ONDRAGDROP EVENT

Declaration

```
{ CONTROLS.PAS }
property OnDragDrop: TDragDropEvent read FOnDragDrop
   write FOnDragDrop;
TDragDropEvent = procedure(Sender, Source: TObject;
   X, Y: Integer) of object;
```

Description

The OnDragDrop event occurs when an object is dropped onto the edit box. Your OnDragDrop event handler should specify what should happen in this situation. Four parameters are passed to your OnDragDrop event handler: Sender (the edit box), Source (the object being dropped), and X and Y (mouse cursor coordinates).

Example

```
{ Allow user to drag other edit boxes onto this edit box }
procedure TForm1.DBEdit1DragDrop(Sender, Source: TObject; X, Y: Integer);
begin
   if Source is TEdit then
```

```
          DBEdit1.Text := (Source as TEdit).Text;
end;
```

See Also

DragCursor property, DragMode property, OnDragOver method

TDBEDIT.ONKEYDOWN EVENT

Declaration

```
{ CONTROLS.PAS }
property OnKeyDown: TKeyEvent read FOnKeyDown write FOnKeyDown;

TKeyEvent = procedure(Sender: TObject; var Key: Word;
    Shift: TShiftState) of object;

{ CLASSES.PAS }
TShiftState = set of (ssShift, ssAlt, ssCtrl,
    ssLeft, ssRight, ssMiddle, ssDouble);
```

Description

The OnKeyDown event occurs when a user presses a key while the edit box has focus. You can write an OnKeyDown event handler to handle special keypresses, including function keys or keypresses combined with the **Shift**, **Alt**, and/or **Ctrl** keys. Parameters passed to your OnKeyDown event handler are Key (the numeric code associated with the keypress) and Shift (status of special keys, such as **Shift**, **Alt**, **Ctrl**, and mouse buttons).

Notes

A complete list of numeric codes associated with these keypresses can be found by searching for the topic "Virtual Key Codes" in the Delphi on-line help file. Alternatively, you can identify a key by its ASCII value if it has one.

Example

```
{ If user presses Alt-Delete, cut all text in edit box to clipboard }
procedure TForm1.DBEdit1KeyDown(Sender: TObject; var Key: Word;
  Shift: TShiftState);
begin
    if Key = vk_Delete then begin
        if Shift = [ssAlt] then begin
            DBEdit1.SelectAll;
            DBEdit1.CutToClipboard;
        end
        else
            Key := 0;   { This nullifies the keypress }
    end;
end;
```

See Also

OnKeyPress event, OnKeyUp event, OnMouseDown event

TDBEDIT.ONMOUSEDOWN EVENT

Declaration

```
{ CONTROLS.PAS }
property OnMouseDown: TMouseEvent read FOnMouseDown
    write FOnMouseDown;

TMouseEvent = procedure(Sender: TObject; Button: TMouseButton;
    Shift: TShiftState; X, Y: Integer) of object;

TMouseButton = (mbLeft, mbRight, mbMiddle);

{ CLASSES.PAS }
TShiftState = set of (ssShift, ssAlt, ssCtrl,
    ssLeft, ssRight, ssMiddle, ssDouble);
```

Description

The OnMouseDown event occurs when the user presses a mouse button while the mouse cursor is over the edit box. The following parameters are passed to your OnMouseDown event handler: Button (identifies which mouse button was pressed), Shift (status of special keys and mouse buttons), and X and Y (screen coordinates of mouse cursor).

Notes

See the OnKeyDown discussion for a list of TShiftState values.

See Also

OnKeyDown event, OnMouseUp event

TDBEDIT.ONMOUSEMOVE EVENT

Declaration

```
{ CONTROLS.PAS }
property OnMouseMove: TMouseMoveEvent read FOnMouseMove
    write FOnMouseMove;

TMouseMoveEvent = procedure(Sender: TObject; Shift: TShiftState;
    X, Y: Integer) of object;

{ CLASSES.PAS }
TShiftState = set of (ssShift, ssAlt, ssCtrl,
    ssLeft, ssRight, ssMiddle, ssDouble);
```

Description

The OnMouseMove event occurs when the user moves the mouse while its cursor is over the edit box. The following parameters are passed to your OnMouseMove event handler: Shift (status of special keys and mouse buttons) and X and Y (screen coordinates of mouse cursor).

Notes

See the OnKeyDown discussion for a list of TShiftState values.

See Also

OnKeyDown event, OnMouseDown event, OnMouseUp event

TDBEdit.OnMouseUp Event

Declaration

```
{ CONTROLS.PAS }
property OnMouseUp: TMouseEvent read FOnMouseUp write FOnMouseUp;

TMouseEvent = procedure(Sender: TObject; Button: TMouseButton;
    Shift: TShiftState; X, Y: Integer) of object;

TMouseButton = (mbLeft, mbRight, mbMiddle);

{ CLASSES.PAS }
TShiftState = set of (ssShift, ssAlt, ssCtrl,
    ssLeft, ssRight, ssMiddle, ssDouble);
```

Description

The OnMouseUp event occurs when the user releases a mouse button while the mouse cursor is over the edit box. The following parameters will be passed to your OnMouseUp event handler: Button (identifies which mouse button was pressed), Shift (status of special keys and mouse buttons), and X and Y (screen coordinates of mouse cursor).

Notes

See the OnKeyDown discussion for a list of TShiftState values.

See Also

OnKeyDown event, OnMouseDown event

TDBEdit.PasswordChar Property

Declaration

```
{ STDCTRLS.PAS }
property PasswordChar: Char read FPasswordChar write SetPasswordChar
    default #0;
```

Description

The PasswordChar property can be used to display alternate characters in the edit box. By default, the text will be displayed as the user enters it. However, changing this property to anything besides ASCII character zero will cause that character to be displayed. The Text property will remain unaffected by this.

Example

```
{ Display question marks instead of text }
DBEdit1.PasswordChar := '?';
```

TDBEdit.PasteFromClipboard Method

Declaration

```
{ STDCTRLS.PAS }
procedure PasteFromClipboard;
```

Description

The PasteFromClipboard method replaces the edit box's selected text (if any) with the contents of the clipboard. If no text is currently selected, the clipboard contents will be inserted at the position of the cursor within the edit box.

See Also

CopyToClipboard method, CutToClipboard method, SelText property

TDBEdit.SelectAll Method

Declaration

```
{ STDCTRLS.PAS }
procedure SelectAll;
```

Description

The SelectAll method is self-explanatory—it selects (highlights) the entire text in the edit box.

See Also

Text property

TDBEdit.SelLength Property

Declaration

```
{ STDCTRLS.PAS }
property SelLength: Integer read GetSelLength write SetSelLength;
```

Description

The SelLength returns the length, in characters, of the currently selected text in the edit box. If it contains zero, then no text is selected.

Notes

The edit box should be focused before you change this property.

Example

```
{ Programmatically highlight first ten characters of text }
DBEdit1.SetFocus;
DBEdit1.SelStart := 0;
DBEdit1.SelLength := 10;
```

See Also

SelStart property, SelText property

TDBEdit.SelStart Property

Declaration

```
{ STDCTRLS.PAS }
property SelStart: Integer read GetSelStart write SetSelStart;
```

Description

The SelStart returns the starting position of the currently selected text, if any, in the edit box.

Notes

The edit box should be focused before you change this property.

Example

See the example provided with the TDBEdit.SelLength property.

See Also

SelStart property, SelText property

TDBEDIT.SELTEXT PROPERTY

Declaration

```
{ STDCTRLS.PAS }
property SelText: String read GetSelText write SetSelText;
```

Description

The SelText returns the currently selected text, if any, in the edit box.

See Also

SelLength property, SelText property

TDBEDIT.SETSELTEXTBUF METHOD

Declaration

```
{ STDCTRLS.PAS }
procedure SetSelTextBuf(Buffer: PChar);
```

Description

The SetSelTextBuf method copies text from a null-terminated string (Buffer) into the edit box and automatically selects it.

Notes

SetSelTextBuf is for manipulating strings that are longer than 255 characters. Most TDBEdit boxes will not be this long, so, therefore, it is unlikely that you will need to use this method.

Example

See example provided with the TDBMemo.SetSelTextBuf method.

See Also

GetTextBuf method, GetSelTextBuf method, GetTextLen method, SelText property

TDBEDIT.TEXT PROPERTY

Declaration

```
{ CONTROLS.PAS }
property Text: TCaption read GetText write SetText;

TCaption = string[255];
```

Description

This property contains the text currently displayed in the edit box.

See Also

SelLength property, SelStart property, SelText property

TDBEDIT.VALIDATEEDIT METHOD

Declaration

```
{ MASK.PAS }
procedure ValidateEdit;
```

Description

The ValidateEdit method checks the EditText property to ensure that all required characters have been entered. If any are missing, Delphi will raise an EDBEditError exception. ValidateEdit also forces any pending paint messages to be processed for the edit box.

Notes

The ValidateEdit method is called automatically when you attempt to leave the edit box.

See Also

EditText property, IsMasked property, OnExit event

TDBGrid

Unit

DBGrids

Inherits from

TCustomDBGrid

Description

The TDBGrid component displays the contents of multiple records in a spreadsheet-like format. In addition to viewing the data, you can allow the user to add, edit, or delete data.

The following tables summarize the properties (Table 3.25), methods (Table 3.26), and events (Table 3.27) for TDBGrid. Items new to Delphi 2.0 are annotated with an asterisk(*).

TABLE 3.25 TDBGRID PROPERTIES

PROPERTY	DATA TYPE	RUN-TIME ONLY	READ-ONLY	DESCRIPTION
BorderStyle	TBorderStyle	No	No	Dictates whether or not grid will have a border.
Brush	TBrush	Yes	No	Brush used to draw grid's background
Canvas	TCanvas	Yes	Yes	Provides access to drawing surface.
ClientHeight	Integer	Yes	No	Vertical size of usable area in grid
ClientOrigin	Integer	Yes	Yes	Top left corner of grid's client area
ClientRect	Integer	Yes	Yes	The bounding rectangle of the usable area within the grid
ClientWidth	Integer	Yes	No	Horizontal size of usable area in grid
Columns*	TDBGridColumns	Yes	No	The columns within the grid
DefaultDrawing	Boolean	No	No	Determines whether cells in grid are drawn automatically (T) or manually (F).
EditorMode	Boolean	No	No	Determines whether automatic cell edit mode is activated (T = yes, F = no).
FieldCount	Integer	Yes	Yes	Number of fields within grid
Fields	TFields	Yes	Yes	Provides direct access to fields in grid.
FixedColor	TColor	No	No	Color used to display nonscrolling rows and columns within grid
Options	TDBGridOptions	No	No	Various options for the grid
SelectedField	TField	Yes	Yes	Currently selected field in grid
SelectedIndex	Integer	Yes	No	Number of currently selected field
TitleFont	TFont	No	No	Font used to display column headings

TABLE 3.26 TDBGRID METHODS

METHOD	DESCRIPTION
Create	Allocates memory to create the grid.

TABLE 3.27 TDBGRID EVENTS

EVENT	DATA TYPE	DESCRIPTION
OnColEnter	TNotifyEvent	Occurs when user enters a column within the grid.
OnColExit	TNotifyEvent	Occurs when user exits any column within the grid.
OnColumnMoved*	TMovedEvent	Occurs when user moves a column in the grid.
OnDblClick	TNotifyEvent	Occurs when user double-clicks upon the grid.
OnDrawColumnCell*	TDrawColumnCellEvent	Occurs whenever a cell in the grid needs to be redrawn.
OnDrawDataCell	TDrawDataCellEvent	Occurs when cell in grid needs to be redrawn (rendered obsolete in version 2.0 by OnDrawColumnCell).
OnEditButtonClick*	TNotifyEvent	Occurs when user clicks on a button in one of the grid columns.
OnKeyDown	TKeyEvent	Occurs when user presses a key while in grid.
OnKeyPress	TKeyPressEvent	Occurs when user presses a character key in grid.
OnStartDrag*	TStartDragEvent	Occurs when user begins a drag-and-drop operation with the grid.

TDBGRID.BORDERSTYLE PROPERTY

Declaration

```
{ STDCTRLS.PAS }
property BorderStyle: TBorderStyle read FBorderStyle
   write SetBorderStyle default bsSingle;
TBorderStyle = (bsSingle, bsNone);
```

Description

The BorderStyle property dictates whether or not the grid should have a discernible border. If set to its default value of bsSingle, the grid will have a border.

See Also

Options property

TDBGRID.BRUSH PROPERTY

Declaration

```
{ CONTROLS.PAS }
property Brush: TBrush read FBrush;
```

Description

Run-time only. The Brush property is used for drawing the background within the grid. However, it is not particularly relevant unless you are handling cell drawing yourself, i.e., setting DefaultDrawing to False and writing an OnDrawDataCell event handler.

Example

See the example provided with TDBGrid.OnDrawDataCell.

See Also

Canvas property, DefaultDrawing property, OnDrawDataCell event

TDBGrid.Canvas Property

Declaration

```
{ STDCTRLS.PAS }
property Canvas: TCanvas read FCanvas;
```

Description

Run-time and read-only. The Canvas property gives you access to a drawing surface within the grid. Although the Canvas itself is read-only, you can change its Brush, Font, and Pen properties to customize drawing for the grid. It is not relevant unless you are drawing the cells in the grid yourself (i.e., by setting DefaultDrawing to False and writing an OnDrawDataCell event handler).

Example

See the example provided with TDBGrid.OnDrawDataCell.

See Also

Brush property, DefaultDrawing property, OnDrawDataCell event

TDBGrid.ClientHeight Property

Declaration

```
{ CONTROLS.PAS }
property ClientHeight: Integer read GetClientHeight
    write SetClientHeight stored False;
```

Description

The ClientHeight property contains the usable vertical size of the grid. It will generally be the value of the Height property less the height of the column headings. This property can be used in lieu of Height to manipulate the size of the grid at run-time.

See Also

ClientWidth property, Height property

TDBGrid.ClientOrigin Property

Declaration

```
{ CONTROLS.PAS }
property ClientOrigin: TPoint read GetClientOrigin;
```

Description

Run-time and read-only. The ClientOrigin property contains a point denoting the top left corner of the grid's usable area, relative to its parent.

See Also

ClientRect property

TDBGrid.ClientRect Property

Declaration

```
{ CONTROLS.PAS }
property ClientRect: TRect read GetClientRect;
```

Description

Run-time and read-only. The ClientRect property contains a TRect object, which delineates the bounding rectangle of the grid's usable area. The coordinates of BoundsRect are relative to the parent of the grid.

See Also

BoundsRect property, SetBounds methods

TDBGrid.ClientWidth Property

Declaration

```
{ CONTROLS.PAS }
property ClientWidth: Integer read GetClientWidth
   write SetClientWidth stored False;
```

Description

The ClientWidth property contains the usable horizontal size of the grid.

See Also

ClientHeight property, Width property

TDBGRID.COLUMNS PROPERTY (NEW IN DELPHI 2.0)

Declaration

```
{ DBCTRLS.PAS }
property Columns: TDBGridColumns read FColumns write SetColumns;
```

Description

Run-time only. The Columns property gives you access to the columns within the grid, thus allowing you to change any of the following column attributes: alignment, color, field name, font, read-only status, title alignment, title caption, title color, title font, and width. You can also attach controls, including push buttons and list boxes, to individual columns.

The TDBGridColumns class has the following properties and methods:

TABLE 3.28 TDBGRIDCOLUMNS PROPERTIES

PROPERTY	DATA TYPE	RUN-TIME ONLY	READ-ONLY	DESCRIPTION
Grid	TCustomDBGrid	Yes	Yes	The grid to which the columns belong
Items	Tcolumn	Yes	No	The column objects for the grid
State	TDBGridColumnsState	No	No	Indicates whether the columns are default (csDefault) or persistent (csCustomized).

TABLE 3.29 TDBGRIDCOLUMNS METHODS

METHOD	DESCRIPTION
Add	Creates a new Tcolumn object and adds it to Items property.
RebuildColumns	Removes all existing columns in Items and rebuilds new columns based on the fields in the dataset attached to the grid.
RestoreDefaults	Nullifies any customization done to the columns in Items property.

The Tcolumn objects held in the TDBGridColumns.Items in turn have the following properties and methods. Although you will generally set these at design-time, there will certainly be times when you will want to manipulate them at run-time.

TABLE 3.30 TCOLUMN PROPERTIES

PROPERTY	DATA TYPE	RUN-TIME ONLY	READ-ONLY	DESCRIPTION
Alignment	Talignment	No	No	Indicates how text should be displayed within the column (left-justified, centered, or right-justified).
AssignedValues	TColumnValues	Yes	Yes	Indicates which values, if any, have been customized for the column.
ButtonStyle	TColumn-ButtonStyle	No	No	Dictates how user can select from a list, if any, in this column (cbsAuto, cbsEllipsis, or cbsNone).
Color	Tcolor	No	No	Background color for column
DropDownRows	Integer	No	No	Number of drop down rows to use for pick list, if any, in this column
Field	Tfield	No	No	Field object tied to this column
FieldName	String	No	No	Name of field tied to this column
Fontq	Tfont	No	No	Font in which to display text in this column
PickList	Tstrings	No	No	List of strings to be displayed in the combo box, if any, for this column
ReadOnly	Boolean	No	No	Dictates whether user can edit data within this column.
Title	TColumnTitle	No	No	Controls attributes for the column's heading, including Alignment, Caption, Color, and Font properties.
Width	Integer	No	No	Width in pixels of this column

TABLE 3.31 TCOLUMN METHODS

METHOD	DESCRIPTION
Assign	Enables you to assign one Tcolumn object to another.
DefaultAlignment	Default alignment of data in this column, which will be taLeftJustify if no field object is attached to this column
DefaultColor	Default background color for this column (same as TDBGrid.Color)
DefaultFont	Default font used to show column heading (same as TDBGrid.TitleFont)
DefaultReadOnly	Default read only setting for this column (False)
DefaultWidth	Default width for this column
RestoreDefaults	Restores all default settings for column, erasing any customization.

Example

```
{ Dynamically add a picklist to the AUTHOR column }
procedure TForm1.FormCreate(Sender: TObject);
```

```
var
   x : Integer;
begin
   { Initialize default columns }
   DBGrid1.Columns.RebuildColumns;
   x := 0;
   { Locate AUTHOR column }
   while (x <= DBGrid1.Columns.Count) and
         (DBGrid1.Columns[x].Fieldname <> 'AUTHOR') do
     Inc(x);
   if x <= g.Columns.Count then    { Found it! }
   begin
      DBGrid1.Columns[x].PickList.Add('Ted Blue');
      DBGrid1.Columns[x].PickList.Add('John Kaster');
      DBGrid1.Columns[x].PickList.Add('Greg Lief');
      DBGrid1.Columns[x].PickList.Add('Loren Scott');
   end;
end;
```

See Also

OnDrawColumnCell event, OnEditButtonClick event

TDBGrid.Create Method

Declaration

```
{ DBCTRLS.PAS }
constructor Create(AOwner: TComponent); override;
```

Description

The Create method can be used to create a grid manually at run-time. If you give the grid an owner, the grid will go to the bit bucket at the same time as its owner.

Note: If you create a grid manually with this method, you must specify its Parent property in order for the grid to be displayed on-screen.

Notes

If you do not want the grid to have an owner, pass Self as the parameter to the Create method. For an example of this logic, see the TDBCheckBox.Free method.

Example

```
{ Create grid on-the-fly and link it to the articles table, which is
  located in C:\AQUARIUM\ARTICLES. this also creates the TTable and
  TDataSource objects on-the-fly. if you have created them at design-time,
  then eliminate that part of the code }
```

```
var
    g : TDBGrid;
    t : TTable;
    d : TDataSource;
begin
    { create TTable object to access Articles table }
    t := TTable.Create(Application);
    t.DatabaseName := 'c:\aquarium\articles';
    t.TableName := 'articles.dbf';
    t.Open;
    { Create TDataSource object to link to Articles table }
    d := TDataSource.Create(Application);
    d.DataSet := t;
    { Now create the grid }
    g := TDBGrid.Create(Form1);
    g.Parent      := Form1;   { Very important! }
    g.Align       := alClient;
    g.DataSource := d;   { Link to DataSource created above }
    { Set font for scrolling area within grid }
    g.Font.Name := 'MS Sans Serif';
    g.Font.Size := 8;
    { Set font for column headings within grid }
    g.TitleFont.Name := 'MS Sans Serif';
    g.TitleFont.Size := 11;
    g.TitleFont.Style := [fsBold];
    g.SetFocus;
end;
```

See Also

Free method

TDBGrid.DefaultDrawing Property

Declaration

```
{ DBGRIDS.PAS }
property DefaultDrawing: Boolean read FDefaultDrawing
    write FDefaultDrawing default True;
```

Description

The DefaultDrawing property determines if the cells within the grid are to be drawn automatically. If set to its default value of True, the cells are drawn automatically. If you set this to False, you must then write an OnDrawDataCell event handler to handle the drawing.

Example

See the example provided with the TDBGrid.OnDrawDataCell discussion.

See Also

Brush property, Canvas property, OnDrawDataCell event

TDBGRID.EDITORMODE PROPERTY

Declaration

```
{ GRIDS.INT }
property EditorMode: Boolean
```

Description

Run-time only. The EditorMode property determines whether or not the grid should be in automatic edit mode. When the grid is in automatic edit mode, the user can start editing by typing into a cell without having to first press **Enter** or **F2**. If the Options property includes dgAlwaysShowEditor, the grid will be in automatic edit mode as if EditorMode was set to True.

If the Options property does not include dgEditing, then the user will be unable to edit and the value of EditorMode will thus be irrelevant. If EditorMode is False and the Options property does include dgEditing, but not dgAlwaysShowEditor, the user will still be able to edit a cell by pressing either **Enter** or **F2**.

See Also

Options property

TDBGRID.FIELDCOUNT PROPERTY

Declaration

```
{ DBGRIDS.PAS }
property FieldCount: Integer read FFieldCount;
```

Description

The FieldCount property contains the number of columns within the grid. This may or may not match the number of fields in the attached dataset, because it is possible to add or delete columns via the Fields Editor.

See Also

Fields property, SelectedField property

TDBGRID.FIELDS PROPERTY

Declaration

```
{ DBGRIDS.PAS }
property Fields[I: Integer]: TField read GetFields;
```

Description

The Fields property is an array that contains all of the TFields currently displayed in the grid. This can be used to manipulate either the field values or the column attributes. The fields are zero-based (i.e., use zero to refer to the first column).

Example

```
{ Find TITLE column and make it leftmost column within the grid }
var
   x : Integer;
begin
   x := 0;
   while (x <= DBGrid1.FieldCount) and
         (DBGrid1.Fields[x].FieldName <> 'TITLE') do
      Inc(x);
   if x < DBGrid1.FieldCount then begin
      DBGrid1.Fields[x].Index := 0;
      { Center the data within this column }
      DBGrid1.Fields[0].Alignment := taCenter;
      { Change the heading for this column }
      DBGrid1.Fields[0].DisplayLabel := 'Article Title';
   end;
end;
```

See Also

FieldCount property, SelectedField property, SelectedIndex property

TDBGRID.FIXEDCOLOR PROPERTY

Declaration

```
{ GRIDS.INT }
property FixedColor: TColor default clBtnFace;
```

Description

The FixedColor property dictates how any fixed (nonscrolling) rows and columns will be drawn within the grid.

See the discussion of TDBCheckBox.Color for a complete list of available color values.

See Also

Color property

TDBGRID.ONCOLENTER EVENT

Declaration

```
{ DBGRIDS.PAS }
property OnColEnter: TNotifyEvent read FOnColEnter write FOnColEnter;
```

```
{ CLASSES.PAS }
TNotifyEvent = procedure(Sender: TObject) of object;
```

Description

The OnColEnter event occurs whenever the user enters a new column, either via keypress or mouse click.

See Also

OnColExit event

TDBGRID.ONCOLEXIT EVENT

Declaration

```
{ DBGRIDS.PAS }
property OnColExit: TNotifyEvent read FOnColExit write FOnColExit;
```

```
{ CLASSES.PAS }
TNotifyEvent = procedure(Sender: TObject) of object;
```

Description

The OnColExit event occurs whenever the user exits a column, either via keypress or mouse click.

See Also

OnColEnter event

TDBGRID.ONCOLUMNMOVED EVENT (NEW IN DELPHI 2.0)

Declaration

```
{ DBGRIDS.PAS }
property OnColumnMoved: TMovedEvent read FOnColumnMoved
    write FOnColumnMoved;
```

```
{ CLASSES.PAS }
TMovedEvent = procedure (Sender: TObject;
                         FromIndex, ToIndex: Longint) of object;
```

Description

The OnColumnMoved event occurs whenever the user moves a column. The parameters passed to this event handler are Sender (the grid), FromIndex (the original position of the column being moved), and ToIndex (the new position of the column).

See Also

OnColEnter event, OnColExit event

TDBGRID.ONDBLCLICK EVENT

Declaration

```
{ CONTROLS.PAS }
property OnDblClick: TNotifyEvent read FOnDblClick write FOnDblClick;

{ CLASSES.PAS }
TNotifyEvent = procedure(Sender: TObject) of object;
```

Description

The OnDblClick event occurs whenever the user double-clicks within the grid.

Example

```
{ Bring up a form view of record currently highlighted in grid and allow
  user to edit }
procedure TForm1.DBGrid1DblClick(Sender: TObject);
var
    f : TFormView;
begin
    f :=TFormView.Create(self);
    f.DataSource1.DataSet := DBGrid1.DataSource.DataSet;
    f.DataSource1.DataSet.Edit;
    if f.Showmodal = mrOK then
        f.DataSource1.DataSet.Post
    else
        f.DataSource1.DataSet.Cancel;
    f.Release;
end;
```

TDBGRID.ONDRAWCOLUMNCELL EVENT (NEW IN DELPHI 2.0)

Declaration

```
{ DBGRIDS.PAS }
property OnDrawColumnCell: TDrawColumnCellEvent
    read FOnDrawColumnCell write FOnDrawColumnCell;

TDrawColumnCellEvent = procedure(Sender: TObject;
    const Rect: TRect; DataCol: Integer; Column: TColumn;
    State: TGridDrawState) of object;
```

```
{ GRIDS.PAS }

TGridDrawState = set of (gdSelected, gdFocused, gdFixed);
```

Description

The OnDrawColumnCell event occurs whenever a cell is redrawn in the grid. If you want more control over the appearance of the cells within the grid, you should set the DefaultDrawing property to False and write an OnDrawColumnCell event handler, which will receive the following parameters: *Sender* (the grid), *Rect* (the rectangular area delineating the cell to be drawn), *DataCol* (the zero-based ordinal position of the column currently being drawn), *Column* (the column in which the drawing is taking place), and *State* (the current state of the cell).

Notes

This is a replacement for the OnDrawDataCell event. The primary difference between these two events is that OnDrawColumnCell supports TDBGrid.Column objects, which in turn leads to far greater flexibility and control. Compare the following example with that accompanying OnDrawDataCell to understand the importance of column support.

Example

```
{ If we are displaying the AUTHOR column, draw any cells containing the word
   'Judy' in a different font and color }
procedure TForm1.DBGrid1DrawColumnCell(Sender: TObject;
   const Rect: Trect; DataCol: Integer; Column: TColumn;
   State: TGridDrawState);
begin
   if (Column.FieldName = 'AUTHOR') and
      (Pos('Judy', Column.Field.AsString) > 0) then
   begin
      if gdSelected in State then
      begin
         DBGrid1.Canvas.Font.Style := Column.Font.Style +
                                       [fsItalic];
         DBGrid1.Canvas.Font.Color := clYellow;
         DBGrid1.Canvas.Brush.Color := clBlue;
      end
      else
         DBGrid1.Canvas.Font.Color := clFuchsia;
   end;
   DBGrid1.Canvas.FillRect(Rect);
   DBGrid1.Canvas.TextOut(Rect.Left + 2, Rect.Top,
                          Column.Field.AsString);
end;
```

See Also

Columns property, DefaultDrawing property

TDBGRID.ONDRAWDATACELL EVENT

Declaration

```
{ DBGRIDS.PAS }
property OnDrawDataCell: TDrawDataCellEvent read FOnDrawDataCell
   write FOnDrawDataCell;

TDrawDataCellEvent = procedure(Sender: TObject; const Rect: TRect;
   Field: TField; State: TGridDrawState) of object;

{ GRIDS.PAS }
TGridDrawState = set of (gdSelected, gdFocused, gdFixed);
```

Description

The OnDrawDataCell event occurs whenever a cell is redrawn in the grid. If you want more control over the appearance of the cells within the grid, you should set the DefaultDrawing property to False and write an OnDrawDataCell event handler, which will receive the following parameters: Sender (the grid), Rect (the rectangular area delineating the cell to be drawn), Field (the field corresponding to the column in which the drawing is to occur), and State (the current state of the cell).

Notes

In Delphi version 2.0, this event has been rendered obsolete by the OnDrawColumnCell event. It is therefore provided only for the purpose of backwards compatibility.

Example

```
{ If we are displaying the PRODUCT column, draw any cells containing the
   word 'Delphi' in a different font and color }
procedure TForm1.DBGrid1DrawDataCell(Sender: TObject;
   const Rect: TRect; Field: TField; State: TGridDrawState);
begin
   if (Field.FieldName = 'PRODUCT') and
      (Pos('Delphi', Field.AsString) > 0) then begin
      if gdSelected in State then begin   { if current cell }
         DBGrid1.Canvas.Font.Style := [fsItalic];
         DBGrid1.Canvas.Font.Color := clYellow;
         DBGrid1.Canvas.Brush.Color := clBlue;
      end
      else
         DBGrid1.Canvas.Font.Color := clFuchsia;
   end;
   DBGrid1.Canvas.FillRect(Rect);
   DBGrid1.Canvas.TextOut(Rect.Left + 2, Rect.Top,
                          Field.AsString);
end;
```

See Also

DefaultDrawing property, OnDrawColumnCell event

TDBGRID.ONEDITBUTTONCLICK EVENT (NEW IN DELPHI 2.0)

Declaration

```
{ CONTROLS.PAS }
property OnEditButtonClick: TNotifyEvent read FOnEditButtonClick
        write FOnEditButtonClick;

{ CLASSES.PAS }
TNotifyEvent = procedure(Sender: TObject) of object;
```

Description

The OnEditButtonClick event occurs whenever the user clicks on a button in one of the grid's columns. This allows you to customize the editing behavior for individual columns completely.

Example

```
{ If the user clicks on the edit button in the NAME column, display a custom
  form for some type of data selection, then retrieve a value from that
  form with its GetValue method and stuff it into this field. }
procedure TForm1.gEditButtonClick(Sender: TObject);
var
    f : TMyForm;
begin
  if g.SelectedField.FieldName = 'NAME' then begin
      f := TMyForm.Create(self);
      try
          if f.ShowModal = mrOK then begin
              g.DataSource.DataSet.Edit;
              g.SelectedField.AsString := f.GetValue;
          end;
      finally
          f.Release;
      end;
  end;
end;
```

TDBGRID.ONKEYDOWN EVENT

Declaration

```
{ CONTROLS.PAS }
property OnKeyDown: TKeyEvent read FOnKeyDown write FOnKeyDown;

TKeyEvent = procedure(Sender: TObject; var Key: Word;
    Shift: TShiftState) of object;
```

```
{ CLASSES.PAS }
TShiftState = set of (ssShift, ssAlt, ssCtrl,
    ssLeft, ssRight, ssMiddle, ssDouble);
```

Description

The OnKeyDown event occurs when a user presses a key while the grid has focus. You can write an OnKeyDown event handler to handle special keypresses, including function keys or keypresses combined with the **Shift, Alt,** and/or **Ctrl** keys. Parameters passed to your OnKeyDown event handler are Key (the numeric code associated with the keypress) and Shift (status of special keys, such as **Shift, Alt, Ctrl,** and mouse buttons).

Example

```
{ If user presses Ctrl-Insert, copy text in currently selected cell to the
  clipboard.  IMPORTANT: In order to use the clipboard variable, you must
  put the CLIPBRD unit in your USES clause }
procedure TForm1.DBGrid1KeyDown(Sender: TObject; var Key: Word;
  Shift: TShiftState);
begin
   if (Shift = [ssCtrl]) and (Key = VK_Insert) then
      Clipboard.AsText := DBGrid1.SelectedField.AsString;
end;
```

See Also

OnKeyPress event, OnKeyUp event, OnMouseDown event

TDBGRID.ONKEYPRESS EVENT

Declaration

```
{ CONTROLS.PAS }
property OnKeyPress: TKeyPressEvent read FOnKeyPress
    write FOnKeyPress;
TKeyPressEvent = procedure(Sender: TObject; var Key: Char) of object;
```

Description

The OnKeyPress event occurs when a user presses a key that has a corresponding ASCII value while the grid has focus. The Key parameter passed to your OnKeyPress event handler is the character that was pressed. If you need to trap special (non-ASCII) keys, you should use the OnKeyDown event.

Example

```
{ If user presses a key within the grid, search for that value. Note: this
  requires that editing be turned off in Options }
procedure TForm1.DBGrid1KeyPress(Sender: TObject; var Key: Char);
begin
```

```
     Table1.FindNearest([Key]);
end;
```

See Also

OnKeyDown event

TDBGrid.OnStartDrag Event (New in Delphi 2.0)

Declaration

```
{ CONTROLS.PAS }
property OnStartDrag: TStartDragEvent read FOnStartDrag
        write FOnStartDrag;
```

```
{ CONTROLS.PAS }
TStartDragEvent = procedure(Sender: TObject;
     var DragObject: TDragObject) of object;
```

Description

The OnStartDrag event occurs whenever the user commences a drag-and-drop operation with the grid.

See Also

DragMode property

TDBGrid.Options Property

Declaration

```
{ CLASSES.PAS }
property Options: TDBGridOptions read FOptions write SetOptions
   default [dgEditing, dgTitles, dgIndicator, dgColumnResize,
   dgColLines, dgRowLines, dgTabs, dgConfirmDelete, dgCancelOnExit];
```

```
TDBGridOption = (dgEditing, dgAlwaysShowEditor, dgTitles,
   dgIndicator, dgColumnResize, dgColLines, dgRowLines,
   dgTabs, dgRowSelect, dgAlwaysShowSelection, dgConfirmDelete,
   dgCancelOnExit);
```

```
TDBGridOptions = set of TDBGridOption;
```

Description

The Options property allows you to control a variety of aesthetic and functional aspects of the grid. Table 3.32 lists the possibilities.

TABLE 3.32 DBGRIDOPTION VALUES

VALUE (* = DEFAULT)	ACTION WHEN ENABLED
dgAlwaysShowEditor	When True, the grid will be in automatic edit mode assuming that dgEditing is also True. When the grid is in automatic edit mode, the user does not have to press **Enter** or **F2** before editing the contents of a cell. When dgAlwaysShowEditor is False and dgEditing is True, the user must press **Enter** or **F2** before editing the contents of a cell. If gdEditing is False, this item has no effect.
dgAlwaysShowSelection	The cell selected in the grid will remain selected even if the grid does not have input focus.
dgCancelOnExit*	If an insert is pending and the user makes no modifications, the insert will be canceled when the user exits the grid. This prevents inadvertent posting of blank records.
dgColLines*	Display separator lines between columns.
dgColumnResize*	User can resize columns at will.
dgConfirmDelete*	Displays a warning box when user attempts to delete a row by pressing **Ctrl-Delete**.
dgEditing*	Allows the user to edit data in the grid. Even if the ReadOnly property is True, the user can still press **Insert** to insert a blank row or press the **down arrow** at the bottom of the grid to append a blank record (even though they will not be able to edit any of the cells in the new row).
dgIndicator*	An indicator is displayed at the left edge of the grid pointing at the currently selected row.
dgRowLines*	Display separator lines between rows.
dgRowSelect	User can select entire rows only rather than individual cells.
dgTabs*	User can press **Tab** and **Shift-Tab** to move between columns.
dgTitles*	Column headings are displayed.

See Also

EditorMode property, Readonly property

TDBGRID.SELECTEDFIELD PROPERTY

Declaration

```
{ DBGRIDS.PAS }
property SelectedField: TField read GetSelectedField
   write SetSelectedField;
```

Description

Run-time and read-only. The SelectedField property contains the field corresponding to the column in which the cursor currently resides. This allows you to manipulate the field directly or any of the column attributes.

Example

```
{ When user double-clicks in grid, make current column leftmost }
procedure TForm1.DBGrid1DblClick(Sender: TObject);
begin
    DBGrid1.SelectedField.Index := 0;
end;
```

See Also

SelectedIndex property

TDBGRID.SELECTEDINDEX PROPERTY

Declaration

```
{ DBGRIDS.PAS }
property SelectedIndex: Integer read GetSelectedIndex
    write SetSelectedIndex;
```

Description

Run-time only. The SelectedIndex property contains the number of the currently selected column.

Example

```
{ When user double-clicks in grid, move to the leftmost column }
procedure TForm1.DBGrid1DblClick(Sender: TObject);
begin
    DBGrid1.SelectedIndex := 0;
end;
```

See Also

SelectedField property

TDBGRID.TITLEFONT PROPERTY

Declaration

```
{ DBGRIDS.PAS }
property TitleFont: TFont read FTitleFont write SetTitleFont;
```

Description

The TitleFont property contains the font used to draw the column headings in the grid.

Example

See the example accompanying TDBGrid.Create.

See Also

Font property

TDBImage

Unit

DBCtrls

Inherits from

TCustomControl

Description

The TDBImage component displays an image that is stored in a Binary Large Object (BLOB) field. The following tables summarize the properties (Table 3.33), methods (Table 3.34), and events (Table 3.35) for TDBImage.

TABLE 3.33 TDBIMAGE PROPERTIES

PROPERTY	DATA TYPE	RUN-TIME ONLY	READ-ONLY	DESCRIPTION
AutoDisplay	Boolean	No	No	Determines whether to display new image automatically when record pointer changes.
BorderStyle	TBorderStyle	No	No	Dictates whether or not image will have a border.
Center	Boolean	No	No	Determines whether image should be centered within the designated area.
Field	TField	Yes	Yes	Field to which the image is linked
Stretch	Boolean	No	No	Determines whether to size the image to fit the designated area.

TABLE 3.34 TDBIMAGE METHODS

METHOD	DESCRIPTION
CopyToClipboard	Copies image to clipboard.
Create	Allocates memory to create the image.
CutToClipboard	Deletes image from screen and copy to clipboard.
LoadPicture	Loads a new image into the control.
PasteFromClipboard	Copies image from clipboard to the control.

TABLE 3.35 TDBIMAGE EVENTS

EVENT	DATA TYPE	DESCRIPTION
OnClick	TNotifyEvent	Occurs when user single-clicks upon the image.
OnDblClick	TNotifyEvent	Occurs when user double-clicks upon the image.
OnDragDrop	TDragDropEvent	Occurs when user drops the image.
OnDragOver	TDragOverEvent	Occurs when user drags an object over the image.
OnMouseDown	TMouseEvent	Occurs when user presses mouse button with mouse pointer over the image.
OnMouseMove	TMouseMoveEvent	Occurs when user moves mouse button if mouse pointer is over the image.
OnMouseUp	TMouseEvent	Occurs when user releases mouse button with mouse pointer over the image.

TDBIMAGE.AUTODISPLAY PROPERTY

Declaration

```
{ DBCTRLS.PAS }
property AutoDisplay: Boolean read FAutoDisplay write SetAutoDisplay
    default True;
```

Description

The AutoDisplay property dictates whether or not the control will display a new image when the record pointer changes in its data source. By default, this behavior is enabled. If you set AutoDisplay to False, the image will be cleared whenever the record pointer moves, and the picture will not be loaded unless the user either double-clicks or presses **Enter** upon the control. You can also load the picture programmatically by calling the LoadPicture method.

Notes

A possible reason to disable this would be in the interest of performance. Depending upon the size of the images and the speed of the target CPU, there may be a momentary pause as the images are loaded.

See Also

LoadPicture method

TDBIMAGE.BORDERSTYLE PROPERTY

Declaration

```
{ STDCTRLS.PAS }
property BorderStyle: TBorderStyle read FBorderStyle
    write SetBorderStyle default bsSingle;

TBorderStyle = (bsSingle, bsNone);
```

Description

The BorderStyle dictates whether or not the image will have a border. Leave this at its default value of bsSingle if you want a border or set it to bsNone if you do not.

TDBImage.Center Property

Declaration

```
{ DBCTRLS.PAS }
property Center: Boolean read FCenter write SetCenter default True;
```

Description

The Center property dictates whether or not the image should be centered within the area of the control. By default, the image will be centered.

See Also

Stretch property

TDBImage.CopyToClipboard Method

Declaration

```
{ DBCTRLS.PAS }
procedure CopyToClipboard;
```

Description

The CopyToClipboard method copies the currently displayed image to the clipboard.

Example

```
{ This logic copies a bit map from a TDBImage to the clipboard, then
  effectively pastes it into another image control on the same form.
  IMPORTANT: In order to use the clipboard variable, you must put the
  CLIPBRD unit in your USES clause }
var
   b : TBitMap;
   p : TPicture;
begin
   DBImage1.CopyToClipboard;
   b := TBitMap.Create;
   b.Assign(Clipboard);   {Copy contents of clipboard to bit map }
   p := TPicture.Create;
   p.Bitmap := b;         { Assign bit map to TPicture object }
   Image1.Picture := p;   { Assign TPicture to image control }
end;
```

See Also

CutToClipboard method, PasteFromClipboard method

TDBImage.Create Method

Declaration

```
{ DBCTRLS.PAS }
constructor Create(AOwner: TComponent); override;
```

Description

The Create method can be used to create an image manually at run-time. If you give the image an owner, the image will automatically be destroyed when its owner is destroyed.

Note: If you create a image manually with this method, you must specify its Parent property in order for the image to be displayed on-screen. If you do not want the image to have an owner, pass Self as the parameter to the Create method. (See the example accompanying the discussion of the TDBCheckBox.Free method.)

Example

```
{ Create image on-the-fly and link it to the Graphic field in the BIOLIFE.DB
  table, which is located in DBDEMOS }
var
    i: TDBImage;
    t : TTable;
    d : TDataSource;
begin
    { Create TTable object }
    t := TTable.Create(Application);
    t.DatabaseName := 'DBDEMOS';
    t.TableName := 'biolife.db';
    t.Open;
    { Create TDataSource object to link to Biolife table }
    d := TDataSource.Create(Application);
    d.DataSet := t;
    { Create the image control }
    i := TDBImage.Create(Form1);
    i.Parent       := Form1;   { Don't forget this!! }
    i.Align        := alClient;
    i.DataSource   := d;
    i.DataField    := 'Graphic';
end;
```

See Also

Free method

TDBImage.CutToClipboard Method

Declaration

```
{ DBCTRLS.PAS }
procedure CutToClipboard;
```

Description

The CutToClipboard method deletes the image from the control and copies it to the clipboard.

Example

See the example provided with TDBImage.CopyToClipboard.

See Also

CopyToClipboard method, PasteFromClipboard method

TDBImage.Field Property

Declaration

```
{ DBCTRLS.PAS }
property Field: TField read GetField;
```

Description

Run-time and read-only. The Field property contains the field to which the DBComboBox is linked. This can be used to manipulate the field directly.

Example

```
{ Assign the JJ.BMP bit map to the field linked to this image }
DBComboBox1.DataSource.DataSet.Edit;
(DBImage1.Field as TBlobField).LoadFromFile('jj.bmp');
DBComboBox1.DataSource.DataSet.Post;
```

See Also

DataField property, DataSource property

TDBImage.LoadPicture Method

Declaration

```
{ DBCTRLS.PAS }
procedure LoadPicture;
```

Description

The LoadPicture method loads the picture from the data field. This would be used if you have set the AutoDisplay property to False.

Example

See example provided with TDBImage.OnClick discussion.

See Also

AutoDisplay property

TDBImage.OnClick Event

Declaration

```
{ CONTROLS.PAS }
property OnClick: TNotifyEvent read FOnClick write FOnClick;

{ CLASSES.PAS }
TNotifyEvent = procedure(Sender: TObject) of object;
```

Description

The OnClick event occurs when the user single-clicks upon the image.

Example

```
{ When user clicks upon image, allow them to select a .BMP file, which will
  then be loaded into the image. IMPORTANT: This requires that the DIALOGS
  unit be in the Form's USES clause. }
procedure TForm1.DBImage1Click(Sender: TObject);
var
   od: TOpenDialog;
begin
   od := TOpenDialog.Create(Form1);
   od.Filter := 'Bitmaps (*.BMP)|*.BMP';
   if od.Execute then begin
      if not (DBImage1.DataSource.State in
            [dsEdit,dsInsert]) then
         DBImage1.DataSource.Edit;
      (DBImage1.Field as TBlobField).
               LoadFromFile(od.FileName);
      DBImage1.LoadPicture;
   end;
end;
```

See Also

OnDblClick event

TDBImage.OnDblClick Event

Declaration

```
{ CONTROLS.PAS }
property OnDblClick: TNotifyEvent read FOnDblClick write FOnDblClick;

{ CLASSES.PAS }
TNotifyEvent = procedure(Sender: TObject) of object;
```

Description

The OnDblClick event occurs whenever the user double-clicks upon the image. By default, this will cause the image to be loaded (i.e., same as the LoadPicture method).

See Also

LoadPicture method, OnClick event

TDBImage.OnDragDrop Event

Declaration

```
{ CONTROLS.PAS }
property OnDragDrop: TDragDropEvent read FOnDragDrop
   write FOnDragDrop;

TDragDropEvent = procedure(Sender, Source: TObject;
   X, Y: Integer) of object;
```

Description

The OnDragDrop event occurs when an object is dropped onto the image. You should write an OnDragDrop event handler to specify what you want to happen in this situation. Four parameters are passed to your OnDragDrop event handler: Sender (the image), Source (the object being dropped), and X and Y (mouse cursor coordinates).

Example

```
{ Allow user to drag a TImage onto the TDBImage. NOTE: This requires that
  the CLIPBRD unit be in the Form's USES clause }
procedure TForm1.DBImage1DragDrop(Sender, Source: TObject;
  X, Y: Integer);
begin
  if Source is TImage then begin
    Clipboard.Assign((Source as TImage).Picture.Bitmap);
    DBImage1.PasteFromClipboard;
  end;
end;
```

See Also

DragCursor property, DragMode property, OnDragOver method

TDBIMAGE.ONDRAGOVER EVENT

Declaration

```
{ CONTROLS.PAS }
property OnDragOver: TDragOverEvent read FOnDragOver
    write FOnDragOver;

TDragOverEvent = procedure(Sender, Source: TObject; X, Y: Integer;
    State: TDragState; var Accept: Boolean) of object;
TDragState = (dsDragEnter, dsDragLeave, dsDragMove);
```

Description

The OnDragOver event occurs when an object is dragged over the image. By writing an OnDragOver event handler, you can determine which objects the image can accept. The parameters passed to your OnDragOver event handler are Sender (the image), Source (the object being dragged), X and Y (mouse cursor coordinates), State (the status of the object being dragged in relation to the image), and Accept, which should be set to a boolean value (True means the image can accept the object, and False means that it cannot).

Example

```
{ Configure image to only accept other TImages }
procedure TForm1.DBImage1DragOver(Sender, Source: TObject;
    X, Y: Integer; State: TDragState; var Accept: Boolean);
begin
    Accept := (Source is TImage);
end;
```

See Also

DragCursor property, OnDragDrop event

TDBIMAGE.ONMOUSEDOWN EVENT

Declaration

```
{ CONTROLS.PAS }
property OnMouseDown: TMouseEvent read FOnMouseDown
    write FOnMouseDown;

TMouseEvent = procedure(Sender: TObject; Button: TMouseButton;
    Shift: TShiftState; X, Y: Integer) of object;

TMouseButton = (mbLeft, mbRight, mbMiddle);
```

```
{ CLASSES.PAS }
TShiftState = set of (ssShift, ssAlt, ssCtrl,
    ssLeft, ssRight, ssMiddle, ssDouble);
```

Description

The OnMouseDown event occurs when the user presses a mouse button while the mouse cursor is over the image. The following parameters are passed to your OnMouseDown event handler: Button (identifies which mouse button was pressed), Shift (status of special keys and mouse buttons), and X and Y (screen coordinates of mouse cursor).

See Also

OnKeyDown event, OnMouseUp event

TDBIMAGE.ONMOUSEMOVE EVENT

Declaration

```
{ CONTROLS.PAS }
property OnMouseMove: TMouseMoveEvent read FOnMouseMove
    write FOnMouseMove;

TMouseMoveEvent = procedure(Sender: TObject; Shift: TShiftState;
    X, Y: Integer) of object;
{ CLASSES.PAS }
TShiftState = set of (ssShift, ssAlt, ssCtrl,
    ssLeft, ssRight, ssMiddle, ssDouble);
```

Description

The OnMouseMove event occurs when the user moves the mouse while the mouse cursor is over the image. The following parameters are passed to your OnMouseMove event handler: Shift (status of special keys and mouse buttons) and X and Y (screen coordinates of mouse cursor).

See Also

OnKeyDown event, OnMouseDown event, OnMouseUp event

TDBIMAGE.ONMOUSEUP EVENT

Declaration

```
{ CONTROLS.PAS }
property OnMouseUp: TMouseEvent read FOnMouseUp write FOnMouseUp;

TMouseEvent = procedure(Sender: TObject; Button: TMouseButton;
    Shift: TShiftState; X, Y: Integer) of object;
```

```
TMouseButton = (mbLeft, mbRight, mbMiddle);

{ CLASSES.PAS }
TShiftState = set of (ssShift, ssAlt, ssCtrl,
    ssLeft, ssRight, ssMiddle, ssDouble);
```

Description

The OnMouseUp event occurs when the user releases a mouse button while the mouse cursor is over the image. The following parameters will be passed to your OnMouseUp event handler: Button (identifies which mouse button was pressed), Shift (status of special keys and mouse buttons), and X and Y (screen coordinates of mouse cursor).

Notes

See the TDBCheckBox.OnKeyDown discussion if you need further explanation of the TShiftState values.

See Also

OnKeyDown event, OnMouseDown event

TDBListBox

Unit

DBCtrls

Inherits from

TCustomListBox

Description

The TDBListBox component allows the user to change the value of a field by making a selection from a list of choices.

The following tables summarize the properties (Table 3.36), methods (Table 3.37), and events (Table 3.38) for TDBListBox.

TABLE 3.36 TDBLISTBOX PROPERTIES

PROPERTY	DATA TYPE	RUN-TIME ONLY	READ-ONLY	DESCRIPTION
BorderStyle	TBorderStyle	No	No	Dictates whether or not list box will have a border.
Brush	TBrush	Yes	No	Brush for drawing list box background
Canvas	TCanvas	Yes	Yes	Provides access to drawing surface.
Field	TField	Yes	Yes	Field to which the list box is linked

Handle	THandle (HWnd)	Yes	Yes	Handle to list box (for Windows API function calls)
IntegralHeight	Boolean	No	No	Determines whether or not to show partial bottom row within list box.
ItemHeight	Integer	No	No	Height (in pixels) of a single item in the drop-down list (applies to fixed owner-draw list boxes only)
ItemIndex	Integer	Yes	No	Ordinal position of currently selected item in the drop-down list
Items	TStrings	No	No	The items that appear in the drop-down list for selection
TopIndex	Integer	Yes	No	Number of item displayed at top of list box

TABLE 3.37 TDBLISTBOX METHODS

METHOD	DESCRIPTION
Clear	Deletes all items from list box.
Create	Allocates memory to create the list box.
ItemAtPos	Returns the index of an item at a given point upon the list box.
ItemRect	Returns the rectangle surrounding a specified item in the list box.

TABLE 3.38 TDBLISTBOX EVENTS

EVENT	DATA TYPE	DESCRIPTION
OnClick	TNotifyEvent	Occurs when user single-clicks upon the list box.
OnDblClick	TNotifyEvent	Occurs when user double-clicks upon the list box.
OnDragDrop	TDragDropEvent	Occurs when user drops the list box.
OnDragOver	TDragOverEvent	Occurs when user drags an object over the list box.
OnMouseDown	TMouseEvent	Occurs when user presses mouse button with mouse pointer over the list box.
OnMouseMove	TMouseMoveEvent	Occurs when user moves mouse button if mouse pointer is over the list box.
OnMouseUp	TMouseEvent	Occurs when user releases mouse button with mouse pointer over the list box.

TDBLISTBOX.BORDERSTYLE PROPERTY

Declaration

```
{ STDCTRLS.PAS }
property BorderStyle: TBorderStyle read FBorderStyle
  write SetBorderStyle default bsSingle;

TBorderStyle = (bsSingle, bsNone);
```

Description

The BorderStyle dictates whether or not the list box should have a border. Leave this at its default value of bsSingle to have a border or set it to bsNone if you do not want a border.

TDBListBox.Brush Property

Declaration

```
{ CONTROLS.PAS }
property Brush: TBrush read FBrush;
```

Description

Run-time only. The Brush property is used for drawing the background area within the list box.

Example

See the example provided with the TDBListBox.Create method.

See Also

Canvas property

TDBListBox.Canvas Property

Declaration

```
{ STDCTRLS.PAS }
property Canvas: TCanvas read FCanvas;
```

Description

Run-time and read-only. The Canvas property gives you access to a drawing surface within the list box. Although the Canvas itself is read-only, you can change its Brush, Font, and Pen properties to customize drawing.

See Also

Brush property

TDBListBox.Clear Method

Declaration

```
{ STDCTRLS.PAS }
procedure Clear;
```

Description

The Clear method removes all items from the list box. It is most useful when you want to fill the list box with a new set of items.

See Also

Items property

TDBListBox.Create Method

Declaration

```
{ DBCTRLS.PAS }
constructor Create(AOwner: TComponent); override;
```

Description

The Create method can be used to create a list box manually at run-time. If you give the combo box an owner, the list box will automatically be destroyed when its owner bites the dust.

Note: If you create a list box manually with this method, you must specify its Parent property in order for the list box to be displayed on-screen.

Notes

If you do not want the list box to have an owner, pass Self as the parameter to the Create method. (A relevant example accompanies the discussion of the TDBCheckBox.Free method.)

Example

```
{ Create list box on-the-fly and link it to the Name field in the Articles
  table, which is located in C:\AQUARIUM\ARTICLES. If your table and data
  source were created at design-time, feel free to delete the appropriate
  sections of code. }
var
   lb : TDBListBox;
   t  : TTable;
   d  : TDataSource;
begin
   { Create TTable object to access Articles table }
   t := TTable.Create(Application);
   t.DatabaseName := 'c:\aquarium\articles';
   t.TableName := 'articles.dbf';
   t.Open;
   { Create TDataSource object to link to Articles table }
   d := TDataSource.Create(Application);
   d.DataSet := t;
   { create the list box }
   lb := TDBListBox.Create(Form1);
   lb.Parent      := Form1;   { Very important! }
```

```
lb.Top          := 50;
lb.Left         := 10;
lb.DataSource   := d;   { Link to DataSource created above }
lb.DataField    := 'NAME';
{ Various aesthetic niceties (or not-so-niceties) }
lb.BorderStyle := bsNone;
lb.Brush.Color := clYellow;
lb.Font.Name    := 'Arial';
lb.Font.Style   := [fsItalic];
lb.Font.Height := 24;
lb.IntegralHeight := True;
lb.Hint := 'This is a list of authors';
lb.ShowHint := True;
{ Fill list box with possible choices }
lb.Items.Add('Ted Blue');
lb.Items.Add('John Kaster');
lb.Items.Add('Greg Lief');
lb.Items.Add('Loren Scott');
end;
```

See Also

Free method

TDBLISTBOX.FIELD PROPERTY

Declaration

```
{ DBCTRLS.PAS }
property Field: TField read GetField;
```

Description

The Field property contains the field to which the list box is linked. This property can be used to manipulate the field directly.

Notes

Run-time and read-only

Example

```
{ Set value of field to the first string in the Items property }
if not (DBListBox1.DataSource.State in [dsEdit, dsInsert]) then
   DBListBox1.DataSource.DataSet.Edit;
DBListBox1.Field.AsString := DBListBox1.Items[0];
DBListBox1.DataSource.DataSet.Post;
```

See Also

DataField property, DataSource property, TField chapter

TDBLISTBOX.HANDLE PROPERTY

Declaration

```
{ CONTROLS.PAS }
property Handle: HWnd read GetHandle;
```

Description

Run-time and read-only. The Handle property is useful should you need to pass the handle of the list box to a Windows API function.

Example

```
{ Delete first item in list box }
SendMessage(DBListBox1.Handle, lb_DeleteString, 0, 0);
```

TDBLISTBOX.ITEMATPOS METHOD

Declaration

```
{ STDCTRLS.PAS }
function ItemAtPos(Pos: TPoint; Existing: Boolean): Integer;
```

Description

The ItemAtPos method returns the ordinal position of the item at a specified screen location. It accepts two parameters. Pos is the point in the list box. If Pos is outside or beyond the list box, the return value will depend upon the Existing parameter. If Existing is True, then the return value will be –1. If Existing is False, then the return value will be the same as the total number of items in the list box.

Example

See the examples provided with the TDBListBox.OnMouseDown and TDBListBox.OnDragDrop events.

See Also

ItemRect method

TDBLᴉsᴛBox.IᴛᴇᴍHᴇɪɢʜᴛ Pʀᴏᴘᴇʀᴛʏ

Declaration

```
{ STDCTRLS.PAS }
property ItemHeight: Integer read GetItemHeight write SetItemHeight;
```

Description

The ItemHeight property contains the display height (in pixels) of an item in the list box. Because data-aware list boxes cannot be owner-drawn, this is not particularly relevant because you will be unable to change it.

See Also

Font property

TDBLᴉsᴛBox.IᴛᴇᴍIɴᴅᴇx Pʀᴏᴘᴇʀᴛʏ

Declaration

```
{ STDCTRLS.PAS }
property ItemIndex: Integer read GetItemIndex
    write SetItemIndex;
```

Description

Run-time only. The ItemIndex property contains the ordinal position of the currently highlighted item in the list box.

Example

```
{ This is the equivalent of the user pressing the down arrow }
DBListBox1.ItemIndex := DBListBox1.ItemIndex + 1;
```

See Also

Items property, TopIndex property

TDBLᴉsᴛBox.IᴛᴇᴍRᴇᴄᴛ Mᴇᴛʜᴏᴅ

Declaration

```
{ STDCTRLS.PAS }
function ItemRect(Item: Integer): TRect;
```

Description

The ItemRect method returns a rectangle surrounding a specified item in the list box.

Example

See the example provided with the TDBListBox.OnMouseDown event.

See Also

ItemAtPos method

TDBLISTBOX.ITEMS PROPERTY

Declaration

```
{ STDCTRLS.PAS }
property Items: TStrings read FItems write SetItems;
```

Description

The Items property contains the strings that will be displayed in the list box. You can manipulate them by using the Add, Exchange, Delete, Insert, and Move methods.

Example

```
{ Example #1: Fill the list box from a table }
DBListBox1.Clear;
Table1.DisableControls;
Table1.First;
while not Table1.EOF do
  begin
      DBListBox1.Items.Add( Table1.FieldByName('NAME').AsString );
      Table1.Next;
    end;
Table1.EnableControls;

{ Example #2: fill the list box with the contents of a memo }
DBListBox1.Items := Memo1.Lines;

{ Example #3: insert a new item at the top of the list box }
DBListBox1.Items.Insert(0, 'New Item');
```

See Also

ItemIndex property, Selected property

TDBLISTBOX.INTEGRALHEIGHT PROPERTY

Declaration

```
{ STDCTRLS.PAS }
property IntegralHeight: Boolean read FIntegralHeight
   write SetIntegralHeight default False;
```

Description

The IntegralHeight property dictates how the bottom row of the list box is drawn. If IntegralHeight is set to its default value of False, the bottom row might not be completely shown. If set to True, the list box will show only items that fit completely into its vertical space, which is usually a better aesthetic alternative.

Example

See example provided with TDBListBox.Create.

See Also

Height property, ItemHeight property

TDBListBox.OnClick Event

Declaration

```
{ CONTROLS.PAS }
property OnClick: TNotifyEvent read FOnClick write FOnClick;

{ CLASSES.PAS }
TNotifyEvent = procedure(Sender: TObject) of object;
```

Description

The OnClick event occurs when the user selects an item in the list box, either by clicking with the mouse or by using one of the navigation keys.

Example

```
{ Change a label to the currently selected item in the list box }
procedure TForm1.DBListBox1Click(Sender: TObject);
begin
    Label1.Caption := DBListBox1.Items[DBListBox1.ItemIndex];
end;
```

See Also

Items property, OnDblClick event

TDBListBox.OnDblClick Event

Declaration

```
{ CONTROLS.PAS }
property OnDblClick: TNotifyEvent read FOnDblClick write FOnDblClick;
```

```
{ CLASSES.PAS }
TNotifyEvent = procedure(Sender: TObject) of object;
```

Description

The OnDblClick event occurs whenever the user double-clicks upon the list box.

Example

```
{ When user double-clicks on the list box, the current item is displayed
  in a message box and then the form is closed }
procedure TForm1.DBListBox1DblClick(Sender: TObject);
begin
   MessageDlg('You selected ' +
              DBListBox1.Items[DBListBox1.ItemIndex],
              mtInformation, [mbOK], 0);
   (DBListBox1.Owner as TForm).Close;
end;
```

See Also

OnClick event

TDBLISTBOX.ONDRAGDROP EVENT

Declaration

```
{ CONTROLS.PAS }
property OnDragDrop: TDragDropEvent read FOnDragDrop
   write FOnDragDrop;

TDragDropEvent = procedure(Sender, Source: TObject;
    X, Y: Integer) of object;
```

Description

The OnDragDrop event occurs when an object is dropped onto the list box. You should write an OnDragDrop event handler to specify what you want to happen in this situation. Four parameters are passed to your OnDragDrop event handler: Sender (the list box), Source (the object being dropped), and X and Y (mouse cursor coordinates).

Example

```
{ If user drops an edit control onto the list box, insert its text at the
  position indicated by the mouse cursor (ItemAtPos). If user drops a memo
  control onto the list box, set its items to the text within the memo. }
procedure TForm1.DBListBox1DragDrop(Sender, Source: TObject;
  X, Y: Integer);
var
```

```
      pos : Integer;
begin
    if Source is TEdit then begin
        pos := DBListBox1.ItemAtPos( Point(X, Y), False );
        DBListBox1.Items.Insert(pos, (Source as TEdit).Text );
    end
    else if Source is TMemo then
        DBListBox1.Items := (Source as TMemo).Lines;
end;
```

See Also

DragCursor property, DragMode property, OnDragOver method

TDBLISTBOX.ONDRAGOVER EVENT

Declaration

```
{ CONTROLS.PAS }
property OnDragOver: TDragOverEvent read FOnDragOver
    write FOnDragOver;

TDragOverEvent = procedure(Sender, Source: TObject; X, Y: Integer;
    State: TDragState; var Accept: Boolean) of object;

TDragState = (dsDragEnter, dsDragLeave, dsDragMove);
```

Description

The OnDragOver event occurs when an object is dragged over the list box. By writing an OnDragOver event handler, you can determine which objects the list box can accept. The parameters passed to your OnDragOver event handler are Sender (the list box), Source (the object being dragged), X and Y (mouse cursor coordinates), State (the status of the object being dragged in relation to the list box), and Accept, which should be set to a boolean value (True means the list box can accept the object, and False means that it cannot).

Example

```
{ Allow list box to accept either edit or memo controls.  also refer to
  example provided with TDBListBox.OnDragDrop event }
procedure TForm1.DBListBox1DragOver(Sender, Source: TObject;
    X, Y: Integer; State: TDragState; var Accept: Boolean);
begin
    Accept := (Source is TEdit) or (Source is TMemo);
end;
```

See Also

DragCursor property, OnDragDrop event

TDBListBox.OnEndDrag Event

Declaration

```
{ CONTROLS.PAS }
property OnEndDrag: TEndDragEvent read FOnEndDrag write FOnEndDrag;

TEndDragEvent = procedure(Sender, Target: TObject;
    X, Y: Integer) of object;
```

Description

The OnEndDrag event occurs whenever the user stops dragging the list box. The drag operation ends either by dropping the list box or by releasing the mouse button. Write an OnEndDrag event handler if you need to implement special processing to occur when the drag operation stops. The parameters passed to your OnEndDrag event handler will be Sender (the combo box), Target (the object upon which you are dropping the combo box), and X and Y (mouse cursor coordinates). If the drag operation is canceled, then Target will have the value of NIL, which can be tested as shown in the following example.

Example

```
{ If list box was dropped on an edit control, change its text to match the
  currently selected item in the list box. If list box was dropped on a
  memo, set the memo's text to all of the items in the list box. }
procedure TForm1.DBListBox1EndDrag(Sender, Target: TObject;
  X, Y: Integer);
begin
   if Target is TEdit then
      (Target as TEdit).Text :=
               DBListBox1.Items[DBListBox1.ItemIndex]
   else if Target is TMemo then
      (Target as TMemo).Lines := DBListBox1.Items;
end;
```

See Also

BeginDrag method, DragCursor property, DragMode property

TDBListBox.OnMouseDown Event

Declaration

```
{ CONTROLS.PAS }
property OnMouseDown: TMouseEvent read FOnMouseDown
    write FOnMouseDown;

TMouseEvent = procedure(Sender: TObject; Button: TMouseButton;
    Shift: TShiftState; X, Y: Integer) of object;
```

```
TMouseButton = (mbLeft, mbRight, mbMiddle);

{ CLASSES.PAS }
TShiftState = set of (ssShift, ssAlt, ssCtrl,
    ssLeft, ssRight, ssMiddle, ssDouble);
```

Description

The OnMouseDown event occurs when the user presses a mouse button while the mouse cursor is over the list box. The following parameters are passed to your OnMouseDown event handler: Button (identifies which mouse button was pressed), Shift (status of special keys and mouse buttons), and X and Y (screen coordinates of mouse cursor).

Notes

See the OnKeyDown discussion for a list of TShiftState values.

Example

```
{ If user right-clicks upon an item in the list box, redisplay it in white
  italics on blue background, using the ItemAtPos and ItemRect methods }
procedure TMyForm.DBListBox1MouseDown(Sender: TObject;
  Button: TMouseButton; Shift: TShiftState; X, Y: Integer);
var
   Temp : integer;
   TempRect : TRect;
begin
   if Button = mbRight then
      with Sender as TListBox do begin
         Temp := ItemAtPos(Point(X, Y), True);
         if Temp <> -1 then begin
            Canvas.Brush.Color := clBlue;
            Canvas.Font.Color := clWhite;
            Canvas.Font.Style := Canvas.Font.Style + [fsItalic];
            TempRect := ItemRect(Temp);
            Canvas.FillRect(TempRect);
            Canvas.TextOut(TempRect.Left, TempRect.Top,
                           Items[Temp]);
         end;
      end;
end;
```

See Also

OnMouseUp event

TDBLISTBOX.ONMOUSEMOVE EVENT

Declaration

```
{ CONTROLS.PAS }
property OnMouseMove: TMouseMoveEvent read FOnMouseMove
```

```
    write FOnMouseMove;

TMouseMoveEvent = procedure(Sender: TObject; Shift: TShiftState;
    X, Y: Integer) of object;

{ CLASSES.PAS }
TShiftState = set of (ssShift, ssAlt, ssCtrl,
    ssLeft, ssRight, ssMiddle, ssDouble);
```

Description

The OnMouseMove event occurs when the user moves the mouse over the list box. The following parameters are passed to your OnMouseMove event handler: Shift (status of special keys and mouse buttons) and X and Y (screen coordinates of mouse cursor).

Notes

See the OnKeyDown discussion for a list of TShiftState values.

See Also

OnKeyDown event, OnMouseDown event, OnMouseUp event

TDBLISTBOX.ONMOUSEUP EVENT

Declaration

```
{ CONTROLS.PAS }
property OnMouseUp: TMouseEvent read FOnMouseUp write FOnMouseUp;

TMouseEvent = procedure(Sender: TObject; Button: TMouseButton;
    Shift: TShiftState; X, Y: Integer) of object;

TMouseButton = (mbLeft, mbRight, mbMiddle);

{ CLASSES.PAS }
TShiftState = set of (ssShift, ssAlt, ssCtrl,
    ssLeft, ssRight, ssMiddle, ssDouble);
```

Description

The OnMouseUp event occurs when the user releases a mouse button while the mouse cursor is over the list box. The following parameters will be passed to your OnMouseUp event handler: Button (identifies which mouse button was pressed),Shift (status of special keys and mouse buttons), and X and Y (screen coordinates of mouse cursor).

Notes

See the OnKeyDown discussion for a list of TShiftState values.

See Also

OnKeyDown event, OnMouseDown event

TDBLISTBOX.TOPINDEX PROPERTY

Declaration

```
{ STDCTRLS.PAS }
property TopIndex: Integer read GetTopIndex write SetTopIndex;
```

Description

Run-time only. The TopIndex property contains the ordinal position of the item currently displayed on the top row of the list box. This can be set at run-time to exercise greater control over the display of the list box.

Example

```
{ Set the 5th item to be displayed at the top of the list box, making sure
  it is highlighted (remember items are zero-based) }
DBListBox1.TopIndex := 4;
DBListBox1.ItemIndex := 4;
```

See Also

ItemIndex property

TDBLookupCombo

Unit

DBLookup

Inherits from

TCustomEdit

Description

The TDBLookupCombo component is similar to TDBComboBox, except that it displays values from a look-up database.

The following tables summarize the properties (Table 3.39), methods (Table 3.40), and events (Table 3.41) for TDBLookupCombo.

TABLE 3.39 TDBLookupCombo Properties

Property	Data Type	Run-Time Only	Read-Only	Description
AutoSelect	Boolean	Yes	No	Determines whether to select text in edit area automatically when combo box gains focus.
DisplayValue	String	Yes	No	Text currently displayed in combo box (same as value of LookupDisplay field)

DropDownCount	Integer	No	No	Number of items to be displayed in the drop-down list
DropDownWidth	Integer	No	No	Determines width of drop-down list box.
Handle	THandle (HWnd)	Yes	Yes	Handle to combo box (for Windows API function calls)
LookupDisplay	String	No	No	Name of field in look-up table whose value will be displayed in combo box
LookupField	String	No	No	Name of field in look-up table which is used for look-ups
LookupSource	TDataSource	No	No	Data source for the look-up table
MaxLength	Integer	No	No	Maximum number of characters that can be entered into edit area
Options	TDBLookup-ListOptions	No	No	Aesthetic choices for displaying multiple columns within combo box
SelLength	Integer	Yes	No	Length (in characters) of selected text in combo box's edit control
SelStart	Integer	Yes	No	Starting position of selected text in combo box's edit control (zero-based)
SelText	String	Yes	No	The selected text, if any, in the combo box's edit control
Style	TDBLookup-ComboStyle	No	No	Determines how combo box will display its items (see details that follow)
Text	String	Yes	No	Text visible in combo box's edit control
Value	String	Yes	No	Current value of the field designated in the combo box's DataField property

TABLE 3.40 TDBLOOKUPCOMBO METHODS

METHOD	DESCRIPTION
Clear	Deletes all items and text from combo box.
CloseUp	Closes the drop-down list.
Create	Allocates memory to create the combo box.
DropDown	Makes the drop-down list visible.
SelectAll	Selects entire text in the combo box's edit control.

TABLE 3.41 TDBLOOKUPCOMBO EVENTS

EVENT	DATA TYPE	DESCRIPTION
OnChange	TNotifyEvent	Occurs when user selects an item in the drop-down list.
OnClick	TNotifyEvent	Occurs when user single-clicks upon the combo box.
OnDblClick	TNotifyEvent	Occurs when user double-clicks upon the combo box.
OnDragDrop	TDragDropEvent	Occurs when user drops the combo box.
OnDragOver	TDragOverEvent	Occurs when user drags an object over the combo box.
OnDropDown	TNotifyEvent	Occurs when user opens the drop-down list.

continued

TABLE 3.41 CONTINUED

EVENT	DATA TYPE	DESCRIPTION
OnChange	TNotifyEvent	Occurs when user selects an item in the drop-down list.
OnEndDrag	TEndDragEvent	Occurs when user stops dragging the combo box.
OnKeyDown	TKeyEvent	Occurs when user presses a key with combo box active.
OnKeyPress	TKeyPressEvent	Occurs when user presses a character key.
OnKeyUp	TKeyEvent	Occurs when user releases a key with combo box active.
OnMouseDown	TMouseEvent	Occurs when user presses mouse button with mouse pointer over the combo box.
OnMouseMove	TMouseMoveEvent	Occurs when user moves mouse button if mouse pointer is over the combo box.
OnMouseUp	TMouseEvent	Occurs when user releases mouse button with mouse pointer over the combo box.

TDBLookupCombo.AutoSelect Property

Declaration

```
{ STDCTRLS.PAS }
property AutoSelect: Boolean read FAutoSelect write FAutoSelect
   default True;
```

Description

The AutoSelect property determines whether or not the text in the edit area will be selected automatically as the combo box is activated. If set to its default value of True, the text will be selected.

See Also

SelText property, Text property

TDBLookupCombo.Clear Method

Declaration

```
{ STDCTRLS.PAS }
procedure Clear;
```

Description

The Clear method removes the entire text from the edit area.

See Also

Text property

TDBLookupCombo.CloseUp Method

Declaration

```
{ DBLOOKUP.PAS }
procedure CloseUp; dynamic;
```

Description

The CloseUp method closes the drop-down list. Along with the DropDown method, this allows you to control manually when the drop-down list is displayed.

See Also

DropDown method

TDBLookupCombo.Create Method

Declaration

```
{ DBLOOKUP.PAS }
constructor Create(AOwner: TComponent); override;
```

Description

The Create method can be used to create a combo box manually at run-time. If you give the combo box an owner, the combo box will automatically be destroyed when its owner is destroyed.

Note: If you create a combo box manually with this method, you must specify its Parent property in order for the combo box to be displayed on-screen.

Notes

If you do not want the combo box to have an owner, pass Self as the parameter to the Create method. (A relevant example accompanies the TDBCheckBox.Free method.)

Example

```
{ Create combo box on-the-fly, which will display the PartNo and Descrip
  fields from the Parts table.  The primary link to the combo box will be
  the PartNo field in the Orders table. }
var
   lc : TDBLookupCombo;
   tMaster, tDetail : TTable;
   dsMaster, dsDetail : TDataSource;
begin
   { Create Master table and data source }
   tMaster := TTable.Create(Application);
   tMaster.DatabaseName := 'c:\data';
```

```
tMaster.TableName := 'orders.dbf';
tMaster.Open;
dsMaster := TDataSource.Create(Application);
dsMaster.DataSet := tMaster;
{ Create Detail table and data source }
tDetail := TTable.Create(Application);
tDetail.DatabaseName := 'c:\data';
tDetail.TableName := 'parts.dbf';
tDetail.IndexName := 'ByPartNo';  { Should match LookupField }
tDetail.Open;
dsDetail := TDataSource.Create(Application);
dsDetail.DataSet := tDetail;
{ Create the look-up combo box }
lc := TDBLookupCombo.Create(Form1);
lc.Parent := Form1;    { Very important! }
lc.SetBounds(10, 100, 75, 25);
{ Attach data sources and select data fields }
lc.DataSource   := dsMaster ;
lc.DataField    := 'PartNo' ;
lc.LookupSource := dsDetail ;
lc.LookupField  := 'PartNo' ;
lc.LookupDisplay:= 'PartNo;Descrip';  { Display two columns }
{ Various forms of "gratuitous puffery" (Long live Basil!) }
lc.DropDownWidth := lc.Width * 3;  { To show all columns }
lc.Hint := 'Click for a list of part numbers/descriptions';
lc.ShowHint := True;
lc.Font.Name := 'Times New Roman';
lc.Font.Size := 12;
lc.Font.Style := [fsItalic];
lc.Options := [loRowLines,loColLines,loTitles];
end;
```

See Also

Free method

TDBLookupCombo.DisplayValue Property

Declaration

```
{ DBLOOKUP.PAS }
property DisplayValue: String read GetDisplayValue
   write SetDisplayValue;
```

Description

Run-time only. The DisplayValue property contains the string currently displayed in the combo box. This is the same as the value of the LookupDisplay field.

See Also

LookupDisplay property, LookupSource property, Value property

TDBLOOKUPCOMBO.DROPDOWN METHOD

Declaration

```
{ DBLOOKUP.PAS }
procedure DropDown; dynamic;
```

Description

The DropDown method opens the drop-down list. This allows you to control manually when the drop-down list is displayed.

Example

See example provided with TDBLookupCombo.OnEnter discussion.

See Also

CloseUp method, OnDropDown event

TDBLOOKUPCOMBO.DROPDOWNCOUNT PROPERTY

Declaration

```
{ DBLOOKUP.PAS }
property DropDownCount: Integer read FDropDownCount
    write FDropDownCount default 8;
```

Description

The DropDownCount property dictates how many items should be visible in the drop-down list. By default, this is set to either 8 or the maximum number of items in the drop-down list, whichever is higher.

Example

```
{ Show a maximum of four items at a time }
DBComboBox1.DropDownCount := 4;
```

See Also

DropDownWidth property

TDBLookupCombo.DropDownWidth Property

Declaration

```
{ DBLOOKUP.PAS }
property DropDownWidth: Integer read FDropDownWidth
    write FDropDownWidth default 0;
```

Description

The DropDownWidth property dictates the width in pixels of the drop-down list. If left to its default value of zero (0), the drop-down list will be of the same width as the combo box. This is particularly useful when you are displaying multiple fields in the LookupDisplay property, so that you can minimize the combo box's screen real estate until the drop-down list makes its appearance.

Example

```
{ Set the show a maximum of four items at a time }
DBComboBox1.DropDownWidth := DBComboBox1.Width * 2;
```

See Also

LookupDisplay property, Width property

TDBLookupCombo.Handle Property

Declaration

```
{ CONTROLS.PAS }
property Handle: HWnd read GetHandle;
```

Description

Run-time and read-only. The Handle property is useful should you need to pass the combo box's handle to a Windows API function.

Example

```
{ Check whether drop-down list is visible, and if not, make it so }
if SendMessage(DBLookupCombo1.Handle,
            cb_GetDroppedState, 0, 0) = 0 then
    DBLookupCombo1.DropDown;
```

TDBLookupCombo.LookupDisplay Property

Declaration

```
{ DBLOOKUP.PAS }
property LookupDisplay: String read GetLookupDisplay
   write SetLookupDisplay;
```

Description

The LookupDisplay property determines which field(s) from the look-up table will be displayed in the combo box. If you want to display multiple fields, specify the field names in a semicolon-delimited list. They will each be displayed in their own column.

Notes

Prior to choosing a LookupDisplay field(s), you must specify a LookupField. If you do not specify a LookupDisplay field, the value of the LookupField will be displayed in the combo box.

Example

See the example provided with the TDBLookupCombo.Create discussion.

See Also

DisplayValue property, Options property, LookupSource property

TDBLookupCombo.LookupField Property

Declaration

```
{ DBLOOKUP.PAS }
property LookupField: String read GetLookupField
   write SetLookupField;
```

Description

The LookupField property serves as your link into the look-up data source (specified in the LookupSource property). The field stored in this property should contain the same value as the field stored in the DataField property, although they are not required to have the same name.

Notes

If you do not specify a LookupDisplay field, the value of the LookupField will be displayed in the combo box.

Example

See the example provided with the TDBLookupCombo.Create discussion.

See Also

LookupDisplay field, LookupSource property

TDBLookupCombo.LookupSource Property

Declaration

```
{ DBLOOKUP.PAS }
property LookupSource: TDataSource read GetLookupSource
   write SetLookupSource;
```

Description

The LookupSource property contains the look-up data source to which the combo box should be linked. The data to be displayed in the combo box will be retrieved from this data source.

Example

See the example provided with the TDBLookupCombo.Create discussion.

See Also

LookupDisplay property, LookupField property

TDBLookupCombo.MaxLength Property

Declaration

```
{ STDCTRLS.PAS }
property MaxLength: Integer read FMaxLength write SetMaxLength
   default 0;
```

Description

The MaxLength property can be used to limit the number of characters entered into the edit box. By default, this value is zero (0), which means that there is no limitation.

See Also

Text property

TDBLookupCombo.OnChange Event

Declaration

```
{ STDCTRLS.PAS }
property OnChange: TNotifyEvent read FOnChange write FOnChange;

{ CLASSES.PAS }
TNotifyEvent = procedure(Sender: TObject) of object;
```

Description

The OnChange event occurs whenever the text in the combo box's edit area is changed. This can be done either by the user (via typing or selecting an item from the drop-down list) or by the developer programmatically.

Example

See the example provided with TDBComboBox.OnChange.

See Also

DisplayValue property

TDBLookupCombo.OnClick Event

Declaration

```
{ CONTROLS.PAS }
property OnClick: TNotifyEvent read FOnClick write FOnClick;

{ CLASSES.PAS }
TNotifyEvent = procedure(Sender: TObject) of object;
```

Description

The OnClick event occurs when the user selects an item from the drop-down list.

Example

See example provided with TDBComboBox.OnChange event discussion.

See Also

OnChange event, OnDblClick event

TDBLOOKUPCOMBO.ONDBLCLICK EVENT

Declaration

```
{ CONTROLS.PAS }
property OnDblClick: TNotifyEvent read FOnDblClick write FOnDblClick;

{ CLASSES.PAS }
TNotifyEvent = procedure(Sender: TObject) of object;
```

Description

The OnDblClick event occurs whenever the user double-clicks upon the combo box.

Example

See example provided with TDBComboBox.OnChange method discussion.

See Also

OnChange event, OnClick event

TDBLOOKUPCOMBO.ONDROPDOWN EVENT

Declaration

```
{ CONTROLS.PAS }
property OnDropDown: TNotifyEvent read FOnDropDown write FOnDropDown;

{ CLASSES.PAS }
TNotifyEvent = procedure(Sender: TObject) of object;
```

Description

The OnDropDown event occurs whenever the drop-down list is made visible, either by the user or programmatically (with the DropDown method).

See Also

DropDown method

TDBLOOKUPCOMBO.ONMOUSEDOWN EVENT

Declaration

```
{ CONTROLS.PAS }
property OnMouseDown: TMouseEvent read FOnMouseDown
    write FOnMouseDown;

TMouseEvent = procedure(Sender: TObject; Button: TMouseButton;
    Shift: TShiftState; X, Y: Integer) of object;
```

```
TMouseButton = (mbLeft, mbRight, mbMiddle);

{ CLASSES.PAS }
TShiftState = set of (ssShift, ssAlt, ssCtrl,
    ssLeft, ssRight, ssMiddle, ssDouble);
```

Description

The OnMouseDown event occurs when the user presses a mouse button while the mouse cursor is over the combo box. The following parameters are passed to your OnMouseDown event handler: Button (identifies which mouse button was pressed), Shift (status of special keys and mouse buttons), and X and Y (screen coordinates of mouse cursor).

Notes

See the OnKeyDown discussion for a list of TShiftState values.

See Also

OnKeyDown event, OnMouseUp event

TDBLookupCombo.OnMouseMove Event

Declaration

```
{ CONTROLS.PAS }
property OnMouseMove: TMouseMoveEvent read FOnMouseMove
    write FOnMouseMove;

TMouseMoveEvent = procedure(Sender: TObject; Shift: TShiftState;
    X, Y: Integer) of object;

{ CLASSES.PAS }
TShiftState = set of (ssShift, ssAlt, ssCtrl,
    ssLeft, ssRight, ssMiddle, ssDouble);
```

Description

The OnMouseMove event occurs when the user moves the mouse while the mouse cursor is over the combo box. The following parameters are passed to your OnMouseMove event handler: Shift (status of special keys and mouse buttons) and X and Y (screen coordinates of mouse cursor).

Notes

See the OnKeyDown discussion for a list of TShiftState values.

See Also

OnKeyDown event, OnMouseDown event, OnMouseUp event

TDBLookupCombo.OnMouseUp Event

Declaration

```
{ CONTROLS.PAS }
property OnMouseUp: TMouseEvent read FOnMouseUp write FOnMouseUp;

TMouseEvent = procedure(Sender: TObject; Button: TMouseButton;
    Shift: TShiftState; X, Y: Integer) of object;

TMouseButton = (mbLeft, mbRight, mbMiddle);

{ CLASSES.PAS }
TShiftState = set of (ssShift, ssAlt, ssCtrl,
    ssLeft, ssRight, ssMiddle, ssDouble);
```

Description

The OnMouseUp event occurs when the user releases a mouse button while the mouse cursor is over the combo box. The following parameters will be passed to your OnMouseUp event handler: Button (identifies which mouse button was pressed), Shift (status of special keys and mouse buttons), and X and Y (screen coordinates of mouse cursor).

Notes

See the TDBCheckBox.OnKeyDown discussion for a list of TShiftState values.

See Also

OnKeyDown event, OnMouseDown event

TDBLookupCombo.Options Property

Declaration

```
{ DBLOOKUP.PAS }
property Options: TDBLookupListOptions read GetOptions
    write SetOptions default [];

TDBLookupListOptions = set of TDBLookupListOption;

TDBLookupListOption = (loColLines, loRowLines, loTitles);
```

Description

The Options property gives you several aesthetic choices. Although these make most sense when displaying multiple columns, they can also be used for single column lists. Table 3.42 describes the possible values.

TABLE 3.42 TDBLOOKUPLISTOPTION VALUES

VALUE	DESCRIPTION
loColLines	Display lines between columns
loRowLines	Display lines between rows
loTitles	Display actual field names as column headings

Example

```
{ This event handler, tied to a check box, allows the user to toggle the
  display of row/column lines within the drop-down list }
procedure TForm1.CheckBox1Click(Sender: TObject);
begin
  if CheckBox1.Checked then
    DBLookupCombo1.Options := [loRowLines,loColLines]
  else
    DBLookupCombo1.Options := [];
end;
```

See Also

LookupDisplay property

TDBLookupCombo.SelLength Property

Declaration

```
{ STDCTRLS.PAS }
property SelLength: Integer read GetSelLength write SetSelLength;
```

Description

The SelLength returns the length, in characters, of the currently selected portion of the combo box's edit area. If it contains zero, then no text is selected.

Example

See example provided with TDBComboBox.SelLength.

See Also

SelStart property, SelText property

TDBLookupCombo.SelStart Property

Declaration

```
{ STDCTRLS.PAS }
property SelStart: Integer read GetSelStart write SetSelStart;
```

Description

The SelStart returns the starting position of the currently selected text, if any, in the combo box's edit area.

Example

See example provided with TDBComboBox.SelStart.

See Also

SelLength property, SelText property

TDBLookupCombo.SelText Property

Declaration

```
{ STDCTRLS.PAS }
property SelText: String read GetSelText write SetSelText;
```

Description

The SelText returns the currently selected text, if any, in the combo box's edit area.

See Also

SelLength property, SelText property

TDBLookupCombo.Style Property

Declaration

```
{ DBLOOKUP.PAS }
property Style: TDBLookupComboStyle read FStyle write SetStyle
    default csDropDown;

TDBLookupComboStyle = (csDropDown, csDropDownList);
```

Description

The Style property determines whether or not the user can type into the edit area. Setting this property to the value csDropDownList prevents the user from doing so. If the LookupField and LookupDisplay are different, this property will automatically be set to csDropDownList.

See Also

LookupDisplay property, LookupField property

TDBLookupCombo.Text Property

Declaration

```
{ CONTROLS.PAS }
property Text: TCaption read GetText write SetText;

TCaption = String[255];
```

Description

Run-time only. The Text property contains the text currently displayed in the combo box's edit area, which will be the value of the field specified by the LookupField property.

See Also

DisplayValue property, SelLength property, SelStart property, SelText property

TDBLookupCombo.Value Property

Declaration

```
{ DBLOOKUP.PAS }
property Value: String read GetValue write SetValue;
```

Description

Run-time only. The Value property contains the contents of the field specified in the DataField property. You can change the contents of the field in the primary data source by changing the Value property directly.

See Also

DataField property, DataSource property, DisplayValue property

TDBLookupList

Unit

DBLookup

Inherits from

TCustomDBGrid

Description

A more apropos name for the TDBLookupList component would be "TDBLookupGrid" because it is actually much closer to a grid than a list box. The user can make selections from a read-only grid made up of multiple rows and columns. This is excellent for showing user-friendly descriptions of (what would otherwise be) obtuse look-up codes.

The following tables summarize the properties (Table 3.43), methods (Table 3.44), and events (Table 3.45 for TDBLookupList.

TABLE 3.43 TDBLookupList Properties

Property	Data Type	Run-Time Only	Read-Only	Description
BorderStyle	TBorderStyle	No	No	Dictates whether or not look-up list will have a border.
DisplayValue	String	Yes	No	Text displayed in current row of look-up list (same as value of LookupDisplay field)
FieldCount	Integer	Yes	Yes	Number of columns in look-up list
Fields	TFields	Yes	Yes	Provides direct access to fields in look-up list.
LookupDisplay	String	No	No	Name of field in look-up table whose value will be displayed in look-up list
LookupField	String	No	No	Name of field in look-up table that is used for look-ups
LookupSource	TDataSource	No	No	Data source for the look-up table
Options	TDBLookup-ListOptions	No	No	Aesthetic choices for displaying multiple columns within look-up list
SelectedField	TField	Yes	Yes	Field currently selected within look-up list
SelectedIndex	Integer	Yes	No	Number of currently selected field
Value	String	Yes	No	Current value of the field designated in the look-up list's DataField property

TABLE 3.44 TDBLookupList Methods

Method	Description
Create	Allocates memory to create the look-up list.

TABLE 3.45 TDBLookupList Events

Event	Data Type	Description
OnClick	TNotifyEvent	Occurs when user single-clicks upon the look-up list.
OnDblClick	TNotifyEvent	Occurs when user double-clicks upon the look-up list.
OnKeyDown	TKeyEvent	Occurs when user presses a key with look-up list active.
OnKeyPress	TKeyPressEvent	Occurs when user presses a character key.
OnKeyUp	TKeyEvent	Occurs when user releases a key with look-up list active.

OnMouseDown	TMouseEvent	Occurs when user presses mouse button with mouse pointer over the look-up list.
OnMouseMove	TMouseMoveEvent	Occurs when user moves mouse button if mouse pointer is over the look-up list.
OnMouseUp	TMouseEvent	Occurs when user releases mouse button with mouse pointer over the look-up list.

TDBLookupList.BorderStyle Property

Declaration

```
{ STDCTRLS.PAS }
property BorderStyle: TBorderStyle read FBorderStyle
   write SetBorderStyle default bsSingle;

TBorderStyle = (bsSingle, bsNone);
```

Description

The BorderStyle dictates whether or not the look-up list should have a border. Leave this at its default value of bsSingle to have a border, or set it to bsNone if you do not want a border.

TDBLookupList.BoundsRect Property

Declaration

```
{ CONTROLS.PAS }
property BoundsRect: TRect read GetBoundsRect write SetBoundsRect;
```

Description

Run-time only. The BoundsRect property contains a TRect object, which delineates the bounding rectangle of the look-up list. The coordinates of BoundsRect are relative to the parent of the look-up list.

See Also

SetBounds methods

TDBLookupList.Create Method

Declaration

```
{ DBLOOKUP.PAS }
constructor Create(AOwner: TComponent); override;
```

Description

The Create method can be used to create a look-up list manually at run-time. If you give the look-up list an owner, it will automatically be destroyed when its owner is destroyed.

Note: If you create a look-up list manually with this method, you must specify its Parent property in order for the look-up list to be displayed on-screen.

Notes

If you do not want the look-up list to have an owner, pass Self as the parameter to the Create method.

Example

```
{ Create look-up list on-the-fly, which will display the PartNo, Descrip,
  and Price fields from the Parts table.  The primary link to the look-up
  list will be the PartNo field in the Orders table. }
var
    ll : TDBLookupList;
    tMaster, tDetail : TTable;
    dsMaster, dsDetail : TDataSource;
begin
    { Create Master table and data source }
    tMaster := TTable.Create(Application);
    tMaster.DatabaseName := 'c:\data';
    tMaster.TableName := 'orders.dbf';
    tMaster.Open;
    dsMaster := TDataSource.Create(Application);
    dsMaster.DataSet := tMaster;
    { Create Detail table and data source }
    tDetail := TTable.Create(Application);
    tDetail.DatabaseName := 'c:\data';
    tDetail.TableName := 'parts.dbf';
    tDetail.IndexName := 'ByPartNo';   { Should match LookupField }
    tDetail.Open;
    dsDetail := TDataSource.Create(Application);
    dsDetail.DataSet := tDetail;
    { Create the look-up list control }
    ll := TDBLookupList.Create(Form1);
    ll.Parent := Form1;   { Very important! }
    ll.Align   := alClient;
    { Attach data sources, select data fields }
    ll.DataSource   := dsMaster ;
    ll.DataField    := 'PartNo' ;
    ll.LookupSource := dsDetail ;
    ll.LookupField  := 'PartNo' ;
    ll.LookupDisplay:= 'PartNo;Descrip;Price'; { Show 3 columns }
    { Miscellaneous aesthetic tweaks }
    ll.BorderStyle := bsNone;
    ll.Hint := 'Double-click to select a part';
```

```
ll.ShowHint := True;
ll.Font.Name := 'Courier New';
ll.Font.Size := 10;
ll.Options := [loRowLines,loColLines,loTitles];
{ Attach double-click event handler--this event handler must
be attached to the form which will hold this look-up list.
See OnDblClick discussion for more information. }
ll.OnDblClick := DBLookupList1DblClick;
end;
```

See Also

Free method

TDBLookupList.DisplayValue Property

Declaration

```
{ DBLOOKUP.PAS }
property DisplayValue: string read GetDisplayValue
   write SetDisplayValue;
```

Description

Run-time only. The DisplayValue property contains the row currently displayed in the look-up list. This is the same as the value of the LookupDisplay field.

See Also

LookupDisplay property, LookupSource property, Value property

TDBLookupList.FieldCount Property

Declaration

```
{ DBGRIDS.PAS }
property FieldCount: Integer read FFieldCount;
```

Description

The FieldCount property contains the number of columns (fields) within the look-up list. This may or may not match the number of fields in the attached data set, because it is possible to add or delete columns via the Fields Editor.

See Also

Fields property, SelectedField property

TDBLookupList.Fields Property

Declaration

```
{ DBGRIDS.PAS }
property Fields[I: Integer]: TField read GetFields;
```

Description

The Fields property is an array that contains all the TFields currently displayed in the look-up list. This can be used to manipulate either the field values or the column attributes. The fields are zero-based (i.e., use zero to refer to the first column).

Example

See the example provided with TDBLookupCombo.Fields.

See Also

FieldCount property, SelectedField property, SelectedIndex property

TDBLookupList.LookupDisplay Property

Declaration

```
{ DBLOOKUP.PAS }
property LookupDisplay: string read GetLookupDisplay
   write SetLookupDisplay;
```

Description

The LookupDisplay property determines which field(s) from the look-up table will be displayed in the look-up list. If you want to display multiple fields, specify the field names in a semicolon-delimited list. They will each be displayed in their own column.

Notes

Prior to choosing a LookupDisplay field(s), you must specify a LookupField. If you do not specify a LookupDisplay field, the value of the LookupField will be displayed in the look-up list.

Example

See the example provided with the TDBLookupList.Create discussion.

See Also

DisplayValue property, Options property, LookupSource property

TDBLookupList.LookupField Property

Declaration

```
{ DBLOOKUP.PAS }
property LookupField: string read GetLookupField
   write SetLookupField;
```

Description

The LookupField property serves as the link into the look-up data source (specified in the LookupSource property). The field stored in this property should contain the same value as the field stored in the DataField property, although they need not have the same name.

Notes

If you do not specify a LookupDisplay field, the value of the LookupField will be displayed in the look-up list.

Example

See the example provided with the TDBLookupList.Create discussion.

See Also

LookupDisplay field, LookupSource property

TDBLookupList.LookupSource Property

Declaration

```
{ DBLOOKUP.PAS }
property LookupSource: TDataSource read GetLookupSource
   write SetLookupSource;
```

Description

The LookupSource property contains the look-up data source to which the look-up list should be linked. The data to be displayed in the look-up list will be retrieved from this data source.

Example

See the example provided with the TDBLookupList.Create discussion.

See Also

LookupDisplay property, LookupField property

TDBLookupList.OnClick Event

Declaration

```
{ CONTROLS.PAS }
property OnClick: TNotifyEvent read FOnClick write FOnClick;

{ CLASSES.PAS }
TNotifyEvent = procedure(Sender: TObject) of object;
```

Description

The OnClick event occurs when the user selects an item in the look-up list, either by clicking upon it or using the navigation keys.

Example

See example provided with TDBComboBox.OnClick event discussion.

See Also

OnDblClick event

TDBLookupList.OnDblClick Event

Declaration

```
{ CONTROLS.PAS }
property OnDblClick: TNotifyEvent read FOnDblClick write FOnDblClick;

{ CLASSES.PAS }
TNotifyEvent = procedure(Sender: TObject) of object;
```

Description

The OnDblClick event occurs whenever the user double-clicks upon the look-up list.

Example

```
{ Set up double-click to alternately maximize and then restore the
  original size of, the look-up list }
var
   OldCoords : TRect;   { To hold previous coordinates }

procedure TForm1.DBLookupList1DblClick(Sender: TObject);
begin
   with Sender as TDBLookupList do
      if Align = alClient then begin
         Align := alNone;
         SetBounds(OldCoords.Left, OldCoords.Top,
```

```
                    OldCoords.Right,OldCoords.Bottom);
      end
      else begin
         OldCoords := BoundsRect;
         Align := alClient;
      end;
end;
```

See Also

OnClick event

TDBLOOKUPLIST.ONMOUSEDOWN EVENT

Declaration

```
{ CONTROLS.PAS }
property OnMouseDown: TMouseEvent read FOnMouseDown
    write FOnMouseDown;

TMouseEvent = procedure(Sender: TObject; Button: TMouseButton;
    Shift: TShiftState; X, Y: Integer) of object;

TMouseButton = (mbLeft, mbRight, mbMiddle);

{ CLASSES.PAS }
TShiftState = set of (ssShift, ssAlt, ssCtrl,
    ssLeft, ssRight, ssMiddle, ssDouble);
```

Description

The OnMouseDown event occurs when the user presses a mouse button while the mouse cursor is positioned over the look-up list. The following parameters are passed to your OnMouseDown event handler: Button (identifies which mouse button was pressed), Shift (status of special keys and mouse buttons), and X and Y (screen coordinates of mouse cursor).

See Also

OnKeyDown event, OnMouseUp event

TDBLOOKUPLIST.ONMOUSEMOVE EVENT

Declaration

```
{ CONTROLS.PAS }
property OnMouseMove: TMouseMoveEvent read FOnMouseMove
  write FOnMouseMove;

TMouseMoveEvent = procedure(Sender: TObject; Shift: TShiftState;
   X, Y: Integer) of object;
```

```
{ CLASSES.PAS }
TShiftState = set of (ssShift, ssAlt, ssCtrl,
    ssLeft, ssRight, ssMiddle, ssDouble);
```

Description

The OnMouseMove event occurs when the user moves the mouse while the mouse cursor is over the look-up list. The following parameters are passed to your OnMouseMove event handler: Shift (status of special keys and mouse buttons) and X and Y (screen coordinates of mouse cursor).

See Also

OnKeyDown event, OnMouseDown event, OnMouseUp event

TDBLookupList.OnMouseUp Event

Declaration

```
{ CONTROLS.PAS }
property OnMouseUp: TMouseEvent read FOnMouseUp write FOnMouseUp;

TMouseEvent = procedure(Sender: TObject; Button: TMouseButton;
    Shift: TShiftState; X, Y: Integer) of object;

TMouseButton = (mbLeft, mbRight, mbMiddle);

{ CLASSES.PAS }
TShiftState = set of (ssShift, ssAlt, ssCtrl,
    ssLeft, ssRight, ssMiddle, ssDouble);
```

Description

The OnMouseUp event occurs when the user releases a mouse button while the mouse cursor is over the look-up list. The following parameters will be passed to your OnMouseUp event handler: Button (identifies which mouse button was pressed), Shift (status of special keys and mouse buttons), and X and Y (screen coordinates of mouse cursor).

See Also

OnKeyDown event, OnMouseDown event

TDBLookupList.Options Property

Declaration

```
{ DBLOOKUP.PAS }
property Options: TDBLookupListOptions read GetOptions
    write SetOptions default [];

TDBLookupListOptions = set of TDBLookupListOption;

TDBLookupListOption = (loColLines, loRowLines, loTitles);
```

Description

The Options property gives you several aesthetic choices for displaying multiple columns. Table 3.46 describes the possible values.

TABLE 3.46 TDBLookupListOption Values

Value	Description
loColLines	Display lines between columns
loRowLines	Display lines between rows
loTitles	Display actual field names as column headings

Example

See example accompanying the TDLookupCombo.Options discussion.

See Also

LookupDisplay property

TDBLookupList.SelectedField Property

Declaration

```
{ DBGRIDS.PAS }
property SelectedField: TField read GetSelectedField
   write SetSelectedField;
```

Description

Run-time and read-only. The SelectedField property contains the field corresponding to the column in which the cursor currently resides. This allows you to manipulate the field directly or any of the columns' attributes.

Example

See example provided with TBLookupCombo.SelectedField discussion.

See Also

SelectedIndex property

TDBLookupList.SelectedIndex Property

Declaration

```
{ DBGRIDS.PAS }
property SelectedIndex: Integer read GetSelectedIndex
   write SetSelectedIndex;
```

348

Description

The SelectedIndex property contains the number of the currently selected column in the look-up list.

Notes

Run-time only

Example

See example provided with TBLookupCombo.SelectedIndex discussion.

See Also

SelectedField property

TDBLOOKUPLIST.VALUE PROPERTY

Declaration

```
{ DBLOOKUP.PAS }
property Value: String read GetValue write SetValue;
```

Description

Run-time only. The Value property contains the contents of the field specified in the DataField property. You can change the contents of the field in the primary data source by changing the Value property directly.

See Also

DataField property, DataSource property, DisplayValue property

TDBMemo

Unit

DBCtrls

Inherits from

TCustomMemo

Description

The TDBMemo component displays the value of a field in a multiline edit control. The user can change the value of the field by typing into the edit control.

The following tables summarize the properties (Table 3.47), methods (Table 3.48, and events (Table 3.49) for TDBMemo.

TABLE 3.47 TDBMEMO PROPERTIES

PROPERTY	DATA TYPE	RUN-TIME ONLY	READ-ONLY	DESCRIPTION
Alignment	TAlignment	No	No	Determines alignment of text within the memo.
AutoDisplay	Boolean	No	No	Determines whether to display new memo automatically when record pointer changes.
BorderStyle	TBorderStyle	No	No	Dictates whether or not memo will have a border.
Field	TField	Yes	Yes	Field to which the memo is linked
Font	TFont	No	No	Font used to display text in memo
Handle	THandle (HWnd)	Yes	Yes	Handle to memo (for Windows API function calls)
Lines	TStrings	Yes	No	Contains text lines displayed in memo.
MaxLength	Integer	No	No	Maximum number of characters that can be entered into the memo
Modified	Boolean	Yes	No	Indicates whether text in memo has been modified.
ScrollBars	TScrollStyle	No	No	Dictates whether memo has horizontal and/or vertical scroll bar
SelLength	Integer	Yes	No	Length (in characters) of selected text in memo's edit control
SelStart	Integer	Yes	No	Starting position of selected text in memo's edit control (zero-based)
SelText	String	Yes	No	The selected text, if any, in the memo's edit control
Text	String	Yes	No	Text displayed in memo's edit control
WantTabs	Boolean	No	No	Determines whether tabs are enabled within the memo.
WordWrap	Boolean	No	No	Determines whether text in memo word-wraps or clips.

TABLE 3.48 TDBMEMO METHODS

METHOD	DESCRIPTION
Clear	Deletes all text in memo.
CopyToClipboard	Copies selected text in memo to the clipboard.
Create	Allocates memory to create the memo.
CutToClipboard	Deletes selected text in memo and copies it to the clipboard.
GetSelTextBuf	Retrieves memo's selected text (for strings longer than 255 characters).

continued

TABLE **3.48** CONTINUED

METHOD	DESCRIPTION
LoadMemo	Loads a text Binary Large Object Field into the memo.
PasteFromClipboard	Copies text in clipboard into memo at current cursor position.
SelectAll	Selects entire text in the memo.
SetSelTextBuf	Sets the memo's highlighted text (for strings longer than 255 characters).

TABLE **3.49** TDBMEMO EVENTS

EVENT	DATA TYPE	DESCRIPTION
OnChange	TNotifyEvent	Occurs when the text in the memo is changed.
OnClick	TNotifyEvent	Occurs when user single-clicks upon the memo.
OnDblClick	TNotifyEvent	Occurs when user double-clicks upon the memo.
OnKeyDown	TKeyEvent	Occurs when user presses a key while in memo.
OnKeyPress	TKeyPressEvent	Occurs when user presses a character key in memo.
OnKeyUp	TKeyEvent	Occurs when user releases a key with memo active.
OnMouseDown	TMouseEvent	Occurs when user presses mouse button with mouse pointer over the memo.
OnMouseMove	TMouseMoveEvent	Occurs when user moves mouse button if mouse pointer is over the memo.
OnMouseUp	TMouseEvent	Occurs when user releases mouse button with mouse pointer over the memo.

TDBMEMO.ALIGNMENT PROPERTY

Declaration

```
{ STDCTRLS.PAS }
property Alignment: TAlignment read FAlignment write SetAlignment
   default taLeftJustify;

{ CLASSES.PAS }
TAlignment = (taLeftJustify, taRightJustify, taCenter);
```

Description

The Alignment property determines how each line of text will be displayed within the memo area. Text can be either left-justified, right-justified, or centered (which looks fairly unusual). Default alignment is left-justified.

Example

See the example provided with TDBMemo.Create.

See Also

Lines property, Text property

TDBMEMO.AUTODISPLAY PROPERTY

Declaration

```
{ DBCTRLS.PAS }
property AutoDisplay: Boolean read FAutoDisplay write SetAutoDisplay
   default True;
```

Description

The AutoDisplay property dictates whether or not the control will display a new memo when the record pointer changes in its data source. By default, this behavior is enabled. If you set AutoDisplay to False, the memo will be cleared whenever the record pointer moves, and it will not be loaded unless the user either double-clicks or presses **Enter** upon the control. You can also load the memo programmatically by calling the LoadMemo method.

Notes

One reason to disable this would be in the interest of performance. Depending upon the size of the memos and the speed of the target CPU, there may be a momentary pause as the memos are loaded.

See Also

LoadMemo method

TDBMEMO.BORDERSTYLE PROPERTY

Declaration

```
{ STDCTRLS.PAS }
property BorderStyle: TBorderStyle read FBorderStyle
   write SetBorderStyle default bsSingle;

TBorderStyle = (bsSingle, bsNone);
```

Description

The BorderStyle dictates whether or not the memo should have a border. If set to its default value of bsSingle, the memo will have a border. Change this to bsNone if you prefer no border.

TDBMEMO.BOUNDSRECT PROPERTY

Declaration

```
{ CONTROLS.PAS }
property BoundsRect: TRect read GetBoundsRect write SetBoundsRect;
```

Description

Run-time only. The BoundsRect property contains a TRect object, which delineates the bounding rectangle of the memo. The coordinates of BoundsRect are relative to the parent of the memo.

See Also

SetBounds methods

TDBMEMO.CLEAR METHOD

Declaration

```
{ STDCTRLS.PAS }
procedure Clear;
```

Description

The Clear method deletes all text from the memo.

See Also

CutToClipboard method, Text property

TDBMEMO.COPYTOCLIPBOARD METHOD

Declaration

```
{ STDCTRLS.PAS }
procedure CopyToClipboard;
```

Description

The CopyToClipboard method copies the selected text in the memo (if any) to the clipboard.

See Also

CutToClipboard method, PasteFromClipboard method, SelText property

TDBMEMO.CREATE METHOD

Declaration

```
{ DBCTRLS.PAS }
constructor Create(AOwner: TComponent); override;
```

Description

The Create method can be used to create a memo manually at run-time. If you give the memo an owner, the memo will automatically be destroyed when its owner is destroyed.

Note: If you create a memo with this method, you must specify its Parent property in order for the memo to be displayed on-screen.

Notes

If you do not want the memo to have an owner, pass Self as the parameter to the Create method. (See the example accompanying the discussion of the TDBCheckBox.Free method.)

Example

```
{ Create memo on-the-fly and link it to the Text field in the Outbox table,
  which is located in C:\AQUARIUM\ARTICLES. This also creates the TTable
  and TDataSource objects on-the-fly. If you have created them at design-
  time, then you can eliminate those sections of code }
var
    m : TDBMemo;
    t : TTable;
    d : TDataSource;
begin
    { Create TTable object to access Messages table }
    t := TTable.Create(Application);
    t.DatabaseName := 'c:\aquarium\messages';
    t.TableName := 'outbox.dbf';
    t.Open;
    { Create TDataSource object to link to Articles table }
    d := TDataSource.Create(Application);
    d.DataSet := t;
    { Create the memo }
    m := TDBMemo.Create(Form1);
    m.Parent := Form1;   { Very important! }
    m.Height := 200;
    m.Align := alTop;
    m.DataSource := d;   { Link to DataSource created above }
    m.DataField   := 'Text';
    m.MaxLength := 150; { Limit user to 150 characters }
    { Aesthetics aesthetics aesthetics! }
    m.ScrollBars := ssBoth;
    m.WantTabs    := True;
    m.Hint := 'This is the text of the message';
    m.ShowHint := True;
    m.Font.Name := 'Arial';
    m.Font.Size := 9;
end;
```

See Also

Free method

TDBMEMO.CUTTOCLIPBOARD METHOD

Declaration

```
{ STDCTRLS.PAS }
procedure CutToClipboard;
```

Description

The CutToClipboard method deletes the memo's selected text (if any) and copies it to the clipboard.

Example

See the comprehensive example provided with the TDBEdit.PopupMenu discussion.

See Also

CopyToClipboard method, PasteFromClipboard method, SelText property

TDBMEMO.FIELD PROPERTY

Declaration

```
{ DBCTRLS.PAS }
property Field: TField read GetField;
```

Description

Run-time and read-only. The Field property contains the field to which the memo is linked. This can be used to manipulate the field directly.

Example

```
{ Assign the contents of some other memo to the field linked to our DBMemo }
if not (DBMemo1.DataSource.State in [dsInsert,dsEdit]) then
   DBMemo1.DataSource.Edit;
(DBMemo1.Field as TMemoField).Assign(SomeOtherMemo.Lines);
DBMemo1.DataSource.DataSet.Post;
```

See Also

DataField property, DataSource property, TField chapter

TDBMEMO.GETSELTEXTBUF METHOD

Declaration

```
{ STDCTRLS.PAS }
function GetSelTextBuf(Buffer: PChar; BufSize: Integer): Integer;
```

Description

The GetSelTextBuf method copies the memo's selected text (if any) into a null-terminated string (Buffer). The BufSize parameter limits the number of characters to be copied. This method returns the number of characters copied.

Notes

GetSelTextBuf's raison d'être is for manipulating strings that are longer than 255 characters. If the selected text in the memo is shorter than that, you will find it easier to manipulate the SelText property directly.

Example

```
{ Copy selected text from one DBMemo to another, then restore the highlight
  in the original memo (note that the HideSelection property that originally
  appeared in the Delphi help file
  would have precluded the need to restore the highlight manually, but it
  does not exist for TDBMemos!) }
var
   buffer : PChar;
   start, bytes  : Integer;
begin
   start := DBMemo1.SelStart;        { For restoring highlight below }
   bytes := DBMemo1.SelLength;
   if bytes > 0 then begin
      Inc(bytes);              {To accommodate null terminator}
      GetMem(buffer, bytes);    {Allocate memory for PChar }
      DBMemo1.GetSelTextBuf(buffer, bytes);
      DBMemo2.Text := StrPas(buffer);
      FreeMem(buffer, bytes); {Free memory allocated to PChar }
      { restore selection }
      DBMemo1.SetFocus;              { Must do this first! }
      DBMemo1.SelStart   := start;
      DBMemo1.SelLength := bytes;
   end;
end;
```

See Also

SelLength property, SelStart property, SelText property, SetSelTextBuf method

TDBMemo.Handle Property

Declaration

356

```
{ CONTROLS.PAS }
property Handle: HWnd read GetHandle;
```

Description

Run-time and read-only. The Handle property is useful should you need to pass the memo's handle to a Windows API function.

Example

```
{ Mini-cornucopia of useful Windows API calls for memos }

{ Determine first visible line in memo }
var
   x : Integer;
...
x := SendMessage(DBMemo1.Handle, em_GetFirstVisibleLine, 0, 0)

{ Scroll the memo vertically five lines (positive values scroll down, negative
  values scroll up -- see help file for details on how to scroll horizontally }
SendMessage(DBMemo1.Handle, em_LineScroll, 0, -5);

{ Undo most recent change to memo }
SendMessage(DBMemo1.Handle, EM_UNDO, 0, 0);
```

TDBMemo.Lines Property

Declaration

```
{ STDCTRLS.PAS }
property Lines: TStrings read FLines write SetLines;
```

Description

The Lines property contains the lines of text to be displayed in the memo. Because these are TString objects, you are free to manipulate them by using the Add, Exchange, Delete, Insert, and Move methods.

Notes

If you would prefer to manipulate the entire text of the memo rather than line by line, use the Text property.

Example

```
{ Append contents of a text file to the end of a memo. The logic to create
  TOpenDialog object dynamically is unnecessary if you have created it at
  design-time, but otherwise remember to put the DIALOGS unit in the USES
  clause for this form. }
var
  Buffer: TStringList;
  od: TOpenDialog;
begin
  od := TOpenDialog.Create(Form1);
  od.Filter := 'Text Files (*.TXT)|*.TXT';
  if od.Execute then
    try   { Exception handling is smart when doing file I/O }
       Buffer := TStringList.Create;
       Buffer.LoadFromFile(od.FileName);
       DBMemo1.DataSource.DataSet.Edit ;
       DBMemo1.Lines.AddStrings(Buffer);
       DBMemo1.DataSource.DataSet.Post ;
    finally
       Buffer.Free;
    end;
end;
```

See Also

Text property

TDBMEMO.LOADMEMO METHOD

Declaration

```
{ DBCTRLS.PAS }
procedure LoadMemo;
```

Description

The LoadMemo method loads the memo into the control from the data field. This would be used if you have set the AutoDisplay property to False.

See Also

AutoDisplay property

TDBMEMO.MAXLENGTH PROPERTY

Declaration

```
{ STDCTRLS.PAS }
property MaxLength: Integer read FMaxLength write SetMaxLength
    default 0;
```

Description

The MaxLength property can be used to limit the number of characters entered into the memo. By default, this value is zero (0), which means that there is no limit.

Example

See the example provided with the TDBMemo.Create discussion.

See Also

Text property

TDBMEMO.MODIFIED PROPERTY

Declaration

```
{ STDCTRLS.PAS }
property Modified: Boolean read GetModified write SetModified;
```

Description

The Modified property indicates whether the user has changed the text in the memo. If Modified contains the value True, then the text has indeed been altered. This can be used, for example, to verify that the user wants to cancel the current edit operation.

Example

```
{ Request confirmation before canceling if memo was modified }
if (DBMemo1.Modified) and (MessageDlg('Are you sure?',
            mtConfirmation, [mbOk,mbCancel], 0) = mrOk) then
   Cancel;
```

TDBMEMO.ONCHANGE EVENT

Declaration

```
{ STDCTRLS.PAS }
property OnChange: TNotifyEvent read FOnChange write FOnChange;
```

```
{ CLASSES.PAS }
TNotifyEvent = procedure(Sender: TObject) of object;
```

Description

The OnChange event occurs whenever the user changes the text in the memo.

See Also

Text property

TDBMEMO.ONCLICK EVENT

Declaration

```
{ CONTROLS.PAS }
property OnClick: TNotifyEvent read FOnClick write FOnClick;
```

```
{ CLASSES.PAS }
TNotifyEvent = procedure(Sender: TObject) of object;
```

Description

The OnClick event occurs when the user single-clicks within the memo.

See Also

OnChange event, OnDblClick event

TDBMEMO.ONDBLCLICK EVENT

Declaration

```
{ CONTROLS.PAS }
property OnDblClick: TNotifyEvent read FOnDblClick write FOnDblClick;
```

```
{ CLASSES.PAS }
TNotifyEvent = procedure(Sender: TObject) of object;
```

Description

The OnDblClick event occurs whenever the user double-clicks within the memo.

Example

```
{ Double-click to alternately maximize then restore original size of memo }
var
   OldCoords : TRect;
```

```
procedure TForm1.DBMemo1DblClick(Sender: TObject);
begin
   with Sender as TDBMemo do
      if Align = alClient then begin
         Align := alNone;
         SetBounds(OldCoords.Left, OldCoords.Top,
                   OldCoords.Right,OldCoords.Bottom);
      end
      else
      begin
         OldCoords := BoundsRect;
         Align := alClient;
      end;
end;
```

See Also

OnChange event, OnClick event

TDBMemo.OnKeyDown Event

Declaration

```
{ CONTROLS.PAS }
property OnKeyDown: TKeyEvent read FOnKeyDown write FOnKeyDown;

TKeyEvent = procedure(Sender: TObject; var Key: Word;
   Shift: TShiftState) of object;

{ CLASSES.PAS }
TShiftState = set of (ssShift, ssAlt, ssCtrl,
   ssLeft, ssRight, ssMiddle, ssDouble);
```

Description

The OnKeyDown event occurs when a user presses a key while the memo has focus. You can write an OnKeyDown event handler to handle special keypresses, including function keys or keypresses combined with the **Shift, Alt**, and/or **Ctrl** keys. Parameters passed to your OnKeyDown event handler are Key (the numeric code associated with the keypress) and Shift (status of special keys, such as **Shift, Alt, Ctrl**, and mouse buttons).

Notes

A complete list of numeric codes associated with these keypresses can be found by searching for the topic "Virtual Key Codes" in the Delphi on-line help file. Alternatively, you can identify a key by its ASCII value if it has one.

Example

```
{ If user presses Alt-Delete, cut all text in memo to clipboard }
procedure TForm1.DBMemo1KeyDown(Sender: TObject; var Key: Word;
  Shift: TShiftState);
begin
    if (Key = vk_Delete) and (Shift = [ssAlt]) then
    begin
        DBMemo1.SelectAll;
        DBMemo1.CutToClipboard;
    end;
end;
```

See Also

OnKeyPress event, OnKeyUp event, OnMouseDown event

TDBMEMO.ONKEYPRESS EVENT

Declaration

```
{ CONTROLS.PAS }
property OnKeyPress: TKeyPressEvent read FOnKeyPress
    write FOnKeyPress;

TKeyPressEvent = procedure(Sender: TObject; var Key: Char) of object;
```

Description

The OnKeyPress event occurs when a user presses a key that has a corresponding ASCII value while the memo has focus. The Key parameter passed to your OnKeyPress event handler is the character that was pressed. If you need to trap special (non-ASCII) keys, you should use the OnKeyDown event.

See Also

OnKeyDown event

TDBMEMO.ONKEYUP EVENT

Declaration

```
{ CONTROLS.PAS }
property OnKeyUp: TKeyEvent read FOnKeyUp write FOnKeyUp;

TKeyEvent = procedure(Sender: TObject; var Key: Word;
    Shift: TShiftState) of object;
```

```
{ CLASSES.PAS }
TShiftState = set of (ssShift, ssAlt, ssCtrl,
    ssLeft, ssRight, ssMiddle, ssDouble);
```

Description

The OnKeyUp event occurs when a user releases a key while the memo has focus. OnKeyUp handles special keypresses, including function keys or keypresses combined with the **Shift**, **Alt**, and/or **Ctrl** keys. Parameters passed to your OnKeyUp event handler are Key (the numeric code associated with the keypress) and Shift (status of special keys, such as **Shift**, **Alt**, **Ctrl**, and mouse buttons).

See Also

OnKeyDown event

TDBMEMO.ONMOUSEDOWN EVENT

Declaration

```
{ CONTROLS.PAS }
property OnMouseDown: TMouseEvent read FOnMouseDown
    write FOnMouseDown;

TMouseEvent = procedure(Sender: TObject; Button: TMouseButton;
    Shift: TShiftState; X, Y: Integer) of object;

TMouseButton = (mbLeft, mbRight, mbMiddle);

{ CLASSES.PAS }
TShiftState = set of (ssShift, ssAlt, ssCtrl,
    ssLeft, ssRight, ssMiddle, ssDouble);
```

Description

The OnMouseDown event occurs when the user presses a mouse button while the mouse cursor is over the memo. The following parameters are passed to your OnMouseDown event handler: Button (identifies which mouse button was pressed), Shift (status of special keys and mouse buttons), and X and Y (screen coordinates of mouse cursor).

Notes

See the OnKeyDown discussion for a list of TShiftState values.

See Also

OnKeyDown event, OnMouseUp event

TDBMEMO.ONMOUSEMOVE EVENT

Declaration

```
{ CONTROLS.PAS }
property OnMouseMove: TMouseMoveEvent read FOnMouseMove
   write FOnMouseMove;

TMouseMoveEvent = procedure(Sender: TObject; Shift: TShiftState;
   X, Y: Integer) of object;

{ CLASSES.PAS }
TShiftState = set of (ssShift, ssAlt, ssCtrl,
   ssLeft, ssRight, ssMiddle, ssDouble);
```

Description

The OnMouseMove event occurs when the user moves the mouse while its cursor is over the memo. The following parameters are passed to your OnMouseMove event handler: Shift (status of special keys and mouse buttons) and X and Y (screen coordinates of mouse cursor).

Notes

See the OnKeyDown discussion for a list of TShiftState values.

See Also

OnKeyDown event, OnMouseDown event, OnMouseUp event

TDBMEMO.ONMOUSEUP EVENT

Declaration

```
{ CONTROLS.PAS }
property OnMouseUp: TMouseEvent read FOnMouseUp write FOnMouseUp;

TMouseEvent = procedure(Sender: TObject; Button: TMouseButton;
   Shift: TShiftState; X, Y: Integer) of object;

TMouseButton = (mbLeft, mbRight, mbMiddle);

{ CLASSES.PAS }
TShiftState = set of (ssShift, ssAlt, ssCtrl,
   ssLeft, ssRight, ssMiddle, ssDouble);
```

Description

The OnMouseUp event occurs when the user releases a mouse button while the mouse cursor is over the memo. The following parameters will be passed to your OnMouseUp event handler: Button (identifies which mouse button was pressed), Shift (status of special keys and mouse buttons), and X and Y (screen coordinates of mouse cursor).

Notes

See the OnKeyDown discussion for a list of TShiftState values.

See Also

OnKeyDown event, OnMouseDown event

TDBMemo.PasteFromClipboard Method

Declaration

```
{ STDCTRLS.PAS }
procedure PasteFromClipboard;
```

Description

The PasteFromClipboard method replaces the memo's selected text (if any) with the contents of the clipboard. If no text is currently selected, the clipboard contents will be inserted at the position of the cursor within the memo.

Example

See the PopupMenu discussion in the Common Attributes section at the beginning of this chapter, which contains a comprehensive example that applies equally well to memos.

See Also

CopyToClipboard method, CutToClipboard method, SelText property

TDBMemo.ScrollBars Property

Declaration

```
{ STDCTRLS.PAS }
property ScrollBars: TScrollStyle read FScrollBars
    write SetScrollBars default ssNone;

TScrollStyle = (ssNone, ssHorizontal, ssVertical, ssBoth);
```

Description

The ScrollBars property determines which, if any, scroll bars will be displayed for the memo. The values listed here should be self-explanatory.

Example

See the example provided with TDBMemo.OnEnter.

See Also

WordWrap property

TDBMemo.SelectAll Method

Declaration

```
{ STDCTRLS.PAS }
procedure SelectAll;
```

Description

The SelectAll method selects (highlights) the entire text in the memo.

Example

See the example provided with TDBMemo.OnKeyDown.

See Also

Text property

TDBMemo.SelLength Property

Declaration

```
{ STDCTRLS.PAS }
property SelLength: Integer read GetSelLength write SetSelLength;
```

Description

The SelLength returns the length, in characters, of the currently selected text in the memo. If it contains zero, then no text is selected.

Notes

The memo should have input focus focused before you change this property.

Example

See the example provided with the TDBMemo.GetSelTextBuf method.

See Also

SelStart property, SelText property

TDBMemo.SelStart Property

Declaration

{ STDCTRLS.PAS }
property SelStart: Integer **read** GetSelStart **write** SetSelStart;

Description

The SelStart returns the starting position of the currently selected text, if any, in the memo.

Notes

The memo should be focused before you change this property.

See Also

SelStart property, SelText property

TDBMemo.SelText Property

Declaration

{ STDCTRLS.PAS }
property SelText: string **read** GetSelText **write** SetSelText;

Description

The SelText returns the currently selected text, if any, in the memo.

See Also

SelLength property, SelText property

TDBMemo.SetSelTextBuf Method

Declaration

{ STDCTRLS.PAS }
procedure SetSelTextBuf(Buffer: PChar);

Description

The SetSelTextBuf method copies text from a null-terminated string (Buffer) into the memo and automatically selects it.

Notes

SetSelTextBuf is for manipulating strings that are longer than 255 characters. If the selected text in the memo is shorter than this, it is easier for you to manipulate the SelText property directly.

Example

See example provided with TDBMemo.GetSelTextBuf.

See Also

GetSelTextBuf method, SelLength property, SelText property

TDBMEMO.TEXT PROPERTY

Declaration

```
{ CONTROLS.PAS }
property Text: TCaption read GetText write SetText;

TCaption = String[255];
```

Description

This property contains the text currently displayed in the memo. If the total length of the memo is longer than 255 characters, you should manipulate it with the GetTextBuf and SetTextBuf methods.

See Also

GetTextBuf method, SelLength property, SelStart property, SelText property, SetTextBuf method

TDBMEMO.WANTTABS PROPERTY

Declaration

```
{ STDCTRLS.PAS }
property WantTabs: Boolean read FWantTabs write FWantTabs
   default False;
```

Description

The WantTabs property determines whether tabs are enabled in the memo. If WantTabs is set to True, tabs will be enabled, but the user will be unable to use the Tab key to navigate to the next control. To turn tabs off, leave WantTabs at its default value of False.

TDBMEMO.WORDWRAP PROPERTY

Declaration

```
{ STDCTRLS.PAS }
property WordWrap: Boolean read FWordWrap write SetWordWrap
    default True;
```

Description

The WordWrap property determines if the text in the memo wraps at the right margin to fit within its area. You can give the user access to clipped text by adding scroll bars (via the ScrollBars property).

Notes

Even if WordWrap is set to True, the memo's height must accommodate at least one line of text in order for the user to be able to edit its contents.

See Also

ScrollBars property

TDBNavigator

Unit

DBCtrls

Inherits from

TCustomPanel

Description

The TDBNavigator component allows the user to move through a data set. You can also permit the user to insert, delete, and edit records with this component.

The following tables summarize the properties (Table 3.50), methods (Table 3.51), and events (Table 3.52) for TDBNavigator.

TABLE 3.50 TDBNAVIGATOR PROPERTIES

PROPERTY	DATA TYPE	RUN-TIME ONLY	READ-ONLY	DESCRIPTION
ConfirmDelete	Boolean	No	No	Determines whether or not to ask the user for confirmation prior to deletion.
Hints	TStrings	No	No	Specific hints for each button
VisibleButtons	TButtonSet	No	No	Determines which buttons will be available upon the navigator.

TABLE 3.51 TDBNAVIGATOR METHODS

METHOD	DESCRIPTION
BtnClick	Simulates a keypress upon one of the navigator's buttons.
Create	Allocates memory to create the navigator.

TABLE 3.52 TDBNAVIGATOR EVENTS

EVENT	DATA TYPE	DESCRIPTION
OnClick	TNotifyEvent	Occurs when user single-clicks upon the navigator.
OnDblClick	TNotifyEvent	Occurs when user double-clicks upon the navigator.
OnMouseDown	TMouseEvent	Occurs when user presses mouse button with mouse pointer over the navigator.
OnMouseMove	TMouseMoveEvent	Occurs when user moves mouse button if mouse pointer is over the navigator.
OnMouseUp	TMouseEvent	Occurs when user releases mouse button with mouse pointer over the navigator.
OnResize	TNotifyEvent	Occurs when navigator's parent form is resized.

TDBNAVIGATOR.BTNCLICK METHOD

Declaration

```
{ DBCTRLS.PAS }
procedure BtnClick(Index: TNavigateBtn);

TNavigateBtn = (nbFirst, nbPrior, nbNext, nbLast, nbInsert,
                nbDelete, nbEdit, nbPost, nbCancel, nbRefresh);
```

Description

The BtnClick method simulates a keypress on one of the navigator buttons, as specified by the Index parameter. All the TNavigateBtn values listed here should be self-explanatory.

Notes

You can simulate keypresses for buttons that are not visible upon the navigator (i.e., not part of the VisibleButtons property).

Example

```
{ Insert a new record in the data set attached to navigator }
DBNavigator.BtnClick(nbInsert);
```

TDBNavigator.ConfirmDelete Property

Declaration

```
{ DBCTRLS.PAS }
property ConfirmDelete: Boolean read FConfirmDelete
    write FConfirmDelete default True;
```

Description

The ConfirmDelete property dictates whether or not the user will be asked for confirmation prior to deleting a record via the navigator. By default, this is set to True, which enables confirmation.

Example

See the example provided for the TDBNavigator.Create method.

TDBNavigator.Create Method

Declaration

```
{ DBCTRLS.PAS }
constructor Create(AOwner: TComponent); override;
```

Description

The Create method can be used to create a navigator manually at run-time. If you give the navigator an owner, the navigator will automatically be destroyed when its owner is destroyed.

Note: If you create a navigator manually with this method, you must specify its Parent property in order for the navigator to be displayed on-screen.

Notes

If you do not want the navigator to have an owner, pass Self as the parameter to the Create method. (See the example accompanying the discussion of the TDBCheckBox.Free method.)

Example

```
{ Create navigator on-the-fly and link it to the Articles table }
var
    n : TDBNavigator;
    t : TTable;
    d : TDataSource;
    sl : TStringList;
    p : TPanel;
begin
    { create TTable object to access Articles table }
    t := TTable.Create(Application);
    t.DatabaseName := 'c:\aquarium\articles';
    t.TableName := 'articles.dbf';
```

```
t.Open;
{ Create TDataSource object to link to Articles table }
d := TDataSource.Create(Application);
d.DataSet := t;
{ Create a panel which will serve as parent to navigator.
This is completely optional -- you could instead set the
navigator's Align property to alTop, and have the form
serve as both its Owner and Parent. Your call... }
p := TPanel.Create(Form1);
p.BevelInner := bvRaised;
p.BevelOuter := bvRaised;
p.BevelWidth := 2;
p.Parent := Form1;          { Very important! }
p.Align := alTop;
{ Create the navigator }
n := TDBNavigator.Create(Form1);
n.Parent := p;             { Change to Form1 if not using panel }
n.Align   := alClient;     { Change to alTop if not using panel }
n.DataSource := d;         { Link to DataSource created above }
n.VisibleButtons := [nbFirst, nbPrior, nbNext, nbLast,
                     nbDelete, nbEdit ];
n.ShowHint := True;
n.ConfirmDelete := False;     { Give them the rope }
{ Create alternate hints for the navigator }
sl := TStringList.Create;
sl.Add('First article');
sl.Add('Previous article');
sl.Add('Next article');
sl.Add('Last article');
sl.Add('Delete this article');
sl.Add('Edit this article');
n.Hints := sl;
end;
```

See Also

Free method

TDBNavigator.Hints Property

Declaration

```
{ DBCTRLS.PAS }
property Hints: TStrings read FHints write SetHints;
```

Description

The Hints property enables you to override the default hints for each navigator button.

Example

See example provided with TDBNavigator.Create discussion.

See Also

Refresh method, Repaint method

TDBNavigator.OnClick Event

Declaration

```
{ CONTROLS.PAS }
property OnClick: TNotifyEvent read FOnClick write FOnClick;

{ CLASSES.PAS }
TNotifyEvent = procedure(Sender: TObject) of object;
```

Description

The OnClick event occurs when the user single-clicks within the navigator. This will be called after the action attached to the relevant button.

See Also

OnDblClick event

TDBNavigator.OnDblClick Event

Declaration

```
{ CONTROLS.PAS }
property OnDblClick: TNotifyEvent read FOnDblClick write FOnDblClick;

{ CLASSES.PAS }
TNotifyEvent = procedure(Sender: TObject) of object;
```

Description

The OnDblClick event occurs whenever the user double-clicks on an inactive button within the navigator.

See Also

OnClick event

TDBNavigator.OnMouseDown Event

Declaration

```
{ CONTROLS.PAS }
property OnMouseDown: TMouseEvent read FOnMouseDown
    write FOnMouseDown;
```

```
TMouseEvent = procedure(Sender: TObject; Button: TMouseButton;
    Shift: TShiftState; X, Y: Integer) of object;

TMouseButton = (mbLeft, mbRight, mbMiddle);

{ CLASSES.PAS }
TShiftState = set of (ssShift, ssAlt, ssCtrl,
    ssLeft, ssRight, ssMiddle, ssDouble);
```

Description

The OnMouseDown event occurs when the user presses a mouse button while the mouse cursor is over the navigator. The following parameters are passed to your OnMouseDown event handler: Button (identifies which mouse button was pressed), Shift (status of special keys and mouse buttons), and X and Y (screen coordinates of mouse cursor).

Notes

See the OnKeyDown discussion for a list of TShiftState values.

See Also

OnKeyDown event, OnMouseUp event

TDBNAVIGATOR.ONMOUSEMOVE EVENT

Declaration

```
{ CONTROLS.PAS }
property OnMouseMove: TMouseMoveEvent read FOnMouseMove
    write FOnMouseMove;

TMouseMoveEvent = procedure(Sender: TObject; Shift: TShiftState;
    X, Y: Integer) of object;

{ CLASSES.PAS }
TShiftState = set of (ssShift, ssAlt, ssCtrl,
    ssLeft, ssRight, ssMiddle, ssDouble);
```

Description

The OnMouseMove event occurs when the user moves the mouse while its cursor is over the navigator. The following parameters are passed to your OnMouseMove event handler: Shift (status of special keys and mouse buttons) and X and Y (screen coordinates of mouse cursor).

Notes

See the OnKeyDown discussion for a list of TShiftState values.

See Also

OnKeyDown event, OnMouseDown event, OnMouseUp event

TDBNavigator.OnMouseUp Event

Declaration

```
{ CONTROLS.PAS }
property OnMouseUp: TMouseEvent read FOnMouseUp write FOnMouseUp;

TMouseEvent = procedure(Sender: TObject; Button: TMouseButton;
    Shift: TShiftState; X, Y: Integer) of object;

TMouseButton = (mbLeft, mbRight, mbMiddle);

{ CLASSES.PAS }
TShiftState = set of (ssShift, ssAlt, ssCtrl,
    ssLeft, ssRight, ssMiddle, ssDouble);
```

Description

The OnMouseUp event occurs when the user releases a mouse button while the mouse cursor is over the navigator. The following parameters will be passed to your OnMouseUp event handler: Button (identifies which mouse button was pressed), Shift (status of special keys and mouse buttons), and X and Y (screen coordinates of mouse cursor).

Notes

See the OnKeyDown discussion for a list of TShiftState values.

See Also

OnKeyDown event, OnMouseDown event

TDBNavigator.OnResize Event

Declaration

```
{ EXTCTRLS.PAS }
property OnResize: TNotifyEvent read FOnResize write FOnResize;

{ CLASSES.PAS }
TNotifyEvent = procedure(Sender: TObject) of object;
```

Description

The OnResize event occurs when the navigator is resized. This will happen when the navigator is first displayed and then again whenever its parent is resized (assuming that its Align property is something other than alNone).

Notes

Depending upon the size of its parent, resize actions may cause part or all the navigator to become hidden. By writing an OnResize event handler, you can add logic to ensure that the navigator will always be visible.

See Also

Parent property

TDBNavigator.VisibleButtons Property

Declaration

```
{ DBCTRLS.PAS }
property VisibleButtons: TButtonSet read FVisibleButtons
    write SetVisible default [nbFirst, nbPrior, nbNext, nbLast,
        nbInsert, nbDelete,nbEdit, nbPost, nbCancel, nbRefresh];

TButtonSet = set of TNavigateBtn;

TNavigateBtn = (nbFirst, nbPrior, nbNext, nbLast, nbInsert,
                nbDelete, nbEdit, nbPost, nbCancel, nbRefresh);
```

Description

The VisibleButtons property dictates which buttons will be included as part of the navigator. By default, all ten buttons will be visible. However, you are always free to hide any or all of these at will.

Example

See the example provided for TDBNavigator.Create.

See Also

BtnClick method

TDBRadioGroup

Unit

DBCtrls

Inherits from

TCustomRadioGroup

Description

The TDBRadioGroup component allows the user to change the value of a field by making a selection from a fixed list of choices.

The following tables summarize the properties (Table 3.53), methods (Table 3.54), and events (Table 3.55) for TDBRadioGroup.

TABLE 3.53 TDBRadioGroup Properties

Property	Data Type	Run-Time Only	Read-Only	Description
Caption	String	No	No	Title for radio group
Columns	Integer	No	No	Number of columns in radio group
Field	TField	Yes	Yes	Field to which the radio group is linked
ItemIndex	Integer	Yes	No	Ordinal position of currently selected item in the radio group
Items	TStrings	No	No	The items that appear in the radio group for selection
Value	String	Yes	No	Current contents of field linked to radio group
Values	TStrings	No	No	Underlying values to match Items (this serves as your link to values in database field)

TABLE 3.54 TDBRadioGroup Methods

Method	Description
Create	Allocates memory to create the radio group.

TABLE 3.55 TDBRadioGroup Events

Event	Data Type	Description
OnChange	TNotifyEvent	Occurs when user selects a button within the radio group.
OnClick	TNotifyEvent	Occurs when user single-clicks upon the radio group.
OnDblClick	TNotifyEvent	Occurs when user double-clicks upon the radio group.

TDBRadioGroup.Caption Property

Declaration

```
{ CONTROLS.PAS }
property Caption: TCaption read GetText write SetText;
```

Description

The Caption property is a string containing text to be displayed as the radio group's title. You may designate an accelerator key by preceding one of the characters within the Caption with an ampersand (&).

Example

See example provided with TDBRadioGroup.Create.

See Also

Font property

TDBRADIOGROUP.COLUMNS PROPERTY

Declaration

```
{ STDCTRLS.PAS }
property Columns: Integer read FColumns write SetColumns default 0;
```

Description

The Columns property dictates how many columns will appear within the radio group. By default, this will be set to one. The items within the radio group will automatically be arranged based upon the number of columns specified.

Example

See example provided with TDBRadioGroup.Create.

See Also

ParentColor property

TDBRADIOGROUP.CREATE METHOD

Declaration

```
{ DBCTRLS.PAS }
constructor Create(AOwner: TComponent); override;
```

Description

The Create method can be used to create a radio group manually at run-time. If you give the combo box an owner, the radio group will automatically be destroyed when its owner bites the dust.

Note: If you create a radio group manually with this method, you must specify its Parent property in order for the radio group to be displayed on-screen.

Notes

If you do not want the radio group to have an owner, pass Self as the parameter to the Create method. (A relevant example accompanies the discussion of the TDBCheckBox.Free method.)

Example

```
{ Create radio group on-the-fly and link it to the Payment field in the Orders
  table, which is located in C:\DATA. If your table and data source were created
  at design-time, feel free to delete the appropriate sections of code. }
var
    rg : TDBRadioGroup;
    t : TTable;
    d : TDataSource;
begin
    { Create TTable object to access Articles table }
    t := TTable.Create(Application);
    t.DatabaseName := 'c:\data';
    t.TableName := 'orders.dbf';
    t.Open;
    { Create TDataSource object to link to Articles table }
    d := TDataSource.Create(Application);
    d.DataSet := t;
    { Create the radio group }
    rg := TDBRadioGroup.Create(Form1);
    rg.Parent := Form2;    { Very important! }
    rg.SetBounds(10, 50, 200, 150);
    rg.DataSource := d;   { Link to DataSource created above }
    rg.DataField := 'PAYMENT';
    rg.Caption := '&Payment Method';
    rg.Columns := 2;
    rg.Font.Name := 'Times New Roman';
    rg.Font.Height := 11;
    { Create items to be displayed within radio group }
    rg.Items.Add('Cash/check');
    rg.Items.Add('VISA');
    rg.Items.Add('Mastercard');
    rg.Items.Add('Amex');
    rg.Items.Add('COD');
    rg.Items.Add('Net 30');
    { Create values to correspond with items above }
    rg.Values.Add('C');
    rg.Values.Add('V');
    rg.Values.Add('M');
    rg.Values.Add('A');
    rg.Values.Add('O');
    rg.Values.Add('N');
    rg.Hint := 'This is the payment method';
    rg.ShowHint := True;
end;
```

See Also

Free method

TDBRadioGroup.Field Property

Declaration

```
{ DBCTRLS.PAS }
property Field: TField read GetField;
```

Description

The Field property contains the field to which the radio group is linked. This property can be used to manipulate the field directly.

Notes

Run-time and read-only

Example

```
{ Set value of field to the value underlying the first button }
if not (DBRadioGroup1.DataSource.State in [dsEdit, dsInsert]) then
   DBRadioGroup1.DataSource.DataSet.Edit;
DBRadioGroup1.Field.AsString := DBRadioGroup1.Values[0];
DBRadioGroup1.DataSource.DataSet.Post;
```

See Also

DataField property, DataSource property

TDBRadioGroup.ItemIndex Property

Declaration

```
{ STDCTRLS.PAS }
property ItemIndex: Integer read GetItemIndex
   write SetItemIndex;
```

Description

Run-time only. The ItemIndex property contains the ordinal position of the currently selected item/button in the radio group.

Example

```
{ Select the last button in the radio group }
DBRadiogroup1.ItemIndex := DBRadiogroup1.Items.Count;
```

See Also
Items property

TDBRadioGroup.Items Property

Declaration

```
{ STDCTRLS.PAS }
property Items: TStrings read FItems write SetItems;
```

Description
The Items property contains the strings that will be displayed in the radio group. You can manipulate them by using the Add, Exchange, Delete, Insert, and Move methods.

Example

```
{ Example #1: Fill the radio group from a table }
DBRadioGroup1.Items.Clear;
DBRadioGroup1.Values.Clear;
Table1.DisableControls;
Table1.First;
while not Table1.EOF do
begin
   DBRadioGroup1.Items.Add(Table1.FieldByName('DESCRIP').AsString);

   DBRadioGroup1.Values.Add(Table1.FieldByName('CODE').AsString );
   Table1.Next;
end;
Table1.EnableControls;

{ Example #2: Fill the radio group with the contents of a memo }
DBRadiogroup1.Items := Memo1.Lines;

{ Example #3: Change the text of the third button }
DBRadiogroup1.Items[2] := 'Something Else';
```

See Also
ItemIndex property, Values property

TDBRadioGroup.OnChange Event

Declaration

```
{ CONTROLS.PAS }
property OnChange: TNotifyEvent read FOnChange write FOnChange;

{ CLASSES.PAS }
TNotifyEvent = procedure(Sender: TObject) of object;
```

Description

The OnChange event occurs when the user selects a button in the radio group, either by clicking with the mouse or by using one of the navigation keys.

Example

```
{ Change a label to the currently selected item in the radio group }
procedure TForm1.DBRadioGroup1Change(Sender: TObject);
begin
   Label1.Caption := DBRadioGroup1.Items[DBRadioGroup1.ItemIndex];
end;
```

See Also

Items property

TDBRadioGroup.OnClick Event

Declaration

```
{ CONTROLS.PAS }
property OnClick: TNotifyEvent read FOnClick write FOnClick;

{ CLASSES.PAS }
TNotifyEvent = procedure(Sender: TObject) of object;
```

Description

The OnClick event occurs when the user single-clicks upon the radio group.

Example

See example provided with TDBRadioGroup.OnChange event.

See Also

OnChange event, OnDblClick event

TDBRadioGroup.OnDblClick Event

Declaration

```
{ CONTROLS.PAS }
property OnDblClick: TNotifyEvent read FOnDblClick write FOnDblClick;

{ CLASSES.PAS }
TNotifyEvent = procedure(Sender: TObject) of object;
```

Description

The OnDblClick event occurs whenever the user double-clicks upon the radio group.

See Also

OnClick event

TDBRadioGroup.Value Property

Declaration

```
{ DBCTRLS.PAS }
property Value: String read GetValue write SetValue;
```

Description

The Value property holds the current contents of the field linked to the radio group. You can manipulate the field directly by changing this property.

See Also

Field property, Values property

TDBRadioGroup.Values Property

Declaration

```
{ DBCTRLS.PAS }
property Values: TStrings read FValues write SetValues;
```

Description

The Values property holds values that correspond to the strings in the Items property. These should contain all the possible values of the DataField linked to the radio group. When the user selects an item in the radio group, the value of the field will be changed to the matching item in the Values property.

Example

See the example accompanying the TDBRadioGroup.Create discussion.

See Also

Items property, Value property

TDBText

Unit

DBCtrls

Inherits from

TCustomLabel

Description

The TDBText component displays the value of a field in a read-only label. If you want the user to be able to change the value of the field, use a TDBEdit or TDBMemo component instead.

The following tables summarize the properties (Table 3.56), methods (Table 3.57), and events (Table 3.58) for TDBText.

TABLE 3.56 TDBTEXT PROPERTIES

PROPERTY	DATA TYPE	RUN-TIME ONLY	READ-ONLY	DESCRIPTION
Alignment	TAlignment	No	No	Determines alignment of text within the label.
AutoSize	Boolean	No	No	Determines whether label automatically resizes to accommodate its text.
Field	TField	Yes	Yes	Field to which the label is linked.
Transparent	Boolean	No	No	Determines whether label should be transparent or opaque.
WordWrap	Boolean	No	No	Determines whether text in label word-wraps or clips.

TABLE 3.57 TDBTEXT METHODS

METHOD	DESCRIPTION
Create	Allocates memory to create the label.

TABLE 3.58 TDBTEXT EVENTS

EVENT	DATA TYPE	DESCRIPTION
OnClick	TNotifyEvent	Occurs when user single-clicks upon the label.
OnDblClick	TNotifyEvent	Occurs when user double-clicks upon the label.
OnDragDrop	TDragDropEvent	Occurs when user drops the label.
OnDragOver	TDragOverEvent	Occurs when user drags an object over the label.
OnEndDrag	TEndDragEvent	Occurs when user stops dragging the label.
OnMouseDown	TMouseEvent	Occurs when user presses mouse button with mouse pointer over the label.
OnMouseMove	TMouseMoveEvent	Occurs when user moves mouse button if mouse pointer is over the label.
OnMouseUp	TMouseEvent	Occurs when user releases mouse button with mouse pointer over the label.

TDBTEXT.ALIGNMENT PROPERTY

Declaration

```
{ STDCTRLS.PAS }
property Alignment: TAlignment read FAlignment write SetAlignment
    default taLeftJustify;
```

```
{ CLASSES.PAS }
TAlignment = (taLeftJustify, taRightJustify, taCenter);
```

Description

The Alignment property determines how the text will be displayed within the label area. Text can be either left-justified, right-justified, or centered. Default is left-justified.

Example

See the example provided with TDBText.Create.

TDBTEXT.AUTOSIZE PROPERTY

Declaration

```
{ STDCTRLS.PAS }
property AutoSize: Boolean read FAutoSize write SetAutoSize
    default True;
```

Description

The AutoSize property determines whether the label should automatically resize itself to fit the text within it. By default, this is enabled. It will also cause the label to react appropriately to any changes with its font.

See Also

Font property

TDBTEXT.CREATE METHOD

Declaration

```
{ DBCTRLS.PAS }
constructor Create(AOwner: TComponent); override;
```

Description

The Create method can be used to create a data-aware label manually at run-time. If you give the label an owner, the label will automatically be destroyed when its owner is destroyed.

Note: If you create a label with this method, you must specify its Parent property in order for the label to be displayed on-screen.

Notes

If you do not want the label to have an owner, pass Self as the parameter to the Create method. (See the example accompanying the discussion of the TDBCheckBox.Free method.)

Example

```
{ Create label on-the-fly and link it to the Title field in the Articles
  table, which is located in C:\AQUARIUM\ARTICLES. This also creates the
  TTable and TDataSource objects on-the-fly. If you have created them at
  design-time, then you can eliminate those sections of code }
var
    tTitle : TDBText;
    t : TTable;
    d : TDataSource;
begin
    { Create TTable object to access Articles table }
    t := TTable.Create(Application);
    t.DatabaseName := 'c:\aquarium\articles';
    t.TableName := 'articles.dbf';
    t.Open;
    { Create TDataSource object to link to Articles table }
    d := TDataSource.Create(Application);
    d.DataSet := t;
    { Create label }
    tTitle := TDBText.Create(Form1);
    tTitle.Parent        := Form1;    { Very important! }
    tTitle.Align         := alTop;
    tTitle.Alignment     := taCenter;
    tTitle.DataSource    := d; { Link to DataSource created above }
    tTitle.DataField     := 'TITLE';
    tTitle.Hint := 'This is the title of the article!';
    tTitle.ShowHint      := True;
    tTitle.Font.Name     := 'Arial';
    tTitle.Font.Style    := [fsBold, fsItalic];
    tTitle.Font.Height   := 12;
    tTitle.Transparent   := True;
end;
```

See Also

Free method

TDBTEXT.FIELD PROPERTY

Declaration

```
{ DBCTRLS.PAS }
property Field: TField read GetField;
```

Description

The Field property contains the field to which the label is linked. This can be used either to manip-ulate the field directly or to retrieve its value.

Notes

Run-time and read-only

Example

```
{ Grab contents of label }
x := DBLabel1.Field.AsString;
```

See Also

DataField property, DataSource property, TField chapter

TDBTEXT.ONCLICK EVENT

Declaration

```
{ CONTROLS.PAS }
property OnClick: TNotifyEvent read FOnClick write FOnClick;
```

```
{ CLASSES.PAS }
TNotifyEvent = procedure(Sender: TObject) of object;
```

Description

The OnClick event occurs when the user single-clicks within the label.

Example

```
{ Change the label to a random color whenever you click on it }
procedure TForm2.DBText1Click(Sender: TObject);
begin
    DBText1.Color := (Random(255) * 256) + (Random(255) * 16) +
                      Random(255);
end;
```

See Also

OnDblClick event

TDBTEXT.ONDBLCLICK EVENT

Declaration

```
{ CONTROLS.PAS }
property OnDblClick: TNotifyEvent read FOnDblClick write FOnDblClick;
```

```
{ CLASSES.PAS }
TNotifyEvent = procedure(Sender: TObject) of object;
```

Description

The OnDblClick event occurs whenever the user double-clicks upon the label.

See Also

OnClick event

TDBTEXT.ONMOUSEDOWN EVENT

Declaration

```
{ CONTROLS.PAS }
property OnMouseDown: TMouseEvent read FOnMouseDown
    write FOnMouseDown;

TMouseEvent = procedure(Sender: TObject; Button: TMouseButton;
    Shift: TShiftState; X, Y: Integer) of object;

TMouseButton = (mbLeft, mbRight, mbMiddle);

{ CLASSES.PAS }
TShiftState = set of (ssShift, ssAlt, ssCtrl,
    ssLeft, ssRight, ssMiddle, ssDouble);
```

Description

The OnMouseDown event occurs when the user presses a mouse button while the mouse cursor is over the label. The following parameters are passed to your OnMouseDown event handler: Button (identifies which mouse button was pressed), Shift (status of special keys and mouse buttons), and X and Y (screen coordinates of mouse cursor).

Notes

See the OnKeyDown discussion for a list of TShiftState values.

See Also

OnKeyDown event, OnMouseUp event

TDBTEXT.ONMOUSEMOVE EVENT

Declaration

```
{ CONTROLS.PAS }
property OnMouseMove: TMouseMoveEvent read FOnMouseMove
    write FOnMouseMove;
```

```
TMouseMoveEvent = procedure(Sender: TObject; Shift: TShiftState;
    X, Y: Integer) of object;

{ CLASSES.PAS }
TShiftState = set of (ssShift, ssAlt, ssCtrl,
    ssLeft, ssRight, ssMiddle, ssDouble);
```

Description

The OnMouseMove event occurs when the user moves the mouse while its cursor is over the label. The following parameters are passed to your OnMouseMove event handler: Shift (status of special keys and mouse buttons) and X and Y (screen coordinates of mouse cursor).

Notes

See the OnKeyDown discussion for a list of TShiftState values.

See Also

OnKeyDown event, OnMouseDown event, OnMouseUp event

TDBTEXT.ONMOUSEUP EVENT

Declaration

```
{ CONTROLS.PAS }
property OnMouseUp: TMouseEvent read FOnMouseUp write FOnMouseUp;

TMouseEvent = procedure(Sender: TObject; Button: TMouseButton;
    Shift: TShiftState; X, Y: Integer) of object;

TMouseButton = (mbLeft, mbRight, mbMiddle);

{ CLASSES.PAS }
TShiftState = set of (ssShift, ssAlt, ssCtrl,
    ssLeft, ssRight, ssMiddle, ssDouble);
```

Description

The OnMouseUp event occurs when the user releases a mouse button while the mouse cursor is over the label. The following parameters will be passed to your OnMouseUp event handler: Button (identifies which mouse button was pressed), Shift (status of special keys and mouse buttons), and X and Y (screen coordinates of mouse cursor).

Notes

See the OnKeyDown discussion for a list of TShiftState values.

See Also

OnKeyDown event, OnMouseDown event

TDBText.Transparent Property

Declaration

```
{ STDCTRLS.PAS }
property Transparent: Boolean read GetTransparent
    write SetTransparent default False;
```

Description

The Transparent property determines whether or not the label will be transparent. This can be useful if, for example, you want to place a label upon a bit map without blocking it. If this property is left to its default value of False, the label will be opaque.

Example

See the example provided with the TDBText.Create method.

TDBText.WordWrap Property

Declaration

```
{ STDCTRLS.PAS }
property WordWrap: Boolean read FWordWrap write SetWordWrap
    default False;
```

Description

The WordWrap property determines if the text in the label wraps at the right margin to fit within its area. If set to its default value of False, the text within the label will not wrap (i.e., will be clipped).

See Also

AutoSize property

CHAPTER 4

The TField Components

OVERVIEW OF TFIELD COMPONENTS

TField components are used to access fields in a database. By default, a set of TField components is created automatically each time a dataset component is activated; the resulting set of TField components is dynamic, mirroring the actual columns in an underlying physical table at that time. At design-time, you can also create TField objects using the Fields Editor, which gives you greater ability to control the individual attributes for each field.

The TField component is itself an abstract component that defines much of the basic functionality for all of its descendants. When you create TField objects in your application using the Fields Editor, the appropriate TField descendant is automatically chosen to match the data stored in the underlying field. These descendants, collectively referred to as TField components, are listed in Table 4.1.

TABLE 4.1 DESCENDANTS OF TFIELD AND THE FIELD TYPES TO WHICH THEY REFER

TFIELD DESCENDANT	FIELD CONTENTS
TBCDField	Binary Coded Decimal (BCD)—fixed decimal floating point values (Paradox only)
TBlobField	Binary data of any length
TBooleanField	Boolean (logical) values
TBytesField	Binary data of any length
TCurrencyField	Currency values
TDateField	Date values
TDateTimeField	Date and time values
TFloatField	Floating-point values
TGraphicField	Graphic (bit-map) values of any length
TIntegerField	Integer values in the range −2,147,483,648..2,147,483,648
TMemoField	Text values of any length
TNumericField	Abstract component that defines the functionality for TFloatField, TBCDField, TCurrencyField, TIntegerField, TSmallIntField and TWordField
TSmallIntField	Integer values in the range −32,768..32,767
TStringField	Text values up to 255 characters
TTimeField	Time values
TVarBytesField	Fixed length binary data up to 65,535 bytes
TWordField	Integer values in the range 0..65,535

The TField Class Heirarchy

An outline of the TField branch of the VCL class hierarchy as it appears in the Object Browser looks something like Figure 4.1.

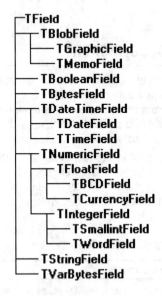

FIGURE 4.1 TFIELD CLASS HEIRARCHY.

COMPONENT REFERENCE

TField

Unit

DB

Inherits from

TComponent

Description

Abstract parent class that supplies much of the basic functionality for all its descendants. All TField components inherit all the functionality of the TField class, although not all the TField components will use all this functionality. The following tables summarize the properties (Table 4.2), methods (Table 4.3), and events (Table 4.4) for the TField class.

TABLE **4.2** TField Properties

Property	Data Type	Run-time Only	Read-Only	Description
Alignment	TAlignment	No	No	Centers or left or right justifies the display of field data in a data-aware component such as DBGrid or DBEdit
AsBoolean	Boolean	Yes	No	Allows access or assignment of a TBooleanField or TStringField field value as a Boolean value
AsDateTime	TDateTime	Yes	No	Allows access or assignment of a TDateField, TDateTimeField, TStringField, or TTimeField field value as a TDateTime value
AsFloat	Double	Yes	No	Allows access or assignment of a TBDCField, TCurrencyField, TFloatField, or TStringField field value as a floating-point value
AsInteger	Longint	Yes	No	Allows access or assignment of a TIntegerField, TSmallIntField, TStringField, or TWordField field value as an integer value
AsString	String	Yes	No	Accesses any TField descendant's field value as a string or converts a string to the field's native data type on assignment (except for TBlobField, TGraphicField, or TMemoField)
Calculated	Boolean	No	No	Specifies whether the field is a calculated field
CanModify	Boolean	Yes	Yes	Specifies whether the field value can be modified
DataSet	TDataSet	Yes	No	Specifies the DataSet to which the TField belongs
DataSize	Word	Yes	Yes	Memory storage requirements of field, in bytes
DataType	TFieldType	Yes	Yes	Specifies the field's data type (ftFloat, ftInteger, etc.)
DisplayLabel	String	No	No	Specifies a column heading label for a DBGrid object (defaults to field name)
DisplayName	PString	Yes	Yes	Field name for display purposes; returns DisplayLabel if not null or FieldName
DisplayText	String	Yes	Yes	Contains the field value as a string, for use by the data-aware controls in non-Edit mode
DisplayWidth	Integer	No	No	Display width for field in a DBGrid object; defaults to 10 or field width for TStringField
EditMask	String	No	No	Mask used for formatted display and data entry of field value

continued

TABLE 4.2 CONTINUED

PROPERTY	DATA TYPE	RUN-TIME ONLY	READ-ONLY	DESCRIPTION
EditMaskPtr	Pointer	Yes	Yes	Pointer to EditMask property string
FieldName	String	No	No	Name of field that a data-aware control is bound to
FieldNo	Integer	Yes	Yes	Ordinal value of the TField object in relation to the other fields in its DataSet
Index	Integer	No	No	Ordinal offset into the Fields property of the TField's DataSet object; also determines display order in a DBGrid object
IsIndexField	Boolean	Yes	Yes	Specifies whether an index exists for a field
IsNull	Boolean	Yes	Yes	Specifies whether a field's value is NULL
ReadOnly	Boolean	No	No	If True, field cannot be written to
Required	Boolean	No	No	If True, field must not be NULL
Size	Integer	Yes	No	Specifies the size of the field
Text	String	Yes	No	Contains the edit-mode string used to display text in some of the data aware controls
Visible	Boolean	No	No	Determines whether a field can be displayed in a DBGrid component

TABLE 4.3 TFIELD METHODS

METHOD	SCOPE	DESCRIPTION
Assign	Public	Copies data from one field to another
AssignValue	Public	Assigns a value of any data type to a field
Clear	Public	Sets a field's value to NULL
FocusControl	Public	Switches focus to the first data-aware control on the form
GetData	Public	Returns raw data from field without conversion
IsValidChar	Public	Determines whether an input character is valid for a particular field type
SetData	Public	Used to assign raw data to the field

TABLE 4.4 TFIELD EVENTS

EVENT	DATA TYPE	DESCRIPTION
OnChange	TFieldNotifyEvent	Activated whenever the data in the field changes or when a bound data-aware control attempts to store changes to the record
OnGetText	TFieldGetTextEvent	Activated when a reference is made to the Text or DisplayText properties
OnSetText	TFieldSetTextEvent	Activated when a reference is made to the Text property
OnValidate	TFieldNotifyEvent	Activated when a field is modified or when a bound data-aware control attempts to store changes to the record

TFIELD.ALIGNMENT PROPERTY

Applies to

TBCDField, TBooleanField, TCurrencyField, TDateField, TDateTimeField, TFloatField, TIntegerField, TSmallintField, TStringField, TTimeField and TWordField components

Declaration

```
{ DB.PAS }
property Alignment: TAlignment read FAlignment write SetAlignment
   default taLeftJustify;
{ CLASSES.PAS }
TAlignment = (taLeftJustify, taRightJustify, taCenter);
```

Description

The Alignment property is used by a TField component to center, or left or right justify the display of field data in data-aware control, such as a DBGrid or DBEdit component. The data in the field are not affected by this setting. The Alignment property is an enumerated type (TAlignment) that can be set to one of the values shown in Table 4.5:

TABLE 4.5 TFIELD.ALIGNMENT VALUES

VALUE	DESCRIPTION
taCenter	Centers the field value
taLeftJustify	Left justifies the field value (default)
taRightJustify	Right justifies the field value

Example

```
{ force a number to be left justified in a data-aware control }
Table1.FieldByName('CREDITBAL').Alignment := taLeftJustify;
```

Notes

Do not confuse this with the Align property of some data-aware controls, which aligns the control within its Parent.

See Also

TNumeric.DisplayFormat, TNumeric.EditFormat

TFIELD.AsBOOLEAN PROPERTY

Applies to

TBooleanField and TStringField components

Declaration

```
{ DB.PAS }
property AsBoolean: Boolean read GetAsBoolean write SetAsBoolean;
```

Description

Run-time only. Allows access or assignment of a TBooleanField or TStringField field value as a Boolean value. When used on a TBooleanField component, conversion is unnecessary—use the Value property instead to reduce overhead. When accessing TStringField components, if the field value begins with 'T', 't', 'Y', or 'y', AsBoolean is set to True; otherwise, it is set to False. Assigning a Boolean value to a TStringField stores a 'T' or 'F' in the field.

Example

```
{ APPROVED is a character field of length 1 or greater }
var
    IsApproved: Boolean;
begin
    { read the string value from the field as a Boolean value }
    IsApproved := Table1.FieldByName('APPROVED').AsBoolean;
    if IsApproved then
        { assign the value 'F' to the field }
        Table1.FieldByName('APPROVED').AsBoolean := False;
end;
```

Notes

This property does not make sense when applied to a TBooleanField component, as its data do not require conversion.

See Also

TField.AsString

TFIELD.AsDATETIME PROPERTY

Applies to

TDateField, TDateTimeField, TStringField and TTimeField components

Declaration

```
{ DB.PAS }
property AsDateTime: TDateTime read GetAsDateTime
   write SetAsDateTime;
```

Description

Run-time only. Allows access or assignment of a TDateField, TDateTimeField, TStringField, or TTimeField field value as a TDateTime value. For TStringField components, converts a TDateTime value to a string on assignment and converts a string to a TDateTime value when accessing. The resulting string is formatted according to the date and time settings currently in effect in Windows.

Example

```
{ NOTE: assumes DATESTRING is a string field that contains the current date
   and time }
var
   RightNow: TDateTime;
begin
   RightNow := Now;
   { example of assignment to a string field }
   Table1.FieldByName('DATESTRING').AsDateTime := RightNow;
   {example of accessing a string field }
   RightNow := Table1.FieldByName('DATESTRING').AsDateTime;
end;
```

Notes

Only makes sense when used on a TStringField component, as the other applicable components do not require conversion.

See Also

TField.AsFloat

TFIELD.ASFLOAT PROPERTY

Applies to

TBCDField, TCurrencyField, TFloatField, and TStringField components.

Declaration

```
{ DB.PAS }
property AsFloat: Double read GetAsFloat write SetAsFloat;
```

Description

Run-time only. Allows access or assignment of a TBDCField, TCurrencyField, TFloatField, or TStringField field value as a floating-point value. For TStringField components, converts a float to a string on assignment and converts a string to a float on access.

Example

```
{ Assumes STRFLOAT is a string field that contains a valid string representation
  of a floating point number }
var
   AFloat: Real;
begin
   AFloat := 123.456;
   { example of assignment to a string field }
   Table1.FieldByName('STRFLOAT').AsFloat := AFloat;
   {example of accessing a string field }
   AFloat := Table1.FieldByName('STRFLOAT').AsFloat;
end;
```

Notes

Makes sense only when used on a TStringField component, as the other applicable components do not require conversion. An exception is raised if the value in a TStringField field is not a valid representation of a floating-point number.

See Also

TField.AsString

TFIELD.ASINTEGER PROPERTY

Applies to

TIntegerField, TSmallIntField, TStringField, and TWordField.

Declaration

```
{ DB.PAS }
property AsInteger: Longint read GetAsInteger write SetAsInteger;
```

Description

Run-time only. Allows access or assignment of a TIntegerField, TSmallIntField, TStringField, or TWordField field value as an integer value. For TStringField components, converts an integer to a string on assignment to the field and converts from a string to an integer when accessing the field.

Example

```
{ Assumes STRINGINT is a string field that contains a valid string representation
  of an integer }
var
   I: Integer;
begin
   I := 123;

   { example of assignment to a string field }
   Table1.FieldByName('STRINGINT').AsInteger := I;

   {example of accessing a string field }
   I := Table1.FieldByName('STRINGINT').AsInteger;
end;
```

Notes

Makes sense only when used with TStringField, as the other applicable components do not require conversion. An exception is raised if the value in a TStringField field is not a valid representation of an integer.

See Also

TField.AsFloat

TFIELD.ASSTRING PROPERTY

Applies to

All TField components for a read operation, all except TBlobField, TBytesField, TBytesField, TGraphicField, TMemoField, and TVarBytesField components for assignment operations.

Declaration

```
{ DB.PAS }
property AsString: string read GetAsString write SetAsString;
```

Description

Run-time only. Accesses any TField component's field value as a string or converts a string to the field's native data type on assignment (except for TBlobField, TGraphicField or TMemoField).

For TBlobField, TBytesField, TGraphicField, TMemoField, and TVarBytesField components, returns the name of the data type in parentheses (e.g., '(Blob)'), and an exception is raised when an attempt to assign a value to any of these component types. Use Assign, LoadFromFile, LoadFromStream, SaveToFile and/or SaveToStream for these components.

For the numeric fields, converts from a string to the appropriate numeric type on assignment, or from the numeric type to a string on access. For Boolean fields, converts True values to 'T' and False values to 'F' on access and returns True only if the text being assigned begins with 'T','t','Y', or 'y'.

Example

```
{ Various examples of assigning and accessing field values }
var
    S: string;
begin
    { examples of valid assignment to fields }
    Table1.FieldByName('BOOLEAN').AsString    := 'T';
    Table1.FieldByName('BCD').AsString        := '123.456';
    Table1.FieldByName('DATE').AsString       := '01/02/03';
    Table1.FieldByName('DATETIME').AsString   := '01/02/03 01:01:01';
    Table1.FieldByName('FLOAT').AsString      := '123.456';
    Table1.FieldByName('INTEGER').AsString    := '12345';
    Table1.FieldByName('SMALLINT').AsString   := '123';
    Table1.FieldByName('STRING').AsString     := 'Redundant!';
    Table1.FieldByName('TIME').AsString       := '01:01:01';
    Table1.FieldByName('WORD').AsString       := '123456';
    {examples of accessing field values }
    S := Table1.FieldByName('BOOLEAN').AsString;      { 'T' }
    S := Table1.FieldByName('BCD').AsString;          { '123.456' }
    S := Table1.FieldByName('DATE').AsString;         { '01/02/03' }
    S := Table1.FieldByName('DATETIME').AsString;     { '01/02/03 01:01:01' }
    S := Table1.FieldByName('FLOAT').AsString;        { '123.456' }
    S := Table1.FieldByName('INTEGER').AsString;      { '12345' }
    S := Table1.FieldByName('SMALLINT').AsString;     { '123' }
    S := Table1.FieldByName('STRING').AsString;       { 'Redundant!' }
    S := Table1.FieldByName('TIME').AsString;         { '01:01:01' }
    S := Table1.FieldByName('WORD').AsString;         { '123456' }
    { these fields are read-only for AsString }
    S := Table1.FieldByName('BYTES').AsString;        { '(Byte)' }
    S := Table1.FieldByName('BLOB').AsString;         { '(Blob)' }
    S := Table1.FieldByName('MEMO').AsString;         { '(Memo)' }
    S := Table1.FieldByName('VARBYTES').AsString;     { '(Varbytes)' }
end;
```

Notes

Does not make sense when used on a TStringField component, as the field value does not require conversion.

See Also

TField.Assign, TMemo.LoadFromFile, TMemo.SaveToFile

TField.Assign Method

Applies to

All TField components

Declaration

```
{ DB.PAS }
procedure Assign(Source: TPersistent); override;
```

Description

Copies data from one compatible field to another, as shown in Table 4.6.

TABLE 4.6 COMPATIBILITY RULES FOR ASSIGN METHOD

FIELD TYPE	COMPATIBILITY RULES FOR SOURCE
All fields except TBlobField, TBytesField, TGraphicField, TMemoField and TVarBytesField	Must be of same DataType and Size values as the field, and the size of Source must be 255 bytes or less.
TBlobField, TBytesField, TGraphicField, TMemoField, and TVarBytesField	Source can be a TBlobField, TBytesField, TMemoField, or TVarBytesField field, or a TGraphic, TStrings or TPicture object

Example

```
{ Copy a graphic image from one table to another }
ImageField.Assign(Table2IMAGE);
{ Copy lines from a TMemo component to a memo field }
MemoField.Assign(Memo1.Lines);
```

Notes

Use Assign instead of Value for TBlobField, TBytesField, TGraphicField, TMemoField, and TVarBytesField. Note that Source is a descendant of TPersistent, which means that you can copy from a variety of components, including TGraphic, TImage, TStrings, TIcon, TMetaFile, and so on.

See Also

TField.AssignValue, TField.DataType, TField.Size

TField.AssignValue Method

Applies to

All TField components

Declaration

```
{ DB.PAS }
procedure AssignValue(const Value: TVarRec);
```

Description

Assigns a value of any data type to a field, using the field's AsString, AsInteger, AsBoolean, or AsFloat methods as appropriate, based on the data type of the Value parameter as specified in and from an array of const parameter. If Value is not a string, boolean, integer, or float value but is an object descended from TObject, the field's Assign method is used instead.

Example

```
{ This incorrect example is shown in DELPHI.HLP, but does not actually
  compile - it generates a 'Type Mismatch' error... }
Field1.AssignValue('new string');
{ This correct example (from DB.PAS) shows passing an array of values, each
  element of which is used as parameter to AssignValue }
procedure TDataSet.SetFields(const Values: array of const);
var
   I: Integer;
begin
   for I := 0 to High(Values) do Fields[I].AssignValue(Values[I]);
end;
{ This example compiles, but generates a run-time error 'Invalid Value for
  Field ...' error on assignment }
var
   VarRec: TVarRec;
begin
   VarRec.VInteger := 123;
   IntegerField.AssignValue(VarRec); { generates run-time error! }
end;
```

Notes

The Delphi 1.0 documentation contains an example (shown previously) that implies that you can pass a parameter of various types to AssignValue and that it will call the appropriate AsXXX method to assign value to the field based on the type of parameter passed. The AssignValue method requires a parameter of type TVarRec, which is generated for you automatically when you pass a parameter of type **array of const** to a procedure, as shown in the preceding example.

Note that although you can pacify the compiler by passing a value of TVarRec to AssignValue, a run-time error will still be generated on assignment. This makes the AssignValue method useful only in situations where you are within a procedure or function that has been passed a parameter of type **array of const** that contains values to be assigned to fields.

See Also

TDataSet.SetFields, TField.AsString, TField.AsInteger, TField.AsBoolean, TField.AsFloat, TField.Assign

TFIELD.CALCULATED PROPERTY

Applies to

All TField components

Declaration

```
{ DB.PAS }
property Calculated: Boolean read FCalculated write SetCalculated
   default False;
```

Description

Specifies whether the field is a calculated (derived) field. Calculated fields are not stored in the data set—they are created dynamically at run-time within the TTable component's OnCalcFields event handler.

Example

```
{ This checks to see if the field is a calculated field prior to assigning
   the value... }
if not Table1TAXTOTAL.Calculated then
   Table1TAXTOTAL.Value := 0;
```

Notes

Do not assign a value to a calculated field outside of the OnCalcFields event handler. Use the Calculated flag as shown in the preceeding example to determine whether the field is calculated prior to assignment.

See Also

TTable.OnCalcFields

TFIELD.CANMODIFY PROPERTY

Applies to

All TField components

Declaration

```
{ DB.PAS }
property CanModify: Boolean read FCanModify;
```

Description

Run-time only, read-only. Specifies whether the field value can be modified.

Example

```
{ assumes CREDITLIMIT is a floating-point field }
if Table1CREDITLIMIT.CanModify then
   Table1CREDITLIMIT.Value := Table1CREDITLIMIT.Value * 1.1;
```

Notes

There are other properties on this and other related components that may also affect the ability to modify a field, such as Enabled, Visible and ReadOnly.

See Also

TField.ReadOnly, TField.IsNull

TFIELD.CLEAR METHOD

Applies to

All TField components

Declaration

```
{ DB.PAS }
procedure Clear; virtual;
```

Description

Sets a field's value to NULL

Example

```
Table1DATEFIELD.Clear;      { result: NULL date ( / / ) }
Table1INTEGERFIELD.Clear;   { result: NULL (not zero!) }
Table1STRINGFIELD.Clear;    { result: NULL (not ''!) }
```

Notes

Do not confuse NULL, which is used only in the context of a field's value (or absence thereof), and the reserved word NIL, which is used to indicate a pointer type that points to nothing.

See Also

TField.ReadOnly

TFIELD.DATASET PROPERTY

Applies to

All TField components

Declaration

```
{ DB.PAS }
property DataSet: TDataSet read FDataSet write SetDataSet
    stored False;
```

Description

Run-time only. Specifies the dataset to which the TField object is attached.

Example

```
{ This example switches a TField from one dataset to another, copying data to
    a similar field in another table }
var
    IDField: TIntegerField;
    ID: Longint;
begin
    { create the TField object }
    IDField := TIntegerField.Create(Self):
    IDField.FieldName := 'ID';
    { bind the field object to the first table }
    IDField.DataSet := Table1;
    { retrieve the ID number stored in this column }
    ID := IDField.Value;
    { bind the field object to the second table }
    IDField.DataSet := Table2;
    { assign the ID value to the field }
    IDField.Value := ID;
end;
```

Notes

This value is automatically initialized when creating TField objects at design-time using the Fields Editor. You can also use it to specify a dataset where you are creating the TField objects dynamically at run-time, as shown in the preceeding example.

See Also

TTable, TDataSource

TFIELD.DATASIZE PROPERTY

Applies to

All TField components

Declaration

```
{ DB.PAS }
property DataSize: Word read FDataSize;
```

Description

Run-time only, read-only. Contains the memory storage requirements of the field, in bytes, as shown in Table 4.7.

TABLE 4.7 STORAGE BYTES RETURNED BY TFIELD.DATASIZE

TFIELD DESCENDANT	BYTES RETURNED
TBCDField	18
TBlobField	Size of field
TBooleanField	2
TBytesField	Size of field
TCurrencyField	8
TDateField	4
TDateTimeField	8
TFloatField	8
TGraphicField	Size of field
TIntegerField	4
TMemoField	Size of field
TSmallIntField	2
TStringField	Max text size + 1 (limited to 255 bytes)
TTimeField	4
TWordField	2
TVarBytesField	Size of field

Example

```
{ retrieve the field's storage requirements }
Size := AnyField.DataSize;
```

Notes

Contrast the DataSize property, which returns the data requirements of the field, to Size, which returns the actual data size of the value that the field contains.

See Also

TField.DataType, TField.Size

TFIELD.DATATYPE PROPERTY

Applies to

All TField components

Declaration

```
{ DB.PAS }
property DataType: TFieldType read FDataType;
TFieldType = (ftUnknown, ftString, ftSmallint, ftInteger, ftWord,
    ftBoolean, ftFloat, ftCurrency, ftBCD, ftDate, ftTime, ftDateTime,
    ftBytes, ftVarBytes, ftBlob, ftMemo, ftGraphic);
```

Description

Run-time only, read-only. Specifies the field's data type as an emunerated constant (ftFloat, ftInteger, etc.). The possible values for the data type constants are listed in Table 4.8.

TABLE 4.8 CONSTANTS FOR USE WITH TFIELD.DATATYPE

CONSTANT	DATA TYPE
ftBCD	Binary Coded Decimal
ftBlob	Binary large object
ftBoolean	Boolean
ftBytes	Binary, undefined length
ftCurrency	Formatted floating point
ftDate	Date
ftDateTime	Date/Time
ftFloat	Floating point
ftGraphic	Bitmapped image
ftInteger	Integer
ftMemo	Memo field (long text)
ftString	String
ftSmallint	Small integer
ftTime	Time
ftUnknown	Unknown data type
ftVarBytes	Binary, fixed length
ftWord	Word

Example

```
{ Determine a field's data type and display it }
case MysteryField.DataType of
    ftBCD       : Label1.Caption := 'BCD';
    ftBlob      : Label1.Caption := 'BLOB';
    ftBoolean   : Label1.Caption := 'Boolean';
    ftBytes     : Label1.Caption := 'Bytes';
    ftCurrency  : Label1.Caption := 'Currency';
    ftDate      : Label1.Caption := 'Date';
    ftDateTime  : Label1.Caption := 'DateTime';
    ftFloat     : Label1.Caption := 'Float';
    ftGraphic   : Label1.Caption := 'Graphic';
    ftInteger   : Label1.Caption := 'Integer';
    ftMemo      : Label1.Caption := 'Memo';
    ftString    : Label1.Caption := 'String';
    ftSmallint  : Label1.Caption := 'SmallInt';
    ftTime      : Label1.Caption := 'Time';
    ftUnknown   : Label1.Caption := 'What the heck is this?';
    ftVarBytes  : Label1.Caption := 'VarBytes';
    ftWord      : Label1.Caption := 'Word';
end;
```

Notes

Many of the fields descended from TField differ from their parent class only in that their DataType property is set to the correct value for that field in the component's Create constructor, thus allowing the field data to be handled correctly internally.

See Also

TField.DataSize

TFIELD.DISPLAYLABEL PROPERTY

Applies to

All TField components

Declaration

```
{ DB.PAS }
property DisplayLabel: string read GetDisplayLabel write
    SetDisplayLabel stored IsDisplayLabelStored;
```

Description

Specifies a column heading label for a TDBGrid object (defaults to field name).

Example

```
{ Lowercase all field column headings }
for x := 0 to Table1.FieldCount - 1 do
   Table1.Fields[x].DisplayLabel :=
      LowerCase(Table1.Fields[x].FieldName);
```

Notes

Affects only the column headings as displayed on a DBGrid object.

See Also

TField.DisplayName, TField.FieldName

TFIELD.DISPLAYNAME PROPERTY

Applies to

All TField components

Declaration

```
{ DB.PAS }
property DisplayName: PString read GetDisplayName;
```

Description

Run-time only, read-only. Field name for display purposes. Returns DisplayLabel if assigned, or FieldName otherwise.

Example

```
{ Display the names of all fields from a table in a listbox }
for x := 0 to Table1.FieldCount - 1 do
   ListBox1.Add(Table1.Fields[x].DisplayName);
```

Notes

Uses the same algorithm that Delphi components use to retrieve the name of a field, allowing a single location for modification of a field's displayed name.

See Also

TField.DisplayLabel, TField.FieldName

TFIELD.DISPLAYTEXT PROPERTY

Applies to

All TField components

Declaration

```
{ DB.PAS }
property DisplayText: String read GetDisplayText;
```

Description

Run-time only, read-only. Contains the field value as a string, for use by data-aware controls in non-Edit mode. The OnGetText event can be used to specify how the value is formatted. The rules for formatting a DisplayText value are shown in Table 4.9.

TABLE 4.9 FORMATTING RULES FOR THE DISPLAYTEXT PROPERTY

FIELD TYPE	FORMATTING RULES
TIntegerField, TsmallIntField, TWordField	Uses DisplayFormat property if assigned, otherwise uses Str
TStringField	Uses EditMask property
TBCDField, TFloatField	Calls FloatToTextFmt with DisplayFormat property
TCurrencyField	Calls FloatToTextFmt with either DisplayFormat (if assigned) or the CurrencyDecimals variable using the ffCurrency flag (if DisplayFormat is not assigned)
TDateTimeField	Calls DateToTimeStr with the DisplayFormat property
TDateField	Calls DateToTimeStr with the DisplayFormat property (if assigned) or with the ShortDateFormat variable (if DisplayFormat is not assigned).
TTimeField	Calls DateToTimeStr with the DisplayFormat property (if assigned) or with the LongTimeFormat variable (if DisplayFormat is not assigned)

Example

```
{ Display the contents of the current record in a list box }
for x := 0 to Table1.FieldCount - 1 do
   ListBox1.Items.Add(Table1.Fields[x].DisplayText);
```

Notes

When a data-aware control is in edit mode, the formatting for data entry is taken from the EditText property with the EditMask value applied to it.

See Also

TNumericField.DisplayFormat, TDateTimeField.DisplayFormat

TFIELD.DISPLAYWIDTH PROPERTY

Applies to

All TField components

Declaration

```
{ DB.PAS }
property DisplayWidth: integer read GetDisplayWidth write
SetDisplayWidth stored IsDisplayWidthStored;
```

Description

Display width in characters for a field in a DBGrid object. Defaults to 10 or the actual field width for a TStringField.

Example

```
{ Dynamically adjust DisplayWidth at run-time to show all or only part of a
  column's data }
if Field.DisplayWidth = 10 then
   Field.DisplayWidth := 30
else
   Field.DisplayWidth := 10;
```

Notes

Applies only to the display of a DBGrid column. Note that the width is specified in *characters*, not in pixels. The column width itself may be larger than the DisplayWidth value if the DisplayLabel width is greater than the DisplayWidth, but the field values will still be displayed only as wide as the DisplayWidth property, even if the field values exceed that width.

See Also

TField.DisplayLabel

TFIELD.EDITMASK PROPERTY

Applies to

All TField components. Also applies to the TMaskEdit component.

Declaration

```
{ DB.PAS }
property EditMask: String read GetEditMask write SetEditMask;
```

Description

Mask used for formatted display and data entry of a field value. The mask restricts data entry to the format specified; invalid inputs are disallowed.

A mask is a string of formatting characters separated into three sections, delimited by the character stored in the MaskFieldSeparator typed constant (defaults to a semicolon). The first section is the mask itself. The second section contains a value of 0 or 1 to indicate whether any literal characters that are part of the mask are saved with the data (1) or not (0—the default value). The initial value of this setting is stored in the MaskNoSave typed constant. The third section of the mask contains the character that will be used for blanks, as defined in the DefaultBlank typed constant (defaults to an underscore character).

The MaskFieldSeparator, MaskNoSave and DefaultBlank typed constants may be reassigned new values at run-time, if desired. For example, you may wish to set the DefaultBlank value to a space, instead of an underscore character.

The possible values for mask formatting characters are shown in Table 4.10.

TABLE 4.10 MASK CHARACTERS FOR USE WITH THE EDITMASK PROPERTY

MASK CHARACTER	DESCRIPTION
!	If present in the mask, leading blanks are supressed. If not present, trailing blanks are supressed.
>	Converts all characters between the > and the end of the mask (or a < character, if it exists in the mask) to uppercase.
<	Converts all characters between the < and the end of the mask (or a > character, if it exists in the mask) to lowercase.
<>	If both characters appear in a mask, suppresses case checking. The value can be entered in uppercase, lowercase, or mixed case.
\	Specifies that the character that immediately follows the \ is a literal character. Allows specification of a mask character as a literal character.
L	Requires that the character in this position is an alphabetic character (A..Z,a..z).
l	Permits, but does not require, an alphabetic character in this position.
A	Requires that the character in this position is an alphanumeric character (A..Z,a..z,0-9).
a	Permits, but does not require, an alphanumeric character in this position.
C	Requires a character in this position.
c	Permits, but does not require, a character in this position.
0	Requires a numeric character in this position.
9	Permits, but does not require, a numeric character in this position.
#	Permits, but does not require, a numeric character or a plus sign (+) or minus sign (-) in this position.

:	Delimiter for hours, minutes and seconds in a time display. Uses the value found in the International settings of the Control Panel if different.
/	Delimiter for months, days and years in a date display. Uses the value found in the International settings of the Control Panel if different.
;	Delimiter for mask sections. This character is defined by the MaskSeparator typed constant.
_ (underscore)	Used to represent a noneditable blank character for spacing. Displayed using the value in the DefaultBlank typed constant.

Example

```
{ Typical date mask }
DateField.EditMask        := '!90/00/00;1;_';
{ Formatted social security number - note that the dashes will not be saved
  with the number, saving two bytes per record }
SocialSecurity.EditMask   := '000\-00\-0000;1;_';
{ Standard US phone mask }
USPhone.EditMask          := '!\(999\)_000-0000;1; ';
{ Alternate US phone mask, room for extension }
USPhone2.EditMask         := '999\-000\-0000ccccccc;1; ';
{ Simple AM/PM time entry }
TimeField.EditMask        := '!90:00:00_<Lm;1; ';
{ Zip code mask, last four digits optional }
ZipCodeField.EditMask     := '00000\-9999;1; ';
```

Notes

Do not confuse the EditMask property string with the DisplayFormat and EditFormat property string, which may contain standard format strings (see Format Strings in **DELPHI.HLP**), Date format strings (see FormatDateTime in **DELPHI.HLP**), or numeric formatting strings (see FormatFloat in **DELPHI.HLP**) depending on the DataType for the TField component.

See Also

Input Mask Editor in **DELPHI.HLP**, TDateTimeField.DisplayFormat, TDateTimeField.EditFormat, TField.DisplayText, TField.EditMaskPtr, TNumericField.DisplayFormat, TNumericField.EditFormat

TFIELD.EDITMASKPTR PROPERTY

Applies to

All TField components

Declaration

```
{ DB.PAS }
property EditMaskPtr: PString read FEditMask;
```

Description

Run-time only, read-only. Pointer to EditMask property string.

Example

```
{ Assign the mask for one field from another field }
Table1FIRSTFIELD.EditMask := Table1SECONDFIELD.EditMaskPtr^;
```

See Also

TField.EditMask

TFIELD.FIELDNAME PROPERTY

Applies to

All TField components

Declaration

```
{ DB.PAS }
property FieldName: String read GetFieldName write SetFieldName;
```

Description

Name of field that a data-aware control is bound to. This value is assigned automatically when you create TField components using the Fields Editor. For noncalculated fields, this corresponds to the physical name of the column in the underlying dataset. For calculated fields, you must assign the FieldName property when you define the field.

Example

```
{ This example defines a TField object at run-time }
var
    StringField: TStringField;
begin
    { Sspecify the table to bind the TField object to }
    StringField.DataSet := Table1;
    { Assign the field name prior to accessing the data }
    StringField.FieldName := 'COMPANY';
    { Assign a value to the field }
    Table1.Edit;
    StringField.Value := 'Acme, Incorporated';
    Table1.Post;
end;
```

Notes

A exception occurs if FieldName does not exist in the underlying dataset for non-calculated fields.

See Also

TField.DisplayName

TFIELD.FIELDNO PROPERTY

Applies to

All TField components

Declaration

```
{ DB.PAS }
property FieldNo: Integer read FFieldNo;
```

Description

Run-time only, read-only. Ordinal value of the TField object in relation to the other fields in its dataset.

Example

```
{ Retrieve and display field positions within the table }
with Table1 do
begin
   for x := 0 to length(Fields) do
      Memo1.Lines.Add('Field ' + Fields[x].FieldName +
         ' is at position ' + IntToStr(Fields[x].FieldNo));
end;
```

Notes

Do not confuse this with the Index property, which specifies the order of the field within a dataset's Fields array.

See Also

TDataSet.Fields, TField.DisplayName, TField.Index

TFIELD.FOCUSCONTROL METHOD

Applies to

All TField components

Declaration

```
{ DB.PAS }
procedure FocusControl;
```

Description

Switches focus to the first data-aware control on the form associated with a TField object.

Example

```
{ This example shows how to force focus to the first data-aware control for
  an invalid zip code entry using the dataset's BeforePost event handler }
procedure Form1.Table1BeforePost(DataSet: TDataSet);
begin
   if ZipCodeField.IsNull then
   begin
      MessageDlg('Zip code required!',mtWarning,[mbOK],0);
      ZipCodeField.FocusControl;
   end;
end;
```

Notes

If there are more than one data-aware controls attached to the TField component, the focus will be set to the first control in tab order.

See Also

TDataset.BeforePost, et al

TFIELD.GETDATA METHOD

Applies to

All TField components, TParam component

Declaration

```
{ DB.PAS }
function GetData(Buffer: Pointer): Boolean;
```

Description

Returns raw data from the field without conversion. Unlike AsString, DisplayText, and Text, GetData does not perform any kind of conversion or translation of data while retrieving it.

Example

```
{ Allocate sufficient memory to contain the data }
GetMem(Buffer, Field.DataSize);
{ Retrieve the data from the field }
Field.GetData(Buffer);
{ Do something with the data... }
{ Deallocate the memory }
FreeMem(Buffer, DataSize);
```

Notes

Buffer must be of sufficient size to contain the data returned. Use the DataSize property to determine the size that Buffer must be, as shown in the preceding example.

See Also

TField.AsString, TField.DisplayText, TField.Text, TQuery.Params

TFIELD.INDEX PROPERTY

Applies to

All TField components

Declaration

```
{ DB.PAS }
property Index: Integer read GetIndex write SetIndex stored False;
```

Description

Ordinal offset into the Fields property of the TField's DataSet object. Also determines display order in a DBGrid object.

Example

```
{ This example uses the Index property to avoid calling the FieldByName
  property repeatedly from within a loop }
with Table1 do
begin
   { Retrieve the Index values }
   FirstNameIndex := Table1.FieldByName('FIRST').Index;
   LastNameIndex := Table1.FieldByName('LAST').Index;
   { Go to top of file }
   First;
   { For each record in this table }
   while not EOF do
```

```
begin
   { Convert the field values to uppercase }
   Fields[FirstNameIndex].Value :=
      UpperCase(Fields[FirstNameIndex].Value);
   Fields[LastNameIndex].Value :=
      UpperCase(Fields[LastNameIndex].Value);
   { Process next record }
   Next;
   end;
end;
```

Notes

Do not confuse this with the FieldNo property, which stores the physical position of the field within the underlying DataSet. The Index property is sometimes used to avoid the overhead of calling FieldByName repeatedly for each field, as shown in the preceeding example.

See Also

TField.FieldNo

TFIELD.ISINDEXFIELD PROPERTY

Applies to

All TField components

Declaration

```
{ DB.PAS }
property IsIndexField: Boolean read GetIsIndexField;
```

Description

Run-time only, read-only. Specifies whether an index exists for a field.

Example

```
{ This example shows a simple search routine that is automatically optimized
  if an active index exists for the current field }
var
   CurrField: TField;
begin
   { Assumes CurrField is a string field }
   CurrField := Table1ZIPCODE;
   { If this is an indexed field, and the index is active... }
   if CurrField.IsIndexField then
   begin
```

```
      { Optimize search by utilizing any existing indexes }
      Table1.SetKey;
      CurrField.Value := Edit1.Text;
      Table1.GotoKey;
   end else
   begin
      { Search each record individually }
      Table1.First;
      while not Table1.EOF do
      begin
         If CurrField.Value = Edit1.Text then break;
         Table1.Next;
      end;
   end;
end;
```

Notes

IsIndexField will return only True if the index is not an expression index and the index is currently active (i.e., the dataset's IndexName or IndexFieldNames properties are set to the name of the index for that field). This is the same list of indexes that displays in the dataset's IndexFieldNames property drop-down list in the Object Inspector.

See Also

TTable.IndexName, TTable.IndexFieldNames

TFIELD.ISNULL PROPERTY

Applies to

All TField components

Declaration

```
{ DB.PAS }
property IsNull: Boolean read GetIsNull;
```

Description

Run-time only, read-only. Specifies whether a field's value is NULL.

Example

```
{ Ensure a field has a valid date value }
if DateField.IsNull then
   DateField.Value := Date;
```

Notes

A field's value is NULL when no data has been assigned to it. This is not the same as having an inert value, such as zero. You can also use the TField.Clear method to set a field's value to NULL.

See Also

TField.Required, TField.Clear

TFIELD.ISVALIDCHAR PROPERTY

Applies to

All TField components

Declaration

```
{ DB.PAS }
function IsValidChar(InputChar: Char): Boolean; virtual;
```

Description

Run-time only. Determines whether an input character is valid for a particular field type.

Example

```
{ This example replaces the annoying beep that you hear on invalid character
  entry with a message }
procedure TForm1.DBEdit1KeyPress(Sender: TObject; var Key: Char);
begin
   { Check the character for validity }
   if not Table1.FieldByName(DBEdit1.DataField).IsValidChar(Key) then
   begin
      { Display a message to inform the user }
      MessageDlg('Invalid input again!',mtInformation,[mbOK],0);
      { Prevent that annoying beep from occuring }
      Key := #0;
   end;
end;
```

Notes

This function is used internally by the data-aware controls to restrict input to specific values. The TInteger, TSmallInt, and TWord field allow only the '0' through '9', '+' and '-' characters. The TBCDField and TFloatField also allow 'E', 'e' and the value of the DecimalSeparator variable. All other fields accept all characters.

See Also

DecimalSeparator in **DELPHI.HLP**

TFIELD.ONCHANGE EVENT

Applies to

All TField components

Declaration

```
{ DB.PAS }
property OnChange: TFieldNotifyEvent read FOnChange write FOnChange;
TFieldNotifyEvent = procedure(Sender: TField) of object;
```

Description

This event is activated whenever the data in the field changes or when a bound data-aware control attempts to store changes to the record.

Example

```
{ Hide unneeded controls depending on the value of a field }
procedure TForm1.PayTypeFieldChange(Sender: TField);
begin
   if PayTypeField.Value = 'CASH' then
   begin
      CardExpireDateEdit.Visible := False;
      CardNumberEdit.Visible := False;
      DriversLicenseEdit.Visible := False;
   end else if PayTypeField.Value = 'CHECK' then
   begin
      CardExpireDateEdit.Visible := False;
      CardNumberEdit.Visible := False;
      DriversLicenseEdit.Visible := True;
   end else if PayTypeField.Value = 'CHARGE' then
   begin
      CardExpireDateEdit.Visible := True;
      CardNumberEdit.Visible := True;
      DriversLicenseEdit.Visible := False;
   end;
end;
```

Notes

The OnChange event will not be activated until the user attempts to leave the edit control.

See Also

TDataSet.OnDataChange, TField.OnValidate

TField.OnGetText Event

Applies to

All TField components

Declaration

```
{ DB.PAS }
property OnGetText: TFieldGetTextEvent read FOnGetText
   write FOnGetText;
TFieldGetTextEvent = procedure(Sender: TField; var Text: string;
   DisplayText: Boolean) of object;
```

Description

Activated when a reference is made to the Text or DisplayText properties. The Text property is supplied in display format if DisplayText property has been assigned a value (in which case, the DisplayText parameter will be True); otherwise, the EditFormat property is used.

Example

```
{ Override the default formatting for a field on reference. This example
  inserts formatting characters into a social security number that was
  stored without them. }
procedure TForm1.Table1SOCIALSECURITYGetText(Sender: TField;
  var Text: OpenString; DisplayText: Boolean);
begin
   if DisplayText then
   begin
      { Stored value: 123456789 }
      Text := Table1SOCIALSECURITY.Value;
      { Add formatting }
      Insert('-',Text,4);
      Insert('-',Text,7);
      { Text is now formatted as: 123-45-6789 }
   end;
end;
```

Notes

If an event handler method has been assigned to OnGetText, the default processing of Text and DisplayText will not be performed. It is assumed that the event handler method will perform all the necessary processing to convert and display the value. Attempts to reference Text in an assignment statement within OnGetText will cause the OnGetText event to be fired again, resulting in a recursive loop.

See Also

TField.DisplayText, TField.OnSetText, TField.Text

TFIELD.ONSETTEXT EVENT

Applies to

All TField components

Declaration

```
{ DB.PAS }
property OnSetText: TFieldSetTextEvent read FOnSetText
   write FOnSetText;
TFieldSetTextEvent = procedure(Sender: TField; const Text: string)
   of object;
```

Description

The OnSetText event is activated when an attempt is made to assign a value to the Text property, which in turn is assigned to the field's Value property.

Example

```
{ Override the default handling of field assignment }
procedure TForm1.Table1ZIPCODESetText(Sender: TField;
   const Text: String);
begin
   { Check for invalid US zip code entry }
   if length(Text) < 10 then
      Sender.AsString := Copy(Text,1,5)
   else
      Sender.AsString := Text;
end;
```

Notes

If an event handling method has been assigned to OnSetText, the default processing will not be performed. In that case, the event handler must store the value of Text in the field's Value property.

See Also

TField.Text, TField.DisplayText, TField.OnGetText

TFIELD.ONVALIDATE EVENT

Applies to

All TField components

Declaration

```
{ DB.PAS }
property OnValidate: TFieldNotifyEvent read FOnValidate
   write FOnValidate;
TFieldNotifyEvent = procedure(Sender: TField) of object;
```

Description

Activated when a field is modified or when a bound data-aware control attempts to store changes to the record.

Example

```
{ Perform field-level validation }
procedure TForm1.Table1PUR_PRICEValidate(Sender: TField);
begin
   { Disallow negative price entries }
   if StrToFloat(PurchPriceEdit.Text) < 0 then
   begin
      MessageDlg('Value must be positive!',mtWarning,[mbOK],0);
      PurchPriceEdit.Text := '0';
      { Force focus back to that control }
      Sender.FocusControl;
   end;
end;
```

Notes

The OnValidate event is a good place to handle field-level validation or formatting of data that will be stored in a field.

See Also

TField.OnChange, TTable.OnDataChange

TFIELD.READONLY PROPERTY

Applies to

All TField components. Also applies to TTable components, Edit and Memo controls and all data-aware controls.

Declaration

```
{ DB.PAS }
property ReadOnly: Boolean read FReadOnly write FReadOnly
    default False;
```

Description

Determines whether a field can be modified or not.

Example

```
{ Disable a field based on the value of another field }
Table1CREDITLIMIT.ReadOnly := (Table1ACTIVE.AsBoolean = False);
```

Notes

Fields that are marked ReadOnly in a DBGrid component are skipped over when the Tab key is pressed.

See Also

TField.Required

TFIELD.REQUIRED PROPERTY

Applies to

All TField components. Also applies to TFieldDef objects

Declaration

```
{ DB.PAS }
property Required: Boolean read FRequired write FRequired
    default False;
```

Description

Determines whether a field is allowed to contain a NULL value or not.

Example

```
{ Perform field-level validation in a data aware control's OnExit event
  handler to insure that the field's value is entered correctly }
procedure TForm1.DBEdit1Exit(Sender: TObject);
begin
   { Check to see if field is required but empty }
   if (Table1COMPANY.Required) and (DBEdit1.Text = '') then
```

```
  begin
    { Display a warning message }
    MessageDlg('Field cannot be left empty!',mtWarning,[mbOK],0);

    { Set focus back to the control }
    DBEdit1.SetFocus;
  end;
end;
```

Notes

This property is enforced at the record level. A user is not notified of the field's read-only status until an attempt is made to post the record or move to another record. Use the data-aware control's OnExit event handler as shown in the preceeding example will enforce field-level validation.

See Also

TField.Clear, TFieldDef

TFIELD.SETDATA METHOD

Applies to

All TField components. Also applies to TParam objects

Declaration

```
{ DB.PAS }
procedure SetData(Buffer: Pointer);
```

Description

Allows assignment of raw data to a field. Does not perform any translation or interpretation of the data.

Example

```
{ Allocate sufficient memory to contain the data }
GetMem(Buffer, Field.DataSize);
{ Initialize the buffer with data to store... }
{ Assign the contents of Buffer to the field }
Field.SetData(Buffer);
{ Deallocate the buffer memory }
FreeMem(Buffer, Field.DataSize);
```

Notes

The Buffer parameter must have sufficient memory allocated to contain the data—use DataSize to determine how much memory to allocate for Buffer.

See Also

TFieldDef, TField.DataSize, TField.GetData

TField.Size Property

Applies to

TBCDField, TBlobField, TBytesField, TGraphicField, TIntegerField, TMemoField, TStringField, TTimeField and TVarBytesField components; also TFieldDef and TFont objects

Declaration

```
{ DB.PAS }
property Size: Word read FSize write SetSize;
```

Description

Run-time only. Specifies the size of the field as illustrated in Table 4.11.

TABLE 4.11 INTERPRETATION OF THE SIZE PROPERTY FOR VARIOUS FIELD TYPES

FIELD TYPE	INTERPRETATION OF SIZE
TBCDField	Number of digits to the right of the decimal point.
TBlobField, TBytesField, TGraphicField, TMemoField, and TVarBytesField	Size of the field as stored in the dataset.
TStringField, TIntegerField, TTimeField	Number of bytes reserved for the field in the field's dataset.

Example

```
{ Reset the Size field - does not affect the underlying data, just the
  interpretation of it }
Table1.Close;
Table1STRINGFIELD.Size := 10;
Table1.Open;
```

Notes

An exception is generated if the value for Size for a TStringField, TBCDField, TBytesField, TVarBytesField, TBlobField, TMemoField or TGraphicField is out of range or invalid (i.e., less than zero). An exception is always generated when an attempt is made to adjust the Size of a TTimeField or a TIntegerField.

See Also

TField.DataType

TField.Text Property

Applies to

TBCDField, TBooleanField, TCurrencyField, TDateField, TDateTimeField, TFloatField, TIntegerField, TSmallintField, TStringField, TTimeField and TWordField components

Declaration

```
{ DB.PAS }
property Text: String read GetEditText write SetEditText;
```

Description

Run-time only. Contains the string value of the field, used to display text in some of the data aware controls in edit mode. If an event handler has been assigned to OnGetText, the Text property relies on whatever formatting is supplied within that event handler. Otherwise, the formatting for the Text string depends on the field type, as shown in Table 4.12.

TABLE 4.12 FORMATTING OF THE TEXT PROPERTY FOR VARIOUS FIELD TYPES

FIELD TYPE	FORMATTING OF TEXT
TBCDField, TFloatField	FloatToTextFmt is called with the value contained in EditFormat (if assigned) or the value of DisplayFormat (if EditFormat is not assigned a value).
TCurrencyField	FloatToTextFmt is called. If a value is assigned to either EditFormat or DisplayFormat, FloatToTextFmt is called with that value. Otherwise, it is called with the ffCurrency flag and the CurrencyDecimals variable.
TDateField	DateTimeToStr is called with either the DisplayFormat value (if assigned) or the ShortDateFormat value (if DisplayFormat is not assigned).
TDateTimeField	DateTimeToStr is called with the DisplayFormat value.
TIntegerField, TSmallIntField, TWordField	If a value is assigned to either EditFormat or DisplayFormat, FloatToTextFmt is called with that value. Otherwise, Str is called.
TStringField	Uses AsString property.
TTimeField	DateTimeToStr is called with either the DisplayFormat value (if assigned) or the LongTimeFormat value (if DisplayFormat is not assigned).

Notes

See the section on DisplayFormat and EditFormat for a complete description of the interaction between Text and those properties.

See Also

TField.OnGetText, TNumericField.DisplayFormats, TDateTimeField.DisplayFormat

TFIELD.VISIBLE PROPERTY

Applies to

All TField components

Declaration

```
{ DB.PAS }
property Visible: Boolean read FVisible write SetVisible
   default True;
```

Description

Determines whether a field can be displayed as a column in a DBGrid component.

Example

```
{ Toggle the display of a given column in a DBGrid based on the value of a
  checkbox - assumes FaxPhoneField is attached to the same dataset as the
  DBGrid in question... }
FaxPhoneField.Visible := HasFaxCheckbox.Checked;
```

Notes

The value of the Visible property does not affect whether the field can be accessed at run-time. It affects only whether the field is displayed on a DBGrid component or not.

See Also

TField.DisplayWidth, TField.DisplayLabel

TBCDField

Unit

DBTABLES

Inherits from

TNumericField

Description

The TBCDField component inherits most of its functionality from TNumericField and TFloatField. A TBCDField component is designed to attach to a binary coded decimal field in a DataSet. There are no additional methods or events other than those defined by TNumericField and TFloatField. The only additional property, Size, is shown in Table 4.13.

TABLE 4.13 TBDCFIELD PROPERTIES

PROPERTY	DATA TYPE	RUN-TIME ONLY	READ-ONLY	DESCRIPTION
Size	Word	No	No	Defines the number of digits following the decimal point

TBCDFIELD.SIZE PROPERTY

Applies to
TBCDField component

Declaration
```
{ DBTABLES.PAS }
property Size default 4;
```

Description
The value of Size represents the number of digits to the right of the decimal point.

Example
```
{ Reset the number of digits from 4 (the default value) to 2 }
BCDField.Size := 2;
```

Notes
The Size property is inherited from TField, where it is initially declared. TBCDField simply redefines the Size field to default to a value of 4.

See Also
TField.DataSize

TBlobField

Unit
DBTABLES

Inherits from
TField

Description

The TBlobField component provides a connection to a binary large object field. A BLOB field contains an undefined number of arbitrary bytes. TBlobField inherits much of its functionality directly from TField. In addition, TBlobField redefines the TField.Size property, and defines several additional methods specifically designed to allow the manipulation of binary large objects. The following tables list the properties (Table 4.14), and methods (Table 4.15) defined by TBlobField.

TABLE 4.14 TBLOBFIELD PROPERTIES

PROPERTY	DATA TYPE	RUN-TIME ONLY	READ-ONLY	DESCRIPTION
Size	Word	No	No	Defines the size of the field as stored in the underlying DataSet

TABLE 4.15 TBLOBFIELD METHODS

METHOD	SCOPE	DESCRIPTION
LoadFromFile	Public	Loads a binary object from a file into the field
LoadFromStream	Public	Copies the contents of a specified stream to the field
SaveToFile	Public	Saves the contents of the field to a file
SaveToStream	Public	Copies the contents of the field to a specified stream

TBLOBFIELD.LOADFROMFILE METHOD

Applies to

TBlobField, TGraphicField and TMemoField components

Declaration

```
{ DBTABLES.PAS }
procedure LoadFromFile(const FileName: String);
```

Description

Loads a binary object from a file into the field.

Example

```
{ Event handler for a button that loads an image from a bitmap file into the
  current record }
procedure TForm1.LoadButtonClick(Sender: TObject);
begin
   if OpenDialog1.Execute then
   begin
```

```
        Table1.Edit;
        Table1BMP.LoadFromFile(OpenDialog1.Filename);
        Table1.Post;
    end;
end;
```

Notes

An exception is generated if the dataset is not in dsEdit or dsInsert mode when LoadFromFile is called.

See Also

TBlobField.SaveToFile

TBLOBFIELD.LOADFROMSTREAM METHOD

Applies to

TBlobField, TGraphicField and TMemoField components

Declaration

```
{ DBTABLES.PAS }
procedure LoadFromStream(Stream: TStream);
```

Description

Copies data from a specified stream to the field

Example

```
{ Event handler for a button that loads an image from a stream into the
  current record }
procedure TForm1.LoadButtonClick(Sender: TObject);
begin
    Table1.Edit;
    Table1BMP.LoadFromFile(OpenDialog1.Filename);
    Table1.Post;
end;
```

Notes

An exception is generated if the dataset is not in dsEdit or dsInsert mode when LoadFromStream is called.

See Also

TBlobField.SaveToStream

TBlobField.SaveToFile Method

Applies to

TBlobField, TGraphicField and TMemoField components

Declaration

```
{ DBTABLES.PAS }
procedure SaveToFile(const FileName: String);
```

Description

Saves the contents of the field to a specified file.

Example

```
{ Event handler for the OnClick event for a button that saves a bit-mapped
  image stored in the current record to a specified file }
procedure TForm1.SaveButtonClick(Sender: TObject);
begin
   if OpenDialog1.Execute then
      Table1BMP.SaveToFile(OpenDialog1.Filename);
end;
```

Notes

The DataSet need not be in dsEdit or dsInsert mode for this read-only operation.

See Also

TBlobField.LoadFromFile

TBlobField.SaveToStream Method

Applies to

TBlobField, TGraphicField, and TMemoField components

Declaration

```
{ DBTABLES.PAS }
procedure SaveToStream(Stream: TStream);
```

Description

Saves the contents of the field to a specified stream.

Example

```
{ Event handler for the OnClick event for a button that saves a bit-mapped
  image stored in the current record to a specified stream }
procedure TForm1.SaveToStreamButtonClick(Sender: TObject);
begin
     if Assigned(BitmapStream) then
   Table1BMP.SaveToStream(BitmapStream);
end;
```

Notes

The DataSet need not be in dsEdit or dsInsert mode for this read-only operation.

See Also

TBlobField.LoadFromStream, TBytesField, TVarBytesField, TGraphicField

TBooleanField

Unit

DBTABLES

Inherits from

TField

Description

The TBooleanField component establishes a connection to a boolean (logical) field. A boolean field is one that contains a value that is interpreted as being either True or False. TBooleanField inherits most of its functionality directly from TField. Two additional properties are defined by TBooleanField, as shown in Table 4.16.

TABLE 4.16 TBOOLEANFIELD PROPERTIES

PROPERTY	DATA TYPE	RUN-TIME ONLY	READ-ONLY	DESCRIPTION
DisplayValues	String	No	No	Determines how the value of the field is displayed in a data-aware control
Value	Boolean	Yes	No	Contains the actual value of the field

TBOOLEANFIELD.DISPLAYVALUES PROPERTY

Applies to

TBooleanField component

Declaration

```
{ DBTABLES.PAS }
property DisplayValues: string read GetDisplayValues
  write SetDisplayValues;
```

Description

The DisplayValues property contains the text that is shown in a data-aware component for a TBooleanField value. The DisplayValues string is stored as a text phrase for each value, in the order True, False separated by a semicolon. The default value is 'True;False'.

Example

```
{ Various examples of setting the DisplayValue property }
BooleanField.DisplayValue := 'T;F';
BooleanField.DisplayValue := '1;0';
BooleanField.DisplayValue := 'Affirmative;Negative';
BooleanField.DisplayValue := 'Yes;No';
BooleanField.DisplayValue := 'Logical;Illogical';
BooleanField.DisplayValue := 'On;Off';
BooleanField.DisplayValue := 'Accepted;Denied';
```

Notes

You can set the DisplayValue to reflect the standard terms for True and False (or any other mutually exclusive pairs of values, such as On and Off) for a given industry or language. By contrast, the TField.AsString method simply returns 'T' or 'F' for True or False, respectively.

See Also

TDBCheckbox, TBooleanField.Value, TField.AsString

TBOOLEANFIELD.VALUE PROPERTY

Applies to

TBooleanField component

Declaration

```
{ DBTABLES.PAS }
property Value: Boolean read GetAsBoolean write SetAsBoolean;
```

Description

Contains the actual boolean value of the field.

Example

```
{ TBooleanField.Value can be accessed or assigned directly. This example
  toggles the current value }
BooleanField.Value := not BooleanField.Value;
```

Notes

The AsBoolean method defined in TField will also work for retrieving and assigning values to and from a TBooleanField, but it does not make sense to do so as a boolean value does not require conversion. Use the Value property instead.

See Also

TDBCheckBox, TBooleanField.DisplayValue, TField.AsString

TBytesField

Unit

DBTABLES

Inherits from

TField

Description

The TBytesField component establishes a connection to a field in a dataset. The field that TBytesField can connect to is composed of arbitrary bytes with no size limit. TBytesField inherits most of its functionality directly from TField. The only additional property defined by TBytesField is Size, which is actually redeclared from TField.Size with a new default value. The Size property is shown in Table 4.17.

TABLE 4.17 TBYTESFIELD PROPERTIES

PROPERTY	DATA TYPE	RUN-TIME ONLY	READ-ONLY	DESCRIPTION
Size	Word	No	No	Defines the size of the field as stored in the underlying DataSet

TBYTESFIELD.SIZE PROPERTY

Applies to

TBytesField component

Declaration

{ DBTABLES.PAS }
property Size **default** 16;

Description

Contains the size of the field as stored in the DataSet.

Example

{ Retrieve the size of a TBytesField field }
HowBig := TBytesField.Size;

Notes

Unlike TBlobField and its descendants, TBytesField does not have methods designed to manage binary files.

See Also

TBlobField, TVarBytesField

TCurrencyField

Unit

DBTABLES

Inherits from

TFloatField

Description

TCurrencyField establishes a connection to a numeric field formatted for currency values. The data are represented as a binary value in the range $5.0 * 10^{-324}$ to $1.7 * 10^{308,}$, accurate to 15 to 16 places. TCurrencyField inherits all its functionality from TFloatField and defines no new properties, methods, or events of its own.

Notes

The difference between TFloatField and TCurrencyField is essentially how the data are handled internally. TCurrencyField overrides the Create method to set the FCurrency field to True and the DataType property to ftCurrency for this purpose.

See Also

TFloatField

TDateField

Unit

DBTABLES

Inherits from

TDateTimeField

Description

TDateField establishes a connection to a date field. TDateField inherits most of its functionality from TDateTimeField. The Create method is overridden solely to set the field's DataType property to ftDate.

See Also

TDateTimeField, TTimeField

TDateTimeField

Unit

DBTABLES

Inherits from

TField

Description

TDateTimeField establishes a connection to a date/time field. A date/time value is represented as a floating-point number where the integral portion of the number represents the date (in days since 01/01/0001) and the decimal portion of the number represents the time (in seconds since midnight). TDateTimeField adds three properties to the properties, events, and methods inherited form TField, as shown in Table 4.18.

TABLE 4.18 TDATETIMEFIELD PROPERTIES

PROPERTY	DATA TYPE	RUN-TIME ONLY	READ-ONLY	DESCRIPTION
DisplayFormat	String	No	No	Formatting string used for display purposes
EditFormat	String	No	No	Formatting string used for edit purposes
Value	TDateTime	Yes	No	Allows access to the value of the field

TDateTimeField.DisplayFormat Property

Applies to

TDateTimeField, TDateField, TTimeField

Declaration

```
{ DBTABLES.PAS }
property DisplayFormat: string read GetDisplayFormat
   write SetDisplayFormat;
```

Description

The DisplayFormat property is used to determine how the field data will be displayed in data-aware controls such as TDBEdit and TDBGrid.

Example

```
{ Set a display format that results in dates that will display similar to the
   following: 'February 29, 1996' }
DateTimeField.DisplayFormat := 'mmmm dd, yyyy';
```

Notes

If DisplayFormat is not assigned a value, the DateTimeToStr function is called for formatting.

See Also

TDateTimeField.EditMask, TDateTimeField.Text

TDateTimeField.EditMask Property

Applies to

TDateField, TDateTimeField, TTimeField components

Declaration

```
{ DBTABLES.PAS }
property EditMask; { redeclared as Published }
```

Description

The EditMask property is used to determine how the field data will be displayed when editing.

Example

```
{ Set EditMask for standard date entry }
DateField.EditMask := '!99/99/00;1;_';
```

440

Notes

In TDateTimeField, the TField.EditMask property is simply redeclared as Published—no other modifications are made. See the TField.EditMask property for a complete description.

See Also

TField.EditMask, TDateField, TTimeField

TDATETIMEFIELD.VALUE PROPERTY

Applies to

TDateField, TDateTimeField, TTimeField components

Declaration

```
{ DBTABLES.PAS }
property Value: TDateTime read GetAsDateTime write SetAsDateTime;
```

Description

The Value property allows direct access to the field value.

Example

```
{ Add 30 days to all dates }
Table1.First
while not Table1.EOF do
begin
   ExpireDate.Value := ExpireDate.Value + 30;
end;
```

Notes

Accessing or assigning values with the AsDateTime method does not make sense, as the field data is in TDateTime format already and does not require conversion.

See Also

TField.AsString, TField.AsFloat

TFloatField

Unit

DBTABLES

Inherits from

TNumericField

Description

TFloatField establishes a connection to a floating-point field. A TFloatField is represented as a binary value within the range $5.0 * 10^{-324}$ to $1.7 * 10^{308}$, accurate to 15 to 16 places. TFloatField inherits most of its numeric handling capabilities from TNumericField and adds several additional properties specifically designed to handle floating-point values. Table 4.19 lists the additional properties defined by the TFloatField component:

TABLE 4.19 TFLOATFIELD PROPERTIES

PROPERTY	DATA TYPE	RUN-TIME ONLY	READ-ONLY	DESCRIPTION
Currency	Boolean	No	No	If True, field is handled as a currency field
MaxValue	Double	No	No	Specifies the maximum allowable value for the field
MinValue	Double	No	No	Specifies the minimum allowable value for the field
Precision	Integer	No	No	Specifies the number of decimals of precision for the field
Value	Double	Yes	No	Allows direct access to the field data.

TFLOATFIELD.CURRENCY PROPERTY

Applies to

TFloatField component

Declaration

```
{ DBTABLES.PAS }
property Currency: Boolean read FCurrency write SetCurrency
   default False;
```

Description

Specifies whether the field is formatted as a currency field or not. If the value of Currency is True, FloatToText is called with the ftCurrency flag for display text, or ftFixed for edit text. If the value of Currency is False, FloatToTextFmt is called.

Example

```
{ Set the Currency flag }
MoneyField.Currency := False;
```

Notes

Formatting via the Currency flag is done only if both the DisplayFormat and EditFormat properties are not assigned.

See Also

TNumericField.DisplayFormat, TNumericField.EditFormat

TFLOATFIELD.MAXVALUE PROPERTY

Applies to

TFloatField component

Declaration

```
{ DBTABLES.PAS }
property MaxValue: Double read FMaxValue write SetMaxValue;
```

Description

Specifies the maximum value allowed for the field. An exception is raised if an attempt is made to assign a value greater than MaxValue.

Example

```
{ Allow only positive values in the field from 0 to 10000 }
FloatField.MaxValue := 10000;
```

Notes

If both MaxValue and MinValue are zero (the default), the maximum value is limited to the maximum value that the field can contain. If MinValue is less than zero and MaxValue is zero, the maximum value of zero will be enforced.

See Also

TFloatField.MinValue

TFLOATFIELD.MINVALUE PROPERTY

Applies to

TFloatField component

Declaration

```
{ DBTABLES.PAS }
property MinValue: Double read FMinValue write SetMinValue;
```

Description

Specifies the minimum value allowed for the field. An exception is raised if an attempt is made to assign a value less than MinValue.

Example

```
{ Allow only negative values in the field from -10000 to 0 }
FloatField.MinValue := -10000;
```

Notes

If both MaxValue and MinValue are zero (the default), the minimum value is limited to the minimum value that the field can contain. If MaxValue is greater than zero and MinValue is zero, the minimum value of zero will be enforced.

See Also

TFloatField.MaxValue

TFLOATFIELD.PRECISION PROPERTY

Applies to

TFloatField component

Declaration

```
{ DBTABLES.PAS }
property Precision: Integer read FPrecision write SetPrecision
   default 15;
```

Description

The Precision property specifies the number of decimal places for formatting purposes.

Example

```
{ Reset Precision to 4 decimal places }
FloatField.Precision := 4;
```

Notes

Defaults to 15 decimal places.

See Also

TNumericField.DisplayFormat, TNumericField.EditFormat

TFLOATFIELD.VALUE PROPERTY

Applies to

TFloatField

Declaration

```
{ DBTABLES.PAS }
property Value: Double read GetAsFloat write SetAsFloat;
```

Description

Allows direct access or assignment of values to the field.

Example

```
{ Double the double }
FloatField.Value := FloatField.Value * 2;
```

Notes

You could also use AsFloat to access a TFloatField value, but this is not necessary since the field requires no conversion.

See Also

TField.AsString, TField.AsNumeric, TField.AsFloat

TGraphicField

Unit

DBTABLES

Inherits from

TBlobField

Description

TGraphicField establishes a connection to a field that contains a graphic. The field value is represented as an arbitrary set of bytes with no size limit. TGraphicField inherits all its functionality from TBlobField and defines no new properties, events, or methods of its own. The Create method is overridden solely to set the component's DataType property to ftGraphic.

TIntegerField

Unit

DBTABLES

Inherits from

TNumericField

Description

TIntegerField establishes a connection to a field that contains an integral (long integer) value in the range -2,147,483,648 to 2,147,483,647. TIntegerField inherits most of its functionality from TNumericField and adds three properties, as shown in Table 4.20.

TABLE 4.20 TINTEGERFIELD PROPERTIES

PROPERTY	DATA TYPE	RUN-TIME ONLY	READ-ONLY	DESCRIPTION
MaxValue	Longint	No	No	Specifies the maximum allowable value for the field
MinValue	Longint	No	No	Specifies the minimum allowable value for the field
Value	Longint	Yes	No	Allows direct access to the field data

TINTEGERFIELD.MAXVALUE PROPERTY

Applies to

TIntegerField, TSmallIntField and TWordField components

Declaration

```
{ DBTABLES.PAS }
property MaxValue: Longint read FMaxValue write SetMaxValue
  default 0;
```

Description

Specifies the maximum value allowed for the field. An exception is raised if an attempt is made to assign a value greater than MaxValue.

Example

```
{ Allow only positive values in the field from 0 to 10000 }
IntegerField.MaxValue := 10000;
```

Notes

If both MaxValue and MinValue are zero (the default), the maximum value is limited to the maximum value that the field can contain. If MinValue is less than zero and MaxValue is zero, the maximum value of zero will be enforced.

See Also

TIntegerField.MinValue

TINTEGERFIELD.MINVALUE PROPERTY

Applies to

TIntegerField, TSmallIntField and TWordField components

Declaration

```
{ DBTABLES.PAS }
property MinValue: Longint read FMinValue write SetMinValue
   default 0;
```

Description

Specifies the minimum value allowed for the field. An exception is raised if an attempt is made to assign a value less than MinValue.

Example

```
{ Allow only negative values in the field from -10000 to 0 }
IntegerField.MinValue := -10000;
```

Notes

If both MaxValue and MinValue are zero (the default), the minimum value is limited to the minimum value that the field can contain. If MaxValue is greater than zero and MinValue is zero, the minimum value of zero will be enforced.

See Also

TIntegerField.MinValue

TINTEGERFIELD.VALUE PROPERTY

Applies to

TIntegerField, TSmallIntField, and TWordField components

Declaration

```
{ DBTABLES.PAS }
property Value: Longint read GetAsInteger write SetAsInteger;
```

Description

Allows direct access or assignment of values to the field.

Example

```
{ Access and assignment of an integer field using Value }
iVar := IntField.Value;
IntField.Value := IntField.Value + iVar;
```

Notes

You could also use AsInteger to access the field data, but it is not necessary since the field does not require conversion.

See Also

TField.AsString, TField.AsInteger, TField.AsFloat

TMemoField

Unit

DBTABLES

Inherits from

TBlobField

Description

TMemoField establishes a connection to a memo field. A memo field contains an arbitrary set of bytes (normally ASCII or ANSI text) of undefined size. Memo fields are commonly used to store long string information, such as notes. TMemoField inherits most of its functionality from TBlobField, including LoadFromFile and SaveToFile. TMemoField also defines an additional property, as shown in Table 4.21.

TABLE 4.21 TMEMOFIELD PROPERTIES

PROPERTY	DATA TYPE	RUN-TIME ONLY	READ-ONLY	DESCRIPTION
Transliterate	Boolean	Yes	No	Specifies whether translations will be done to the DataSet's Source locale and from the DataSet's Destination locale.

TMEMOFIELD.TRANSLITERATE PROPERTY

Applies to

TMemoField component

Declaration

```
{ DBTABLES.PAS }
property Transliterate: Boolean read FTransliterate
    write FTransliterate default True;
```

Description

Specifies whether translations will be done to and from the DataSet's Source and Destination locales, respectively.

Example

```
{ Disable translation between Source and Destination }
MemoField.Transliterate := False;
```

Notes

Translations are done using the AnsiToNative and NativeToAnsi functions.

See Also

TDataSet.DBLocale, TBatchMove, AnsiToNative and NativeToAnsi in **DELPHI.HLP**

TNumericField

Unit

DBTABLES

Inherits from

TField

Description

TNumericField is an abstract class defined to supply additional functionality for its descendants, which are divided into two categories: floating point and integer fields. TNumericField inherits all of the functionality of TField and defines the additional properties shown in Table 4.22.

TABLE 4.22 TNUMERICFIELD PROPERTIES

PROPERTY	DATA TYPE	RUN-TIME ONLY	READ-ONLY	DESCRIPTION
Alignment	TAlignment	No	No	Determines how data is aligned when displayed
DisplayFormat	String	No	No	Formatting string used for display purposes
EditFormat	String	No	No	Formatting string used for edit purposes

TNUMERICFIELD.ALIGNMENT PROPERTY

Applies to

TBCDField, TCurrencyField, TFloatField, TIntegerField, TSmallIntField and TWordField components

Declaration

```
{ DBTABLES.PAS }
property Alignment default taRightJustify;
```

Description

Specifies how the field data is displayed in a data-aware control.

Example

```
{ Left align a numeric field's text }
Table1BALANCE.Alignment := taLeftJustify
```

Notes

Unlike nonnumeric fields, TNumericField and its descendants display numeric data right justified. The Create constructor is overridden so that the Alignment property can be redeclared to default to taRightJustify.

See Also

TField.Alignment, TNumericField.DisplayFormat, TNumericField.EditFormat

TNumericField.DisplayFormat Property

Applies to

TBCDField, TCurrencyField, TFloatField, TIntegerField, TSmallIntField and TWordField components

Declaration

```
{ DBTABLES.PAS }
property DisplayFormat: String read GetDisplayFormat
    write SetDisplayFormat;
```

Description

The DisplayFormat property is used to determine how the field data will be displayed in data-aware controls such as TDBEdit and TDBGrid.

Example

```
{ Format numbers so that negative numbers are shown in parentheses }
MoneyField.DisplayFormat := '#,##0.00;(#,##0.00)';
```

Notes

The actual format of the string contained in DisplayFormat is dependent on the type of data for the field. For TNumericField descendants, the format string must be compatible with the FloatToTextFmt function.

See Also

TNumericField.EditFormat, FormatFloat in **DELPHI.HLP**

TNumericField.EditFormat Property

Applies to

TBCDField, TCurrencyField, TFloatField, TIntegerField, TSmallIntField and TWordField components

Declaration

```
{ DBTABLES.PAS }
property EditFormat: String read GetEditFormat write SetEditFormat;
```

Description

The EditFormat property is used to format a string for editing purposes.

Example

```
{ An editing format for percentages }
PercentField.EditFormat := '000.00%';
```

Notes

If EditFormat has not been assigned a value and DisplayFormat has, DisplayFormat is used. If neither EditFormat nor DisplayFormat are assigned a value, Str is used for formatting.

See Also

TNumericField.DisplayFormat

TSmallIntField

Unit

DBTABLES

Inherits from

TIntegerField

Description

TSmallIntField establishes a connection to an integer field in the range -32,768 to 32,767. TSmallIntField inherits all its functionality from TIntegerField, and defines no new properties, events or methods of its own. The Create constructor is overridden solely to set the field's DataType property to ftSmallInt and to set the minimum and maximum values allowed to match those of an integer on the current system.

TStringField

Unit

DBTABLES

Inherits from

TField

Description

TStringField establishes a connection to a field that contains up to 255 characters. TStringField inherits most of its functionality directly from TField, and defines several additional properties. as shown in Table 4.23.

TABLE 4.23 TStringField Properties

Property	Data Type	Run-time Only	Read-Only	Description
EditMask	String	No	No	Used to format display value for editing purposes
Size	Word	No	No	Contains the size of the field
Transliterate	Boolean	Yes	No	Determines whether values are translated between the dataset's Source and Destination
Value	String	No	No	Allows direct access to the field's data

TStringField.EditMask Property

Applies to

TStringField component

Declaration

```
{ DBTABLES.PAS }
property EditMask; { redeclared as Published }
```

Description

EditMask controls how the field data is formatted during editing.

Example

```
{ Standard US phone mask }
USPhone.EditMask := '!\(999\)_000-0000;1; ';
```

Notes

This field is defined in TField as a Public variable. It is redefined here in order to make it Published. See TField.EditMask for a complete description of this property.

See Also

TField.EditMask, TStringField.DisplayFormat

TStringField.Size Property

Applies to

TStringField component

Declaration

```
{ DBTABLES.PAS }
property Size default 20; { redeclared as Published }
```

Description

The Size property specifies the number of bytes reserved for the field in the DataSet.

Example

```
{ Determine the size of the string as stored in the dataset, and use it to set
  the DisplayWidth property for a DBGrid component }
StrField.DisplayWidth := StrField.Size;
```

Notes

TStringField.Size is defined in TField as a Public property. It has been redeclared in TStringField in order to reset the default value to 20. See TField.Size for a complete description of this property.

See Also

TField.Size

TStringField.Transliterate Property

Applies to

TStringField component

Declaration

```
{ DBTABLES.PAS }
property Transliterate: Boolean read FTransliterate
  write FTransliterate default True;
```

Description

Specifies whether translations will be done to and from the DataSet's Source and Destination locales, respectively.

Example

```
{ Disable translation between Source and Destination }
StringField.Transliterate := False;
```

Notes

Translations are done using the AnsiToNative and NativeToAnsi functions.

See Also

TDataSet.DBLocale, TBatchMove, AnsiToNative, and NativeToAnsi in **DELPHI.HLP**

TStringField.Value Property

Applies to

TStringField component

Declaration

```
{ DBTABLES.PAS }
property Value: String read GetAsString write SetAsString;
```

Description

Allows direct access to the field's data.

Example

```
{ Lowercase all the text in the field }
StringField.Value := lowercase(StringField.Value);
```

Notes

You could also use the AsString property to access and assign values for a TStringField, but it is not necessary since the field data does not require conversion.

See Also

TField.AsString

TTimeField

Unit

DBTABLES

Inherits from

TDateTimeField

Description

TTimeField establishes a connection to a Time field. TTimeField inherits all its functionality from TDateTimeField and defines no new properties, events, or methods of its own. The Create constructor is overridden solely to set the component's DataType property to ftTime.

See Also

TDateField, TDateTimeField

TVarBytesField

Unit

DBTABLES

Inherits from

TField

Description

TVarBytesField establishes a connect to a field that contains an arbitrary set of up to 65,535 bytes, where the first 2 bytes define the actual length of the field. TVarBytesField inherits most of its functionality from TField, and redefines the Size property as shown in Table 4.24.

TABLE 4.24 TVARBYTESFIELD PROPERTIES

PROPERTY	DATA TYPE	RUN-TIME ONLY	READ-ONLY	DESCRIPTION
Size	Word	No	No	Specifies the size of the field

TVARBYTESFIELD.SIZE PROPERTY

Applies to

TVarBytesField component

Declaration

```
{ DBTABLES.PAS }
property Size default 16;
```

Description

Defines the size of the field in bytes.

Example

```
{ Allocate sufficient memory to contain the data }
GetMem(Buffer, Field.Size);
```

Notes

The Size property is defined in TField as Public and redeclared in TVarBytesSize as a Published property, with a new default of 16. A TVarBytesField stores the size of the field in the first 2 bytes of the data.

See Also

TField.Size, TField.DataSize

TWordField

Unit

DBTABLES

Inherits from

TIntegerField

Description

TWordField establishes a connection to a field that contains a numeric value in the range 0 to 65535. TWordField inherits all its functionality from TIntegerField and defines no new properties, events or methods of its own. The Create constructor is overridden solely to set the component's DataType property to ftWord, and to set the minimum and maximum values for the field to match the definition of a Word on the current system.

BDE Function Reference

The same Borland Database Engine (BDE) is used to power several of Borland's database products and database development platforms, including Paradox for Windows, Visual dBASE, and Delphi.

The BDE was previously referred to as IDAPI, which is short for Integrated Development Application Programming Interface. This is as low level as it gets when dealing with Delphi's database handling features.

From within Delphi, a good majority of the database-related tasks can be handled via pure Delphi calls. For example, when you use a TTable method or property, you are still connecting to the BDE. It is generally much easier to achieve a task through Delphi's objects, if possible, than using BDE functions directly. There may be times, however, when a certain feature you need in the BDE is not accessible via pure Delphi functions or objects. It is in cases like this when you must go directly to the BDE's API functions to get the job done.

The following section contains the complete alphabetical BDE function reference for use by Delphi developers. Under Delphi 1.x, the prototypes for these functions can be found in **DBIPROCS.INT**. This file would have been installed, by default, to your **\DELPHI\DOC** subdirectory. Furthermore, some of the routines use structures defined in **DBITYPES.INT** in this same directory. Constants for the various error codes that DBIResult may contain are in **DBIERRS.INT**. Under Delphi 2.0, the same information is combined within **BDE.INT**.

The majority of the source code examples assume that certain units are being used for that source module. The most commonly required of these will be DbiProcs, DbiTypes, and when using BDE error-handling functions, DbiErrs. For Delphi 2.0, these three units are replaced by the single Bde unit. Examples using the WriteLn function will also require WinCRT and examples using Check require the DB unit.

For the sake of clarity and brevity, we have attempted to make every example a meaningful procedure or function. You will also notice that some examples are used repeatedly to illustrate multiple routines. This is intentional.

All the examples in this chapter can be found on the CD-ROM at the back of this book.

Some examples in this section use the following IsDbiOk function as a generic error-handling routine. This function is also contained in the **BDEREF.PAS** file on the CD-ROM at the back of this book.

```
function IsDbiOk( iResult : DBIResult ) : Boolean;
var
  szErrorStr: DBIMsg;
begin
  Result := iResult = DBIERR_NONE;
  if not Result then
  begin
    DbiGetErrorString( iResult, szErrorStr );
    ShowMessage( 'Error ' + IntToStr(iResult) + ': ' +
                 StrPas( szErrorStr ));
  end; { a DBI Error code }
end; { IsDbiOk() }
```

Another frequently used routine is GetTableCursor, which is included here.

```
function GetTableCursor( oTable : TTable ) : hDBICur;
var
  szTable : Array[0..78] of Char;
begin
  StrPCopy( szTable, oTable.TableName );
  DbiGetCursorForTable( oTable.DBHandle, szTable, nil, Result );
end; { GetTableCursor() }
```

DbiAcqPersistTableLock

Declaration

```
function DbiAcqPersistTableLock ( { Get a persistent lock }
    hDb           : hDBIDb;      { Database handle }
    pszTableName  : PChar;       { Table name }
    pszDriverType : PChar        { Optional Driver type / nil }
  ): DBIResult;
```

Parameters

PARAMETER NAME	DESCRIPTION
hDb	The handle of the database to be locked.
pszTableName	An optional PChar referencing a buffer that holds the table name.
	Paradox: If this parameter is a fully qualified name of a table, including the **.DB** file extension, the pszDriverType parameter is not required.
	If no path is specified, it will be derived from directory where the database associated with hDb is located.
	SQL: This parameter can be a fully qualified name that includes the owner name.

pszDriverType	An optional PChar referencing a buffer holding the driver type. Unless SQL is being used, this will usually be the literal value 'PARADOX' or the equivalent constant value szPARADOX.
	Since this function can be used only on Paradox or SQL tables, the literal 'DBASE' and constant szDBASE are not valid values for this function.
	Paradox: This parameter is required if pszTableName does not include the file extension or if the client application will be overwriting the default file extension (.**DB**).
	If pszTableName does not use the default extension for the table type, and if pszDriverType is NIL, DbiOpenTable will attempt to open the table with the default file extension of all file-based drivers listed in the configuration file in the order that the drivers are listed.
	SQL: This parameter is ignored if the database associated with hDb is an SQL database.

Description

Acquires an exclusive persistent lock on the specified table. This prevents other users from using the table or creating a table of the same name until the lock is released.

When creating a new table, this function can be used to acquire an exclusive table lock as a way to reserve the table name. If the function fails, a table of this name is already in use.

The acquired persistent lock must be explicitly released by the client application by calling DbiRelPersistTableLock.

dBASE. This function is not supported for dBASE tables.

SQL. The behavior of this function will depend on the capabilities of the server being used. Some servers provide non-blocking table locks. Others provide blocking table locks only, while others do not provide table locking at all. Under SQL, table locking is never truly persistent anyway. If the server supports table locking, but locks are not held across transactions, the lock is automatically reacquired after the transaction commits.

Note: The client application must have exclusive access to the table for this function to succeed. If another user is accessing the table, the attempt to lock the table will fail.

DBIResult Return Values

DBIERR_NONE	The persistent lock was acquired successfully.
DBIERR_INVALIDHNDL	The specified database handle is invalid or NIL.
DBIERR_INVALIDPARAM	pszTableName is NIL.
DBIERR_INVALIDFILENAME	An invalid file name was specified by pszTableName.
DBIERR_NOSUCHTABLE	pszTableName is invalid.
DBIERR_UNKNOWNTBLTYPE	The driver type specified by pszTableType is invalid.
DBIERR_LOCKED	The table is already opened by another user, or another session.
DBIERR_NOTSUPPORTED	This function is not supported for dBASE tables.

Example

```
function TableLockOp( ATable : TTable; pOp : OpTableProc ) : Boolean;
var
  iResult : DBIResult;
  bActive : Boolean;
begin
  if not ATable.Active then
  begin
    bActive := False;
    ATable.Active := True;
  end;
  Result := False;
  { Apply the lock }
  iResult := DbiAcqPersistTableLock( ATable.DBHandle, nil, PChar( szPARADOX ));
  if IsDbiOk( iResult ) then
  begin
    { Do the passed operation }
    pOp( ATable );
    { Then, Release the lock }
    iResult := DbiRelPersistTableLock( ATable.DBHandle, nil, PChar( szPARADOX ));
    Result := IsDbiOk( iResult );
  end;
  if not ATable.Active then
    ATable.Active := False;
end; { TableLockOp() }
```

Xbase Equivalent

FLOCK()

See Also

DbiRelPersistTableLock, DbiOpenLockList

DbiAcqTableLock

Declaration

```
function DbiAcqTableLock (        { Lock a table }
    hCursor      : hDBICur;       { Cursor handle }
    eLockType    : DBILockType    { Lock type }
): DBIResult;
```

Parameters

Parameter Name	Description
hCursor	The cursor handle.

eLockType	The table lock type. eLockType can be either dbiWRITELOCK or dbiREADLOCK.
	dbiWRITELOCK When a write lock is placed, it prevents other sessions from placing any locks.
	SQL: A write lock is the same as a read lock. The locking behavior varies depending on the server being used.
	dbiREADLOCK When a read lock is placed, it prevents other users from placing a write lock.
	dBASE: Read locks are automatically upgraded to write lock.
	SQL: Write locks are the same as a read lock. The locking behavior varies depending on the server being used.

Description

Acquires a table-level lock on the table associated with the specified cursor. This function is used to prevent other users from updating a table until the lock is released. This ensures that the data being read by the application is not changed by another user until the lock is released.

If the lock cannot be acquired, an error is returned.

This function is used to acquire a lock of higher precedence than the lock acquired when the cursor was opened. This function is of use only on tables that have not already been opened in exclusive mode.

Multiple, redundant locks can be acquired on the same table. For each lock acquired, a separate call to DbiRelTableLock is required to release it.

- **dBASE.** READ locks are not supported. If a READ lock is attempted, it will automatically be upgraded to a WRITE lock.
- **Paradox.** Both READ and WRITE locks are supported.
- **SQL.** The behavior of this function will depend on the capabilities of the server being used. Some servers provide nonblocking table locks. Others provide blocking table locks only, while others do not provide table locking at all. Under SQL, table locking is never truly persistent anyway. If the server supports table locking, but locks are not held across transactions, the lock is automatically reacquired after the transaction commits.

DBIResult Return Values

DBIERR_NONE	The lock was acquired successfully.
DBIERR_INVALIDHNDL	The specified cursor handle is invalid or NIL.
DBIERR_LOCKED	The requested lock is not available.
DBIERR_TBLLOCKLIMIT	The lock limit has been reached.

Example

```
function dbFLock( oTable : TTable ) : Boolean;
begin
  Result := oTable.Exclusive;
  try
    if not oTable.Exclusive then
      if DbiAcqTableLock( oTable.Handle,
                          dbiWRITELOCK ) = DBIERR_NONE then
        Result := True;
  except
    on E : EDBEngineError do
      ShowMessage( 'Engine Error: ' + E.Message );
    on E : Exception do
      ShowMessage( 'Exception Error: ' + E.Message );
  end;
end;
```

Pure Delphi Equivalent

TTable.Exclusive := True

Xbase Equivalent

SET EXCLUSIVE ON, FLOCK()

See Also

DbiRelTableLock, DbiIsTableLocked, DbiOpenLockList, DbiAcqPersistTableLock, DbiOpenTable

DbiActivateFilter

Declaration

```
function DbiActivateFilter (       { Activate a Filter }
    hCursor        : hDBICur;      { Cursor handle }
    hFilter        : hDBIFilter    { Filter handle / nil }
  ): DBIResult;
```

Parameters

PARAMETER NAME	DESCRIPTION
hCursor	The cursor handle of the cursor for which the filter is to be activated.
hFilter	The filter handle of the filter to be activated, or NIL to activate all filters.

Description

Activates a filter that was previously added with DbiAddFilter.

Multiple filters can be associated with the same cursor. If hFilter is NIL, all filters for the specified cursor are activated.

After activating a filter, only records that meet the filter criteria will be visible for standard database operations such as browses. When skipping through records in the table, those that do not meet the filter condition will be skipped over.

DBIResult Return Values

DBIERR_NONE	The filter was activated successfully.
DBIERR_INVALIDHNDL	The specified cursor handle is invalid or nil.
DBIERR_NOSUCHFILTER	The specified filter handle is invalid.

Example

```
{ This function is used to set up two filters. The first (Table1) is for all
  records where the TYPE field is equal to 'IN'. The second (Table2) is for
  all records where the TYPE field is not equal to 'IN'. }
procedure TfrmDispInv.SetupFilter;
type
  TmyFilter = Record
    Expr     : CANExpr;
    Nodes    : Array[0..2] of CANNode;
    literals : Array[0..7] of Char;
  end;
const
  myFilter : TMyFilter =
    (Expr :
      (iVer : 1; iTotalSize : SizeOf(TMyFilter); iNodes : 3;
       iNodeStart : SizeOf(CANExpr); iLiteralStart :
       SizeOf(CANExpr) + 3 * SizeOf(CANNode));
    Nodes :
      ((canBinary : (nodeClass : nodeBinary; canOP : canEQ;
        iOperand1 : SizeOf(CANNode); iOperand2 :
        2 * SizeOf(CANNode))),
       (canField : (nodeClass : nodeField; canOP : canField2;
        iFieldNum : 0; iNameOffset : 0)),
       (canConst : (nodeClass : nodeConst; canOP : canCONST2;
        iType : fldZSTRING; iSize : 3; iOffset : 5)));
    literals :
      ('T', 'Y', 'P', 'E', #0, 'I', 'N', #0));
var
  dbResult : DBIResult;
  hFilter, hFilter1 : hDBIFilter;
```

```
begin
  dbResult := DbiAddFilter( Table1.Handle, 1, 1, False,
                            Addr( myFilter ), nil, hFilter );
  dbResult := DbiActivateFilter( Table1.Handle, hFilter );
  Table1.First;
  myFilter.nodes[0].canBinary.canOp := canNE;
  dbResult := DbiAddFilter( Table2.Handle, 1, 1, False,
                            Addr(myFilter), nil, hFilter1 );
  dbResult := DbiActivateFilter( Table2.Handle, hFilter1 );
  Table2.First;
  myFilter.nodes[0].canBinary.canOp := canEQ;
end;
```

Pure Delphi Equivalent

TQuery

Xbase Equivalent

SET FILTER

See Also

DbiAddFilter, DbiDeactivateFilter, DbiDropFilter

DbiAddAlias

Declaration

```
function DbiAddAlias (              { Add a new alias }
     hCfg            : hDBICfg;     { nil }
     pszAliasName    : PChar;       { Alias name }
     pszDriverType   : PChar;       { Driver type for alias }
     pszParams       : PChar;       { Optional parameters }
     bPersist        : Bool         { Persistent or session relative }
  ): DBIResult;
```

Parameters

PARAMETER NAME	DESCRIPTION
hCfg	Handle to the configuration file to be updated.
	This parameter must be NIL, which indicates that the configuration handle is the configuration for the current session. No other values are supported for this parameter.
pszAliasName	Buffer holding the name of the new alias to be added.

pszDriverType	Buffer holding the driver type for the new alias that is to be added.
	If this parameter is nil, the alias will be for the STANDARD database. If szPARADOX, szDBASE, or szASCII are passed, this will add an entry in the STANDARD database alias generated to indicate that this will be the preferred driver type.
	If a driver name is passed in, it must reference a driver name that exists in the configuration file being modified.
pszParams	Pointer to a list of optional parameters. This list is defined as follows: "AliasOption: Option Data[;AliasOption: Option Data][;...]"
	AliasOption must correspond to a value retrieved by DbiOpenCfgInfoList.
	For a STANDARD database alias, the only valid parameter is PATH, all others will be ignored (no errors).
bPersist	Determines the scope of the new alias. If True, the Alias is stored in the configuration file for future sessions. If False, the Alias will be used only in this session and is deleted when the session ends (or the program exits).

Description

Creates a new Alias in the configuration file associated with the current session.

The alias created by this function will have as default parameters the values stored in the driver's "DB OPEN" parameter list, unless they are specifically overridden in the pszParams parameter. You can use DbiOpenCfgInfoList to modify the default values after adding an alias with DbiAddAlias.

DbiInit must be called before calling this function.

Note: Use DbiAddAlias to create a permanent alias (i.e. stored in IDAPI.CFG). To create a temporary alias, one that disappears when the application shuts down, use a TDatabase component instead.

DBIResult Return Values

DBIERR_INVALIDPARAM	Nul alias name, or one of the following, was encountered as in pszDriverType: szASCII, szDBASE, szPARADOX. In the case of the latter, use a nil pszDriverType to indicate a STANDARD database.
DBIERR_NONE	The alias was added successfully.
DBIERR_NAMENOTUNIQUE	Another alias with the same name already exists (only applicable when bPersistent is TRUE).
DBIERR_OBJNOTFOUND	One (or more) of the optional parameters passed in through pszParams was not found as a valid type in the driver section of the configuration file.
DBIERR_UNKNOWNDRIVER	No driver name found in configuration file matching pszDriverType.

Example

```
{ This procedure will create an Alias in the IDAPI.CFG file. }
procedure SetAlias( sAlias, sPath: String; PersistentAlias : Boolean );
var
  zAlias, zPath : PChar;
  dbEnv         : DBIEnv;
  dbRes         : DBIResult;
begin
  {Set initialization params for the DB Environment}
  with dbEnv do
  begin
    StrPCopy( szWorkDir, sPath );
    StrPCopy( szIniFile, " );
    bForceLocalInit := True;
    StrPCopy( szLang, " );
    StrPCopy( szClientName, 'dbClientName' );
  end;
  {Initialize the database}
  if DbiInit( @dbEnv ) <> DBIERR_NONE then
  begin
    raise Exception.Create('Error initializing BDE.' +
                             'Alias not set.');
    Exit;
  end
  else
    begin
      zAlias := StrAlloc( Length( sAlias ) + 1 );
      zPath  := StrAlloc( Length( sPath ) + 1 );
      {Add the alias}
      dbRes :=  DbiAddAlias( nil, StrPCopy( zAlias, sAlias ),
                             nil, StrPCopy( zPath, 'PATH:' +
                             sPath ), PersistentAlias );

      case dbRes of
        DBIERR_NONE :
          ShowMessage( 'Alias: ' + sAlias +
                        ' added successfully.' );
        DBIERR_INVALIDPARAM :
        begin
          raise Exception.Create( 'A DriverType was ' +
                                  'specified, but you ' +
                                  'supplied a nil alias.' );
          exit;
        end;
        DBIERR_NAMENOTUNIQUE :
        begin
          raise Exception.Create( sAlias + ' already exists. ' +
                                  'Use another name for the ' +
                                  'alias.' );
          exit;
        end;
        DBIERR_UNKNOWNDRIVER :
        begin
```

```
            raise Exception.Create( 'No driver name found in ' +
                                    'configuration file ' +
                                    'matching pszDriverType.' );
            exit;
         end;
      end;
      if DbiExit <> DBIERR_NONE then
      begin
         raise Exception.Create( 'Alias set, but there was an ' +
                                 'error closing the BDE. ' +
                                 'Shutdown and restart.' );
         exit;
      end;
      StrDispose( zPath );
      StrDispose( zAlias );
   end;
end;
```

Pure Delphi Equivalent

Database Desktop Add Alias

See Also

DbiDeleteAlias, DbiInit, DbiOpenCfgInfoList

DBIADDFILTER

Declaration

```
function DbiAddFilter (            { Add a filter to the cursor }
      hCursor      : hDBICur;      { Cursor handle }
      lClientData  : Longint;      { Client supplied data (opt) }
      iPriority    : Word;         { 1..N with 1 being highest (opt) }
      bCanAbort    : Bool;         { True if pfFilter can return ABORT }
      pcanExpr     : pCANExpr;     { Expression tree (opt) }
      pfFilter     : pfGENFilter;  { Pointer to filter function }
var   hFilter      : hDBIFilter    { Returns filter handle }
   ): DBIResult;
```

Parameters

PARAMETER NAME	DESCRIPTION
hCursor	The handle of the table for which the filter is being applied.
lClientData	Optional pointer to client-supplied data.
iPriority	Priority rating when used with other filters. 1 is the highest priority.
bCanAbort	Set to True if the function referenced by pfFilter can abort the filter operation.
pcanExpr	Pointer to the CANExpr structure, which describes the filter condition as a boolean expression in prefix format.

continued

PARAMETER NAME	DESCRIPTION
pfFilter	Optional pointer to a user-defined function to use in evaluating records for inclusion in the result record set.
hFilter	Pointer to the filter handle.

Description

Adds a new filter to a table. When activated with DbiActivateFilter, only those records in the table that meet the filter condition will be visible.

The specified filter expression must evaluate into a logical return value (True or False).

Multiple filters are allowed per table. If multiple filters are active, any record that does not meet any of the active filter conditions will not be included in the result set. DbiActivateFilter and DbiDeactivateFilter are used to activate and deactivate any or all of the filters associated with the table.

Closing the table automatically clears all filters.

Paradox. DbiGetSeqNo is not affected by filters. The sequence number returned is that of the record in the original table.

DbiGetRecordCount does not respect the active filter condition, and will generally not be accurate when a filter is active. In this case, DbiGetExactRecordCount should be used instead.

Note: Pass-through SQL query cursors do not currently support this function.

DBIResult Return Values

DBIERR_NONE	The filter has been successfully added.
DBIERR_INVALIDHNDL	The specified cursor handle is invalid or NIL.
DBIERR_NA	The filter condition described by the filter expression could not be handled by the driver.

Example

```
{ This function is used to set up two filters. The first (Table1) is for all
  records where the TYPE field is equal to 'IN'. The second (Table2) is
  for all records where the TYPE field is not equal to 'IN'. }
procedure TfrmDispInv.SetupFilter;
type
  TmyFilter = Record
    Expr     : CANExpr;
    Nodes    : Array[0..2] of CANNode;
    literals : Array[0..7] of Char;
  end;
const
  myFilter : TMyFilter =
    (Expr :
      (iVer : 1; iTotalSize : SizeOf(TMyFilter); iNodes : 3;
       iNodeStart : SizeOf(CANExpr);
```

```
       iLiteralStart : SizeOf(CANExpr) + 3 * SizeOf(CANNode));
     Nodes :
       ((canBinary : (nodeClass : nodeBinary; canOP : canEQ;
         iOperand1 : SizeOf(CANNode);
         iOperand2 : 2 * SizeOf(CANNode)))),
        (canField : (nodeClass : nodeField; canOP : canField2;
         iFieldNum : 0; iNameOffset : 0)),
        (canConst : (nodeClass : nodeConst; canOP : canCONST2;
         iType : fldZSTRING; iSize : 3; iOffset : 5))));
     literals :
       ('T', 'Y', 'P', 'E', #0, 'I', 'N', #0));
var
  dbResult : DBIResult;
  hFilter, hFilter1 : hDBIFilter;
begin
  dbResult := DbiAddFilter( Table1.Handle, 1, 1, False,
                            Addr( myFilter ), nil, hFilter );
  dbResult := DbiActivateFilter( Table1.Handle, hFilter );
  Table1.First;
  myFilter.nodes[0].canBinary.canOp := canNE;
  dbResult := DbiAddFilter( Table2.Handle, 1, 1, False,
                            Addr(myFilter), nil, hFilter1 );
  dbResult := DbiActivateFilter( Table2.Handle, hFilter1 );
  Table2.First;
  myFilter.nodes[0].canBinary.canOp := canEQ;
end;
```

Pure Delphi Equivalent

TQuery, TTable.SetRange

Xbase Equivalent

SET FILTER

See Also

DbiActivateFilter, DbiDeactivateFilter, DbiDropFilter

DBIADDINDEX

Declaration

```
function DbiAddIndex (              { Add a new index }
     hDb                : hDBIDb;   { Database handle }
     hCursor            : hDBICur;  { Cursor (OR) }
     pszTableName       : PChar;    { Table name including any path }
     pszDriverType      : PChar;    { Driver type /nil }
var  pIdxDesc           : IDXDesc;  { Description of the index }
     pszKeyviolName     : PChar     { Keyviol table name (optional) }
   ): DBIResult;
```

Parameters

Parameter Name	Description
hDb	The database handle.
hCursor	Optional table cursor. If specified, the operation is performed on the table associated with the cursor. If NIL, pszTableName and pszTableType determine the table to be used.
pszTableName	Optional pointer to the table name.
	If NIL, pszTableName and pszDriverType determine the table to be used. (If both *pszTableName* and *hCursor* are specified, *pszTableName* is ignored.)
	Paradox and dBASE: If *pszTableName* is a fully qualified name of a table, the *pszDriverType* parameter need not be specified. If the path is not included, the path name is taken from the current directory of the database associated with *hDb*.
	SQL: This parameter can be a fully qualified name that includes the owner name.
pszDriverType	Optional pointer to the driver type. If specified, this can be either szDBASE or szPARADOX.
	Paradox and dBASE: This parameter is required if pszTableName does not include a file extension.
	SQL: If the database associated with hDb is an SQL database, this parameter is ignored.
pIdxDesc	Reference to the index descriptor structure. The IDXDesc elements required vary by database driver.
pszKeyviolName	Optional key violation table name.

Description

Creates a new index on an existing table specified by pszTableName or associated with the cursor handle specified by hCursor. The application must open or switch to the newly created index before the cursor will reflect the order of the new index.

dBASE. The client application must be able to open the table in exclusive mode to create new indexes.

SQL. The client application must have the appropriate privileges to add indexes.

Paradox. Adding a primary index sets the cursor position to the beginning of the file. The client application must open or have permission to lock the table exclusively. If adding a nonmaintained Paradox index, only a read lock is required.

DBIResult Return Values

DBIERR_NONE	The index was successfully added.
DBIERR_INVALIDHNDL	The specified database handle or the cursor handle (if specified) is invalid or NIL.
DBIERR_INVALIDPARAM	Neither hCursor nor pszTableName was specified.
DBIERR_UNKNOWNTBLTYPE	The parameter, pszDriverType is invalid.
DBIERR_PRIMARYKEYREDEFINE	The primary index already exists; it is illegal to define another.

DBIERR_INVALIDINDEXTYPE	The index descriptor is invalid.
DBIERR_INVALIDIDXDESC	The index descriptor is invalid.
DBIERR_INVALIDFLDTYPE	Attempting to index an invalid field type (that is, BLOB field).
DBIERR_INVALIDINDEXNAME	The index name or tag name is invalid (usually for dBASE tables).
DBIERR_NAMEREQUIRED	Index name is required.
DBIERR_NAMENOTUNIQUE	Index name was not unique.
DBIERR_MUSTUSBASEORDER	The default order must be used when adding an index.
DBIERR_NEEDEXCLACCESS	Table is opened in share mode when creating a maintained or primary index.

Example

```
function xbCreateIndex(        { Create an index tag }
  dbHandle     : HDBIDB;       { Data file handle }
  hCursor      : HDBICur;      { Cursor for file }
  sOrdBagName  : String;       { Name of index file }
  sOrdName     : String;       { Name of index tag }
  sExpKey      : String;       { Index expression }
  bUnique      : Boolean;      { True for unique index, False is default }
  bDescend     : Boolean;      { True for descending index. False is default }
  sCondition   : String        { Conditional subset for index }
  )            : Boolean;
var
  idx : IDXDesc;
begin
  FillChar( idx, SizeOf( IDXDesc ), 0 ); { zero-out structure }
  with idx do
  begin { Assign index descriptors for creating file }
    bCaseInsensitive := False;
    bExpIdx := not IsValidIdent( sExpKey ); { more than symbol? }
    if bExpIdx then
      iFldsInKey := 0
    else
      iFldsInKey := 1;
    bMaintained := True;
    bSubSet      := Length( sCondition ) > 0;
    if bSubSet then
      StrPCopy( szKeyCond, sCondition );
    StrPCopy( szName, sOrdBagName );
    StrPCopy( szTagName, sOrdName );
    StrPCopy( szKeyExp, sExpKey );
  end; { with idx }
  idx.bUnique      := bUnique;
  idx.bDescending  := bDescend;
  if IsDbiOk( DbiAddIndex( dbHandle, hCursor, nil, nil, idx, nil )) then
    Result := True;
end; { xbCreateIndex() }
```

Pure Delphi Equivalent

TTable.AddIndex

Xbase Equivalent

INDEX ON, dbCreateIndex(), OrdCreate()

See Also

DbiOpenIndexList, DbiGetIndexDesc, DbiSetToKey, DbiRegenIndex, DbiRegenIndexes, DbiDeleteIndex, DbiOpenIndex, DbiCloseIndex, DbiSwitchToIndex, DbiCreateTable, DbiDoRestructure

DBIADDPASSWORD

Declaration

```
function DbiAddPassword (    { Add a password to current session }
    pszPassword : PChar    { Password }
    ): DBIResult;
```

Parameters

PARAMETER NAME	DESCRIPTION
pszPassword	Pointer to the password to be added.

Description

Adds a password to the current session, providing access to a table that has been previously encrypted with DbiCreateTable or DbiDoRestructure. The password is removed from the session using DbiDropPassword. This function is supported for Paradox tables only.

dBASE. This function is not supported for dBASE tables.

SQL. This function is not supported with SQL tables. Access rights for SQL drivers are controlled when the database is opened.

DBIResult Return Values

DBIERR_NONE	The password was successfully added.
DBIERR_PASSWORDLIMIT	Maximum number of passwords have already been added.
DBIERR_INVALIDPASSWORD	The specified password is invalid (for example, it is too long or contains invalid characters).

Example

```
function AddPassword( sPassword : String ) : Boolean;
var
```

```
  iResult    : DBIResult;
  szPassword : Array[0..40] of Char;
begin
  StrPCopy( szPassWord, sPassword );
  Result := IsDbiOk( DbiAddPassWord( szPassWord ));
end; { AddPassword() }
```

Pure Delphi Equivalent

TSession.AddPassword

Xbase Equivalent

SET PASSWORD (Clipper RDD-specific)

See Also

DbiDropPassword, DbiCreateTable, DbiDoRestructure

DBIANSITONATIVE

Declaration

```
function DbiAnsiToNative (   { Convert from ANSI to Native }
      pLdObj     : Pointer; { Language driver }
      pNativeStr : PChar;   { Optional destination buffer }
      pAnsiStr   : PChar;   { Source buffer }
      iLen       : Word;    { Optional length of buffer }
var   pbDataLoss : Bool     { Returns True if conversion will lose
                              data (Optional) }
    ): DBIResult;
```

Parameters

Parameter Name	Description
pLdObj	Pointer to the language driver object returned from *DbiGetLdObj*.
pNativeStr	Pointer to the client buffer where the translation string is placed. If *pNativeStr* is the same as *pAnsiStr*, the conversion occurs in place.
pAnsiStr	Pointer to the client buffer containing the ANSI data.
iLen	Optional length of the buffer to be converted. If this value is 0, it is assumed that the string is null-terminated.
pbDataLoss	Optional reference to a logical variable to be set. If specified, this will be set to True if the ANSI string cannot map to a character in the native character set. Otherwise, it will contain False.

Description

Translates strings from ANSI to the language drivers native character set. If the native character set is ANSI, no translation takes place.

Works on drivers with both ANSI and OEM native character sets.

Does not handle multibyte character sets, such as Japanese **Shift+JIS**. If the native character set is ANSI, no translation takes place.

DBIResult Return Values

DBIERR_NONE	Translation completed successfully.

Example

```
function Ansi2Native( oTable : TTable; sSource : String ) : String;
var
  szNative,
  szAnsi    : Array[0..255] of Char;
  bDataLoss : Bool;
begin
  StrPCopy( szAnsi, sSource );

  if IsDbiOk( DbiAnsiToNative( GetLangDriverObj( oTable ), szNative,
                               szAnsi, 255, bDataLoss )) then
    Result := StrPas( szNative )
  else
    Result := ";
end; { Ansi2Native() }
```

Pure Delphi Equivalent

AnsiToNative

Xbase Equivalent

None

See Also

DbiNativeToAnsi, DbiGetLdObj

DBIAPPENDRECORD

Declaration

```
function DbiAppendRecord (       { Inserts a new record }
    hCursor         : hDBICur; { Cursor handle }
    pRecBuf         : Pointer  { New Record (client) }
  ): DBIResult;
```

Parameters

PARAMETER NAME	DESCRIPTION
hCursor	The cursor handle for the table being appended to. A valid cursor handle must be specified.
pRecBuf	The pointer to the record buffer containing the data to be appended. This record buffer should be initialized with DbiInitRecord. The record data can be filled in using DbiPutField.

Description

Appends a new record to the end of the table associated with the specified cursor. The new record will contain the data referenced by pRecBuf.

If another user has a write lock on the table, this function will fail.

This function leaves the cursor positioned on the inserted record. If there is an active range and the inserted record falls outside the range, the cursor might be positioned at the beginning or end of the file.

dBASE. This function is the same as calling DbiSetToEnd followed by DbiInsertRecord.

Paradox. For tables with a primary index, where physical reordering of records is forced, DbiAppendRecord is equivalent to DbiInsertRecord.

Technically, the new record data is actually added to the physical end of the table. However, the linked-list sequence numbers of the records just prior and just after the new record's position are updated to create an insert effect.

If referential integrity or validity checks are applied to the Paradox table, the data are verified prior to appending the record. If any of the checks fail, an error is returned, and the operation is not completed.

SQL. This function behaves the same as DbiInsertRecord.

DBIResult Return Values

DBIERR_NONE	The data were successfully appended.
DBIERR_INVALIDHNDL	The specified cursor is invalid or NIL.
DBIERR_INVALIDPARAM	The record buffer is NIL.
DBIERR_KEYVIOL	The table has a unique index and the inserted key value conflicts with an existing records key value.
DBIERR_FOREIGNKEYERR	A linking field value does not exist in the corresponding master table (Paradox only).
DBIERR_MINVALERR	The specified data is less than the required minimum value.
DBIERR_MAXVALERR	The specified data are greater than the required maximum value.
DBIERR_LOOKUPTABLEERR	One or more of the fields in the record buffer have failed an existing validity check (Paradox only).
DBIERR_REQDERR	A required field in the record buffer was left blank (not applicable to dBASE).

continued

DBIERR_TABLEREADONLY	Table access denied; the cursor does not have write access to the table.
DBIERR_NOTSUFFTABLERIGHTS	Insufficient table rights to append a record (Paradox only).
DBIERR_NOTSUFFSQLRIGHTS	Insufficient SQL rights for operation.
DBIERR_NODISKSPACE	The record cannot be appended because there is insufficient disk space.

Example

```
{ Duplicates a record }
function DupeRecord( oTable : TTable ): Boolean;
var
  curProp : CURProps;
  pRecBuf : PChar;
begin
  Result := False;
  try
    { Read cursor properties }
    Check( DbiGetCursorProps( oTable.Handle, curProp ));

    { Allocate memory for the record buffer }
    GetMem( pRecBuf, curProp.iRecBufSize );

    { Initialise record buffer }
    if Assigned( pRecBuf ) then
      Check( DbiInitRecord( oTable.Handle, pRecBuf ));

    { Read current record }
    Result := oTable.GetCurrentRecord( pRecBuf ) and
          IsDbiOk( DbiAppendRecord( GetTableCursor( oTable ),
                                    pRecBuf ));

  finally
    if Assigned( pRecBuf ) then
      FreeMem( pRecBuf, curProp.iRecBufSize );
  end;
end; { DupeRecord() }
```

Pure Delphi Equivalent

TTable.AppendRecord, TQuery.AppendRecord

Xbase Equivalent

APPEND, APPENDBLANK

See Also

DbiGetNextRecord, DbiGetPriorRecord, DbiGetRecord, DbiGetCursorProps, DbiGetRelativeRecord, DbiOpenTable, DbiInitRecord, DbiPutBlob, DbiPutField, DbiVerifyField

DBIAPPLYDELAYEDUPDATES (DELPHI 2.0 ONLY)

Declaration

```
function DbiApplyDelayedUpdates(     { Apply cached updates }
     hCursor: hDBICur;               { Cursor handle }
     eUpdCmd: DBIDelayedUpdCmd       { Operation to be performed }
  ): DBIResult stdcall;

type
  DBIDelayedUpdCmd = (               { Op types for DelayedUpdate }
    dbiDelayedUpdCommit,             { Commit the updates }
    dbiDelayedUpdCancel,             { Rollback the updates }
    dbiDelayedUpdCancelCurrent,      { Cancel the Current Rec Change }
    dbiDelayedUpdPrepare             { Phase1 of 2 phase commit }
  );
```

Parameters

PARAMETER NAME	DESCRIPTION
hCursor	The cached updates cursor handle.
eUpdCmd	The operation to be performed on the cached updates cursor.

Description

When in cached updates mode, DbiApplyDelayedUpdates commits or rolls back any modifications made on cached data to the underlying database since the last time it was called.

After calling DbiApplyDelayedUpdates, you can continue modifying data in the cached updates mode. When finished making changes to the data in cached updates mode, call DbiEndDelayedUpdates to close the cached updates mode.

DbiApplyDelayedUpdates must be used in a two-phase process involving the use of the operation types for the cached updates cursor:

Phase 1. The dbiDelayedUpdPrepare operation causes all changes in the cache to be applied to the underlying data. Unless being used in a single-user environment, this operation should always be used within the context of a transaction to allow for error-recovery in the event of an error during the update. Any errors encountered during this phase should be handled through callback functions.

Phase 2. The dbiDelayedUpdateCommit operation performs the second phase. After successfully calling dbiDelayedUpdPrepare directly, follow it with the dbiDelayedUpdateCommit operation. The internal cache is updated to reflect the fact that the updates were successfully applied to the underlying database (that is, the successfully applied records are removed from the cache).

There are two ways to cancel changes made while cached updates are enabled. The dbiDelayedUpdCancel operation clears the cache and restores the dataset to the state it was in when:

- the table was opened,
- cached updates were enabled, or
- updates were last successfully applied.

The dbiDelayedUpdCancelCurrent operation restores the current record in the data set to an unmodified state. If the record was not modified this call has no effect. This operation is similar to the dbiDelayedUpdCancel operation but operates only on the current record.

Standard. All non-BLOB fields are used in determining the record modifications.

DBIResult Return Values

DBIERR_NONE	The update information in the temporary cache was successfully written to the database.

Example

```
function CachedUpdatesToggle( oTable : TTable; bToggle : Boolean;
                   eCommitCmd : DBIDelayedUpdCmd ) : Boolean;
var
  hCur : hDBICur;
begin
  try
    hCur := GetTableCursor( oTable );
    if bToggle then
      Check( DbiBeginDelayedUpdates( hCur ))
    else
    begin
      Check( DbiApplyDelayedUpdates( hCur, eCommitCmd ));
      Check( DbiEndDelayedUpdates( hCur ));
    end; { Turn off caching }
    Result := True;
  except
    Result := False;
  end; { try .. except }
end; { CachedUpdatesToggle() }
```

See Also

DbiBeginDelayedUpdates, DbiEndDelayedUpdates

DBIBATCHMOVE

Declaration

```
function DbiBatchMove (          { Copy records to destination table }
     pSrcTblDesc : pBATTblDesc; { Source table identification, }
     hSrcCur     : hDBICur;     {  OR source cursor (one must be nil)}
     pDstTblDesc : pBATTblDesc; { Dest table identification }
     hDstCur     : hDBICur;     {  OR dest cursor (one must be nil)}
     ebatMode    : eBATMode;    { Batch mode }
     iFldCount   : Word;        { Size of field maps }
     pSrcFldMap  : PWord;       { Array of source field numbers }
     pszIndexName: PChar;       { If update mode, used to match records }
     pszIndexTagName: PChar;    { Index tag name }
     iIndexId    : Word;        { Index ID }
     pszKeyviolName: PChar;     { Key Violation table name (optional) }
     pszProblemsName: PChar;    { Problems table name (optional) }
     pszChangedName: PChar;     { Changed table name (optional) }
var  lProbRecs    : Longint;    { Number of records added to Problems
                                  table }
var  lKeyvRecs    : Longint;    { Number of records added to Key
                                  Violations table }
var  lChangedRecs: Longint;     { Number of records added to
                                  Changed table }
     bAbortOnFirstProb: Bool;   { If True, abort on first problem record }
     bAbortOnFirstKeyviol: Bool;{ If True, abort on first
                                  key violation record }
var  lRecsToMove : Longint;     { Number of records to read from
                                  source table }
     bTransliterate: Bool       { If True, transliterate character data }
  ): DBIResult;
```

Parameters

Parameter Name	Description
pSrcTblDesc	Optional pointer to the source table descriptor (BATTblDesc).
	If NIL, then hSrcCur is used to identify the source table.
	If not NIL, the specified table is opened, and the entire table is processed.
	In-memory tables are not supported as source tables.
hSrcCur	Optional cursor handle of the source table. This value is used only if pSrcTblDesc is NIL. The source table is processed from the current position of the cursor.
	If this value is not passed in, a read lock will be acquired on the source table. If this value is passed in, the client is responsible for controlling locking behavior.
pDstTblDesc	Optional pointer to the destination table descriptor (BATTblDesc).
	If NIL, then hDstCur is used to identify the destination table.
	If not NIL, the specified table is opened, and the entire table is processed. This parameter is required if the ebatMode is batchCOPY.

continued

479

Parameter Name	Description
hDstCur	Optional cursor handle of the destination table. This value is used only if pDstTblDesc is NIL. The destination table is processed from the current position of the cursor.
	If this value is not passed in, a write lock is acquired on the destination table. If this value is passed in, the client is responsible for controlling locking behavior.
ebatMode	The batch mode to be used. Valid mode values and their effects are:
	• **batchAPPEND.** Adds records from the source table to the destination table.
	• **batchUPDATE.** Overwrites matching records in the destination table. Records from the source table that don't match are not added.
	• **batchAPPENDUPDATE.** Adds nonmatching records to the destination table and overwrites matching records.
	• **batchSUBTRACT.** Deletes matching records from the destination table.
	• **batchCOPY.** Copies a table to a new table of a different driver type. This creates the destination table with a record structure that minimizes potential data loss.
	Important: For batAPPEND and batCOPY, no index is required on the destination table. The other three mode options require an index on the destination table.
iFldCount	Optional number of fields in pSrcFldMap. This will usually be set to 0.
pSrcFldMap	Optional pointer to an array of field numbers in the source table to be copied. The number of fields in the array must be equal to iFldCount.
	If set to NIL, the fields in the source are matched from left to right with the fields in the destination.
	This array is indexed by the destination field position (0 to n-1) and contains either the source field number (1 to n) to be matched with the destination or zero to leave the destination field blank or unmodified.
pszIndexName	Optional pointer to the index name. This parameter is used only when ebatMode is batUPDATE, batAPPENDUPDATE, or batSUBTRACT to specify the index used by the destination table to define matching records.
pszIndexTagName	Optional pointer to the index tag name. This parameter is used only when ebatMode is batUPDATE, batAPPENDUPDATE, or batSUBTRACT to specify the index used by the destination table to define matching records.
iIndexId	Optional index identification number. This parameter is used only when ebatMode is batUPDATE, batAPPENDUPDATE, or batSUBTRACT to specify the index used by the destination table to define matching records.
pszKeyviolName	Optional pointer to the Key Violation table name. All records that cause an integrity violation when inserted or updated into the destination table can be placed here.
	If NIL, no Key Violation table is created. If the user supplies a table name, that name is used.
	If not NIL and a pointer to a nil character is specified, the BDE generates a name for the auxiliary table and copies the name back to the location specified by the pointer; therefore, this area must be at least DBIMAXPATHLEN+1 bytes. If no auxiliary table is created, this area is set to all NIL.

.pszProblemsName	Optional pointer to the Problems table name. Unless the user has overridden the default behavior with a callback, records are placed in a Problems table if they cannot be placed into the destination table without trimming data.
	If NIL, no Problems table is created. If the user supplies a table name, that name is used.
	If not NIL and a pointer to a nil character is specified, the BDE generates a name for the auxiliary table and copies the name back to the location specified by the pointer; therefore, this area must be at least DBIMAXPATHLEN+1 bytes. If no auxiliary table is created, this area is set to all NILs.
pszChangedName	Optional pointer to the Changed table name. All records that are updated or subtracted from the source table are placed here.
	If NIL, no Changed table is created. If the user supplies a table name, that name is used.
	If not NIL and a pointer to a nil character is specified, the BDE generates a name for the auxiliary table and copies the name back to the location specified by the pointer; therefore, this area must be at least DBIMAXPATHLEN+1 bytes. If no auxiliary table is created, this area is set to all NILs.
lProbRecs	Optional pointer to the client variable that receives the number of records that were added, or would have been added to the Problems table.
	When pszProblemsName is NIL, the Problems table is not actually created. In that case, lProbRecs reports the number of records that would have been added to the Problems table.
	If lProbRecs is NIL, the number of records is not returned.
lKeyvRecs	Optional pointer to the client variable that receives the number of records that were added or would have been added to the Key Violations table.
	If pszKeyViolName is NIL, the Key Violations table is not actually created. In that case, lKeyvRecs reports the number of records that would have been added to the Key Violations table.
	If lKeyvRecs is NIL, the number of records is not returned.
lChangedRecs	Optional pointer to the client variable that receives the number of records that were added or would have been added to the Changed table.
	If pszChangedName is NIL, the Changed table is not actually created. In that case, lChangedRecs reports the number of records that would have been added to the Changed table.
	If lChangedRecs is NIL, the number of records is not returned.
bAbortOnFirstProb	Indicates whether to cancel as soon as a record is encountered that would be written to the Problems table.
	If True, the operation is canceled and DBIERR_NONE is returned.
bAbortOnFirstKeyviol	Indicates whether to cancel as soon as a record is encountered that would be written to the Key Violations table.
	If True, the operation is canceled and DBIERR_NONE is returned.
lRecsToMove	On input, indicates the number of records to be read from the source table. On output, represents a pointer to the client variable that receives the actual number of records read from the source table.
	If lRecsToMove contains 0 or is NIL, all of the records in the table are processed.

continued

PARAMETER NAME	DESCRIPTION
bTransliterate	Indicates whether to transliterate character data from one character set to another, when the source and destination character sets differ.
	If True, all data in character fields of the source table will be transliterated into the character set of the destination table.

Description

Depending on the mode specified in ebatMode, this function can be used to append, update, or subtract records from a source table to a destination table. It can also be used to copy an entire table to a table of a different driver type.

In cases where an index is required on the destination table, the index is used to find matching records.

When the source and destination record structures differ in the field size or type, data from the source table is converted to the size or type of the destination table. If the conversion is not allowed, an error is returned, and no data are transferred.

DBIResult Return Values

DBIERR_NONE	The operation was performed successfully.
DBIERR_INVALIDPARAM	Either the source or the destination table identification is invalid.
DBIERR_INVALIDFILENAME	The source table name provided is an empty string.

Example

```
{ Although the following sample is quite a bit longer than the average
  sample in this book, it is required for completeness. The field and index
  description structures at the top of the unit are the keys to everything
  below running smoothly. For complete information on the contents of
  these structures, see the BDE Types Appendix. }

unit Batty;

interface

function BatchMoveTest : Boolean;

implementation

uses WinTypes, WinProcs, DbiProcs, DbiTypes, DbiErrs, Db, BdeRef,
SysUtils;

const
  NAMELEN  = 10; { Set the length of the name fields }
  PLACELEN = 20; { Set the length of the POB field }
  DATELEN  = 11; { Length that a date will be displayed: mm\dd\yyyy }

  szDBTblName = 'DBFData';   { Name of table to be created. }
  szDBTblType = szDBASE;     { Table type to use. }
```

```
{ Field Descriptor used in creating a table }
dbFldDesc: Array[0..2] of FLDDesc = (
        ( { First Name }
        iFldNum:      1;              { Field Number }
        szName:       'Name';         { Field Name }
        iFldType:     fldZSTRING;     { Field Type }
        iSubType:     fldUNKNOWN;     { Field Subtype }
        iUnits1:      NAMELEN;        { Field Size }
        iUnits2:      0;              { Decimal places ( 0 ) }
        iOffset:      0;              { Offset in record ( 0 ) }
        iLen:         0;              { Length in Bytes  ( 0 ) }
        iNullOffset: 0;              { For Null Bits    ( 0 ) }
        efldvVchk:    fldvNOCHECKS;   { Validity checks  ( 0 ) }
        efldrRights: fldrREADWRITE    { Rights }
        ),
        ( { Current Location }
        iFldNum:      2;
        szName:       'LOCATION';
        iFldType:     fldZSTRING;
        iSubType:     fldUNKNOWN;
        iUnits1:      PLACELEN;
        iUnits2:      0;
        iOffset:      0;
        iLen:         0;
        iNullOffset: 0;
        efldvVchk:    fldvNOCHECKS;
        efldrRights: fldrREADWRITE
        ),
        ( { Date of Birth }
        iFldNum:      3;
        szName:       'BORN';
        iFldType:     fldDBDATE;
        iSubType:     fldUNKNOWN;
        iUnits1:      DATELEN;
        iUnits2:      0;
        iOffset:      0;
        iLen:         0;
        iNullOffset: 0;
        efldvVchk:    fldvNOCHECKS;
        efldrRights: fldrREADWRITE
        )
    );

    szPDTblName = 'PDData'; { Name of table to be created. }
    szPDTblType = szPARADOX;  { Table type to use }

    { Field Descriptor used in creating Paradox table }
    PDfldDesc: Array[0..4] of FLDDesc = (
        ( { First Name }
        iFldNum:      1;              { Field Number }
        szName:       'First Name'; { Field Name }
        iFldType:     fldZSTRING;     { Field Type }
        iSubType:     fldUNKNOWN;     { Field Subtype }
```

```
      iUnits1:      NAMELEN;        { Field Size }
      iUnits2:      0;              { Decimal places ( 0 ) }
      iOffset:      0;              { Offset in record ( 0 ) }
      iLen:         0;              { Length in Bytes  ( 0 ) }
      iNullOffset: 0;              { For Null Bits    ( 0 ) }
      efldvVchk:    fldvNOCHECKS;   { Validiy checks   ( 0 ) }
      efldrRights: fldrREADWRITE    { Rights }
   ),
   ( { Middle Name }
      iFldNum:      2;
      szName:       'Middle Name';
      iFldType:     fldZSTRING;
      iSubType:     fldUNKNOWN;
      iUnits1:      NAMELEN;
      iUnits2:      0;
      iOffset:      0;
      iLen:         0;
      iNullOffset: 0;
      efldvVchk:    fldvNOCHECKS;
      efldrRights: fldrREADWRITE
   ),
   ( { Last Name }
      iFldNum:      3;
      szName:       'Last Name';
      iFldType:     fldZSTRING;
      iSubType:     fldUNKNOWN;
      iUnits1:      NAMELEN;
      iUnits2:      0;
      iOffset:      0;
      iLen:         0;
      iNullOffset: 0;
      efldvVchk:    fldvNOCHECKS;
      efldrRights: fldrREADWRITE
   ),
   ( { Date of Birth }
      iFldNum:      4;
      szName:       'BORN';
      iFldType:     fldDATE;
      iSubType:     fldUNKNOWN;
      iUnits1:      0;
      iUnits2:      0;
      iOffset:      0;
      iLen:         0;
      iNullOffset: 0;
      efldvVchk:    fldvNOCHECKS;
      efldrRights: fldrREADWRITE
   ),
   ( { Location }
      iFldNum:      5;
      szName:       'Location';
      iFldType:     fldZSTRING;
      iSubType:     fldUNKNOWN;
      iUnits1:      PLACELEN;
```

```
         iUnits2:      0;
         iOffset:      0;
         iLen:         0;
         iNullOffset: 0;
         efldvVchk:    fldvNOCHECKS;
         efldrRights: fldrREADWRITE
      )
   );

{ Index Descriptor - Describes the Indexes associated with the table }
PDidxDesc: Array[0..2] of idxDesc = (
   ( { Primary Index - Full Name }
         szName:            'Full Name';   { Name }
         iIndexId:          1;             { Number }
         szTagName:         '';            { Tag Name (for dBase) }
         szFormat:          '';            { Optional Format}
         bPrimary:          True;          { Primary? }
         bUnique:           True;          { Unique? }
         bDescending:       False;         { Descending? }
         bMaintained:       True;          { Maintained? }
         bSubset:           False;         { SubSet? }
         bExpIdx:           False;         { Expression index? }
         iCost:             0;             { for QBE only }
         iFldsInKey:        3;             { Fields in key }
         iKeyLen:           1;             { Length in bytes }
         bOutofDate:        False;         { Index out of date? }
         iKeyExpType:       0;             { Key Type of Expr }
         aiKeyFld:          (1,2,3,0,0,0,0,0,0,0,0,0,0,0,0,0);
                                           { Array of field numbers
                                             - index on all 3 name
                                               fields }
         szKeyExp:          '';            { Key expression }
         szKeyCond:         '';            { Key Condition }
         bCaseInsensitive: True;           { Case insensitive }
         iBlockSize:        0;             { Block size in bytes }
         iRestrNum:         0;             { Restructure number }
         iUnUsed:           (0,0,0,0,0,0,0,0,0,0,0,0,0,0,0,0)
   ),
   ( { Secondary Index 1 - Single-Field - Maintained, Case
        insensitive }
         szName:            'Last Name';
         iIndexId:          2;
         szTagName:         '';
         szFormat:          '';
         bPrimary:          False;
         bUnique:           False;
         bDescending:       False;
         bMaintained:       True;
         bSubset:           False;
         bExpIdx:           False;
         iCost:             0;
         iFldsInKey:        1;
         iKeyLen:           1;
```

```
            bOutofDate:        False;
            iKeyExpType:       0;
            aiKeyFld:          (3,0,0,0,0,0,0,0,0,0,0,0,0,0,0,0);
            szKeyExp:          '';
            szKeyCond:         '';
            bCaseInsensitive: True;
            iBlockSize:        0;
            iRestrNum:         0;
            iUnUsed:           (0,0,0,0,0,0,0,0,0,0,0,0,0,0,0,0)
        ),
      ( { Secondary Index 2 - Single Field - Not Maintained }
            szName:            'Location';
            iIndexId:          3;
            szTagName:         '';
            szFormat:          '';
            bPrimary:          False;
            bUnique:           False;
            bDescending:       False;
            bMaintained:       False;
            bSubset:           False;
            bExpIdx:           False;
            iCost:             0;
            iFldsInKey:        1;
            iKeyLen:           1;
            bOutofDate:        False;
            iKeyExpType:       0;
            aiKeyFld:          (5,0,0,0,0,0,0,0,0,0,0,0,0,0,0,0);
            szKeyExp:          '';
            szKeyCond:         '';
            bCaseInsensitive: False;
            iBlockSize:        0;
            iRestrNum:         0;
            iUnUsed:           (0,0,0,0,0,0,0,0,0,0,0,0,0,0,0,0)
        )
    );

{ DbiGetCursorProps(), DbiInitRecord(), DbiPutField(), DbiInsertRecord() }
function DBFAddRecord( hCursor : hDBICur; szName, szLocation :
                       PChar; dBorn : TDateTime ): Boolean;
var
  TblProps: CURProps;    { Table Properties }
  pRecBuf: PChar;        { Record Buffer }
begin
  Result := False;
  try
    try
      Check( DbiGetCursorProps( hCursor, TblProps ));

      { Allocate the record buffer }
      pRecBuf := StrAlloc( TblProps.iRecBufSize );
      Check( DbiInitRecord( hCursor, pRecBuf ));
      Check( DbiPutField( hCursor, 1, pRecBuf, szName ));
      Check( DbiPutField( hCursor, 2,  pRecBuf, szLocation ));
      Check( DbiPutField( hCursor, 3,  pRecBuf, @dBorn ));
```

```
        Check( DbiInsertRecord( hCursor, dbiNOLOCK, pRecBuf ));
        Result := True;
    except
    end; { try .. except }
  finally
    if Assigned( pRecBuf ) then
      StrDispose( pRecBuf );
  end; { try .. finally }
end;

{ DbiCreateTable(), DbiOpenTable(), DbiCloseCursor() }
function DBFCreateTable( hDb: hDBIDb ): Boolean;
var
  hCursor: hDBICur;        { Cursor handle for the table that is created }
  crTblDes: CRTblDesc;     { Table Descriptor }
const
  { The number of fields in the table - fldDesc is global }
  iNumFields: Integer = trunc( SizeOf( DBfldDesc ) / SizeOf( DBfldDesc[0] ));

begin
  Result := False;
  try
    { Initialize the table create descriptor }
    FillChar( crTblDes, SizeOf( CRTblDesc ), #0 ); { Clear the buffer }
    StrCopy( crTblDes.szTblName, szDBTblName );     { Table Name }
    StrCopy( crTblDes.szTblType, szDBTblType );     { Table Type }
    crTblDes.iFldCount := iNumFields;               { # of fields }
    crTblDes.pfldDesc := @dbFldDesc;                { Field desc }

    if IsDbiOk( DbiCreateTable( hDb, True, crTblDes )) and
      IsDbiOk( DbiOpenTable( hDb, szDBTblName, szDBTblType, nil,
              nil, 0, dbiREADWRITE, dbiOPENSHARED, xltFIELD, False,
              nil, hCursor )) then
      begin
        { Add records to the table }
        Result := DBFAddRecord( hCursor, 'Sue', 'Redondo Beach',
                              StrToDate( '12/05/1967' )) and
                DBFAddRecord( hCursor, 'Joshua', 'Bellflower',
                              StrToDate( '2/24/1992') ) and
                DBFAddRecord( hCursor, 'Samantha', 'Seoul',
                              StrToDate( '6/11/1987' ) ) and
                DBFAddRecord( hCursor, 'Brandon', 'Temecula',
                              StrToDate( '9/19/1994' ));
      end
    finally
      DbiCloseCursor( hCursor );
    end;
end;

{ DbiGetCursorProps(), DbiInitRecord(), DbiPutfield(), DbiDateEncode(),
  DbiInsertRecord() }
function AddRecord( hCursor: hDBICur; szFirst, szMiddle, szLast:
                   PChar; wMonth, wDay, wYear: Word; szLocation:
                   PChar ) : Boolean;
```

```
var
  dDate: Longint;       { Because of SysUtils, Date is declared as a function }
  TblProps: CURProps;   { Table Properties }
  pRecBuf: PChar;       { Record Buffer }
begin
  Result := False;
  try
    try
      Check( DbiGetCursorProps( hCursor, TblProps ));

      { Allocate the record buffer }
      pRecBuf := StrAlloc( TblProps.iRecBufSize );
      Check( DbiInitRecord( hCursor, pRecBuf ));
      Check( DbiPutField( hCursor, 1, pRecBuf, szFirst ));
      Check( DbiPutField( hCursor, 2, pRecBuf, szMiddle ));
      Check( DbiPutField( hCursor, 3, pRecBuf, szLast ));
      Check( DbiDateEncode( wMonth, wDay, wYear, dDate ));
      Check( DbiPutField( hCursor, 4, pRecBuf, @dDate ));
      Check( DbiPutField( hCursor, 5, pRecBuf, szLocation ));
      Check( DbiInsertRecord( hCursor, dbiNOLOCK, pRecBuf ));
      Result := False;
    except
    end; { try .. except }
  finally
    if Assigned( pRecBuf ) then
      StrDispose( pRecBuf );
  end; { try .. finally }
end;

{ DbiCreateTable(), DbiOpenTable(), DbiCloseCursor() }
function PDCreateTable( hDb: hDBIDb ) : Boolean;
var
  hCursor  : hDBICur;     { Cursor handle for the table that is created }
  crTblDes : CRTblDesc;   { Table Descriptor }
const
  { The number of fields in the table - fldDesc is global }
  iNumFields: Integer = trunc( SizeOf( PDFldDesc )/SizeOf( PDFldDesc[0] ));

  { Number of indexes to be created with the table - idxDesc global }
  iNumIndexes: Integer = trunc( SizeOf( PDIdxDesc )/SizeOf( PDIdxDesc[0] ));

begin
  Result := False;
  try
    {Initialize the table create descriptor.}
    FillChar( crTblDes, sizeof( CRTblDesc ), #0 );   { Clear Buffer }
    StrCopy( crTblDes.szTblName, szPDTblName );       { Table Name }
    StrCopy( crTblDes.szTblType, szPDTblType );       { Table Type }
    crTblDes.iFldCount := iNumFields;                 { # of Fields }
    crTblDes.pfldDesc  := @PDfldDesc;                 { Field Desc }
    crTblDes.iIdxCount := iNumIndexes;                { # of Indexes }
    crTblDes.pidxDesc  := @PDidxDesc;                 { Index Desc }
```

```
    { Create the table using information supplied in the Table
      Descriptor above }

    if IsDbiOk( DbiCreateTable( hDb, True, crTblDes) ) and
       IsDbiOk( DbiOpenTable( hDb, szPDTblName, szPDTblType, nil,
                nil, 0, dbiREADWRITE, dbiOPENSHARED, xltFIELD,
                False, nil, hCursor )) then
    begin
      Result := AddRecord( hCursor, 'Mortimer', 'Wesley', 'Snerd',
                         7, 28, 1968, 'Chicago') and
               AddRecord( hCursor, 'Bond', 'James', 'Bond', 1, 1,
                         1933, 'London') and
               AddRecord( hCursor, 'Marlin', 'Dolphin', 'Perkins',
                         2, 7, 1954, 'Omaha' ) and
               AddRecord( hCursor, 'Donald', 'The', 'Duck', 4, 13,
                         1950, 'Disneyland' );
    end; { Created the table ok }
  finally
    DbiCloseCursor( hCursor );
  end;
end; { PDCreateTable() }

{ DbiSetDirectory(), DbiOpenTable(), DbiSetToBegin(), DbiBatchMove(),
  DbiCloseCursor(), DbiDeleteTable(), DbiCloseDatabase() }
function BatchMoveTest : Boolean;
var
  hDb: hDBIDb;                  { Handle to the database }
  DBhCur: hDBICur;             { dBASE Cursor handle }
  PDhCur: hDBICur;             { PARADOX Cursor handle }
const
  lNumRecs: Longint = 0;       { # of records moved in Batch move }
  lChangedRecs: Longint = 0;   { # of records changed in Batch move }
  lKeyViolRecs: Longint = 0;   { # of key violations in Batch move }
  lProbRecs: Longint = 0;      { # of problem recs in Batch move }
  waSrcRecs: Array[0..2] of Word = (1,5,4);
                               { Fields to use in the source table }
  szKeyViol: DBIPATH = 'KEYVIOL';
  szProblems: DBIPATH = 'PROBLEMS';
  szChanged: DBIPATH = 'CHANGED'; { Names of temporary tables. }

begin
  Result := False;
  try
    { Set directory, create dBase table, and open it }
    Check( DbiSetDirectory( hDb, '\DELPHI\DEMOS\DATA' ));
    if DBFCreateTable( hDb ) then
    begin
      Check( DbiOpenTable( hDb, szDBTblName, szDBTblType, nil, nil,
             0, dbiREADWRITE, dbiOPENSHARED, xltFIELD, False, nil,
             DBhCur ));
      { Go to the top of the dBASE file }
      Check( DbiSetToBegin( DBhCur ));

      { Create Paradox table, and open it }
```

```
      if PDCreateTable( hDb ) then
      begin
        Check( DbiOpenTable( hDb, szPDTblName, szPDTblType, nil,
                             nil, 0, dbiREADWRITE, dbiOPENSHARED,
                             xltFIELD, False, nil, PDhCur ));
        Check( DbiSetToBegin( PDhCur ));
        Result := IsDbiOk( DbiBatchMove( nil, PDhCur, nil, DBhCur,
                           batchAPPEND, 3, @waSrcRecs, nil, nil, 0,
                           szKeyViol, szProblems, szChanged,
                           @lProbRecs, @lKeyViolRecs,
                           @lChangedRecs, False, False, lNumRecs,
                           True ));
      end; { Created Paradox table }
    end; { Created dBASE table }
  except
    if Assigned( PDhCur ) then
    begin
      DbiCloseCursor( PDhCur );
      DbiDeleteTable( hDb, szPDTblName, szPDTblType );
    end; { Close and clean up paradox table }
    if Assigned( DBhCur ) then
      DbiCloseCursor( DBhCur );
    DbiCloseDatabase( hDb );
  end; { try .. finally }
end; { BatchMove() }

end.
```

Pure Delphi Equivalent

TBatchMove

Xbase Equivalent

APPEND FROM, COPY TO

See Also

DbiOpenTable, DbiCreateTable, DbiRegisterCallBack, DbiDoRestructure

DbiBcdFromFloat

Declaration

```
function DbiBcdFromFloat (    { Converts FLOAT number into FMTBcd format }
var    iVal        : Double;  { Float to convert }
       iPrecision  : Word;    { Precision of BCD }
       iPlaces     : Word;    { Number of decimals }
var    Bcd         : FMTBcd   { returns BCD number (length = iPrecision+2) }
   ): DBIResult;
```

Parameters

Parameter Name	Description
iVal	The FLOAT data to convert.
iPrecision	The precision of the BCD number. This number must be 32.
IPlaces	The number of decimals of the BCD number.
Bcd	Pointer to the client buffer that receives the BCD number. The BDE logical BCD format has a length which equals (iPrecision +2).

Description

Converts a number in the BDE logical FLOAT format into the BDE logical BCD format.

DBIResult Return Values

DBIERR_NONE	The operation was performed successfully.

Example

```
procedure BcdToAndFro;
var
  dVal    : Double;
  bcdVal  : FMTBcd;
begin
  dVal := 10 * 10 * 10 * 10.0; { Make a Double value }
  if IsDbiOk( DbiBcdFromFloat( dVal, 32, 6, bcdVal )) and
     IsDbiOk( DbiBcdToFloat( bcdVal, dVal )) then
    ShowMessage( 'Double converted to BCD and back Ok!' );
end;
```

Pure Delphi Equivalent

TParam.AsBCD

See Also

DbiBcdToFloat

DbiBcdToFloat

Declaration

```
function DbiBcdToFloat (    { Converts FMTBcd number to FLOAT }
var    Bcd      : FMTBcd; { BCD number to convert }
var    dVal     : Double  { Returns converted float }
  ): DBIResult;
```

Parameters

PARAMETER NAME	DESCRIPTION
Bcd	The BCD data to convert.
dVal	Pointer to the client buffer that receives the FLOAT number.

Description

Converts a number in the BDE logical binary coded decimal format to the BDE FLOAT format.

DBIResult Return Values

DBIERR_NONE	The operation was performed successfully.

Example

```
procedure BcdToAndFro;
var
  dVal    : Double;
  bcdVal : FMTBcd;
begin
  dVal := 10 * 10 * 10 * 10.0; { Make a Double value }
  if IsDbiOk( DbiBcdFromFloat( dVal, 32, 6, bcdVal )) and
     IsDbiOk( DbiBcdToFloat( bcdVal, dVal )) then
    ShowMessage( 'Double converted to BCD and back Ok!' );
end;
```

Pure Delphi Equivalent

TField.AsFloat

See Also

DbiBcdFromFloat

DBIBEGINBATCH

Declaration

```
function DbiBeginBatch(          { Place CSL on Paradox Table }
    hDBCur       : hDBICur      { Cursor Handle }
  ): DBIResult;
```

Parameters

Parameter Name	Description
hCursor	The handle of the cursor to which the lock is to be applied.

Description

Places a Critical Section Lock (CSL) on the specified table.

This function is applicable only to Paradox tables.

A CSL is a short-term nonblockable lock that prevents any other user from changing the status of the table until the lock has been released with DbiEndBatch. Applying a CSL is similar to acquiring short-term exclusive access to the specified table. During this period, other network users cannot place new record locks or release any locks they have previously applied.

This type of locking ability is central to the referential integrity mechanism and is the only reliable way to implement "cascading delete" operations.

Warning: This function is not documented by Borland and may not be supported in future updates to the BDE. In order to use DbiBeginBatch, you must remember to declare it and its **.DLL** (**IDAPI01.DLL** or **IDAPI32.DLL**) at the beginning of the unit. (*Special thanks to Eryk Bottomley for providing information regarding this entry.)

DBIResult Return Values

DBIERR_NONE	The CSL was successfully applied to the specified cursor.
DBIERR_INVALIDHNDL	The specified cursor handle is invalid or NIL.

Example

```
interface
  function DbiBeginBatch( hDBCur : hDBICur ): DBIResult;
.

.

implementation
        { Change the external below to 'IDAPI32' for Delphi 2.0 }
        function DbiBeginBatch; external 'IDAPI01';
.

.

function ApplyCSL( oTable : TTable ): Boolean;
begin
  Result := ( DbiBeginBatch( oTable.Handle ) = DBIERR_NONE );
end;
```

See Also

DbiEndBatch

DBIBEGINDELAYEDUPDATES (DELPHI 2.0 ONLY)

Declaration

```
function DbiBeginDelayedUpdates(    { Begin cached updates mode }
var    hCursor : hDBICur              { In/Out : returns new cursor }
    ): DBIResult stdcall;
```

Parameters

PARAMETER NAME	DESCRIPTION
hCursor	On input, specifies the original cursor. On output, returns the new cursor; the old cursor is no longer valid.

Description

Converts a cursor to a cached updates cursor layer and activates the cached updates mode. This allows users to make extended changes to cached table data temporarily without writing to the actual table. This can minimize resource locking.

Changes to the data can be saved to the actual table by calling DbiApplyDelayedUpdates.

The record buffer (RecBuffsize) and the bookmark (BookMarksize) increase in size upon completion of DbiBeginDelayedUpdates. You should call DbiGetCursorProps and reallocate memory properties for bookmark and record buffers accordingly.

DBIResult Return Values

DBIERR_NONE	The cached updates mode was initiated and the new cached updates cursor handle was successfully created.

Example

```
function CachedUpdatesToggle( oTable : TTable; bToggle : Boolean;
                        eCommitCmd : DBIDelayedUpdCmd ) : Boolean;
var
  hCur : hDBICur;
begin
  try
    hCur := GetTableCursor( oTable );
    if bToggle then
      Check( DbiBeginDelayedUpdates( hCur ))
    else
    begin
```

```
      Check( DbiApplyDelayedUpdates( hCur, eCommitCmd ));
      Check( DbiEndDelayedUpdates( hCur ));
    end; { Turn off caching }
    Result := True;
  except
    Result := False;
  end; { try .. except }
end; { CachedUpdatesToggle() }
```

See Also

DbiEndDelayedUpdates, DbiApplyDelayedUpdates

DBIBEGINLINKMODE

Declaration

```
function DbiBeginLinkMode (   { Convert cursor to a link cursor }
var    hCursor      : hDBICur  { In/Out : returns new cursor }
   ): DBIResult;
```

Parameters

PARAMETER NAME	DESCRIPTION
hCursor	On input, the original cursor. On output, returns the new cursor; the old cursor is no longer valid.

Description

Converts a standard cursor to a link cursor for relating tables. This function prepares the specified cursor for linked access and returns a new cursor. The original cursor will no longer be valid.

This function enables linking between tables using DbiLinkDetail. Both master and detail cursors must be link-enabled before calling DbiLinkDetail. DbiEndLinkMode must be called to end Link mode before the cursor is closed.

Warning: Using the original cursor (supplied as input to hCursor) will result in an error.

DBIResult Return Values

DBIERR_NONE	The cursor was successfully converted to a linked cursor.

Example

```
{ The ExpressionLength function used in this example can be found in
  BDEREF.PAS on the CD-ROM at the back of the book. This ExpressionLength
  function utilizes the incredibly cool ExtractFields, StringToStringList,
  and AllTrim functions, which are also found in that same file. }
```

```
function MakeTheLink( oMaster, oDetail : TTable; sExp : String ) :
Boolean;
var
  hMaster,
  hDetail : hDBICur;
  szExp   : DBIMsg;
  iLen    : Integer;
begin
  Result := False;
  try
    { You may want to break any existing link before doing this }
    BreakTheLink( oMaster, oDetail );
    hMaster := GetTableCursor( oMaster );
    hDetail := GetTableCursor( oDetail );
    if IsDbiOk( DbiBeginLinkMode( hMaster )) and
       IsDbiOk( DbiBeginLinkMode( hDetail )) then
    begin
      StrPCopy( szExp, sExp );
      iLen := ExpressionLength( oMaster, sExp );
      DbiLinkDetailToExp( hMaster, hDetail, iLen, szExp );
      DbiSetToBegin( hDetail );
      oDetail.First; { Go to first record in set }
      Result := True;
    end; { if links can be set }
  except
    Result := False;
  end;
end; { MakeTheLink() }

function BreakTheLink( oMaster, oDetail : TTable ) : Boolean;
var
  hMaster,
  hDetail : hDBICur;
begin
  Result := False;
  try
    hMaster := GetTableCursor( oMaster );
    hDetail := GetTableCursor( oDetail );
    if DbiUnlinkDetail( hDetail ) = DBIERR_NONE then
    begin
      DbiEndLinkMode( hMaster );
      DbiEndLinkMode( hDetail );
      oDetail.CursorPosChanged;
      oDetail.Refresh;
      Result := True;
    end;
  except
    Result := False;
  end;
end; { BreakTheLink() }
```

Pure Delphi Equivalent
TTable.MasterFields, Field Link Designer

Xbase Equivalent
SET RELATION

See Also
DbiEndLinkMode, DbiLinkDetail, DbiLinkDetailToExp, DbiUnlinkDetail, DbiGetLinkStatus

DBIBEGINTRAN

Declaration
```
function DbiBeginTran (        { Begin a transaction }
      hDb        : hDBIDb;    { Database handle }
      eXIL       : eXILType;  { Transaction isolation level }
var   hXact      : hDBIXact   { Returned Xact handle }
   ): DBIResult;
```

Parameters

PARAMETER NAME	DESCRIPTION
hDb	A valid database handle, obtained from an SQL server.
eXIL	The transaction isolation level.
hXact	Pointer to the transaction handle.

Description
Begins a transaction on the specified database for an SQL server. Operations are not committed automatically for the duration of the transaction, giving the client control over transaction behavior. The transaction remains active until a call to DbiEndTran is made to end the transaction.

Some servers do not allow Data Definition Language (DDL) statements within a transaction, or implicitly commit the transaction when a DDL statement is issued. For such servers, DDL operations are not allowed within a transaction. If table lock release requests cause implicit commits, a request for a table lock release is held until the transaction is ended.

Servers vary in the availability and behavior of isolation and read repeatability capabilities. Some SQL drivers support only the server default isolation level. To check the isolation level actually used, call DbiGetTranInfo after a successful call to DbiBeginTran.

Nested transactions are not supported. If a previously requested transaction is still active, this function returns an error.

DBIResult Return Values

DBIERR_NONE	The transaction has begun successfully.
DBIERR_ACTIVETRAN	There is already an active transaction.

Example

```
function DirtyTableOp( oTable : TTable; pDo : OpTableProc ) : Boolean;
var
  hXact : hDBIXAct;
begin
  try
    { Turn on Dirty read for speed }
    Result := IsDbiOk( DbiBeginTran( oTable.DBHandle, xilDIRTYREAD, hXact ));
    if Result then
    begin
      pDo( oTable );
      Result := IsDbiOk( DbiEndTran( oTable.DBHandle, hXact, xendCOMMIT ));
    end;
  except
    Result := False;
  end;
end; { DirtyTableOp() }
```

Pure Delphi Equivalent

TDatabase.StartTransaction

See Also

DbiEndTran, DbiGetTranInfo

DBICHECKREFRESH

Declaration

```
function DbiCheckRefresh: DbiResult; { Check refresh for session }
```

Description

Checks for remote updates to tables for all cursors in the current session and refreshes the cursors if changed. This is useful for implementing an auto-refresh function that periodically refreshes client data. It can be called when a specified time period for the client process auto-refresh timer has elapsed.

To receive a notification on the cursors that were actually refreshed, install a callback of the type cbTABLECHANGED.

SQL. This function is not supported for SQL drivers.

DBIResult Return Values

DBIERR_NONE	All cursors in the current session have been successfully refreshed.

Example

```
if bTimerExpired then
  DbiCheckRefresh;
```

Pure Delphi Equivalent

TTable.Refresh, TQuery.Refresh, TStoredProc.Refresh

See Also

DbiForceReread, DbiForceRecordReread, DbiRegisterCallBack

DbiCloneCursor

Declaration

```
function DbiCloneCursor (          { Return a duplicate cursor }
    hCurSrc          : hDBICur;   { Source cursor }
    bReadOnly        : Bool;      { If True, read-only mode }
    bUniDirectional  : Bool;      { If True, Unidirectional }
var hCurNew          : hDBICur    { Destination cursor address }
  ): DBIResult;
```

Parameters

PARAMETER NAME	DESCRIPTION
hCurSrc	The cursor handle of the source cursor.
bReadOnly	Indicates whether the cloned cursor access mode is to be read-only or read-write. True specifies read-only and False specifies read-write. The client is able to choose the access mode of the cloned cursor only if the access mode of the source cursor is dbiREADWRITE. If the access mode of the source cursor is dbiREADONLY, then the access mode of the cloned cursor must be read-only.
bUniDirectional	Applies to SQL tables only. If True, the cloned cursor movement is unidirectional. If False, the cloned cursor movement is bidirectional. Bidirectional movement is generally preferable. However, if the client application knows that the cloned cursor is to access data solely from beginning to end, unidirectional movement may result in better performance.
hCurNew	Pointer to the cursor handle for the cloned cursor.

The following table illustrates the effect that the access mode of the source cursor has on the cloned cursor access mode.

SOURCE CURSOR ACCESS MODE	CLONED CURSOR bReadOnly VALUE	CLONED CURSOR ACCESS MODE
Read-only	True	Read-only
Read-only	False	Read-only
Read-write	True	Read-only
Read-write	False	Read-write

The following table lists the effect of the source cursors direction on the cloned cursors direction.

SOURCE CURSOR DIRECTION	CLONED CURSOR bUniDirectional VALUE	RESULTING CLONED CURSOR DIRECTION
Unidirectional	True	Unidirectional
Unidirectional	False	Unidirectional
Bidirectional	True	Unidirectional
Bidirectional	False	Bidirectional

Description

Creates a duplicate of the specified cursor. The source cursor can be opened on a table or a query. The cloned cursor can then be used as a regular cursor, inheriting certain properties from the source cursor but remaining completely independent in terms of position and ordering.

- The cloned cursor must be closed separately.
- The cloned cursor inherits the following properties from the source cursor:
  - Current Index
  - Position
  - Range
  - Field maps
  - Translate mode
  - Filters
  - Share mode

The source cursor is not affected when placing a field map or a filter on the cloned cursor. The filter handles of a cloned cursor are not the same as the original cursor. However, the filter ID (obtained with DbiGetFilterInfo) is equal to that of the clone. This can be used to obtain the new filter handle for a given filter.

Positional commands (for example, DbiGetNextRecord) performed on the source cursor have no effect on the cloned cursor and vice versa.

dBASE. All indexes open on the source cursor are open on the clone.

DBIResult Return Values

DBIERR_NONE	The cloned cursor was created successfully.
DBIERR_CURSORLIMIT	The maximum number of cursors has been exceeded.
DBIERR_INVALIDHNDL	The specified source cursor handle is invalid or NIL, or the new cursor handle is NIL.

Example

```
function CursorClone( hCursor : hDBICur ) : hDBICur;
begin
  IsDbiOk( DbiCloneCursor( hCursor, True, False, Result ));
end; { CursorClone() }
```

See Also

DbiOpenTable, DbiGetFilterInfo

DBICLOSECURSOR

Declaration

```
function DbiCloseCursor (        { Closes cursor }
var   hCursor   : hDBICur     { Pointer to cursor handle }
  ): DBIResult;
```

Parameters

PARAMETER NAME	DESCRIPTION
hCursor	Pointer to the cursor handle to be closed.

Description

Closes a cursor, releasing all associated resources, including record locks, filters, and all indexes that have been opened by DbiOpenIndex. This function can be used to close all types of cursors. For temporary tables, DbiCloseCursor removes the table from memory.

If the cursor closed is the last remaining cursor for the table in the current session, then all locks acquired with DbiAcqTableLock are released.

After calling DbiCloseCursor, the cursor handle is no longer valid, even if an error occurs.

If the given cursor is valid, the cursor is closed even if an error message is returned. Any error returned is to inform the client of a potential problem (for example, a network problem).

DBIResult Return Values

DBIERR_NONE	The table cursor was successfully closed.
DBIERR_INVALIDHNDL	The specified cursor handle is invalid or NIL.
DBIERR_NODISKSPACE	Table could not be saved to disk due to lack of space.

Example

```
{ Original code by Brian Cook, bcook@metronet.com }
procedure MakeLocalShareTrue;
var
  hCursor   : HDBICur;
  ConfigDesc: CFGDesc;
begin
  { Open the configuration tree that contains LOCAL SHARE }
  Check( DbiOpenCfgInfoList( nil, dbiREADWRITE, cfgPERSISTENT,
                             '\SYSTEM\INIT', hCursor ));
  try
    { For each record in our new cursor }
    while DbiGetNextRecord(hCursor,dbiNOLOCK,@ConfigDesc,nil)=0 do
      { If we've landed upon the LOCAL SHARE entry }
      with ConfigDesc do
        if StrComp( szNodeName, 'LOCAL SHARE' ) = 0 then
        begin
          { Change the value to TRUE }
          StrPLCopy( szValue, 'TRUE', sizeof(szValue) );
          AnsiToOem( szValue, szValue ); { Needs WinProcs }
          Check( DbiModifyRecord( hCursor, @ConfigDesc, True ));
          break;
        end; { if }
  finally
    DbiCloseCursor( hCursor );
  end;
end; { MakeLocalShareTrue() }
```

Pure Delphi Equivalent

TTable.Close, TTable.Active := False

Xbase Equivalent

CLOSE

See Also

DbiOpenTable, DbiCreateTempTable, DbiCreateInMemTable, DbiQExec, DbiQExecDirect, DbiOpenTableList, DbiOpenFileList, DbiOpenIndexList, DbiOpenFieldList, DbiOpenVchkList, DbiOpenRintList, DbiOpenSecurityList, DbiOpenFamilyList, DbiCloneCursor, DbiCloseDatabase

DbiCloseDatabase

Declaration

```
function DbiCloseDatabase (    { Close a database }
var    hDb           : hDBIDb    { Pointer to database handle }
    ): DBIResult;
```

Parameters

Parameter Name	Description
hDb	Pointer to the database handle returned by DbiOpenDatabase.

Description

Closes a database and all cursors associated with the database handle, releasing all associated resources. After closing the specified database, the client handle (hDb) is set to NIL.

> **SQL.** Each database represents one or more connections to a specific SQL server. Closing the database will also close those connections and will release other client database resources that have been acquired.

DBIResult Return Values

DBIERR_NONE	The database specified by hDb was closed successfully.
DBIERR_INVALIDHNDL	The specified database handle is invalid or NIL.

Examples

```
{ Example #1:  Creates a second empty table of the same structure. }
function DupeTableStructure( sInFile, sOutFile : String ) : Boolean;
var
  iResult    : DbiResult;
  hDB        : hDBIDB;
  hTbl       : hDBICur;
  pFields    : Pointer;
  szInFile,
  szOutFile : Array[0..78] of Char;
  curProp    : CURProps;
  tblDesc    : CRTblDesc;
begin
  try
    Result := False;
    StrPCopy( szInFile, sInFile );
    if ( IsDbiOk( DbiOpenDataBase( 'MYALIAS', 'STANDARD',
                 dbiREADWRITE, dbiOPENSHARED, nil, 0, nil, nil,
                 hDB ))) and
```

```
      ( IsDbiOk( DbiOpenTable( hDB, szInFile, nil, nil, nil, 0,
                dbiREADONLY, dbiOPENSHARED, xltFIELD, False, nil,
                hTbl ))) then
    begin
      DbiGetCursorProps( hTbl, curProp ); { Load cursor properties }
      pFields := StrAlloc( curProp.iFields * SizeOf( FLDDesc )+1 );
      if IsDbiOk( DbiGetFieldDescs( hTbl, pFields )) then
      begin
        FillChar( tblDesc, sizeof(CRTblDesc), #0);
        StrCopy( TblDesc.szTblName, szOutFile );
        StrCopy( TblDesc.szTblType, szDBASE );
        TblDesc.iFldCount := curProp.iFields;
        TblDesc.pfldDesc := pFields;
        Result := IsDbiOk( DbiCreateTable( hDb, True, TblDesc ));
      end;
    end
  finally
    DbiCloseDatabase( hDB );
    if Assigned( pFields ) then
      StrDispose( pFields );
  end;
end; { DupeTableStructure() }


{ Example #2:  Displays the contents of the second field for each record of
  CUSTOMER.DB within a scrolling window. Requires WinCRT unit. }
procedure ListDatabase(Sender: TObject);
var
  hDB     : hDBIDB;
  hTbl    : hDBICur;
  iResult: DBIResult;
  szBuf,
  szFld   : PChar;
  cProp   : CURProps;
  bBlank : Bool; { Changed from WordBool for Delphi 2.0 }
begin
  DbiInit( nil );
  DbiOpenDataBase( 'DBDEMOS', 'STANDARD', dbiREADWRITE,
                  dbiOPENSHARED, nil, 0, nil, nil, hDB );
  DbiOpenTable( hDB, 'CUSTOMER.DB', nil, nil, nil, 0, dbiREADONLY,
              dbiOPENSHARED, xltFIELD, False, nil, hTbl );
  DbiGetCursorProps( hTbl, cProp );
  szBuf := AllocMem( cProp.iRecBufSize * SizeOf( Byte ));
  szFld := AllocMem( 255 * SizeOf( Byte ));
  DbiSetToBegin( hTbl );
  iResult := 0;
  repeat
    iResult := DbiGetNextRecord( hTbl, dbiNOLOCK, szBuf, nil );
    DbiGetField( hTbl, 2, szBuf, szFld, bBlank );
    WriteLn( StrPas( szFld ));
  until iResult <> DBIERR_NONE;
  FreeMem( szBuf, ( cProp.iRecBufSize * SizeOf( Byte )));
  FreeMem( szFld, ( 255 * SizeOf( Byte )));
```

```
  DbiCloseDatabase( hDB );
  WriteLn( 'Finished' );
  DbiExit;
end; { ListDatabase }
```

Pure Delphi Equivalent

TSession.CloseDatabase

Xbase Equivalent

CLOSE

See Also

DbiOpenDatabase, DbiExit, DbiCloseCursor

DBICLOSEFIELDXLT

Declaration

```
function DbiCloseFieldXlt (      { Close translation object }
    hXlt          : hDBIXlt      { Translation handle }
  ): DBIResult;
```

Parameters

PARAMETER NAME	DESCRIPTION
hXlt	The field translation handle.

Description

Closes a field translation object that was previously opened with DbiOpenFieldXlt.

DBIResult Return Values

DBIERR_NONE	The translation object was closed successfully.
DBIERR_INVALIDHNDL	The specified translation handle is invalid.

Example

```
function CloseFieldXlt( hXlt : hDBIXlt ) : DBIResult;
begin
  Result := DbiCloseFieldXlt( hXlt );
end;
```

See Also

DbiOpenFieldXlt, DbiTranslateField

DBICLOSEINDEX

Declaration

```
function DbiCloseIndex (          { Close an index }
     hCursor       : hDBICur;     { Cursor handle }
     pszIndexName  : PChar;       { Index Name }
     iIndexId      : Word         { Index number }
  ): DBIResult;
```

Parameters

PARAMETER NAME	DESCRIPTION
hCursor	The cursor handle.
pszIndexName	Optional pointer to the index name. This value cannot be the name of the current active index of the cursor or a maintained index. This parameter can be NIL if iIndexId is specified.
iIndexId	Optional position of the index to be closed within the index list. This should be zero (0) if pszIndexName is specified.

Description

Closes the specified index for this cursor. This function is for use on dBASE tables only. It is used primarily to manipulate nonmaintained indexes. An index order that is currently active and maintained indexes cannot be closed. To close the currently active index, DbiSwitchToIndex must be called first, to make another index (or no index) current.

This function does not affect the order of the records or the current position of the cursor.

DBIResult Return Values

DBIERR_NONE	The index was successfully closed.
DBIERR_NA	Operation is not applicable.
DBIERR_INVALIDHNDL	The specified cursor handle is invalid or NIL.
DBIERR_CANNOTCLOSE	The given index is a maintained index and must stay open.
DBIERR_ACTIVEINDEX	The given index is currently used by the cursor to order the result set.
DBIERR_NOSUCHINDEX	The given index is either not opened or no such index exists for the table.

Example

```
{ Close TEMP.NDX }
StrPCopy( cpIdxName, 'TEMP.NDX' );
DbiCloseIndex( Table1.Handle, cpIdxName, 0 );

{ Close .NDX file that is in order 2 }
DbiCloseIndex( Table1.Handle, nil, 2 );
```

Pure Delphi Equivalent

TTable.DeleteIndex

Xbase Equivalent

SET INDEX TO <nothing>

See Also

DbiSwitchToIndex, DbiOpenTable, DbiOpenIndex

DBICLOSESESSION

Declaration

```
function DbiCloseSession (      { Close the current session }
    hSes         : hDBISes    { Session }
  ): DBIResult;
```

Parameters

PARAMETER NAME	DESCRIPTION
hSes	The session handle.

Description

Closes the session associated with the given session handle, releasing all attached resources (database handles, cursors, table level locks, and record level locks). Any buffers that the BDE has allocated that are specific to the session are also released.

If hSes is the session handle of the current session, the client application is set to the default session after DbiCloseSession is completed. The client application cannot close the default session without exiting the client.

DBIResult Return Values

DBIERR_NONE	The session specified by hSes was closed successfully.
DBIERR_INVALIDSESHANDL	The specified session handle is invalid or NIL, or the session has already been closed.

Example

```
function CloseSession( Session : TSession ): DBIResult;
begin
  Result := DbiCloseSession( Session.Handle );
end;
```

Pure Delphi Equivalent

TSession.DropConnections

See Also

DbiGetCurrSession, DbiSetCurrSession, DbiStartSession, DbiGetSysInfo, DbiGetSesInfo

DBICOMPAREBOOKMARKS

Declaration

```
function DbiCompareBookMarks (   { Compare two Book-marks }
     hCur          : hDBICur;    { Cursor handle }
     pBookMark1    : Pointer;    { Book mark 1 }
     pBookMark2    : Pointer;    { Book mark 2 }
var  CmpBkmkResult : Word        { Compare result }
   ): DBIResult;
```

Parameters

PARAMETER NAME	DESCRIPTION
hCur	The cursor handle.
pBookMark1	The pointer to the first bookmark.
pBookMark2	The pointer to the second bookmark.
CmpBkmkResult	Reference to the client-allocated variable that receives the comparison result. • **CMPLess.** pBookmark1 is before pBookmark2 in the result set. • **CMPEql.** pBookmark1 is the same as pBookmark2. • **CMPGtr.** pBookmark1 is after pBookmark2 in the result set. • **CMPKeyEql.** Bookmark1 and pBookmark2 have the same key value. Used in cases involving nonunique keys when it is uncertain if two bookmarks represent the same record.

Description

Compares the relative positions of two bookmarks associated with the cursor. Both bookmarks must be placed on cursors opened on the same table with the same order. Valid bookmarks must have been obtained with DbiGetBookMark.

Note: Comparing bookmarks from cursors with different index orders or that are not stable may lead to unpredictable results.

DBIResult Return Values

DBIERR_NONE	Bookmarks were compared successfully.
DBIERR_INVALIDHNDL	The specified cursor is invalid or NIL.
DBIERR_INVALIDPARAM	pBookMark1 and/or pBookMark2 were NIL.
DBIERR_INVALIDBOOKMARK	Bookmarks are incompatible or corrupt.

Example

```
procedure CompareBookMarks( hCur: hDBICur; pBookMark1, pBookMark2: Pointer );
var
  bmResult : CMPBkMkRslt; { Changed from Word type for Delphi 2.0 }
  sRelation : String;
begin
  Check( DbiCompareBookMarks( hCur, pBookMark1, pBookMark2, bmResult ));
  case Integer( bmResult ) of
    CMPLess  : sRelation := 'comes before';
    CMPEql   : sRelation := 'is equal to';
    CMPGtr   : sRelation := 'comes after';
    CMPKeyEql: sRelation := 'has the same key as';
  end; { case }
  ShowMessage( 'The first bookmark ' + sRelation +
               ' the second bookmark' );
end;
```

See Also

DbiGetCursorProps, DbiGetBookMark, DbiSetToBookMark

DBICOMPAREKEYS

Declaration

```
function DbiCompareKeys (      { Compare two keys }
     hCursor      : hDBICur;   { Cursor handle }
     pKey1        : Pointer;   { Key buffer 1 to compare }
     pKey2        : Pointer;   { Key buffer 2 (Or nil) }
     iFields      : Word;      { Fields to compare in full }
     iLen         : Word;      { Partial key to compare }
var  iResult      : Integer    { Compare result }
   ): DBIResult;
```

Parameters

PARAMETER NAME	DESCRIPTION
hCursor	The cursor handle.
pKey1	Pointer to the first key value. The key is assumed to be in physical format.
pKey2	Optional pointer to the second key value. If pKey2 is NIL, the key value is extracted from the current record. If the key is specified, it is assumed to be in physical format.
iFields	The number of fields to be used for composite keys. iFields and iLen together indicate how much of the key is to be used for matching. If both are 0, the entire key is used.
	If a match is required on a given field of the key, all the key fields preceding it in the composite key must also be supplied for a match. Only character fields can be matched for a partial key; all other field types must be fully matched.
	For partial key matches, iFields must be equal to the number of key fields preceding (if any) the field being partially matched.
iLen	Specifies a partial length in the last field to be used for composite keys; works in conjunction with iFields. The last field of the composite key must be a character type if iLen not equal to 0.
iResult	Pointer to the client variable that receives the compared result. The result can be one of the following values:
	-1 : pKey1 < pKey2
	0 : pkey1 = pKey2
	1 : pKey1 > pKey2

Description

Compares two key values based on the current index of the cursor. The keys can be obtained using DbiExtractKey. An index must be active to use this function.

DBIResult Return Values

DBIERR_NONE	The key fields were compared successfully.
DBIERR_NOCURREC	pKey2 is NIL and the current record is invalid.

Example

```
procedure CompareKey( hCur: hDBICur; pKey : Pointer );
var
  bmResult : SmallInt; { Changed from Word type for Delphi 2.0 }
  sRelation : String;
begin
  Check( DbiCompareKeys( hCur, pKey, nil, 0, 0, bmResult ));
```

```
  case Integer( bmResult ) of
    CMPLess  : sRelation := 'comes before';
    CMPEql   : sRelation := 'is equal to';
    CMPGtr   : sRelation := 'comes after';
    CMPKeyEql  : sRelation := 'has the same key as'';
  end; { case }
  ShowMessage( 'The passed key ' + sRelation + ' the current key' );
end; { CompareKey() }
```

See Also

DbiExtractKey

DBICOPYTABLE

Declaration

```
function DbiCopyTable (           { Copy one table to another }
      hDb              : hDBIDb; { Database handle }
      bOverWrite       : Bool;   { True overwrites existing file }
      pszSrcTableName  : PChar;  { Source table name }
      pszSrcDriverType : PChar;  { Source driver type }
      pszDestTableName : PChar   { Destination table name }
   ): DBIResult;
```

Parameters

PARAMETER NAME	DESCRIPTION
hDb	The database handle.
bOverwrite	Indicates whether to overwrite an existing destination table or not.
	If True, the table is overwritten. If False, an error is returned if the destination table already exists.
pszSrcTableName	Pointer to the name of the table to be copied. pszSrcTblName can include a file extension, in which case pszSrcDriverType is ignored.
pszSrcDriverType	Pointer to the driver type.
	Paradox and dBASE: This parameter is required if no table extension is specified in pszSrcTableName.
pszDestName	Pointer to the name of the destination table.

Description

Copies the source table to a destination table, using the same driver type. A table of one driver type cannot be copied to a different driver type. To copy data from one driver type to another, you would use DbiBatchMove.

DBIResult Return Values

DBIERR_NONE	The table was successfully copied.
DBIERR_INVALIDHNDL	The specified database handle is invalid or NIL.
DBIERR_INVALIDPARAM	The source or destination table name was not specified.
DBIERR_INVALIDFILENAME	An empty string or invalid file name was specified for the source or destination table name.
DBIERR_FILEEXISTS	The table already exists, and bOverwrite specifies not to overwrite it.
DBIERR_FAMFILEINVALID	The family file is corrupt.
DBIERR_NOSUCHTABLE	The source table does not exist.
DBIERR_NOTSUFFTABLERIGHTS	The user does not have permission to delete the existing destination table (Paradox only).
DBIERR_NOTSUFFFAMILYRIGHTS	The user does not have rights to family members (Paradox only).
DBIERR_LOCKED	The table is locked by another user.

Example

```
function CopyTable( oTable : TTable; sDest : String ) : Boolean;
var
  szSrc,
  szDest   : Array[0..DBIMAXTBLNAMELEN] of Char;
  iResult : DBIResult;
begin
  Result := False;
  StrPCopy( szDest, sDest);
  with oTable do
    begin
    try
      DisableControls;
      StrPCopy( szSrc, TableName );
      iResult := DbiCopyTable( DBHandle, True, szSrc, nil, szDest );
      Result := IsDbiOk( iResult );
    finally
      Refresh;
      EnableControls;
    end;
  end;
end; { CopyTable() }
```

Pure Delphi Equivalent

TBatchMove

Xbase Equivalent

COPY TO

See Also

DbiBatchMove

DbiCreateInMemTable

Declaration

```
function DbiCreateInMemTable (    { Create a temporary table }
     hDb          : hDBIDb;       { Database handle }
     pszName      : PChar;        { Logical name }
     iFields      : Word;         { Number of fields }
     pfldDesc     : pFLDDesc;     { Array of field descriptors }
var  hCursor      : hDBICur       { Returned cursor handle }
   ): DBIResult;
```

Parameters

PARAMETER NAME	DESCRIPTION
hDb	The database handle.
pszName	Pointer to the table name.
iFields	The number of fields in the table.
pfldDesc	Pointer to an array of field descriptor (FLDDesc) structures.
hCursor	Reference to the cursor handle.

Description

Creates a temporary in-memory table, returning the cursor in hCursor. The table is deleted when the cursor is closed.

Only logical BDE field types are supported by the in-memory table. Physical field types are not supported. In-memory tables do not support Logical Autoincrement and BLOB fields.

The table is kept in memory if possible, but may be swapped to disk if the table becomes too large.

The maximum table size is 512MB. The maximum record size is 16KB, and can have no more than 1024 fields.

DBIResult Return Values

DBIERR_NONE	The table was created successfully.
DBIERR_NODISKSPACE	The table could not be saved to disk due to lack of space.

Example

```pascal
procedure TTempTable.CreateMemTable;
var
  I, J          : Integer;
  FieldDescs    : PFLDDesc;
  ValCheckPtr   : PVCHKDesc;
  DriverTypeName: DBINAME;
  TableDesc     : CRTblDesc;
begin
  CheckInactive;
  if FieldDefs.Count = 0 then
    for I := 0 to FieldCount - 1 do
      with Fields[I] do
        if not Calculated then
          FieldDefs.Add( FieldName, DataType, Size, Required );
  FieldDescs := nil;
  FillChar( TableDesc, SizeOf( TableDesc ), 0 );
  with TableDesc do
  begin
    SetDBFlag( dbfTable, True );
    try
      AnsiToNative( Locale, TableName, szTblName,
                    SizeOf( szTblName )-1 );
      iFldCount := FieldDefs.Count;
      FieldDescs := AllocMem( iFldCount * SizeOf( FLDDesc ));
      for I := 0 to FieldDefs.Count - 1 do
        with FieldDefs[I] do
        begin
          EncodeFieldDesc( PFieldDescList( FieldDescs )^[ I ], Name,
                           DataType, Size);
          if Required then Inc( iValChkCount );
        end;
      pFldDesc := AllocMem( iFldCount * SizeOf( FLDDesc ));
      Check( DbiTranslateRecordStructure( nil, iFldCount,
                            FieldDescs, nil, nil, pFLDDesc ));
      iIdxCount := IndexDefs.Count;
      pIdxDesc := AllocMem( iIdxCount * SizeOf( IDXDesc ));
      for I := 0 to IndexDefs.Count - 1 do
        with IndexDefs[ I ] do
          EncodeIndexDesc( PIndexDescList( pIdxDesc )^[ I ],
                           Name, Fields, Options );
      if iValChkCount <> 0 then
      begin
        pVChkDesc := AllocMem( iValChkCount * SizeOf( VCHKDesc ));
        ValCheckPtr := pVChkDesc;
        for I := 0 to FieldDefs.Count - 1 do
          if FieldDefs[ I ].Required then
          begin
            ValCheckPtr^.iFldNum := I + 1;
            ValCheckPtr^.bRequired := True;
            Inc( ValCheckPtr );
```

```
            end;
        end;
        Check( DbiCreateInMemTable( DBHandle, 'MemTemp', FieldCount,
                                    FieldDescs, hCursor ));
        Check( DbiSetProp( hDBIObj( hCursor ), curXLTMODE,
                                    LongInt( xltFIELD )));
    finally
        if pVChkDesc <> nil then
            FreeMem( pVChkDesc, iValChkCount * SizeOf( VCHKDesc ));
        if pIdxDesc <> nil then
            FreeMem( pIdxDesc, iIdxCount * SizeOf( IDXDesc ));
        if pFldDesc <> nil then
            FreeMem( pFldDesc, iFldCount * SizeOf( FLDDesc ));
        if FieldDescs <> nil then
            FreeMem( FieldDescs, iFldCount * SizeOf( FLDDesc ));
        SetDBFlag( dbfTable, False );
    end;
  end;
end;
```

See Also

DbiCreateTempTable, DbiCreateTable

DBICREATETABLE

Declaration

```
function DbiCreateTable (        { Create a new table }
      hDb           : hDBIDb;     { Database handle }
      bOverWrite    : Bool;       { True, to overwrite existing file }
var   crTblDsc      : CRTblDesc   { Table description }
   ): DBIResult;
```

Parameters

Parameter Name	Description
hDb	The database handle.
bOverWrite	Indicates whether to overwrite an existing table or not.
	If True is specified, and there is an existing table, it will be overwritten.
	If False is specified, and there is an existing table, an error is returned.
crTblDsc	Pointer to the table descriptor structure (CRTblDesc).

Description

Creates a table and any files in the database associated with the given database handle. If an existing table is to be overwritten, the existing table must be closed.

516

ASCII Text. DbiCreateTable can be used to create a text file for exporting the data to. For text file creation, only szTblName and szTblType values in the CRTblDesc will be used. The rest of the values are ignored (szTblType is specified as ASCIIDRV). A text file is created with the given name; no field Descriptions are necessary.

Paradox. Referential integrity can be created only when creating or restructuring the detail table. The master table must already exist and must be in the same directory as the table being created. A lookup table may exist in any accessible directory, but it must exist at the time this table is created.

SQL. All indexes are maintained; there are no nonmaintained indexes.

DBIResult Return Values

DBIERR_NONE	The table was created successfully.
DBIERR_INVALIDFILEEXTN	The driver type or file extension is invalid.
DBIERR_INVALIDOPTION	The index Description is invalid.
DBIERR_INVALIDINDEXSTRUCT	Invalid index structure. For SQL servers, all indexes are maintained; verify that bMaintained in pidxDesc specifies True.
DBIERR_FILEEXISTS	The table already exists (returned when bOverWrite is False).
DBIERR_INVALIDHNDL	The specified database handle is invalid or nil.
DBIERR_UNKNOWNTABLETYPE	The specified driver type is invalid.
DBIERR_MULTILEVELCASCADE	An illegal attempt was made to create a referential integrity link that is already in use as a link to a higher level cascade update (Paradox only).
DBIERR_FLDLIMIT	iFldCount exceeds maximum number of fields.
DBIERR_INVALIDFIELDNAME	An invalid field name was specified.
DBIERR_NAMENOTUNIQUE	The specified field name or index name is not unique.
DBIERR_INVALIDFLDTYPE	The specified field type is unknown or not allowed.
DBIERR_RECTOOBIG	The record size exceeds the maximum allowed.
DBIERR_INVALIDINDEXNAME	The specified index name is invalid.
DBIERR_INVALIDINDEXTYPE	The specified index type is invalid.
DBIERR_INDEXNAMEREQUIRED	No index name was specified.
DBIERR_LOOKUPTBLOPENERR	The specified lookup table could not be opened.

Example

```
{ Creates a second empty table of the same structure. }
function DupeTableStructure( sInFile, sOutFile : String ) : Boolean;
var
  iResult    : DbiResult;
  hDB        : hDBIDB;
  hTbl       : hDBICur;
  pFields    : Pointer;
  szInFile,
  szOutFile  : Array[0..78] of Char;
  curProp    : CURProps;
```

```
tblDesc    : CRTblDesc;
begin
  try
    Result := False;
    StrPCopy( szInFile, sInFile );
    if ( IsDbiOk( DbiOpenDataBase( 'MYALIAS', 'STANDARD', dbiREADWRITE,
          dbiOPENSHARED, nil, 0, nil, nil, hDB ))) and
       ( IsDbiOk( DbiOpenTable( hDB, szInFile, nil, nil, nil, 0,
          dbiREADONLY, dbiOPENSHARED, xltFIELD, False, nil,
          hTbl ))) then
    begin
      DbiGetCursorProps( hTbl, curProp ); { Load cursor properties }
      pFields := StrAlloc( curProp.iFields * SizeOf( FLDDesc )+1 );
      if IsDbiOk( DbiGetFieldDescs( hTbl, pFields )) then
      begin
        FillChar( tblDesc, sizeof(CRTblDesc), #0);
        StrCopy( TblDesc.szTblName, szOutFile );
        StrCopy( TblDesc.szTblType, szDBASE );
        TblDesc.iFldCount := curProp.iFields;
        TblDesc.pfldDesc := pFields;
        Result := IsDbiOk( DbiCreateTable( hDb, True, TblDesc ));
      end;
    end
  finally
    DbiCloseDatabase( hDB );
    if Assigned( pFields ) then
      StrDispose( pFields );
  end;
end; { DupeTableStructure() }
```

Pure Delphi Equivalent

TTable.TableCreate, SQL's CREATE TABLE

Xbase Equivalent

CREATE, dbCreate()

See Also

DbiCopyTable, DbiSortTable, DbiDoRestructure

DBiCreateTempTable

Declaration

```
function DbiCreateTempTable (    { Create temporary table }
    hDb         : hDBIDb;        { Database handle }
var crTblDsc    : CRTblDesc;     { Table Description }
var hCursor     : hDBICur       { Returned cursor on table }
  ): DBIResult;
```

Parameters

PARAMETER NAME	DESCRIPTION
hDb	The database handle.
crTblDsc	Pointer to the table descriptor structure (CRTblDesc). This parameter is used in the same way as in DbiCreateTable except that referential integrity cannot be created for a temporary table.
	See DbiGetFieldTypeDesc and DbiGetIndexTypeDesc for additional information on the legal values for these structures for each BDE driver.
hCursor	Pointer to the cursor handle for the table.

Description

Creates a temporary table that is deleted when the cursor is closed, unless the call is followed by a call to DbiMakePermanent or DbiSaveChanges. Physical as well as logical field types are supported by the temporary table.

SQL. This function is not supported with SQL tables.

DBIResult Return Values

DBIERR_NONE	The table was created successfully.

Example

```
procedure TTempTable.CreateTable;
var
  I, J          : Integer;
  FieldDescs    : PFLDDesc;
  ValCheckPtr   : PVCHKDesc;
  DriverTypeName: DBINAME;
  TableDesc     : CRTblDesc;
begin
  CheckInactive;
  if FieldDefs.Count = 0 then
    for I := 0 to FieldCount - 1 do
      with Fields[I] do
        if not Calculated then
          FieldDefs.Add( FieldName, DataType, Size, Required );
  FieldDescs := nil;
  FillChar( TableDesc, SizeOf( TableDesc ), 0 );
  with TableDesc do
  begin
    SetDBFlag(dbfTable, True);
    try
      AnsiToNative( Locale, TableName, szTblName,
                    SizeOf( szTblName )-1 );
```

```
    iFldCount := FieldDefs.Count;
    FieldDescs := AllocMem(iFldCount * SizeOf(FLDDesc));
    for I := 0 to FieldDefs.Count - 1 do
      with FieldDefs[I] do
      begin
        EncodeFieldDesc( PFieldDescList( FieldDescs )^[I], Name,
                         DataType, Size );
        if Required then Inc( iValChkCount );
      end;
    pFldDesc := AllocMem( iFldCount * SizeOf( FLDDesc ) );
    Check( DbiTranslateRecordStructure( nil, iFldCount,
                    FieldDescs, nil, nil, pFLDDesc ) );
    iIdxCount := IndexDefs.Count;
    pIdxDesc := AllocMem( iIdxCount * SizeOf( IDXDesc ) );
    for I := 0 to IndexDefs.Count - 1 do
      with IndexDefs[I] do
        EncodeIndexDesc( PIndexDescList( pIdxDesc )^[I], Name,
                         Fields, Options );
    if iValChkCount <> 0 then
    begin
      pVChkDesc := AllocMem( iValChkCount * SizeOf( VCHKDesc ) );
      ValCheckPtr := pVChkDesc;
      for I := 0 to FieldDefs.Count - 1 do
        if FieldDefs[I].Required then
        begin
          ValCheckPtr^.iFldNum := I + 1;
          ValCheckPtr^.bRequired := True;
          Inc( ValCheckPtr );
        end;
    end;
    Check( DbiCreateTempTable( DBHandle, TableDesc, hCursor ) );
    Check( DbiSetProp( hDBIObj( hCursor ), curXLTMODE,
                              LongInt( xltFIELD )));
  finally
    if pVChkDesc <> nil then FreeMem( pVChkDesc, iValChkCount *
                            SizeOf( VCHKDesc ) );
    if pIdxDesc <> nil then FreeMem( pIdxDesc, iIdxCount *
                            SizeOf( IDXDesc ) );
    if pFldDesc <> nil then FreeMem( pFldDesc, iFldCount *
                            SizeOf( FLDDesc ) );
    if FieldDescs <> nil then FreeMem( FieldDescs, iFldCount *
                            SizeOf( FLDDesc ) );
    SetDBFlag( dbfTable, False );
  end;
  end;
end;
```

See Also

DbiMakePermanent, DbiCreateTable, DbiCreateInMemTable

DBIDATEDECODE

Declaration

```
function DbiDateDecode (      { Decode Date into components }
      dateD      : Date;      { Encoded Date }
var   iMon       : Word;      { Month }
var   iDay       : Word;      { Day }
var   iYear      : Integer    { Year }
   ): DBIResult;
```

Parameters

PARAMETER NAME	DESCRIPTION
dateD	The encoded date.
iMon	Pointer to the client variable that receives the decoded month component. Valid values range from 1 through 12.
iDay	Pointer to the client variable that receives the decoded day component. Valid values range from 1 through 31.
iYear	Pointer to the client variable that receives the decoded year component. Valid values range from -9999 to 9999.

Description

Decodes Date into separate month, day, and year components. This call enables the client to interpret date information returned from a call to DbiGetField.

DBIResult Return Values

DBIERR_NONE	The date was decoded successfully.
DBIERR_INVALIDHNDL	At least one of the following Parameters is NIL: iMon, iDay, iYear.

Example

```
{=================================================================
   Function:
         FormatDate( dDate Date, PChar szDate )

   Input:  dDate    - Date which needs to be formatted
           szDate   - String to contain the formatted date

   Return: Result returned from DbiDateDecode().

   Description:
         Formats DATE fields according to the settings in the
         IDAPI.CFG file.
   =================================================================}
function FormatDate( dDate: Date; szDate: PChar ): DBIResult;
```

```pascal
var
  rslt    : DbiResult;         { Return Value from IDAPI }
  dfmtDate: FMTDate;           { Date Format }
  uDay    : Word;              { Day portion of date }
  uMonth  : Word;              { Month portion of date }
  iYear   : Integer;           { Year portion of date }
  sDay, sMonth, sYear: String;
begin
  { Get the formatting of the Date }
  DbiGetDateFormat( dfmtDate );

  { Decode the date }
  rslt := DbiDateDecode( dDate, uMonth, uDay, iYear );

  { Determine if date should be displayed Year-based }
  if (( not (dfmtDate.bFourDigitYear)) and
            (dfmtDate.bYearBiased) ) then
    iYear := iYear + 1900;

  if ( not (dfmtDate.bFourDigitYear )) then
  begin
    iYear := iYear - 1900;
    Str( iYear:2, sYear );
  end
  else
    Str( iYear:4, sYear );

  { Make certain the seperator is not the escape character. }
  if (StrComp( dfmtDate.szDateSeparator, '\') <> 0) then
    StrCopy( dfmtDate.szDateSeparator, '/' );

  Str( uDay:2, sDay );
  Str( uMonth:2, sMonth );

  { Format the date }
  case Byte( dfmtDate.iDateMode ) of
    { MM/DD/YY - Month, Day, Year }
    0:
      StrPCopy( szDate, sMonth + StrPas(dfmtDate.szDateSeparator) +
                        sDay + StrPas(dfmtDate.szDateSeparator) +
                        sYear );

    { DD/MM/YY - Day, Month, Year }
    1:
      StrPCopy( szDate, sDay + StrPas(dfmtDate.szDateSeparator) +
                        sMonth + StrPas(dfmtDate.szDateSeparator) +
                        sYear );

    { YY/MM/DD - Year, Month, Day }
    2:
      StrPCopy( szDate, sYear + StrPas(dfmtDate.szDateSeparator) +
                        sMonth + StrPas(dfmtDate.szDateSeparator) +
                        sDay );
  end;
  FormatDate := rslt;
end;
```

Pure Delphi Equivalent

DecodeDate

Xbase Equivalent

MONTH(), DAY(), YEAR()

See Also

DbiGetField, DbiDateEncode, DbiTimeEncode, DbiTimeDecode, DbiTimeStampEncode, DbiTimeStampDecode

DBIDATEENCODE

Declaration

```
function DbiDateEncode (        { Encode Date components into Date }
     iMon       : Word;         { Month    (1..12) }
     iDay       : Word;         { Day      (1..31) }
     iYear      : Integer;      { Year     (0..2**16-1) }
var  dateD      : Date          { Encoded date }
   ): DBIResult;
```

Parameters

PARAMETER NAME	DESCRIPTION
iMon	The month. Valid values range from 1 through 12.
iDay	The day. Valid values range from 1 through 31.
iYear	The year. Valid values range from -9999 to 9999.
dateD	Pointer to the client buffer that receives the encoded date.

Description

Encodes separate date components into Date for use by DbiPutField and other functions.

DBIResult Return Values

DBIERR_NONE	The date was encoded successfully.
DBIERR_INVALIDHNDL	dateD is NIL.
DBIERR_INVALIDPARAM	The ranges of month and day Parameters are wrong, according to the rules of the Gregorian calendar. iMon is zero or iMon is greater than 12 or iDay is zero or *iDay* is greater than 31.

Example

```
{ This routine is part of the complete Example listing for DbiBatchMove }
function AddRecord( hCursor: hDBICur; szFirst, szMiddle, szLast:
                    PChar; wMonth, wDay, wYear: Word; szLocation:
                    PChar ) : Boolean;
var
  dDate: Longint;      { Because of SysUtils, Date is declared as
                         a function }
  TblProps: CURProps;  { Table Properties }
  pRecBuf : PChar;     { Record Buffer }
begin
  Result := False;
  try
    try
      Check( DbiGetCursorProps( hCursor, TblProps ));

      { Allocate the record buffer }
      pRecBuf := StrAlloc( TblProps.iRecBufSize );
      Check( DbiInitRecord( hCursor, pRecBuf ));
      Check( DbiPutField( hCursor, 1, pRecBuf, szFirst ));
      Check( DbiPutField( hCursor, 2,  pRecBuf, szMiddle ));
      Check( DbiPutField( hCursor, 3,  pRecBuf, szLast ));
      Check( DbiDateEncode( wMonth, wDay, wYear, dDate ));
      Check( DbiPutField( hCursor, 4, pRecBuf, @dDate ));
      Check( DbiPutField( hCursor, 5, pRecBuf, szLocation ));
      Check( DbiInsertRecord( hCursor, dbiNOLOCK, pRecBuf ));
      Result := False;
    except
  end; { try .. except }
finally
  if Assigned( pRecBuf ) then
    StrDispose( pRecBuf );
  end; { try .. finally }
end;
```

Pure Delphi Equivalent

EncodeDate

Xbase Equivalent

CTOD(), STOD()

See Also

DbiDateDecode, DbiTimeEncode, DbiTimeDecode, DbiTimeStampEncode, DbiTimeStampDecode

DBIDEACTIVATEFILTER

Declaration

```
function DbiDeactivateFilter (      { Deactivate Filter }
    hCursor       : hDBICur;        { Cursor handle }
    hFilter       : hDBIFilter      { Filter handle / NIL }
): DBIResult;
```

Parameters

PARAMETER NAME	DESCRIPTION
hCursor	The valid cursor handle from an open table.
hFilter	Optional filter handle of the filter to deactivate. If NIL, then all filters for this cursor are deactivated.

Description

Temporarily disables the specified filter from affecting the record set by turning the filter off. The filter must have been previously added and activated. If a non-NIL filter is applied, it must be activated.

Once a filter has been activated, that filter controls what is contained in the record set, and all operations on the associated cursor are affected. Once a filter is deactivated, all the records that were excluded by the filter are now accessible, subject to other active filters.

DBIResult Return Values

DBIERR_NONE	The filter specified by hFilter was successfully deactivated. If NIL was passed for the filter handle, all filters were deactivated.
DBIERR_INVALIDHNDL	The specified cursor handle is invalid or NIL.
DBIERR_NOSUCHFILTER	The specified filter handle is invalid.
DBIERR_NA	The filter was already deactivated.

Example

```
{ Deactivate only hFilter1 for Table1 }
Result := DbiDeactivateFilter( Table1.Handle, hFilter1 );
Table1.Refresh;

{ Deactivate all filters for Table1 }
Result := DbiDeactivateFilter( Table1.Handle, nil );
Table1.Refresh;
```

Pure Delphi Equivalent

TQuery.SQL.Clear, TQuery.Unprepare

Xbase Equivalent

SET FILTER TO <nothing>

See Also

DbiAddFilter, DbiDeactivateFilter, DbiDropFilter

DBIDEBUGLAYEROPTIONS

Declaration

```
function DbiDebugLayerOptions (      { Get SDK debug layer options }
    iOption     : Word;              { Option }
    pDebugFile  : PChar              { Trace File Name }
  ): DBIResult;
```

Parameters

PARAMETER NAME	DESCRIPTION
iOption	Specifies the debug layer options.
pDebugFile	Specxifies a trace file into which trace information is written. (This parameter is valid only if the option OUTPUTTOFILE is specified.)

The possible debug layer options follow:

OPTION	RESULT
DEBUGON	If specified, the debug layer is activated. (*Note:* The debug layer .**DLL** must be in place.) If this option is not specified, the debug layer is deactivated.
OUTPUTTOFILE	If specified, debug layer trace information is directed to the file specified by pDebugFile. If pDebugfile is not specified, a default trace file is created.
FLUSHEVERYOP	If specified, flushes trace information to the trace file every time a BDE function is called. Using this option dramatically slows processing. If not specified, trace information is flushed periodically.
APPENDTOLOG	If specified, the trace output is appended to the end of the existing pDebugFile file. If not specified, the trace output overwrites the existing pDebugFile.

Description

Used to activate, deactivate, or set options for the BDE debug layer.

The debug layer has two purposes:

- It provides a more advanced level of parameter checking.
- It enables the application to output trace information, giving a detailed breakdown of the Parameters passed into BDE functions. The trace includes error messages that are generated when variables contain invalid data.

526

The trace file name is specified in pDebugFile as <filename.ext>. If that file reaches 500KB, then the contents will be rolled over to a <filename.old> file. The total trace file capacity is limited to 1MB. When the new trace file reaches 500KB, its contents are rolled over, overwriting the <filename.old> file.

Before calling DbiDebugLayerOptions, the proper dynamic link library must be made available to the core file, **IDAPI01.DLL** (for Delphi 1.x) or **IDAPI32.DLL** (for Delphi 2.x). This can be done by running the standalone utility **DLLSWAP.EXE,** which is used to swap between **DBG.DLL** and **NODBG.DLL. DLLSWAP.EXE** makes it known which **DLL** is currently available.

To accomplish the same task without the use of **DLLSWAP.EXE,** locate the directory where the BDE DLLs are installed. **IDAPI01.DLL** is the main entry point to the BDE for Delphi 1.x. Under Delphi 2.x, this file is called **IDAPI32.DLL.**

If DBG.DLL is listed in the directory, the debug layer is not enabled. To enable the debug layer, rename **IDAPI01.DLL** to **NODBG.DLL**, and rename **DBL.DLL** to **IDAPI01.DLL.**

If **NODBG.DLL** is listed in the directory, the debug layer is enabled. To disable the debug layer, rename **IDAPI01.DLL** to **DBG.DLL**, and rename **NODBG.DLL** to **IDAPI01.DLL.**

Note: for delphi 2.x, substitute **idapi32.dll** for **idapi01.dll** in the above two paragraphs.

Special care should be taken when using the debug layer in a multisession environment. Debug layer state is shared by all concurrent sessions. For Example, if one session has set the debug layer on for tracing, all sessions are traced.

Tracing imposes a considerable overhead. For this reason, when you are trying to isolate a problem, avoid tracing within long loops.

DBIResult Return Values

DBIERR_NONE	The debug layer options have been successfully specified.

Example

```
{===================================================================
  Function:
          InitStuff( phDb );

  Input:  phDb - Pointer to the database handle

  Return: BDE return code after DbiInit() and DbiOpenDatabase().

  Description:
          Initialize the BDE.
  ===================================================================}
function InitStuff( var phDb: hDBIDb ): DBIResult;
var
  rslt : DBIResult;
begin
```

```
{ Initialize the BDE with a an empty environment structure }
rslt := DbiInit( nil );
if (rslt = DBIERR_NONE) then
begin
  Check( DbiDebugLayerOptions( DEBUGON or OUTPUTTOFILE,
                               'FOOBAR.DBG' ));

  { Open Standard database by using a NIL database type }
  rslt := DbiOpenDatabase( nil, nil, dbiREADWRITE, dbiOPENSHARED,
                           nil, 0, nil, nil, phDb );

  { Exit BDE if connect did not work }
  if (rslt <> DBIERR_NONE) then
    Check( DbiExit );

end;
  InitStuff := rslt;
end;
```

DBIDELETEALIAS

Declaration

```
function DbiDeleteAlias(      { Deletes a BDE Alias }
    hCfg: hDBICfg;            { Config file handle / NIL }
    pszAliasName: PChar       { Alias name }
  ): DBIResult stdcall;
```

Parameters

PARAMETER NAME	DESCRIPTION
hCfg	The configuration file handle. This parameter must be NIL, indicating that the alias is to be removed from the configuration file for the current session.
pszAliasName	Reference to the buffer holding the name of the alias to be removed.

Description

Deletes a BDE alias from a BDE configuration file.

Note: This function was added in the Delphi 1.02 release and is not found in any releases of **IDAPI01.DLL** dated prior to June 22, 1995.

DBIResult Return Values

DBIERR_INVALIDPARAM	Null alias name passed.
DBIERR_NONE	The alias was successfully deleted.
DBIERR_OBJNOTFOUND	No alias was found matching pszAliasName.

Example

```
procedure DeleteAlias( sAliasName: String );
begin
  Check( DbiDeleteAlias( nil, PChar( sAliasName )));
end;
```

See Also

DbiAddAlias

DbiDeleteIndex

Declaration

```
function DbiDeleteIndex (              { Delete index }
    hDb               : hDBIDb;        { Database handle }
    hCursor           : hDBICur;       { Cursor (OR) }
    pszTableName      : PChar;         { Table name }
    pszDriverType     : PChar;         { Driver type /NIL }
    pszIndexName      : PChar;         { Index name }
    pszIndexTagName   : PChar;         { Index tagname (dBASE .MDX) }
    iIndexId          : Word           { Index number }
  ): DBIResult;
```

Parameters

Parameter Name	Description
hDb	The database handle.
hCursor	Optional cursor handle.
	If hCursor is specified, the operation is performed on the table associated with that cursor and does not affect the order or the position of the cursor.
	If hCursor is NIL, pszTableName and pszDriverType determine the table to be used.
pszTableName	Optional pointer to the table name.
	If hCursor is NIL, pszTableName and pszDriverType determine the table to be used. (If both pszTableName and hCursor are specified, pszTableName is ignored.)
	Paradox and dBASE: If pszTableName is a fully qualified name of a table, the pszDriverType parameter need not be specified. If the path is not included, the path name is taken from the current directory of the database associated with hDb.
	SQL. This parameter can be a fully qualified name that includes the owner name.
pszDriverType	Optional pointer to the driver type. If specified, this value can either be szDBASE or szPARADOX.
	Paradox and dBASE. This parameter is required if pszTableName has no extension.
	SQL. This parameter is ignored if the database associated with hDb is an SQL database.

pszIndexName	Pointer to the name of the index to be dropped.
pszIndexTagName	Pointer to the index tag name. Used only to identify dBASE **.MDX** indexes.
	This parameter is ignored for Paradox and SQL tables.
iIndexId	The index identifier, which is the number of the index to be used. The range for the index identifier is 1 to 511. Used for Paradox tables only and is ignored if pszIndexName is specified.

Description

Deletes a single-order index file or a tag within a dBASE **.MDX** index file. The client application can either specify the table by name or by opening a cursor on the table. If a cursor is specified, it must not be opened with the index to be deleted.

If hCursor is specified, an exclusive cursor handle must be supplied. See the following driver specific information for locking requirements. A currently active index cannot be dropped. If the table name is specified, the table must be able to be opened exclusively.

dBASE. The table must be opened exclusively on behalf of the client application.

Paradox. The table must be opened exclusively on behalf of the client application. (The client application must have permission to lock the table exclusively.)

SQL. The table must be open exclusively where table locking is supported by the driver.

DBIResult Return Values

DBIERR_NONE	The index was successfully deleted.
DBIERR_INDEXNAMEREQUIRED	An index name is required.
DBIERR_INDEXREADONLY	An illegal attempt was made to delete a read-only index.
DBIERR_ACTIVEINDEX	An illegal attempt was made to delete an active, primary index.
DBIERR_MUSTUSEBASEORDER	An illegal attempt was made to delete an active, secondary index.
DBIERR_INVALIDHNDL	Handle was invalid or NIL.
DBIERR_NEEDEXCLACCESS	Exclusive access is required to delete the index.
DBIERR_NOSUCHINDEX	The specified index does not exist.

Example

```
function DeleteNDX( oTable : TTable; sNDXname : String ): DBIResult;
var
  szNDXName : Array[0..127] of Char;
begin
  StrPCopy( szNDXName, sNDXName );
  Result := DbiDeleteIndex( oTable.DBHandle, oTable.Handle, nil,
                            PChar( szDBASE ), szNDXname, nil, 0 );
end;
```

Pure Delphi Equivalent

TTable.DeleteIndex, TQuery.SQL's DROP INDEX

Xbase Equivalent

DELETE TAG

See Also

DbiAddIndex, DbiCloseIndex, DbiOpenIndex, DbiSwitchToIndex, DbiDoRestructure

DBIDELETERECORD

Declaration

```
function DbiDeleteRecord (      { Deletes the current record }
    hCursor      : hDBICur;    { Cursor handle }
    pRecBuf      : Pointer     { Copy of deleted record }
  ): DBIResult;
```

Parameters

PARAMETER NAME	DESCRIPTION
hCursor	The cursor handle.
pRecBuf	Optional pointer to the client buffer that receives the deleted record.

Description

Deletes the current record of the given cursor. The cursor must be positioned on a record, not on a crack, beginning of file, or end of file. The user must have read/write access to the table. The record must not be locked by another session.

Following a successful call to DbiDeleteRecord, the cursor is positioned on the crack between the records before and after the deleted record. Subsequently calling DbiGetNextRecord returns the record after the deleted record. A subsequent call to DbiGetPriorRecord returns the record before the deleted record.

dBASE. DbiDeleteRecord simply marks the record for deletion. The record is not physically removed from the table until the table is packed with DbiPackTable.

Paradox. After a record is deleted and committed, it cannot be recalled. The record is not deleted if the deletion would cause violation of referential integrity. For Example, if the cursor is validly positioned on a record within the master table and that record has linked values in a detail table, then the call to DbiDeleteRecord fails, and the position of the cursor remains unchanged.

Deleting a record does not reduce table size until a call to DbiDoRestructure is made.

SQL. Record deletions are done via optimistic locking. Unless a transaction is explicitly started using DbiBeginTran, a successful deletion is immediately committed.

DBIResult Return Values

DBIERR_NONE	The record was successfully deleted.
DBIERR_INVALIDHNDL	The specified cursor handle is invalid or NIL.
DBIERR_BOF	The cursor is not positioned on a record.
DBIERR_EOF	The cursor is not positioned on a record.
DBIERR_KEYORRECDELETED	The cursor is not positioned on a record.
DBIERR_NOCURRREC	The cursor is not positioned on a record.
DBIERR_RECLOCKED	The record or table is locked by another session.
DBIERR_NOTABLESUPPORT	A deletion cannot be made from a view. Some SQL drivers do not support deletions from non-uniquely indexed tables.
DBIERR_TABLEREADONLY	Table access denied; the cursor does not have write access to the table.
DBIERR_DETAILRECORDSEXIST	The table is the master table in a referential integrity link and the record to be deleted has associated detail records (Paradox only).
DBIERR_NOTSUFFTABLERIGHTS	Insufficient table rights to delete a record (Paradox only).
DBIERR_NOTSUFFSQLRIGHTS	Insufficient SQL rights to delete a record (SQL only).
DBIERR_MULTIPLEUNIQRECS	Attempt to delete a record that has a duplicate (SQL only).

Example

```
{ Deletes record at current position, copying record contents into pRecBuf }
function dbDelete( oTable : TTable; pRecBuf : Pointer ): Boolean;
begin
  Result := ( DbiDeleteRecord( oTable.Handle, pRecBuf ) =  DBIERR_NONE );
end;
```

Pure Delphi Equivalent

TTable.Delete

Xbase Equivalent

DELETE

See Also

DbiGetRecord, DbiDoRestructure, DbiGetNextRecord, DbiGetPriorRecord, DbiGetRelativeRecord, DbiPackTable (dBASE only), DbiUndeleteRecord (dBASE only)

DbiDeleteTable

Declaration

```
function DbiDeleteTable (          { Delete a table }
    hDb          : hDBIDb;        { Database handle }
    pszTableName : PChar;         { Name including any path }
    pszDriverType : PChar         { Driver type / NIL }
): DBIResult;
```

Parameters

PARAMETER NAME	DESCRIPTION
hDb	The handle of the database containing the table to be deleted.
pszTableName	Pointer to the name of the table to delete.
	Paradox and dBASE: If pszTableName is a fully qualified name of a table, the pszDriverType parameter need not be specified. If the path is not included, the path name is taken from the current directory of the database associated with hDb.
	SQL: This parameter can be a fully qualified name that includes the owner name. This function cannot be used to delete SQL views.
pszDriverType	Optional pointer to the driver type of the table being deleted. If specified, pszDriverType can be one of the following values: szDBASE or szPARADOX.
	Paradox and dBASE: This parameter is required if pszTableName does not include a file extension.
	SQL: This parameter is ignored if the database associated with hDb is an SQL database.

Description

Deletes the table given in pszTableName and all associated family members. For Example, all files with <tablename>.* will be deleted. The client application must have permission to lock the table exclusively to use this function.

Paradox. If the table has been encrypted, the master password must have been registered (using DbiAddPassword) prior to calling this function.

DBIResult Return Values

DBIERR_NONE	The table was successfully deleted.
DBIERR_INVALIDHNDL	The specified database handle is invalid or NIL.
DBIERR_NOSUCHFILE	The table does not exist.
DBIERR_NOSUCHTABLE	The table does not exist.
DBIERR_UNKNOWNTBLTYPE	The specified driver type is invalid.
DBIERR_NOTSUFFTABLERIGHTS	The user has insufficient rights to the table (Paradox only).

DBIERR_NOTSUFFFAMILYRIGHTS	The user has insufficient rights to family members (Paradox only).
DBIERR_LOCKED	The table is locked by another user.

Example

```
{ Delete the CUST.DBF table }
StrPCopy( szTable, 'CUST.DBF' );
DbiDeleteTable( hDb, szTable, PChar( szDBASE ));
```

Pure Delphi Equivalent

TTable.DeleteTable

Xbase Equivalent

ERASE, FErase()

See Also

DbiCreateTable, DbiCopyTable, DbiAddPassword

DBIDORESTRUCTURE

Declaration

```
function DbiDoRestructure (       { Restructure a table }
     hDb               : hDBIDb;    { Database handle }
     iTblDescCount     : Word;      { Number of table descriptors (1) }
     pTblDesc          : pCRTblDesc; { Array of table descs }
     pszSaveAs         : PChar;     { Restructure to this table }
     pszKeyviolName    : PChar;     { Key violation table name (Opt) }
     pszProblemsName   : PChar;     { Problems table name (Optional) }
     bAnalyzeOnly      : Bool       { Analyze restructure }
  ): DBIResult;
```

Parameters

PARAMETER NAME	DESCRIPTION
hDb	The database handle.
iTblDescCount	The number of table descriptors. Currently, only one table descriptor can be processed per call, so this value must be set to 1.
pTblDesc	Pointer to the client-allocated CRTblDesc structure, which identifies the source table, describes the new record structure (if modified), and lists all other changes to the table.
pszSaveAs	Optional new name for the restructured table.
	If not NIL, creates a restructured table with this name and leaves the original unchanged.

continued

Parameter Name	Description
pszKeyviolName	Optional pointer to the Key Violation table name. All records that cause an integrity violation are placed here.
	If NIL, no Key Violation table is created.
	If the user supplies a table name, that name is used.
	If a pointer to an empty string is specified, the table name created is returned in the users area (must be at least DBIMAXPATHLEN+1 bytes).
pszProblemsName	Optional pointer to the Problems table name.
	If NIL, no Problems table is created.
	If the user supplies a table name, that name is used. If the user has overridden the default behavior with a callback, records are placed in a Problems table if they cannot be placed into the destination table without trimming data.
	If a pointer to an empty string is specified, the table name created is returned in the users area (must be at least DBIMAXPATHLEN+1 bytes).
bAnalyzeOnly	If True, analyze restructure.

Description

For use with Paradox tables only. Changes the properties of a table such as modifying field types or sizes, adding, deleting, or rearranging fields, changing indexes, changing passwords, and so on.

After a successful table restructuring, the following tables might be created:

- A Key Violations table (if pszKeyviolName was specified integrity violations occurred)
- A Problems table (if pszProblemsName was specified and there was data loss that the client disallowed by a callback)

The most common cause of failures are invalid descriptors or invalid transformations.

DBIResult Return Values

DBIERR_NONE	A table was successfully generated with the new structure.

Example

```
procedure dbPack( oTable : TTable );
var
  iResult: DBIResult;
  szErrMsg: DBIMSG;
  pTblDesc: pCRTblDesc;
  bExclusive: Boolean;
  bActive: Boolean;
begin
  { Save current state of table }
  with oTable do
  begin
```

```
    bExclusive := Exclusive;
    bActive := Active;
    DisableControls;
    Close;
    Exclusive := True;
  end;

{ For dBASE tables, use DbiPackTable; For Paradox, use DbiDoRestructure }
case oTable.TableType of
  ttdBASE:
    begin
      oTable.Open;
      iResult := DbiPackTable( oTable.DBHandle, oTable.Handle,
                               nil, nil, True );
      if iResult <> DBIERR_NONE then
      begin
        DbiGetErrorString( iResult, szErrMsg );
        MessageDlg( szErrMsg, mtError, [mbOk], 0 );
      end;
    end;
  ttParadox:
    begin
      if MaxAvail < SizeOf( CRTblDesc ) then
        MessageDlg( 'Cannot pack table. Insufficient memory!',
                    mtError, [mbOk], 0 )
      else
        begin
          GetMem( pTblDesc, SizeOf( CRTblDesc ));
          FillChar( pTblDesc^, SizeOf( CRTblDesc ), 0 );
          with pTblDesc^ do
          begin
            StrPCopy( szTblName, oTable.TableName );
            StrPCopy( szTblType, szParadox );
            bPack := True;
          end;
          iResult := DbiDoRestructure( oTable.DBHandle, 1,
                       pTblDesc, nil, nil, nil, False );
          if iResult <> DBIERR_NONE then
          begin
            DbiGetErrorString( iResult, szErrMsg );
            MessageDlg( szErrMsg, mtError, [mbOk], 0 );
          end;
          FreeMem( pTblDesc, SizeOf( CRTblDesc ));
        end;
    end;
  else
    MessageDlg( 'Cannot pack this table type!',
                mtError, [mbOk], 0 );
end;

{ Restore previously saved table state }
with oTable do
begin
  Close;
```

```
    Exclusive := bExclusive;
    Active := bActive;
    EnableControls;
  end;
end; { dbPack() }
```

Pure Delphi Equivalent

The Database Desktop's Restructure Table Dialog

Xbase Equivalent

MODIFY STRUCTURE

See Also

DbiRegisterCallBack, DbiBatchMove for use of pszKeyviolName and pszProblemsName

DBIDROPFILTER

Declaration

```
function DbiDropFilter (        { Drop a filter }
    hCursor      : hDBICur;     { Cursor handle }
    hFilter      : hDBIFilter   { Filter handle }
  ): DBIResult;
```

Parameters

PARAMETER NAME	DESCRIPTION
hCursor	The cursor handle.
hFilter	Optional filter handle.
	If NIL, all filters are dropped for this cursor. If no filters are activated and NIL has been specified for the filter handle, no error condition is returned.

Description

Drops the specified filter and frees all resources associated with the filter.

Filters are automatically deactivated before being dropped and automatically dropped when the cursor is closed.

DBIResult Return Values

DBIERR_NONE	The filter specified by the filter handle was successfully dropped. If NIL is passed for the filter handle, all filters, if any, were dropped.
DBIERR_INVALIDHNDL	The specified cursor handle is invalid or NIL.
DBIERR_NOSUCHFILTER	The filter handle (hFilter) is invalid.

Example

```
{ Drop only hFilter1 for Table1 }
Result := DbiDropFilter( Table1.Handle, hFilter1 );
Table1.Refresh;

{ Drop all filters for Table1 }
Result := DbiDropFilter( Table1.Handle, nil );
Table1.Refresh;
```

Pure Delphi Equivalent

TQuery.SQL.Close

Xbase Equivalent

SET FILTER TO <nothing>

See Also

DbiActivateFilter, DbiDeactivateFilter, DbiAddFilter

DBIDROPPASSWORD

Declaration

```
function DbiDropPassword (    { Drop password from current session }
    pszPassword : PChar    { password/NIL }
  ): DBIResult;
```

Parameters

PARAMETER NAME	DESCRIPTION
pszPassword	Optional pointer to the password to be dropped. If NIL, all passwords for the session are dropped.

Description

Removes a password from the current session. This function is used by the Paradox driver only.

This function removes the rights to access previously encrypted tables with that password; it does not cause tables to become decrypted.

DBIResult Return Values

DBIERR_NONE	The password specified by pszPassword was successfully dropped.
DBIERR_INVALIDPASSWORD	The specified password is empty or too long.
DBIERR_OBJNOTFOUND	pszPassword was not found.

Example

```
var
  iResult    : DBIResult;
  szPassword : Array[0..15] of Char;
begin
  { Add password }
  StrPCopy( szPassWord, 'FooBar' );
  Result := IsDbiOk( DbiAddPassWord( szPassWord ));

  … {Do some stuff } …

  { Drop Password }
  Result := IsDbiOk( DbiDropPassWord( szPassWord ));
end;
```

Pure Delphi Equivalent

TSession.RemoveAllPasswords

Xbase Equivalent

SET PASSWORD TO <nothing> (Clipper RDD-specific)

See Also

DbiAddPassword

DBIEMPTYTABLE

Declaration

```
function DbiEmptyTable (          { Deletes all records }
    hDb            : hDBIDb;      { Database handle }
    hCursor        : hDBICur;     { Cursor (OR) }
    pszTableName   : PChar;       { Table name }
    pszDriverType  : PChar        { Driver type /NIL }
  ): DBIResult;
```

Parameters

Parameter Name	Description
hDb	The database handle.
hCursor	Optional cursor for the table.
	If hCursor is specified, the operation is performed on the table associated with the cursor, which must have been opened in exclusive mode.
	If hCursor is NIL, pszTableName and pszDriverType determine the table to be used.

538

pszTableName	Optional pointer to the table name.
	If hCursor is NIL, pszTableName and pszDriverType determine the table to be used. If both pszTableName and hCursor are specified, pszTableName is ignored.
	Paradox and dBASE. If pszTableName is a fully qualified name of a table, the EpszDriverType parameter need not be specified. If the path is not included, the path name is taken from the current directory of the database associated with hDb.
	SQL, This parameter can be a fully qualified name that includes the owner name.
pszDriverType	Optional pointer to the driver type. This value can be either szDBASE or szPARADOX.
	Paradox and dBASE. This parameter is required if pszTableName has no extension.
	SQL. This parameter is ignored if the database associated with hDb is an SQL database.

Description

Deletes all records from the specified table. However, all resources (for Example, indexes and validity checks) remain. After calling this function, the table and index should now be at their respective minimum sizes.

Paradox. The operation is not performed if there are any conflicting referential integrity constraints on the table. If the table is encrypted, a table-level password with prvINSDEL or prvFULL rights must have been registered.

DBIResult Return Values

DBIERR_NONE	The table was successfully emptied.
DBIERR_INVALIDHNDL	The specified database handle or the specified cursor handle is invalid or NIL.
DBIERR_NEEDEXCLACCESS	The table was not emptied because the user does not have exclusive access to this table.
DBIERR_NOSUCHTABLE	The table specified in pszTableName and pszDriverType does not exist.
DBIERR_INVALIDPARAM	The pointer to the table name is NIL, or the table name is an empty string.
DBIERR_NOTSUFFTABLERIGHTS	The user does not have permission to perform this operation (Paradox only).
DBIERR_NOTSUFFSQLRIGHTS	Insufficient SQL rights to perform this operation (SQL only).
DBIERR_DETAILREEXISTEMPTY	There are conflicting referential integrity constraints on the table (Paradox only).

Example

```
function dbZAP( oTable : TTable ): Boolean;
begin
  Result := IsDbiOk( DbiEmptyTable( oTable.DBHandle, oTable.Handle,
                                nil, PChar( szDBASE )));
end; { dbZAP() }
```

Pure Delphi Equivalent

TTable.EmptyTable

Xbase Equivalent

ZAP

See Also

DbiOpenTable, DbiAddPassword

DBIENDBATCH

Declaration

```
function DbiEndBatch(        { Release a CSL on a Paradox Table }
     hDBCur      : hDBICur    { Cursor Handle }
  ): DBIResult;
```

Parameters

PARAMETER NAME	DESCRIPTION
hCursor	The handle of the cursor to which the lock is to be released.

Description

Releases a Critical Section Lock (CSL) on the specified table. This lock must have been previously applied using DbiBeginBatch.

This function is applicable only to Paradox tables.

Warning: This function is not documented by Borland and may not be supported in future updates to the BDE. In order to use DbiEndBatch, you must remember to declare it and its **.DLL (IDAPI01.DLL** under Delphi 1.x or **IDAPI32.DLL** under Delphi 2.x) at the beginning of the unit. (Special thanks to Eryk Bottomley for providing information regarding this entry.)

DBIResult Return Values

DBIERR_NONE	The CSL was successfully released from the specified cursor.
DBIERR_INVALIDHNDL	The specified cursor handle is invalid or NIL.

Example

```
interface
  function DbiEndBatch( hDBCur : hDBICur ): DBIResult;
.
.
.
implementation
  { Change the external below to 'IDAPI32' for Delphi 2.0 }
  function DbiEndBatch; external 'IDAPI01';
.
.
.
function ReleaseCSL( oTable : TTable ): Boolean;
begin
  Result := ( DbiEndBatch( oTable.Handle ) = DBIERR_NONE );
end;
```

See Also

DbiBeginBatch

DbiEndDelayedUpdates (Delphi 2.0 Only)

Declaration

```
function DbiEndDelayedUpdates(    { Ends cached updates mode }
var   hCursor : hDBICur          { In/Out : returns new cursor }
  ): DBIResult stdcall;
```

Parameters

Parameter Name	Description
hCursor	On input, specifies the original cursor. On output, returns the new cursor; the old cursor is no longer valid.

Description

Takes the cursor out of cached updates mode following a call to DbiBeginDelayedUpdates, and returns a new cursor handle.

DBIResult Return Values

DBIERR_NONE	The cached updates mode was ended and a standard cursor handle was successfully created.

Example

```
function CachedUpdatesToggle( oTable : TTable; bToggle : Boolean;
                              eCommitCmd : DBIDelayedUpdCmd ) : Boolean;
var
  hCur : hDBICur;
begin
  try
    hCur := GetTableCursor( oTable );
    if bToggle then
      Check( DbiBeginDelayedUpdates( hCur ))
    else
    begin
      Check( DbiApplyDelayedUpdates( hCur, eCommitCmd ));
      Check( DbiEndDelayedUpdates( hCur ));
    end; { Turn off caching }
    Result := True;
  except
    Result := False;
  end; { try .. except }
end; { CachedUpdatesToggle() }
```

See Also

DbiBeginDelayedUpdates, DbiApplyDelayedUpdates

DBiEndLinkMode

Declaration

```
function DbiEndLinkMode (  { Convert cursor back to normal cursor }
var    hCursor    : hDBICur { In/Out : returns original cursor }
  ): DBIResult;
```

Parameters

PARAMETER NAME	DESCRIPTION
hCursor	The linked cursor handle, and returns a new cursor handle.

Description

Takes the specified cursor out of link mode, and returns a new cursor handle. For Example, if a detail cursor is taken out of link mode, it is no longer constrained by the master cursor.

A previous call to DbiBeginLinkMode must have been made. DbiUnlinkDetail should be called to unlink the cursor before DbiEndLinkMode is called.

Warning: The cursor handle passed in as input can no longer be used.

DBIResult Return Values

DBIERR_NONE	Linked cursor mode was successfully ended.

Example

```
{ The ExpressionLength function used in this Example can be found in
  BDEREF.PAS on the CD-ROM at the back of this book. This ExpressionLength
  function utilizes the incredibly cool ExtractFields, StringToStringList,
  and AllTrim functions, which are also found in that same file. }

function BreakTheLink( oMaster, oDetail : TTable ) : Boolean;
var
  hMaster,
  hDetail : hDBICur;
begin
  Result := False;
     try
    hMaster := GetTableCursor( oMaster );
    hDetail := GetTableCursor( oDetail );
    if DbiUnlinkDetail( hDetail ) = DBIERR_NONE then
    begin
      DbiEndLinkMode( hMaster );
      DbiEndLinkMode( hDetail );
      oDetail.CursorPosChanged;
      oDetail.Refresh;
      Result := True;
    end;
       except
    Result := False;
       end;
end; { BreakTheLink() }

function MakeTheLink( oMaster, oDetail : TTable; sExp : String ) : Boolean;
var
  hMaster,
  hDetail  : hDBICur;
  szExp    : DBIMsg;
  iLen     : Integer;
begin
  Result := False;
       try
    { You may want to break any existing link before doing this }
    BreakTheLink( oMaster, oDetail );
    hMaster := GetTableCursor( oMaster );
    hDetail := GetTableCursor( oDetail );
    if IsDbiOk( DbiBeginLinkMode( hMaster )) and
       IsDbiOk( DbiBeginLinkMode( hDetail )) then
    begin
      StrPCopy( szExp, sExp );
      iLen := ExpressionLength( oMaster, sExp );
      DbiLinkDetailToExp( hMaster, hDetail, iLen, szExp );
```

```
      DbiSetToBegin( hDetail );
      oDetail.First; { Go to first record in set }
      Result := True;
    end; { if links can be set }
  except
    Result := False;
  end;
end; { MakeTheLink() }
```

Pure Delphi Equivalent

TTable.MasterField

Xbase Equivalent

SET RELATION TO <nothing>

See Also

DbiBeginLinkMode, DbiLinkDetail, DbiUnlinkDetail

DBIENDTRAN

Declaration

```
function DbiEndTran (           { End a transaction }
    hDb         : hDBIDb;       { Database handle }
    hXact       : hDBIXact;     { Transaction handle }
    eEnd        : eXEnd         { Transaction end type }
  ): DBIResult;
```

Parameters

PARAMETER NAME	DESCRIPTION
hDb	The database handle.
hXact	The transaction handle.
eEnd	The transaction end type. Valid transaction end type values are:
	• **xendCOMMIT**. Commit the transaction.
	• **xendCOMMITKEEP**. Commit the transaction and keep cursors.
	• **xendABORT**. Roll back the transaction.

Description

Ends a transaction that was previously requested. DbiBeginTran must have been called first.

If a commit is done, all changes performed within the transaction against the associated database are made permanent. If an abort is done, all changes performed against the associated database are undone.

xendCOMMIT and xendABORT currently keep cursors if the driver and the database can support it. For xendCOMMIT and xendABORT, if the database cannot support keeping cursors, four possibilities exist for each server cursor opened on behalf of the BDE user:

- A cursor for an open query with pending results is buffered locally. Other than prematurely reading the data, no visible effect remains.

- A cursor opened on a table supporting direct positioning is closed. No other behavior is affected.

- A cursor opened on a table that does not support direct positioning is opened initially in a different transaction or connection context, if the database supports this. This cursor remains open because it exists in a different context from the requested transaction.

- If none of the previous possibilities apply, the cursor is closed and subsequent access to the BDE objects associated with the server cursor returns an error.

SQL. This function is supported with SQL server databases only.

DBIResult Return Values

DBIERR_NONE	The transaction has ended successfully.

Example

```
function DirtyTableOp( oTable : TTable; pDo : OpTableProc ) : Boolean;
var
  hXact : hDBIXAct;
begin
  try
    { Turn on Dirty read for speed }
    Result := IsDbiOk( DbiBeginTran( oTable.DBHandle,
                                     xilDIRTYREAD, hXact ));

    if Result then
    begin
      pDo( oTable );
      Result := IsDbiOk( DbiEndTran( oTable.DBHandle, hXact,
                                     xendCOMMIT ));

    end;
  except
    Result := False;
  end;
end; { DirtyTableOp() }
```

Pure Delphi Equivalent

TDataBase.Commit, TDatabase.Rollback

Xbase Equivalent

COMMIT

See Also

DbiBeginTran

DBIEXIT

Declaration

```
function DbiExit: DBIResult;        { Exit engine }
```

Description

DbiExit uninitializes the engine for use by this client and releases all resources allocated by the client application. DbiExit should be the last Dbi* (BDE) function call made by the client application.

After calling DbiExit, all databases and cursors are closed, and any temporary tables are removed. If the exit is done while in an SQL transaction, the active transaction is usually rolled back. (Some SQL drivers commit.)

The user must reinitialize the BDE with DbiInit before any BDE functions can be called.

DBIResult Return Values

DBIERR_NONE	The connection to the engine has been successfully removed.

Example

```
{ Displays the contents of the second field for each record of CUSTOMER.DB
within a scrolling window. }
procedure ListDatabase;
var
  hDB     : hDBIDB;
  hTbl    : hDBICur;
  iResult: DBIResult;
  szBuf,
  szFld   : PChar;
  cProp   : CURProps;
       bBlank : Bool; { Changed from WordBool for Delphi 2.0 }
begin
  DbiInit(nil);
  DbiOpenDataBase( 'DBDEMOS', 'STANDARD', dbiREADWRITE, dbiOPENSHARED, nil,
                  0, nil, nil, hDB );
  DbiOpenTable( hDB, 'CUSTOMER.DB', nil, nil, nil, 0, dbiREADONLY,
               dbiOPENSHARED, xltFIELD, False, nil, hTbl );
  DbiGetCursorProps( hTbl, cProp );
```

```
szBuf := AllocMem( cProp.iRecBufSize * SizeOf( Byte ));
szFld := AllocMem( 255 * SizeOf( Byte ));
DbiSetToBegin( hTbl );
iResult := 0;
repeat
  iResult := DbiGetNextRecord( hTbl, dbiNOLOCK, szBuf, nil );
  DbiGetField( hTbl, 2, szBuf, szFld, bBlank );
  WriteLn( StrPas( szFld ));
until iResult <> DBIERR_NONE;
FreeMem( szBuf, ( cProp.iRecBufSize * SizeOf( Byte )));
FreeMem( szFld, ( 255 * SizeOf( Byte )));
DbiCloseDatabase( hDB );
WriteLn( 'Finished' );
DbiExit;
end; { ListDatabase }
```

See Also

DbiInit

DBIEXTRACTKEY

Declaration

```
function DbiExtractKey (       { Get the key value of current record }
    hCursor      : hDBICur; { Cursor handle }
    pRecBuf      : Pointer; { Record buffer (optional) }
    pKeyBuf      : Pointer  { Returned. Key bytes }
  ): DBIResult;
```

Parameters

PARAMETER NAME	DESCRIPTION
hCursor	The cursor handle. The cursor must be opened with an active index.
pRecBuf	Optional pointer to the record buffer from which to extract the key.
	If NIL, DbiExtractKey extracts the key from the current record.
pKeyBuf	Pointer to the client buffer receiving the key value. The length of the key value can be determined by retrieving the Index Descriptor (IDXDesc) and using iKeyLen or iKeySize in the CURProps structure.

Description

Retrieves the index key value for the current record of the given cursor or from the supplied record buffer. This function requires an index to be active. To retrieve the key from the current record, the cursor must be on a valid record.

The extracted key value is returned in pKeyBuf. The returned key can be used as input to functions such as DbiSetToKey, DbiSetRange, and DbiCompareKey.

DBIResult Return Values

DBIERR_NONE	The key value was retrieved successfully.
DBIERR_INVALIDHNDL	The specified cursor handle is invalid or NIL.
DBIERR_NOASSOCINDEX	The cursor does not have an index active.
DBIERR_NOCURRREC	The cursor is not positioned on a record.

Example

```
function OrdKeyVal( ATable : TTable ) : String;
var
  pszBuf : PChar;
begin
  try
    pszBuf := StrAlloc( 255 );
    { Uses GetTableCursor() from DbiGetCursorForTable() }
    if DbiExtractKey( GetTableCursor( ATable ), nil, pszBuf )
                                   <> DBIERR_NONE then
      Result := ''
    else
      Result := StrPas( pszBuf );
  finally
    StrDispose( pszBuf );
  end;
end; { OrdKeyVal() }
```

Pure Delphi Equivalent

TIndexDef.Expression (Returns expression only, not the evaluated value)

Xbase Equivalent

&IndexKey()

See Also

DbiGetCursorProps, DbiSetToKey, DbiSetRange, DbiCompareKeys, DbiGetRecordForKey

DBIFORCEREREAD

Declaration

```
function DbiForceReread (        { Force buffer reread from Disk }
    hCursor     : hDBICur        { Cursor handle }
  ): DBIResult;
```

Parameters

PARAMETER NAME	DESCRIPTION
hCursor	The cursor handle.

Description

Forces all buffers to be refreshed for the table associated with the cursor. This process causes the record data to be reread from the disk, reflecting the current state of the disk data in case remote updates have taken place.

In order to notify the client application that the table data was actually changed by a remote user, a callback of the type cbTABLECHANGED can be installed. This callback will be invoked whenever a change is detected.

SQL. The table must have a unique row identifier such as an index.

DBIResult Return Values

DBIERR_NONE	Buffers were refreshed successfully.
DBIERR_INVALIDHNDL	The specified cursor handle is invalid or NIL.

Example

```
IsDbiOk( DbiForceReread( GetTableCursor( oTable )));
```

Pure Delphi Equivalent

TTable.Refresh, TQuery.Refresh, TStoredProc.Refresh

Xbase Equivalent

SKIP 0, GOTO RecNo()

See Also

DbiCheckRefresh, DbiForceRecordReread, DbiRegisterCallback

DBIFORCERECORDREREAD (DELPHI 2.0 ONLY)

Declaration

```
function DbiForceRecordReread(    { Refresh a data row }
    hCursor  : hDBICur;           { Cursor handle }
    pRecBuff : Pointer            { Record buffer }
  ): DBIResult;
```

Parameters

PARAMETER NAME	DESCRIPTION
hCursor	The cursor handle.
pRecBuff	Record buffer to refresh.

Description

This routine refreshes only one row of the data table rather than clearing the local cache. This routine is more efficient than DbiForceReread, which executes the query on the server to refresh the cursor and causes the entire local cache to be updated. Based on the optimistic record-locking method, individual records (rows) may be reread from the server if a record lock is requested. However, this is based on a number of factors, including record age (how long since the record has been retrieved from the server).

When this routine is called, a valid record based on the index or record address is reread from the server. pRecBuf is used to contain the refreshed record. The behavior of this routine varies from DbiGetRecord in that an optimistic lock is not obtained, and the record is always reread from the server. The record is reread with the current index (or record address), which has to be unique.

DBIResult Return Values

DBIERR_NONE	Buffers were refreshed successfully.
DBIERR_INVALIDHNDL	The specified cursor handle is invalid or NIL.

Example

```
function SafeDupeRecord( oTable : TTable ): Boolean;
var
  curProp : CURProps;
  pRecBuf : PChar;
begin
  Result := False;
  try
    { Read cursor properties }
    Check( DbiGetCursorProps( oTable.Handle, curProp ));

    { Allocate memory for the record buffer }
    GetMem( pRecBuf, curProp.iRecBufSize );

    { Initialise record buffer }
    if Assigned( pRecBuf ) then
      Check( DbiForceRecordReread( oTable.Handle, pRecBuf ));

    { Read current record }
    Result := oTable.GetCurrentRecord( pRecBuf ) and
              IsDbiOk( DbiAppendRecord( GetTableCursor( oTable ),
                                        pRecBuf ));
```

```
  finally
    if Assigned( pRecBuf ) then
      FreeMem( pRecBuf, curProp.iRecBufSize );
  end;
end; { SafeDupeRecord() }
```

Pure Delphi Equivalent

TTable.Refresh, TQuery.Refresh, TStoredProc.Refresh

Xbase Equivalent

SKIP 0, GOTO RecNo()

See Also

DbiCheckRefresh, DbiForceReread, DbiRegisterCallback

DBIFORMFULLNAME

Declaration

```
function DbiFormFullName (         { Form Full Name }
      hDb          : hDBIDb;       { Database handle }
      pszTableName : PChar;        { Table name }
      pszDriverType : PChar;       { Driver type /NIL }
      pszFullName  : PChar         { Returns full name }
  ): DBIResult;
```

Parameters

PARAMETER NAME	DESCRIPTION
hDb	The database handle.
pszTableName	Pointer to the table name.
pszDriverType	Pointer to the driver type.
pszFullName	Pointer to the client buffer that receives the fully qualified table name.

Description

Returns the fully qualified table name, using the directory associated with the supplied database handle. DbiSetDirectory can be used to change this directory

If the specified table name contains the drive letter and colon, this function simply returns the same table name that was passed in without changing it.

DBIResult Return Values

DBIERR_NONE	The table name has been successfully returned.
DBIERR_INVALIDFILENAME	The specified table name is invalid.

Example

```
function FullTableName( oTable : TTable ) : String;
var
  szTableName,
  szFullName   : Array[0..78] of Char;
begin
  StrPCopy( szTableName, oTable.TableName );
  if IsDbiOk( DbiFormFullName( oTable.DBHandle, szTableName, #0,
                               szFullName )) then
    Result := StrPas( szFullName );
end; { FullTableName() }
```

Pure Delphi Equivalent

TTable.DatabaseName + TTable.TableName

See Also

DbiSetDirectory

DBIFREEBLOB

Declaration

```
function DbiFreeBlob (              { Closes the BLOB }
      hCursor     : hDBICur;        { Cursor handle }
      pRecBuf     : Pointer;        { Record Buffer }
      iField      : Word           { Field number of blob (0..n) }
    ): DBIResult;
```

Parameters

PARAMETER NAME	DESCRIPTION
hCursor	The cursor handle for the table. The table must contain a BLOB field.
pRecBuf	The pointer to the record buffer containing the BLOB handle. DbiOpenBlob sets the BLOB handle in the record buffer.
iField	The valid field number of the open BLOB field. If set to 0, the DbiFreeBlob call closes all open BLOBs associated with the record buffer.

Description

Closes the BLOB handle previously obtained with DbiOpenBlob, releasing all resources allocated to it.

The BLOB handle is located within the specified record buffer.

This function must be called after calling DbiModifyRecord, DbiInsertRecord, or DbiAppendRecord (only if a BLOB has been opened), in order to free BLOB resources. DbiModifyRecord, DbiInsertRecord, or DbiAppendRecord do not automatically release BLOB resources after record modification. However, if DbiFreeBlob is called prior to calling DbiModifyRecord, DbiInsertRecord, or DbiAppendRecord, then any changes made to the BLOB are lost.

This function does not affect the contents of the BLOB on disk.

DBIResult Return Values

DBIERR_NONE	The BLOB field was freed successfully.
DBIERR_INVALIDHNDL	The specified cursor handle is invalid or NIL.
DBIERR_INVALIDPARAM	The specified record buffer is NIL.
DBIERR_OUTOFRANGE	The number specified in iField is greater than the number of fields in the table.
DBIERR_BLOBNOTOPENED	The specified BLOB field has not been opened via a call to DbiOpenBlob. This error is returned if the BLOB has already been freed with a previous DbiFreeBlob call.
DBIERR_INVALIDBLOBHANDLE	The logical BLOB handle in the record buffer is invalid.
DBIERR_NOTABLOB	The specified field number does not correspond to a BLOB field.

Example

```
{ Truncates the specified BLOB field to zero length. Then commits the
  changes and releases any record lock (if Shared mode) }
procedure TruncateBlob( oTable : TTable; pRec : Pointer;
                        iFieldNo : Word );
begin
  if oTable.Active then
  begin
    try
      Check( DbiOpenBlob( oTable.Handle, pRec, iFieldNo,
                          dbiREADWRITE ));
      Check( DbiTruncateBlob( oTable.Handle, pRec, iFieldNo, 0 ));
      Check( DbiModifyRecord( oTable.Handle, pRec, True ));
    finally
      if Assigned( pRec ) then
        Check( DbiFreeBlob( oTable.Handle, pRec, iFieldNo ));
    end;
  end;
end;
```

Pure Delphi Equivalent

TBlobField.Free

See Also

DbiOpenTable, DbiOpenBlob, DbiPutBlob, DbiTruncateBlob, DbiGetBlob, DbiGetBlobSize, DbiInsertRecord, DbiAppendRecord, DbiModifyRecord

DBIGETBLOB

Declaration

```
function DbiGetBlob (          { Read bytes from blob }
     hCursor   : hDBICur;      { Cursor handle }
     pRecBuf   : Pointer;      { Record buffer }
     iField    : Word;         { Field number of blob (1..n) }
     iOffSet   : Longint;      { Starting position }
     iLen      : Longint;      { Number of bytes to be read }
     pDest     : Pointer;      { Destination }
var  iRead     : Longint       { Actual number of bytes read }
   ): DBIResult;
```

Parameters

PARAMETER NAME	DESCRIPTION
hCursor	The cursor handle.
pRecBuf	Pointer to the record buffer containing the BLOB handle. The record buffer is returned from a call to DbiGetNextRecord, DbiGetPriorRecord, DbiGetRelativeRecord, or DbiGetRecord. DbiOpenBlob sets the BLOB handle in the record buffer.
iField	The ordinal number of the BLOB field in the record.
iOffSet	The start location for retrieval within the BLOB field. If 0 is specified, retrieval starts from the beginning of the field. If the value exceeds the length of the BLOB field, an error is returned. If any value greater than 0 is specified, then only a portion of the BLOB field is retrieved.
iLen	The number of bytes to retrieve. iLen must be between 0 and the length of the BLOB field. iLen must also be less than 64K.
pDest	Pointer to the client buffer that receives the BLOB data.
iRead	Pointer to the client variable that receives the actual number of bytes read. The actual number can be less than the number of bytes requested if the end of the BLOB is reached.

Description

Retrieves data from the specified BLOB field. Any portion of the data within the BLOB field can be retrieved, starting from the position specified in iOffSet, and extending to the number of bytes specified in iLen. pRecBuf should contain a BLOB handle obtained by calling DbiOpenBlob.

After calling this function, iRead points to the number of bytes of BLOB data retrieved, and pDest points to the retrieved BLOB data.

DBIResult Return Values

DBIERR_NONE	The BLOB field was successfully retrieved.
DBIERR_BLOBNOTOPENED	The specified BLOB field has not been opened via call to DbiOpenBlob.
DBIERR_INVALIDBLOBHANDLE	The logical BLOB handle supplied in the record buffer is invalid.
DBIERR_NOTABLOB	The specified field number does not correspond to a BLOB field.
DBIERR_INVALIDBLOBOFFSET	The start location specified in iOffSet is greater than the length of the BLOB field.
DBIERR_ENDOFBLOB	The end of the BLOB has been reached. Check iRead to see if any data was returned.

Example

```
{====================================================================
   Code:    DispBlob();

   Input:   hCur     -    Table Cursor.
            pRecBuf  -    Record Buffer.
            iOff     -    Which record to display.

   Return: None.

   Desc:    This function displays the BLOB field that is pointed to
            by the Cursor and which resides in the record buffer.
            The function displays the whole BLOB and then half of the
            BLOB. It uses DbiGetBlob with and without a range to
            accomplish this functionality.

   Note:    Requires WinCRT unit for the WriteLn function.
 ================================================================ }
procedure DispBlob( hCur: hDBICur; pRecBuf: Pointer;
                    iOff, iFieldNum : Integer );
var
  BlobSize  : Longint;  { Size of the BLOB }
  ActualSize: Longint;  { Actual size of the BLOB as read from the
                          table }
const
  phBlob     : PChar = nil;  { Pointer to BLOB data }
  phHalfBlob: PChar = nil;  { Pointer to BLOB data }
begin
  { Clear the Record buffer. }
  FillChar( pRecBuf^, SizeOf( pRecBuf ), #0 );

  { Get the record from the table }
  Check( DbiGetRecord( hCur, dbiWRITELOCK, pRecBuf, nil ));

  { Open the BLOB.  The BLOB must be opened before reading or
    writing from a BLOB. If the BLOB is opened in ReadWrite mode,
    the table also has to be open in ReadWrite mode. }
  Check( DbiOpenBlob( hCur, pRecBuf, iFieldNum, dbiREADONLY ));
```

```
{ Get the size of the BLOB }
Check( DbiGetBlobSize( hCur, pRecBuf, iFieldNum, BlobSize ));

{ Allocate the memory for the BLOB buffer }
GetMem( phBlob, ( SizeOf( Char ) * Integer( BlobSize )));

{ Allocate memory for the pHalfBlob buffer }
GetMem( phHalfBlob, (( SizeOf( Char ) *
        trunc( Integer( BlobSize ) / 2 )) + 2 ));

{ Initialize the buffers to 0 }
FillChar( phBlob^, Integer( BlobSize ), #0 );
FillChar( phHalfBlob^, trunc( Integer( BlobSize )/2 ) + 2, #0 );

{ Get the BLOB from the table }
Check( DbiGetBlob( hCur, pRecBuf, iFieldNum, 0, BlobSize,
                   phBlob, ActualSize ));

WriteLn('');
WriteLn('    This is the BLOB information in Record# ' +
        IntToStr( iOff ));
WriteLn('');
WriteLn('    This is the whole BLOB Field');
WriteLn('');
WriteLn( phBlob );

{ Now we are going to get Half the BLOB and display that.  To get
  half the BLOB we start at half the total size BlobSize/2 and
  retrieve BlobSize/2 bytes. }
Check( DbiGetBlob( hCur, pRecBuf, iFieldNum,
        trunc( (BlobSize)/2 ), trunc(( BlobSize )/2 ),
        phHalfBlob, ActualSize ));

WriteLn('    This is half of the BLOB Field');
WriteLn('');
WriteLn( StrPas( phHalfBlob ));

{ Free the BLOB from memory }
Check( DbiFreeBlob( hCur, pRecBuf, iFieldNum ));

{ Free the BLOB and half BLOB buffer form the program's memory }
FreeMem( phBlob, ( SizeOf( Byte ) * Integer( BlobSize )));
FreeMem( phHalfBlob, (( SizeOf( Byte ) *
                       trunc( Integer( BlobSize )/2 )) + 2 ));
end;
```

Pure Delphi Equivalent

TBlobField.GetData

See Also

DbiOpenBlob, DbiPutBlob, DbiFreeBlob, DbiTruncateBlob, DbiGetBlobSize

DBIGETBLOBHEADING

Declaration

```
function DbiGetBlobHeading (      { Get BLOBHeading }
     hCursor      : hDBICur;      { Cursor handle }
     iField       : Word;         { Field number of blob (1..n) }
     pRecBuf      : Pointer;      { Record buffer of owner record }
     pDest        : Pointer       { Destination buffer }
) : DBIResult;
```

Parameters

PARAMETER NAME	DESCRIPTION
hCursor	The cursor handle.
iField	The ordinal number of the BLOB field within the record.
pRecBuf	Pointer to the client buffer containing the BLOB heading.
pDest	Pointer to the client buffer that receives the retrieved BLOB heading. The client buffer must be large enough to accommodate the retrieved information.

Description

Retrieves information about a BLOB field from the BLOB heading in the record buffer. This call does not require a prior call to DbiOpenBlob. This function is the functional equivalent of a DbiGetField call for BLOB fields).

This function is valid only for Paradox table types, since only they support BLOB headings. When the table is created, the client can specify the number of bytes of the BLOB field information to be stored in the record itself. This information is also duplicated in the normal storage area of the BLOB. The benefit of storing some of the BLOB field in the record is that the BLOB field does not have to be opened to retrieve this information. If the BLOB is small, it can be contained fully in the record making access faster.

Paradox. With formatted BLOB fields, the formatting information in the first eight bytes of the field is not stored within the record. It is functionally the same as if DbiGetBlob were called with an iOffSet of 8 and an iLen the length of the record buffer.

dBASE. This function is not supported for dBASE tables.

SQL. This function is not supported for SQL tables.

DBIResult Return Values

DBIERR_NONE	The BLOB heading was retrieved successfully.
DBIERR_NOTABLOB	The specified field number does not correspond to a BLOB field.
DBIERR_NOTSUFFFIELDRIGHTS	The application does not have sufficient rights to this field.
DBIERR_NOTSUPPORTED	This function is not supported by SQL or dBASE.

Example

```
{ DbiOpenBlob(), DbiGetBlobSize(), DbiGetBlobHeading(), DbiFreeBlob() }
procedure BlobHeader( InDataSet: TDataSet; sField : String;
                      var P: PChar);
var
  iBlobPos    : Integer;
  iBlobSize   : Longint;
begin
  { Get ordinal position of blob for field in file }
  iBlobPos := InDataSet.FieldByName( sField ).Index + 1;
  InDataSet.UpdateCursorPos;
  Check( DbiOpenBlob( InDataSet.Handle, InDataSet.ActiveBuffer,
                     iBlobPos, dbiReadOnly ));
  Check( DbiGetBlobSize( InDataSet.Handle, InDataSet.ActiveBuffer,
                        iBlobPos, iBlobSize ));
  Check( DbiGetBlobHeading( InDataSet.Handle, iBlobPos,
                           InDataSet.ActiveBuffer, P ));
  Check( DbiFreeBlob( InDataSet.Handle, InDataSet.ActiveBuffer,
                     iBlobPos ));
end; { BlobHeader() }
```

See Also

DbiPutBlob, DbiTruncateBlob, DbiFreeBlob, DbiGetBlob, DbiGetBlobSize

DBIGETBLOBSIZE

Declaration

```
function DbiGetBlobSize (          { Gets the size of a blob }
      hCursor    : hDBICur;        { Cursor handle }
      pRecBuf    : Pointer;        { Record Buffer }
      iField     : Word;           { Field number of blob (1..n) }
var   iSize      : Longint         { Blob size in bytes }
   ): DBIResult;
```

Parameters

PARAMETER NAME	DESCRIPTION
hCursor	The cursor handle.
pRecBuf	Pointer to the record buffer containing the BLOB handle. The client application must first allocate the buffer and fetch a valid record. A call to DbiOpenBlob then obtains the BLOB handle.
iField	The ordinal number of the BLOB field within the specified record buffer.
iSize	Pointer to the client variable that receives the BLOB size in bytes.

Description

Retrieves the size of the specified BLOB field in bytes.

In order to call this function, the current record buffer must contain a BLOB field which has been opened by a call to DbiOpenBlob.

After calling this function, *iSize* points to the retrieved size of the BLOB field.

DBIResult Return Values

DBIERR_NONE	The BLOB size was successfully retrieved.
DBIERR_BLOBNOTOPENED	The specified BLOB field has not been opened with a call to DbiOpenBlob.
DBIERR_INVALIDBLOBHANDLE	The logical BLOB handle supplied in the record buffer is invalid.
DBIERR_NOTABLOB	The specified field number does not correspond to a BLOB field.

Example

```
{=================================================================
    Code:    DispBlob();

    Input:   hCur     -   Table Cursor.
             pRecBuf  -   Record Buffer.
             iOff     -   Which record to display.

    Return: None.

    Desc:   This function displays the BLOB field that is pointed to
            by the Cursor and which resides in the record buffer.
            The function displays the whole BLOB and then half of the
            BLOB. It uses DbiGetBlob with and without a range to
            accomplish this functionality.

    Note:   Requires WinCRT unit for the WriteLn function.

 ================================================================= }
procedure DispBlob( hCur: hDBICur; pRecBuf: Pointer;
                    iOff, iFieldNum : Integer );
var
  BlobSize  : Longint;  { Size of the BLOB }
  ActualSize: Longint;  { Actual size of the BLOB as read from the
                          table }
const
  phBlob    : PChar = nil;  { Pointer to BLOB data }
  phHalfBlob: PChar = nil;  { Pointer to BLOB data }
begin
  { Clear the Record buffer. }
  FillChar( pRecBuf^, SizeOf( pRecBuf ), #0 );

  { Get the record from the table }
  Check( DbiGetRecord( hCur, dbiWRITELOCK, pRecBuf, nil ));
```

```
{ Open the BLOB.  The BLOB must be opened before reading or
  writing from a BLOB. If the BLOB is opened in ReadWrite mode,
  the table also has to be open in ReadWrite mode. }
Check( DbiOpenBlob( hCur, pRecBuf, iFieldNum, dbiREADONLY ));

{ Get the size of the BLOB }
Check( DbiGetBlobSize( hCur, pRecBuf, iFieldNum, BlobSize ));

{ Allocate the memory for the BLOB buffer }
GetMem( phBlob, ( SizeOf( Char ) * Integer( BlobSize )));

{ Allocate memory for the pHalfBlob buffer }
GetMem( phHalfBlob, (( SizeOf( Char ) *
        trunc( Integer( BlobSize ) / 2 )) + 2 ));

{ Initialize the buffers to 0 }
FillChar( phBlob^, Integer( BlobSize ), #0 );
FillChar( phHalfBlob^, trunc( Integer( BlobSize )/2 ) + 2, #0 );

{ Get the BLOB from the table }
Check( DbiGetBlob( hCur, pRecBuf, iFieldNum, 0, BlobSize,
                   phBlob, ActualSize ));

WriteLn('');
WriteLn('    This is the BLOB information in Record# ' +
        IntToStr( iOff ));
WriteLn('''');
WriteLn('    This is the whole BLOB Field');
WriteLn('');
WriteLn( phBlob );

{ Now we are going to get Half the BLOB and display that. To get half
  the BLOB we start at half the total size BlobSize/2 and retrieve
  BlobSize/2 bytes. }
Check( DbiGetBlob( hCur, pRecBuf, iFieldNum,
       trunc( (BlobSize)/2 ), trunc(( BlobSize )/2 ),
       phHalfBlob, ActualSize ));

WriteLn('    This is half of the BLOB Field');
WriteLn('');
WriteLn( StrPas( phHalfBlob ));

{ Free the BLOB from memory }
Check( DbiFreeBlob( hCur, pRecBuf, iFieldNum ));

{ Free the BLOB and half BLOB buffer form the program's memory }
FreeMem( phBlob, ( SizeOf( Byte ) * Integer( BlobSize )));
FreeMem( phHalfBlob, (( SizeOf( Byte ) *
                       trunc( Integer( BlobSize )/2 )) + 2 ));
end;
```

Pure Delphi Equivalent

TBlobField.DataSize

See Also

DbiOpenBlob, DbiPutBlob, DbiGetBlob, DbiFreeBlob, DbiTruncateBlob

DBiGetBookMark

Declaration

```
function DbiGetBookMark (        { Get a bookmark }
    hCur          : hDBICur;     { Cursor handle }
    pBookMark     : Pointer      { Pointer to bookmark }
): DBIResult;
```

Parameters

PARAMETER NAME	DESCRIPTION
hCur	The cursor handle.
pBookMark	Pointer to the client-allocated bookmark buffer.

Description

Saves the current position of a cursor in the client-supplied bookmark buffer. This position is called a bookmark. DbiGetCursorProps should be called to retrieve the iBookMarkSize property and the bookmark buffer should be allocated to accommodate the bookmark.

A bookmark contains internal information about the current position of the cursor. This information can be passed to DbiSetToBookMark to reposition the same or compatible cursor. If a bookmark is stable, it is guaranteed that the cursor can be repositioned there. Whether or not the bookmark is stable can be determined from the bBookMarkStable property returned by DbiGetCursorProps.

dBASE. For dBASE tables, the bookmark is always stable.

Paradox. For Paradox tables, the bookmark is stable only if the table has a primary key.

SQL. For SQL tables, the bookmark is stable only if the table has a unique index or unique row identifier.

Note: The size of a bookmark depends on the current index and can change if DbiSwitchToIndex is called.

DBIResult Return Values

DBIERR_NONE	The bookmark was returned successfully.
DBIERR_INVALIDHNDL	The specified cursor handle is invalid or NIL, or the pointer to the bookmark is NIL.

Example

```
function GrabBookmark( oTable : TTable ): Pointer;
begin
  Result := StrAlloc( TableProperties( oTable ).iBookmarkSize );
  IsDbiOk( DbiGetBookmark( oTable.Handle, Result ));
end;
```

Pure Delphi Equivalent

TTable.GetBookMark, TQuery.GetBookMark

Xbase Equivalent

RecNo(), OrdKeyData()

See Also

DbiSetToBookMark, DbiCompareBookMarks, DbiGetCursorProps

DBIGETCALLBACK

Declaration

```
function DbiGetCallBack (            { Register a call back function }
      hCursor      : hDBICur;        { Cursor (Optional) }
      ecbType      : CBType;         { Type of call back }
var   iClientData  : Longint;        { Pass-thru client data }
var   iCbBufLen    : Word;           { Callback buffer len }
var   pCbBuf       : Pointer;        { Pointer to callback buffer }
      ppfCb        : ppfDBICallBack  { Call back function being
                                       registered }
    ): DBIResult;
```

Parameters

PARAMETER NAME	DESCRIPTION
hCursor	The cursor handle. If NIL, the callback is session-wide rather than cursor-level.
ecbType	The type of callback.
iClientData	Reference to the pass-through client data (used by the client function).
iCbBufLen	Reference to the callback buffer length.
pCbBuf	Reference to the callback buffer pointer.
ppfCb	Pointer to the client variable that receives a pointer to the callback function that was previously registered for this type. The buffer receives a NIL pointer if no function was registered.

Description

Returns a pointer to the function previously registered by the client (using DbiRegisterCallBack) for the given callback type.

This function is typically used to find out whether the specified callback function was registered for the given cursor handle or the currently active session.

DBIResult Return Values

DBIERR_NONE	The callback function for the given cursor handle has been successfully retrieved.

Example

```
const
  StartTime   : LongInt = 0;
  ServerTimer : Word = 0;
var
  dbiCallBack : TCallBack;
  pServerData : Pointer;

{ Timer callback function }
procedure TimerCallBack( hWnd: HWND; Message: Word; TimerID: Word;
                         SysTime: LongInt); export;

begin
  KillTimer( 0, TimerID );
  ServerTimer := 0;
  StartTime := 0;
end;

function ServerCallBack( CallType: CBType; Data: Longint;
                         var Info: Pointer): CBRType; export;
const
  MinWait = 500;
var
  CallInfo: CBSCType;
begin
  Result := cbrUSEDEF;
  if CallType = cbSERVERCALL then
  begin
    CallInfo := CBSCType( Info );
    if CallInfo = cbscSQL then
      if StartTime = 0 then
      begin
        ServerTimer := SetTimer( 0, 0, 1000, @TimerCallBack );
        StartTime := GetTickCount;
      end;
    with dbiCallBack do
      if ChainedFunc <> nil then
        Result := pfDBICallBack( ChainedFunc )( cbSERVERCALL, Data,
                                                Buffer )
```

```
    end;
end;

function InitializeSession : Boolean;
var
  dbEnv        : DbiEnv;
  callBack     : TCallBack;
  ServerData   : Pointer;
begin
  Result := False;
  try
    FillChar( dbEnv, SizeOf( dbEnv ), 0 );
    StrPLCopy( dbEnv.szLang, LoadStr( SIDAPILangID ),
             SizeOf( dbEnv.szLang )-1 );
    if IsDbiOk( DbiInit( @dbEnv )) then
    begin
      pServerData := AllocMem( SizeOf( CBSCType ));
      with dbiCallback do
        DbiGetCallBack( nil, cbSERVERCALL, Data, BufLen, Buffer,
                        @ChainedFunc );
        DbiRegisterCallBack( nil, cbSERVERCALL, 0,
                             SizeOf( CBSCType ),
                             pServerData, ServerCallBack );
      Result := True;
    end;
  except
  end;
end;
```

See Also

DbiRegisterCallBack

DbiGetClientInfo

Declaration

```
function DbiGetClientInfo (          { Get Client info }
var    clientInfo : CLIENTInfo
  ): DBIResult;
```

Parameters

PARAMETER NAME	DESCRIPTION
clientInfo	Reference to the client-allocated CLIENTInfo structure.

Description

Retrieves system-level information about the client application in clientInfo.

This function can be used to determine if other sessions are present when exclusive access is required to a table. It can also be used to determine the current language driver and to get the working directory.

DBIResult Return Values

DBIERR_NONE	Client application information was returned successfully.

Example

```
function BDEClientInfo : CLIENTInfo;
begin
  IsDbiOk( DbiGetClientInfo( Result ));
end; { BDEClientInfo() }
```

See Also

DbiGetSysVersion, DbiGetSysConfig, DbiGetSysInfo

DBIGETCURRSESSION

Declaration

```
function DbiGetCurrSession (      { Get the current session }
var   hSes        : hDBISes      { Session handle }
    ): DBIResult;
```

Parameters

PARAMETER NAME	DESCRIPTION
hSes	Pointer to the current session handle.

Description

Returns the handle associated with the current session. If no sessions have been started explicitly by the client application (with DbiStartSession), the handle of the default session is returned.

DBIResult Return Values

DBIERR_NONE	The current session handle has been retrieved successfully.
DBIERR_INVALIDHNDL	hSes is NIL.

Example

```
function CurrentSession : HDBISes;
begin
  if not IsDbiOk( DbiGetCurrSession( Result )) then Result := nil;
end;
```

Pure Delphi Equivalent

TSession.Handle

See Also

DbiSetCurrSession, DbiStartSession, DbiCloseSession, DbiGetSysInfo, DbiGetSesInfo

DBIGETCURSORFORTABLE

Declaration

```
function DbiGetCursorForTable (     { Find cursor for a given table }
     hDb             : hDBIDb;      { Database handle }
     pszTableName    : PChar;       { Table name }
     pszDriverType   : PChar;       { Driver type / NIL }
var  hCursor          : hDBICur     { Returned cursor }
   ): DBIResult;
```

Parameters

PARAMETER NAME	DESCRIPTION
hDb	Optional database handle. If supplied, DbiFormFullName is called to create a fully qualified table name.
pszTableName	Pointer to the table name.
pszDriverType	Optional pointer to the driver type. If supplied, used with hDb in a call to DbiFormFullName.
hCursor	Pointer to the returned cursor handle.

Description

Returns an existing cursor for the given table within the current session. If more than one cursor is opened on the table, the first cursor found on the table is returned. There is no implied ordering of cursors on a table.

DBIResult Return Values

DBIERR_NONE	The cursor for the table was retrieved successfully.
DBIERR_INVALIDHNDL	The specified database handle is invalid or NIL.
DBIERR_INVALIDPARAM	The specified table name or the pointer to the table name is NIL.
DBIERR_NOSUCHTABLE	The specified table name is invalid.
DBIERR_OBJNOTFOUND	A valid cursor could not be found.

Example

```
function GetTableCursor( oTable : TTable ) : hDBICur;
var
  pszTable : Array[0..78] of Char;
begin
  StrPCopy( pszTable, oTable.TableName );
  DbiGetCursorForTable( oTable.DBHandle, pszTable, nil, Result );
end; { GetTableCursor() }
```

Pure Delphi Equivalent

TTable.Handle

Xbase Equivalent

Select(), Alias()

See Also

DbiFormFullName

DBIGETCURSORPROPS

Declaration

```
function DbiGetCursorProps (      { Get Cursor properties }
     hCursor    : hDBICur;        { Cursor handle }
var  curProps   : CURProps        { Cursor properties }
   ): DBIResult;
```

Parameters

PARAMETER NAME	DESCRIPTION
hCursor	The cursor handle.
curProps	Reference to the client-allocated CURProps structure to be filled.

Description

Retrieves the most commonly used cursor properties. Additional properties can be obtained using DbiGetProp. This function can be called immediately after opening a table to retrieve information necessary to allocate the record buffer and the array for the field descriptors in the table.

The Parameters for this routine are deceptively simple. The structure of CURProps (as found in **DBITYPES.INT** under Delphi 1.x) provides extensive details about the data cursor, as shown in the following:

```
pCURProps = ^CURProps;
CURProps = record                           { Virtual Table properties }
  szName            : DBITBLNAME;           { Table name (no extension, if it
                                              can be derived) }
  iFNameSize        : Word;                 { Full file name size }
  szTableType       : DBINAME;              { Driver type }
  iFields           : Word;                 { No of fields in Table }
  iRecSize          : Word;                 { Record size (logical record) }
  iRecBufSize       : Word;                 { Record size (physical record) }
  iKeySize          : Word;                 { Key size }
  iIndexes          : Word;                 { Number of indexes }
  iValChecks        : Word;                 { Number of val checks }
  iRefIntChecks     : Word;                 { Number of Ref Integrity constraints }
  iBookMarkSize     : Word;                 { Bookmark size }
  bBookMarkStable   : Bool;                 { Stable book marks }
  eOpenMode         : DBIOpenMode;          { ReadOnly / ReadWrite }
  eShareMode        : DBIShareMode;         { Exclusive / Shared }
  bIndexed          : Bool;                 { Index is in use }
  iSeqNums          : Integer;              { 1: Has Seqnums; 0: Has Record# }
  bSoftDeletes      : Bool;                 { Supports soft deletes }
  bDeletedOn        : Bool;                 { If above, deleted recs seen }
  iRefRange         : Word;                 { Not used }
  exltMode          : XLTMode;              { Translate Mode }
  iRestrVersion     : Word;                 { Restructure version number }
  bUniDirectional   : Bool;                 { Cursor is uni-directional }
  eprvRights        : Word;                 { Table rights }
  iFmlRights        : Word;                 { Family rights }
  iPasswords        : Word;                 { Number of Aux passwords }
  iCodePage         : Word;                 { Codepage (0 if unknown) }
  bProtected        : Bool;                 { Table is protected by password }
  iTblLevel         : Word;                 { Driver dependent table level }
  szLangDriver      : DBINAME;              { Language driver name }
  bFieldMap         : Bool;                 { Field map active }
  iBlockSize        : Word;                 { Physical file blocksize in K }
  bStrictRefInt     : Bool;                 { Strict referential integrity }
  iFilters          : Word;                 { Number of filters }
  bTempTable        : Bool;                 { Table is a temporary table }
  iUnUsed           : Array[0..15] of Word;
end;
```

DBIResult Return Values

DBIERR_NONE	Cursor properties for hCursor were successfully retrieved.
DBIERR_INVALIDHNDL	The specified cursor handle is invalid or NIL.

Example

```
{ A single Recno function that works with dBASE or Paradox tables }
function Recno( oTable : TTable ): LongInt;
var
  CursorProps: CurProps;
  RecordProps: RECProps;
begin
  result := 0;
  with oTable do
  begin
    if State = dsInactive then
      DBError( SDataSetClosed );
    Check( DbiGetCursorProps( Handle, CursorProps ));
    UpdateCursorPos;
    Check( DbiGetRecord( Handle, dbiNOLOCK, nil, @RecordProps ));
    case CursorProps.iSeqNums of
      0: result := RecordProps.iPhyRecNum;
      1: result := RecordProps.iSeqNum;
    end;
  end;
end;
```

See Also

DbiGetProp, DbiSetProp

DBIGETDATABASEDESC

Declaration

```
function DbiGetDatabaseDesc (    { Get a Description of a logical db }
      pszName       : PChar;      { Name of logical database }
      pdbDesc       : pDBDesc     { Database Description }
  ): DBIResult;
```

Parameters

PARAMETER NAME	DESCRIPTION
pszName	Specifies the database name.
pdbDesc	Specifies the client-allocated DBDesc structure to be filled.

Description

Retrieves the Description of the specified database from the configuration file.

DBIResult Return Values

DBIERR_NONE	The database Description for pszName was retrieved successfully.
DBIERR_OBJNOTFOUND	The database named in pszName was not found.

Example

```
procedure DatabaseDescList( const sAliasName : String; List: TStrings );
var
  szAlias : Array[0..31] of Char;
  Desc : DBDesc;
begin
  List.BeginUpdate;
  try
    List.Clear;
    StrPCopy( szAlias, sAliasName );
    AnsiToOem( szAlias, szAlias );
    Check( DbiGetDatabaseDesc( szAlias, @Desc ) );
    if StrIComp( Desc.szDbType, 'STANDARD' ) = 0 then
      with Desc do
      begin
        OemToAnsi( szName, szName );
        List.Add( Format( 'NAME=%s', [ szName ] ));
        OemToAnsi( szText, szText );
        List.Add( Format( 'TEXT=%s', [ szText ] ));
        OemToAnsi( szPhyName, szPhyName );
        List.Add( Format( 'PATH=%s', [ szPhyName ] ));
        OemToAnsi( szDbType, szDbType );
        List.Add( Format( 'DbType=%sv,' [ szDbType ] ));
      end; { with Desc }
  finally
    List.EndUpdate;
  end;
end;
```

See Also

DbiOpenDatabaseList

DBIGETDATEFORMAT

Declaration

```
function DbiGetDateFormat (     { Get current date format }
var    fmtDate    : FMTDate
   ): DBIResult;
```

Parameters

PARAMETER NAME	DESCRIPTION
pfmtDate	Reference to the client-allocated FMTDate structure to be filled.

Description

Gets the date format for the current session. The date format is used by QBE for input and wildcard character matching. It is also used by batch operations such as DbiDoRestructure and DbiBatchMove to handle data type coercion between character and date types. The default date format can be changed by editing the system configuration file. The date format for the current session can be changed using DbiSetDateFormat.

DBIResult Return Values

DBIERR_NONE	The date format was successfully retrieved.
DBIERR_INVALIDHNDL	pfmtDate is NIL.

Example

```
function BDEDateFormat : FMTDate;
begin
  IsDbiOk( DbiGetDateFormat( Result ));
end; { BDEDateFormat }
```

Pure Delphi Equivalent

LongDateFormat, ShortDateFormat

Xbase Equivalent

Set(_SET_DATEFORMAT)

See Also

DbiGetNumberFormat, DbiGetTimeFormat, DbiSetDateFormat

DBIGETDIRECTORY

Declaration

```
function DbiGetDirectory (    { Get the current/default directory }
    hDb         : hDBIDb;    { Universal database handle }
    bDefault    : Bool;      { True for default }
    pszDir      : PChar      { Returned directory }
  ): DBIResult;
```

Parameters

PARAMETER NAME	DESCRIPTION
hDb	The database handle. Must be associated with a standard database.
bDefault	Indicates whether to retrieve the default directory (True) or the current working directory (False).
pszDir	Pointer to the client-allocated buffer which receives the directory string. The buffer must be large enough to hold the directory string (DBIMAXPATHLEN + 1).

Description

Retrieves the current directory or the default directory, depending on the value specified in bDefault.

This function is valid only for a standard database. The default directory can be set when DbiInit is called as part of the DBIEnv structure. If DbiSetDirectory is not called, then the default directory is the same as the application startup directory.

SQL. DbiGetDirectory is not applicable to SQL databases.

DBIResult Return Values

DBIERR_NONE	The directory was returned successfully.
DBIERR_INVALIDHNDL	The specified database handle is invalid or NIL.

Example

```
function GetAliasPath( sAlias: String ): String;
var
  Database : TDatabase;
  pszDir   : PChar;
begin
  try
    Database := TDatabase.Create(nil);
    with Database do
    begin
      pszDir := StrAlloc( 255 );
      AliasName := sAlias;
      DatabaseName := 'TEMP';
      Connected := True;
      DbiGetDirectory( Handle, True, pszDir );
      GetAliasPath := StrPas( pszDir );
      Connected := False;
    end; { with Database }
  finally
    Database.Free;
    StrDispose( pszDir );
  end;
end; { GetAliasPath() }
```

Pure Delphi Equivalent

TTable.DataBaseName (when not used as an alias)

Xbase Equivalent

Set(_SET_DEFAULT)

See Also

DbiSetDirectory, DbiInit, DbiOpenDatabase

DbiGetDriverDesc

Declaration

```
function DbiGetDriverDesc (      { Get Description for a given type }
     pszDriverType : PChar;      { Symbolic name for driver type }
var    drvType       : DRVType   { Driver type Description }
   ): DBIResult;
```

Parameters

PARAMETER NAME	DESCRIPTION
pszDriverType	Pointer to the string containing the driver name.
drvType	Pointer to the client-allocated DRVType structure.

Description

Retrieves a driver Description in a DRVType structure.

DBIResult Return Values

DBIERR_NONE	The driver Description was retrieved successfully.

Example

```
constructor TDriverList.Create;
var
  hDb: hDBIDb;              { Database handle }
  hTblTypeCur: hDBICur;    { In-memory table cursor for table types }
  hFldTypeCur: hDBICur;    { In-memory table cursor for field types }
  hIdxTypeCur: hDBICur;    { In-memory table cursor for index types }
  rslt: DBIResult;         { Return value from IDAPI functions }
  TblProps: CURProps;      { Table Properties }
  pRecBuf: PChar;          { Record Buffer }
  szDriver: Array[0..DBIMAXNAMELEN+1] of Char; { Driver name }
```

```
  bIsBlank: Bool;          { Is the field blank? }
  drType: DRVType;         { Driver type information }
begin
  inherited Create;
  try
    Check( DbiOpenDataBase( 'DEMOS', 'STANDARD', dbiREADWRITE,
           dbiOPENSHARED, NIL, 0, NIL, NIL, hDB ));
    Check( DbiSetDirectory( hDb, '\DELPHI\DEMOS' ));

    { Get a list of all available drivers }
    Check( DbiOpenDriverList( Cursor ));

    { Get the size of the record buffer }
    Check( DbiGetCursorProps( Cursor, TblProps ));

    { Allocate record buffer }
    pRecBuf := StrAlloc( TblProps.iRecBufSize );
    Check( DbiSetToBegin( Cursor ));

    { Iterate through all available drivers in the configuration file. }
    while DbiGetNextRecord( Cursor, dbiNOLOCK, pRecBuf, nil )
                                        = DBIERR_NONE do
    begin
      { Get the driver name }
      Check( DbiGetField( Cursor, 1, pRecBuf, @szDriver,
                          bIsBlank ));
      Check( DbiGetDriverDesc( szDriver, drType ));

      { Retrieve all usable table types for the driver }
      Check( DbiOpenTableTypesList( szDriver, hTblTypeCur ));

      { Retrieve all usable field types for the driver }
      Check( DbiOpenFieldTypesList( szDriver, nil, hFldTypeCur ));

      { Retrieve all usable Index types for the driver }
      Check( DbiOpenIndexTypesList( szDriver, hIdxTypeCur ));
      Add( TDriverInfo.Create( StrPas( szDriver ), drType,
           hTblTypeCur, hFldTypeCur, hIdxTypeCur ));
    end; { while }
  finally
    if Assigned( pRecBuf ) then
      StrDispose( pRecBuf );
  end; { try .. finally }
end; { TDriverList.Create }
```

Pure Delphi Equivalent

TTable.TableType

Xbase Equivalent

RDDName()

See Also

DbiOpenDriverList

DBIGETERRORCONTEXT

Declaration

```
function DbiGetErrorContext (   { Get specific Context if available }
    eContext    : Integer;   { Context type }
    pszContext  : PChar      { Context string (MAXMSGLEN +1) }
): DBIResult;
```

Parameters

PARAMETER NAME	DESCRIPTION
eContext	The context type (see below).
pszContext	Pointer to the client-allocated buffer that receives the context string. Memory allocated for this parameter must be at least as large as (DBIMAXMSGLEN + 1).

eContext can be one of the following values:

VALUE	DESCRIPTION
ecALIAS	Alias
ecCAPABILITY	Capability
ecDIRNAME	Directory name
ecDRIVENAME	Drive name, including colon (C:)
ecFIELDNAME	Field name
ecFILENAME	File name
ecIMAGEROW	Image row (For QBE only)
ecINDEXNAME	Index name
ecKEYNAME	Key name
ecLINENUMBER	Line number
ecNATIVECODE	Native error code
ecNATIVEMSG	Native error message
ecTABLENAME	Table name, including drive/path
ecTOKEN	Token (For QBE only)
ecUSERNAME	For Example, in locking conflicts, the name of the user involved.

Description

Allows the client to query the BDE for additional, more detailed information regarding a just received error code. Besides error-handling functions, no other calls can be made after the call that produced the error.

If a simple, formatted error message is all that is required, DbiGetErrorInfo is a simpler function to use.

DBIResult Return Values

DBIERR_NONE	The error context was successfully returned.

Example

```
procedure OpenDatabase;
var
  iResult : DBIResult;
  hDB     : hDBIDB;
  hTbl    : hDBICur;
  cpBuf   : Array[0..DBIMAXMSGLEN + 1] of Char;
begin
  try
    DbiOpenDataBase( 'MYALIAS', 'STANDARD', dbiREADWRITE,
                     dbiOPENSHARED, nil, 0, nil, nil, hDB );
    iResult := DbiOpenTable( hDB, 'PRODUCTS.DBF', nil, nil, nil, 0,
                             dbiREADONLY, dbiOPENSHARED, xltFIELD,
                             False, nil, hTbl );
  except
    if iResult = DBIERR_NOSUCHFILE then
    begin
      DbiGetErrorContext( ecTABLENAME, cpBuf );
      MessageDlg( 'File Not Found: ' + StrPas( cpBuf ),
                  mtError,[mbOk], 0 );
    end;
  end;
end; { OpenDatabase() }
```

See Also

DbiGetErrorInfo, DbiGetErrorEntry, DbiGetErrorString

DBIGETERRORENTRY

Declaration

```
function DbiGetErrorEntry (        { Get error entry }
     uEntry         : Word;        { Error stack entry }
var  ulNativeError  : Longint;     { Returned. Native error code, if any )
     pszError       : PChar        { Returned. Error string, if any }
   ): DBIResult;
```

Parameters

PARAMETER NAME	DESCRIPTION
uEntry	The error stack entry. Error stack entries begin with 1.
ulNativeError	Optional reference to the client variable that receives the native error code (if any). This is generally for use with SQL systems and will otherwise generally return a zero (0).

pszError	Optional pointer to the client-allocated buffer that receives the error string (if any). Memory allocated for this parameter must be at least as large as (DBIMAXMS-GLEN + 1).

Description

Retrieves the error description of a specified error stack entry.

If error entry 1 returns DBIERR_NONE, there are no additional errors on the stack. To view all errors on the stack, the client can call DbiGetErrorEntry in a loop that starts uEntry at 1, and increments it for each iteration of the loop. When DbiGetErrorEntry returns DBIERR_NONE, no additional errors are on the stack to view.

The stack can be traversed multiple times, or combined with other error interface calls, but non-error routine BDE calls reset the error stack.

DBIResult Return Values

DBIERR_NONE	The error stack entry is empty. Any other error return value indicates what the error code is that is contained in the error stack entry.

Example

```
function LastErrorEntry : String;
var
  lErrCode : Longint;
  pszError : Array[0..DBIMAXMSGLEN + 1] of Char;
begin
  if DbiGetErrorEntry( 1, lErrCode, pszError ) = DBIERR_NONE then
    Result := 'No Error'
  else
    Result := IntToStr( lErrCode ) + ': ' + StrPas( pszError );
end; { LastErrorEntry }
```

Xbase Equivalent

ON ERROR, ERRORSYS()

See Also

DbiGetErrorInfo, DbiGetErrorEntry, DbiGetErrorString

DBIGETERRORINFO

Declaration

```
function DbiGetErrorInfo (          { Return info on last error }
    bFull       : Bool;            { If Full details }
var ErrInfo     : DBIErrInfo       { Error Info }
  ): DBIResult;
```

Parameters

PARAMETER NAME	DESCRIPTION
bFull	Set to True if full error details are desired or False for terse information.
ErrInfo	Reference to the client DBIErrInfo structure to be filled.

Description

Retrieves descriptive information about the last error that occurred, and error contexts for up to four error messages on the error stack.

The error information consists of:

- The DBIResult error code.
- An error message in ANSI characters corresponding to the code.
- Up to four associated error contexts.

Unlike DbiGetErrorContext, the client does not need to be concerned about the different types of error contexts. If the client wishes to interpret certain error codes and contexts, DbiGetErrorContext should be used instead.

DBIResult Return Values

DBIERR_NONE	Error information was retrieved successfully

Example

```
{ Fills TEdit boxes with error information regarding last error }
procedure LastErrorInfo;
var
  eErrInfo : DBIErrInfo;
begin
  DbiGetErrorInfo( True, eErrInfo );

  { Last Error Code }
  edErrInfo1.Text := IntToStr( eErrInfo.iError );

  { Last Error Message }
  edErrInfo2.Text := StrPas( eErrInfo.szErrCode );

  { Error Context #1 }
  edErrInfo3.Text := StrPas( eErrInfo.szContext[1] );

  { Error Context #2 }
  edErrInfo4.Text := StrPas( eErrInfo.szContext[2] );

  { Error Context #3 }
  edErrInfo5.Text := StrPas( eErrInfo.szContext[3] );

  { Error Context #4 }
```

```
    edErrInfo6.Text := StrPas( eErrInfo.szContext[4] );
end;

{ Example use of the LastErrorInfo procedure above }
procedure TForm1.OpenTableClick(Sender: TObject);
var
  Table1 : TTable;
begin
  Table1 := TTable.Create(nil);
  Table1.DatabaseName := 'c:\data';
  Table1.TableName := 'XXX.DBF';
  try
    Table1.Open;
  except
    LastErrorInfo;
  end;
end;
```

See Also

DbiGetErrorContext

DBIGETERRORSTRING

Declaration

```
function DbiGetErrorString (        { Get message for error code }
     iResult         : DBIResult;   { Engine error code }
     pszError        : PChar        { Error string for the error }
  ): DBIResult;
```

Parameters

PARAMETER NAME	DESCRIPTION
iResult	The error code.
pszError	Pointer to the client buffer that receives the message string for the given error code. Memory allocated for this parameter must be at least as large as (DBIMAXMSGLEN + 1).

Description

Returns the message associated with a given error code. This function has no context, so it is not limited to error codes that were returned by previous BDE calls, as is the case with DbiGetErrorInfo.

DBIResult Return Values

DBIERR_NONE	The error string was retrieved successfully.

Examples

```
{ Example #1 - Generic Error Checking Function }
function IsDbiOk( iResult : DBIResult ) : Boolean;
var
  szErrorStr: DBIMsg;
begin
  Result := iResult = DBIERR_NONE;
  if not Result then
  begin
    DbiGetErrorString( iResult, szErrorStr );
    ShowMessage( 'Error ' + IntToStr(iResult) + ': ' +
                 StrPas( szErrorStr ));
  end;
end; { IsDbiOk() }

{ Example #2 - Creates Complete Listing Of All BDE Errors Codes }
procedure GenErrMsgTable;
var
  F: TextFile;
  OutString: String;
  ErrCat,
  SubCode: Byte;
  Code: Word;
  ErrString: Array[ 0.. DBIMAXMSGLEN + 1 ] of Char;
begin
  DbiInit( nil );
  AssignFile( F, 'BDE_ERRS.TXT' );
  Rewrite( F );
  for ErrCat := ERRCAT_NONE to ERRCAT_RC do
    for SubCode := 0 to 255 do
    begin
      Code := SubCode + ( ErrCat shl 8 );
      DbiGetErrorString( Code, ErrString );
      if StrLen( ErrString ) > 0 then
      begin
        OutString := Format('%6d : $%0.4x : %s',
                     [Code,Code,ErrString]);
        WriteLn( F, OutString );
      end;
  end;
  CloseFile( F );
  DbiExit;
end; { GenErrMsgTable }
```

See Also

DbiGetErrorInfo, DbiGetErrorEntry, DbiGetErrorContext

DBIGETEXACTRECORDCOUNT

Declaration

```
function DbiGetExactRecordCount (   { Get the current # of records }
     hCursor      : hDBICur;        { Cursor handle }
var  iRecCount    : Longint         { Number of records }
   ): DBIResult;
```

Parameters

PARAMETER NAME	DESCRIPTION
hCursor	The cursor handle.
iRecCount	Pointer to the client variable that receives the number of records associated with the cursor.

Description

This function is meant to get the exact number of records associated with the cursor, respecting any active DbiAddFilter constraints. This differs from DbiGetRecordCount, which does not respect any active filter.

DbiGetExactRecordCount is effectively an optimized version of a 'While not Eof' loop with a counter variable.

Paradox. If a range is active, the record count returned is the number of records in the range.

Warning: This function is not documented by Borland and may not be supported in future updates to the BDE. In order to use DbiGetExactRecord, you must remember to declare it and its **.DLL** (**IDAPI01.DLL** under Delphi 1.x or **IDAPI32.DLL** under Delphi 2.x) at the beginning of the unit.

DBIResult Return Values

DBIERR_NONE	The record count was retrieved successfully.
DBIERR_INVALIDHNDL	The specified cursor handle is invalid or NIL.

Example

```
interface
  function DbiGetExactRecordCount ( hCursor: hDBICur;
                                  var iRecCount: Longint
    ): DBIResult;
  .
  .
  .

implementation
{ For Delphi 2.0, change the external below to 'IDAPI32' }
function DbiGetExactRecordCount; external 'IDAPI01';
```

```
{$R *.DFM}

.
. { Other application code }
.
procedure ShowExactRecCount( oTable : TTable );
var
  lRecCount : Longint;
begin
  if IsDbiOk( DbiGetExactRecordCount( oTable.Handle, lRecCount )) then
    ShowMessage( IntToStr( lRecCount ) + ' records are in scope.' );
end; { ShowExactRecCount() }
```

Xbase Equivalent

COUNT

See Also

DbiGetRecordCount

DBIGETFIELD

Declaration

```
function DbiGetField (                    { Get Field value }
      hCursor        : hDBICur;      { Cursor }
      iField         : Word;         { Field # (1..n) }
      pRecBuff       : Pointer;      { Record buffer }
      pDest          : Pointer;      { Destination field buffer }
var   bBlank         : Bool          { Returned : Is field blank? }
    ): DBIResult;
```

Parameters

PARAMETER NAME	DESCRIPTION
hCursor	The cursor handle.
iField	The ordinal number of the field within the record. Field numbers start with 1.
pRecBuf	Pointer to the record buffer.
pDest	Optional pointer to the client buffer that receives the data from the requested field.
bBlank	Optional pointer to the client variable. Set to True if the field is blank; otherwise, False.

Description

Retrieves the data contents of the requested field from the record buffer. The output buffer pointed to by pDest (if supplied) will contain the requested field. The output buffer pointed to by bBlank (if supplied) will indicate whether or not the field is blank.

The data that DbiGetField returns is based on the current translation mode of the cursor. If the record translation is set to xltNONE, DbiGetField returns the raw data in the drivers physical format. This is called a BDE physical type. If the translation mode is set to xltFIELD, the data are returned in a generic form (for Example, a Paradox numeric value is returned as an 8-byte Double). This is called a BDE logical type.

DbiGetField cannot be used to return the data contents of a BLOB field, although it can be used to determine if the BLOB field is empty.

DBIResult Return Values

DBIERR_NONE	Data contents were retrieved successfully.
DBIERR_INVALIDHNDL	The specified cursor handle is invalid or NIL.

Example

```
{ Displays the contents of the second field for each record of CUSTOMER.DB
  within a scrolling window. }
procedure ListDatabase(Sender: TObject);
var
  hDB : hDBIDB;
  hTbl : hDBICur;
  iResult: DBIResult;
  szBuf,
  szFld : PChar;
  cProp : CURProps;
  bBlank : Bool; { Changed from WordBool for Delphi 2.0 }
begin
  DbiInit(nil);
  DbiOpenDataBase( 'DBDEMOS', 'STANDARD', dbiREADWRITE,
                   dbiOPENSHARED, nil, 0, nil, nil, hDB );
  DbiOpenTable( hDB, 'CUSTOMER.DB', nil, nil, nil, 0, dbiREADONLY,
                dbiOPENSHARED, xltFIELD, False, nil, hTbl );
  DbiGetCursorProps( hTbl, cProp );
  szBuf := AllocMem( cProp.iRecBufSize * SizeOf( Byte ));
  szFld := AllocMem( 255 * SizeOf( Byte ));
  DbiSetToBegin( hTbl );
  iResult := 0;
  repeat
    iResult := DbiGetNextRecord( hTbl, dbiNOLOCK, szBuf, nil );
    DbiGetField( hTbl, 2, szBuf, szFld, bBlank );
    WriteLn( StrPas( szFld ));
  until iResult <> DBIERR_NONE;
  FreeMem( szBuf, ( cProp.iRecBufSize * SizeOf( Byte )));
  FreeMem( szFld, ( 255 * SizeOf( Byte )));
  DbiCloseDatabase( hDB );
  WriteLn( 'Finished' );
  DbiExit;
end; { ListDatabase }
```

Pure Delphi Equivalent

TTable.Fields

Xbase Equivalent

GET, FieldGet()

See Also

DbiPutField, DbiInsertRecord, DbiGetNextRecord, DbiGetPriorRecord, DbiGetRelativeRecord, DbiGetRecord

DBIGETFIELDDESCS

Declaration

```
function DbiGetFieldDescs (        { Get field Descriptions }
    hCursor      : hDBICur;        { Cursor handle }
    pfldDesc     : pFLDDesc        { Array of field descriptors }
  ): DBIResult;
```

Parameters

PARAMETER NAME	DESCRIPTION
hCursor	The cursor handle.
pfldDesc	Pointer to the client FLDDesc structures, one for each of the fields in the table associated with the specified cursor.

Description

Retrieves a list of descriptors for all the fields in the table associated with hCursor.

The type of field descriptors returned depend on which translation mode is set for the cursor. If the translation mode is xltNONE, the physical field descriptors are returned. If the translation mode is xltFIELD, the logical field descriptors are returned.

DbiGetCursorProps can be used to get the number of field in the table.

DBIResult Return Values

DBIERR_NONE	The field Descriptions were returned successfully.
DBIERR_INVALIDHNDL	The specified cursor handle is invalid or NIL.

Examples

```
{ Example #1:  Returns a pointer to the field descriptor structure for the
  specified table. Uses StrAlloc() so StrDispose() may be used to dispose the
  pointer, which means the length of the pointer doesn't have to be passed
  by reference }
function TableFieldDescs( oTable : TTable ) : Pointer;
var
  curProp : CURProps;
begin
  Result := nil;
  try
    if IsDbiOk( DbiGetCursorProps( oTable.Handle, curProp )) then
    begin
      Result := StrAlloc( curProp.iFields * SizeOf( FLDDesc ) + 1 );
      if not IsDbiOk( DbiGetFieldDescs( GetTableCursor( oTable ),
                                                        Result)) then

      begin
        StrDispose( Result );
        Result := nil;
      end;
    end;
  except
    if Assigned( Result ) then
      StrDispose( Result );
    Result := nil;
  end;
end; { TableFieldDescs() }


{ Example #2: Creates a new, empty table of the same structure }
function DupeTableStructure( sInFile, sOutFile : String ) : Boolean;
var
  iResult    : DbiResult;
  hDB        : hDBIDB;
  hTbl       : hDBICur;
  pFields    : Pointer;
  szInFile,
  szOutFile : Array[0..78] of Char;
  curProp    : CURProps;
  tblDesc    : CRTblDesc;
begin
  try
    Result := False;
    StrPCopy( szInFile, sInFile );
    if ( IsDbiOk( DbiOpenDataBase( 'MYALIAS', 'STANDARD',
                  dbiREADWRITE, dbiOPENSHARED, nil, 0, nil, nil,
                  hDB ))) and
       ( IsDbiOk( DbiOpenTable( hDB, szInFile, nil, nil, nil, 0,
                  dbiREADONLY, dbiOPENSHARED, xltFIELD, False, nil,
                  hTbl ))) then
```

585

```
  begin
    DbiGetCursorProps( hTbl, curProp ); { Load cursor properties }
    pFields := StrAlloc( curProp.iFields * SizeOf( FLDDesc )+1 );
    if IsDbiOk( DbiGetFieldDescs( hTbl, pFields )) then
    begin
      FillChar( tblDesc, SizeOf(CRTblDesc), #0);
      StrCopy( TblDesc.szTblName, szOutFile );
      StrCopy( TblDesc.szTblType, szDBASE );
      TblDesc.iFldCount := curProp.iFields;
      TblDesc.pfldDesc := pFields;
      Result := IsDbiOk( DbiCreateTable( hDb, True, TblDesc ));
    end;
  end
finally
  DbiCloseDatabase( hDB );
  if Assigned( pFields ) then
    StrDispose( pFields );
  end;
end; { DupeTableStructure() }
```

Pure Delphi Equivalent

TField

See Also

DbiGetCursorProps

DBIGETFIELDTYPEDESC

Declaration

```
function DbiGetFieldTypeDesc (      { Get list of field types }
      pszDriverType : PChar;        { Driver type }
      pszTableType  : PChar;        { Table type }
      pszFieldType  : PChar;        { Field type  (Physical only) }
var   fldType       : FLDType       { Field type Description }
    ): DBIResult;
```

Parameters

PARAMETER NAME	DESCRIPTION
pszDriverType	Pointer to the driver type. Use DbiOpenDriverList to find the valid driver types.
pszTableType	Pointer to the table type. Use DbiOpenTableTypesList to find the valid table types.
pszFieldType	Pointer to the field type. Use DbiOpenFieldTypesList to find the valid field types.
fldType	Pointer to the client FLDType structure.

Description
Retrieves a description of the specified field type.

DBIResult Return Values

DBIERR_NONE	The field type description was retrieved successfully.

Example

```
function GetFieldTypeDesc( szDriver, szTable, szField : PChar ) :  FLDType;
begin
  IsDbiOk( DbiGetFieldTypeDesc( szDriver, szTable, szField, Result ));
end; { GetFieldTypeDesc() }
```

Pure Delphi Equivalent
TFieldDef.DataType

See Also
DbiOpenFieldTypesList, DbiOpenTableTypesList, DbiOpenDriverList

DBIGETFILTERINFO

Declaration

```
function DbiGetFilterInfo (          { Get filter information }
     hCur          : hDBICur;        { Cursor handle }
     hFilter       : hDBIFilter;     { Filter handle    /NIL }
     iFilterId     : Word;           { Filter ID  /0 }
     iFilterSeqNo  : Word;           { Filter sequence number /0 }
var  Filterinfo    : FILTERInfo      { Returns filter info }
  ): DBIResult;
```

Parameters

PARAMETER NAME	DESCRIPTION
hCursor	The cursor handle.
hFilter	Optional filter handle.
iFilterId	Optional filter identification number. A filter handle, filter identification number, or filter sequence number may be used to identify the filter. The default is 0.
iFilterSeqNo	Optional filter sequence number. A filter handle, filter identification number, or filter sequence number may be used to identify the filter. The default is 0.
Filterinfo	Reference to the client FILTERInfo structure to be filled.

Description

Retrieves information about a specified filter. This information is returned in the FILTERInfo structure, which has the following structure:

```
pFILTERInfo = ^FILTERInfo;
FILTERInfo = record
  iFilterId    : Word;         { ID for the filter }
  hFilter      : hDBIFilter;   { Filter handle }
  iClientData  : Longint;      { Client supplied data }
  iPriority    : Word;         { Priority; 1..N with 1 being highest }
  bCanAbort    : Bool;         { If True, pfFilter can return ABORT }
  pfFilter     : pfGENFilter;  { Client filter function }
  pCanExpr     : Pointer;      { Supplied expression }
  bActive      : Bool;         { If True, the filter is active }
end;
```

DBIResult Return Values

DBIERR_NONE	Filter information was retrieved successfully.
DBIERR_INVALIDHNDL	The specified cursor handle is invalid or NIL.

Example

```
function TableFilterInfo( oTable : TTable ) : FILTERInfo;
begin
  IsDbiOk( DbiGetFilterInfo( GetTableCursor( oTable ), nil,
                            0, 0, Result ));
end; { TableFilterInfo() }
```

DbiGetIndexDesc

Declaration

```
function DbiGetIndexDesc (         { Get index properties }
     hCursor       : hDBICur;      { Cursor handle }
     iIndexSeqNo   : Word;         { Index number }
var  idxDesc       : IDXDesc       { Returned index Description }
   ): DBIResult;
```

Parameters

Parameter Name	Description
hCursor	The cursor handle.
iIndexSeqNo	The ordinal number of the index in the list of open indexes of the cursor. DbiGetIndexSeqNo can be called to obtain this number for a given index. If iIndexSeqNo is 0, the properties of the active index are returned.
idxDesc	Reference to the client-allocated IDXDesc structure to be filled.

Description

Retrieves the properties of the given index associated with hCursor.

This function is used to find the properties of an open index for this cursor. Use DbiGetCursorProps to get the number of open indexes (iIndexes). iIndexSeqNo must be between zero and iIndexes.

Note: If a field map is active, the field numbers in aiKeyFld list the mapped field numbers. However, if a key field is not part of the field map, it is a negative number.

DBIResult Return Values

DBIERR_NONE	The properties of the specified index were returned successfully.
DBIERR_INVALIDHNDL	The specified handle is invalid or NIL.
DBIERR_NOTINDEXED	Table has no associated indexes.
DBIERR_NOSUCHINDEX	iIndexSeqNo is invalid.

Example

```
function OrdGetDesc( oTable : TTable; iOrder : Integer ) : IDXDesc;
begin
  IsDbiOk( DbiGetIndexDesc( GetTableCursor( oTable ), iOrder, Result ));
end; { OrdGetDesc() }
```

Pure Delphi Equivalent

TTable.IndexDefs

See Also

DbiGetIndexDescs, DbiOpenIndex, DbiCloseIndex, DbiGetCursorProps, DbiGetIndexSeqNo

DBIGETINDEXDESCS

Declaration

```
function DbiGetIndexDescs (          { Get index properties }
     hCursor        : hDBICur;       { Cursor handle }
var  idxDesc        : IDXDesc        { Returned index descriptors }
   ): DBIResult;
```

Parameters

PARAMETER NAME	DESCRIPTION
hCursor	The cursor handle.
idxDesc	Reference to the client-allocated IDXDesc structure to be filled.

Description

Retrieves the index properties for all the indexes associated with the specified cursor.

The client application must allocate a buffer large enough to hold all of the index descriptors. DbiGetCursorProps can be used to get the indexes count by examining the iIndexes property.

DBIResult Return Values

DBIERR_NONE	Index Descriptions were returned successfully.
DBIERR_INVALIDHNDL	The specified handle is invalid or NIL.

Example

```
function OrdGetDescs( oTable : TTable ) : pIDXDesc;
var
  iSize : Integer;
begin
  try
    iSize := oTable.IndexDefs.Count * SizeOf( IDXDesc );
    GetMem( Result, iSize );
    IsDbiOk( DbiGetIndexDescs( GetTableCursor( oTable ), Result^ ));
  except
    if Assigned( Result ) then
      FreeMem( Result, iSize );
    Result := nil;
  end;
end; { OrdGetDescs() }
```

Pure Delphi Equivalent

TTable.IndexDefs

See Also

DbiGetIndexDesc, DbiOpenIndex, DbiCloseIndex, DbiGetIndexSeqNo, DbiGetCursorProps

DBiGetIndexForField

Declaration

```
function DbiGetIndexForField (    { Get index desc for given field }
     hCursor       : hDBICur;      { Cursor handle }
     iFld          : Word;         { Field Number (1..N) }
     bProdTagOnly  : Bool;         { If True, only xBASE production
                                     tags will be returned }
var  idxDesc       : IDXDesc       { Optional; Returned index descriptors }
   ): DBIResult;
```

Parameters

PARAMETER NAME	DESCRIPTION
hCursor	The cursor handle.
iFld	The field number.
bProdTagOnly	For use with dBASE tables only. If set to True, only dBASE production tags are searched.
idxDesc	Optional reference to the IDXDesc structure to be filled.

Description

Returns the Description of any useful index on the specified field. It can also be used just to check if an index exists for the given field.

This function does not work on queries or in-memory or temporary tables.

Paradox. If multiple indexes exist on the field, the following order of precedence is followed: primary index, secondary index on the specified field only, and secondary composite index with the specified field as the first component.

dBASE. Only simple indexes are considered because there are no composite indexes. Expression indexes are not considered.

SQL. If multiple indexes are created for the field, the first useful index is returned. An will be made to return the unique index with the least number of fields in the key. If there is no unique index, an index with the least number of fields in the key is returned.

DBIResult Return Values

DBIERR_NONE	The index descriptors were returned successfully.
DBIERR_INVALIDHNDL	The specified handle is invalid or NIL.
DBIERR_NOSUCHINDEX	No index on this field.

Example

```
function GetFieldIndex( oTable : TTable; iField : Word; bProd :
                        Boolean ) : IDXDesc;
begin
  IsDbiOk( DbiGetIndexForField( GetTableCursor( oTable ), iField,
                        bProd, Result ));
end; { GetFieldIndex() }
```

Pure Delphi Equivalent

TIndexDefs.FindIndexForField

See Also

DbiOpenIndex, DbiCloseIndex, DbiDeleteIndex, DbiAddIndex

DɪʙɪGᴇᴛIɴᴅᴇxSᴇǫNᴏ

Declaration

```
function DbiGetIndexSeqNo (        { Get index sequence number }
      hCursor        : hDBICur;    { Cursor handle }
      pszIndexName   : PChar;      { Index name }
      pszTagName     : PChar;      { Tag name (if applicable) }
      iIndexId       : Word;       { Index number }
var   iIndexSeqNo    : Word        { Index number }
   ): DBIResult;
```

Parameters

PARAMETER NAME	DESCRIPTION
hCursor	The cursor handle.
pszIndexName	Pointer to the index name.
pszTagName	For use with dBASE only. Pointer to the index tag name.
iIndexId	The index ID, if required to identify an index.
iIndexSeqNo	Reference to the client variable to receive the index sequence number.

Description

Retrieves the ordinal position of the specified index within the list of indexes for the specified cursor.

dBASE. The ordinal position of the index in the list of indexes can be affected by the opening and closing of indexes on the cursor. pszIndexName and pszTagName are used to specify the index.

Paradox. The index can be specified by name or ID.

SQL. The index must be specified by name.

DBIResult Return Values

DBIERR_NONE	The index sequence number was returned successfully.
DBIERR_INVALIDHNDL	The specified handle is invalid or NIL.
DBIERR_NOSUCHINDEX	The index is not open, or does not exist.

Example

```
function GetIndexSeqNo( oTable : TTable; sIndex, sTag : String ) : Word;
var
  szIndex,
  szTag    : DBINAME;
```

```
begin
  StrPCopy( szIndex, sIndex );
  StrPCopy( szTag, sTag );
  IsDbiOk( DbiGetIndexSeqNo( GetTableCursor( oTable ), szIndex,
                             szTag, 0, Result ));
end; { GetIndexSeqNo() }
```

Pure Delphi Equivalent

TIndexDefs.IndexOf

Xbase Equivalent

OrdNumber()

See Also

DbiGetIndexDesc

DBIGETINDEXTYPEDESC

Declaration

```
function DbiGetIndexTypeDesc (    { Get desc of given index type }
       pszDriverType : PChar;     { Driver type }
       pszIndexType  : PChar;     { Index type }
var    idxType       : IDXType    { Index Description }
   ): DBIResult;
```

Parameters

PARAMETER NAME	DESCRIPTION
pszDriverType	Pointer to the driver type.
pszIndexType	Pointer to the index type. Use DbiOpenIndexTypesList to find the valid index types.
idxType	Reference to the IDXType structure to be filled.

Description

Retrieves a description of the index type.

DBIResult Return Values

DBIERR_NONE	The index type Description was returned successfully.

Example

```
function BDEGetIndexTypeDesc( sDriverType, sIndexType : String ) : IDXType;
var
  szDriverType,
  szIndexType  : DBINAME;
begin
  StrPCopy( szDriverType, sDriverType );
  StrPCopy( szIndexType, sIndexType );
  IsDbiOk( DbiGetIndexTypeDesc( szDriverType, szIndexType, Result ));
end; { BDEGetIndextypeDesc() }
```

Pure Delphi Equivalent

TTable.IndexDefs

Xbase Equivalent

None

See Also

DbiOpenIndexTypesList

DBIGETLDNAME

Declaration

```
function DbiGetLdName (        { Get language driver name from table }
      pszDriver   : PChar;     { Driver name }
      pObjName    : PChar;     { Name of object, i.e. table name }
      pLdName     : PChar      { Returned language driver name }
   ): DBIResult;
```

Parameters

PARAMETER NAME	DESCRIPTION
pszDriver	Pointer to the driver name.
pObjName	Optional pointer to the table name.
	If NIL, the name of the drivers default language driver will be returned.
	SQL: If this parameter is specified, it must be of the form: dbaAlias:objName.
pLdName	Pointer to the client buffer that receives the language driver name associated with the specified table. This buffer should be at least (DBIMAXNAMELEN + 1) in size.

Description

Retrieves the name of the language driver associated with the specified object name (table name).

The returned language driver name can be used as an optional parameter for DbiCreateTable as a way to override the default language driver at create time.

DBIResult Return Values

DBIERR_NONE	The name of the language driver was retrieved successfully.

Example

```
function LanguageDriverName( sDriver : String ) : String;
var
  szDriver,
  szLdName : DBINAME;
begin
  StrPCopy( szDriver, sDriver );
  if IsDbiOk( DbiGetLdName( szDriver, nil, szLdName )) then
    Result := StrPas( szLdName )
  else
    Result := '';
end; { DataDriverName() }
```

Pure Delphi Equivalent

TTable.DBLocale, BDE Configuration Utility

See Also

DbiCreateTable

DBIGETLDOBJ

Declaration

```
function DbiGetLdObj (          { Get language driver }
    hCursor      : hDBICur;     { Cursor handle }
var pLdObj       : Pointer      { Returned language driver object }
  ): DBIResult;
```

Parameters

PARAMETER NAME	DESCRIPTION
hCursor	Optional cursor handle.
	If NIL, a pointer to the system language driver is returned. Otherwise, the returned object pointer has a lifetime equivalent to the cursors lifetime.
pLdObj	Reference to the client variable that receives the pointer to the language driver.

Description

Returns the language driver object associated with the specified cursor. The object pointer returned in this function can be used with DbiNativeToAnsi and DbiAnsiToNative.

If a specified cursor is closed, and if no other cursors are open on the same table, the language driver object is destroyed and can no longer be accessed through this object pointer.

This pointer is valid for the duration of the session and can be used regardless of which cursors are opened or closed.

DBIResult Return Values

DBIERR_NONE	The language driver object was returned successfully.

Example

```
function GetLangDriverObj( oTable : TTable ) : Pointer;
begin
  IsDbiOk( DbiGetLdObj( GetTableCursor( oTable ), Result ));
end; { GetLangDriverObj() }
```

Pure Delphi Equivalent

TTable.DBLocale, BDE Configuration Utility

See Also

DbiNativeToAnsi, DbiAnsiToNative

DBIGETLINKSTATUS

Declaration

```
function DbiGetLinkStatus (    { Query linkage info for table }
      hCursor     : hDBICur; { Cursor handle }
  var hCursorMstr : hDBICur; { Returns master cursor, if any }
  var hCursorDet  : hDBICur; { Returns 1st detail cursor, if any }
  var hCursorSib  : hDBICur  { Returns next sibling detail cursor, if any }
  ): DBIResult;
```

Parameters

PARAMETER NAME	DESCRIPTION
hCursor	The cursor handle.
hCursorMstr	Optional reference to the master cursor, if any.
hCursorDet	Optional reference to the first detail cursor, if any.
hCursorSib	Optional reference to the next sibling detail cursor.

Description

Returns the master, detail, and sibling cursors, if any, of the specified linked cursor.

Used to find all links for the given cursor. If the cursor has a master, the master is returned. If the cursor has one or more details, the first detail is returned. If the cursor has siblings, the next sibling is returned. The master, detail, and sibling cursor handle can be used as an input to this function. If handle is not applicable, NIL is returned.

The cursor must be a linked cursor. A linked cursor is created with DbiBeginLinkMode, DbiLinkDetail, or DbiLinkDetailToExp.

DBIResult Return Values

DBIERR_NONE	The linked cursor status was returned successfully.
DBIERR_INVALIDHNDL	The specified handle is invalid, not a linked cursor, or NIL.

Example

```
function TableIsLinked( oTable : TTable ) : Boolean;
var
  hCursor,
  hMaster,
  hDetail,
  hSibling : hDBICur;
begin
  try
    hCursor := GetTableCursor( oTable );
    Result := DbiGetLinkStatus( hCursor, hMaster, hDetail,
                                hSibling ) = DBIERR_NONE;
  except
    Result := False;
  end;
end;
```

Pure Delphi Equivalent

TTable.MasterFields

Xbase Equivalent

dbRelation()

See Also

DbiBeginLinkMode, DbiLinkDetail, DbiLinkDetailToExp

DBIGETNETUSERNAME

Declaration

```
function DbiGetNetUserName (         { Get network user name }
      pszNetUserName : PChar         { Returns user name }
    ): DBIResult;
```

Parameters

PARAMETER NAME	DESCRIPTION
pszNetUserName	Pointer to the client variable that receives the user network login name string.

Description

Returns the user's network login name. User names are available for all networks supported by Microsoft Windows.

DBIResult Return Values

DBIERR_NONE	The user network login name was successfully retrieved.
DBIERR_INVALIDHNDL	pszNetUserName is NIL.

Example

```
function GetNetName: String;
var
  cpNetName: Array[0..48] of Char;
  iResult: DBIResult;
begin
  iResult := DbiGetNetUserName( cpNetName );
  if iResult <> DBIERR_NONE then
    DbiError( iResult );
  Result := StrPas( cpNetName );
end;
```

DBIGETNEXTRECORD

Declaration

```
function DbiGetNextRecord (          { Find/Get the next record }
      hCursor          : hDBICur;    { Cursor handle }
      eLock            : DBILockType; { Optional lock request }
      pRecBuff         : Pointer;    { Record buffer(client) }
      pRecProps        : pRecProps   { Optional record properties }
    ): DBIResult;
```

Parameters

PARAMETER NAME	DESCRIPTION
hCursor	The cursor handle.
eLock	Optional lock request type. Valid types are: dbiNOLOCK, dbiREADLOCK, or dbiWRITELOCK.
pRecBuf	Optional pointer to the client buffer that receives the record data. If NIL, no data is returned.
pRecProps	Optional pointer to the client-allocated RECProps structure. For dBASE and Paradox drivers only. If NIL, no record properties are returned.

Description

Retrieves the next record in the table associated with hCursor and, if a record buffer was provided, reads the data for the record into the record buffer.

If filters are active, the next record that meets the filter criteria is retrieved. The record can be locked if an explicit lock is specified (using eLock), and the function call fails if the requested lock cannot be acquired.

Field data can be retrieved using DbiGetField or DbiOpenBlob/DbiGetBlob for BLOB fields.

If the cursor is at the beginning of a table, after a opening a table or calling DbiSetToBegin, calling this function positions the cursor on the first record of the table. If the cursor is currently positioned on the last record in the table, DbiGetNextRecord returns an EOF error.

dBASE. If the pRecProps argument is supplied, the record number can be retrieved for the record (via the iPhyRecNum field of pRecProps). dBASE does not support the concept of sequence number. If the pRecProps argument is supplied, record properties are returned.

Paradox. If the pRecProps argument is supplied, the sequence number can be retrieved for the record (via the iSeqNum field of RECProps). Paradox does not support the concept of record number. If the pRecProps argument is supplied, record properties are returned.

SQL. Record properties are not supported for SQL drivers. If *pRecProps* is supplied, no properties are returned.

DBIResult Return Values

DBIERR_NONE	The next record was successfully retrieved.
DBIERR_EOF	The cursor was positioned at the crack at the end of the file or on the last record. It is now positioned at the crack at the end of the file.
DBIERR_INVALIDHNDL	The specified cursor handle is invalid or NIL.
DBIERR_ALREADYLOCKED	The record is already locked by the same user in the same session.
DBIERR_FILELOCKED	The table is already locked by another user (Paradox and dBASE only).

Example

```
{ Displays the contents of the second field for each record of CUSTOMER.DB
  within a scrolling window. }
```

```
procedure ListDatabase;
var
  hDB    : hDBIDB;
  hTbl   : hDBICur;
  iResult: DBIResult;
  szBuf,
  szFld  : PChar;
  cProp  : CURProps;
      bBlank : Bool; { Changed from WordBool for Delphi 2.0 }
begin
  DbiInit(nil);
  DbiOpenDataBase( 'DBDEMOS', 'STANDARD', dbiREADWRITE,
                  dbiOPENSHARED, nil, 0, nil, nil, hDB );
  DbiOpenTable( hDB, 'CUSTOMER.DB', nil, nil, nil, 0, dbiREADONLY,
              dbiOPENSHARED, xltFIELD, False, nil, hTbl );
  DbiGetCursorProps( hTbl, cProp );
  szBuf := AllocMem( cProp.iRecBufSize * SizeOf( Byte ));
  szFld := AllocMem( 255 * SizeOf( Byte ));
  DbiSetToBegin( hTbl );
  iResult := 0;
  repeat
    iResult := DbiGetNextRecord( hTbl, dbiNOLOCK, szBuf, nil );
    DbiGetField( hTbl, 2, szBuf, szFld, bBlank );
    WriteLn( StrPas( szFld ));
  until iResult <> DBIERR_NONE;
  FreeMem( szBuf, ( cProp.iRecBufSize * SizeOf( Byte )));
  FreeMem( szFld, ( 255 * SizeOf( Byte )));
  DbiCloseDatabase( hDB );
  WriteLn( 'Finished' );
  DbiExit;
end; { ListDatabase }
```

Pure Delphi Equivalent

TTable.Next

Xbase Equivalent

SKIP

See Also

DbiGetRecord, DbiGetPriorRecord, DbiGetRelativeRecord

DBIGETNUMBERFORMAT

Declaration

```
function DbiGetNumberFormat (        { Get current number format }
var    fmtNumber   : FMTNumber
  ): DBIResult;
```

Parameters

PARAMETER NAME	DESCRIPTION
fmtNumber	Reference to the FMTNumber structure to be filled.

Description

Returns the number format for the current session.

The number format is used by QBE for input and wildcard character matching. It is also used by batch operations (such as DbiDoRestructure and DbiBatchMove) to handle data type coercion between character and numeric types.

Here is the Declaration for FMTNumber.

```
FMTNumber = record                       {Date Format }
  cDecimalSeparator    : Char;    { Default ''.'' }
  cThousandSeparator   : Char;    { Default '','' }
  iDecimalDigits       : Byte;    { Default 2 }
  bLeadingZero         : Boolean; { Default True }
end;
```

DBIResult Return Values

DBIERR_NONE	The number format was successfully retrieved.
DBIERR_INVALIDHNDL	fmtNumber is NIL.

Example

```
procedure ShowNumberFormat;
var
  fmtNum : FMTNumber;

  function TrueOrFalse( bVal : Boolean ) : String;
  begin
    if bVal then
      Result := 'True'
    else
      Result := 'False';
  end; { TrueOrFalse() }

begin
  if IsDbiOk( DbiGetNumberFormat( fmtNum )) then
  with fmtNum do
    ShowMessage( 'Decimals use "' + cDecimalSeparator + '"' + #13 +
      'Thousands are separated by "' + cThousandSeparator + '"' +
      #13 + 'Decimal precision is ' + IntToStr(iDecimalDigits) +
      ' digits' + #13 + 'and leading zeros is set to ' +
      TrueOrFalse( bLeadingZero ));
end; { ShowNumberFormat() }
```

Pure Delphi Equivalent

DecimalSeparator, ThousandSeparator

Xbase Equivalent

SET DECIMALS TO

See Also

DbiGetDateFormat, DbiGetTimeFormat, DbiSetNumberFormat

DBIGETOBJFROMNAME

Declaration

```
function DbiGetObjFromName (        { Get object from name }
     eObjType      : DBIOBJType;    { Object handle }
     pszObjName    : PChar;         { Name of object /NIL }
var  hObj          : hDBIObj        { Returned object handle }
   ): DBIResult;
```

Parameters

PARAMETER NAME	DESCRIPTION
eObjType	The type of object.
pszObjName	Optional pointer to the name of the object.
hObj	Reference to hold the object handle.

The following table lists the supported object types and whether or not the object name is required.

EOBJTYPE	NAME
objSYSTEM	Not needed
objSESSION	Optional
objDRIVER	Required
objDATABASE	Optional
objCURSOR	Required
objCLIENT	Not needed

Description

Returns an object handle of the specified type or with the given name, if any.

Some handles can be retrieved only by name, such as handles associated with cursors. For those, pszObjName is not optional. There can be more than one cursor open for a given table name; DbiGetObjFromName returns the handle to one of those cursors. To get a session handle, the session name need not be specified; by default, a handle to the currently active session is returned.

DBIResult Return Values

DBIERR_NONE	The object handle was returned successfully.
DBIERR_NOTSUPPORTED	Object is not supported for this function.
DBIERR_OBJNOTFOUND	Named object was not found.

Example

```
function BDEGetActiveSession : hDBIObj;
begin
  IsDbiOk( DbiGetObjFromName( objSYSTEM, '', Result ));
end; { BDEGetActiveSession }

function BDEGetDbaseDriverObj : hDBIObj;
begin
  IsDbiOk( DbiGetObjFromName( objDRIVER, szDBASE, Result ));
end; { BDEGetDbaseDriverObj }
```

Pure Delphi Equivalent

<ObjectName>.Handle

DbiGetObjFromObj

Declaration

```
function DbiGetObjFromObj (          { Get associated object }
      hObj            : hDBIObj;     { Object handle }
      eObjType        : DBIOBJType;  { Type of associated object }
var   hObj            : hDBIObj      { Returns object of eObjType }
    ): DBIResult;
```

Parameters

PARAMETER NAME	DESCRIPTION
hObj	The object.
eObjType	The type of object.
hObj	Reference to hold the object handle.

Description

Returns an object of the specified object type associated with or derived from a given object.

The following table summarizes the relationship between eObjType and hObj:

EObjType	Type of hObj Allowed
objCURSOR	None
objDRIVER	objCURSOR, objDATABASE
objDATABASE	objCURSOR
objSESSION	objCURSOR, objDATABASE, NIL (active)
objCLIENT	Any or NIL
objSYSTEM	Any or NIL
objSTATEMENT	None

DBIResult Return Values

DBIERR_NONE	The object handle was returned successfully.
DBIERR_INVALIDPARAM	hObj is NIL or invalid.
DBIERR_NA	No associated object.

Example

```
procedure GetObjFromObj( hTmpDb: hDBIDb; TblName: String );
var
  hCursor: hDBICur;
  szName: Array[0..DBIMAXPATHLEN] of Char;
  nLen: Word;
  hObj: hDBIObj;
  rslt: DBIResult;
begin
  { Open the specified table }
  Check( DbiOpenTable( hTmpDb, PChar( TblName ), nil, nil, nil, 0,
         dbiREADONLY, dbiOPENSHARED, xltFIELD, True, nil, hCursor));

  { Retrieve driver handle given cursor handle }
  Check( DbiGetObjFromObj( hDBIObj( hCursor ),
                           DBIOBJType( objDRIVER ), hObj ));

  { Display driver name associated with the object handle }
  rslt := DbiGetProp( hObj, drvDRIVERTYPE, @szName,
                      SizeOf( DBIPATH ), nLen );
  if (rslt <> DBIERR_NONE) then
    Check( DbiCloseCursor( hCursor ))
  else
    ShowMessage( 'Drive type: ' + szName );
  { Close table }
  Check( DbiCloseCursor( hCursor ));
end;
```

DBIGETPRIORRECORD

Declaration

```
function DbiGetPriorRecord (        { Find/Get the prior record }
    hCursor      : hDBICur;         { Cursor handle }
    eLock        : DBILockType;     { Optional lock request }
    pRecBuff     : Pointer;         { Record buffer (client) }
    pRecProps    : pRecProps        { Optional record properties }
): DBIResult;
```

Parameters

PARAMETER NAME	DESCRIPTION
hCursor	The cursor handle.
eLock	Optional lock request type. Valid types are: dbiNOLOCK, dbiREADLOCK, or dbiWRITELOCK. If a lock is requested, the call returns DBIERR_NONE only if the lock is granted.
pRecBuf	Optional pointer to the client buffer that receives the record data. If NIL, no data are returned.
pRecProps	Optional pointer to the client-allocated RECProps structure. For dBASE and Paradox drivers only. If NIL, no record properties are returned.

Description

Retrieves the previous record in the table associated with the given cursor. If the cursor is currently positioned on the first record in the table and the user calls DbiGetPriorRecord, then a BOF error is returned.

If a record buffer is provided, DbiGetPriorRecord reads the data for the record into the record buffer. If the pRecProps argument is supplied, record properties are returned (for dBASE and Paradox only). If filters are active, only records that meet the filters criteria are retrieved. The record can be locked if an explicit lock is specified (using eLock), and the function call fails if the requested lock cannot be acquired.

dBASE. If the pRecProps argument is supplied, the record number can be retrieved for the prior record (the iPhyRecNum field of the RECProps structure). dBASE does not support the concept of sequence numbers.

Paradox. If the pRecProps argument is supplied, the sequence number can be retrieved for the prior record (via the iSeqNum field of pRecProps). Paradox does not support the concept of record numbers.

SQL. Record properties are not supported for SQL drivers (pRecProps is NIL). If pRecProps is supplied, no properties are returned. An error is returned if the cursor is not bidirectional.

DBIResult Return Values

DBIERR_NONE	The prior record was retrieved successfully.
DBIERR_BOF	The cursor was positioned in the crack before the beginning of the file or on the first record after the crack. The cursor is now positioned in the crack at the beginning of the file.
DBIERR_INVALIDHNDL	The specified cursor handle is invalid or NIL.
DBIERR_ALREADYLOCKED	The record is already locked by the same user in the same session.
DBIERR_FILELOCKED	The table is already locked by another user (Paradox and dBASE only).
DBIERR_NA	Cursor is unidirectional.

Example

```
function PriorRecord( oTable : TTable ) : Pointer;
begin
   Result := StrAlloc( TableProperties( oTable ).iRecBufSize );
   IsDbiOk( DbiGetPriorRecord( GetTableCursor( oTable ), dbiNoLock,
      Result, nil ) );
end; { PriorRecord() }
```

Pure Delphi Equivalent

TTable.Prior

Xbase Equivalent

SKIP -1

See Also

DbiGetRecord, DbiGetNextRecord, DbiGetPriorRecord, DbiGetRelativeRecord, DbiGetField, DbiModifyRecord

DBIGETPROP

Declaration

```
function DbiGetProp (              { Get property }
      hObj       : hDBIObj;        { Object handle }
      iProp      : Longint;        { Property to retrieve }
      pPropValue : Pointer;        { If NIL, validate iProp for retrieval }
      iMaxLen    : Word;           { Length of buffer pPropValue }
var   iLen       : Word            { Returns required length }
   ): DBIResult;
```

Parameters

Parameter Name	Description
hObj	The system, session, client, driver, database, cursor, or statement object.
iProp	The property to retrieve.
pPropValue	Optional pointer to the client variable that receives the value of the property. If NIL, validates *iProp* for retrieval.
iMaxLen	The length of the *pPropValue* buffer.
iLen	Reference to variable to receive the buffer length.

Description

Retrieves the properties of an object. The specified object does not necessarily have to match the type of property as long as the object is associated with the object type of the property. For Example, the property drvDRIVERTYPE assumes an object of type objDRIVER, but because a cursor is derived from a driver, a cursor handle (objCURSOR) could also be specified.

DBIResult Return Values

DBIERR_NONE	The properties were retrieved successfully.
DBIERR_BUFFTOOSMALL	Required buffer length is bigger than *iMaxLen*.
DBIERR_NOTSUPPORTED	Property is not supported for this object.

Example

```
procedure GetDatabaseName( oTable : TTable );
var
  szFileName : Array[0..127] of Char;
  iLen       : Word;
begin
  DbiGetProp( HDBIobj(oTable.DBHandle), dbDATABASENAME, @szFileName,
                          SizeOf(szFileName), iLen );
  ShowMessage( 'The database name ' + StrPas( szFileName ) +
               ' is ' + IntToStr( iLen ) + ' bytes long.' );
end; { GetDatabaseName() }
```

See Also

DbiSetProp, DbiGetCursorProps, DbiGetObjFromObj

DBIGETRECORD

Declaration

```
function DbiGetRecord (          { Gets the current record }
    hCursor      : hDBICur;      { Cursor handle }
    eLock        : DBILockType;  { Optional lock request }
    pRecBuff     : Pointer;      { Record buffer(client) }
    pRecProps    : pRecProps     { Optional record properties }
): DBIResult;
```

Parameters

PARAMETER NAME	DESCRIPTION
hCursor	The cursor handle.
eLock	Optional lock request type. Valid types are dbiNOLOCK, dbiREADLOCK, or dbiWRITELOCK.
pRecBuf	Optional pointer to the client buffer that receives the record data. If NIL, no data is returned.
pRecProps	Optional pointer to the client-allocated RECProps structure. For dBASE and Paradox drivers only. If NIL, no record properties are returned.

Description

Retrieves the current record, if any, in the table associated with hCursor.

If NIL pointers are supplied for pRecBuf and pRecProps, DbiGetRecord can be used to validate the current cursor position (on a current record, or on a crack).

If filters are active, the record is retrieved only if it meets the filters criteria. The record can be locked if an explicit lock is specified (using eLock), and the function call fails if the requested lock cannot be acquired.

If the cursor is currently positioned on a record and that record is subsequently deleted or the records key value is changed, then the cursor is left on a crack between records. At this point, a call to DbiGetRecord returns the DBIERR_KEYORRECDELETED error.

dBASE. If pRecProps is supplied, the record number can be retrieved for the current record (via the iPhyRecNum field of pRecProps). dBASE does not support the concept of sequence numbers.

Paradox. If pRecProps is supplied, the sequence number can be retrieved for the current record (via the iSeqNum field of pRecProps). Paradox does not support the concept of record numbers.

SQL. Record properties are not supported for SQL drivers (pRecProps is NIL). If pRecProps is supplied, no properties are returned.

DBIResult Return Values

DBIERR_NONE	The record was successfully retrieved.
DBIERR_BOF	At beginning of file.
DBIERR_EOF	At end of file.
DBIERR_NOCURRREC	No current record.
DBIERR_KEYORRECDELETED	The cursor is positioned on a record that has been deleted, or the key value was changed.
DBIERR_INVALIDHNDL	The specified cursor handle is invalid or NIL.
DBIERR_ALREADYLOCKED	The record is already locked by the same user in the same session.
DBIERR_LOCKED	The table is already locked by another user (Paradox and dBASE only).

Example

```
{ A single Recno function that works with dBASE or Paradox tables }
function Recno( oTable : TTable ): LongInt;
var
  CursorProps: CurProps;
  RecordProps: RECProps;
begin
  result := 0;
  with oTable do
  begin
    if State = dsInactive then
      DBError( SDataSetClosed );
    Check( DbiGetCursorProps( Handle, CursorProps ));
    UpdateCursorPos;
    Check( DbiGetRecord( Handle, dbiNOLOCK, nil, @RecordProps ));
    case CursorProps.iSeqNums of
      0: result := RecordProps.iPhyRecNum;
      1: result := RecordProps.iSeqNum;
    end;
  end;
end;
```

Pure Delphi Equivalent

TTable.Edit

Xbase Equivalent

GATHER

See Also

DbiGetField, DbiGetNextRecord, DbiGetPriorRecord, DbiGetRelativeRecord

DBIGETRECORDCOUNT

Declaration

```
function DbiGetRecordCount (    { Get the current number of records }
     hCursor      : hDBICur;    { Cursor handle }
var  lRecCount    : Longint     { Number of records }
   ): DBIResult;
```

Parameters

PARAMETER NAME	DESCRIPTION
hCursor	The cursor handle.
iRecCount	Reference to the client variable that receives the number of records associated with the cursor. This number may be approximate.

Description

Retrieves the current number of records associated with the cursor. The count is the number of physical records in the table, without regard to filters or range settings.

Paradox. If a range is active, the record count returned is the number of records in the range.

DBIResult Return Values

DBIERR_NONE	The record count was retrieved successfully.
DBIERR_INVALIDHNDL	The specified cursor handle is invalid or NIL.

Example

```
function GetRecordCount( oTable : TTable ) : Longint;
begin
  IsDbiOk( DbiGetRecordCount( oTable.Handle, Result ));
end;
```

Pure Delphi Equivalent

TTable.RecordCount

Xbase Equivalent

LastRec(), RecCount()

See Also

DbiGetExactRecordCount

DBIGETRECORDFORKEY

Declaration

```
function DbiGetRecordForKey ( { Find a record matching key }
     hCursor       : hDBICur;   { Cursor handle }
     bDirectKey    : Bool;      { Key is supplied directly }
     iFields       : Word;      { No of full fields to match }
     iLen          : Word;      { Partial key len of last field }
     pKey          : Pointer;   { Either Record buffer or Key itself }
     pRecBuff      : Pointer    { (Optional) Record buffer }
  ): DBIResult;
```

Parameters

PARAMETER NAME	DESCRIPTION
hCursor	The cursor handle.
bDirectKey	Determines whether pKey is used to specify the key directly or not.
	If True, the value in pKey is used to specify the key directly. If False, pKey specifies the record buffer.
iFields	The number of fields to be used for composite keys. If iFields and iLen are both 0, the entire key is used.
iLen	The length into the last field to be used for composite keys. If not 0, the last field to be used must be a character type.
pKey	If bDirectKey is True, pKey specifies the pointer to the record key. Otherwise, pKey specifies the pointer to the record buffer.
	DbiExtractKey can be used to construct the record key when bDirectKey is True.
	The iFields and iLen Parameters together indicate how much of the key should be used for matching. If both are 0, the entire key is used. If a match is required on a given field of the key, all the key fields preceding it in the composite key must also be supplied for a match. Only character fields can be matched for a partial key; all other field types must be fully matched.
	For partial key matches, iFields must be equal to the number of key fields preceding the field being partially matched. iLen specifies the number of characters in the partial key to be matched.
pRecBuf	Optional pointer to the record buffer where the new current record is returned.

Description

Finds a record matching pKey and positions the cursor on that record. After the operation, the cursor will be positioned on the found record. If pRecBuf is supplied, it will be filled with the contents of the new current record. If there is no key in the index that matches the given key, an error is returned.

SQL. For SQL tables, if the active index is not unique, DbiGetRecordForKey may return different records with the same key value.

DBIResult Return Values

DBIERR_NOCURRREC	The cursor is not positioned on a record.
DBIERR_RECNOTFOUND	No record with the specified key value was found.

Example

```
function SeekRecord( oTable : TTable; sKey : String ) : Boolean;
var
  szKey : Array[0..255] of Char;
begin
  StrPCopy( szKey, sKey );
  { Finds a full match on szKey }
  Result := IsDbiOk( DbiGetRecordForKey( GetTableCursor( oTable ),
                                 True, 0, 0, @szKey, nil ));
end; { SeekRecord() }
```

Pure Delphi Equivalent

TTable.FindKey, TTable.GotoKey

Xbase Equivalent

SEEK, dbSeek()

See Also

DbiSetToKey, DbiExtractKey

DBIGETRELATIVERECORD

Declaration

```
function DbiGetRelativeRecord (    { Find/Get a record by record # }
    hCursor        : hDBICur;      { Cursor handle }
    iPosOffset     : Longint;      { Offset from current position }
    eLock          : DBILockType;  { Optional lock request }
    pRecBuff       : Pointer;      { Record buffer(client) }
    pRecProps      : pRECProps     { Optional record properties }
): DBIResult;
```

Parameters

PARAMETER NAME	DESCRIPTION
hCursor	The cursor handle.
iPosOffset	The (signed) offset from current record.

eLock	Optional lock request type. Valid types are: dbiNOLOCK, dbiREADLOCK, or dbiWRITELOCK.
pRecBuff	Optional pointer to the client buffer that receives the record data. If NIL, no data are returned.
pRecProps	Optional pointer to the client-allocated RECProps structure. If specified, record properties are returned.

Description

Positions the cursor on a record in the table relative to the current position of the cursor.

The record offset (iPosOffset) can be positive or negative. If the cursor is currently positioned between records, the next or prior (depending on the direction) record is counted as 1. If the filter is active, only those records that meet the filter condition are included.

If a record buffer is provided, DbiGetRelativeRecord reads the data for the record into the record buffer. The record can be locked if an explicit lock is specified (using eLock), and the function call returns an error if the requested lock cannot be acquired.

If not enough records exist in the result set to move to the relative record location, a beginning of file/end of file (BOF/EOF) error is returned.

dBASE. If Soft Delete is off, only undeleted records are included. If the pRecProps argument is supplied, the record number can be retrieved for the record (the iPhyRecNum field of the RECProps structure). dBASE does not support the concept of sequence numbers.

Paradox. If the pRecProps argument is supplied, the sequence number can be retrieved for the record (via the iSeqNum field of pRecProps). Paradox does not support the concept of record numbers.

SQL. Record properties are not supported for SQL drivers (pRecProps is NIL). If pRecProps is supplied, no properties are returned. An error is returned if the cursor is not bidirectional, and the cursor is moving backwards.

DBIResult Return Values

DBIERR_NONE	The record was retrieved successfully.
DBIERR_BOF	The beginning of the file was reached.
DBIERR_EOF	The end of the file was reached.
DBIERR_INVALIDHNDL	The specified cursor handle is invalid or NIL.
DBIERR_KEYORRECDELETED	The cursor is positioned in a crack other than BOF or EOF.
DBIERR_ALREADYLOCKED	The record is already locked by the same user in the same session.
DBIERR_FILELOCKED	The table is already locked by another user.

Example

```
function GoRelative( oTable : TTable; iPosOffset : Longint ) : Boolean;
begin
```

```
     Result := IsDbiOk( DbiGetRelativeRecord( GetTableCursor( oTable ),
                              iPosOffset, dbiNoLock, nil, nil ));
  end; { GoRelative() }
```

Pure Delphi Equivalent

TTable.MoveBy

Xbase Equivalent

GO, dbGoto(), SKIP

See Also

DbiGetField, DbiGetNextRecord, DbiGetPriorRecord

DBIGETRINTDESC

Declaration

```
function DbiGetRintDesc (      { Get referential integrity descriptor }
    hCursor      : hDBICur;    { Cursor handle }
    iRintSeqNo   : Word;       { Rint sequence number }
    printDesc    : pRINTDesc   { Returned rint description }
  ): DBIResult;
```

Parameters

PARAMETER NAME	DESCRIPTION
hCursor	The cursor handle.
IRintSeqNo	The referential integrity sequence number. This number is between 1 and the value of iRefIntChecks. The value of iRefIntChecks can be obtained from the cursor properties (CURProps) structure.
PrintDesc	Pointer to the client variable that receives the referential integrity descriptor.

Description

Retrieves the referential integrity descriptor identified by the referential integrity sequence number and the cursor.

If a field map is associated with the cursor, the aiThisTabFld array in the referential integrity descriptor reflects the field map. If any of the fields are not part of the field-mapped record, a negative number is listed.

DBIResult Return Values

DBIERR_NONE	The descriptor was returned successfully.

Example

```
function RefIntegDesc( oTable : TTable; wRefInt : Word ) : pRINTDesc;
begin
  try
    GetMem( Result, SizeOf( RINTDesc ));
    IsDbiOk( DbiGetRintDesc( GetTableCursor( oTable ), wRefInt, Result ));
  except
    if Assigned( Result ) then
      FreeMem( Result, SizeOf( RINTDesc ));
    Result := nilyt;
  end; { try .. except }
end; { RefIntegDesc() }
```

See Also

DbiGetCursorProps

DBIGETSEQNO

Declaration

```
function DbiGetSeqNo (              { Get logical record number }
     hCursor      : hDBICur;       { Cursor handle }
var  iSeqNo       : Longint        { Pointer to sequence number }
   ): DBIResult;
```

Parameters

PARAMETER NAME	DESCRIPTION
hCursor	The cursor handle.
iSeqNo	Pointer to the client variable that receives the logical sequence number of the current record in the table associated with *hCursor*.

Description

Retrieves the sequence number of the current record in the Paradox table associated with the cursor. The sequence number is the relative position of a record with respect to the beginning of the file. A sequence number for a given record, therefore, depends on the current index in use. An active range also affects the sequence numbers, the sequence number is relative to the beginning of the range. Filters do not affect sequence numbers, so there might seem to be gaps in the sequence numbers.

Paradox. This function is only supported for Paradox tables.

dBASE. This function is not supported by the dBASE driver.

SQL. This function is not supported by SQL drivers.

DBIResult Return Values

DBIERR_NOTSUPPORTED	This call is not supported for the given table.
DBIERR_NONE	The sequence number was returned successfully.
DBIERR_BOF	beginning of the file.
DBIERR_EOF	The cursor must be positioned on a record; it is positioned at the end of the file.
DBIERR_KEYORRECDELETED	The cursor is positioned on a deleted record.
DBIERR_NOCURRREC	No record is current.

Example

```
function RecordSequence( oTable : TTable ) : Longint;
begin
  IsDbiOk( DbiGetSeqNo( GetTableCursor( oTable ), Result ));
end; { RecordSequence() }
```

Xbase Equivalent

RecNo()

See Also

DbiSetToSeqNo, DbiGetCursorProps

DBIGETSESINFO

Declaration

```
function DbiGetSesInfo (            { Get current session info }
var    sesInfo     : SESInfo
   ): DBIResult;
```

Parameters

PARAMETER NAME	DESCRIPTION
sesInfo	Reference to the client-allocated SESInfo structure to be filled.

Description

Retrieves the environment settings for the current session.

This function provides the client with information about the resources attached to the current session, including the number of database handles and open cursors (when the session is closed, these resources are released). This function also returns the session ID and name, the current private directory, and the lock retry time for repeated attempts to lock a table. The lock retry time is specified by DbiSetLockRetry.

DBIResult Return Values

DBIERR_NONE	The session information was returned successfully.
DBIERR_INVALIDHNDL	sesInfo is NIL.

Example

```
function BDEGetSesInfo : SESInfo;
begin
  IsDbiOk( DbiGetSesInfo( Result ));
end; { BDEGetSesInfo() }
```

Pure Delphi Equivalent

TSession.<Various properties>

See Also

DbiSetLockRetry, DbiStartSession, DbiCloseSession, DbiGetCurrSession, DbiSetCurrSession

DbiGetSysConfig

Declaration

```
function DbiGetSysConfig (          { System configuration }
var    sysConfig  : SYSConfig
   ): DBIResult;
```

Parameters

PARAMETER NAME	DESCRIPTION
sysConfig	Reference to the client-allocated SYSConfig structure to be filled.

Description

Retrieves BDE system configuration information. After the call, the SYSConfig structure pointed to by sysConfig will contain the retrieved system configuration information.

DBIResult Return Values

DBIERR_NONE	System configuration information was returned successfully.

Example

```
function BDESysConfig : SYSConfig;
begin
  IsDbiOk( DbiGetSysConfig( Result ));
end; { BDESysConfig }
```

See Also

DbiGetSysVersion, DbiGetClientInfo, DbiGetSysInfo

DBIGETSYSINFO

Declaration

```
function DbiGetSysInfo (          { Get system status/info }
var    sysInfo      : SYSInfo
   ): DBIResult;
```

Parameters

PARAMETER NAME	DESCRIPTION
sysInfo	Reference to the client-allocated SYSInfo structure to be filled.

Description

Retrieves system status and information. After the call, the SYSInfo structure referenced by sysInfo will contain the retrieved system status and information.

DBIResult Return Values

DBIERR_NONE	System status information was returned successfully.

Example

```
function BDESysInfo : SYSInfo;
begin
  IsDbiOk( DbiGetSysInfo( Result ));
end; { BDESysInfo }
```

See Also

DbiGetSysVersion, DbiGetSysConfig, DbiGetClientInfo

DbiGetSysVersion

Declaration

```
function DbiGetSysVersion (          { Get system version info }
var   sysVersion   : SYSVersion
   ): DBIResult;
```

Parameters

Parameter Name	Description
sysVersion	Reference to the client-allocated SYSVersion structure to be filled.

Description

Retrieves the system version information, including the engine version number, date, and time; and the client interface version number. After the call, the SYSVersion structure returned in sysVersion will contain the system version information.

DBIResult Return Values

DBIERR_NONE	The system version information was returned successfully.

Example

```
function BDESysVersion : SYSVersion;
begin
  IsDbiOk( DbiGetSysVersion( Result ));
end; { BDESysVersion }
```

See Also

DbiGetSysConfig, DbiGetClientInfo, DbiGetSysInfo

DbiGetTableOpenCount

Declaration

```
function DbiGetTableOpenCount (      { Get local cursor count }
      hDb          : hDBIDb;         { Database handle }
      pszTableName : PChar;          { Table name }
      pszDriverType : PChar;         { Driver type /NIL }
var   iOpenCount   : Word            { returned number of cursors }
   ): DBIResult;
```

Parameters

PARAMETER NAME	DESCRIPTION
hDb	The database handle.
pszTableName	Pointer to the name of the table.
	Paradox and dBASE: If pszTableName is a fully qualified name of a table, the pszDriverType parameter need not be specified. If the path is not included, the path name is taken from the current directory of the database associated with hDb.
	SQL: This parameter can be a fully qualified name that includes the owner name.
pszDriverType	Optional pointer to the table type. Valid driver types are: szDBASE or szPARADOX.
	Paradox and dBASE: This parameter is required if pszTableName has no extension.
	SQL: This parameter is ignored if the database associated with hDb is an SQL database.
iOpenCount	Reference to the client variable that receives the number of cursors opened on the table.

Description

Returns the total number of cursors that are open on the specified table by this instance of the BDE, irrespective of database and current session.

Most of the functions that operate on tables require a cursor, which is obtained by calling DbiOpenTable. A table can be opened more than once, resulting in more than one cursor for that table. Some functions, such as DbiDoRestructure, require that no cursors be opened on the table. Use this function to check for this requirement.

This name of the table (not the cursor) is input to DbiGetTableOpenCount, which returns a count of how many cursors are opened on the table. This function is useful for determining whether a table is in use.

Paradox. The number of open cursors includes any cursors opened implicitly by referential integrity or look up tables.

DBIResult Return Values

DBIERR_NONE	The table open count was returned successfully.
DBIERR_INVALIDHNDL	The specified database handle is invalid or NIL.
DBIERR_INVALIDPARAM	The specified table name or the pointer to the table name is NIL.
DBIERR_NOSUCHTABLE	The specified table name is invalid.
DBIERR_UNKNOWNTBLTYPE	The specified driver type is invalid or NIL, or the pointer to the driver type is NIL.

Example

```
function BDEGetTableOpenCount( oTable : TTable ) : Word;
var
  szTableName : DBITBLNAME;
begin
  StrPCopy( szTableName, oTable.TableName );
```

```
IsDbiOk( DbiGetTableOpenCount( oTable.DBHandle, szTableName, '',
                               Result ));
end; { BDEGetTableOpenCount() }
```

See Also

DbiOpenTable

DBiGetTableTypeDesc

Declaration

```
function DbiGetTableTypeDesc (      { Get Table capabilities }
     pszDriverType : PChar;         { Driver type }
     pszTableType  : PChar;         { Table type }
var  tblType       : TBLType        { Table Capabilities }
  ): DBIResult;
```

Parameters

PARAMETER NAME	DESCRIPTION
pszDriverType	Pointer to the driver type.
pszTableType	Pointer to the table type. Use *DbiOpenTableTypesList* to get a list of valid table types.
tblType	Reference to the client-allocated TBLType structure to be filled.

Description

Returns a description of the capabilities of the table type given in pszTableType for the driver type given in pszDriverType.

SQL. The table type distinguishes between views, queries, and tables. It does not identify the driver type.

DBIResult Return Values

DBIERR_NONE	The table type description was returned successfully.
DBIERR_INVALIDHNDL	The pointer to the driver type is NIL, or the pointer to the table type is NIL, or *tblType* is NIL.
DBIERR_UNKNOWNDRVTYPE	The specified driver type is invalid or NIL, or the specified table type is invalid or NIL.

Example

```
function BDEGetTableTypeDesc( szDriver, szTable : PChar ) : TBLType;
begin
```

```
    IsDbiOk( DbiGetTableTypeDesc( szDriver, szTable, Result ));
end; { BDEGetTableTypeDesc() }
```

See Also

DbiOpenTableTypesList

DBIGETTIMEFORMAT

Declaration

```
function DbiGetTimeFormat (          { Get current time format }
var     fmtTime      : FMTTime
    ): DBIResult;
```

Parameters

PARAMETER NAME	DESCRIPTION
fmtTime	Reference to the client-allocated FMTTime structure to be filled.

Description

Retrieves the time format for the current session. The time format is used by QBE for input and wildcard character matching. It is also used by batch operations (such as DbiDoRestructure and DbiBatchMove) to handle data-type coercion between character and datetime or time types.

DBIResult Return Values

DBIERR_NONE	The time format was successfully retrieved.
DBIERR_INVALIDHNDL	fmtTime is NIL.

Example

```
{==================================================================
   Function:
          FormatTime( tTime Time, PChar szTime )

   Input:  tTime    - Time which needs to be formatted
           szTime   - String to contain the formatted time

   Return: Result returned from DbiTimeDecode().

   Description:
          This function is used to format time fields according to
          the settings in the IDAPI.CFG file.
   ================================================================ }

function FormatTime( tTime: Time; szTime: PChar ): DBIResult;
```

```
var
  rslt    : DBIResult;        { Return value from BDE functions }
  timeFmt : FMTTime;          { Time format }
  uHour   : Word;             { Hour portion of the time }
  uMinute : Word;             { Minute portion of the time }
  uMilSec : Word;             { Second portion (in ms) of the time }
  uIsAM   : Word;             { Is Time AM? }
  szTemp  : Array[0..10] of Char; { Temp buffer, used for AM, PM
                                    string }
  sHour, sMinute, sSec, sMilSec: String;
begin
  { Get the formatting of the Time }
  Check( DbiGetTimeFormat( timeFmt ));

  { Decode the time }
  rslt := DbiTimeDecode( tTime, uHour, uMinute, uMilSec );

  { Make certain the seperator is not the escape character }
  if ( timeFmt.cTimeSeparator = '\' ) then
    timeFmt.cTimeSeparator  := '/';

  { Check if time should be displayed in 12 or 24 hour format }
  if ( timeFmt.bTwelveHour ) then
  begin
    { Temporary variable used to determine if the time is AM or PM }
    uIsAm := uHour;
    uHour := uHour mod 12;
    if (uHour = 0) then
      uHour := 12;
      { If AM, set uIsAm to TRUE, else set uIsAm to 0 }
      if (uIsAm = uHour) then
        uIsAm := 1
      else
        uIsAm := 0;
  end;
  Str( uHour:2, sHour );
  Str( uMinute:2, sMinute );
  Str( (round(uMilsec/1000)):2, sSec );
  Str( (round(uMilSec mod 1000)):2, sMilsec );

  { Format the hour and minute of the time }
  StrPCopy( szTime, sHour+timeFmt.cTimeSeparator+sMinute );

  { Determine if seconds are to be displayed }
  if (timeFmt.bSeconds) then
  begin
    StrPCopy(szTemp, timeFmt.cTimeSeparator+sSec);
    StrCat( szTime, szTemp );

    { Determine if milliseconds are to be displayed }
    if ( timeFmt.bMilSeconds ) then
    begin
      StrPCopy( szTemp, timeFmt.cTimeSeparator+sMilsec );
      StrCat( szTime, szTemp );
    end;
```

```
      end;

      { Add a string to the time if the time is 12-hour }
      if ( timeFmt.bTwelveHour ) then
      begin
        { Add a space to the format }
        StrCat( szTime, ' ' );

        { If AM }
        if (uIsAm = 1) then
          { Copy the AM string }
          StrCat( szTime, timeFmt.szAmString )
        else { otherwise it's PM }
          { Copy the PM string }
          StrCat( szTime, timeFmt.szPmString );
    end;
    FormatTime := rslt;
  end;
```

Pure Delphi Equivalent

ShortTimeFormat and LongTimeFormat variables

See Also

DbiGetNumberFormat, DbiGetDateFormat, DbiSetTimeFormat

DBIGETTRANINFO

Declaration

```
function DbiGetTranInfo (      { Get transaction info }
     hDb         : hDBIDb;     { Database handle }
     hXact       : hDBIXact;   { Xact handle }
     pxInfo      : pXInfo      { Xact info }
   ): DBIResult;
```

Parameters

PARAMETER NAME	DESCRIPTION
hDb	The database handle.
hXact	Optional transaction handle. If NIL, hDb is used. Otherwise, hDb is ignored.
pxInfo	Pointer to the client-allocated XInfo structure.

Description

Retrieves transaction information. If the DbiBeginTran request is successful, the transaction state is active. The state remains active until DbiEndTran is called. While the transaction is active, the actual isolation level being used can be retrieved with this function.

This is an Information function only and does not affect transaction processing.

DBIResult Return Values

DBIERR_NONE	The transaction information was returned successfully.

Example

```
function TableTransactionInfo( oTable : TTable ) : pXInfo;
begin
  try
    GetMem( Result, SizeOf( XInfo ));
    { Use FreeMem( Result, SizeOf( XInfo )) when done }
    IsDbiOk( DbiGetTranInfo( oTable.DBHandle, nil, Result ));
  except
    if Assigned( Result ) then
      FreeMem( Result, SizeOf( XInfo ));
    Result := nil;
  end; { try .. except }
end; { TableTransactionInfo() }
```

DBIGETVCHKDESC

Declaration

```
function DbiGetVchkDesc (        { Get valcheck descriptor }
    hCursor      : hDBICur;      { Cursor handle }
    iValSeqNo    : Word;         { Valcheck sequence number }
    pvalDesc     : pVCHKDesc     { Returned valcheck Description }
  ): DBIResult;
```

Parameters

PARAMETER NAME	DESCRIPTION
hCursor	The cursor handle.
iValSeqNo	The validity check sequence number. This number is between 1 and the value of iValChecks. The value of iValChecks can be obtained from the cursor properties (CURProps) structure.
pvalDesc	Pointer to the client-allocated VCHKDesc structure.

Description

Retrieves the validity check descriptor identified by the validity check sequence number and the cursor.

If a field map is active, the iFldNum in the validity check descriptor reflects the field map. If any of the fields are not part of the field-mapped record, a negative number is listed.

DBIResult Return Values

DBIERR_NONE	The descriptor was returned successfully.

Example

```
function TableVchkDesc( oTable : TTable; iCheck : integer ) : pVCHKDesc;
var
  iMaxChecks : integer;
begin
  try
    GetMem( Result, SizeOf( VCHKDesc ));
    { Use FreeMem( Result, SizeOf( VCHKDesc ) ) when done }
    iMaxChecks := TableProperties( oTable ).iValChecks;
    if iCheck < 1 then
      iCheck := 1
    else if iCheck > iMaxChecks then
      iCheck := iMaxChecks;
    IsDbiOk( DbiGetVchkDesc( GetTableCursor( oTable ), iCheck, Result ));
  except
    if Assigned( Result ) then
      FreeMem( Result, SizeOf( VCHKDesc ));
    Result := nil;
  end; { try .. except }
end; { TableTransactionInfo() }
```

See Also

DbiGetCursorProps

DBIINIT

Declaration

```
function DbiInit(         { Initialize the BDE environment }
    pEnv: PDbiEnv         { Pointer to DBIEnv struct (Opt) }
  ): DBIResult;
```

Parameters

PARAMETER NAME	DESCRIPTION
pEnv	Optional pointer to the DBIEnv structure. Can be used to change the working directory and the location of the configuration file, to set up the language driver, and to supply the BDE with the client name.
	If NIL, the BDE assumes that the start-up directory is the working directory, szClientName will be empty and bForceLocalInit will be False.

Description

Initializes the BDE environment. DbiInit must be called once by each client application before any other BDE calls are made. However, if the application is using a TTable component, the DbiInit call is already handled under the hood.

Default settings can be overwritten by supplying the appropriate settings.

DBIResult Return Values

DBIERR_NONE	The engine environment was initialized successfully.
DBIERR_MULTIPLEINIT	Illegal attempt to initialize the engine more than once.

Example

```
function DBInitEnv : Boolean;
var
  dbEnv : DBIEnv;
begin
  {Set initialization params for the DB Environment}
  with dbEnv do
  begin
    StrPCopy( szWorkDir, 'c:\data' );
    StrPCopy( szIniFile, '' );
    bForceLocalInit := True;
    StrPCopy( szLang, '' );
    StrPCopy( szClientName, 'dbClientName' );
  end;

  {Initialize the database}
  Result := IsDbiOk( DbiInit( @dbEnv ));
end; { DBInitEnv }
```

See Also

DbiExit

DBIINITRECORD

Declaration

```
function DbiInitRecord (          { Initialize record area }
    hCursor      : hDBICur;       { Cursor handle }
    pRecBuff     : Pointer        { Record buffer }
  ): DBIResult;
```

Parameters

PARAMETER NAME	DESCRIPTION
hCursor	The cursor handle.
pRecBuf	Pointer to the client buffer that receives the initialized record buffer.

Description

Initializes a record buffer with blank fields or default values. This operation is required before composing a new record for insertion.

The position of the given cursor is not affected.

The client application can use the BDE field-level functions to fill the record buffer with the appropriate values.

Paradox. If the table has associated default values with any of the fields, the default values are used to initialize the fields.

DBIResult Return Values

DBIERR_NONE	The initialization was successful.
DBIERR_INVALIDHNDL	The specified cursor handle is invalid or NIL.
DBIERR_INVALIDPARAM	The specified record buffer is NIL.

Example

```
function InitRecord( oTable : TTable; pRecBuf : PChar ) : Boolean
begin
  Result := IsDbiOk( DbiInitRecord( oTable.Handle, pRecBuf ));
end;
```

Pure Delphi Equivalent

TTable.AppendRecord

Xbase Equivalent

APPEND BLANK

See Also

DbiAppendRecord, DbiGetRecord, DbiGetNextRecord, DbiGetPriorRecord, DbiModifyRecord, DbiInsertRecord, DbiPutField, DbiSetToKey, DbiGetBlob, DbiPutBlob, DbiOpenBlob, DbiFreeBlob, DbiGetField

DbiInsertRecord

Declaration

```
function DbiInsertRecord (        { Inserts a new record }
    hCursor       : hDBICur;      { Cursor handle }
    eLock         : DBILockType;  { Optional lock on this record }
    pRecBuff      : Pointer       { New Record (client) }
): DBIResult;
```

Parameters

PARAMETER NAME	DESCRIPTION
hCursor	The cursor handle.
eLock	Optional lock request type. Valid types are: dbiNOLOCK, dbiREADLOCK, or dbiWRITELOCK.
pRecBuff	Pointer to the record buffer.

Description

Inserts a new record into the table associated with the given cursor, using the data contained in pRecBuff. The client application can optionally acquire a lock on the newly inserted record by specifying the lock type in eLock.

In order for this function to succeed, no other user can have a write lock, or greater, on the table. The record buffer should be initialized with DbiInitRecord, and data filled in using DbiPutField or DbiOpenBlob and DbiPutBlob.

After successful completion, the cursor is positioned on the new record. If the function fails, the record is not inserted and the current position of the cursor is not affected.

If the cursor has a filter or a range associated with it, the cursor might be positioned on a crack or BOF/EOF and the operation will fail if a record lock was requested.

dBASE. There is no difference between DbiAppendRecord and DbiInsertRecord. The record is inserted at the end of the table. The cursor is positioned at the inserted record. If an active range exists, the cursor might be positioned at the beginning or end of the file.

Paradox. Before inserting the record, the function verifies any referential integrity requirements or validity checks that may be in place. If either fails, an error is returned and the insert operation is canceled. If a primary index is in place, the record is physically placed at a location that conforms to the primary index order. With non-indexed tables, the record is inserted before the current position.

SQL. The table must be opened for write access. After the insert, the cursor is always positioned on the inserted record.

DBIResult Return Values

DBIERR_NONE	The record was successfully inserted.
DBIERR_INVALIDHNDL	The specified cursor handle is invalid or NIL.
DBIERR_INVALIDPARAM	The specified record buffer is NIL.
DBIERR_FOREIGNKEYERR	The target table is a detail table in a referential integrity link, and the linking value cannot be found in the master table.
DBIERR_MINVALERR	The specified data are less than the required minimum value.
DBIERR_MAXVALERR	The specified data are greater than the required maximum value.
DBIERR_REQDERR	The field cannot be blank.
DBIERR_LOOKUPTABLEERR	The specified value was not found in the assigned look-up table.
DBIERR_KEYVIOL	The table has a unique index, and the inserted key value conflicts with an existing records key value.
DBIERR_FILELOCKED	The table is locked by another user.
DBIERR_TABLEREADONLY	Table access denied; the specified cursor handle is read-only.
DBIERR_NOTSUFFTABLERIGHTS	Insufficient table rights to insert a record (Paradox only).
DBIERR_NODISKSPACE	Insert failed due to insufficient disk space.
DBIERR_RECLOCKFAILED	Insert failed because the record could not be locked due to range or filter constraint.

Example

```
function RecInsert( oTable : TTable ) : Boolean;
var
  pRecBuf : Pointer;
begin
  Result := False;
  try
    pRecBuf := StrAlloc( TableProperties( oTable ).iRecBufSize+1 );
    if IsDbiOk( DbiGetRecord( oTable.Handle, dbiNOLOCK, nil,
                                                  pRecBuf )) then
      Result := IsDbiOk( DbiInsertRecord( GetTableCursor( oTable ),
                                    dbiNOLOCK, pRecBuf ));
  finally
    if Assigned( pRecBuf ) then
      StrDispose( pRecBuf );
  end;
end; { RecInsert() }
```

Pure Delphi Equivalent

TTable.Insert

Xbase Equivalent

INSERT

See Also

DbiPutField, DbiGetNextRecord, DbiGetRecord, DbiGetRelativeRecord, DbiAppendRecord

DbiIsRecordLocked

Declaration

```
function DbiIsRecordLocked (          { Check if current record is locked }
     hCursor          : hDBICur;      { Cursor handle }
var  bLocked          : Bool          { Record lock status }
   ): DBIResult;
```

Parameters

PARAMETER NAME	DESCRIPTION
hCursor	The cursor handle.
bLocked	Reference to the client variable. It will be set to True if the record is locked, and to False if not.

Description

Used to check if the session for this cursor has the current record lock. Record locks differ from table locks in that they only have two states: locked or not locked.

Table locks have four states:

- No Lock
- Read Lock
- Write Lock
- Exclusive Lock

The lock status is returned in bLocked, and indicates whether the record is locked by anybody.

SQL. For SQL, the lock status returned in *bLocked* indicates whether the record is locked by you.

DBIResult Return Values

DBIERR_NONE	The lock status was returned successfully.
DBIERR_NOCURRREC	There is no current record.
DBIERR_BOF	Positioned at beginning of file.
DBIERR_EOF	Positioned at end of file.
DBIERR_KEYORRECDELETED	Key or record is deleted.
DBIERR_INVALIDHNDL	The specified cursor handle is invalid or NIL.
DBIERR_INVALIDPARAM	*bLocked* is NIL.

Example

```
function dbIsRLock( oTable : TTable ) : Boolean;
var
  bBlank : Bool; { Changed from WordBool for Delphi 2.0 }
begin
  bLocked := False;
  try
    DbiIsRecordLocked( oTable.Handle, bLocked );
  except
    on E : EDBEngineError do
      ShowMessage( 'Engine Error:' + E.Message );
    on E : Exception do
      ShowMessage( 'Exception: ' + E.Message );
  end;
  Result := bLocked;
end; { dbIsRLock() }
```

See Also

DbiGetNextRecord, DbiGetPriorRecord, DbiGetRecord, DbiGetRelativeRecord, DbiRelRecordLock, DbiIsTableLocked, DbiAcqTableLock, DbiRelTableLock

DbiIsTableLocked

Declaration

```
function DbiIsTableLocked (          { Verify if Table is locked }
    hCursor        : hDBICur;        { Cursor handle }
    epdxLock       : DBILockType;    { Lock type to verify }
var iLocks         : Word            { Number of locks of the given type }
  ): DBIResult;
```

Parameters

Parameter Name	Description
hCursor	The cursor handle.
edbiLock	The lock type to verify: dbiNOLOCK, dbiREADLOCK, or dbiWRITELOCK.
iLocks	Reference to the client variable that receives the number of locks of the given lock type.

Description

Returns the number of locks of type edbiLock acquired on the table associated with the given session.

dBASE. dbiREADLOCKs are upgraded to dbiWRITELOCKs. If the value of edbiLock is dbiREADLOCK, then the number of write locks are returned in iLocks.

DBIResult Return Values

DBIERR_NONE	The number of locks was returned successfully.
DBIERR_INVALIDHNDL	The specified cursor handle is invalid or NIL.
DBIERR_INVALIDPARAM	*iLocks* is NIL.

Example

```
function dbIsFLock( oTable : TTable ) : Boolean;
var
  iLocks  : Word;
begin
  Result := False;
  try
  if IsDbiOk( DbiIsTableLocked( GetTableCursor( oTable ),
                                dbiWRITELOCK, iLocks )) then
    Result := True
  else
  Result := iLocks > 0;
  except
    on E : EDBEngineError do
      ShowMessage( 'Engine Error: ' + E.Message );
    on E : Exception do
      ShowMessage( 'Exception: ' + E.Message );
  end;
end; { dbIsFLock() }
```

See Also

DbiAcqTableLock, DbiRelTableLock, DbiOpenLockList

DBIISTABLESHARED

Declaration

```
function DbiIsTableShared (      { Verify if this is a shared table }
     hCursor        : hDBICur; { Cursor handle }
var  bShared        : Bool     { Shared status }
   ): DBIResult;
```

Parameters

PARAMETER NAME	DESCRIPTION
hCursor	The cursor handle.
bShared	Reference to the client variable to hold shared status. Will be set to True if the table is physically shared, False if not.

Description

Determines whether the table is physically shared or not.

Standard. The table is physically shared if it is placed on a shared drive (network, or local drive when LOCALSHARE in the configuration is True), and the table is not opened exclusively. If a table is shared, dirty data is not buffered. The table is available to all users in the session, unless acquired table or record locks have been placed since the table was opened.

DBIResult Return Values

DBIERR_NONE	The table shared status was returned successfully.
DBIERR_INVALIDHNDL	The specified cursor handle is invalid or NIL.
DBIERR_INVALIDPARAM	bShared is NIL.

Example

```
function IsShared( oTable : TTable ) : Boolean;
var
  bShared : Bool;
begin
  if IsDbiOk( DbiIsTableShared( GetTableCursor( oTable ), bShared )) then
    Result := bShared
  else
    Result := False; { Bad table — default to not shared }
end; { IsShared() }
```

Pure Delphi Equivalent

(**not** TTable.Exclusive)

See Also

DbiOpenTable, DbiAcqTableLock, DbiAcqPersistTableLock, DbiRelTableLock, DbiRelPersist-TableLock, DbiForceReread, DbiForceRecordReread, DbiCheckRefresh

DBILINKDETAIL

Declaration

```
function DbiLinkDetail (          { Link detail to master }
    hMstrCursor    : hDBICur;     { Master cursor }
    hDetlCursor    : hDBICur;     { Detail cursor }
    iLnkFields     : Word;        { Number of link fields }
    piMstrFields   : PWord;       { Array of fields in master }
    piDetlFields   : PWord        { Array of fields in detail }
): DBIResult;
```

Parameters

PARAMETER NAME	DESCRIPTION
hMstrCursor	The cursor handle associated with the master table. The cursor does not have to be opened on an index.
hDetlCursor	The cursor handle associated with the detail table. The cursor must be opened on an index corresponding to all the link fields.
iLnkFields	The number of link fields.
piMstrFields	Pointer to the array of field numbers of link fields in the master table.
piDetlFields	Pointer to the array of field numbers of link fields in the detail table.

Description

Establishes a relation between two cursors so that the view in the child cursor has its record set limited to the set of records matching the linking key values of the master cursor.

A master cursor can have more than one detail cursor; a detail cursor can have only one master cursor. A detail cursor can also be a master cursor.

Links apply to all available driver types and can be established between cursors of the same or different driver types. The effect is equivalent to setting a range using DbiSetRange on the detail table and using the linking fields of the master table.

In order for the cursors to be linked, both cursors must be enabled with DbiBeginLinkMode. The data types of linked fields in master and detail records must be compatible. The detail cursor must be opened on an index corresponding to all of the linking fields.

DbiLinkDetailToExp performs the equivalent operation for expression links on dBASE tables.

DBIResult Return Values

DBIERR_NONE	The link between the detail cursor (*hDetlCursor*) and the master cursor (hMstrCursor) was successfully established.
DBIERR_INVALIDHNDL	One or more of the specified cursor handles is invalid or NIL.

Example

```
function DetailLinkTest( oMaster, oDetail : TTable ) : Boolean;
var
  hCurDetail,
  hCurMaster    : hDBICur;
  wMastFields,
  wDetailFields : Word;
begin
  Result := False;
  try
    hCurMaster := GetTableCursor( oMaster );
    hCurDetail := GetTableCursor( oDetail );
```

```
{ Switch to the second index in Detail }
Check( DbiSwitchToIndex( hCurDetail, nil, nil, 2, False ));
Check( DbiBeginLinkMode( hCurMaster ));
Check( DbiBeginLinkMode( hCurDetail ));
wMastFields := 2;
wDetailFields := 3;

{ Link the 2nd field of Master to the third field of Details }
Check( DbiLinkDetail( hCurMaster, hCurDetail, 1, @wMastFields,
                      @wDetailFields ));
Result := True;
except
  DbiUnlinkDetail( hCurDetail );
  DbiEndLinkMode( hCurMaster );
  DbiEndLinkMode( hCurDetail );
end; { try .. except }
end; { DetailLinkTest() }
```

Pure Delphi Equivalent

TTable.MasterFields, TTable.MasterSource

Xbase Equivalent

SET RELATION

See Also

DbiLinkDetailToExp, DbiUnlinkDetail, DbiSetRange

DBILINKDETAILTOEXP

Declaration

```
function DbiLinkDetailToExp (   { Link detail to master using an
                                  expression }
    hCursorMstr   : hDBICur; { Master cursor }
    hCursorDetl   : hDBICur; { Detail cursor }
    iKeyLen       : Word;    { Key length to match }
    pszMstrExp    : PChar    { Expression string }
  ): DBIResult;
```

Parameters

PARAMETER NAME	DESCRIPTION
hCursorMstr	The cursor handle associated with the master table. Must be a cursor on a dBASE table. The cursor does not have to be opened on an index.
hCursorDetl	The cursor handle associated with the detail table. The cursor must be ordered on an index corresponding to the provided expression, and the cursor must be open on a dBASE table.

iKeyLen	The length of the key to match.
pszMstrExp	Pointer to the expression string. Must be a valid dBASE expression whose key type is the same as the active index of the detail table.

Description

Used to establish one-to-many or one-to-one relationships on dBASE tables, using expressions. Unlike a relationship set using DbiLinkDetail, this function is used to create linked cursors so that the master cursor is on a dBASE table and the link is a dBASE-style expression, not a set of fields.

This function is supported by the dBASE driver only.

hCursorMstr and hCursorDetl must be link cursors. This is done by calling DbiBegin-LinkMode for both master and detail cursor. For the tables to be linked, both cursor handles must be obtained on a dBASE table.

Paradox. This function is not supported for Paradox tables.

SQL. This function is not supported for SQL tables.

DBIResult Return Values

DBIERR_NONE	The specified detail cursor was successfully linked to the specified master cursor.
DBIERR_INVALIDHNDL	One or more of the specified cursor handles is invalid or NIL.
DBIERR_INVALIDLINKEXPR	The expression used was invalid.

Example

```
{ The ExpressionLength function used in this Example can be found in
  BDEREF.PAS on the CD-ROM at the back of the book. This ExpressionLength
  function utilizes the incredibly cool ExtractFields, StringToStringList,
  and AllTrim functions, which are also found in that same file. }

function MakeTheLink( oMaster, oDetail : TTable; sExp : String ) : Boolean;
var
  hMaster,
  hDetail  : hDBICur;
  szExp    : DBIMsg;
  iLen     : Integer;
begin
  Result := False;
  try
    { You may want to break any existing link before doing this }
    BreakTheLink( oMaster, oDetail );
    hMaster := GetTableCursor( oMaster );
    hDetail := GetTableCursor( oDetail );
    if IsDbiOk( DbiBeginLinkMode( hMaster )) and
       IsDbiOk( DbiBeginLinkMode( hDetail )) then
    begin
      StrPCopy( szExp, sExp );
      iLen := ExpressionLength( oMaster, sExp );
```

```
        DbiLinkDetailToExp( hMaster, hDetail, iLen, szExp );
        DbiSetToBegin( hDetail );
        oDetail.First; { Go to first record in set }
        Result := True;
      end; { if links can be set }
    except
      Result := False;
    end;
end; { MakeTheLink() }

function BreakTheLink( oMaster, oDetail : TTable ) : Boolean;
var
  hMaster,
  hDetail : hDBICur;
begin
  Result := False;
  try
    hMaster := GetTableCursor( oMaster );
    hDetail := GetTableCursor( oDetail );
    if DbiUnlinkDetail( hDetail ) = DBIERR_NONE then
    begin
      DbiEndLinkMode( hMaster );
      DbiEndLinkMode( hDetail );
      oDetail.CursorPosChanged;
      oDetail.Refresh;
      Result := True;
    end;
  except
    Result := False;
  end;
end; { BreakTheLink() }
```

Pure Delphi Equivalent

TTable.MasterFields, TTable.MasterSource

Xbase Equivalent

SET RELATION

See Also

DbiLinkDetail, DbiUnlinkDetail

DBILOADDRIVER

Declaration

```
function DbiLoadDriver (        { Load a given data driver }
     pszDriverType : PChar     { Driver name }
   ): DBIResult;
```

Parameters

Parameter Name	Description
pszDriverType	Pointer to the driver name.

Description

Loads a given data driver. Use *DbiOpenDriverList* to get list of valid drivers.

DBIResult Return Values

DBIERR_NONE	The driver has been loaded successfully.

Example

```
function DbaseAvailable : Boolean;
begin
  Result := DbiLoadDriver( 'DBASE' ) = DBIERR_NONE;
end; { DbaseAvailable }

function ParadoxAvailable : Boolean;
begin
  Result := DbiLoadDriver( 'PARADOX' ) = DBIERR_NONE;
end; { ParadoxAvailable }

function InterbaseAvailable : Boolean;
begin
  Result := DbiLoadDriver( 'INTRBASE' ) = DBIERR_NONE;
end; { InterbaseAvailable }
```

Xbase Equivalent

REQUEST <RDDname> (Clipper only)

See Also

DbiOpenDriverList

DBIMAKEPERMANENT

Declaration

```
function DbiMakePermanent (        { Make temporary table permanent }
     hCursor       : hDBICur;      { Cursor handle }
     pszName       : PChar;        { Rename temporary table }
     bOverWrite    : Bool          { Overwrite existing file }
   ): DBIResult;
```

Parameters

PARAMETER NAME	DESCRIPTION
hCursor	The cursor handle.
pszName	Pointer to the name of the permanent table.
bOverWrite	If set to True, overwrites the existing file.

Description

Change a temporary table, created with DbiCreateTempTable, into a permanent table, that is, one that will not be deleted when the cursor is closed with DbiCloseCursor. The table is renamed to pszName if not NIL. The table is saved to disk when the cursor is closed.

DbiSaveChanges can also be used to make the temporary table permanent, but the table is flushed out to disk immediately.

With DbiMakePermanent, buffers are flushed to disk when convenient, or when the cursor is closed.

SQL. This function is not supported by SQL drivers.

DBIResult Return Values

DBIERR_NONE	The temporary table has been designated as a permanent table.

Example

```
function TTempTable.Save( sPermanent : String ) : Boolean;
var
  szFile : Array[0..78] of Char;
begin
  StrPCopy( szFile, sPermanent );
  Result := IsDbiOk( DbiMakePermanent( hCursor, szFile, True ));
end; { TTempTable.Save() }
```

See Also

DbiSaveChanges, DbiCreateTempTable

DBIMODIFYRECORD

Declaration

```
function DbiModifyRecord (        { Updates the current record }
      hCursor      : hDBICur;     { Cursor handle }
      pRecBuf      : Pointer;     { Modified record }
      bFreeLock    : Bool        { Free record lock }
   ): DBIResult;
```

Parameters

PARAMETER NAME	DESCRIPTION
hCursor	The cursor handle for the table. The cursor must be positioned on a valid record.
pRecBuf	Pointer to the client buffer where the modified record is stored.
bFreeLock	Indicates whether to release locks on completion.
	If set to True, the lock is released on the updated record when DbiModifyRecord completes.
	If set to False, the lock is not released.

Description

Modifies the current record of the table associated with hCursor with the data supplied in pRecBuf.

If the record is locked (using dbiREADLOCK or dbiWRITELOCK), and the user tries to modify the record after another user has deleted the record or changed the key value for the record, DbiModifyRecord returns a DBIERR_KEYORRECDELETED error.

Before calling this function, the cursor must be positioned on a record, not on a crack, beginning of file, or end of file. The user must have read-write access to the table. The record must not be locked by another session.

After calling this function, the cursor will be positioned on the updated record. An error is returned if there is no current record for the cursor. If the key has changed, DbiModifyRecord is equivalent to calling first DbiDeleteRecord then DbiInsertRecord. When a record is modified in a table that has an active index, the position of the modified record may change if the key value was modified.

If the client requests to keep a lock on a modified record and the record flies outside a current range or filter condition, the function returns DBIERR_RECLOCKFAILED and the operation fails.

Paradox. Before the table is updated, any referential integrity requirements or validity checks in place are verified. If any fail, an error is returned and the operation is canceled.

SQL. Tables must be opened with write access. If the table has no unique index or server row ID (this includes views), DbiModifyRecord can be used to modify records if the server supports it. However, if you attempt to modify a record that has a duplicate, you will receive an error.

DBIResult Return Values

DBIERR_NONE	The record was modified successfully.
DBIERR_KEYVIOL	The table has a unique index, and the modified key value conflicts with another records key value.
DBIERR_BOF/EOF	The cursor is not positioned on a valid record; it is positioned at the beginning or the end of the table.
DBIERR_FILELOCKED	The table is locked by another user.

continued

DBIERR_INVALIDHNDL	The specified cursor handle is invalid or NIL.
DBIERR_INVALIDPARAM	The specified record buffer is NIL.
DBIERR_KEYORRECDELETED	The specified cursor is not positioned on a valid record.
DBIERR_FOREIEGNKEYERR	The target table is a detail table in a referential integrity link, and the linking value cannot be found in the master table (Paradox only).
DBIERR_MINVALERR	The specified data are less than the required minimum value.
DBIERR_MAXVALERR	The specified data are greater than the required maximum value.
DBIERR_REQDERR	The field cannot be blank.
DBIERR_LOOKUPTABLEERR	The specified value cannot be located in the assigned look-up table.
DBIERR_NOTSUFFTABLERIGHTS	Insufficient table rights to update table.
DBIERR_TABLEREADONLY	The specified cursor is read-only.
DBIERR_RECLOCKFAILED	The record lock failed.
DBIERR_MULTIPLUNIQRECS	Attempt to modify a record that has a duplicate (SQL).

Example

```
procedure MakeLocalShareTrue;
var
  hCursor    : HDBICur;
  ConfigDesc : CFGDesc;
begin
  { Open the configuration tree that contains LOCAL SHARE }
  Check( DbiOpenCfgInfoList( nil, dbiREADWRITE, cfgPERSISTENT,
                             '\SYSTEM\INIT', hCursor ));

  try
    { For each record in our new cursor }
    while DbiGetNextRecord( hCursor, dbiNOLOCK, @ConfigDesc,
                            nil ) = 0 do
      { If we've landed upon the LOCAL SHARE entry }
      with ConfigDesc do
      if StrComp( szNodeName, 'LOCAL SHARE' ) = 0 then
        begin
        { Change the value to TRUE }
          StrPLCopy( szValue, 'TRUE', sizeof(szValue));
          AnsiToOem( szValue, szValue ); { Needs WinProcs }
          Check( DbiModifyRecord( hCursor, @ConfigDesc, True ));
          break;
        end;
  finally
    DbiCloseCursor( hCursor );
  end;
end; { MakeLocalShareTrue() }
```

Pure Delphi Equivalent

TTable.Post

Xbase Equivalent

REPLACE

See Also

DbiDeleteRecord, DbiInitRecord, DbiPutField, DbiGetNextRecord, DbiGetRecord, DbiGetField, DbiAppendRecord, DbiInsertRecord, DbiGetBlob, DbiPutBlob, DbiOpenBlob, DbiFreeBlob

DBINATIVETOANSI

Declaration

```
function DbiNativeToAnsi (     { Convert from native to Ansi }
     LdObj      : Pointer;    { Language driver }
     pAnsiStr   : PChar;      { Destination buffer (opt) }
     pNativeStr : PChar;      { Source buffer }
     iLen       : Word;       { Length of buffer (opt) }
var  bDataLoss  : Bool        { Returns True if conversion will loose data }
   ): DBIResult;
```

Parameters

PARAMETER NAME	DESCRIPTION
LdObj	Pointer to the language driver object returned from DbiGetLdObj.
pAnsiStr	Pointer to the client buffer that returns the ANSI data. If pAnsiStr equals pOemStr, conversion occurs in place.
pNativeStr	Pointer to the buffer containing data to be translated.
iLen	If iLen equals 0, assumes null-terminated string; otherwise, iLen The length of the buffer to convert.
bDataLoss	Reference to a client variable. Will be set to True if a character cannot map to an ANSI character.

Description

Translates strings from the language driver's native character set to ANSI. If the native character set is ANSI, no translation takes place.

This function works on drivers having both ANSI and OEM native character sets, but it does not deal with multibyte character sets such as Japanese **Shift+JIS**. If the native character set is ANSI, no translation takes place.

DBIResult Return Values

DBIERR_NONE	Translation completed successfully.

Example

```
function Native2Ansi( oTable : TTable; sSource : String ) : String;
var
  szAnsi,
  szNative  : Array[0..255] of Char;
  bDataLoss : Bool;
begin
  StrPCopy( szNative, sSource );

  if IsDbiOk( DbiNativeToAnsi( GetLangDriverObj( oTable ), szAnsi,
                               szNative, 255, bDataLoss )) then
    Result := StrPas( szAnsi )
  else
    Result := '';
end; { Native2Ansi() }
```

Pure Delphi Equivalent

NativeToAnsi

See Also

DbiAnsiToNative, DbiGetLdObj

DBIOPENBLOB

Declaration

```
function DbiOpenBlob (            { Open a BLOB for access }
      hCursor    : hDBICur;       { Cursor handle }
      pRecBuf    : Pointer;       { Record Buffer }
      iField     : Word;          { Field number (1..n) }
      eOpenMode  : DBIOpenMode    { Open for Read or RW }
    ): DBIResult;
```

Parameters

PARAMETER NAME	DESCRIPTION
hCursor	The cursor handle.
pRecBuf	Pointer to the record buffer.
IField	The ordinal number of the BLOB field within the record.
eOpenMode	The BLOB open mode. If dbiREADWRITE is specified, both the database and the table must be opened in dbiREADWRITE mode.

Description

Prepares the cursors record buffer to access a BLOB field. The BLOB is opened and the BLOB handle is stored in the record buffer, which can then be passed to DbiGetBlob, DbiPutBlob, and other BLOB functions.

DbiOpenBlob opens the BLOB and stores the supplied BLOB handle in pRecBuf so that all or portions of the BLOB field can be retrieved, modified, deleted, or inserted, and the size of the field can be determined. The BLOB field can be opened in either read-only or read-write mode, depending on the value specified in eOpenMode.

DbiOpenBlob must be called prior to calling the BLOB functions DbiGetBlobSize, DbiGetBlob, DbiPutBlob, DbiTruncateBlob, or DbiFreeBlob.

Standard. It is advisable to lock the record before opening the BLOB in read-write mode. This ensures that another client application does not lock the record or update the BLOB, preventing the record from being updated.

SQL. This function is supported by SQL drivers. However, for SQL servers that do not support BLOB handles for random reads and writes, full BLOB support requires uniquely identifiable rows. Most SQL servers limit a single sequential BLOB read to less than the maximum size of a BLOB. In cases with no row uniqueness and without BLOB handles, an entire BLOB may not be available.

DBIResult Return Values

DBIERR_NONE	The BLOB field was successfully opened.
DBIERR_INVALIDHNDL	The specified cursor handle is invalid or NIL.
DBIERR_INVALIDPARAM	The specified record buffer is NIL.
DBIERR_OUTOFRANGE	The specified field number is equal to zero, or is greater than the number of fields in the table.
DBIERR_BLOBOPENED	The specified BLOB field is already open.
DBIERR_NOTABLOB	The specified field number does not correspond to a BLOB field.
DBIERR_OPENBLOBLIMIT	The allowed number of open BLOB handles for the current driver has been exceeded.
DBIERR_TABLEREADONLY	The BLOB cannot be opened in read-write mode; the table is read-only.

Example

```
{ Truncates the specified BLOB field to zero length. Then commits the changes
  and releases any record lock (if Shared mode) }
procedure TruncateBlob( oTable : TTable; pRec : Pointer;
                        iFieldNo : Word );
begin
  if oTable.Active then
  begin
    try
      Check( DbiOpenBlob( oTable.Handle, pRec, iFieldNo,
                          dbiREADWRITE ));
      Check( DbiTruncateBlob( oTable.Handle, pRec, iFieldNo, 0 ));
      Check( DbiModifyRecord( oTable.Handle, pRec, True ));
    finally
      if Assigned( pRec ) then
        Check( DbiFreeBlob( oTable.Handle, pRec, iFieldNo ));
    end;
```

```
    end;
end;
```

Pure Delphi Equivalent

TBlobStream.Create

See Also

DbiGetBlob, DbiPutBlob, DbiTruncateBlob, DbiFreeBlob, DbiGetBlobSize

DBIOpenCfgInfoList

Declaration

```
function DbiOpenCfgInfoList (          { Open a cursor on "Config" }
     hCfg          : hDBICfg;          { Config file handle / NIL }
     eOpenMode     : DBIOpenMode;      { ReadWrite or readonly }
     eConfigMode   : CFGMode;          { Config mode }
     pszCfgPath    : PChar;            { Path }
var  hCur          : hDBICur          { Returned cursor }
   ): DBIResult;
```

Parameters

Parameter Name	Description
hCfg	Optional configuration file handle. If NIL, the default config file is assumed.
eOpenMode	The open mode. Valid types are dbiREADWRITE or dbiREADONLY.
eConfigMode	The configuration mode. Currently, this must be cfgPersistent.
pszCfgPath	Pointer to the configuration file path name used to locate a piece of information within the configuration file. The path name starts at the root, denoted by a backslash (\). As many levels as necessary to locate the target piece of information may be specified. Each node specified in the path name must have at least one subnode, or an error results. The path name must be null-terminated.
hCur	Reference to the client-allocated CFGDesc structure to be filled.

Description

Returns a handle to a list of all the nodes in the BDE configuration file accessible by the specified path. By supplying a known path in pszConfigPath, information can be retrieved from the configuration file that includes the list of available BDE drivers, internal buffer sizes, and aliases.

This function accesses the same configuration file that was used when the BDE was initialized. If no configuration file was used during DbiInit, an empty table is returned.

The full path name is supplied by pszConfigPath, starting at the root, and then subsequently specifying the name of a node, a backslash (\), one of the nodes subnodes, and so on until the desired level is reached. For Example, to retrieve the values used to initialize the BDE, the pszConfigPath passed in would be:

\system\init

hCur will then receive the handle to a table containing a list of records, each representing a node accessible by the specified path name. The cursor is used by subsequent record manipulation calls such as DbiGetNextRecord and DbiGetPriorRecord. DbiGetCursorProps can be used to allocate the proper record size or the client application can allocate the size of the CFGDesc structure.

DbiModifyRecord can also be used with the cursor with the following restrictions:

- *szValue* is the only field that can be updated.
- Only leaf nodes can be modified.

This function can also be used to build a path name to a target piece of information within the configuration file, when the path name is not known. In that case, the first call to DbiOpenCfgInfoList is passed with pszConfigPath set to backslash (\). The table returned lists all the nodes accessible to the root. If these nodes do not contain the target information (in szText[MAXSCFLDLEN]), subsequent calls to DbiOpenCfgInfoList can be made, each one extending the path name to access one level deeper in the configuration file.

Here is the structure of CFGDesc.

```
CFGDesc = record                        { Config Description }
   szNodeName     : DBINAME;            { Node name }
                                        { Node Description }
   szDescription : Array[0..DBIMAXSCFLDLEN-1] of Char;
   iDataType     : Word;               { Value type }
   szValue       : Array[0..DBIMAXSCFLDLEN-1] of Char; { Value }
   bHasSubnodes  : Bool;               { True, if not leaf node }
end;
```

DBIResult Return Values

DBIERR_NONE	The handle to the table listing configuration file information was returned successfully.

Example

```
{ Fills an outline with all BDE information.
  Contributed by Brian Cook }

function RecurseCfgInfo( theOutline: TOutline; Path, Node: PChar;
                         Level: Word ) : Word;
var
  Cursor     : HDBICur;
  SPath      : Array[0..63] of Char;
  ConfigDesc : CFGDesc;
  I          : Word;
begin
  { If this is the first or second level of recursion }
  if Path = nil then
    { Build the root '\' or first level '\PATH' path name }
    StrLFmt( SPath, SizeOf(SPath) - 1, '\%s', [Node] )
```

```
  else
  {Otherwise, we can simply append the new node name '\PATH\SUB' }
  StrLFmt( SPath, SizeOf(SPath) - 1, '%s\%s', [Path,Node] );

  { Open a cursor on the newly created path }
  Check( DbiOpenCfgInfoList( nil, dbiREADONLY, cfgPERSISTENT,
                             SPath, Cursor ));
  { Track the AddChild for the most previous call to
      RecurseCfgInfo }
  I := 0;
  try
    { For each record in our new cursor }
    while DbiGetNextRecord( Cursor, dbiNOLOCK, @ConfigDesc, nil ) = 0 do
      with ConfigDesc do
      begin
        Inc( I );

        { If the record / node has levels below }
        if bHasSubnodes then
        begin

          { First add the node to the outline }
          theOutline.AddChild( Level, StrPas( szNodeName ));

          { And recursively call to handle the lower levels }
          if Level = 0 then
            Inc( I, RecurseCfgInfo( theOutline, nil, szNodeName,
                                    Level+I ))
          else
            Inc( I, RecurseCfgInfo( theOutline, SPath, szNodeName,
                                    Level+I ));
          { Otherwise }
        end
        else
        begin
          { Convert the value to ANSI }
          OemToAnsi( szValue, szValue );

          { And add it to the outline }
          theOutline.AddChild( Level, Format('%s=%s', [szNodeName,
                                                szValue]));
        end;
      end;
  finally
    DbiCloseCursor( Cursor );
  end;
  { Return the index of last item this call added to the outline }
  Result := I;
end;
```

See Also

DbiInit, DbiOpenDatabaseList, DbiOpenDriverList

DBIOPENDATABASE

Declaration

```
function DbiOpenDatabase (            { Open a database }
        pszDbName       : PChar;      { Database name }
        pszDbType       : PChar;      { Database type (NIL:
                                        Universal) }
        eOpenMode       : DBIOpenMode; { Open type }
        eShareMode      : DBIShareMode; { Share type }
        pszPassword     : PChar;      { Password }
        iOptFlds        : Word;       { Number of optional Params }
        pOptFldDesc     : pFLDDesc;   { Optional Field Descriptors }
        pOptParams      : Pointer;    { Optional Params }
var     hDb             : hDBIDb      { Returned database handle }
    ): DBIResult;
```

Parameters

PARAMETER NAME	DESCRIPTION
pszDbName	Optional pointer to the alias name string defined in the configuration file. If NIL, the standard database is opened. If pszDbName specifies an SQL database, pszDbType can be NIL.
pszDbType	Optional pointer to the database type string. If both pszDbName and pszDbType are nil, a standard database is opened. Examples of database types include: • Standard • Oracle • Sybase • Interbase • Informix
eOpenMode	The open mode. This can be either dbiREADWRITE (Read-write) or dbiREADONLY (Read-only).
eShareMode	The share mode. This can be either dbiOPENSHARED (Shared) or dbiOPENEXCL (Exclusive).
pszPassword	Optional pointer to the password string (SQL only).
iOptFlds	The number of optional Parameters.
pOptFldDesc	Pointer to an array of field descriptors for the optional Parameters. See DbiCreateTable for use of optional parameters.
pOptParams	Pointer to the optional Parameters required by the database.
hDb	Pointer to the database handle.

Description

Opens a database in the current session. If successful, a database handle is returned. The database must be opened before a table can be opened in the database.

DbiInit must be called prior to calling DbiOpenDatabase. The database must be successfully opened before any other calls can be made to access or manipulate data. If the database requires login, a password must be supplied.

The database handle is passed into several functions. The values in pszDbName and pszDbType determine which database is opened. The eOpenMode and eShareMode parameters determine the access modes of the cursors within each database. For Example, if eOpenMode is set to dbiREADONLY, its associated cursors are also READONLY.

SQL. SQL configuration file settings might override the eOpenMode setting.

OptFields, pOptFldDesc and pOptParams are the optional Parameters. The optional parameters passed by this function vary depending on the driver. They can be identified by calling the DbiOpenCfgInfoList function.

Standard: Connecting to a standard database:

- If pszDbName and pszDBType are both set to NIL, the unnamed standard database is opened.

- If pszDbName specifies an alias for a standard database in the configuration file, this database is opened.

SQL: Connecting to an SQL database

DBIResult Return Values

DBIERR_NONE	The database was successfully opened.
DBIERR_UNKNOWNDB	The specified database or database type is invalid.
DBIERR_NOCONFIGFILE	The configuration file was not found.
DBIERR_INVALIDDBSPEC	When using an alias from the configuration file, the specification is invalid.
DBIERR_DBLIMIT	The maximum number of databases have been opened.

Example

```
{ Displays the contents of the second field for each record of CUSTOMER.DB
  within a scrolling window. }
procedure ListDatabase;
var
  hDB     : hDBIDB;
  hTbl    : hDBICur;
  iResult : DBIResult;
  szBuf,
  szFld   : PChar;
  cProp   : CURProps;
  bBlank  : Bool; { Changed from WordBool for Delphi 2.0 }
```

```
begin
  DbiInit(nil);
  DbiOpenDataBase( 'DBDEMOS', 'STANDARD', dbiREADWRITE,
                   dbiOPENSHARED, nil, 0, nil, nil, hDB );
  DbiOpenTable( hDB, 'CUSTOMER.DB', nil, nil, nil, 0, dbiREADONLY,
                dbiOPENSHARED, xltFIELD, False, nil, hTbl );
  DbiGetCursorProps( hTbl, cProp );
  szBuf := AllocMem( cProp.iRecBufSize * SizeOf( Byte ));
  szFld := AllocMem( 255 * SizeOf( Byte ));
  DbiSetToBegin( hTbl );
  iResult := 0;
  repeat
    iResult := DbiGetNextRecord( hTbl, dbiNOLOCK, szBuf, nil );
    DbiGetField( hTbl, 2, szBuf, szFld, bBlank );
    WriteLn( StrPas( szFld ));
  until iResult <> DBIERR_NONE;
  FreeMem( szBuf, ( cProp.iRecBufSize * SizeOf( Byte )));
  FreeMem( szFld, ( 255 * SizeOf( Byte )));
  DbiCloseDatabase( hDB );
  WriteLn( 'Finished' );
  DbiExit;
end;
```

Pure Delphi Equivalent

TDatabase.Open

Xbase Equivalent

USE

See Also

DbiOpenTableList, DbiGetDatabaseDesc

DBIOPENDATABASELIST

Declaration

```
function DbiOpenDatabaseList (    { Get list of registered databases }
var    hCur        : hDBICur     { Returned cursor }
   ): DBIResult;
```

Parameters

PARAMETER NAME	DESCRIPTION
hCur	Reference to an in-memory table.

Description

Returns a cursor on a list of accessible databases (and all aliases) found in the configuration file. The cursor is positioned before the first record. Accessible databases are those that are defined within the configuration file.

Be sure to close the cursor after you are done using it. To find out about the cursor, use DbiGetCursorProps.

DBIResult Return Values

DBIERR_NONE	The table was created successfully.
DBIERR_INVALIDHNDL	hCur is NIL.

Example

```
function GetOpenDatabaseList : hDBICur;
begin
  IsDbiOk( DbiOpenDatabaseList( Result ));
end; { GetOpenDatabaseList }
```

See Also

DbiGetDatabaseDesc

DbiOpenDriverList

Declaration

```
function DbiOpenDriverList (      { Get a list of driver names }
var    hCur        : hDBICur      { Returned cursor }
   ): DBIResult;
```

Parameters

Parameter Name	Description
hCur	Reference to the cursor handle.

Description

Creates a list of driver names available to the client application.

The list of drivers is obtained from the BDE configuration file and can be used as input to other functions. If no configuration file was available at initialization time, or if no drivers were configured, an error is returned. The table contains only one CHAR field. Use DbiGetCursorProps() to examine the cursor.

DBIResult Return Values

DBIERR_NONE	The table containing a list of the available drivers was successfully created.
DBIERR_INVALIDHNDL	*hCur* is NIL.
DBIERR_NOCONFIGFILE	No configuration file was available at initialization time.
DBIERR_OBJNOTFOUND	No drivers were configured at initialization time.

Example

```
constructor TDriverList.Create;
var
    hDb: hDBIDb;              { Database handle }
    hTblTypeCur: hDBICur; { In-memory table cursor for table types }
    hFldTypeCur: hDBICur; { In-memory table cursor for field types }
    hIdxTypeCur: hDBICur; { In-memory table cursor for index types }
    rslt: DBIResult;         { Return value from IDAPI functions }
    TblProps: CURProps;      { Table Properties }
    pRecBuf: PChar;          { Record Buffer }
    szDriver: Array[0..DBIMAXNAMELEN+1] of Char; { Driver name }
    bIsBlank: Bool;          { Is the field blank? }
    drType: DRVType;         { Driver type information }

begin
    inherited Create;
    try
        Check( DbiOpenDataBase( 'DEMOS', 'STANDARD', dbiREADWRITE,
                        dbiOPENSHARED, NIL, 0, NIL, NIL, hDB ));
        Check( DbiSetDirectory( hDb, '\DELPHI\DEMOS' ));

        { Get a list of all available drivers }
        Check( DbiOpenDriverList( Cursor ));

        { Get the size of the record buffer }
        Check( DbiGetCursorProps( Cursor, TblProps ));

        { Allocate record buffer }
        pRecBuf := StrAlloc( TblProps.iRecBufSize );
        Check( DbiSetToBegin( Cursor ));

        { Iterate through all available drivers in the config file. }
        while DbiGetNextRecord( Cursor, dbiNOLOCK, pRecBuf, nil )
                            = DBIERR_NONE do
        begin
            { Get the driver name }
            Check( DbiGetField( Cursor, 1, pRecBuf, @szDriver,
                                            bIsBlank ));
            Check( DbiGetDriverDesc( szDriver, drType ));

            { Retrieve all usable table types for the driver }
            Check( DbiOpenTableTypesList( szDriver, hTblTypeCur ));

            { Retrieve all usable field types for the driver }
```

```
        Check( DbiOpenFieldTypesList( szDriver, nil,
                                      hFldTypeCur ));

        { Retrieve all usable Index types for the driver }
        Check( DbiOpenIndexTypesList( szDriver, hIdxTypeCur ));
        Add( TDriverInfo.Create( StrPas( szDriver ), drType,
                        hTblTypeCur, hFldTypeCur, hIdxTypeCur ));
    end; { while }
  finally
    if Assigned( pRecBuf ) then
      StrDispose( pRecBuf );
  end; { try .. finally }
end; { TDriverList.Create }
```

Xbase Equivalent

RDDList() (Clipper only)

See Also

DbiGetDriverDesc

DbiOpenFamilyList

Declaration

```
function DbiOpenFamilyList (         { Return family members }
      hDb           : hDBIDb;        { Database handle }
      pszTableName  : PChar;         { Table name }
      pszDriverType : PChar;         { Driver type }
var   hFmlCur       : hDBICur        { Returned cursor on "Family" }
    ): DBIResult;
```

Parameters

PARAMETER NAME	DESCRIPTION
hDb	The database handle.
pszTableName	Pointer to the table name. If pszTableName is a fully qualified name of a table, the pszTableType parameter need not be specified. If the path is not included, the path name is taken from the current directory of the database associated with hDb.
pszDriverType	Optional pointer to the table type. This parameter is required if pszTableName has no extension. pszDriverType can be one of the following values: szDBASE or szPARADOX.
hFmlCur	Reference to the family list table.

Description

Creates a table listing the family members associated with a specified table. Family members include default members, as specified by the driver, and registered family members.

dBASE. For dBASE tables, the table can include maintained index files (.MDX files), BLOBs (.DBT files), and tables (**.DBF** files).

Paradox. For Paradox tables, the table can include index files (**.PX, .X??, .Y??** files), BLOBs (.MB files), and validity check and referential integrity files (**.VAL** files).

SQL. This function is not supported with SQL tables. With SQL databases, this function returns an empty table.

The user must have full password rights to the table. Any required passwords to get prvFULL rights must have been added to the current session prior to calling this function.

DBIResult Return Values

DBIERR_NONE	The table of family members was successfully created.
DBIERR_INVALIDHNDL	The specified database handle is invalid or NIL, or hFmlCur is NIL.
DBIERR_INVALIDPARAM	The specified table name or the pointer to the table name is NIL.
DBIERR_NOSUCHTABLE	The specified table is invalid.
DBIERR_UNKNOWNDRIVER	The table type or the pointer to the table type is NIL, or the table type is invalid.

Example

```
function TableFamilyCursor( oTable : TTable ) : hDBICur;
var
  szTable  : DBINAME;
begin
  try
    StrPCopy( szTable, oTable.TableName );
    IsDbiOk( DbiOpenFamilyList( oTable.DBHandle, szTable, nil, Result ));
  except
    Result := nil;
  end; { try .. except }
end; { TableFamilyCursor() }
```

See Also

DbiOpenFileList, DbiOpenFieldList, DbiOpenIndexList, DbiOpenRintList, DbiOpenSecurityList

DBIOPENFIELDLIST

Declaration

```
function DbiOpenFieldList(      { Return "Fields" for a table }
      hDb            : hDBIDb;   { Database handle }
      pszTableName   : PChar;    { Table name }
      pszDriverType  : PChar;    { Driver type }
      bPhyTypes      : Bool;     { True, for physical types }
var   hCur           : hDBICur   { Returned cursor on "Fields" }
    ) : DBIResult;
```

Parameters

PARAMETER NAME	DESCRIPTION
hDb	The database handle.
pszTableName	Pointer to the table name.
	Paradox and dBASE. If pszTableName is a fully qualified name of a table, the pszDriverType parameter need not be specified. If the path is not included, the path name is taken from the current directory of the database associated with hDb.
	SQL. This parameter can be a fully qualified name that includes the owner name.
pszDriverType	Optional pointer to the table type. This can be either szDBASE or szPARADOX.
	Paradox and dBASE. This parameter is required if pszTableName has no extension.
	SQL. This parameter is ignored if the database associated with *hDb* is an SQL database.
bPhyTypes	Indicates whether physical or logical field types are returned. If set to True, native physical types are returned. If set to False, BDE logical types are returned.
	Physical types represent the data in its native state, specific to each driver.
	Logical types are the generic, derived BDE translations of the native data types.
hCur	Reference to the field list table.

Description

Retrieves field information from a closed table, as opposed to DbiGetFldDescs which uses an opened table.

DBIResult Return Values

DBIERR_NONE	The cursor to the table was returned successfully.
DBIERR_INVALIDHNDL	The specified database handle is invalid or NIL.
DBIERR_INVALIDPARAM	The specified table name or the pointer to the table name is NIL.
DBIERR_UNKNOWNTBLTYPE	The specified driver type is not known.
DBIERR_NOSUCHTABLE	The specified table is invalid.

Example

```
function TableFieldsCursor( oTable : TTable ) : hDBICur;
var
  szTable  : DBINAME;
  bPhys    : Bool;
begin
  try
    StrPCopy( szTable, oTable.TableName );
    bPhys := True;
    IsDbiOk( DbiOpenFieldList( oTable.DBHandle, szTable, nil, bPhys,
                               Result ));
  except
```

```
    Result := nil;
  end; { try .. except }
end; { TableFieldsCursor() }
```

See Also

DbiOpenFileList, DbiOpenTableList, DbiGetNextRecord, DbiGetPriorRecord, DbiOpenFamilyList, DbiSetDirectory, DbiGetCursorProps, DbiGetFieldDescs

DBIOPENFIELDTYPESLIST

Declaration

```
function DbiOpenFieldTypesList (      { Get a list of field types }
      pszDriverType : PChar;          { Driver type }
      pszTblType    : PChar;          { Table type (Optional) }
var   hCur          : hDBICur         { Returned cursor }
   ): DBIResult;
```

Parameters

PARAMETER NAME	DESCRIPTION
pszDriverType	Pointer to the driver type.
pszTblType	Optional pointer to the table type. If not specified, the default table type is used. Use DbiOpenTableTypesList to retrieve table type information.
hCur	Reference to the cursor handle.

Description

Creates a table containing a list of field types supported by the table type for the driver type.

This function can be used to determine the legal field types, sizes, and other field-level attributes for a particular driver and table type. This allows configurable table creation user interfaces and allows for validation of Field Descriptors (FLDDesc) without creating a table.

DBIResult Return Values

DBIERR_NONE	The table with the list of field types was created successfully.

Example

```
constructor TDriverList.Create;
var
  hDb: hDBIDb;              { Database handle }
  hTblTypeCur: hDBICur;    { In-memory table cursor for table types }
  hFldTypeCur: hDBICur;    { In-memory table cursor for field types }
```

```
    hIdxTypeCur: hDBICur;    { In-memory table cursor for index types }
    rslt: DBIResult;         { Return value from IDAPI functions }
    TblProps: CURProps;      { Table Properties }
    pRecBuf: PChar;          { Record Buffer }
    szDriver: Array[0..DBIMAXNAMELEN+1] of Char; { Driver name }
    bIsBlank: Bool;          { Is the field blank? }
    drType: DRVType;         { Driver type information }
begin
  inherited Create;
  try
    Check( DbiOpenDataBase( 'DEMOS', 'STANDARD', dbiREADWRITE,
           dbiOPENSHARED, nil, 0, nil, nil, hDB ));
    Check( DbiSetDirectory( hDb, '\DELPHI\DEMOS' ));

    { Get a list of all available drivers }
    Check( DbiOpenDriverList( Cursor ));

    { Get the size of the record buffer }
    Check( DbiGetCursorProps( Cursor, TblProps ));

    { Allocate record buffer }
    pRecBuf := StrAlloc( TblProps.iRecBufSize );
    Check( DbiSetToBegin( Cursor ));

    { Iterate through all available drivers in the config file. }
    while DbiGetNextRecord( Cursor, dbiNOLOCK, pRecBuf, nil )
             = DBIERR_NONE do
    begin
      { Get the driver name }
      Check( DbiGetField( Cursor, 1, pRecBuf, @szDriver, bIsBlank ));
      Check( DbiGetDriverDesc( szDriver, drType ));

      { Retrieve all usable table types for the driver }
      Check( DbiOpenTableTypesList( szDriver, hTblTypeCur ));

      { Retrieve all usable field types for the driver }
      Check( DbiOpenFieldTypesList( szDriver, nil, hFldTypeCur ));

      { Retrieve all usable Index types for the driver }
      Check( DbiOpenIndexTypesList( szDriver, hIdxTypeCur ));
      Add( TDriverInfo.Create( StrPas( szDriver ), drType,
                     hTblTypeCur, hFldTypeCur, hIdxTypeCur ));
    end; { while }
  finally
    if Assigned( pRecBuf ) then
      StrDispose( pRecBuf );
  end; { try .. finally }
end; { TDriverList.Create }
```

Pure Delphi Equivalent

TField.FieldDefs

See Also

DbiGetFieldTypeDesc

DbiOpenFieldXlt

Declaration

```
function DbiOpenFieldXlt (          { Open translation object }
     pszSrcTblType  : PChar;        { nil for Logical }
     pszSrcLangDrv  : PChar;        { nil if no tranliteration }
     pfldSrc        : pFLDDesc;     { Source field descriptor }
     pszDestTblType : PChar;        { nil for Logical }
     pszDstLangDrv  : PChar;        { nil if no tranliteration }
     pfldDest       : pFLDDesc;     { Source field descriptor }
var  bDataLoss      : Bool;         { Set to True for data loss }
var  hXlt           : hDBIXlt       { Returned translate handle }
   ): DBIResult;
```

Parameters

Parameter Name	Description
pszSrcDriverType	Pointer to the source driver type. Set to NIL for logical.
pszSrcLangDrv	Pointer to the language driver name of the source. Set to NIL if no character set transliteration is desired. Ignored if both source and destination are not character types.
pfldSrc	Pointer to the source field descriptor.
pszDesDriverType	Pointer to the destination driver type. Set to NIL for logical.
pszDstLangDrv	Pointer to the language driver name of the destination. Set to NIL if no character set transliteration is desired. Ignored if both source and destination are not character types.
pfldDest	Pointer to the destination field descriptor.
bDataLoss	Reference to a client variable used to indicate both the possibility of data loss and actual data loss for each field translated when DbiTranslateField is called. If NIL, no data loss detection is done.
hXlt	Reference to the translation object handle.

Description

Builds a field translation object that can be used to translate a logical or physical field type into any other compatible logical or physical field type.

Used in conjunction with DbiTranslateField, this function allows clients to convert any logical or physical field data to any compatible logical or physical field data. The client supplies a pair of logical or physical field descriptors. These descriptors can be obtained from a call to DbiGetFieldDescs or DbiOpenFieldList.

If bDataLoss is supplied, this client indicator variable is set to True when the translation object is built if there is the potential for data loss when converting between the source and destination field types. For Example, if the user requests a translation object to convert a dBASE character field to a BDE logical TDateTime field, the data loss indicator is set to True, because the character field may not contain a legal TDateTime string according to the current sessions Date and Time conventions. Additionally, each time DbiTranslateField is called, this client flag is set to True if that particular field conversion caused data loss. If supplied, this client variable must remain addressable until the translation object is closed with DbiCloseFieldXlt. For BLOB fields, this function provides a translation object that does nothing.

DBIResult Return Values

DBIERR_NONE	The translation object was successfully built.
DBIERR_NOTSUPPORTED	The requested field conversion is not considered legal.

Example

```
function OpenFieldXlt( hSource, hDest : hDBICur; hXlt : hDBIXlt )
                     : DBIResult;
var
  pSourceFldDesc,
  pDestFldDesc : pFLDDesc;
  sCurProps,
  dCurProps    : CURProps;
  bDataLoss    : Bool;
begin
  Check( DbiGetCursorProps( hSource, sCurProps ));
  Check( DbiGetCursorProps ( hDest, dCurProps ));
  GetMem( pSourceFldDesc,  ( SizeOf( FLDDesc )) *
                           ( sCurProps.iFields ));
  GetMem( pDestFldDesc,    ( SizeOf( FLDDesc )) *
                           ( dCurProps.iFields ));

  Check( DbiGetFieldDescs ( hSource, pSourceFldDesc ));
  Check( DbiGetFieldDescs ( hDest, pDestFldDesc ));
  Result := DbiOpenFieldXlt( szDBASE, '', pSourceFldDesc, szDBASE,
                          '', pDestFldDesc, bDataLoss, hXlt );
  FreeMem( pSourceFldDesc );
  FreeMem( pDestFldDesc );
end; { OpenField() }
```

See Also

DbiTranslateField, DbiCloseFieldXlt

DbiOpenFileList

Declaration

```
function DbiOpenFileList (          { Open a cursor on "Files" }
    hDb             : hDBIDb;       { Universal database handle }
    pszWild         : PChar;        { Wildcard name }
var hCur            : hDBICur       { Returned cursor }
  ): DBIResult;
```

PARAMETERS

PARAMETER NAME	DESCRIPTION
hDb	The database handle.
pszWild	Pointer to the search string for retrieving a selective list of tables. Two wild-card characters can be used: the asterisk (*) and the question mark (?). The asterisk expands to any number of characters; the question mark expands to a single character.
hCur	Reference to the file list table.

Description

Opens a cursor on a list of files contained within the database.

Standard. DbiOpenFileList provides an efficient way to retrieve all the names of files in a database directory. This function returns a list of all files that match the wildcard criteria, if any.

SQL. This function returns information similar to that returned by DbiOpenTableList. Some fields, such as szExt, bDir, and iSize, are not applicable for SQL databases.

DBIResult Return Values

DBIERR_NONE	The cursor on the table was opened successfully.
DBIERR_INVALIDHNDL	The specified database handle is invalid or NIL, or hCur is NIL.

Example

```
function BDEFileList( oTable : TTable; sMatch : String ) : hDBICur;
var
  szMatch : DBIName;
begin
  try
    StrPCopy( szMatch, sMatch );
    IsDbiOk( DbiOpenFileList( oTable.DBHandle, szMatch, Result ));
```

```
    except
      Result := nil;
    end;
end; { BDEFileList() }
```

Pure Delphi Equivalent

TDatabase.DataSets

See Also

DbiOpenDatabase, DbiOpenTableList

DBIOPENFUNCTIONARGLIST (DELPHI 2.0 ONLY)

Declaration

```
function DbiOpenFunctionArgList(    { Return "Arguments" for a function }
      hDb        : hDBIDb          { Database handle }
      pszFuncName:                 { function name }
      uOverload  :                 { Overload number }
      phCur      :                 { Returned cursor on "Arguments" }
    ): DBIResult stdcall;
```

Parameters

Parameter Name	Description
hDb	Specifies the universal database handle.
pszFuncName	Name of data source function.
uOverload	Overload number, used with functions that take different sets of arguments.
hCur	Reference to the returned cursor on the schema table "Arguments"

Description

Opens a cursor to a schema table for the data source function defined by pszFuncName for the driver associated with the database handle (hDb). The Record Description is of type DBIFUNCDesc.

```
type
  DBIFUNCOpts = (
    fnDummy,
    fnListINCL_USER_DEF  { Include user-defined functions }
  );

  pDBIFUNCDesc = ^DBIFUNCDesc;
  DBIFUNCDesc  = packed record
    szName   : DBINAME;                              { Function name }
    szDesc   : packed Array[0..254] of Char; { Short Description }
    uOverload: Word;                      { Number of function overloads }
    eStdFn   : DBISTDFuncs; { Corresponds to DBI standard function }
```

```
  end;

pDBIFUNCArgDesc = ^DBIFUNCArgDesc;
DBIFUNCArgDesc  = packed record
  uArgNum    : Word;  { Arg position #; 0 for function return }
  uFldType   : Word;  { Field type }
  uSubType   : Word;  { Field subtype (if applicable) }
  ufuncFlags : Word;  { Function flags }
end;
```

When calling DbiOpenFunctionList, you get the number of overloads it can have. By passing the corresponding overload number (uOverload) to DbiOpenFunctionArgList, you get the list of arguments that function takes with that particular overload number.

A cursor with the function argument data is returned. This cursor must be closed using DbiCloseCursor. If pszFunctionName is not a valid function associated for the driver associated with hDb, the cursor points to an empty table.

If the hDb is associated with a local table, a "not applicable" error is returned.

DBIResult Return Values

DBIERR_NONE	The cursor on the table was opened successfully.
DBIERR_INVALIDHNDL	The specified database handle is invalid or NULL, or hCur is NULL.

Example

Available on the CD-ROM at the back of the book.

See Also

DbiOpenFunctionList

DBIOPENFUNCTIONLIST (DELPHI 2.0 ONLY)

Declaration

```
function DbiOpenFunctionList(  { Open list of functions }
     hDb       : hDBIDb;        { Universal database handle }
     eoptBits  : DBIFUNCOpts;   { Function options }
var  hCur      : hDBICur        { Returned function cursor handle }
   ): DBIResult stdcall;
```

Parameters

PARAMETER NAME	DESCRIPTION
hDb	Specifies the universal database handle.
eoptBits	Set to True to include user-defined functions. (InterBase only)
hCur	Reference to the returned cursor on functions

Description

Opens a cursor to a schema table containing a list of all the functions for the driver associated with hDb. The returned record Description is type DBIFUNCDesc.

This function is for use with SQL data sources only.

When used for building SQL queries, this cursor must be closed by calling to DbiCloseCursor.

DBIResult Return Values

DBIERR_NOTSUPPORTED	*DbiOpenFunctionList* returns an error if *hDb* is associated with a local table.

Example

Available on the CD-ROM at the back of the book.

See Also

DbiOpenFunctionArgList

DBIOPENINDEX

Declaration

```
function DbiOpenIndex (          { Open an index }
     hCursor        : hDBICur;   { Cursor handle }
     pszIndexName   : PChar;     { Index Name }
     iIndexId       : Word       { Index number (if applicable) }
): DBIResult;
```

Parameters

PARAMETER NAME	DESCRIPTION
hCursor	The cursor handle.
pszIndexName	Pointer to the index name.
iIndexId	The index identifier, which is the number of the index to be used. The range for the index identifier is 1 to 511. Used for Paradox tables only and is ignored if pszIndexName is specified.

Description

Opens the specified index or indexes for the table associated with the cursor. This does not alter the current record order of the result set or the currency of the cursor. To change the current index order, use DbiSwitchToIndex.

dBASE. This function is used to open nonproduction dBASE indexes. The open index is maintained, but only in the context of this cursor. That is, only updates applied during the use of this cursor maintain the index. If the index is a **.MDX** index, all tags in that index are opened and maintained.

Paradox. This function can be used only to verify that the specified index exists; it does not open the index. If the index does not exist, an error is returned. With Paradox tables, indexes are automatically opened when the table is opened.

DBIResult Return Values

DBIERR_NONE	The index was successfully opened on a dBASE table or the index exists on a Paradox table.
DBIERR_INVALIDHNDL	The specified handle is invalid or NIL.
DBIERR_ALREADYOPENED	The index is already opened, either implicitly or explicitly.
DBIERR_NOSUCHINDEX	No such index exists for the table.

Example

```
function OrdListAdd( oTable : TTable; sOrdBagName,
                     sOrderName : String ) : Boolean;
var
  szIndex : Array[0..78]of Char;
begin
  Result := False;
  StrPCopy( szIndex, sOrdBagName );    { Convert to 0-delim string }
  Result := IsDbiOk( DbiOpenIndex( GetTableCursor( oTable ), szIndex, 0 ));
  if Result then
    if Length( sOrderName ) > 0 then
      oTable.IndexName := sOrderName;
end; { OrdListAdd() }
```

Xbase Equivalent

```
SET INDEX TO, dbSetIndex()
```

See Also

DbiAddIndex, DbiCloseIndex, DbiSwitchToIndex

DBIOPENINDEXLIST

Declaration

```
function DbiOpenIndexList (        { Return "Indexes" for a table }
     hDb           : hDBIDb;       { Database handle }
     pszTableName  : PChar;        { Table name }
     pszDriverType : PChar;        { Driver type }
var  hCur          : hDBICur       { Returned cursor on "Indexes" }
  ): DBIResult;
```

Parameters

Parameter Name	Description
hDb	The database handle.
pszTableName	Pointer to the table name for which indexes are to be listed.
	Paradox and dBASE: If pszTableName is a fully qualified name of a table, the pszDriverType parameter need not be specified. If the path is not included, the path name is taken from the current directory of the database associated with hDb.
	SQL: This parameter can be a fully qualified name that includes the owner name.
pszDriverType	Optional pointer to the driver type. This parameter can be one of the following values: szDBASE or szPARADOX.
	Paradox and dBASE: This parameter is required if pszTableName has no extension.
	SQL: This parameter is ignored if the database associated with hDb is an SQL database.
hCur	Reference to the cursor handle.

Description

Opens a cursor on a table listing the indexes on a specified table, along with their Descriptions. If there are no indexes, a cursor to an empty table is returned.

This function retrieves index information from a closed table, as opposed to DbiGetIndexDescs and DbiGetIndexDesc that use an open table.

DBIResult Return Values

DBIERR_NONE	The table listing indexes for the table has been created.
DBIERR_INVALIDHNDL	The specified database handle is invalid or NIL, or hCur is NIL.
DBIERR_INVALIDPARAM	The specified table name or the pointer to the table name is NIL.
DBIERR_NOSUCHTABLE	The specified table name is invalid.
DBIERR_UNKNOWNTBLTYPE	The specified driver type is invalid.

Example

```
function TableIndexList( oTable : TTable ) : hDBICur;
var
  szTableName : DBIName;
begin
  try
    StrPCopy( szTableName, oTable.TableName );
    IsDbiOk( DbiOpenIndexList( oTable.DBHandle, szTableName, nil,
                               Result ));
  except
    Result := nil;
  end; { try .. except }
end; { TableIndexList() }
```

See Also

DbiGetNextRecord, DbiGetCursorProps, DbiGetIndexDesc, DbiGetIndexDescs

DBIOPENINDEXTYPESLIST

Declaration

```
function DbiOpenIndexTypesList (    { Get list of index types }
     pszDriverType : PChar;         { Driver type }
var    hCur          : hDBICur     { Returned cursor }
   ): DBIResult;
```

Parameters

PARAMETER NAME	DESCRIPTION
pszDriverType	Pointer to the driver type.
hCur	Reference to the cursor handle.

Description

Creates a table containing a list of all supported index types for the driver type. Each of the index-type Description records can be retrieved using DbiGetNextRecord.

DbiGetCursorProps can be used to allocate the proper record size.

DBIResult Return Values

DBIERR_NONE	The list of all supported index types was returned successfully.
DBIERR_UNKNOWNTABLETYPE	The specified driver type is unknown.
DBIERR_INVALIDHNDL	The specified handle is invalid.

Example

```
constructor TDriverList.Create;
var
  hDb: hDBIDb;             { Database handle }
  hTblTypeCur: hDBICur;    { In-memory table cursor for table types }
  hFldTypeCur: hDBICur;    { In-memory table cursor for field types }
  hIdxTypeCur: hDBICur;    { In-memory table cursor for index types }
  rslt: DBIResult;         { Return value from IDAPI functions }
  TblProps: CURProps;      { Table Properties }
  pRecBuf: PChar;          { Record Buffer }
  szDriver: Array[0..DBIMAXNAMELEN+1] of Char; { Driver name }
  bIsBlank: Bool;          { Is the field blank? }
  drType: DRVType;         { Driver type information }
begin
```

```
    inherited Create;
    try
      Check( DbiOpenDataBase( 'DEMOS', 'STANDARD', dbiREADWRITE,
                              dbiOPENSHARED, nil, 0, nil, nil, hDB ));
      Check( DbiSetDirectory( hDb, '\DELPHI\DEMOS' ));

      { Get a list of all available drivers }
      Check( DbiOpenDriverList( Cursor ));

      { Get the size of the record buffer }
      Check( DbiGetCursorProps( Cursor, TblProps ));

      { Allocate record buffer }
      pRecBuf := StrAlloc( TblProps.iRecBufSize );
      Check( DbiSetToBegin( Cursor ));

      { Iterate through all available drivers in the configuration
        file. }
      while DbiGetNextRecord( Cursor, dbiNOLOCK, pRecBuf, nil )
                                          = DBIERR_NONE do
      begin
        { Get the driver name }
        Check( DbiGetField( Cursor, 1, pRecBuf, @szDriver,
                            bIsBlank ));
        Check( DbiGetDriverDesc( szDriver, drType ));

        { Retrieve all usable table types for the driver }
        Check( DbiOpenTableTypesList( szDriver, hTblTypeCur ));

        { Retrieve all usable field types for the driver }
        Check( DbiOpenFieldTypesList( szDriver, nil, hFldTypeCur ));

        { Retrieve all usable Index types for the driver }
        Check( DbiOpenIndexTypesList( szDriver, hIdxTypeCur ));
        Add( TDriverInfo.Create( StrPas( szDriver ), drType,
             hTblTypeCur, hFldTypeCur, hIdxTypeCur ));
      end; { while }
    finally
      if Assigned( pRecBuf ) then
        StrDispose( pRecBuf );
    end; { try .. finally }
  end; { TDriverList.Create }
```

See Also

DbiGetIndexDesc

DBIOPENLDLIST

Declaration

```
function DbiOpenLdList (                { Get a list of Lang Drivers }
var   hCur           : hDBICur          { Returned cursor }
    ): DBIResult;
```

Parameters

PARAMETER NAME	DESCRIPTION
hCur	Reference to the cursor handle.

Description

Creates a table containing a list of available language drivers. Each of the language driver records can be retrieved using DbiGetNextRecord. DbiGetCursorProps can be used to allocate the proper record size.

DBIResult Return Values

DBIERR_NONE	The list of available language drivers was returned successfully.
DBIERR_INVALIDHNDL	hCur is NIL.

Example

```
function LanguageDrivers : hDBICur;
begin
  IsDbiOk( DbiOpenLdList( Result ));
end; { LanguageDrivers }
```

DBIOPENLOCKLIST

Declaration

```
function DbiOpenLockList (        { Get a list of locks }
      hCursor       : hDBICur;    { Cursor handle }
      bAllUsers     : Bool;       { True, for all Users locks }
      bAllLockTypes : Bool;       { True, for all lock types }
var   hLocks        : hDBICur     { Returned cursor on Lock list }
   ): DBIResult;
```

Parameters

PARAMETER NAME	DESCRIPTION
hCursor	The cursor handle.
bAllUsers	Indicates whether to list locks acquired in the current session only, or to list locks acquired by all sessions.
	Paradox: bAllUsers can be either True or False. If bAllUsers is set to True, users for all sessions are listed; if it is set to False, only users for the current session are listed.
	dBASE and **SQL:** bAllUsers must be set to False. For dBASE, only users for the current session are listed. For SQL, only locks for the current database connection are listed.

continued

PARAMETER NAME	DESCRIPTION
bAllLockTypes	Indicates whether to include all locks of all types or to record locks only. If set to False, only record locks are listed. If set to True, locks of all types are listed.
hLocks	Reference to the cursor handle.

Description

Creates a table containing a list of locks acquired on the table associated with hCursor. This function is not applicable to query cursors or in-memory or temporary table cursors.

The cursor is returned in hLocks. Lock types returned can include both table and record locks or only record locks, as specified in bAllLockTypes.

Paradox. For Paradox tables, the locks on the table are returned, including those placed by the current session and those placed by other users, depending on the value of bAllUsers.

dBASE. For dBASE tables, only the locks placed by the current session are returned.

SQL. For SQL tables, only the locks placed by the current database connection are returned.

DBIResult Return Values

DBIERR_NONE	The requested lock list was returned successfully.
DBIERR_INVALIDHNDL	The specified cursor handle is invalid or NIL, or hLocks is NIL.

Example

```
function GetAllLocks( oTable : TTable ) : hDBICur;
begin
  IsDbiOk( DbiOpenLockList( GetTableCursor( oTable ), True, True,
                            Result ));
end; { GetAllLocks() }
```

See Also

DbiOpenTable, DbiAcqTableLock, DbiAcqPersistTableLock

DbiOpenRintList

Declaration

```
function DbiOpenRintList (          { Return Integrity checks }
    hDb            : hDBIDb;        { Database handle }
    pszTableName   : PChar;        { Table name }
    pszDriverType  : PChar;        { Driver type }
var hChkCur        : hDBICur       { Returned cursor on "Ref Int". }
  ): DBIResult;
```

Parameters

PARAMETER NAME	DESCRIPTION
hDb	The database handle.
pszTableName	Pointer to the table name. If pszTableName is a fully qualified name of a table, the pszDriverType parameter need not be specified. If the path is not included, the path name is taken from the current directory of the database associated with hDb.
pszDriverType	Pointer to the driver type; required only if no extension is specified by pszTableName. Currently, the only valid type is szPARADOX.
hChkCur	Reference to the cursor handle.

Description

Creates a table listing the referential integrity links for a specified table, along with their Descriptions. Each of the referential integrity records can be retrieved using DbiGetNextRecord. DbiGetCursorProps can be used to allocate the proper record size.

Note: This function is supported only with Paradox tables.

DBIResult Return Values

DBIERR_NONE	The cursor to the table was successfully returned.
DBIERR_INVALIDPARAM	The specified table name or pointer to the table name is NIL.
DBIERR_INVALIDHNDL	The specified database handle is invalid or NIL, or hChkCur is NIL.
DBIERR_UNKNOWNTBLTYPE	The specified table type is invalid.
DBIERR_NOSUCHTABLE	The specified table does not exist.

Example

```
function TableRefIntList( oTable : TTable ) : hDBICur;
var
  szTableName : DBIName;
begin
  try
    StrPCopy( szTableName, oTable.TableName );
    IsDbiOk( DbiOpenRintList( oTable.DBHandle, szTableName, nil, Result ));
  except
    Result := nil;
  end; { try .. except }
end; { TableRefIntList() }
```

See Also

DbiOpenVchkList, DbiCreateTable, DbiGetRintDesc

DBIOPENSECURITYLIST

Declaration

```
function DbiOpenSecurityList ( { Return security Descriptions }
      hDb          : hDBIDb;   { Database handle }
      pszTableName : PChar;    { Table name }
      pszDriverType : PChar;   { Driver type }
var   hSecCur      : hDBICur   { Returned cursor on security list }
   ): DBIResult;
```

Parameters

PARAMETER NAME	DESCRIPTION
hDb	The database handle.
pszTableName	Pointer to the table name. If pszTableName is a fully qualified name of a table, the pszDriverType parameter need not be specified. If the path is not included, the path name is taken from the current directory of the database associated with hDb.
pszDriverType	Pointer to the driver type. Required only if pszTableName did not specify an extension. Currently, the only valid driver type is szPARADOX.
hSecCur	Reference to the cursor handle.

Description

Creates a table listing record-level security information about a specified table. Each of the security information records can be retrieved via DbiGetNextRecord. DbiGetCursorProps can be used to allocate the proper record size.

Table- and field-level security is applied with the functions DbiDoRestructure and DbiCreateTable.

Note: This function is supported only with Paradox tables.

DBIResult Return Values

DBIERR_NONE	The cursor was returned successfully.
DBIERR_INVALIDHNDL	The specified database handle is invalid or NIL, or hSecCur is NIL.
DBIERR_INVALIDPARAM	The specified table name or the pointer to the table name is NIL.
DBIERR_NOSUCHTABLE	The specified table name does not exist.
DBIERR_UNKNOWNTBLTYPE	The specified table type is invalid.

Example

```
function TableSecurityList( oTable : TTable ) : hDBICur;
var
```

```
     szTableName : DBIName;
begin
  try
    StrPCopy( szTableName, oTable.TableName );
    IsDbiOk( DbiOpenSecurityList( oTable.DBHandle, szTableName, nil,
                                  Result ));

  except
    Result := nil;
  end; { try .. except }
end; { TableSecurityList() }
```

See Also

DbiCreateTable, DbiDoRestructure

DBIOPENTABLE

Declaration

```
function DbiOpenTable (            { Open a table }
      hDb                 : hDBIDb; { Database handle }
      pszTableName    : PChar;  { Table name or file name }
      pszDriverType   : PChar;  { Driver type /nil }
      pszIndexName    : PChar;  { Index to be used for access /nil }
      pszIndexTagName : PChar;  { Index tag name /nil }
      iIndexId        : Word;   { Index number /0 }
      eOpenMode       : DBIOpenMode;  { ReadOnly or ReadWrite }
      eShareMode      : DBIShareMode; { Exclusive or Shared }
      exltMode        : XLTMode;      { Translate mode }
      bUniDirectional : Bool;         { Uni- or Bi-directional }
      pOptParams      : Pointer;      { Optional Parameters /nil }
var   hCursor         : hDBICur       { Returns Cursor handle }
    ): DBIResult;
```

Parameters

PARAMETER NAME	DESCRIPTION
hDb	The database handle associated with the database where the table exists.
pszTableName	Pointer to the table name.
	Paradox and dBASE: If pszTableName is a fully qualified name of a table, the pszDriverType parameter need not be specified. If the path is not included, the path name is taken from the current directory of the database associated with hDb.
	SQL: pszTableName can be a fully qualified name that includes the owner name, in the form <owner>.<tablename>.
	If not specified, <owner> is supplied from the database handle. Extensions are not valid for SQL table names.

continued

PARAMETER NAME	DESCRIPTION
pszDriverType	Optional pointer to the driver type. pszDriverType can be one of the following values. szDBASE, szPARADOX, or szASCII.
	Paradox and dBASE: This parameter is required if pszTableName has no extension or if the client application wants to overwrite the default file extension, including the situation where pszTableName is terminated with a period (.). If pszTableName does not supply the default extension, and pszDriverType is NIL, DbiOpenTable tries to open the table with the default file extension of all file-based drivers listed in the configuration file in the order that the drivers are listed.
	SQL: This parameter is ignored if the database associated with hDb is an SQL database.
pszIndexName	Optional pointer to the name of the index to be used to order the records in the result set.
	SQL: The index name does not have to be qualified with the owner for servers supporting naming conventions with owner qualification.
pszIndexTagName	Optional pointer to the tag name of the index in a **.MDX** file used to order the records in the result set.
	dBASE: This parameter is use for dBASE tables only. This parameter is ignored if the index given by pszIndexName is an **.NDX** index.
iIndexId	Optional index identifier, which is the number of the index to be used to order the records in the result set.
	Paradox and SQL: This parameter is used by Paradox and SQL tables only.
	Paradox: The range for the index identifier is 1 to 511. This parameter is ignored if pszIndexName is specified.
	SQL: This field is used only to specify that the table should be opened with no default index. This is done by setting iIndexId to NODEFAULTINDEX and is useful when opening a table read-only to speed up record access time.
eOpenMode	The open mode. This can be either dbiREADWRITE (read-write) or dbiREADONLY (read-only). If the mode is read-only, updates to the table are not permitted.
eShareMode	The share mode, and determines whether other users or other cursors are able to open the table. This can be either dbiOPENSHARED (Shared) or dbiOPENEXCL (Exclusive).
	dBASE and Paradox: If eShareMode is set to dbiOPENEXCL, then only this session can open the table. If the table is already opened (shared or exclusive) by another session, an attempt to open the table exclusively results in an error.
exltMode	The data translation mode. This parameter can be one of the following values.
	xltNONE. No translation. Data are returned from the table in physical format. Field descriptors returned from DbiGetFieldDescs are physical field descriptors.
	xltFIELD. Field translation. Data are returned from the table in physical format. Field level operations are performed in logical format. Field descriptors returned from DbiGetFieldDescs are logical field descriptors.
bUniDirectional	The scan mode of the cursor for SQL only. This parameter can be one of the following values.
	True. Unidirectional. The cursor can only be advanced forward.
	False. Bidirectional. The cursor can be advanced forward and backward.
pOptParams	Optional pointer to Parameters.
hCursor	Reference to the cursor handle for the opened table.

The following table shows the interaction between the database open mode and eOpenMode.

DATABASE	EOPENMODE	RESULT
Read-only	Read-only	Read-only
Read-only	Read-write	Error
Read-write	Read-only	Read-only
Read-write	Read-write	Read-write

The following table shows the results of different combinations of the database share mode and eShareMode

DATABASE	ESHAREMODE	RESULT
Exclusive	Exclusive	Exclusive
Exclusive	Share	Exclusive
Share	Exclusive	Exclusive
Share	Share	Share

Description

Opens the given table for access and associates a cursor handle with the opened table. If the database is opened read-only, the table cannot be opened read-write.

After the table has been successfully opened, the cursor is opened and positioned on the crack at the beginning of the file. A valid cursor is returned.

Text. The DbiOpenTable call can be used to open a text file for import/export of data. The pszDriverType argument is used differently to indicate whether the fields in the text file are fixed length or delimited. The field separator and delimiter are passed through the pszDriverType argument.

dBASE. If no index is specified, the table is opened in physical order. If pszIndexTagName specifies an index tag, the table is opened with that tag active. The index name and the tag name are specified to open the index.

Paradox. If all index Parameters are NIL, the table is opened in primary key order, if a primary key exists. If a secondary key is specified, the table is opened in that key. Either pszIndexName or iIndexId can be used to specify a composite or noncomposite secondary index. A single-field index that is case-insensitive is classified as a composite index.

SQL. An index can be specified only in pszIndexName. The index name can be qualified or unqualified. SQL provides limited support for exclusive opens, depending on the level of server explicit lock support.

DBIResult Return Values

DBIERR_NONE	The table was successfully opened.
DBIERR_INVALIDFILENAME	The specified file name is not valid.

continued

DBIERR_NOSUCHFILE	The specified file could not be found.
DBIERR_TABLEREADONLY	This table cannot be opened for read-write access.
DBIERR_NOTSUFFTABLERIGHTS	The client application does not have sufficient rights to open this table.
DBIERR_INVALIDINDEXNAME	The specified index name is invalid.
DBIERR_INVALIDHNDL	The specified database handle is invalid or NIL.
DBIERR_INVALIDPARAM	The specified table name or the pointer to the table name is NIL, or hCursor is NIL.
DBIERR_UNKNOWNTBLTYPE	The specified table type is invalid.
DBIERR_NOSUCHTABLE	The specified table name is invalid.
DBIERR_NOSUCHINDEX	The specified index is not available.
DBIERR_LOCKED	The table is locked by another user.
DBIERR_DIRBUSY	Invalid attempt to open a table in private directory (Paradox only).
DBIERR_OPENTBLLIMIT	The maximum number of tables is already opened.

Example

```
{ Displays the contents of the second field for each record of CUSTOMER.DB
  within a scrolling window. }
procedure ListDatabase;
var
  hDB    : hDBIDB;
  hTbl   : hDBICur;
  iResult: DBIResult;
  szBuf,
  szFld  : PChar;
  cProp  : CURProps;
        bBlank : Bool; { Changed from WordBool for Delphi 2.0 }
begin
  DbiInit(nil);
  DbiOpenDataBase( 'DBDEMOS', 'STANDARD', dbiREADWRITE,
                   dbiOPENSHARED, nil, 0, nil, nil, hDB );
  DbiOpenTable( hDB, 'CUSTOMER.DB', nil, nil, nil, 0, dbiREADONLY,
                dbiOPENSHARED, xltFIELD, False, nil, hTbl );
  DbiGetCursorProps( hTbl, cProp );
  szBuf := AllocMem( cProp.iRecBufSize * SizeOf( Byte ));
  szFld := AllocMem( 255 * SizeOf( Byte ));
  DbiSetToBegin( hTbl );
  iResult := 0;
  repeat
    iResult := DbiGetNextRecord( hTbl, dbiNOLOCK, szBuf, nil );
    DbiGetField( hTbl, 2, szBuf, szFld, bBlank );
    WriteLn( StrPas( szFld ));
  until iResult <> DBIERR_NONE;
  FreeMem( szBuf, ( cProp.iRecBufSize * SizeOf( Byte )));
  FreeMem( szFld, ( 255 * SizeOf( Byte )));
  DbiCloseDatabase( hDB );
  WriteLn( 'Finished' );
  DbiExit;
end; { ListDatabase() }
```

Pure Delphi Equivalent

TTable.Open, TTable.Active := True

Xbase Equivalent

USE, dbUseArea()

See Also

DbiCloseCursor

DbiOpenTableList

Declaration

```
function DbiOpenTableList (          { Open a cursor on "Tables" }
      hDb            : hDBIDb;       { Database handle }
      bExtended      : Bool;         { True for extended info }
      bSystem        : Bool;         { True to include system tables }
      pszWild        : PChar;        { Wild card name }
var   hCur           : hDBICur      { Returned cursor }
   ) : DBIResult;
```

Parameters

PARAMETER NAME	DESCRIPTION
hDb	The database handle.
bExtended	If False, returns only the standard table information; If True, returns extended table information as well. The default is False (standard information only).
bSystem	If True, includes system tables; If False, does not. SQL only.
pszWild	Pointer to the search string for retrieving a selective list of tables. Two wild-card characters can be used: the asterisk (*) and the question mark (?). The asterisk expands to any number of characters; the question mark expands to a single character.
hCur	Reference to the cursor handle.

Description

Creates a table with information about all the tables associated with the database.

The client application can request either standard or extended information for the table. The bExtended parameter must be set to True to request extended information.

After calling this function, hCur will contain the returned cursor handle. The table contains information about all the tables in the database associated with the specified database handle. If the associated database is a standard database, only the tables in the current directory of the database are listed in the table. The record Description for the table is TBLDesc/TBLFullDesc.

Standard. The table includes tables in the directory associated with hDb.

SQL. For SQL servers, bSystem must be set to True to include system tables.

DBIResult Return Values

DBIERR_NONE	The cursor to the table was returned successfully.
DBIERR_INVALIDHNDL	The specified database handle is invalid or NIL.

Example

```
function ListAllTables( oTable : TTable; sWild : String ) : hDBICur;
var
  szWild : DBIName;
begin
  StrPCopy( szWild, sWild );
  if not IsDbiOk( DbiOpenTableList( oTable.DBHandle, True, False,
                  szWild, Result )) then
    Result := nil;
end; { TableRefIntList() }
```

See Also

DbiOpenCfgInfoList, DbiOpenDriverList, DbiOpenFieldTypesList, DbiOpenIndexTypesList, DbiOpenLdList, DbiOpenTableTypesList, DbiOpenUserList

DBIOPENTABLETYPESLIST

Declaration

```
function DbiOpenTableTypesList (    { Get a list of table types }
     pszDriverType : PChar;         { Driver type }
var  hCur          : hDBICur       { Returned cursor }
   ): DBIResult;
```

Parameters

PARAMETER NAME	DESCRIPTION
pszDriverType	Pointer to the driver type.
hCur	Reference to the cursor handle.

Description

Creates a table listing table type names for the given driver.

Each of the table type records can be retrieved via DbiGetNextRecord. DbiGetCursorProps can be used to allocate the proper record size.

DBIResult Return Values

DBIERR_NONE	The list of table type names was returned successfully.
DBIERR_INVALIDHNDL	The specified handle is invalid.
DBIERR_DRIVERNOTLOADED	The driver was not initialized.

Example

```
constructor TDriverList.Create;
var
  hDb: hDBIDb;           { Database handle }
  hTblTypeCur: hDBICur; { In-memory table cursor for table types }
  hFldTypeCur: hDBICur; { In-memory table cursor for field types }
  hIdxTypeCur: hDBICur; { In-memory table cursor for index types }
  rslt: DBIResult;       { Return value from IDAPI functions }
  TblProps: CURProps;   { Table Properties }
  pRecBuf: PChar;        { Record Buffer }
  szDriver: Array[0..DBIMAXNAMELEN+1] of Char; { Driver name }
  bIsBlank: Bool;        { Is the field blank? }
  drType: DRVType;       { Driver type information }
begin
  inherited Create;
  try
    Check( DbiOpenDataBase( 'DEMOS', 'STANDARD', dbiREADWRITE,
           dbiOPENSHARED, nil, 0, nil, nil, hDB ));
    Check( DbiSetDirectory( hDb, '\DELPHI\DEMOS' ));

    { Get a list of all available drivers }
    Check( DbiOpenDriverList( Cursor ));

    { Get the size of the record buffer }
    Check( DbiGetCursorProps( Cursor, TblProps ));

    { Allocate record buffer }
    pRecBuf := StrAlloc( TblProps.iRecBufSize );
    Check( DbiSetToBegin( Cursor ));

    { Iterate through all available drivers in the configuration file. }
    while DbiGetNextRecord( Cursor, dbiNOLOCK, pRecBuf, nil )
                = DBIERR_NONE do
    begin
      { Get the driver name }
      Check( DbiGetField( Cursor, 1, pRecBuf, @szDriver, bIsBlank ));
      Check( DbiGetDriverDesc( szDriver, drType ));

      { Retrieve all usable table types for the driver }
      Check( DbiOpenTableTypesList( szDriver, hTblTypeCur ));

      { Retrieve all usable field types for the driver }
      Check( DbiOpenFieldTypesList( szDriver, nil, hFldTypeCur ));

      { Retrieve all usable Index types for the driver }
      Check( DbiOpenIndexTypesList( szDriver, hIdxTypeCur ));
```

```
        Add( TDriverInfo.Create( StrPas( szDriver ), drType,
             hTblTypeCur, hFldTypeCur, hIdxTypeCur ) );
      end; { while }
  finally
    if Assigned( pRecBuf ) then
      StrDispose( pRecBuf );
  end; { try .. finally }
end; { TDriverList.Create }
```

See Also

DbiGetTableTypeDesc

DBIOPENUSERLIST

Declaration

```
function DbiOpenUserList (          { Get a list of users logged in }
var   hUsers          : hDBICur     { Returned cursor on user list }
    ): DBIResult;
```

Parameters

PARAMETER NAME	DESCRIPTION
hUsers	Reference to the cursor handle.

Description

Creates a table containing a list of users sharing the same network file. Each of the user records can be retrieved using DbiGetNextRecord. DbiGetCursorProps can be used to allocate the proper record size.

Note: This function is supported for Paradox only.

DBIResult Return Values

DBIERR_NONE	The user list was returned successfully.
DBIERR_INVALIDHNDL	hUsers is NIL.

Example

```
function GetUserList : hDBICur;
begin
  IsDbiOk( DbiOpenUserList( Result ));
end; { GetUserList() }
```

DbiOpenVchkList

Declaration

```
function DbiOpenVchkList (          { Return "Checks" for a table }
      hDb            : hDBIDb;      { Database handle }
      pszTableName   : PChar;       { Table name }
      pszDriverType  : PChar;       { Driver Type }
var   hChkCur        : hDBICur      { Returned cursor on "Checks" }
   ): DBIResult;
```

Parameters

Parameter Name	Description
hDb	The database handle.
pszTableName	Pointer to the table name. If pszTableName is a fully qualified name of a table, the pszDriverType parameter need not be specified. If the path is not included, the path name is taken from the current directory of the database associated with hDb.
	For SQL databases, this parameter can be a fully qualified name that includes the owner name.
pszDriverType	Pointer to the driver type. For Paradox, required only if no extension is specified by pszTableName. The only valid type is szPARADOX. This parameter is ignored if the database associated with hDb is an SQL database.
hChkCur	Reference to the cursor handle.

Description

Creates a table containing records with information about validity checks for fields within the specified table. hChkCur points to the returned cursor handle on the table. Once the cursor is returned, the client application can retrieve information about validity checks from the table. The cursor is read-only.

dBASE. This function is not supported for dBASE tables.

Paradox. This function returns information about validity checks including required fields, minimum/maximum settings for fields, look-up tables, picture specifications, and default values.

SQL. The only validity check that can be created for SQL tables is bRequired (required fields). However, some drivers support reporting of fields with default values.

DBIResult Return Values

DBIERR_NONE	The cursor to the table was returned successfully.
DBIERR_INVALIDHNDL	The specified database handle is invalid or NIL, or hChkCur is NIL.
DBIERR_INVALIDPARAM	The specified table name or the pointer to the table name is NIL.
DBIERR_NOSUCHTABLE	The specified table name does not exist.
DBIERR_UNKNOWNTBLTYPE	The specified driver type is invalid.

Example

```
function TableVChkList( oTable : TTable ) : hDBICur;
var
  szTableName : DBIName;
begin
  try
    StrPCopy( szTableName, oTable.TableName );
    IsDbiOk( DbiOpenVChkList( oTable.DBHandle, szTableName, nil, Result ));
  except
    Result := nil;
  end; { try .. except }
end; { TableVChkList() }
```

See Also

DbiOpenRintList, DbiCreateTable

DbiPackTable

Declaration

```
function DbiPackTable (            { Pack a table }
     hDb            : hDBIDb;      { Database handle }
     hCursor        : hDBICur;     { Cursor (OR) }
     pszTableName   : PChar;       { Table name }
     pszDriverType  : PChar;       { Driver type /nil }
     bRegenIdxs     : Bool         { Regenerate indexes? }
     ): DBIResult;
```

Parameters

PARAMETER NAME	DESCRIPTION
hDb	The valid database handle.
hCursor	Optional cursor on the table to be packed.
	If NIL, pszTableName and pszDriverType determine the table to be used.
	If specified, the operation is performed on the table associated with the cursor.
pszTableName	Optional pointer to the table name.
	If hCursor is NIL, pszTblName and pszTblType determine the table to be used. (If both pszTableName and hCursor are specified, pszTableName is ignored.)
	If pszTableName is a fully qualified name of a table, the pszDriverType parameter need not be specified.
	If the path is not included, the path name is taken from the current directory of the database associated with hDb.
pszDriverType	Optional pointer to the driver type. The only valid pszDriverType is szDBASE.
	This parameter is required if pszTableName has no extension.

| bRegenIdxs | Indicates whether or not to regenerate out-of-date table indexes. |
| | If True, all out-of-date table indexes are regenerated (applies to maintained indexes only). Otherwise, out-of-date indexes are not regenerated. |

Description

Purges all records that have been marked for deletion from the table. Exclusive access to the table is required in order to perform a Pack. Once a Pack has been performed on a table, the purged records can no longer be recalled (undeleted) or recovered.

Packing a table reduces it to its minimum size, and, if bRegenIdxs is True, rebuilds all associated indexes. If you intend to use the existing indexes after the Pack, you should always select to have them rebuilt for this process.

dBASE. dBASE allows users to mark a record for deletion (as opposed to actually removing it from the table). The only way to remove marked records permanently is with DbiPackTable.

Paradox. This function is not valid for Paradox tables. Use DbiDoRestructure with the bPack option, instead.

SQL. This function is not valid for SQL tables.

DBIResult Return Values

DBIERR_NONE	The table was successfully rebuilt.
DBIERR_INVALIDPARAM	The specified table name or the pointer to the table name is NIL.
DBIERR_INVALIDHNDL	The specified database handle or cursor handle is invalid or NIL.
DBIERR_NOSUCHTABLE	Table name does not exist.
DBIERR_UNKNOWNTBLTYPE	Table type is unknown.
DBIERR_NEEDEXCLACCESS	The table is not open in exclusive mode.

Example

```
procedure dbPack( oTable : TTable );
var
  iResult: DBIResult;
  szErrMsg: DBIMSG;
  pTblDesc: pCRTblDesc;
  bExclusive: Boolean;
  bActive: Boolean;
begin
  { Save current state of table }
  with oTable do
  begin
    bExclusive := Exclusive;
    bActive := Active;
    DisableControls;
    Close;
    Exclusive := True;
```

```
        end;

        { For dBASE tables, use DbiPackTable; For Paradox, use DbiDoRestructure }
        case oTable.TableType of
          ttdBASE:
            begin
              oTable.Open;
              iResult := DbiPackTable( oTable.DBHandle, oTable.Handle,
                                       nil, nil, True );
              if iResult <> DBIERR_NONE then
                begin
                  DbiGetErrorString( iResult, szErrMsg );
                  MessageDlg( szErrMsg, mtError, [mbOk], 0 );
                end;
            end;
          ttParadox:
            begin
              if MaxAvail < SizeOf( CRTblDesc ) then
                MessageDlg( 'Cannot pack table. Insufficient memory!',
                            mtError, [mbOk], 0 )
              else
                begin
                  GetMem( pTblDesc, SizeOf( CRTblDesc ) );
                  FillChar( pTblDesc^, SizeOf( CRTblDesc ), 0 );
                  with pTblDesc^ do
                  begin
                    StrPCopy( szTblName, oTable.TableName );
                    StrPCopy( szTblType, szParadox );
                    bPack := True;
                  end;
                  iResult := DbiDoRestructure( oTable.DBHandle, 1,
                                 pTblDesc, nil, nil, nil, False );
                  if iResult <> DBIERR_NONE then
                  begin
                    DbiGetErrorString( iResult, szErrMsg );
                    MessageDlg( szErrMsg, mtError, [mbOk], 0 );
                  end;
                  FreeMem( pTblDesc, SizeOf( CRTblDesc ) );
                end;
            end;
          else
            MessageDlg( 'Cannot pack this table type!', mtError, [mbOk], 0 );
        end;

        { Restore previously saved table state }
        with oTable do
        begin
          Close;
          Exclusive := bExclusive;
          Active := bActive;
          EnableControls;
        end;
      end; { dbPack() }
```

Xbase Equivalent

PACK

See Also

DbiOpenTable, DbiDeleteRecord, DbiDoRestructure

DBIPUTBLOB

Declaration

```
function DbiPutBlob (          { Write bytes to BLOB }
     hCursor       : hDBICur;  { Cursor handle }
     pRecBuf       : Pointer;  { Record Buffer }
     iField        : Word;     { Field number of BLOB (1..n) }
     iOffSet       : Longint;  { Starting position }
     iLen          : Longint;  { Number of bytes to put }
     pSrc          : Pointer   { Pointer to Source }
): DBIResult;
```

Parameters

PARAMETER NAME	DESCRIPTION
hCursor	The cursor handle.
pRecBuf	Pointer to the record buffer.
iField	The ordinal number of a BLOB field within the record buffer.
iOffSet	The starting position, offset from the beginning of the BLOB, where the data are to be written. This value must not exceed the length of the BLOB. Valid values of iOffset range from 0 to the BLOB fields length. If iOffset is less than the BLOB fields length, part of the existing BLOB field is overwritten. If iOffset is equal to the length of the BLOB field, the data are appended to the existing BLOB field.
	If the BLOB field also has a BLOB header (BLOB tuple area) and iOffset falls within that header area, the information in the tuple is also updated when DbiModifyRecord, DbiAppendRecord, or DbiInsertRecord is called.
iLen	The number of bytes to write to the BLOB field. iLen should be less than 64KB.
pSrc	Pointer to the data to be written to the BLOB field.

Description

Writes data into an open BLOB field. The BLOB field must be opened in read-write mode. The block of data supplied in pSrc is transferred to the BLOB field, based on the values specified in iOffset and iLen. Performs the equivalent of DbiPutField, for a BLOB field.

Note: This does not update the underlying table. The client application must call DbiAppendRecord, DbiModifyRecord, or DbiInsertRecord, using this record buffer, to update the table with the BLOB field.

DBIResult Return Values

DBIERR_NONE	The data was successfully written to the BLOB field.
DBIERR_BLOBNOTOPENED	The specified BLOB field was not opened via a call to DbiOpenBlob.
DBIERR_INVALIDBLOBHANDLE	The record buffer supplied contains an invalid BLOB handle.
DBIERR_NOTABLOB	The specified field number does not correspond to a BLOB field.
DBIERR_INVALIDBLOBOFFSET	The specified iOffSet is greater than the length of the BLOB field.
DBIERR_READONLYFLD	The BLOB field was opened in dbiREADONLY mode and cannot be modified.

Example

```
procedure PutTheBlob( oTable : TTable; pTmpRecBuf: pBYTE;
                      sField, sInput : String );
var
  hCur   : hDBICur;
  iField : Integer;
begin
  hCur := GetTableCursor( oTable );
  iField := oTable.FieldByName( sField ).Index + 1;
  Check( DbiOpenBlob( hCur, pTmpRecBuf, iField, dbiREADWRITE ));
  Check( DbiPutBlob( hCur, pTmpRecBuf, iField, 0,
         StrLen( PChar( sInput )) + 1, PChar( sInput )));
  Check( DbiModifyRecord( hCur, pTmpRecBuf, True ));
  Check( DbiFreeBlob( hCur, pTmpRecBuf, iField ));
end; { PutTheBlob() }
```

Pure Delphi Equivalent

TBlobField.SetData

See Also

DbiAppendRecord, DbiModifyRecord, DbiInsertRecord, DbiGetBlob, DbiOpenBlob, DbiTruncateBlob, DbiFreeBlob, DbiGetBlobSize

DBiPutField

Declaration

```
function DbiPutField (       { Put a value in the record buffer }
    hCursor    : hDBICur;    { Cursor handle }
    iField     : Word;       { Field # (1..n) }
    pRecBuff   : Pointer;    { Record buffer }
    pSrc       : Pointer     { Source field buffer }
): DBIResult;
```

Parameters

PARAMETER NAME	DESCRIPTION
hCursor	The cursor handle.
iField	The ordinal number of the field to be updated.
pRecBuf	Pointer to the record buffer, which is updated upon success.
pSrc	Pointer to the new field value.

Description

Update a record one field at a time. If a NIL pointer is supplied, the field is set to NIL or blank. After using DbiPutField one or more times, the client application must call DbiInsertRecord, DbiAppendRecord, or DbiModifyRecord to update the table with the record buffer. If the function fails, the record buffer is not affected.

If the xltMODE for the cursor is xltFIELD, pSrc is assumed to contain field data in BDE logical format. These data are translated to the drivers physical type by this function. If xltMODE is xltNONE, pSrc is assumed to contain field data in physical format.

This function is not supported with BLOB fields.

DBIResult Return Values

DBIERR_NONE	The field was updated successfully.
DBIERR_INVALIDHNDL	The specified cursor handle is invalid or NIL.
DBIERR_OUTOFRANGE	iField is equal to zero, or is greater than the number of fields in the table.
DBIERR_INVALIDXLATION	A translation error has occurred.

Example

```
{ This function is part of the larger Example used for the DbiBatchMove
  example }
function DBFAddRecord( hCursor : hDBICur; szName, szLocation :
                       PChar; dBorn : TDateTime ): Boolean;
var
  TblProps: CURProps;    { Table Properties }
  pRecBuf: PChar;        { Record Buffer }
begin
  Result := False;
  try
    try
      Check( DbiGetCursorProps( hCursor, TblProps ));

      { Allocate the record buffer }
      pRecBuf := StrAlloc( TblProps.iRecBufSize );
      Check( DbiInitRecord( hCursor, pRecBuf ));
```

```
    Check( DbiPutField( hCursor, 1, pRecBuf, szName ));
    Check( DbiPutField( hCursor, 2,  pRecBuf, szLocation ));
    Check( DbiPutField( hCursor, 3,  pRecBuf, @dBorn ));
    Check( DbiInsertRecord( hCursor, dbiNOLOCK, pRecBuf ));
    Result := True;
  except
  end; { try .. except }
finally
  if Assigned( pRecBuf ) then
    StrDispose( pRecBuf );
  end; { try .. finally }
end;
```

Pure Delphi Equivalent

TField.Assign

Xbase Equivalent

REPLACE, FieldPut()

See Also

DbiVerifyField, DbiAppendRecord, DbiInsertRecord, DbiModifyRecord, DbiSetToKey, DbiGetField, DbiPutBlob

DbiQAlloc

Declaration

```
function DbiQAlloc(              { Execute prepared query }
     hDb       : hDBIDb;         { Database handle }
     eQryLang  : DBIQryLang;     { Query language }
  var hStmt    : hDBIStmt        { Statement handle }
     ): DBIResult stdcall;
```

Parameters

PARAMETER NAME	DESCRIPTION
hDb	The database handle.
eQryLang	The query language to use. Can be qryLangSQL or qryLangQBE.
hStmt	The statement handle to be allocated.

Description

Allocates a statement handle used by other DbiQ*() routines.

DBIResult Return Values

DBIERR_NONE	The prepared query was executed successfully.

Example

```
function QueryHandler( hDb: hDBIDB; sTable, sSQL : String;
          var hOrigCols : hDBICur; var lRecCount : Longint ) : hDBICur;
var
  hStmt    : hDBIStmt;
  hQryCur  : hDBICur;
begin
  Result   := nil;
  hQryCur  := nil;
  hStmt    := nil;

  try
    Check( DbiQAlloc( hDb, qrylangSQL, hStmt ));
    Check( DbiQPrepare( hStmt, PChar( sSQL )));
    Check( DbiQGetBaseDescs( hStmt, @hOrigCols ));
    Check( DbiQExec( hStmt, @hQryCur ));
    Check( DbiQInstantiateAnswer( hStmt, hQryCur, PChar( sTable ),
                          szPARADOX, True, Result ));
    { Make sure to DbiQFree() the return value of the cursor! }
    Check( DbiGetRecordCount( Result, lRecCount ));
  finally
    if hStmt <> nil then
      Check( DbiQFree( hStmt ));
  end;
end; { QueryHandler() }
```

Pure Delphi Equivalent

TTable.Filter (Delphi 2.0 only)

See Also

DbiQPrepare, DbiQExecDirect, DbiQExecProcDirect, DbiQFree, DbiQSetParams

DBIQEXEC

Declaration

```
function DbiQExec (              { Execute prepared query }
    hStmt        : hDBIStmt;     { Statement handle }
    phCur        : phDBICur      { Returned handle on result set }
  ): DBIResult;
```

Parameters

Parameter Name	Description
hStmt	The statement handle.
hCur	Reference to the cursor handle.

Description

Executes the previously prepared query identified by the supplied statement handle and returns a cursor to the result set, if one is generated.

This function is used to execute a prepared query. If the query returns a result set, the cursor handle to the result set is returned into the address given by hCur. If the query does not generate a result set, the returned cursor handle is zero. If no cursor handle address is given and a result set would be returned, the result set is discarded.

SQL. For SQL, the same prepared query can be executed several times, but only after the returned cursor has been closed.

DBIResult Return Values

DBIERR_NONE	The prepared query was executed successfully.

Example

```
function QueryHandler( hDb: hDBIDB; sTable, sSQL : String;
         var hOrigCols : hDBICur; var lRecCount : Longint ) : hDBICur;
var
  hStmt    : hDBIStmt;
  hQryCur  : hDBICur;
begin
  Result  := nil;
  hQryCur := nil;
  hStmt   := nil;

  try
    Check( DbiQAlloc( hDb, qrylangSQL, hStmt ));
    Check( DbiQPrepare( hStmt, PChar( sSQL )));
    Check( DbiQGetBaseDescs( hStmt, @hOrigCols ));
    Check( DbiQExec( hStmt, @hQryCur ));
    Check( DbiQInstantiateAnswer( hStmt, hQryCur, PChar( sTable ),
                              szPARADOX, True, Result ));
    { Make sure to DbiQFree() the return value of the cursor! }
    Check( DbiGetRecordCount( Result, lRecCount ));
  finally
    if hStmt <> nil then
      Check( DbiQFree( hStmt ));
  end;
end; { QueryHandler() }
```

Pure Delphi Equivalent

TQuery.ExecSQL, TTable.Filter (Delphi 2.0 only)

Xbase Equivalent

SET FILTER

See Also

DbiQPrepare, DbiQExecDirect, DbiQExecProcDirect, DbiQFree, DbiQSetParams

DBIQEXECDIRECT

Declaration

```
function DbiQExecDirect (        { Execute query }
     hDb          : hDBIDb;      { Database handle }
     eQryLang     : DBIQryLang;  { Query language }
     pszQuery     : PChar;       { Query }
     phCur        : phDBICur     { Returned cursor on result set }
   ): DBIResult;
```

Parameters

Parameter Name	Description
hDb	The database handle.
eQryLang	The query language, QBE or SQL.
pszQuery	Pointer to the query, formulated in the appropriate language.
hCur	Reference to the cursor handle.

Description

Immediately prepares and executes an SQL or QBE query. If the query returns a result set, the cursor handle to the result set is returned into the address given by hCur. If the query does not generate a result set, the returned cursor handle is zero. If no cursor handle address is given and a result set would be returned, the result set is discarded.

SQL. If the database handle given does not refer to a server database, the BDE SQL dialect is recognized. Otherwise, the appropriate server dialect is expected. Heterogeneous data access and cross-server data access can be achieved by using the BDE SQL dialect and referencing tables qualified with database alias names.

QBE. The BDE QBE Syntax is expected. Heterogeneous data access and cross-server data access can be achieved.

DBIResult Return Values

DBIERR_NONE	The query was successfully prepared and executed.

Example

```
function QueryTable( oTable : TTable; szQuery : PChar ) : hDBICur;
begin
  IsDbiOk( DbiQExecDirect( oTable.DBHandle, qrylangSQL, szQuery,
                           @Result ));
end; { QueryTable() }
```

Pure Delphi Equivalent

TQuery.Prepare, TQuery.ExecSQL, TTable.Filter (Delphi 2.0 only)

See Also

DbiQExec, DbiQExecProcDirect, DbiQFree, DbiQPrepare, DbiQSetParams

DBIQEXECPROCDIRECT

Declaration

```
function DbiQExecProcDirect (          { Direct execution of stored
                                        procedure }
      hDb           : hDBIDb;         { Database handle }
      pszProc       : PChar;          { Stored procedure name }
      uParamDescs   : Word;           { Number of parameter
                                        descriptors }
      paParamDescs  : pSPParamDesc;   { Array of param descriptors }
      pRecBuff      : Pointer;        { Record buffer }
var   hCur          : hDBICur        { Returned handle on result set }
    ): DBIResult;
```

Parameters

PARAMETER NAME	DESCRIPTION
hDb	The database handle.
pszProc	The stored procedure name.
uParamDescs	Number of parameter descriptors.
paParamDescs	Array of parameter descriptors.
pRecBuff	Pointer to a record buffer.
hCur	Reference to the returned cursor handle.

Description

Executes a stored procedure and returns a cursor to the result set, if any.

All Parameters must be set before the statement is executed, including any output parameters. After execution, any output parameter values will be placed in the specified offset of the client-supplied pRecBuf.

If there is no output parameter value (NULL) or if it is truncated, then indNULL or indTRUNC will be stored in the iNulloffset of the client-supplied pRecBuf. The indNULL and indTRUNC values are enums defined by eINDValues.

Sybase. Output parameter values will not available until all rows have been fetched from the result set.

InterBase. All input Parameters must be specified before output parameters.

DBIResult Return Values

DBIERR_NONE	The stored procedure was executed without error.

Example

Available on the CD-ROM at the back of the book.

See Also

DbiQExec, DbiQExecDirect, DbiQFree, DbiQPrepare, DbiQSetParams

DBIQFREE

Declaration

```
function DbiQFree (              { Free statement handle }
var    hStmt        : hDBIStmt   { Statement handle }
   ): DBIResult;
```

Parameters

PARAMETER NAME	DESCRIPTION
hStmt	Reference to the statement handle.

Description

Release the resources acquired during preparation and use of a query. If cursors are associated with an outstanding result set produced by execution of the statement, the cursors remain valid, and the dependent statement resources are not released until the last cursor has been closed or the result set is read to completion, whichever happens first.

DBIResult Return Values

DBIERR_NONE	The query's resources were released successfully.

Example

```
function QueryHandler( hDb: hDBIDB; sTable, sSQL : String;
         var hOrigCols : hDBICur; var lRecCount : Longint ) : hDBICur;
var
  hStmt   : hDBIStmt;
  hQryCur : hDBICur;
begin
  Result  := nil;
  hQryCur := nil;
  hStmt   := nil;

  try
    Check( DbiQAlloc( hDb, qrylangSQL, hStmt ));
    Check( DbiQPrepare( hStmt, PChar( sSQL )));
    Check( DbiQGetBaseDescs( hStmt, @hOrigCols ));
    Check( DbiQExec( hStmt, @hQryCur ));
    Check( DbiQInstantiateAnswer( hStmt, hQryCur, PChar( sTable ),
                                  szPARADOX, True, Result ));
    { Make sure to DbiQFree() the return value of the cursor! }
    Check( DbiGetRecordCount( Result, lRecCount ));
  finally
    if hStmt <> nil then
      Check( DbiQFree( hStmt ));
  end;
end; { QueryHandler() }
```

Pure Delphi Equivalent

TQuery.Free

See Also

DbiQExec, DbiQExecDirect, DbiQPrepare

DBIQGETBASEDESCS (DELPHI 2.0 ONLY)

Declaration

```
function DbiQGetBaseDescs(    { Get base desc names for query }
         hStmt : hDBIStmt;    { Statement handle }
var      phCur : phDBICur;    { Returned cursor }
    ): DBIResult stdcall;
```

Parameters

PARAMETER NAME	DESCRIPTION
hStmt	Statement handle.
phCur	Returned cursor of type StatementBaseDesc.

Description

Returns the original database, table, and field names of the fields that make up the result set of a query.

This function gives the client the original columns upon which the result set is based. In other words, the original columns from the SQL select list along with their table and database names. By associating the base or original field attributes with the result set, Delphi users can obtain a complete picture.

As with other BDE functions that return a cursor, the cursor must be closed by the client. The normal calling sequence to use is DbiQAlloc, DbiQPrepare, DbiQGetBaseDescs, DbiQExec, DbiQFree, DbiCloseCursor(StmtBaseCur).

DBIResult Return Values

DBIERR_NONE	The query's resources were released successfully.
DBIERR_NOTSUPPORTED	A QBE language query could processed.

Example

```
function DbiQGetBaseDescs( hStmt : hDBIStmt; phCur : phDBICur )
    : DBIResult; external 'IDAPI32';

function QueryHandler( hDb: hDBIDB; sTable, sSQL : String;
        var hOrigCols : hDBICur; var lRecCount : Longint ) : hDBICur;
var
  hStmt   : hDBIStmt;
  hQryCur : hDBICur;
begin
  Result   := nil;
  hQryCur := nil;
  hStmt   := nil;

  try
    Check( DbiQAlloc( hDb, qrylangSQL, hStmt ));
    Check( DbiQPrepare( hStmt, PChar( sSQL )));
    Check( DbiQGetBaseDescs( hStmt, @hOrigCols ));
    Check( DbiQExec( hStmt, @hQryCur ));
    Check( DbiQInstantiateAnswer( hStmt, hQryCur, PChar( sTable ),
                                  szPARADOX, True, Result ));
    { Make sure to DbiQFree() the return value of the cursor! }
    Check( DbiGetRecordCount( Result, lRecCount ));
  finally
    if hStmt <> nil then
      Check( DbiQFree( hStmt ));
  end;
end; { QueryHandler() }
```

See Also

DbiQAlloc, DbiQPrepare, DbiQGetBaseDescs, DbiQExec, DbiQFree, DbiCloseCursor

DBiQINSTANTIATEANSWER

Declaration

```
function DbiQInstantiateAnswer ( { Create answer table }
       hStmt          : hDBIStmt;  { Statement Handle }
       hCur           : hDBICur;   { Cursor Handle }
       pszAnswerName  : PChar;     { Answer Table Name/nil }
       pszAnswerType  : PChar;     { Answer Table Type/nil }
       bOverWrite     : Bool;      { Overwrite Flag }
var    hCur           : hDBICur    { Optional Cursor to instantiated
                                     table }
   ): DBIResult;
```

Parameters

Parameter Name	Description
hStmt	The statement handle.
hCur	The cursor handle
pszAnswerName	Optional name of the answer table.
pszAnswerType	Optional type of the answer table.
bOverWrite	Overwrite flag. If True, any existing answer table of the name specified in pszAnswerName will be overwritten.
hCur	Optional reference to variable to receive the instantiated table cursor handle.

Description

Creates a permanent answer table in a Paradox or dBASE format from the specified statement or cursor handle. This handle must first be generated by calling DbiQPrepare.

By default, the newly created answer table will be named **ANSWER.DB** or **ANSWER.DBF**, depending on the table type. The pszAnswerName and pszAnswerType flag values may be used in renaming and changing the type, respectively. If bOverWrite is set to True, then it any existing pszAnswerTable will be overwritten.

DBIResult Return Values

DBIERR_NONE	The temporary table has been designated as a permanent table.

Example

```
function QueryHandler( hDb: hDBIDB; sTable, sSQL : String;
          var hOrigCols : hDBICur; var lRecCount : Longint ) : hDBICur;
var
  hStmt    : hDBIStmt;
  hQryCur  : hDBICur;
begin
```

```
  Result   := nil;
  hQryCur := nil;
  hStmt    := nil;

  try
    Check( DbiQAlloc( hDb, qrylangSQL, hStmt ));
    Check( DbiQPrepare( hStmt, PChar( sSQL )));
    Check( DbiQGetBaseDescs( hStmt, @hOrigCols ));
    Check( DbiQExec( hStmt, @hQryCur ));
    Check( DbiQInstantiateAnswer( hStmt, hQryCur, PChar( sTable ),
                                  szPARADOX, True, Result ));
    { Make sure to DbiQFree() the return value of the cursor! }
    Check( DbiGetRecordCount( Result, lRecCount ));
  finally
    if hStmt <> nil then
      Check( DbiQFree( hStmt ));
  end;
end; { QueryHandler() }
```

See Also

DbiPrepare, DbiQExec, DbiQExecDirect, DbiQFree, DbiQSetParams

DBiQPREPARE

Declaration

```
function DbiQPrepare (                 { Prepare a query }
      hDb          : hDBIDb;           { Database handle }
      eQryLang     : DBIQryLang;       { Query language }
      pszQuery     : PChar;            { Query }
var   hStmt        : hDBIStmt          { Returned statment handle }
    ): DBIResult;
```

Parameters

PARAMETER NAME	DESCRIPTION
hDb	The database handle.
eQryLang	The query language, QBE or SQL.
pszQuery	Pointer to the query, formulated in the appropriate language.
hStmt	Reference to variable to receive the statement handle.

Description

Prepares an SQL or QBE query for execution, and returns a handle to a statement containing the prepared query.

SQL. If the database handle given does not refer to a server database, the BDE SQL dialect is recognized. Otherwise, the appropriate server dialect is expected. Heterogeneous data access and cross-server data access can be achieved by using the BDE SQL dialect and referencing tables qualified with database alias names.

QBE. The BDE QBE Syntax is expected. Heterogeneous data access and cross-server data access can be achieved.

DBIResult Return Values

DBIERR_NONE	The query was successfully prepared for execution.
DBIERR_ALIASNOTOPEN	One of the aliases used in the query was not opened prior to preparing the query. The alias name can be found on the error context stack.

Example

```
function QueryHandler( hDb: hDBIDB; sTable, sSQL : String;
          var hOrigCols : hDBICur; var lRecCount : Longint ) : hDBICur;
var
  hStmt    : hDBIStmt;
  hQryCur : hDBICur;
begin
  Result   := nil;
  hQryCur := nil;
  hStmt    := nil;

  try
    Check( DbiQAlloc( hDb, qrylangSQL, hStmt ));
    Check( DbiQPrepare( hStmt, PChar( sSQL )));
    Check( DbiQGetBaseDescs( hStmt, @hOrigCols ));
    Check( DbiQExec( hStmt, @hQryCur ));
    Check( DbiQInstantiateAnswer( hStmt, hQryCur, PChar( sTable ),
                                  szPARADOX, True, Result ));
    { Make sure to DbiQFree() the return value of the cursor! }
    Check( DbiGetRecordCount( Result, lRecCount ));
  finally
    if hStmt <> nil then
      Check( DbiQFree( hStmt ));
  end;
end; { QueryHandler() }
```

Pure Delphi Equivalent

TQuery.Prepare

See Also

DbiQExec, DbiQExecDirect, DbiQFree, DbiQSetParams

DBiQPrepareProc

Declaration

```
function DbiQPrepareProc (          { Prepare a stored procedure }
      hDb         : hDBIDb;         { Database handle }
      pszProc     : PChar;          { Stored procedure name }
      uParamDescs : Word;           { Number of param descriptors }
      paParamDescs : pSPParamDesc;  { Array of param descriptors }
      pRecBuff    : Pointer;        { Record buffer }
var   hStmt       : hDBIStmt        { Returned statment handle }
  ): DBIResult;
```

Parameters

Parameter Name	Description
hDb	The database handle.
pszProc	The stored procedure name.
uParamDescs	Number of parameter descriptors.
paParamDescs	Array of parameter descriptors.
pRecBuff	Pointer to a record buffer. If NULL, then the Parameters are not bound.
hCur	Reference to the returned cursor handle.

Description

Prepares and optionally binds Parameters for a stored procedure. This function is for use with *DbiQExec* and *DbiQFree*.

DBIResult Return Values

DBIERR_NONE	The stored procedure was successfully prepared for execution.

Example

Available on the CD-ROM at the back of the book.

See Also

DbiPrepare, DbiPrepareExt, DbiQExec, DbiQExecDirect, DbiQFree, DbiQSetParams

DBIQSETPARAMS

Declaration

```
function DbiQSetParams (       { Set query options }
     hStmt          : hDBIStmt; { Statement handle }
     uFldDescs      : Word;     { Number of param field descriptors }
     paFldDescs     : pFLDDesc; { Array of param field descriptors }
     pRecBuff       : Pointer   { Record buffer }
  ): DBIResult;
```

Parameters

Parameter Name	Description
hStmt	The statement handle.
uFldDescs	The number of parameter field descriptors given.
paFldDescs	Pointer to the array of parameter field descriptors.
pRecBuf	Pointer to the client buffer containing data for the specified fields.

Description

Sets the value of parameter markers in a prepared query before the query execution. This function is currently supported only for pass-through SQL queries processed on SQL server tables.

The field descriptor array and record buffer is constructed by the client and passed to the BDE, which uses each specified field, along with the record buffer, to locate the data and set the specified parameter. Each field may be either a BDE type or a driver type for the database that the query is prepared for.

Parameter markers are either ? or :name. The field descriptor for a ? parameter marker must contain no name and must contain a field number that matches the position of the ? marker within the query, beginning with marker number one. The field descriptor for a :name marker must contain the name of the marker and a field number of zero.

Parameter settings are retained from statement execution to statement execution. However, all Parameters must be set before execution can occur.

dBASE. This function is not supported for dBASE tables.

Paradox. This function is not supported for Paradox tables.

DBIResult Return Values

DBIERR_NONE	The value of parameter markers was successfully set.
DBIERR_OBJNOTFOUND	A field descriptor references a parameter marker that does not exist.

Example

```pascal
function QueryParams( hDb : hDBIDb; pRecBuf : PChar; sTable,
                      sSQL : String ) : DBIResult;
var
  hStmt   : hDBIStmt;
  hQuery,
  hNew    : hDBICur;
  Fields : FLDDesc;
begin
  hQuery := nil;
  hNew   := nil;
  try
    { Create a Field Descriptor for the parameter }
    FillChar( Fields, 0, SizeOf( Fields ));
    with Fields do
    begin
      iFldNum  := 1;
      iFldType := fldFLOAT;
      iUnits1  := 1;
      iLen     := StrLen( pRecBuf );
    end; { FldDesc }

    { Allocate a statement handle }
    Check( DbiQAlloc( hDb, qryLangSQL, hStmt ));
    Check( DbiQPrepare( hStmt, PChar( sSQL )));
    Check( DbiQSetParams( hStmt, 1, @Fields, pRecBuf ));

    { Execute the SQL statement }
    Check( DbiQExec( hStmt, @hQuery ));

    { Save the Result set to disk and close the result query
      (hQryCur). Now there is an open cursor on the result set
      on disk. }
    Check( DbiQInstantiateAnswer( hStmt, hQuery, PChar( sTable ),
                                  szPARADOX, True, hNew ));

    if ( hNew <> nil) then
      Check( DbiCloseCursor( hNew ));
  finally
    { De-Allocate the statement handle }
    DbiQFree( hStmt );
  end;
end; { QueryParams() }
```

See Also

DbiQExec, DbiQExecDirect, DbiQFree, DbiQPrepare

DBIQSETPROCPARAMS

Declaration

```
function DbiQSetProcParams (         { Set procedure params }
    hStmt        : hDBIStmt;         { Statement handle }
    uParamDescs  : Word;             { Number of param descriptors }
    paParamDescs : pSPParamDesc;     { Array of param descriptors }
    pRecBuff     : Pointer           { Record buffer }
) : DBIResult;
```

Parameters

PARAMETER NAME	DESCRIPTION
hStmt	The statement handle.
uFldDescs	The number of parameter field descriptors given.
paFldDescs	Pointer to the array of parameter field descriptors.
pRecBuf	Pointer to the client buffer containing data for the specified fields.

Description

Binds Parameters for a stored procedure prepared with DbiQPrepareProc.

All Parameters must be set before the statement is executed, including any output parameters. After execution, any output parameter values will be placed in the specified offset of the client-supplied pRecBuf.

If there is no output parameter value (NULL) or if it is truncated, then indNULL or indTRUNC will be stored in the iNulloffset of the client-supplied pRecBuf. The indNULL and indTRUNC values are enums defined by eINDValues.

Sybase. Output parameter values will not be available until all rows have been fetched from the result set.

InterBase: All input Parameters must be specified before output parameters.

DBIResult Return Values

DBIERR_NONE	The value of parameter markers was successfully set.
DBIERR_OBJNOTFOUND	A field descriptor references a parameter marker that does not exist.

Example

Available on the CD-ROM at the back of the book.

See Also

DbiSetParams, DbiQExecProcDirect

DBIREADBLOCK

Declaration

```
function DbiReadBlock (           { Read a block of records }
      hCursor        : hDBICur;   { Cursor handle }
var   iRecords       : Longint;   { Number of records to read }
      pBuf           : Pointer    { Buffer }
   ): DBIResult;
```

Parameters

PARAMETER NAME	DESCRIPTION
hCursor	The cursor handle to the table.
iRecords	On input, The number of records to read. On output, reference to the client variable that receives the number of actual records that were read.
pBuf	Pointer to the client buffer that receives the record data.

Description

Reads a specified number of records (starting from the current position of the cursor) into a buffer. This function is equivalent to doing a loop with DbiGetNextRecord for the specified number in iRecords, though it can be considered significantly faster than a DbiGetNextRecord loop.

If filters are active, DbiReadBlock reads only the records that meet filter criteria. All other records are skipped. The records are not locked. The number of records read may differ from the number of records requested due to conditions such as end of table.

The variable, iRecords, contains the number of actual records read after the function completes. The cursor position is updated according to the actual number of records read.

DBIResult Return Values

DBIERR_NONE	The block of records was successfully read.
DBIERR_INVALIDHNDL	The specified cursor handle is invalid or NIL, or iRecords is NIL, or pBuf is NIL.
DBIERR_EOF	An attempt was made to read beyond the end of the file. The cursor is positioned in the crack at the end of the file. IRecords contains the number of records, if any, that were read before the end of file was reached.

Example

```
{ Requires WinCRT in the 'uses' section }
procedure BlockCopy( hSource, hDest: hDBICUR; lRecsToCopy: Longint );
var
  rslt: DBIResult;            { Return value from BDE functions }
  CurProp: CURProps;          { Properties of the Cursor }
  pRecBuf: Pointer;           { Pointer to the record buffer }
```

```
  iRecNo: Integer;                 { Loop counter - current record # }
  iRecOffset: Integer;             { Offset into the block of recs }
  DestBuf: Array[0..20] of Char;   { New value to write to table }
  TempBuf: Array[0..20] of Char;   { Field value read from the table }
  bBlank: Bool;                    { True if a field is blank }
begin

  WriteLn('*** Block Read/Write Example ***');
  WriteLn('');

  { Get the size of the record buffer }
  Check( DbiGetCursorProps( hSource, CurProp ));

  { Allocate space for the Record Buffer }
  GetMem( pRecBuf, CurProp.iRecBufSize * SizeOf( Byte ) *
                                 lRecsToCopy );
  if not Assigned( pRecBuf ) then
  begin
    WriteLn(' Error - Out of memory.');
    exit;
  end;

  WriteLn(' Go to the beginning of the source table...');
  Check( DbiSetToBegin( hSource ));

  WriteLn(' Read 10 records from the source table...');
  rslt := DbiReadBlock( hSource, lRecsToCopy, pRecBuf );

  { Getting an EOF error is ok - just means that an attempt was
    made to read more records than are currently in the table. }
  if ((rslt <> DBIERR_EOF) and (rslt <> DBIERR_NONE)) then
  begin
    Check( rslt );
  end;

  for iRecNo := 1 to lRecsToCopy do
  begin
    { Calculate the record offset. }
    iRecOffset := (iRecNo-1) * CurProp.iRecBufSize;

    { Get the value in the second field for each record }
    Check( DbiGetField( hSource, 2, PChar( pRecBuf ) + iRecOffset,
                        @TempBuf, bBlank ));

    { UpperCase field #2 buffer }
    StrPCopy( DestBuf, UpperCase( StrPas( TempBuf )));

    { Update the buffer value }
    Check( DbiPutField( hSource, 2, PChar( pRecBuf ) + iRecOffset,
                        @DestBuf ));

    WriteLn(' Modified record ' + IntToStr( iRecNo ) +
            ' with field #2 as "' + StrPas( DestBuf ) + '"' );
  end;

  { Write lRecsToCopy records to the table }
  WriteLn('');
```

```
WriteLn(' Writing 10 records to the destination table...');
Check( DbiWriteBlock( hDest, lRecsToCopy, pRecBuf ));

{ Release allocated memory }
FreeMem( pRecBuf, CurProp.iRecBufSize * SizeOf( Byte ) *
                                        lRecsToCopy );

WriteLn('');
WriteLn('*** End of Example ***');
end;
```

Pure Delphi Equivalent

BlockRead

See Also

DbiWriteBlock, DbiGetNextRecord

DbiRegenIndex

Declaration

```
function DbiRegenIndex (              { Regenerate an index }
     hDb             : hDBIDb;        { Database handle }
     hCursor         : hDBICur;       { Cursor (OR) }
     pszTableName    : PChar;         { Table name }
     pszDriverType   : PChar;         { Driver type /nil }
     pszIndexName    : PChar;         { Index name }
     pszIndexTagName : PChar;         { Index tagname (xbase MDX) }
     iIndexId        : Word           { Index number }
  ): DBIResult;
```

Parameters

PARAMETER NAME	DESCRIPTION
hDb	The database handle associated with the database where the table exists.
hCursor	Optional table cursor.
	If hCursor is specified, the operation is performed on the table associated with the cursor.
	f hCursor is NIL, pszTblName and pszDriverType determine the table to be used.
pszTableName	Optional pointer to the table name.
	If hCursor is NIL, pszTableName and pszDriverType determine the table to be used. If both pszTableName and hCursor are specified, pszTableName is ignored.
	Paradox and dBASE: If pszTableName is a fully qualified name of a table, the pszDriverType parameter need not be specified. If the path is not included, the path name is taken from the current directory of the database associated with hDb.

continued

PARAMETER NAME	DESCRIPTION
pszDriverType	Optional pointer to the table type.
	Paradox and dBASE: This parameter is required if pszTableName has no extension. pszDriverType can be either szDBASE or szPARADOX.
pszIndexName	Pointer to the name of the index.
pszIndexTagName	Pointer to the tag name of the index in a .MDX file. Used for dBASE tables only. This parameter is ignored if the index given by pszIndexName is not a .MDX index.
iIndexId	The index number.

Description

Regenerates an index to ensure that it is up to date (all records currently in the table are included in the index and are in the index order). It can also be used to pack the index on disk.

The table name must be provided and the index must already exist. When regenerating a maintained index, the table must be opened exclusively. When regenerating a nonmaintained index, the engine must be able to obtain a write lock on the table.

iIndexId, pszIndexName, and pszIndexTagName are used in various combinations to specify the index to regenerate.

Note: A maintained index is automatically updated when the table is updated. A nonmaintained index must use DbiRegenIndex to update the index after the table is modified before it can be used to access data.

Paradox. The effect of regenerating a maintained index is that it becomes more efficient and compact. (Frequent updates can fragment an index.)

SQL. An SQL index cannot be regenerated.

dBASE. DbiRegenIndex is normally used to update a nonmaintained dBASE index. However, there may be situations when a maintained index needs to be regenerated. Since a nonproduction index is maintained only when it is in use, it is not actually maintained at all times. If the index is not up to date, DbiRegenIndex can be used to synchronize the index with the current data.

DBIResult Return Values

DBIERR_NONE	The index specified by pszIdxName was successfully regenerated.
DBIERR_NOSUCHINDEX	The given index (pszIdxName) does not exist.
DBIERR_INVALIDPARAM	A cursor was not provided for the table, and the table name is either empty or not provided.
DBIERR_INVALIDHNDL	The specified handle was invalid or NIL.
DBIERR_NEEDEXCLACCESS	A cursor was provided for the table, but it was not opened in exclusive mode when regenerating a maintained index.
DBIERR_FILEBUSY	Exclusive access could not be obtained on table.
DBIERR_FILELOCKED	Write lock could not be obtained on table.
DBIERR_NOTSUPPORTED	An SQL index cannot be regenerated.

Example

```
function TableReindex( oTable : TTable; sIndex, sTag : String ) :
Boolean;
var
  szIndex,
  szTag    : DBINAME;
begin
  try
    StrPCopy( szIndex, sIndex );
    StrPCopy( szTag, sTag );
    Result := IsDbiOk( DbiRegenIndex( oTable.DBHandle,
            GetTableCursor( oTable ), nil, nil, szIndex,
            szTag, 0 ));
  except
    Result := False;
  end; { try .. except }
end; { TableReindex() }
```

Xbase Equivalent

INDEX, REINDEX

See Also

DbiRegenIndexes

DbiRegenIndexes

Declaration

```
function DbiRegenIndexes (         { Regenerate all indexes }
    hCursor         : hDBICur     { Cursor }
  ): DBIResult;
```

Parameters

Parameter Name	Description
hCursor	The cursor handle for the table to be regenerated.

Description

Regenerates all indexes associated with a cursor. A maintained index is automatically updated when the table is updated. There can be more than one index open on a table. A valid cursor handle must be obtained, the table must be opened exclusively, and the index must already exist.

dBASE. All open indexes are regenerated.

Paradox. All maintained and nonmaintained indexes are regenerated.

SQL. SQL indexes cannot be regenerated.

DBIResult Return Values

DBIERR_NONE	All the indexes for the table associated with the specified cursor have been successfully regenerated.
DBIERR_INVALIDHNDL	The specified cursor handle is invalid or NIL.
DBIERR_NEEDEXCLACCESS	The table associated with hCursor is opened in open shared mode.
DBIERR_NOTSUPPORTED	SQL indexes cannot be regenerated.

Example

```
function dbReindex( oTable : TTable ): DBIResult;
begin
  Result := DbiRegenIndexes( oTable.Handle );
end;
```

Xbase Equivalent

REINDEX

See Also

DbiRegenIndex

DBIREGISTERCALLBACK

Declaration

```
function DbiRegisterCallBack (      { Register a callback function }
     hCursor      : hDBICur;        { Cursor (Optional) }
     ecbType      : CBType;         { Type of callback }
     iClientData  : Longint;        { Pass-through client data }
     iCbBufLen    : Word;           { Callback buffer len }
     CbBuf        : Pointer;        { Pointer to callback buffer }
     pfCb         : pfDBICallBack   { Call back fn being registered }
   ): DBIResult;
```

Parameters

PARAMETER NAME	DESCRIPTION
hCursor	Optional cursor handle to which the callback is being registered. If hCursor is NIL, the callback is registered to the current session. If a cursor is supplied, any previous callbacks for the given cursor are overwritten.
ecbType	The type of callback. ecbType can be cbGENPROGRESS, cbBATCHRESULT, cbRESTRUCTURE, or cbTABLECHANGED.
iClientData	Pass-through data specified by the client. This is used to help the client establish the context of the callback (such as a pointer to a client structure, a window handle, and so on.) These data are passed back to the client as a parameter to the callback function.
iCbBufLen	The callback buffer length.

CbBuf	Pointer to the buffer where the callback data are to be returned. Points to an instantiated callback descriptor, which varies depending upon the type of callback. For Example, the cbGENPROGRESS callback type creates a pointer to the CBPROGRESSDesc structure.
	The data that are written to CbBuf is the percentage completed or a message string.
pfCb	Optional pointer to the desired callback function. If NIL, the previously registered callback function is unregistered.

Description

Registers a callback function for the client application. Callbacks are used when a client application needs clarification about a given engine function before completing an operation or to return information to the client.

DbiRegisterCallBack allows the client to instruct the database engine about what further actions should be taken by the engine upon the occurrence of an event. The engine calls the client-registered function when the pertinent event occurs, and the client responds to the callback by telling the engine what to do with the appropriate return code (cbrABORT, cbrCONTINUE, and so on). Advantages of this mechanism are that clients do not have to check every return code on every function call, and the engine can get a user's response without interrupting the normal client process flow.

Under Delphi 1.0, callback function declarations and associated parameter lists, function return types, and callback data types are defined in the file **DBITYPES.INT**, which is the client interface to the engine. Under Delphi 2.0, this same information is defined in **BDE.INT**.

All callbacks are applicable to the current session only. The callback is valid only while the cursor is open. Closing the cursor automatically unregisters any cursor-specific callbacks.

All callback functions use the following prototype:

```
type
  ppfDBICallBack = ^pfDBICallBack;
  pfDBICallBack  = function (    { Call-back function pointer type }
      ecbType         : CBType;  { Callback type }
      iClientData     : Longint; { Client callback data }
var   CbInfo          : Pointer  { Call back info/Client Input }
    ): CBRType;
```

For each different callback type, the CbInfo parameter serves a different purpose:

- cbGENPROGRESS
- cbRESTRUCTURE
- cbBATCHRESULT
- cbTABLECHANGED

DBIResult Return Values

| DBIERR_NONE | The callback was registered successfully. |
| DBIERR_OBJIMPLICITLYDROPPED | The field name was modified. |

continued

DBIERR_OBJMAYBETRUNCATED	The field width was reduced.
DBIERR_VALFIELDMODIFIED	Inserted field in position pointed to by an existing VCHKDesc.
DBIERR_VALIDDATEDATE	An existing VCHKDesc was modified.
DBIERR_INVALIDFLDXFORM	The field type was modified.
DBIERR_KEYVIOL	An existing IDXDesc was modified.
DBIERR_NOMEMORY	Insufficient memory was allocated for CbBuf.

Example

```
unit BdeCallB;

{ Place one TTable (Table1), one TButton (Reindex1), and one TGauge (Gauge1)
  component onto a form (Form1) }
interface

uses
  Forms, DbiTypes, DbiErrs, DbiProcs, DB, DBTables, Controls, Gauges, Classes,
  StdCtrls;
type
  TForm1 = class(TForm)
    Reindex1: TButton;
    Gauge1: TGauge;
    Table1: TTable;
    procedure Reindex1Click(Sender: TObject);
  public
    InfoBuff : cbProgressDesc;
  end;
  Procedure RemoveMDXByte(dbFile : String);
var
  Form1: TForm1;

function ShowProg( ecbType    : CBType;
                   iClientData : Longint;
                   { var for Delphi 1.0 } CbInfo : Pointer )
                            : cbrType; export;

implementation
uses SysUtils;

{$R *.DFM}

{Callback Function to show progress.}
function ShowProg( ecbType : CBType; iClientData : Longint;
                   var CbInfo : Pointer): CBRType;
begin
  if Form1.InfoBuff.iPercentDone >= 0 then
  begin
    Form1.Gauge1.Visible := True;
    Form1.Gauge1.Progress := Form1.InfoBuff.iPercentDone;
  end;
  Result := cbrUSEDEF;
end;

{This procedure takes a DBF file name as a parameter. It will patch
 the DBF header, so that it no longer requires the MDX file.}
```

```
procedure RemoveMDXByte( dbFile : String );
const
  Value: Byte = 0;
var
  F: File of Byte;
begin
  AssignFile( F, dbFile );
  Reset( F );
  Seek( F, 28 );
  Write( F, Value );
  CloseFile( F );
end;

procedure TForm1.Reindex1Click(Sender: TObject);
begin
  { Rebuild Index }
  Table1.Close;
  Table1.Exclusive := True;
  Table1.IndexName := '';
  if FileExists( 'C:\DATA\CUSTOMER.MDX') then
    DeleteFile( 'C:\DATA\CUSTOMER.MDX');
  try
    Table1.Open;
  except
    RemoveMDXByte( 'C:\DATA\CUSTOMER.DBF' );
    Table1.Open;
  end;

  Gauge1.Progress := 0;
  Form1.Refresh;

  { Register Callback Progress Function with BDE }
  {$IFDEF DELPHI_10}
  Check( DbiRegisterCallBack( Table1.Handle, cbGENPROGRESS,
                           Longint(0), 130, @InfoBuff, ShowProg ));
  {$ELSE}
  Check( DbiRegisterCallBack( GetTableCursor( Table1 ),cbGENPROGRESS,
                           0,130, @InfoBuff,@ShowProg ));
    {$ENDIF}
  Table1.AddIndex( 'CUST', 'STR(CUSTNO,6)+LNAME+FNAME', [ixExpression] );

  { UnRegister CallBack Progress Function with BDE }
  Check( DbiRegisterCallBack( Table1.Handle, cbGENPROGRESS,
                           Longint(0), 130, @InfoBuff, nil ));
  Gauge1.Progress := 0;
  Table1.IndexName := 'CUST';
  Table1.Close;
end;

end.
```

See Also

DbiGetCallBack, DbiBatchMove, DbiDoRestructure, DbiForceRecordReread, DbiForceReread

DbiRelPersistTableLock

Declaration

```
function DbiRelPersistTableLock (     { Releases a persistent lock }
        hDb          : hDBIDb;        { Database handle }
        pszTableName : PChar;         { Table name }
        pszDriverType : PChar         { Driver type / nil }
    ): DBIResult;
```

Parameters

PARAMETER NAME	DESCRIPTION
hDb	The handle of the database to be unlocked.
pszTableName	A PChar referencing a buffer that holds the table name.
	Paradox: If no path is specified, it will be derived from directory where the database associated with hDb is located.
	SQL: This parameter can be a fully qualified name that includes the owner name.
pszDriverType	An optional PChar referencing a buffer that holds the driver type.
	Paradox: If pszTableName does not include the file extension, this parameter is required and must be the constant szPARADOX or the literal 'PARADOX'.
	SQL: This parameter is ignored if the database associated with hDb is an SQL database.

Description

Attempts to release a previously-applied persistent table lock on the specified table for the associated session. This lock would have been applied with DbiAcqPersistTableLock.

If multiple locks have been applied, this function decrements the number of persistent locks on the table. If this is the last persistent lock on the table, the lock is released.

This function applies only to Paradox and SQL tables, since only Paradox and SQL tables can have persistent locks placed on them.

dBASE. This function is not supported with dBASE tables.

DBIResult Return Values

DBIERR_NONE	The persistent lock was acquired successfully.
DBIERR_INVALIDHNDL	The specified database handle is invalid or NIL.
DBIERR_INVALIDPARAM	Either pszTableName or *pszTableName is NIL.
DBIERR_NOTLOCKED	The specified table does not have a persistent lock placed on it.

Example

```
function TableLockOp( ATable : TTable; pOp : OpTableProc ) : Boolean;
var
  iResult : DBIResult;
  bActive : Boolean;
begin
  if not ATable.Active then
  begin
    bActive := False;
    ATable.Active := True;
  end;
  Result := False;

  { Apply the lock }
  iResult := DbiAcqPersistTableLock( ATable.DBHandle, nil,
                                     PChar( szPARADOX ));
  if IsDbiOk( iResult ) then
  begin
    { Do the passed operation }
    pOp( ATable );
    { Then, Release the lock }
    iResult := DbiRelPersistTableLock( ATable.DBHandle, nil,
                                       PChar( szPARADOX ));
    Result := IsDbiOk( iResult );
  end;
  if not ATable.Active then
    ATable.Active := False;
end; { TableLock() }
```

Xbase Equivalent

UNLOCK, dbUnlock()

See Also

DbiAcqPersistTableLock

DbiRelRecordLock

Declaration

```
function DbiRelRecordLock (      { Releases record level locks }
    hCursor        : hDBICur;  { Cursor handle }
    bAll           : Bool      { True for ALL; False for Current }
  ): DBIResult;
```

Parameters

PARAMETER NAME	DESCRIPTION
hCursor	The cursor handle.
bAll	Specifies which record locks to release. If set to True, all record locks acquired in the current session are released. If set to False, hCursor must be positioned on a record in order to release the lock for that record.

Description

Releases the record lock on either the current record of *hCursor* or all the record locks acquired in the current session.

    SQL. Optimistic locks are released by this function. The SQL drivers always perform optimistic record locking; therefore, a record lock request does not explicitly attempt to lock the record on the server.

DBIResult Return Values

DBIERR_NONE	Locks were successfully released.
DBIERR_INVALIDHNDL	The specified cursor handle is invalid or NIL.
DBIERR_NOTLOCKED	The current record is not locked (this error is returned only when bAll is False).
DBIERR_NOCURREC	The cursor is not positioned on a record.

Example

```
function dbUnlock( oTable : TTable ) : Boolean;
begin
  Result := IsDbiOk( DbiRelRecordLock( GetTableCursor( oTable ),
                                       True ));
end; { dbUnlock() }
```

Pure Delphi Equivalent

TTable.Post

Xbase Equivalent

UNLOCK, dbUnlock()

See Also

DbiGetNextRecord, DbiGetPriorRecord, DbiGetRecord, DbiGetRelativeRecord, DbiIsRecordLocked

DBIRELTABLELOCK

Declaration

```
function DbiRelTableLock (          { Unlocks table level locks }
    hCursor       : hDBICur;        { Cursor handle }
    bAll          : Bool;           { True for all table level locks }
    eLockType     : DBILockType     { Specific lock type }
): DBIResult;
```

Parameters

PARAMETER NAME	DESCRIPTION
hCursor	The cursor handle.
bAll	Determines which table locks to release. If set to True, all locks on the table associated with hCursor are released, and eLockType is ignored.
eLockType	The table lock type. eLockType can be either dbiWRITELOCK (Write lock) or dbiREADLOCK (Read lock). eLockType is ignored if bAll is True.
	dBASE and SQL: dbiREADLOCK is upgraded to dbiWRITELOCK. In that case, if eLockType specifies dbiREADLOCK, the write lock is released.

Description

Releases table locks of the specified type associated with the session in which hCursor was created.

There must be an existing table lock of the type specified in eLockType. However, an existing table lock is not required if all locks are being released (bAll is True).

Only locks acquired by calling DbiAcqTableLock can be released. A separate call to DbiRelTableLock is required to release each lock acquired by DbiAcqTableLock, if bAll is not set to True.

dBASE. See the eLockType parameter Description.

SQL. See the eLockType parameter Description.

DBIResult Return Values

DBIERR_NONE	Locks were successfully released.
DBIERR_INVALIDHNDL	The specified cursor handle is invalid or NIL.
DBIERR_NOTLOCKED	The table is not locked with the specified lock type (this error is returned only when bAll is False).

Example

```
function dbFUnlock( oTable : TTable ) : Boolean;
begin
```

```
    Result := IsDbiOk( DbiRelTableLock( GetTableCursor( oTable ),
                                        False, dbiWRITELOCK ));
end; { dbFUnlock() }
```

Xbase Equivalent

UNLOCK

See Also

DbiAcqTableLock, DbiIsTableLocked, DbiOpenLockList

DbiRenameTable

Declaration

```
function DbiRenameTable (          { Rename table & family }
    hDb             : hDBIDb;      { Database handle }
    pszOldName      : PChar;       { Old name }
    pszDriverType   : PChar;       { Driver type /nil }
    pszNewName      : PChar        { New name }
): DBIResult;
```

Parameters

Parameter Name	Description
hDb	The database handle.
pszOldName	Pointer to the name of existing table. For Paradox and dBASE tables only, if pszOldName contains an extension, pszDriverType is not needed. The source driver type determines the destination driver type.
pszDriverType	Optional pointer to the table type. Valid types are szPARADOX or szDBASE.
	Paradox and dBASE: This parameter is required if pszOldName has no extension.
	SQL: This parameter is ignored if the database associated with hDb is an SQL database.
pszNewName	Pointer to the new name for the table.

Description

Renames the table given in pszOldName and all its resources to the new name specified by pszNewName. When the table is renamed, other resources are also renamed, depending on the database driver. The client application must have permission to lock the table exclusively.

Paradox. The following files are renamed:

- The table (**.DB** extension)
- BLOB files (**.MB** extension)

- All indexes
- Validity check and referential integrity files (**.VAL** extension)

If the table is encrypted, the master password must be specified, or the DbiRenameTable call fails. A master table in a referential integrity link, the table cannot be renamed. If it is a detail table and the table is renamed into the same directory, the function automatically maintains the link to its master table. If it is a detail table and the table is renamed into the different directory, referential integrity is dropped. Exclusive access to the master table is required.

dBASE. The following files are renamed:

- The table (**.DBF** extension)
- BLOB files (**.DBT** extension)
- The production index (**.MDX** extension)

SQL. All indexes are renamed with the table. Some SQL servers do not support DbiRenameTable.

DBIResult Return Values

DBIERR_NONE	The table was renamed successfully.
DBIERR_INVALIDHNDL	The specified database handle is invalid or NIL.
DBIERR_NOSUCHTABLE	The source table does not exist.
DBIERR_UNKNOWNTBLTYPE	The driver type is unknown.
DBIERR_NOTSUFFTABLERIGHTS	The client application has insufficient rights to the table (Paradox only).
DBIERR_NOTSUFFFAMILYRIGHTS	The client application has insufficient rights to family members (Paradox only).
DBIERR_LOCKED	The table is already in use.

Example

```
function RenameDataTable( szSource, szDest : PChar ) : Boolean;
var
  DB : TDatabase;
begin
  try
    DB := Session.OpenDatabase( 'NetPdox' );
    Result := IsDbiOk( dbiRenameTable( DB.Handle, szSource, nil,
                                       szDest ));
  finally
    Session.CloseDatabase( DB );
  end;
end; { RenameDataTable() }
```

See Also

DbiAddPassword, DbiCopyTable, DbiDeleteTable

DBIRESETRANGE

Declaration

```
function DbiResetRange (              { Reset range }
    hCursor        : hDBICur    { cursor handle }
  ): DBIResult;
```

Parameters

PARAMETER NAME	DESCRIPTION
hCursor	The cursor handle of the table with the range to be removed.

Description

Removes the specified cursor's limited range previously established by the function DbiSetRange.

This function has no effect on existing filters.

The current position of the cursor is preserved. If the cursor was positioned on a valid record before the call, it is left on the same record. If it was positioned on a crack, it is positioned there after the call.

DBIResult Return Values

DBIERR_NONE	The range was reset successfully.
DBIERR_INVAIDHNDL	hCursor is not valid.
DBIERR_NOASSOCINDEX	The specified table does not have an index open.

Example

```
function ClearRange( oTable : TTable ) : Boolean;
begin
  Result := IsDbiOk( DbiResetRange( GetTableCursor( oTable )));
end; { ClearRange() }
```

Pure Delphi Equivalent

TTable.SetRange

Xbase Equivalent

SET SCOPE

See Also

DbiSetRange

DbiSaveChanges

Declaration

```
function DbiSaveChanges (              { Flush all buffered changes }
    hCursor         : hDBICur     { Cursor handle }
): DBIResult;
```

Parameters

PARAMETER NAME	DESCRIPTION
hCursor	The cursor handle.

Description

Forces all updated records associated with hCursor to disk.

If the table associated with hCursor is a temporary table (created with DbiCreateTempTable), DbiSaveChanges saves all buffered changes to disk and makes the table permanent. This table will not be removed when the cursor is closed.

SQL. This function is not supported with SQL tables.

DBIResult Return Values

DBIERR_NONE	All changes have been saved successfully.
DBIERR_INVALIDHNDL	The specified cursor is invalid or NIL.
DBIERR_NODISKSPACE	The changes could not be saved because there is no disk space available.
DBIERR_NOTSUPPORTED	This function is not supported for SQL tables.

Example

```
function FlushRecBuffers( oTable : TTable ): DBIResult;
begin
  Result := DbiSaveChanges( oTable.Handle );
end;
```

Xbase Equivalent

COMMIT, dbCommit()

See Also

DbiMakePermanent

DBISETCURRSESSION

Declaration

```
function DbiSetCurrSession (         { Set the current session }
    hSes            : hDBISes       { Session/nil }
  ): DBIResult;
```

Parameters

PARAMETER NAME	DESCRIPTION
hSes	Optional session handle. If NIL, the default session becomes the current session.

Description

Sets the current session of the client application to the session associated with hSes.

All subsequent operations that do not require an object handle (such as cursor, database, or statement) are associated with this session. Any functions that take an explicit database, query, or cursor handle as an argument are not affected by DbiSetCurrSession. Any resources required by these functions are allocated in the context of the session set by DbiSetCurrSession.

DBIResult Return Values

DBIERR_NONE	The session has been successfully set to the session associated with hSes.
DBIERR_INVALIDSESHANDLE	The specified session handle is invalid.

Example

```
function ActivateDefaultSession : Boolean;
begin
 Result := IsDbiOk( DbiSetCurrSession( nil ));
end; { ActivateDefaultSession() }
```

Pure Delphi Equivalent

TSession.Handle

See Also

DbiGetCurrSession, DbiStartSession, DbiCloseSession, DbiGetSysInfo, DbiGetSesInfo

DbiSetDateFormat

Declaration

```
function DbiSetDateFormat (      { Set current date format }
var    fmtDate      : FMTDate
   ): DBIResult;
```

Parameters

PARAMETER NAME	DESCRIPTION
fmtDate	Reference to the date format structure to be filled.

Description

Sets the date format for the current session. The date format is used by QBE for input and wildcard character matching. It is also used by batch operations (such as DbiDoRestructure and DbiBatchMove) to handle data-type coercion between character and date types.

DBIResult Return Values

DBIERR_NONE	The date format was successfully set.
DBIERR_INVALIDHNDL	The reference to the date format structure is NIL.
DBIERR_INVALIDPARAM	Data within the date format structure is invalid.

Example

```
function ModifyDateFormat : Boolean;
var
  DateFormat : FMTDate;
begin
  with DateFormat do
  begin
    iDateMode := 2; { Set to Y, M, D }
    bFourDigitYear := True;
    bYearBiased := False;
    bMonthLeadingZero := False;
    bDayLeadingZero := False;
  end; { DateFormat }
  Result := IsDbiOk( DbiSetDateFormat( DateFormat ));
end; { ModifyDateFormat }
```

Pure Delphi Equivalent

FormatDateTime

Xbase Equivalent

SET DATE, SET DATE FORMAT

See Also

DbiGetDateFormat

DBISETDIRECTORY

Declaration

```
function DbiSetDirectory (          { Set the current directory }
    hDb              : hDBIDb;      { Universal database handle }
    pszDir           : PChar        { Directory/nil }
): DBIResult;
```

Parameters

PARAMETER NAME	DESCRIPTION
hDb	Specifies a standard database handle.
pszDir	Optional pointer to the client buffer specifying the new current directory path. If NIL, the current directory becomes the default directory.

Description

Sets the current directory for a standard database. After setting the directory, any TblList or FileList cursors opened on this handle are restricted to this directory, and any call to DbiOpenTable without a specified path is limited to searching to this directory. Any resources acquired before DbiSetDirectory is called, such as opened tables, are not affected by the change.

Before calling DbiSetDirectory, the directory is set to whatever was specified as the working directory in the DBIEnv structure in DbiInit. The default directory is the applications start-up directory. If an alias was used to open the database, the path that was specified in the alias is used as the current directory.

SQL. This function is not supported for SQL databases.

DBIResult Return Values

DBIERR_NONE	The current directory has been successfully set.
DBIERR_NOTSUPPORTED	This function is not supported with a nonstandard database.
DBIERR_INVALIDHNDL	The specified database handle is invalid or NIL.

Example

```
{ Set default directory to C:\DATA }
DbiSetDirectory( Table1.DBHandle, PChar('C:\DATA'));

{ Set default directory to the current directory }
DbiSetDirectory( Table1.DBHandle, PChar(''));
```

Pure Delphi Equivalent

TDatabase.DatabaseName

Xbase Equivalent

SET PATH, SET DEFAULT

See Also

DbiGetDirectory, DbiInit, DbiOpenTable

DBISETFIELDMAP

Declaration

```
function DbiSetFieldMap (              { Set a field map }
    hCur            : hDBICur;         { Cursor handle }
    iFields         : Word;           { Number of fields }
    pFldDesc        : pFLDDesc        { Array of field Descriptions }
  ): DBIResult;
```

Parameters

PARAMETER NAME	DESCRIPTION
hCur	The cursor handle.
iFields	The number of fields to map.
pFldDesc	Pointer to an array of FLDDesc structures.

Description

Sets a field map of the table associated with the given cursor. The underlying table is not affected. All the original fields still exist; they are simply not visible. (To drop fields in the underlying table, use DbiDoRestructure.) Setting iFields to 0 removes any existing field map and allows the underlying fields to become visible again.

A field map allows the user to effectively reorder the fields of a table or to drop some of the fields from view. This function does not produce a new cursor, but it does modify the existing one. The client application specifies a field map by building an array of field descriptors. The order of field descriptors in the array is the order in which the cursor presents the fields.

DbiGetFieldDescs must be called to retrieve the array of field descriptors for the table.

dBASE and Paradox. All data retrieval functions map the returned records as specified in the field Description; no type conversions are allowed. When a record is updated in a table with a field map, the unmapped fields are left unchanged. When a record is inserted in a table with a field map, the unmapped fields are set to blank.

Paradox. When a record is inserted in a table with a field map, the unmapped fields are set to blank or set to any defined default value.

Text: Since no Description of the fields are available when the text file is created with DbiCreateTable, it is a good practice to set a field map on the cursor that is opened on that text file. The text driver uses this field map to interpret the data types of the fields in that text file. The DbiTranslateRecordStructure call can be used to convert the logical or physical fields of a given driver type (such as Paradox or dBASE) to the physical fields of the text driver. These resulting physical text fields can be used in the DbiSetFieldMap call. When a field map is set on a text table, iFldType, iFldNum, iUnits1, and iUnits2 must be set correctly in all the field descriptors.

DBIResult Return Values

DBIERR_NONE	The field map was set successfully.
DBIERR_NA	The field number in the field descriptor is greater than the number of fields in the table, or the specified field name does not exist. Some drivers return this error if the user tried to set a field map on a table that already has a field map set.

Example

```
function ClearFieldMaps( oTable : TTable ) : Boolean;
begin
  Result := IsDbiOk( DbiSetFieldMap( GetTableCursor( oTable ),
                                     0, nil ));
end; { ClearFieldMaps }
```

See Also

DbiGetFieldDescs

DBISETLOCKRETRY

Declaration

```
function DbiSetLockRetry (      { Set Lock wait time }
     iWait        : Integer     { Time in seconds }
   ): DBIResult;
```

Parameters

PARAMETER NAME	DESCRIPTION
iWait	The lock retry time in seconds. A negative value causes infinite retries. A zero results in no retry at all. The default setting is 5 seconds.

Description

Sets the table and record lock retry time for the current session.

Paradox or dBASE. Whenever a table or record lock fails, the lock will be attempted until the retry time limit is reached. If iWait is 0, no retry is performed, resulting in the immediate failure of any unsuccessful lock request. The default setting is 5 seconds.

SQL. This function is not supported with SQL tables.

The following functions retry locking if the lock fails:

- Record locks.
  - DbiGetNextRecord
  - DbiGetRelativeRecord
  - DbiGetPriorRecord
  - DbiGetRecord
- Table locks.
  - DbiAcqTableLock
  - DbiAcqPersistTableLock

The following functions do not retry locking if the lock fails:

- DbiOpenDatabase
- DbiOpenTable
- DbiSetDirectory
- DbiSetPrivateDir

DBIResult Return Values

DBIERR_NONE	The lock retry time was successfully set for the session.

Example

```
{ Make locks retry for 10 seconds before failing }
DbiSetLockRetry( 10 );

{ Attempt lock only once with no retry before failing }
DbiSetLockRetry( 0 );
```

See Also

DbiGetNextRecord, DbiGetPriorRecord, DbiGetRelativeRecord, DbiGetRecord, DbiAcqTableLock, DbiAcqPersistTableLock, DbiSetPrivateDir, DbiSetDirectory, DbiOpenTable

DBISETNUMBERFORMAT

Declaration

```
function DbiSetNumberFormat (        { Set current number format }
var    fmtNumber     : FMTNumber
   ): DBIResult;
```

Parameters

PARAMETER NAME	DESCRIPTION
fmtNumber	Reference to the client-allocated FMTNumber structure to be filled.

Description

Sets the number format for the current session. The number format is used by QBE for input and wildcard character matching. It is also used by batch operations (such as *DbiDoRestructure* and *DbiBatchMove*) to handle data type coercion between character and numeric types.

DBIResult Return Values

DBIERR_NONE	The number format was set successfully.
DBIERR_INVALIDHNDL	The reference to the number format structure is NIL.
DBIERR_INVALIDPARAM	Data within the number format structure is invalid.

Example

```
function SetNumFormatAmerican : Boolean;
var
   fmtNum    : FMTNumber;
begin
   with fmtNum do
   begin
     cDecimalSeparator := '.';
     cThousandSeparator := ',';
     bLeadingZero := False;
   end; { with fmtNum }
   Result := IsDbiOk( DbiSetNumberFormat( fmtNum ));
end; { SetNumFormatAmerican() }
```

Pure Delphi Equivalent

FormatFloat

See Also
DbiGetNumberFormat

DbiSetPrivateDir

Declaration

```
function DbiSetPrivateDir (     { Set Private Directory for session }
    pszDir          : PChar    { Directory name / nil }
    ): DBIResult;
```

Parameters

Parameter Name	Description
pszDir	Optional pointer to the full path name of the new private directory. If NIL, then the private directory is reset to the default start-up directory.

Description

Sets the private directory for the current session. The directory must be available for exclusive access. No other BDE users can access the private directory.

Although DbiSetPrivateDir is specific to Paradox tables, it has one important use for all drivers. all temporary or auxiliary files are created in this directory by default. If no private directory is specified, then all temporary or auxiliary tables are created in the default start-up directory. Examples of functions that may create temporary or auxiliary tables are DbiDoRestructure and DbiBatchMove.

DBIResult Return Values

DBIERR_NONE	The private directory was successfully set.
DBIERR_DIRBUSY	The specified directory is currently in use.

Example

```
function SetPrivateDir( sPrivDir : String ): DBIResult;
var
  szPrivDir : Array[0..127] of Char;
begin
  StrPCopy( szPrivDir, sPrivDir );
  Result := DbiSetPrivateDir( szPrivDir );
end;
```

Pure Delphi Equivalent

TSession.PrivateDir

See Also

DbiGetSesInfo

DBISETPROP

Declaration

```
function DbiSetProp (              { Set property }
        hObj            : hDBIObj;    { Object handle }
        iProp           : Longint;    { Property to set }
        iPropValue      : Longint     { Property value }
    ): DBIResult;
```

Parameters

PARAMETER NAME	DESCRIPTION
hObj	The object handle to a system, client, session, driver, database, cursor, or statement object.
iProp	The property to set.
iPropValue	The value of the property.

Description

Sets the specified property of an object to a given value. The specified object does not necessarily have to match the type of property as long as the object is associated with the object type of the property. For Example, the property drvDRIVERTYPE assumes an object of type objDRIVER, but because a cursor is derived from a driver, a cursor handle (objCURSOR) could also be specified.

The following Examples shows how you can use DbiSetProp to specify your preference for live or canned result sets during query execution. A canned result set is like a snapshot or a copy of the original data selected by the query. In contrast, a live result set is a view of the original data. Specifically, if you modify a live result set, the changes are reflected in the original data.

```
DbiSetProp( hCursor, stmtLIVENESS, Longint( wantLIVE ));
```

To set the translation mode of a cursor to xltNONE (see DbiOpenTable), use

```
DbiSetProp( hCursor, curXLTMODE, Longint( xltNONE ));
```

For properties wider than 32 bits, pass a pointer to the property and cast the pointer to Longint.

See DbiGetObjFromObj for details about associated objects.

DBIResult Return Values

DBIERR_NONE	The property of the object was successfully set.
DBIERR_NOTSUPPORTED	Property is not supported for this object.

Example

```
{
QueryHandler2()

Adapted from C code supplied from:
  Albert Dayes Compuserve: 70007,3615

Prepares SQL statements and tests the SQL Syntax and finally executes SQL
query and stores results in the named answer table if no errors occur.

Inputs:
   hDBIDb  = Database session handle
   hDBICur = Cursor Handle
   PChar   = SQL Query Text
   PChar   = Answer table name
}

function QueryHandler2( hDb : hDBIDb; hCur : hDBICur; szSQLText :
                        PChar; szAnswerTable : PChar ) : Boolean;
var
  hStmt : hDBIStmt;    { Query Statement Handle }
begin
  try
     Result := IsDbiOk( DbiQPrepare( hDb, qrylangSQL, szSQLText,
                              hStmt ))
           and IsDbiOk( DbiSetProp( hDBIObj( hStmt ), stmtANSNAME,
                                  LongInt( szAnswerTable )))
           and IsDbiOk( DbiQExec( hStmt, @hCur ));
  finally
    if not Result then
      DbiQFree( hStmt );
  end;

  { There is now an answer table named the value of szAnswerTable
    in the current database BDE private directory. This is a
    temporary table. }

end; { QueryHandler() }
```

See Also

DbiOpenTable, DbiGetProp

DBISETRANGE

Declaration

```
function DbiSetRange (          { Set cursor to a range }
      hCursor         : hDBICur; { Cursor }
      bKeyItself      : Bool;    { Whether Key or Record buffer }
      iFields1        : Word;    { Key fields to be mathced in full }
      iLen1           : Word;    { Key length to compare }
      pKey1           : Pointer; { Top/Left key in Range }
      bKey1Incl       : Bool;    { If Inclusive of Key1 }
      iFields2        : Word;    { Key fields to be matched in full }
      iLen2           : Word;    { Key length to compare }
      pKey2           : Pointer; { Bottom/Right key in Range }
      bKey2Incl       : Bool     { If Inclusive of Key2 }
   ): DBIResult;
```

Parameters

PARAMETER NAME	DESCRIPTION
hCursor	The cursor handle.
bKeyItself	Defines the key buffer type.
	If set to True, pKey1 and pKey2 contain the keys directly.
	If set to False, pKey1 and pKey2 point to record buffers from which the keys can be extracted.
iFields1	Optional number of fields to be used for composite keys, for the beginning of the range.
	The iFields1 and iLen1 Parameters together indicate how much of the key is to be used for matching. If both are zero, the entire key is used. If a partial match is required on a given field of the key, all the key fields preceding it in the composite key must be included.
	Only character fields can be matched for a partial key; all other field types must be fully matched.
	For partial key matches, iFields1 must be equal to the number (if any) of key fields preceding the field being partially matched. iLen1 indicates the number of characters in the partial key to be matched.
iLen1	The length into the last field to be used for composite keys. If not zero, the last field to be used must be a character type.
pKey1	Optional pointer to the key value or record buffer for the beginning of the range. If NIL, no low limit is set.
bKey1Incl	Indicates whether to include the beginning key value in the range. bKey1Incl can be either True or False.

iFields2	Optional number of fields to be used for composite keys, for the end of the range. The iFields2 and iLen2 Parameters together indicate how much of the key is to be used for matching. If both are zero, the entire key is used.
	If a match is required on a given field of the key, all the key fields preceding it in the composite key must also be supplied. Only character fields can be matched for a partial key; all other field types must be fully matched.
	For partial key matches, iFields2 must be equal to the number (if any) of key fields preceding the field being partially matched. iLen2 The number of characters in the partial key to be matched.
iLen2	The length into the last field to be used for composite keys. If not zero, the last field to be used must be a character type.
pKey2	Optional pointer to the key value or record buffer for the end of the range. If NIL, no high limit is set.
bKey2Incl	Indicates whether to include the end key value in the range. bKey2Incl can be either True or False.

Description

Limits the result set to the contiguous index keys bounded by the specified low and high values. There must be an active index. DbiSetRange positions the cursor at the beginning of the range, not on the first record in the range.

After this function is called, the cursor allows access only to records in the table that fall within the defined range. Any attempt to reference records outside the range results in a BOF or EOF error condition.

Paradox. DbiGetRecCount now reflects only the records in the range. DbiGetSeqNo is relative to the beginning of the range, rather than the beginning of the table.

DBIResult Return Values

DBIERR_NONE	The range was set successfully.
DBIERR_INVALIDHNDL	The specified cursor handle is invalid or NIL.
DBIERR_OUTOFRANGE	(iField + iLen) is less than the whole key.
DBIERR_NOASSOCINDEX	The specified cursor does not have an active index.

Example

```
function SetRangeInclusive( oTable : TTable; sLow, sHigh : String )
                           : Boolean;
var
  szLow,
  szHigh : PChar;
begin
  Result := False;
  try
    if sLow <> sHigh then { the values are not the same }
```

732

```
  begin
    if Length( sLow ) > 0 then
    begin
      szLow := StrAlloc( Length( sLow ) + 1 );
      StrPCopy( szLow, sLow );
    end
    else
      szLow := nil;

    if Length( sHigh ) > 0 then
    begin
      szHigh := StrAlloc( Length( sHigh ) + 1 );
      StrPCopy( szHigh, sHigh );
    end
    else
      szHigh := nil;

    Result := IsDbiOk( DbiSetRange( GetTableCursor( oTable ),
                       True, 0, 0, szLow, True, 0, 0, szHigh,
                       True ));
    if Assigned( szLow ) then
      StrDispose( szLow );

    if Assigned( szHigh ) then
      StrDispose( szHigh );
  end;
except
  Result := False;
end;
end; { SetRangeInclusive() }
```

Pure Delphi Equivalent

TTable.SetRange

Xbase Equivalent

SET SCOPE

See Also

DbiResetRange, DbiExtractKey, DbiSetToKey, DbiGetRecordCount, DbiGetSeqNo

DBISETTIMEFORMAT

Declaration

```
function DbiSetTimeFormat (          { Set current time format }
var    fmtTime        : FMTTime
  ): DBIResult;
```

Parameters

PARAMETER NAME	DESCRIPTION
fmtTime	Reference to the client-allocated FMTTime structure to be filled.

Description

Sets the time format for the current session. The time format is used by QBE for input and wildcard character matching. It is also used by batch operations (such as *DbiDoRestructure* and *DbiBatchMove*) to handle data-type coercion between character and time or datetime types.

DBIResult Return Values

DBIERR_NONE	The time format was successfully set.
DBIERR_INVALIDHNDL	The pointer to the time format structure is NIL.
DBIERR_INVALIDPARAM	Data within the time format structure is invalid.

Example

```
function TimeShowSeconds( iTog : Integer ) : Boolean;
var
  fmTime    : FMTTime;
begin
  Result := False;
  if IsDbiOk( DbiGetTimeFormat( fmTime )) then
  begin
    with fmTime do
    begin
      Result := bSeconds and bMilSeconds;
      case iTog of
        0, 1 :
          begin
            bSeconds := iTog = 1;
            bMilSeconds := iTog = 1;
            Result := IsDbiOk( DbiSetTimeFormat( fmTime ));
          end;
      end; { case }
    end; { with }
  end; { if }
end; { TimeShowSeconds() }
```

Pure Delphi Equivalent

FormatDateTime

See Also

DbiGetTimeFormat

DBISETTOBEGIN

Declaration

```
function DbiSetToBegin (          { Reset cursor to beginning }
    hCursor      : hDBICur        { Cursor handle }
  ): DBIResult;
```

Parameters

PARAMETER NAME	DESCRIPTION
hCursor	The cursor handle.

Description

Position the cursor to the *crack* before the first record in the table.

Crack semantics allow for the current location of the cursor to be before the first record, between records, or after the last record. One of the reasons for having crack semantics is to allow the use of one function to access all records in a table. For Example, instead of having to use DbiGetRecord the first time, and DbiGetNextRecord each subsequent time, DbiGetNextRecord itself can be used to get all records in a table.

DBIResult Return Values

DBIERR_NONE	The cursor was successfully set to BOF.
DBIERR_INVALIDHNDL	The specified cursor handle is invalid or NIL.

Example

```
{ Displays the contents of the second field for each record of CUSTOMER.DB
  within a scrolling window. }
procedure ListDatabase( Sender: TObject );
var
  hDB    : hDBIDB;
  hTbl   : hDBICur;
  iResult: DBIResult;
  szBuf,
  szFld  : PChar;
  cProp  : CURProps;
  bBlank : Bool;   { Changed from WordBool for Delphi 2.0 }
begin
  DbiInit(nil);
```

```
DbiOpenDataBase( 'DBDEMOS', 'STANDARD', dbiREADWRITE,
                dbiOPENSHARED, nil, 0, nil, nil, hDB );
DbiOpenTable( hDB, 'CUSTOMER.DB', nil, nil, nil, 0, dbiREADONLY,
             dbiOPENSHARED, xltFIELD, False, nil, hTbl );
DbiGetCursorProps( hTbl, cProp );
szBuf := AllocMem( cProp.iRecBufSize * SizeOf( Byte ));
szFld := AllocMem( 255 * SizeOf( Byte ));
DbiSetToBegin( hTbl );
iResult := 0;
repeat
  iResult := DbiGetNextRecord( hTbl, dbiNOLOCK, szBuf, nil );
  DbiGetField( hTbl, 2, szBuf, szFld, bBlank );
  WriteLn( StrPas( szFld ));
until iResult <> DBIERR_NONE;
FreeMem( szBuf, ( cProp.iRecBufSize * SizeOf( Byte )));
FreeMem( szFld, ( 255 * SizeOf( Byte )));
DbiCloseDatabase( hDB );
WriteLn( 'Finished' );
DbiExit;
end; { ListDatabase }
```

Pure Delphi Equivalent

TTable.First

Xbase Equivalent

GO TOP, dbGoTop()

See Also

DbiGetNextRecord, DbiGetPriorRecord, DbiGetRelativeRecord, DbiSetToEnd, DbiSetToCursor

DBISETTOBOOKMARK

Declaration

```
function DbiSetToBookMark (        { Position to a bookmark }
     hCur          : hDBICur;     { Cursor handle }
     pBookMark     : Pointer      { Pointer to bookmark }

  ): DBIResult;
```

Parameters

PARAMETER NAME	DESCRIPTION
hCur	The cursor handle. hCur must be compatible with the cursor used when the bookmark was obtained.
pBookMark	Pointer to the bookmark. The bookmark is obtained by a prior call to DbiGetBookMark.

Description

Positions the cursor to the position saved in the specified bookmark. To determine if the bookmark is stable, DbiGetCursorProps can be called, and the bBookMarkStable property examined. If the record pointed to by the bookmark has been deleted, the cursor is positioned on a crack where the original record was.

DbiGetBookMark must have been called to retrieve a valid bookmark. The supplied cursor can be different from the one used to retrieve the bookmark information, but the cursor must be opened on the same table, with the same index order, if any.

Note: DbiSwitchToIndex may make bookmarks obtained under a different index order unusable with the new order.

DBIResult Return Values

DBIERR_NONE	The call was successful; however, the position may not be the expected one if the record has been deleted, or if the bookmark was unstable.
DBIERR_INVALIDHNDL	The specified cursor handle is invalid or NIL, or the pointer to the bookmark is NIL, or the specified bookmark is NIL.
DBIERR_INVALIDBOOKMARK	The specified bookmark is not from the same table, or the bookmark is corrupt.

Example

```
function dbGoToBookMark( oTable : TTable; pBookMark : Pointer ) : Boolean;
begin
  Result := IsDbiOk( DbiSetToBookMark( oTable.Handle, pBookMark ));
end; { dbGoToBookMark() }
```

Pure Delphi Equivalent

TTable.GotoBookmark, TQuery.GotoBookmark, TStoredProc.GotoBookmark

Xbase Equivalent

GO, dbGoto()

See Also

DbiOpenTable, DbiGetCursorProps, DbiGetBookMark, DbiCompareBookMarks

DBISETTOCURSOR

Declaration

```
function DbiSetToCursor (          { Set cursor to another cursor position }
    hDest          : hDBICur;     { Destination cursor }
    hSrc           : hDBICur      { Source cursor }
): DBIResult;
```

Parameters

PARAMETER NAME	DESCRIPTION
hDest	The destination cursor handle.
hSrc	The source cursor handle.

Description

Sets the position of one cursor (the destination cursor) to the position of the source cursor. After DbiSetToCursor executes, the destination cursor is positioned on the same record as the source cursor. They remain independent of each other; they do not track each other.

Source and destination cursors must be opened on the same table in the same session, and both must be valid. If both cursors are opened on a single table, they do not have to have the same current index. The source cursor must have a current record if the index order is different.

DBIResult Return Values

DBIERR_NONE sor.	The destination cursor was successfully set to the record of the source cursor.
DBIERR_INVALIDHNDL	The specified source cursor or destination cursor is invalid or NIL.
DBIERR_NOCURRREC	The source cursor has no current record.

Example

```
function SyncTables( oDest, oSource : TTable ) : Boolean;
begin
  Result := IsDbiOk( DbiSetToCursor( GetTableCursor( oDest ),
                 GetTableCursor( oSource )));
  if Result then
    oDest.UpdateCursorPos;
end; { SyncTables() }
```

Pure Delphi Equivalent

TTable.GotoCurrent

Xbase Equivalent

GO, dbGoto()

See Also

DbiGetBookMark, DbiSetToBookMark, DbiCloneCursor, DbiOpenTable

DBISETTOEND

Declaration

```
function DbiSetToEnd (          { Reset cursor to ending }
    hCursor      : hDBICur     { Cursor handle }
  ): DBIResult;
```

Parameters

PARAMETER NAME	DESCRIPTION
hCursor	The cursor handle.

Description

Positions the cursor on the crack after the end of the result set. DbiGetPriorRecord or DbiGetRelativeRecord can be called to position the cursor on the last valid record of the result set.

There is no current record after DbiSetToEnd completes. (DbiGetRecord returns DBIERR_EOF.)

DBIResult Return Values

DBIERR_NONE	The cursor was successfully set to the EOF position.
DBIERR_INVALIDHNDL	The specified cursor handle is invalid or NIL.

Example

```
function dbGoBottom( oTable : TTable ) : Boolean;
begin
  Result := IsDbiOk( DbiSetToEnd( oTable.Handle )) and
                   ( DbiGetRecord( oTable.Handle, dbiNOLOCK,
                     nil, nil ) = DBIERR_EOF );
end; { dbGoBottom() }
```

Pure Delphi Equivalent

TTable.Last

Xbase Equivalent

GO BOTTOM, dbGoBottom()

See Also

DbiSetToBegin, DbiGetNextRecord, DbiGetPriorRecord, DbiGetRelativeRecord, DbiSetToCursor

DBISETTOKEY

Declaration

```
function DbiSetToKey (            { Set key condition }
     hCursor      : hDBICur;      { Cursor handle }
     eSearchCond  : DBISearchCond; { Search cond (default is =) }
     bDirectKey   : Bool;         { Key is supplied directly }
     iFields      : Word;         { Number of full flds to match }
     iLen         : Word;         { Partial key len of last field }
     pBuff        : Pointer       { Either Rec buf or Key itself }
  ): DBIResult;
```

Parameters

PARAMETER NAME	DESCRIPTION
hCursor	The cursor handle.
eSearchCond	The search condition: keySEARCHEQ, keySEARCHGT, or keySEARCHGEQ.
bDirectKey	Indicates whether the key is supplied directly in pBuf or not. If set to True, pBuf The pointer to the key in physical format; if set to False, pBuf The pointer to the record buffer.
iFields	Optional number of complete fields to be used for composite keys. If iFields and iLen are both 0, the entire key is used.
iLen	The length into the last field to be used for composite keys. If not zero, the last field to be used must be a character type.
pBuf	Pointer to either the record buffer or the key itself, determined by bDirectKey.

Description

Positions an ordered cursor based on the given key value. The search always results in the cursor being positioned on the crack just prior to the specified key. If no index is currently associated with the cursor, an error is generated, and no cursor movement occurs.

There are three possible search conditions: keySEARCHEQ, keySEARCHGT, and keySEARCHGEQ. Searches always result in the cursor being positioned on the crack before the record of the specified key value. Assuming all the arguments are specified correctly, only the (=) search condition can return a DBIERR_RECNOTFOUND error.

(> or >=) always succeeds.

The key can be specified either by setting the key fields in a record buffer and supplying the record buffer or by specifying the key buffer directly as a string of bytes. To construct the key buffer, use DbiExtractKey.

The iFields and iLen Parameters together indicate how much of the key is to be used for matching. If both are 0, the entire key is used. If a partial match is required on a given field of the key, all the key fields preceding it in the composite key must also be specified for match. Only character fields can be matched for a partial key; all other field types must be fully matched.

DBIResult Return Values

DBIERR_NONE	The record was successfully found.
DBIERR_NOASSOCINDEX	There is no index to search on.
DBIERR_INVALIDPARAM	One of the specified parameters is invalid (for Example, iLen is invalid for the current index).
DBIERR_RECNOTFOUND	No record matches the key value.

Example

```
function dbSeek(          { Seek an index key value }
    oTable: TTable;       { Table to seek in }
    sVal  : String;       { Value to seek in index }
    bSoft : Boolean;      { Perform a soft seek? }
    bExact: Boolean;      { Get an exact match? }
    bLast : Boolean       { Position at last matching key? }
    )     : Boolean;      { True if index key value is found }
var
  eSearchCond : DBISearchCond;
  iMatchLen   : Integer;
  szVar       : PChar;
begin
  Result := False;
  try
    try
      oTable.DisableControls;
      if bLast then
        eSearchCond := keySEARCHGT
      else if bSoft then
        eSearchCond := keySEARCHGEQ
      else
        eSearchCond := keySEARCHEQ;

      szVar := StrAlloc( 256 );
      StrPCopy( szVar, sVal );
```

```
    if bExact then
      iMatchLen := 0 { Match entire key }
    else
      iMatchLen := StrLen( szVar );

    Result := IsDbiOk( DbiSetToKey( GetTableCursor( oTable ),
                  eSearchCond, True, 0, iMatchLen, szVar ));
    if Result then
    begin
      oTable.UpdateCursorPos;
      oTable.Refresh;
    end
    else
    begin
      DbiExtractKey( GetTableCursor( oTable ), nil, szVar );
      ShowMessage( 'Seek Failed.  Current Key: ' + StrPas( szVar ));
    end;
  except
    on E : EDBEngineError do
      ShowMessage( 'Engine Error: ' + E.Message );
    on E : Exception do
      ShowMessage( 'Exception: ' + E.Message );
  end;
  finally
    oTable.EnableControls;
    if Assigned( szVar ) then
      StrDispose( szVar );
  end;
end; { dbSeek() }
```

Pure Delphi Equivalent

TTable.FindKey

Xbase Equivalent

SEEK, dbSeek()

See Also

DbiSetRange, DbiSwitchToIndex, DbiSetToBookMark, DbiGetNextRecord, DbiGetPriorRecord

DBISETTORECORDNO

Declaration

```
function DbiSetToRecordNo (        { Position to Physical Rec# }
    hCursor       : hDBICur;      { Cursor handle }
    iRecNo        : Longint       { Physical record number }
  ): DBIResult;
```

Parameters

PARAMETER NAME	DESCRIPTION
hCursor	The cursor handle.
iRecNo	The physical record number.

Description

Positions the cursor to the given physical record number. This function is currently valid only with dBASE tables. For Paradox tables see the *DbiSetToSeqNo* function.

The physical record number can be retrieved from the iPhyRecNum field of the RECProps structure in calls to DbiGetRecord, DbiGetNextRecord, DbiGetPriorRecord, or DbiGetRelativeRecord.

If the given record number is beyond the valid range for the cursor, the cursor is set to the beginning or end of the file (BOF/EOF).

DBIResult Return Values

DBIERR_NONE	The cursor was successfully set to the record specified by iRecNo.
DBIERR_INVALIDHNDL	The specified cursor handle is invalid or NIL.
DBIERR_BOF	The specified record number is zero.
DBIERR_EOF	The specified record number is greater than the number of records in the table.
DBIERR_NOTSUPPORTED	This function is not supported for Paradox and SQL tables.

Example

```
function dbGoTo( oTable : TTable; lRecNo : Longint ) : Boolean;
begin
  Result := IsDbiOk( DbiSetToRecordNo( oTable.Handle, lRecNo ));
end; { dbGoTo() }
```

Pure Delphi Equivalent

TTable.GotoBookmark

Xbase Equivalent

GO, dbGoto()

See Also

DbiSetToSeqNo

DBISETTOSEQNO

Declaration

```
function DbiSetToSeqNo (      { Position to a logical record number }
    hCursor    : hDBICur;    { Cursor handle }
    iSeqNo     : Longint     { Sequence number }
): DBIResult;
```

Parameters

Parameter Name	Description
hCursor	The cursor handle.
iSeqNo	The logical record number.

Description

Positions the cursor to the specified sequence number of a table. This function is currently valid only with Paradox tables. For dBASE tables, see the DbiSetToRecordNo function.

The sequence number can be retrieved by calling DbiGetSeqNo or from the iSeqNo field of the RECProps structure in calls to DbiGetRecord, DbiGetNextRecord, DbiGetPriorRecord, or DbiGetRelativeRecord.

A sequence number is the position of a record in the result set associated with hCursor. If the given sequence number is beyond the valid sequence number for the cursor, the cursor is set to the beginning or end of the file (BOF/EOF).

For Example, if the table is empty, this function leaves the cursor positioned at BOF and returns DBIERR_BOF. If the table is not empty and the user attempts to position the cursor beyond a valid sequence number, the cursor is set to EOF, and DBIERR_EOF is returned.

Note: The sequence number for a given record is not stable. If a record is inserted or deleted before the given index order, the sequence number for the record changes.

DBIResult Return Values

DBIERR_NONE	The Paradox cursor was successfully set to the sequence number specified by iSeqNo.
DBIERR_INVALIDHNDL	The specified cursor handle is invalid or NIL.
DBIERR_EOF	The specified record number is greater than the number of records in the table.
DBIERR_BOF	The specified record number is zero.
DBIERR_NOTSUPPORTED	This function is not supported for SQL or dBASE drivers.

Example

```
function PDXGoTo( oTable : TTable; lRecNo : Longint ) : Boolean;
begin
  Result := IsDbiOk( DbiSetToSeqNo( oTable.Handle, lRecNo ));
end; { PDXGoTo() }
```

Pure Delphi Equivalent

TTable.GotoBookmark

Xbase Equivalent

GO, dbGoto()

See Also

DbiGetSeqNo, DbiSetToRecordNo

DBISORTTABLE

Declaration

```
function DbiSortTable (          { Sort table }
     hDb             : hDBIDb;    { Database handle }
     pszTableName  : PChar;     { Table name of source }
     pszDriverType : PChar;     { Driver type /nil }
     hSrcCur         : hDBICur;   { OR cursor of table to sort }
     pszSortedName : PChar;     { Destination table (nil if sort to
                                     self) }
     phSortedCur   : phDBICur;  { If non-null, return cursor on
                                     destination }
     hDstCur         : hDBICur;   { OR cursor of destination }
     iSortFields   : Word;      { Number of sort fields }
     piFieldNum    : PWord;     { Array of field numbers }
     pbCaseInsensitive : PBool;  { Which fields should sort case-
                                     insensitive (Optional) }
     pSortOrder    : pSORTOrder; { Array of Sort orders (Opt) }
     ppfSortFn     : ppfSORTCompFn; { Array of compare function
                                     pointers (Optional) }
     bRemoveDups   : Bool;      { If True, remove duplicates }
     hDuplicatesCur : hDBICur;  { Cursor to duplicates table (Opt) }
var  lRecsSort     : Longint    { in/out parameter - sort this
                                     number }
   ): DBIResult;
```

Parameters

PARAMETER NAME	DESCRIPTION
hDb	Optional database handle when pszTableName and pszDriverType are used to identify the source table. Not used when hSrcCur is supplied. Must be a valid database handle.
pszTableName	Optional pointer to the table name. Must be a defined table name and the table must exist. If hDb, pszTableName, and pszTableType are supplied, hSrcCur should be NIL. A valid extension may be specified.
pszDriverType	Optional pointer to the driver type. Required only when hDb and pszTableName are supplied. Must be a defined driver type.
hSrcCur	Optional parameter supplied when an opened source table is to be sorted to a destination table, as specified in pszSortedName. When the table is to be sorted into itself, hDb, pszTableName, and pszDriverType must be used to identify the table instead of hSrcCur.
pszSortedName	Optional pointer to the file name to be used as the sorted destination table. The table must be closed. The extension must match that of the source table.
	To specify a destination table of a different driver type, hDstCur must be used.
	If this parameter is specified, phSortedCur, and hDstCur are all NIL, the source table is sorted into itself.
phSortedCur	Optional pointer to a cursor handle on the sorted destination table, with the name specified by pszSortedName. If NIL, the cursor handle is not returned.
hDstCur	Optional handle to a destination table. This parameter is used instead of pszSortedName to specify the sorted destination table when the destination table is already open. If this parameter and pszSortedName are NIL, the source table is sorted into itself.
iSortFields	The number of sort fields to be used.
piFieldNum	Pointer to an array of the field numbers on which to sort. The number of elements in the array must equal the number specified in iSortFields.
pbCaseInsensitive	Optional pointer to an array of values indicating whether the sort is to be case-insensitive for each sort field. True specifies case-insensitive. The number of elements in the array must equal the number specified in iSortFields.
	If a NIL pointer is given, the default is case-sensitive. Only text fields are affected.
pSortOrder	Optional pointer to an array of the sort order for each field, either ascending or descending. If a NIL pointer is given, the order is ascending. The number of elements in the array must equal the number specified in iSortFields.
ppfsortFn	Optional pointer to an array of pointers to client-supplied compare functions. The number of elements in the array must be equal to the number specified in iSortFields.
bRemoveDups	Indicates whether duplicates are to be removed during sorting or not. If True, duplicates are removed from the destination table. Duplicates may be written to a table associated with hDuplicatesCur.
hDuplicatesCur	Optional handle to a Duplicates table. If specified, duplicates removed from the table are placed in a Duplicates table associated with the specified cursor. The structure of this table must be the same as the source table.
lRecsSort	Optional number of records to sort, from the current position of the source table cursor (on Input), or a reference to the client variable that receives the actual number of records sorted into the destination table (on Output).
	Used only when the source table is identified by hSrcCur.

746

Description

Sorts an opened or closed table, either into itself or into a destination table. There are options to remove duplicates, to enable case-insensitive sorts and special sort functions, and to control the number of records sorted.

The records in the destination table will be ordered according to the sort criteria. If lRecSort is specified, only lRecSort records are sorted, starting from the current position in the table, otherwise, the whole table is sorted.

As the table is sorted, the records are physically ordered according to the specified sort criteria. Source and destination tables can be of different driver types; if so, the destination table must be specified by hDstCur.

Paradox. A Paradox table with a primary key cannot be sorted into itself. Auto-increment fields cannot be sorted.

SQL. DbiSortTable is not supported with SQL tables as the destination.

DBIResult Return Values

DBIERR_NONE	The sort was successful.
DBIERR_INVALIDHNDL	The specified database handle is invalid or NIL.
DBIERR_INVALIDFILENAME	The source table name was not provided.
DBIERR_UNKNOWNTBLTYPE	The source driver type was not provided.
DBIERR_INVALIDPARAM	The specified number of sort fields is invalid.
DBIERR_NOTSUPPORTED	This function is not supported for sort to self on a Paradox table with a primary index.

Example

Available on the CD-ROM at the back of the book.

Xbase Equivalent

SORT

See Also

DbiBatchMove, DbiCreateTable, DbiDoRestructure, DbiCopyTable, DbiSortOpenedTable

DBISTARTSESSION

Declaration

```
function DbiStartSession (   { Start a new session }
    pszName    : PChar;      { Name (Optional) }
var hSes       : hDBISes;    { Session }
    pNetDir    : PChar       { Netfile directory for session (opt) }
    ): DBIResult;
```

Parameters

PARAMETER NAME	DESCRIPTION
pszName	Optional pointer to the session name.
hSes	Reference to the session handle. Used to identify the session.
pNetDir	Optional pointer to the network file directory for the session.

Description

Starts a new session for the client application. This function can be used to create different concurrency schemes.

DBIResult Return Values

DBIERR_NONE	The session was successfully started.
DBIERR_INVALIDHNDL	hSes is NIL.
DBIERR_SESSIONSLIMIT	The maximum number of sessions are open.

Example

```
procedure SessionIO;
var
  rslt: DBIResult;          { Value returned from BDE functions }
  I   : Integer;            { Loop variable }
const
  phSession     : ^hDBISes = nil; { Handle to the session }
  pSesInf       :  pSESInfo = nil; { Session descriptor }
  uNumOfSessions: Integer = 4;     { The # of sessions to open }
begin
  { Inform user that the Example is running }
  WriteLn('*** Session I/O Example ***');
  WriteLn('   Initializing BDE...');

  rslt := DbiInit( nil );
  if (rslt <> DBIERR_NONE) then { Check if successful }
  begin
    WriteLn('');
    WriteLn('*** End of Example ***');
    exit;
  end;

  { Allocate memory for the uNumOfSessions amount of sessions.
    These will be pointers to sessions once we start them. }
  GetMem( phSession, uNumOfSessions * SizeOf( hDBISes ));
  if not Assigned( phSession ) then
  begin
    WriteLn('    Error - Out of memory.');
    Check( DbiExit );
    WriteLn('');
```

```
    WriteLn('*** End of Example ***');
    exit;
  end;

  { Allocate memory for the session info pointers }
  GetMem( pSesInf, uNumOfSessions * SizeOf( SESInfo ));
  if not Assigned( pSesInf ) then
  begin
    WriteLn('    Error - Out of memory.');
    Check( DbiExit );
    WriteLn('');
    WriteLn('*** End of Example ***');
    exit;
  end;

  { Acquire the initial session handle. A session is started for
    you when the engine is initialized.  }
  WriteLn('    Getting session #1 (opened automatically by DbiInit)...');
  Check( DbiGetCurrSession( (phSession^ ) ));

  { Starts new sessions and display the number of open sessions on
    the WriteLn. Having already opened the first one, start the
    second session through the uNumOfSessions - 1 session. }
  WriteLn('');
  for i := 1 to (uNumOfSessions - 1) do
  begin
    Inc( phSession );
    WriteLn('    Opening session #' + IntToStr( i + 1 ));
    Check( DbiStartSession( '', phSession^, nil ));
  end;
  Dec( phSession, i );
  WriteLn('');

  { Now iterate through each of the sessions and will get the
    current settings.  The settings include the session number, the
    number of open databases and the number of open cursors among
    other things. }
  for i := 1 to uNumOfSessions do
  begin
    WriteLn('    Setting session #' + IntToStr( i ) +
            ' as the current session...');
    Check( DbiSetCurrSession( phSession^ ));
    WriteLn('    Getting Session information...');
    Check( DbiGetSesInfo( pSesInf^ ));
    WriteLn('    Open databases: ' +
            IntToStr( pSesInf^.iDatabases ) +
            ',    Open Cursors: ' + IntToStr( pSesInf^.iCursors ));
    Inc( phSession );
  end;
  Dec( phSession, i );

  { Close all the session and then close BDE }
```

```
WriteLn('   We cannot yet close session #1 as it is ' +
        'the default session.');
WriteLn('   We will therefore close all other sessions ' +
        'and then close session #1.');
WriteLn('');
for i := 1 to (uNumOfSessions-1) do
begin
  { We cannot close Session #1 so we will close session #2 and
    on.  We cannot close session #1 because it is the default
    session (created with DbiInit.) }
  Inc( phSession );
  WriteLn('   Closing session #' + IntToStr( i + 1 ) + '...' );
  Check( DbiCloseSession( phSession^ ));
end;

{ Release the memory used to hold the session handles }
FreeMem( phSession, uNumOfSessions * SizeOf( hDBISes ));

{ Release the memory used to store information about the session }
FreeMem( pSesInf, uNumOfSessions * SizeOf( SESInfo ));

WriteLn('   Closing session #1 (done during DbiExit)');
WriteLn('   Clean up BDE...');
Check( DbiExit );

WriteLn('');
WriteLn('*** End of Example ***');
  exit;
end;
```

Pure Delphi Equivalent

TSession.Create(**NIL**)

See Also

DbiSetCurrSession, DbiCloseSession

DBISWITCHTOINDEX

Declaration

```
function DbiSwitchToIndex (      { Change index order of access }
var    hCursor       : hDBICur;  { Cursor handle (In/Out) }
       pszIndexName  : PChar;    { Index name }
       pszTagName    : PChar;    { Tag name (if applicable) }
       iIndexId      : Word;     { Index number }
       bCurrRec      : Bool      { Position at current record }
   ): DBIResult;
```

Parameters

Parameter Name	Description
hCursor	On input, hCursor The original cursor handle; on output, pointer to the new cursor handle.
pszIndexName	Pointer to the index name string.
pszTagName	Pointer to the tag name string. Used for dBASE tables only.
iIndexId	The index ID.
	bCurrRec If True, positions the new cursor on the current record of the original cursor.

Description

Changes the active index order of the given cursor without closing the cursor and opening another cursor. The original cursor is passed into the function, and a new cursor handle is returned with the new ordering. The original cursor handle becomes invalid and cannot be used.

Setting pszIndexName, pszTagName, and iIndexId to NIL is equivalent to changing the order to the default order. As a result, the cursor is set to one of the following orders:

- Relational order for dBASE and SQL tables.
- Primary index order for a keyed Paradox table or physical order for a Paradox heap table.

If *bCurr*Rec is set to True, the new cursor is positioned on the same record as the original cursor. If bCurrRec is set to False, the new cursor is positioned at BOF. If the original cursor is not positioned on a valid record (for Example, the current record has been deleted and the cursor has not been advanced), this function with bCurrRec set to True fails. If this function is used to switch to the same index, then no action is taken.

Note: The size of a bookmark buffer may change after a call to DbiSwitchToIndex.

A valid cursor handle must be obtained on a table, not on a query or an in-memory table. If the given index is not open, it is automatically opened by this function before switching to that index order. (Therefore, all error return codes for DbiOpenIndex apply.)

Switching the index may change some properties of the cursor, such as bookmark size. Existing bookmarks on the original cursor cannot be used in the new cursor, so any saved positions will no longer be applicable to the new cursor.

DBIResult Return Values

DBIERR_NONE	The index was successfully changed.
DBIERR_NOCURRREC	Cannot position to the current record because the original cursor is not positioned on a valid record. (Applicable only if bCurrRec is set to True.)
DBIERR_NOSUCHINDEX	No such index exists for the table.
DBIERR_INVALIDHNDL	The specified handle was invalid or NIL.
DBIERR_INDEXOUTOFDATE	An attempt was made to switch to a nonmaintained index that is out of date.

Example

```
function DetailLinkTest( oMaster, oDetail : TTable ) : Boolean;
var
  hCurDetail,
  hCurMaster   : hDBICur;
  wMastFields,
  wDetailFields : Word;
begin
  Result := False;
  try
    hCurMaster := GetTableCursor( oMaster );
    hCurDetail := GetTableCursor( oDetail );

    { Switch to the second index in Detail }
    Check( DbiSwitchToIndex( hCurDetail, nil, nil, 2, False ));
    Check( DbiBeginLinkMode( hCurMaster ));
    Check( DbiBeginLinkMode( hCurDetail ));
    wMastFields := 2;
    wDetailFields := 3;

    { Link the 2nd field of Master to the 3rd field of Details }
    Check( DbiLinkDetail( hCurMaster, hCurDetail, 1, @wMastFields,
                          @wDetailFields ));
    Result := True;
  except
    DbiUnlinkDetail( hCurDetail );
    DbiEndLinkMode( hCurMaster );
    DbiEndLinkMode( hCurDetail );
  end; { try .. except }
end; { DetailLinkTest() }
```

Pure Delphi Equivalent

TTable.IndexName

Xbase Equivalent

SET ORDER, dbSetOrder(), OrdSetFocus()

See Also

DbiAddIndex, DbiOpenIndex, DbiRegenIndex, DbiRegenIndexes, DbiOpenTable

DBITIMEDECODE

Declaration

```
function DbiTimeDecode (        { Decode TIME into components }
      timeT        : Time;      { Encoded Time }
var   iHour        : Word;      { Hours (0..23) }
```

```
var    iMin       : Word;     { Minutes (0..59) }
var    iMilSec    : Word      { Milliseconds (0..59999) }
  ): DBIResult;
```

Parameters

PARAMETER NAME	DESCRIPTION
timeT	The encoded time.
iHour	Reference to the client variable that receives the decoded hours. Valid values range from 0 through 23.
iMin	Reference to the client variable that receives the decoded minutes. Valid values range from 0 through 59.
iMilSec	Reference to the client variable that receives the decoded milliseconds. Valid values range from 0 through 59999.

Description

Decodes Time into separate components (hours, minutes, milliseconds), enabling the client application to interpret time values obtained from DbiGetField.

This function is a non-driver related service function and works for all drivers.

DBIResult Return Values

DBIERR_NONE	The time was decoded successfully.
DBIERR_INVALIDHNDL	The pointer to the decoded hours, minutes, or milliseconds is NIL.
DBIERR_INVALIDTIME	The specified encoded time is invalid.

Example

```
{===================================================================
   Function:
           FormatTime( tTime Time, PChar szTime )

   Input:  tTime    - Time that needs to be formatted
           szTime   - String to contain the formatted time

   Return: Result returned from DbiTimeDecode().

   Description.
           This function is used to format time fields according to
           the settings in the IDAPI.CFG file.
   =================================================================== }
function FormatTime( tTime: Time; szTime: PChar ): DBIResult;
var
   rslt    : DBIResult;        { Return value from BDE functions }
   timeFmt : FMTTime;          { Time format }
   uHour   : Word;             { Hour portion of the time }
   uMinute : Word;             { Minute portion of the time }
```

```
  uMilSec : Word;              { Second portion (in ms) of the time }
  uIsAM   : Word;              { Is Time AM? }
  szTemp  : Array[0..10] of Char;  { Temp buffer, used for AM, PM
                                     string }
  sHour, sMinute, sSec, sMilSec: String;
begin
  { Get the formatting of the Time }
  Check( DbiGetTimeFormat( timeFmt ));

  { Decode the time  }
  rslt := DbiTimeDecode( tTime, uHour, uMinute, uMilSec );

  { Make certain the seperator is not the escape character }
  if ( timeFmt.cTimeSeparator = '\' ) then
    timeFmt.cTimeSeparator  := '/';

  { Check if time should be displayed in 12- or 24-hour format }
  if ( timeFmt.bTwelveHour ) then
  begin
    { Temporary variable used to determine if the time is AM or PM }
    uIsAm := uHour;
    uHour := uHour mod 12;
    if (uHour = 0) then
      uHour := 12;
      { If AM, set uIsAm to TRUE, else set uIsAm to 0 }
      if (uIsAm = uHour) then
        uIsAm := 1
      else
        uIsAm := 0;
  end;
  Str( uHour:2, sHour );
  Str( uMinute:2, sMinute );
  Str( (round(uMilsec/1000)):2, sSec );
  Str( (round(uMilSec mod 1000)):2, sMilsec );

  { Format the hour and minute of the time }
  StrPCopy( szTime, sHour+timeFmt.cTimeSeparator+sMinute );

  { Determine if seconds are to be displayed }
  if (timeFmt.bSeconds) then
  begin
    StrPCopy(szTemp, timeFmt.cTimeSeparator+sSec);
    StrCat( szTime, szTemp );

    { Determine if milliseconds are to be displayed }
    if ( timeFmt.bMilSeconds ) then
    begin
      StrPCopy( szTemp, timeFmt.cTimeSeparator+sMilsec );
      StrCat( szTime, szTemp );
    end;
  end;

  { Add a string to the time if the time is 12 hour }
  if ( timeFmt.bTwelveHour ) then
  begin
```

```
        { Add a space to the format }
        StrCat( szTime, ' ' );

        { If AM }
        if (uIsAm = 1) then
          { Copy the AM string }
          StrCat( szTime, timeFmt.szAmString )
        else { otherwise it's PM }
          { Copy the PM string }
          StrCat( szTime, timeFmt.szPmString );
  end;
  FormatTime := rslt;
end;
```

Pure Delphi Equivalent

DecodeTime()

See Also

DbiTimeEncode, DbiDateDecode, DbiDateEncode, DbiTimeStampDecode, DbiTimeStampEncode

DBITIMEENCODE

Declaration

```
function DbiTimeEncode (      { Encode Time components into TIME }
      iHour      : Word;      { Hours (0..23) }
      iMin       : Word;      { Minutes (0..59) }
      iMilSec    : Word;      { Milliseconds (0..59999) }
var   timeT      : Time       { Encoded Time }
    ): DBIResult;
```

Parameters

PARAMETER NAME	DESCRIPTION
iHour	Specifies hours. Valid values range from 0 through 23.
iMin	Specifies minutes. Valid values range from 0 through 59.
iMilSec	Specifies milliseconds. Valid values range from 0 through 59999.
timeT	Reference to the client variable that receives the encoded time.

Description

Encodes separate time components into Time for use by DbiPutField and other functions, enabling the client application to construct a time value for use by DbiPutField.

This function is a nondriver-related service function and works for all drivers.

DBIResult Return Values

DBIERR_NONE	The time was successfully encoded.
DBIERR_INVALIDHNDL	timeT is NIL.
DBIERR_INVALIDTIME	Ranges of hour, minute, and millisecond Parameters are invalid.

Example

```
{ Generates and returns a random Time value }
function GetRandomTime: Time;
var
  tTime: Time;
  hour : Word;
  min  : Word;
  sec  : Word;
begin
  hour := random(23) + 1;
  min := random(59) + 1;
  sec := random(59999);
  Check( DbiTimeEncode( hour, min, sec, tTime ));
  GetRandomTime := tTime;
end;
```

Pure Delphi Equivalent

EncodeTime()

See Also

DbiDateEncode, DbiDateDecode, DbiTimeStampDecode, DbiTimeStampEncode, DbiPutField

DBITIMESTAMPDECODE

Declaration

```
function DbiTimeStampDecode ( { Decode Date & Time from Date+Time }
     tsTS      : TimeStamp; { Encoded Date+Time }
var  dateD     : Date;      { Encoded Date }
var  timeT     : Time       { Encoded Time }
   ): DBIResult;
```

Parameters

PARAMETER NAME	DESCRIPTION
tsTS	The encoded Date+Time timestamp.
dateD	Reference to the client variable that receives the encoded Date component.
timeT	Reference to the client variable that receives the encoded Time component.

Description

Extracts separate encoded Date and Time components from the TDateTime, enabling the client to interpret TDateTime values obtained from DbiGetField.

This function is a nondriver-related service function and works for all drivers.

DateDecode and TimeDecode must be called in order to further decode the date and time elements into their individual components (for Example, month, day, year/hours, minutes, milliseconds).

DBIResult Return Values

DBIERR_OK	The timestamp was successfully decoded.
DBIERR_INVALIDHNDL	dateD or timeT is NIL.

Example

```
function FormatTimeStamp( tStamp: TimeStamp; szTimeStamp: PChar): DBIResult;
var
  rslt  : DBIResult;    { Return value from IDAPI functions }
  tTime : Time;         { Time portion of the TimeStamp }
  dDate : Date;         { Date portion of the TimeStamp }
  szDate: PChar;        { Date string }
  szTime: pChar;        { Time string }
begin
  { Get the date and time components }
  rslt := Check( DbiTimeStampDecode( tStamp, dDate, tTime ));
  GetMem( szDate, 16 * SizeOf( Char ));
  GetMem( szTime, 21 * SizeOf( Char ));

  { Get the Date format }
  FormatDate( dDate, szDate );      {See DbiDateDecode Example}

  { Get the Time format }
  FormatTime( tTime, szTime );      {See DbiTimeDecode Example}

  { Format the TimeStamp }
  szTime := StrCat( szTime, ', ' );
  StrCopy( szTimeStamp, StrCat( szTime, szDate ));
  FormatTimeStamp := rslt;
end;
```

Pure Delphi Equivalent

DecodeDate(), DecodeTime()

See Also

DbiTimeStampEncode, DbiGetField

DBITIMESTAMPENCODE

Declaration

```
function DbiTimeStampEncode ( { Encode Date & Time into Date+Time }
     dateD       : Date;       { Encoded Date }
     timeT       : Time;       { Encoded Time }
var  tsTS        : TimeStamp   { Encoded Date+Time }
   ): DBIResult;
```

Parameters

PARAMETER NAME	DESCRIPTION
dateD	The encoded date.
timeT	The encoded time.
tsTS	Reference to the client variable that receives the encoded timestamp.

Description

Encodes the encoded Date and encoded Time into a TDateTime, enabling the client application to construct a TDateTime value for use in *DbiPutField*.

This function is a nondriver-related service function and works for all drivers.

DBIResult Return Values

DBIERR_NONE	The timestamp was successfully encoded.
DBIERR_INVALIDHNDL	tsTS is NIL.
DBIERR_INVALIDTIMESTAMP	The range of date and time Parameters is invalid.

Example

```
{=================================================================
  Function:
          FormatTimeStamp( tStamp, szTime )

  Input:  tStamp   - Time that needs to be formatted
          szTime   - String to contain the formatted time

  Return: Result returned from DbiTimeStampDecode().

  Description.
          This function is used to format TimeStamp fields
          according to the settings in the IDAPI.CFG file. It
          calls the FormatDate and FormatTime functions, which can
          be found in the Example code for DbiDateDecode and
          DbiTimeDecode, respectively.
  ================================================================ }
```

```
function FormatTimeStamp( tStamp: TimeStamp; szTimeStamp: PChar):
DBIResult;
var
  rslt    : DBIResult;    { Return value from BDE functions }
  tTime   : Time;         { Time portion of the TimeStamp }
  dDate   : Date;         { Date portion of the TimeStamp }
  szDate  : PChar;        { Date string }
  szTime  : PChar;        { Time String }
begin
  { Get the date and time components }
  rslt := DbiTimeStampDecode( tStamp, dDate, tTime );
  GetMem( szDate, 16 * SizeOf(Char));
  GetMem( szTime, 21 * SizeOf(Char));

  { Get the Date format }
  FormatDate( dDate, szDate );

  { Get the Time format }
  FormatTime( tTime, szTime );

  { Format the TimeStamp }
  szTime := StrCat( szTime,', ' );
  StrCopy( szTimeStamp, Strcat( szTime, szDate ));
  FormatTimeStamp := rslt;
end;
```

Pure Delphi Equivalent

EncodeDate(), EncodeTime()

See Also

DbiTimeStampDecode, DbiPutField

DBITRANSLATEFIELD

Declaration

```
function DbiTranslateField (     { Translate a field }
    hXlt        : hDBIXlt;       { Translation handle }
    pSrc        : Pointer;       { Source field }
    pDest       : Pointer;       { Destination field }
  ): DBIResult;
```

Parameters

PARAMETER NAME	DESCRIPTION
hXlt	The translate handle.
pSrc	Pointer to the source field.
pDest	Pointer to the destination field.

Description

Translates a logical or physical field value to any compatible logical or physical field value.

SQL. This function can be used only on fields that are contained with a valid SQL record buffer. The translation object must be built using a BDE-supplied field descriptor because each field descriptor contains an offset to a NIL indicator, and each field translation must read or write this NIL indicator. The offset from the field buffer to the NIL indicator is stored when the translation object is built.

DBIResult Return Values

DBIERR_NONE	The field was translated successfully.

Example

```
function FieldTranslate( hCur : hDBICur; hXlt : hDBIXlt;
                         pTransField : pBYTE ) : DBIResult;
var
  pFieldBuf,
  pRecBuf      : pBYTE;
  CursorProps : CURProps;
  bBlank       : Bool;
begin
  Result := DBIERR_NONE + 1;
  bBlank := False;
  try
    Check( DbiGetCursorProps( hCur, CursorProps ));
    GetMem( pRecBuf, CursorProps.iRecBufSize );
    GetMem( pFieldBuf, 1024 );
    GetMem( pTransField, 1024 );
    Check( DbiSetToBegin( hCur ) );
    Check( DbiGetNextRecord( hCur, dbiNOLOCK, pRecBuf, nil ));
    Check( DbiGetField( hCur, 1, pRecBuf, pFieldBuf, bBlank ));
    Result := DbiTranslateField( hXlt, pFieldBuf, pTransField );
  finally
    FreeMem( pRecBuf );
    FreeMem( pFieldBuf );
    FreeMem( pTransField );
  end; { try .. finally }
end; { FieldTranslate() }
```

See Also

DbiOpenFieldXlt, DbiCloseFieldXlt

DBITRANSLATERECORDSTRUCTURE

Declaration

```
function DbiTranslateRecordStructure (  { Translate a record }
    pszSrcDriverType : PChar;     { Source driver type }
```

```
         iFlds              : Word;      { Number of fields }
         pfldsSrc           : pFLDDesc;  { Array of source fields }
         pszDstDriverType   : PChar;     { Destination driver type }
         pszLangDriver      : PChar;     { Lang driver for destination }
         pfldsDst           : pFLDDesc   { Array of dest flds returned }
       ): DBIResult;
```

Parameters

Parameter Name	Description
pszSrcDriverType	Pointer to the source driver type. If NIL, it is assumed that the source fields are logical.
iFlds	The number of fields.
pfldsSrc	Pointer to an array of the logical or physical types of the source fields.
pszDstDriverType	Optional pointer to the destination driver type. If NIL, it is assumed that the destination fields are logical.
pszLangDriver	Pointer to the destination drivers language driver name. This language driver is used to validate the destination field names after the translation.
pfldsDst	Pointer to an array of the destination fields.

Description

Takes the logical or physical fields of the source driver and attempts to map them to equivalent logical or physical fields of the destination driver. If an exact match is not found, the function attempts to map to the closest possible logical or physical fields of the destination driver. If a close match is not found, this returns the error DBIERR_NOTSUPPORTED.

DBIResult Return Values

DBIERR_NONE	The translation was successfully completed.
DBIERR_NOTSUPPORTED	Returned if source fields cannot be translated into equivalent destination fields.

Example

```
procedure TTempTable.CreateTable;
var
  I, J            : Integer;
  FieldDescs      : PFLDDesc;
  ValCheckPtr     : PVCHKDesc;
  DriverTypeName: DBINAME;
  TableDesc       : CRTblDesc;
begin
  CheckInactive;
  if FieldDefs.Count = 0 then
    for I := 0 to FieldCount - 1 do
      with Fields[I] do
        if not Calculated then
```

```
        FieldDefs.Add( FieldName, DataType, Size, Required );
FieldDescs := nil;
FillChar( TableDesc, SizeOf( TableDesc ), 0 );
with TableDesc do
begin
  SetDBFlag(dbfTable, True);
  try
    AnsiToNative( Locale, TableName, szTblName,
                  SizeOf( szTblName ) - 1 );
    iFldCount := FieldDefs.Count;
    FieldDescs := AllocMem(iFldCount * SizeOf(FLDDesc));
    for I := 0 to FieldDefs.Count - 1 do
      with FieldDefs[I] do
      begin
        EncodeFieldDesc( PFieldDescList( FieldDescs )^[I], Name,
                         DataType, Size );
        if Required then Inc( iValChkCount );
      end;
    pFldDesc := AllocMem( iFldCount * SizeOf( FLDDesc ));
    Check( DbiTranslateRecordStructure( nil, iFldCount,
                        FieldDescs, nil, nil, pFLDDesc ));
    iIdxCount := IndexDefs.Count;
    pIdxDesc := AllocMem( iIdxCount * SizeOf( IDXDesc ));
    for I := 0 to IndexDefs.Count - 1 do
      with IndexDefs[I] do
        EncodeIndexDesc( PIndexDescList( pIdxDesc )^[I], Name,
                         Fields, Options );
    if iValChkCount <> 0 then
    begin
      pVChkDesc := AllocMem( iValChkCount * SizeOf( VCHKDesc ));
      ValCheckPtr := pVChkDesc;
      for I := 0 to FieldDefs.Count - 1 do
        if FieldDefs[I].Required then
        begin
          ValCheckPtr^.iFldNum := I + 1;
          ValCheckPtr^.bRequired := True;
          Inc( ValCheckPtr );
        end;
    end;
    Check( DbiCreateTempTable( DBHandle, TableDesc, hCursor ));
    Check( DbiSetProp( hDBIObj( hCursor ), curXLTMODE,
                                   LongInt( xltFIELD )));
  finally
    if pVChkDesc <> nil then FreeMem( pVChkDesc, iValChkCount *
                                SizeOf( VCHKDesc ));
    if pIdxDesc <> nil then FreeMem( pIdxDesc, iIdxCount *
                                SizeOf( IDXDesc ));
    if pFldDesc <> nil then FreeMem( pFldDesc, iFldCount *
                                SizeOf( FLDDesc ));
    if FieldDescs <> nil then FreeMem( FieldDescs, iFldCount *
                                SizeOf( FLDDesc ));
    SetDBFlag( dbfTable, False );
  end;
```

```
  end;
end;
```

DbiTruncateBlob

Declaration

```
function DbiTruncateBlob (          { Reduces the blob size }
     hCursor       : hDBICur;       { Cursor handle }
     pRecBuf       : Pointer;       { Record Buffer }
     iField        : Word;          { Field number of blob (1..n) }
     iLen          : Longint        { New BLOB length }
  ): DBIResult;
```

Parameters

Parameter Name	Description
hCursor	The cursor handle.
pRecBuf	Pointer to the record buffer.
iField	The ordinal number of BLOB field within the record buffer.
iLen	The new shorter length of the BLOB. If zero is specified, the whole BLOB is truncated.

Description

Shortens the size of the contents of a BLOB field or deletes the contents of a BLOB field from the record by shortening it to zero. This is the only way to delete a BLOB without deleting the entire record. The BLOB field must be open in dbiREADWRITE mode by a call to DbiOpenBlob.

Standard. It is advisable to lock the record before opening the BLOB in read-write mode to ensure that another client application does not lock the record.

After shortening the BLOB field, DbiModifyRecord must be called to post the altered record to the table.

DBIResult Return Values

DBIERR_NONE	The BLOB field was successfully truncated.
DBIERR_BLOBNOTOPENED	The specified BLOB field was not opened via a call to DbiOpenBlob.
DBIERR_INVALIDBLOBHANDLE	The BLOB handle supplied in the record buffer is invalid.
DBIERR_NOTABLOB	The specified field number does not correspond to a BLOB field.
DBIERR_INVALIDBLOBOFFSET	The specified iOffSet is greater than the length of the BLOB field.
DBIERR_READONLYFLD	The BLOB field was opened in dbiREADONLY mode and cannot be modified.

Example

```
{ Truncates the specified BLOB field to zero length. Then commits the changes
  and releases any record lock (if Shared mode) }
```

```
procedure TruncateBlob( oTable : TTable; pRec : Pointer; iFieldNo : Word );
begin
  if oTable.Active then
  begin
    try
      Check( DbiOpenBlob( oTable.Handle, pRec, iFieldNo,
                          dbiREADWRITE ));
      Check( DbiTruncateBlob( oTable.Handle, pRec, iFieldNo, 0 ));
      Check( DbiModifyRecord( oTable.Handle, pRec, True ));
    finally
      if Assigned( pRec ) then
        Check( DbiFreeBlob( oTable.Handle, pRec, iFieldNo ));
    end;
  end;
end;
```

Pure Delphi Equivalent

TBlobStream.Truncate

Xbase Equivalent

REPLACE

See Also

DbiGetBlob, DbiOpenBlob, DbiPutBlob, DbiFreeBlob, DbiModifyRecord

DBIUNDELETERECORD

Declaration

```
function DbiUndeleteRecord (      { Undeletes the current record }
    hCursor      : hDBICur        { Cursor handle }
  ): DBIResult;
```

Parameters

PARAMETER NAME	DESCRIPTION
hCursor	The dBASE cursor handle.

Description

Undeletes, or "recalls," a dBASE record that has been marked for deletion (a soft delete). This function is supported with dBASE tables only. The cursor must be positioned on a record. The cursor must have the property bDeletedOn set to True.

DBIResult Return Values

DBIERR_NONE	The dBASE record was successfully undeleted.
DBIERR_INVALIDHNDL	The specified cursor handle is invalid or NIL.
DBIERR_BOF	The cursor is positioned on the crack at the beginning of the file.
DBIERR_EOF	The cursor is positioned on the crack at the end of the file.
DBIERR_NA	The specified record was not deleted; cannot undelete the record.
DBIERR_TABLEREADONLY	The specified table is read-only; cannot undelete the record.
DBIERR_FILELOCKED	The table is locked by another user; cannot undelete the record.
DBIERR_NOTSUPPORTED	The function is supported only for dBASE tables.
DBIERR_NOCURRREC	The cursor is not positioned on a valid record.

Example

```
function GetTableCursor( oTable : TTable ) : hDBICur;
var
  szTable : Array[0..78] of Char;
begin
  StrPCopy( szTable, oTable.TableName );
  DbiGetCursorForTable( oTable.DBHandle, szTable, nil, Result );
end; { GetTableCursor() }

function dbRecall( oTable : TTable ) : Boolean;
begin
  Result := IsDbiOk( DbiUndeleteRecord( GetTableCursor( oTable )));
end; { dbRecall() }
```

Xbase Equivalent

RECALL

See Also

DbiDeleteRecord, DbiPackTable

DBIUNLINKDETAIL

Declaration

```
function DbiUnlinkDetail (        { Unlink detail from master }
    hDetlCursor   : hDBICur    { Detail cursor to unlink }
  ): DBIResult;
```

Parameters

PARAMETER NAME	DESCRIPTION
hDetlCursor	The detail cursor handle.

Description

Removes the link from a detail cursor and its master. Links should be removed before calling DbiEndLinkMode. The cursors will no longer be related to each other but will remain in the linked cursor mode.

A call to DbiLinkDetail or DbiLinkDetailToExp must be made prior to calling DbiUnlinkDetail.

DBIResult Return Values

DBIERR_NONE	The link between the detail and master cursors was removed successfully.
DBIERR_INVALIDHNDL	The specified cursor handle is invalid or NIL.

Example

```
{ The ExpressionLength function used in this Example can be found in
  BDEREF.PAS on the included CD-ROM at the back of the book. This
  ExpressionLength function utilizes the incredibly cool ExtractFields,
  StringToStringList, and AllTrim functions, which are also found in that
  same file.}

function BreakTheLink( oMaster, oDetail : TTable ) : Boolean;
var
  hMaster,
  hDetail : hDBICur;
begin
  Result := False;
  try
    hMaster := GetTableCursor( oMaster );
    hDetail := GetTableCursor( oDetail );
    if DbiUnlinkDetail( hDetail ) = DBIERR_NONE then
    begin
      DbiEndLinkMode( hMaster );
      DbiEndLinkMode( hDetail );
      oDetail.CursorPosChanged;
      oDetail.Refresh;
      Result := True;
    end;
    except
    Result := False;
    end;
end; { BreakTheLink() }

function MakeTheLink( oMaster, oDetail : TTable; sExp : String ) : Boolean;
var
  hMaster,
  hDetail  : hDBICur;
  szExp    : DBIMsg;
  iLen     : Integer;
begin
  Result := False;
```

```
try
  { You may want to break any existing link before doing this }
  BreakTheLink( oMaster, oDetail );
  hMaster := GetTableCursor( oMaster );
  hDetail := GetTableCursor( oDetail );
  if IsDbiOk( DbiBeginLinkMode( hMaster )) and
     IsDbiOk( DbiBeginLinkMode( hDetail )) then
  begin
    StrPCopy( szExp, sExp );
    iLen := ExpressionLength( oMaster, sExp );
    DbiLinkDetailToExp( hMaster, hDetail, iLen, szExp );
    DbiSetToBegin( hDetail );
    oDetail.First; { Go to first record in set }
    Result := True;
  end; { if links can be set }
except
  Result := False;
end;
end; { MakeTheLink() }
```

Pure Delphi Equivalent

TTable.MasterField := ''

See Also

DbiLinkDetail, DbiLinkDetailToExp, DbiBeginLinkMode, DbiEndLinkMode

DBIUSEIDLETIME

Declaration

```
function DbiUseIdleTime: DBIResult;   { Use Idle time }
```

DBIResult Return Values

DBIERR_NONE	This function always returns DBIERR_NONE.

Description

Allows the BDE to accomplish background tasks during times when the client application is idle.

This function is primarily used for writing dirty buffers to disk. This can make the client application more reliable during power failure or machine lockups in another application (recoverable by Ctrl+Alt+Delete). Likewise, client applications can set up a timer and call this function periodically when the timer event is generated.

Example

IsDbiOk(DbiUseIdleTime);

DBIVALIDATEPROP (DELPHI 2.0 ONLY)

Declaration

```
function DbiValidateProp(    { Validate a property for an object }
    hObj      : hDBIObj;   { Object handle }
    iProp     : Longint;   { Property to validate }
    bSetting  : Bool       { Get or set property? }
): DBIResult stdcall;
```

Parameters

PARAMETER NAME	DESCRIPTION
hObj	The object handle.
iProp	The property ID to validate for the passed object handle.
bBlank	Reference to the client variable that is set to True if the field is blank; otherwise, it is set to False.

Description

This routine validates a property for a given object handle. You can use it to determine whether a given property can be changed or retrieved from the provided object handle.

DBIResult Return Values

DBIERR_NONE	The data meet all the requirements for the specified field.
DBIERR_NOTSUPPORTED	The property is invalid for the given object.

Example

Example on the CD-ROM at the back of the book.

See Also

DbiOpenTable, DbiPutField, DbiInsertRecord, DbiModifyRecord, DbiAppendRecord

DBIVERIFYFIELD

Declaration

```
function DbiVerifyField (        { Verifies the field value }
    hCursor   : hDBICur;      { Cursor handle }
    iField    : Word;         { Field # (1..n) }
    pSrc      : Pointer;      { Field Value }
var bBlank    : Bool          { Field is Blank (Returned) }
    ): DBIResult;
```

Parameters

PARAMETER NAME	DESCRIPTION
hCursor	The cursor handle.
iField	The ordinal number of the field in the record.
pSrc	Pointer to the buffer containing the data to be verified. If NIL, the function verifies whether a blank value is allowed.
bBlank	Reference to the client variable that is set to True if the field is blank; otherwise, it is set to False.

Description

Verifies that the data specified in pSrc is a valid data type for the field specified by iField, and that all validity checks specified for the field are satisfied. It can also be used to check if a field is blank.

If the field is blank, the variable pointed to by bBlank is set to True. If any field-level validity check has failed, an error message is returned, indicating which type of validity check the field has failed.

If the translation mode of the cursor is xltFIELD, pSrc is assumed to contain field data in BDE logical format; otherwise, it is considered to be the drivers physical format.

Using the validity-checking abilities of this function enables the client application to report errors without actually attempting to write the data. It can also be used to check if a field is blank. If pSrc is NIL, the function verifies whether or not a blank value is allowed.

DbiVerifyField is not supported with BLOB fields.

dBASE. For dBASE tables, this function can be used only to determine if a field is blank.

Paradox. For Paradox tables, this function evaluates field-level validity checks; it does not evaluate referential integrity constraints.

DBIResult Return Values

DBIERR_NONE	The data meet all the requirements for the specified field.
DBIERR_MINVALERR	The data are less than the required minimum value.
DBIERR_MAXVALERR	The data are greater than the required maximum value.
DBIERR_REQDERR	The field cannot be blank.
DBIERR_LOOKUPTABLEERR	The value cannot be located in the assigned look-up table.

Example

```
procedure VerifyFieldNumberTen;
var
  rslt     : DBIResult;
  lVal     : Longint;
  bIsBlank : Bool;
begin
```

```
{ Get proposed value from user input }
lVal := StrToInt( Edit1.Text );
rslt := DbiVerifyField( Table1.Handle, 10, @lVal, bIsBlank );

case rslt of
  DBIERR_NONE:
  ShowMessage( 'The data meets all the requirements for ' +
               'the specified field.' );
  DBIERR_MINVALERR:
  ShowMessage( 'The data is less than the required ' + 'minimum value.' );
  DBIERR_MAXVALERR:
  ShowMessage( 'The data is greater than the required ' +
               'maximum value.' );
  DBIERR_REQDERR:
  ShowMessage( 'The field cannot be blank.' ); DBIERR_LOOKUPTABLEERR:
  ShowMessage( 'The value cannot be located in the ' +
               'assigned look-up table.' );
  end;
end;
```

See Also

DbiOpenTable, DbiPutField, DbiInsertRecord, DbiModifyRecord, DbiAppendRecord

DBIWRITEBLOCK

Declaration

```
function DbiWriteBlock (        { Write a block of records }
      hCursor     : hDBICur; { Cursor handle }
var   iRecords    : Longint; { Number of records to write/written }
      pBuf        : Pointer  { Buffer }
   ): DBIResult;
```

Parameters

PARAMETER NAME	DESCRIPTION
hCursor	The cursor handle to the table.
iRecords	On input, iRecords is a reference to the client variable containing the number of records to be written. On output, it is a reference to the client variable that receives the actual number of records written. The number actually written may be less than requested if an integrity violation or other error occurred.
pBuf	Pointer to the buffer containing the records to be written.

Description

Writes a block of records to the table associated with hCursor. This function is similar to calling DbiAppendRecord for the specified number of iRecords.

After the operation completes, the cursor will be positioned at the last record that was inserted.

Paradox. This function verifies any referential integrity requirements or validity checks that may be in place. If either fails, the write operation is canceled.

Note: This function does not work for records containing nonempty BLOBs.

DBIResult Return Values

DBIERR_NONE	The block of records contained in pBuf has been successfully written to the table specified by hCursor.
DBIERR_INVALIDHNDL	The specified cursor handle is invalid or NIL, or iRecords is NIL, or pBuf is NIL.
DBIERR_TABLEREADONLY	The table is opened read-only; cannot write to it.
DBIERR_NOTSUFFTABLERIGHTS	Insufficient table rights to insert a record (Paradox only).
DBIERR_NODISKSPACE	Insertion failed due to insufficient disk space.

Example

```
{ Requires WinCRT in the 'uses' section }
procedure BlockCopy( hSource, hDest: hDBICUR; lRecsToCopy: Longint );
var
  rslt       : DBIResult;           { Return value from BDE functions }
  CurProp    : CURProps;            { Properties of the Cursor }
  pRecBuf    : Pointer;             { Pointer to the record buffer }
  iRecNo     : Integer;             { Loop counter - current record number }
  iRecOffset : Integer;             { Offset into the block of records }
  DestBuf    : Array[0..20] of Char; { New field value to write to the table }
  TempBuf    : Array[0..20] of Char; { Field value read from table }
  bBlank     : Bool;                { Contains True if a field is blank }
begin
  WriteLn('*** Block Read/Write Example ***');
  WriteLn('');

  { Get the size of the record buffer }
  Check( DbiGetCursorProps( hSource, CurProp ));

  { Allocate space for the Record Buffer }
  GetMem( pRecBuf, CurProp.iRecBufSize * SizeOf( Byte ) *lRecsToCopy );
  if not Assigned( pRecBuf ) then
  begin
    WriteLn(' Error - Out of memory.');
    exit;
  end;

  WriteLn(' Go to the beginning of the source table...');
  Check( DbiSetToBegin( hSource ));

  WriteLn(' Read 10 records from the source table...');
  rslt := DbiReadBlock( hSource, lRecsToCopy, pRecBuf );

  { Getting an EOF error is ok - just means that an attempt was
    made to read more records than are currently in the table. }
```

```
if ((rslt <> DBIERR_EOF) and (rslt <> DBIERR_NONE)) then
begin
  Check( rslt );
end;

for iRecNo := 1 to lRecsToCopy do
begin
  { Calculate the record offset. }
  iRecOffset := (iRecNo-1) * CurProp.iRecBufSize;

  { Get the value in the second field for each record }
  Check( DbiGetField( hSource, 2, PChar( pRecBuf ) + iRecOffset,
                      @TempBuf, bBlank ));

  { UpperCase field #2 buffer }
  StrPCopy( DestBuf, UpperCase( StrPas( TempBuf )));

  { Update the buffer value }
  Check( DbiPutField( hSource, 2, PChar( pRecBuf ) + iRecOffset,
                      @DestBuf ));

  WriteLn(' Modified record ' + IntToStr( iRecNo ) +
          ' with field #2 as "' + StrPas( DestBuf ) + '"' );
end;

{ Write lRecsToCopy records to the table }
WriteLn('');
WriteLn(' Writing 10 records to the destination table...');
Check( DbiWriteBlock( hDest, lRecsToCopy, pRecBuf ));

{ Release allocated memory }
FreeMem( pRecBuf, CurProp.iRecBufSize * SizeOf( Byte ) *
                                        lRecsToCopy );

WriteLn('');
WriteLn('*** End of Example ***');
end;
```

Pure Delphi Equivalent

BlockWrite

See Also

DbiReadBlock, DbiAppendRecord, DbiInsertRecord

BDE Error Return Codes

Each BDE function returns an error code indicating either success (DBIERR_NONE) or failure (anything else). The error description attached to those anything else's is what gives the developer a clue as to the exact cause of the failure within their application.

DUMPING ALL ERROR CODES AND MESSAGES TO A FILE

The following code snippet, used in this case with a TButton control, will roll through all the error categories and types, passing the resulting calculated error value to DbiGetErrorString. This function returns the description string associated with the specified error code. This description string, along with the original error code (in both decimal and hex representations), is then written out to a text file called **BDE_ERRS.TXT**. Any error code value that results in a null string return value from DbiGetErrString is omitted from the **BDE_ERRS.TXT** file.

In Delphi 1.0, be sure to include DbiProcs, DbiTypes, and DbiErrs to the uses section of the unit. For Delphi 2.0, simply include the Bde unit.

```
procedure TForm1.Button1Click(Sender: TObject);
var
  F: TextFile;
  OutString: String;
  ErrCat, SubCode: Byte;
  Code: Word;
  ErrString: Array[0..DBIMAXMSGLEN + 1] of Char;
begin
  DbiInit( nil );
  AssignFile( F, 'BDE_ERRS.TXT' );
  Rewrite( F );
  Screen.Cursor := crHourGlass;
  for ErrCat := ERRCAT_NONE to ERRCAT_RC do
    for SubCode := 0 to 255 do
    begin
      Code := SubCode + (ErrCat shl 8);
      DbiGetErrorString( Code, ErrString );
      if StrLen( ErrString ) > 0 then
      begin
        OutString := Format( '%6d : $%0.4x : %s', [Code, Code, ErrString] );
        WriteLn( F, OutString );
      end;
```

```
    end;
  CloseFile( F );
  Screen.Cursor := crDefault;
  DbiExit;
end;
```

This code should produce a text file that begins something, if not exactly, like this:

```
 0 : $0000 : Successful completion
33 : $0021 : System Error
34 : $0022 : Object of Interest Not Found
35 : $0023 : Physical Data Corruption
36 : $0024 : I/O Related Error
37 : $0025 : Resource or Limit Error
38 : $0026 : Data Integrity Violation
39 : $0027 : Invalid Request
40 : $0028 : Lock Violation
41 : $0029 : Access/Security Violation
42 : $002A : Invalid Context
43 : $002B : OS Error
44 : $002C : Network Error
45 : $002D : Optional Parameter
46 : $002E : Query Processor
47 : $002F : Version Mismatch
48 : $0030 : Capability Not Supported
49 : $0031 : System Configuration Error
50 : $0032 : Warning
51 : $0033 : Miscellaneous
52 : $0034 : Compatibility Error
62 : $003E : Driver Specific Error
63 : $003F : Internal Symbol
   .
   . {And so on...}
   .
```

Now, whenever Borland releases new maintenance updates for Delphi, you can just run this code with the new version, and it will produce an updated BDE error message list for you. This will ensure that your list of BDE error messages is always accurate and up to date.

ERRORS CODES BY CATEGORY

The following is an accurate listing of the current BDE error return codes and messages, under Delphi 1.02, separated into categories. Included in the list are the return code constant, the actual code value in both decimal and hex formats, and the description of the error.

No Error (Success)

DBIERR_NONE	0	$0000	Successful completion of operation.

System Errors

DBIERR_SYSFILEOPEN	8449	$2101	Cannot open a system file.
DBIERR_SYSFILEIO	8450	$2102	I/O error on a system file.
DBIERR_SYSCORRUPT	8451	$2103	Data structure corruption.
DBIERR_NOCONFIGFILE	8452	$2104	Cannot find Engine configuration file.
DBIERR_CFGCANNOTWRITE	8453	$2105	Cannot write to Engine configuration file.
DBIERR_CFGMULTIFILE	8454	$2106	Cannot initialize with different configuration file.
DBIERR_REENTERED	8455	$2107	System has been illegally reentered.
DBIERR_CANTFINDODAPI	8456	$2108	Cannot locate IDAPI01.DLL.
DBIERR_CANTLOADODAPI	8457	$2109	Cannot load IDAPI01.DLL.
DBIERR_CANTLOADLIBRARY	8458	$210A	Cannot load an IDAPI service library.

Object of Interest Not Found

DBIERR_BOF	8705	$2201	At beginning of table.
DBIERR_EOF	8706	$2202	At end of table.
DBIERR_RECMOVED	8707	$2203	Record moved because key value changed.
DBIERR_RECDELETED	8708	$2204	Record deleted.
DBIERR_KEYORRECDELETED	8708	$2204	Record or Key deleted.
DBIERR_NOCURRREC	8709	$2205	No current record.
DBIERR_RECNOTFOUND	8710	$2206	Could not find record.
DBIERR_ENDOFBLOB	8711	$2207	End of BLOB.
DBIERR_OBJNOTFOUND	8712	$2208	Could not find object.
DBIERR_FMLMEMBERNOTFOUND	8713	$2209	Could not find family member.
DBIERR_BLOBFILEMISSING	8714	$220A	BLOB file is missing.
DBIERR_LDNOTFOUND	8715	$220B	Could not find language driver.

Physical Data Corruption Errors

DBIERR_HEADERCORRUPT	8961	$2301	Corrupt table/index header.
DBIERR_FILECORRUPT	8962	$2302	Corrupt file—other than header.
DBIERR_MEMOCORRUPT	8963	$2303	Corrupt Memo/BLOB file.
DBIERR_BMPCORRUPT	8964	$2304	Corrupt bitmap (internal error).
DBIERR_INDEXCORRUPT	8965	$2305	Corrupt index.
DBIERR_CORRUPTLOCKFILE	8966	$2306	Corrupt lock file.
DBIERR_FAMFILEINVALID	8967	$2307	Corrupt family file.
DBIERR_VALFILECORRUPT	8968	$2308	Corrupt or missing .VAL file.
DBIERR_FOREIGNINDEX	8969	$2309	Foreign index file format.

File I/O Related Errors

DBIERR_READERR	9217	$2401	Read failure.
DBIERR_WRITEERR	9218	$2402	Write failure.
DBIERR_DIRNOACCESS	9219	$2403	Cannot access directory.
DBIERR_FILEDELETEFAIL	9220	$2404	File Delete operation failed.
DBIERR_FILENOACCESS	9221	$2405	Cannot access file.
DBIERR_ACCESSDISABLED	9222	$2406	Access to table disabled because of previous error.

Resource or Limit Errors

DBIERR_NOMEMORY	9473	$2501	Insufficient memory for this operation.
DBIERR_NOFILEHANDLES	9474	$2502	Not enough file handles.
DBIERR_NODISKSPACE	9475	$2503	Insufficient disk space.
DBIERR_NOTEMPTBLSPACE	9476	$2504	Temporary table resource limit.
DBIERR_RECTOOBIG	9477	$2505	Record size is too big for table.
DBIERR_CURSORLIMIT	9478	$2506	Too many open cursors.
DBIERR_TABLEFULL	9479	$2507	Table is full.
DBIERR_WSSESLIMIT	9480	$2508	Too many sessions from this workstation.
DBIERR_SERNUMLIMIT	9481	$2509	Serial number limit (Paradox).
DBIERR_INTERNALLIMIT	9482	$250A	Some internal limit (see context).
DBIERR_OPENTBLLIMIT	9483	$250B	Too many open tables.
DBIERR_TBLCURSORLIMIT	9484	$250C	Too many cursors per table.
DBIERR_RECLOCKLIMIT	9485	$250D	Too many record locks on table.
DBIERR_CLIENTSLIMIT	9486	$250E	Too many clients.
DBIERR_INDEXLIMIT	9487	$250F	Too many indexes on table.
DBIERR_SESSIONSLIMIT	9488	$2510	Too many sessions.
DBIERR_DBLIMIT	9489	$2511	Too many open databases.
DBIERR_PASSWORDLIMIT	9490	$2512	Too many passwords.
DBIERR_DRIVERLIMIT	9491	$2513	Too many active drivers.
DBIERR_FLDLIMIT	9492	$2514	Too many fields in Table Create.
DBIERR_TBLLOCKLIMIT	9493	$2515	Too many table locks.
DBIERR_OPENBLOBLIMIT	9494	$2516	Too many open BLOBs.
DBIERR_LOCKFILELIMIT	9495	$2517	Lock file has grown too large.
DBIERR_OPENQRYLIMIT	9496	$2518	Too many open queries.
DBIERR_THREADLIMIT	9497	$2519	Too many threads for client.
DBIERR_BLOBLIMIT	9498	$251A	Too many BLOBs.

Data Integrity Violation Errors

DBIERR_KEYVIOL	9729	$2601	Key violation.
DBIERR_MINVALERR	9730	$2602	Minimum validity check failed.
DBIERR_MAXVALERR	9731	$2603	Maximum validity check failed.
DBIERR_REQDERR	9732	$2604	Field value required.
DBIERR_FOREIGNKEYERR	9733	$2605	Master record missing.
DBIERR_DETAILRECORDSEXIST	9734	$2606	Master has detail records. Cannot delete or modify.
DBIERR_MASTERTBLLEVEL	9735	$2607	Master table level is incorrect.
DBIERR_LOOKUPTABLEERR	9736	$2608	Field value out of lookup table range.
DBIERR_LOOKUPTBLOPENERR	9737	$2609	Lookup Table Open operation failed.
DBIERR_DETAILTBLOPENERR	9738	$260A	Detail Table Open operation failed.
DBIERR_MASTERTBLOPENERR	9739	$260B	Master Table Open operation failed.
DBIERR_FIELDISBLANK	9740	$260C	Field is blank.
DBIERR_MASTEREXISTS	9741	$260D	Link to master table already defined.
DBIERR_MASTERTBLOPEN	9742	$260E	Master table is open.
DBIERR_DETAILTABLESEXIST	9743	$260F	Detail table(s) exist.
DBIERR_DETAILRECEXISTEMPTY	9744	$2610	Master has detail records. Cannot empty it.
DBIERR_MASTERREFERENCEERR	9745	$2611	Self-referencing ref-erential integrity must be entered one at a time with no other changes to the table.
DBIERR_DETAILTBLOPEN	9746	$2612	Detail table is open.
DBIERR_DEPENDENTSMUSTBEEMPTY	9747	$2613	Cannot make this master a detail of another table if its details are not empty.
DBIERR_RINTREQINDEX	9748	$2614	Referential integrity fields must be indexed.
DBIERR_LINKEDTBLPROTECTED	9749	$2615	A table linked by referential integrity requires password to open.
DBIERR_FIELDMULTILINKED	9750	$2616	Field(s) linked to more than one master.

Invalid Request Errors

DBIERR_OUTOFRANGE	9985	$2701	Number is out of range.
DBIERR_INVALIDPARAM	9986	$2702	Invalid parameter.
DBIERR_INVALIDFILENAME	9987	$2703	Invalid file name.
DBIERR_NOSUCHFILE	9988	$2704	File does not exist.
DBIERR_INVALIDOPTION	9989	$2705	Invalid option.
DBIERR_INVALIDHNDL	9990	$2706	Invalid handle to the function.
DBIERR_UNKNOWNTBLTYPE	9991	$2707	Unknown table type.

continued

DBIERR_UNKNOWNFILE	9992	$2708	Cannot open file.
DBIERR_PRIMARYKEYREDEFINE	9993	$2709	Cannot redefine primary key.
DBIERR_INVALIDRINTDESCNUM	9994	$270A	Cannot change this RINTDesc.
DBIERR_KEYFLDTYPEMISMATCH	9995	$270B	Foreign and primary key do not match.
DBIERR_INVALIDMODIFYREQUEST	9996	$270C	Invalid modify request.
DBIERR_NOSUCHINDEX	9997	$270D	Index does not exist.
DBIERR_INVALIDBLOBOFFSET	9998	$270E	Invalid offset into the BLOB.
DBIERR_INVALIDDESCNUM	9999	$270F	Invalid descriptor number.
DBIERR_INVALIDFLDTYPE	10000	$2710	Invalid field type.
DBIERR_INVALIDFLDDESC	10001	$2711	Invalid field descriptor.
DBIERR_INVALIDFLDXFORM	10002	$2712	Invalid field transfor-mation.
DBIERR_INVALIDRECSTRUCT	10003	$2713	Invalid record structure.
DBIERR_INVALIDDESC	10004	$2714	Invalid descriptor.
DBIERR_INVALIDINDEXSTRUCT	10005	$2715	Invalid array of index descriptors.
DBIERR_INVALIDVCHKSTRUCT	10006	$2716	Invalid array of validity check descriptors.
DBIERR_INVALIDRINTSTRUCT	10007	$2717	Invalid array of referential integrity descriptors.
DBIERR_INVALIDRESTRTBLORDER	10008	$2718	Invalid ordering of tables during restructure.
DBIERR_NAMENOTUNIQUE	10009	$2719	Name not unique in this context.
DBIERR_INDEXNAMEREQUIRED	10010	$271A	Index name required.
DBIERR_INVALIDSESHANDLE	10011	$271B	Invalid session handle.
DBIERR_INVALIDRESTROP	10012	$271C	Invalid restructure operation.
DBIERR_UNKNOWNDRIVER	10013	$271D	Driver not known to system.
DBIERR_UNKNOWNDB	10014	$271E	Unknown database.
DBIERR_INVALIDPASSWORD	10015	$271F	Invalid password given.
DBIERR_NOCALLBACK	10016	$2720	No callback function.
DBIERR_INVALIDCALLBACKBUFLEN	10017	$2721	Invalid callback buffer length.
DBIERR_INVALIDDIR	10018	$2722	Invalid directory.
DBIERR_INVALIDXLATION	10019	$2723	Translate error—value out of bounds.
DBIERR_DIFFERENTTABLES	10020	$2724	Cannot set cursor of one table to another.
DBIERR_INVALIDBOOKMARK	10021	$2725	Bookmarks do not match table.
DBIERR_INVALIDINDEXNAME	10022	$2726	Invalid index/tag name.
DBIERR_INVALIDIDXDESC	10023	$2727	Invalid index descriptor.
DBIERR_NOSUCHTABLE	10024	$2728	Table does not exist.
DBIERR_USECOUNT	10025	$2729	Table has too many users.
DBIERR_INVALIDKEY	10026	$272A	Cannot evaluate Key or Key does not pass filter condition.
DBIERR_INDEXEXISTS	10027	$272B	Index already exists.
DBIERR_INDEXOPEN	10028	$272C	Index is open.
DBIERR_INVALIDBLOBLEN	10029	$272D	Invalid BLOB length.
DBIERR_INVALIDBLOBHANDLE	10030	$272E	Invalid BLOB handle in record buffer.
DBIERR_TABLEOPEN	10031	$272F	Table is open.
DBIERR_NEEDRESTRUCTURE	10032	$2730	Need to do (hard) restructure.

DBIERR_INVALIDMODE	10033	$2731	Invalid mode.
DBIERR_CANNOTCLOSE	10034	$2732	Cannot close index.
DBIERR_ACTIVEINDEX	10035	$2733	Index is being used to order table.
DBIERR_INVALIDUSRPASS	10036	$2734	Unknown user name or password.
DBIERR_MULTILEVELCASCADE	10037	$2735	Multilevel cascade is not supported.
DBIERR_INVALIDFIELDNAME	10038	$2736	Invalid field name.
DBIERR_INVALIDTABLENAME	10039	$2737	Invalid table name.
DBIERR_INVALIDLINKEXPR	10040	$2738	Invalid linked cursor expression.
DBIERR_NAMERESERVED	10041	$2739	Name is reserved.
DBIERR_INVALIDFILEEXTN	10042	$273A	Invalid file extension.
DBIERR_INVALIDLANGDRV	10043	$273B	Invalid language driver.
DBIERR_ALIASNOTOPEN	10044	$273C	Alias is not currently opened.
DBIERR_INCOMPATRECSTRUCTS	10045	$273D	Incompatible record structures.
DBIERR_RESERVEDOSNAME	10046	$273E	Name is reserved by DOS.
DBIERR_DESTMUSTBEINDEXED	10047	$273F	Destination must be indexed.
DBIERR_INVALIDINDEXTYPE	10048	$2740	Invalid index type.
DBIERR_LANGDRVMISMATCH	10049	$2741	Language drivers of table and index do not match.
DBIERR_NOSUCHFILTER	10050	$2742	Filter handle is invalid.
DBIERR_INVALIDFILTER	10051	$2743	Invalid filter.
DBIERR_INVALIDTABLECREATE	10052	$2744	Invalid table create request.
DBIERR_INVALIDTABLEDELETE	10053	$2745	Invalid table delete request.
DBIERR_INVALIDINDEXCREATE	10054	$2746	Invalid index create request.
DBIERR_INVALIDINDEXDELETE	10055	$2747	Invalid index delete request.
DBIERR_INVALIDTABLE	10056	$2748	Invalid table specified.
DBIERR_MULTIRESULTS	10057	$2749	Multiple results.
DBIERR_INVALIDTIME	10058	$274A	Invalid time.
DBIERR_INVALIDDATE	10059	$274B	Invalid date.
DBIERR_INVALIDTIMESTAMP	10060	$274C	Invalid datetime.
DBIERR_DIFFERENTPATH	10061	$274D	Tables in different directories
DBIERR_MISMATCHARGS	10062	$274E	Mismatch in the number of arguments
DBIERR_FUNCTIONNOTFOUND	10063	$274F	Function not found in service library.
DBIERR_MUSTUSEBASEORDER	10064	$2750	Must use baseorder for this operation.
DBIERR_INVALIDPROCEDURENAME	10065	$2751	Invalid procedure name.

Lock Violation Errors

DBIERR_LOCKED	10241	$2801	Record locked by another user.
DBIERR_UNLOCKFAILED	10242	$2802	Unlock failed.
DBIERR_FILEBUSY	10243	$2803	Table is busy.
DBIERR_DIRBUSY	10244	$2804	Directory is busy.

continued

DBIERR_FILELOCKED	10245	$2805	File is locked.
DBIERR_DIRLOCKED	10246	$2806	Directory is locked.
DBIERR_ALREADYLOCKED	10247	$2807	Record already locked by this session.
DBIERR_NOTLOCKED	10248	$2808	Object not locked.
DBIERR_LOCKTIMEOUT	10249	$2809	Lock time out.
DBIERR_GROUPLOCKED	10250	$280A	Key group is locked.
DBIERR_LOSTTBLLOCK	10251	$280B	Table lock was lost.
DBIERR_LOSTEXCLACCESS	10252	$280C	Exclusive access was lost.
DBIERR_NEEDEXCLACCESS	10253	$280D	Table cannot be opened for exclusive use.
DBIERR_RECGROUPCONFLICT	10254	$280E	Conflicting record lock in this session.
DBIERR_DEADLOCK	10255	$280F	A deadlock was detected.
DBIERR_ACTIVETRAN	10256	$2810	A user transaction is already in progress.
DBIERR_NOACTIVETRAN	10257	$2811	No user transaction is currently in progress.
DBIERR_RECLOCKFAILED	10258	$2812	Record lock failed.
DBIERR_OPTRECLOCKFAILED	10259	$2813	Couldn't perform the edit because another user changed the record.
DBIERR_OPTRECLOCKRECDEL	10260	$2814	Couldn't perform the edit because another user deleted or moved the record.

Access/Security Violation Errors

DBIERR_NOTSUFFFIELDRIGHTS	10497	$2901	Insufficient field rights for operation.
DBIERR_NOTSUFFTABLERIGHTS	10498	$2902	Insufficient table rights for operation. Password required.
DBIERR_NOTSUFFFAMILYRIGHTS	10499	$2903	Insufficient family rights for operation.
DBIERR_READONLYDIR	10500	$2904	This directory is read-only.
DBIERR_READONLYDB	10501	$2905	Database is read-only.
DBIERR_READONLYFLD	10502	$2906	Trying to modify read-only field.
DBIERR_TBLENCRYPTED	10503	$2907	Encrypted dBASE tables not supported.
DBIERR_NOTSUFFSQLRIGHTS	10504	$2908	Insufficient SQL rights for operation.

Invalid Context Errors

DBIERR_NOTABLOB	10753	$2A01	Field is not a BLOB.
DBIERR_BLOBOPENED	10754	$2A02	BLOB already opened.
DBIERR_BLOBNOTOPENED	10755	$2A03	BLOB not opened.
DBIERR_NA	10756	$2A04	Operation not applicable.
DBIERR_NOTINDEXED	10757	$2A05	Table is not indexed.
DBIERR_NOTINITIALIZED	10758	$2A06	Engine not initialized.
DBIERR_MULTIPLEINIT	10759	$2A07	Attempt to reinitialize engine.

DBIERR_NOTSAMESESSION	10760	$2A08	Attempt to mix objects from different sessions.
DBIERR_PDXDRIVERNOTACTIVE	10761	$2A09	Paradox driver not active.
DBIERR_DRIVERNOTLOADED	10762	$2A0A	Driver not loaded.
DBIERR_TABLEREADONLY	10763	$2A0B	Table is read-only.
DBIERR_NOASSOCINDEX	10764	$2A0C	No associated index.
DBIERR_HASOPENCURSORS	10765	$2A0D	Table(s) open. Cannot perform this operation.
DBIERR_NOTABLESUPPORT	10766	$2A0E	Table does not support this operation.
DBIERR_INDEXREADONLY	10767	$2A0F	Index is read-only.
DBIERR_NOUNIQUERECS	10768	$2A10	Table does not support this operation because it is not uniquely indexed.
DBIERR_NOTCURSESSION	10769	$2A11	Operation must be performed on the current session.
DBIERR_INVALIDKEYWORD	10770	$2A12	Invalid use of keyword.
DBIERR_CONNECTINUSE	10771	$2A13	Connection is in use by another statement.
DBIERR_CONNECTNOTSHARED	10772	$2A14	Passthrough SQL connection must be shared.

OS Errors

DBIERR_OSEINVFNC	11009	$2B01	Invalid function number.
DBIERR_OSENOENT	11010	$2B02	File or directory does not exist.
DBIERR_OSENOPATH	11011	$2B03	Path not found.
DBIERR_OSEMFILE	11012	$2B04	Too many open files. You may need to increase MAXFILEHANDLE limit in IDAPI configuration.
DBIERR_OSEACCES	11013	$2B05	Permission denied.
DBIERR_OSEBADF	11014	$2B06	Bad file number.
DBIERR_OSECONTR	11015	$2B07	Memory blocks destroyed.
DBIERR_OSENOMEM	11016	$2B08	Not enough memory.
DBIERR_OSEINVMEM	11017	$2B09	Invalid memory block address.
DBIERR_OSEINVENV	11018	$2B0A	Invalid environment.
DBIERR_OSEINVFMT	11019	$2B0B	Invalid format.
DBIERR_OSEINVACC	11020	$2B0C	Invalid access code.
DBIERR_OSEINVDAT	11021	$2B0D	Invalid data.
DBIERR_OSENODEV	11023	$2B0F	Device does not exist.
DBIERR_OSECURDIR	11024	$2B10	Attempt to remove current directory.
DBIERR_OSENOTSAM	11025	$2B11	Not same device.
DBIERR_OSENMFILE	11026	$2B12	No more files.
DBIERR_OSEINVAL	11027	$2B13	Invalid argument.
DBIERR_OSE2BIG	11028	$2B14	Argument list is too long.
DBIERR_OSENOEXEC	11029	$2B15	Execution format error.
DBIERR_OSEXDEV	11030	$2B16	Cross-device link.
DBIERR_OSEDOM	11041	$2B21	Math argument.

continued

DBIERR_OSERANGE	11042	$2B22	Result is too large.
DBIERR_OSEEXIST	11043	$2B23	File already exists.
DBIERR_OSUNKNOWN	11047	$2B27	Unknown internal operating system error.
DBIERR_OSSHAREVIOL	11058	$2B32	Share violation.
DBIERR_OSLOCKVIOL	11059	$2B33	Lock violation.
DBIERR_OSNETERR	11060	$2B34	Critical DOS error.
DBIERR_OSINT24FAIL	11061	$2B35	Drive not ready.
DBIERR_OSDRIVENOTREADY	11108	$2B64	Not exact read/write.
DBIERR_NOTEXACT	11109	$2B65	Operating system network error.
DBIERR_OSUNKNOWNSRVERR	11110	$2B66	Error from NOVELL file server.
DBIERR_SERVERNOMEMORY	11111	$2B67	NOVELL server out of memory.
DBIERR_OSALREADYLOCKED	11112	$2B68	Record already locked by this workstation.
DBIERR_OSNOTLOCKED	11113	$2B69	Record not locked.
DBIERR_NOSERVERSW	11114	$2B70	Server software not running the workstation/server.

Network Errors

DBIERR_NETINITERR	11265	$2C01	Network initialization failed.
DBIERR_NETUSERLIMIT	11266	$2C02	Network user limit exceeded.
DBIERR_NETFILEVERSION	11267	$2C03	Wrong .NET file version.
DBIERR_NETFILELOCKED	11268	$2C04	Cannot lock network file.
DBIERR_DIRNOTPRIVATE	11269	$2C05	Directory is not private.
DBIERR_NETMULTIPLE	11270	$2C06	Multiple .NET files in use.
DBIERR_NETUNKNOWN	11271	$2C07	Unknown network error.
DBIERR_SHAREDFILE	11272	$2C08	Not initialized for accessing network files.
DBIERR_SHARENOTLOADED	11273	$2C09	SHARE not loaded. It is required to share local files.
DBIERR_NOTONANETWORK	11274	$2C0A	Not on a network. Not logged in or wrong network driver.
DBIERR_SQLCOMMLOST	11275	$2C0B	Lost communication with SQL server.
DBIERR_SERVERCOMMLOST	11276	$2C0C	Lost communication with IDAPI server.

Optional Parameter Errors

DBIERR_REQOPTPARAM	11521	$2D01	Optional parameter is required.
DBIERR_INVALIDOPTPARAM	11522	$2D02	Invalid optional parameter.

Query Processor Errors

DBIERR_AMBJOASY	11777	$2E01	Obsolete
DBIERR_AMBJOSYM	11778	$2E02	Obsolete
DBIERR_AMBOUTEX	11779	$2E03	Ambiguous use of ! (inclusion operator).
DBIERR_AMBOUTPR	11780	$2E04	Obsolete
DBIERR_AMBSYMAS	11781	$2E05	Obsolete
DBIERR_ASETOPER	11782	$2E06	A SET operation cannot be included in its own grouping.
DBIERR_AVENUMDA	11783	$2E07	Only numeric and date/time fields canx be averaged.
DBIERR_BADEXPR1	11784	$2E08	Invalid expression.
DBIERR_BADFLDOR	11785	$2E09	Invalid OR expression.
DBIERR_BADVNAME	11786	$2E0A	Obsolete
DBIERR_BITMAPER	11787	$2E0B	Bitmap
DBIERR_CALCBADR	11788	$2E0C	CALC expression cannot be used in INSERT, DELETE, CHANGETO, and SET rows.
DBIERR_CALCTYPE	11789	$2E0D	Type error in CALC expression.
DBIERR_CHGTO1TI	11790	$2E0E	CHANGETO can be used in only one query form at a time.
DBIERR_CHGTOCHG	11791	$2E0F	Cannot modify CHANGED table.
DBIERR_CHGTOEXP	11792	$2E10	A field can contain only one CHANGETO expression.
DBIERR_CHGTOINS	11793	$2E11	A field cannot contain more than one expression to be inserted.
DBIERR_CHGTONEW	11794	$2E12	Obsolete
DBIERR_CHGTOVAL	11795	$2E13	CHANGETO must be followed by the new value for the field.
DBIERR_CHKMRKFI	11796	$2E14	Check mark or CALC expressions cannot be used in FIND queries.
DBIERR_CHNAMBIG	11797	$2E15	Cannot perform operation on CHANGED table together with a CHANGETO query.
DBIERR_CHUNKERR	11798	$2E16	Chunk
DBIERR_COLUM255	11799	$2E17	More than 255 fields in ANSWER table.
DBIERR_CONAFTAS	11800	$2E18	AS must be followed by the name for the field in the ANSWER table.
DBIERR_DEL1TIME	11801	$2E19	DELETE can be used in only one query form at a time.
DBIERR_DELAMBIG	11802	$2E1A	Cannot perform operation on DELETED table together with a DELETE query.
DBIERR_DELFRDEL	11803	$2E1B	Cannot delete from the DELETED table.

continued

DBIERR_EGFLDTYP	11804	$2E1C	Example element isused in two fields with incompatible types or with a BLOB.
DBIERR_EXAMINOR	11805	$2E1D	Cannot use example elements in an OR expression.
DBIERR_EXPRTYPS	11806	$2E1E	Expression in this field has the wrong type.
DBIERR_EXTRACOM	11807	$2E1F	Extra comma found.
DBIERR_EXTRAORO	11808	$2E20	Extra OR found.
DBIERR_EXTRAQRO	11809	$2E21	One or more query rows do not contribute to the ANSWER.
DBIERR_FIND1ATT	11810	$2E22	FIND can be used in only one query form at a time.
DBIERR_FINDANST	11811	$2E23	FIND cannot be used with the ANSWER table.
DBIERR_GRPNOSET	11812	$2E24	A row with GROUPBY must contain SET operations.
DBIERR_GRPSTROW	11813	$2E25	GROUPBY can be used only in SET rows.
DBIERR_IDFINLCO	11814	$2E26	Use only INSERT, DELETE, SET, or FIND in leftmost column.
DBIERR_IDFPERLI	11815	$2E27	Use only one INSERT, DELETE, SET, or FIND per line.
DBIERR_INANEXPR	11816	$2E28	Syntax error in expression.
DBIERR_INS1TIME	11817	$2E29	INSERT can be used in only one query form at a time.
DBIERR_INSAMBIG	11818	$2E2A	Cannot perform operation on INSERTED table together with an INSERT query.
DBIERR_INSDELCH	11819	$2E2B	INSERT, DELETE, CHANGETO, and SET rows may not be checked.
DBIERR_INSEXPRR	11820	$2E2C	Field must contain an expression to insert (or be blank).
DBIERR_INSTOINS	11821	$2E2D	Cannot insert into the INSERTED table.
DBIERR_ISARRAY	11822	$2E2E	Variable is an array and cannot be accessed.
DBIERR_LABELERR	11823	$2E2F	Label
DBIERR_LINKCALC	11824	$2E30	Rows of example elements in CALC expression must be linked.
DBIERR_LNGVNAME	11825	$2E31	Variable name is too long.
DBIERR_LONGQURY	11826	$2E32	Query may take a long time to process.
DBIERR_MEMVPROC	11827	$2E33	Reserved word or one that can't be used as a variable name.
DBIERR_MISNGCOM	11828	$2E34	Missing comma.
DBIERR_MISNGRPA	11829	$2E35	Missing).
DBIERR_MISSRTQU	11830	$2E36	Missing right quote.
DBIERR_NAMTWICE	11831	$2E37	Cannot specify duplicate column names.
DBIERR_NOCHKMAR	11832	$2E38	Query has no checked fields.
DBIERR_NODEFOCC	11833	$2E39	Example element has no defining occurrence.
DBIERR_NOGROUPS	11834	$2E3A	No grouping is defined for SET operation.

DBIERR_NONSENSE	11835	$2E3B	Query makes no sense.
DBIERR_NOPATTER	11836	$2E3C	Cannot use patterns in this context.
DBIERR_NOSUCHDA	11837	$2E3D	Date does not exist.
DBIERR_NOVALUE	11838	$2E3E	Variable has not been assigned a value.
DBIERR_ONLYCONS	11839	$2E3F	Invalid use of example element in summary expression.
DBIERR_ONLYSETR	11840	$2E40	Incomplete query statement. Query contains only a SET definition.
DBIERR_OUTSENS1	11841	$2E41	Example element with ! makes no sense in expression.
DBIERR_OUTTWIC1	11842	$2E42	Example element cannot be used more than twice with a ! query.
DBIERR_PAROWCNT	11843	$2E43	Row cannot contain expression.
DBIERR_PERSEPAR	11844	$2E44	Obsolete
DBIERR_PROCPLSW	11845	$2E45	Obsolete
DBIERR_PWINSRTS	11846	$2E46	No permission to insert or delete records.
DBIERR_PWMODRTS	11847	$2E47	No permission to modify field.
DBIERR_QBEFLDFOUND	11848	$2E48	Field not found in table.
DBIERR_QBENOFENCE	11849	$2E49	Expecting a column separator in table header.
DBIERR_QBENOFENCET	11850	$2E4A	Expecting a column separator in table.
DBIERR_QBENOHEADERT	11851	$2E4B	Expecting column name in table.
DBIERR_QBENOTAB	11852	$2E4C	Expecting table name.
DBIERR_QBENUMCOLS	11853	$2E4D	Expecting consistent number of columns in all rows of table.
DBIERR_QBEOPENTAB	11854	$2E4E	Cannot open table.
DBIERR_QBETWICE	11855	$2E4F	Field appears more than once in table.
DBIERR_QRYNOANSWER	11856	$2E50	This DELETE, CHANGE, or INSERT query has no ANSWER.
DBIERR_QRYNOTPREP	11857	$2E51	Query is not prepared. Properties unknown.
DBIERR_QUAINDEL	11858	$2E52	DELETE rows cannot contain quantifier expression.
DBIERR_QUAININS	11859	$2E53	Invalid expression in INSERT row.
DBIERR_RAGININS	11860	$2E54	Invalid expression in INSERT row.
DBIERR_RAGINSET	11861	$2E55	Invalid expression in SET definition.
DBIERR_ROWUSERR	11862	$2E56	Row use
DBIERR_SETEXPEC	11863	$2E57	SET keyword expected.
DBIERR_SETVAMB1	11864	$2E58	Ambiguous use of example element.
DBIERR_SETVBAD1	11865	$2E59	Obsolete
DBIERR_SETVDEF1	11866	$2E5A	Obsolete
DBIERR_SUMNUMBE	11867	$2E5B	Only numeric fields can be summed.
DBIERR_TBLISWP3	11868	$2E5C	Table is write-protected.
DBIERR_TOKENNOT	11869	$2E5D	Token not found.

continued

DBIERR_TWOOUTR1	11870	$2E5E	Cannot use example element with ! more than once in a single row.
DBIERR_TYPEMISM	11871	$2E5F	Type mismatch in expression.
DBIERR_UNRELQ1	11872	$2E60	Query appears to ask two unrelated questions.
DBIERR_UNUSEDST	11873	$2E61	Unused SET row.
DBIERR_USEINSDE	11874	$2E62	INSERT, DELETE, FIND, and SET can be used only in the leftmost column.
DBIERR_USEOFCHG	11875	$2E63	CHANGETO cannot be used with INSERT, DELETE, SET, or FIND.
DBIERR_VARMUSTF	11876	$2E64	Expression must be followed by an example element defined in a SET.
DBIERR_REGISTER	11877	$2E65	Lock failure.
DBIERR_LONGEXPR	11878	$2E66	Expression is too long.
DBIERR_REFRESH	11879	$2E67	Refresh exception during query.
DBIERR_CANCEXCEPT	11880	$2E68	Query canceled.
DBIERR_DBEXCEPT	11881	$2E69	Unexpected database engine error.
DBIERR_MEMEXCEPT	11882	$2E6A	Not enough memory to finish operation.
DBIERR_FATALEXCEPT	11883	$2E6B	Unexpected exception.
DBIERR_QRYNIY	11884	$2E6C	Feature not implemented yet in query.
DBIERR_BADFORMAT	11885	$2E6D	Query format is not supported.
DBIERR_QRYEMPTY	11886	$2E6E	Query string is empty.
DBIERR_NOQRYTOPREP	11887	$2E6F	Attempted to prepare an empty query.
DBIERR_BUFFTOOSMALL	11888	$2E70	Buffer too small to contain query string.
DBIERR_QRYNOTPARSE	11889	$2E71	Query was not previously parsed or prepared.
DBIERR_NOTHANDLE	11890	$2E72	Function called with bad query handle.
DBIERR_QRYSYNTERR	11891	$2E73	QBE syntax error.
DBIERR_QXFLDCOUNT	11892	$2E74	Query extended syntax field count error.
DBIERR_QXFLDSYMNOTFOUND	11893	$2E75	Field name in sort or field clause not found.
DBIERR_QXTBLSYMNOTFOUND	11894	$2E76	Table name in sort or field clause not found.
DBIERR_BLOBTERM	11895	$2E77	Operation is not supported on BLOB fields.
DBIERR_BLOBERR	11896	$2E78	General BLOB error.
DBIERR_RESTARTQRY	11897	$2E79	Query must be restarted.
DBIERR_UNKNOWNANSTYPE	11898	$2E7A	Unknown answer table type.
DBIERR_BLOBGROUP	11926	$2E96	BLOB cannot be used as grouping field.
DBIERR_QRYNOPROP	11927	$2E97	Query properties have not been fetched.
DBIERR_ANSTYPNOTSUP	11928	$2E98	Answer table is of unsuitable type.
DBIERR_ANSALIASNOTSUP	11929	$2E99	Answer table is not yet supported under server alias.
DBIERR_INSBLOBREQ	11930	$2E9A	Non-null BLOB field required. Cannot insert records.
DBIERR_CHGUNIQUENDXREQ	11931	$2E9B	Unique index required to perform CHANGETO.
DBIERR_DELUNIQUENDXREQ	11932	$2E9C	Unique index required to delete records.

DBIERR_SQLNOFULLUPDATE	11933	$2E9D	Update of table on the server failed.
DBIERR_CANTEXECREMOTE	11934	$2E9E	Cannot process this query remotely.
DBIERR_UNEXPECTEDEOC	11935	$2E9F	Unexpected end of command.
DBIERR_SQLPARAMNOTSET	11936	$2EA0	Parameter not set in query string.
DBIERR_QUERYTOOLONG	11937	$2EA1	Query string is too long.

Version Mismatch Errors

DBIERR_INTERFACEVER	12033	$2F01	Interface mismatch. Engine version different.
DBIERR_INDEXOUTOFDATE	12034	$2F02	Index is out of date.
DBIERR_OLDVERSION	12035	$2F03	Older version (see context).
DBIERR_VALFILEINVALID	12036	$2F04	.VAL file is out of date.
DBIERR_BLOBVERSION	12037	$2F05	BLOB file version is too old.
DBIERR_ENGQRYMISMATCH	12038	$2F06	Query and Engine DLLs are mismatched.
DBIERR_SERVERVERSION	12039	$2F07	Server is incompatible version.

Capability Not Supported Errors

DBIERR_NOTSUPPORTED	12289	$3001	Capability not supported.
DBIERR_NIY	12290	$3002	Not implemented yet.
DBIERR_TABLESQL	12291	$3003	SQL replicas not supported.
DBIERR_SEARCHCOLREQD	12292	$3004	Non-BLOB column in table required to perform operation.
DBIERR_NOMULTCONNECT	12293	$3005	Multiple connections not supported.

System Configuration Errors

DBIERR_INVALIDDBSPEC	12545	$3101	Invalid database alias specification.
DBIERR_UNKNOWNDBTYPE	12546	$3102	Unknown database type.
DBIERR_INVALIDSYSDATA	12547	$3103	Corrupt system configuration file.
DBIERR_UNKNOWNNETTYPE	12548	$3104	Network type unknown.
DBIERR_NOTONTHATNET	12549	$3105	Not on the network.
DBIERR_INVALIDCFGPARAM	12550	$3106	Invalid configuration parameter.

Warnings

| DBIERR_OBJIMPLICITLYDROPPED | 12801 | $3201 | Object implicitly dropped. |
| DBIERR_OBJMAYBETRUNCATED | 12802 | $3202 | Object may be truncated. |

continued

DBIERR_OBJIMPLICITLYMODIFIED	12803	$3203	Object implicitly modified.
DBIERR_VALIDATEDATA	12804	$3204	Should field constraints be checked?
DBIERR_VALFIELDMODIFIED	12805	$3205	Validity check field modified.
DBIERR_TABLELEVELCHANGED	12806	$3206	Table level changed.
DBIERR_COPYLINKEDTABLES	12807	$3207	Copy linked tables?
DBIERR_OBJIMPLICITLYTRUNCATED	12809	$3209	Object implicitly truncated.
DBIERR_VCHKMAYNOTBEENFORCED	12810	$320A	Validity check will not be enforced.
DBIERR_MULTIPLEUNIQRECS	12811	$320B	Multiple records found, but only one was expected.
DBIERR_FIELDMUSTBETRIMMED	12812	$320C	Field will be trimmed; cannot put master records into PROBLEM table.

Miscellaneous Errors

DBIERR_FILEEXISTS	13057	$3301	File already exists.
DBIERR_BLOBMODIFIED	13058	$3302	BLOB has been modified.
DBIERR_UNKNOWNSQL	13059	$3303	General SQL error.
DBIERR_TABLEEXISTS	13060	$3304	Table already exists.
DBIERR_PDX10TABLE	13061	$3305	Paradox 1.0 tables are not supported.

Compatibility Errors

DBIERR_DIFFSORTORDER	13313	$3401	Different sort order.
DBIERR_DIRINUSEBYOLDVER	13314	$3402	Directory in use by earlier version of Paradox.
DBIERR_PDX35LDDRIVER	13315	$3403	Needs Paradox 3.5-compatible language driver.

Driver Specific Errors

DBIERR_WRONGDRVNAME	15873	$3E01	Wrong driver name.
DBIERR_WRONGSYSVER	15874	$3E02	Wrong system version.
DBIERR_WRONGDRVVER	15875	$3E03	Wrong driver version.
DBIERR_WRONGDRVTYPE	15876	$3E04	Wrong driver type.
DBIERR_CANNOTLOADDRV	15877	$3E05	Cannot load driver.
DBIERR_CANNOTLOADLDDRV	15878	$3E06	Cannot load language driver.
DBIERR_VENDINITFAIL	15879	$3E07	Vendor initialization failed.

BDE Constants, Types, and Data Structures

This appendix contains information regarding the defined constants, types, and data structures (also referred to as records) used by the BDE. In Delphi 1.0, these are declared in **DBITYPES.INT**. This file would have been installed, by default, to your **\DELPHI\DOC** subdirectory. Since the final release of Delphi 2.0 was not available at the time this appendix was written, the information contained here is specific to Delphi 1.0. In Delphi 2.0, all BDE-specific declarations are contained in **BDE.INT**, normally found in the **\Program Files\Borland\Delphi 2.0\DOC** subdirectory. The changes and additions to the BDE structures are also documented in the BDE API help file (**BDE32.HLP**) that is installed with Delphi 2.0.

CONSTANTS

```
DBIMAXNAMELEN        = 31;     { Name limit (table, field etc) }
DBIMAXTBLNAMELEN     = 127;    { Maximum table name length }
DBIMAXSPNAMELEN      = 64;     { Maximum stored procedure name length }
DBIMAXFLDSINKEY      = 16;     { Maximum fields in a key }
DBIMAXKEYEXPLEN      = 220;    { Maximum key expression length }
DBIMAXPATHLEN        = 81;     { Maximum path+file name length (allocate 82) }
DBIMAXEXTLEN         = 3;      { Maximum file extension length, omitting dot }
DBIMAXDRIVELEN       = 2;      { Maximum drive length }
DBIMAXMSGLEN         = 127;    { Maximum message length (allocate 128) }
DBIMAXVCHKLEN        = 255;    { Maximum validity check length }
DBIMAXPICTLEN        = 175;    { Maximum picture length }
DBIMAXFLDSINSEC      = 256;    { Maximum fields in security spec }
DBIMAXSCFIELDS       = 16;     { Maximum number of fields in a config section }
DBIMAXSCFLDLEN       = 128;    { Maximum field length }
DBIMAXSCRECSIZE      = 2048;   { Maximum record size }
DBIMAXUSERNAMELEN    = 14;     { Maximum user name (general) }
DBIMAXXBUSERNAMELEN  = 12;     { Maximum user name length (xBASE) }
DBIMAXBOOKMARKLEN    = 4104;   { Maximum bookmark length }
```

Types

General

```
DATE        = Longint;
TIME        = Longint;
TIMESTAMP   = Double;
DBIResult   = Word;
WordEnum    = Word;
PLocale     = Pointer;
```

Handle Types

```
_hDBIObj    = Record end;    { Dummy structure to create "typed" handles }
hDBIObj     = ^_hDBIObj;      { Generic object handle }
hDBIDb      = ^_hDBIObj;      { Database handle }
hDBIQry     = ^_hDBIObj;      { Query handle }
hDBIStmt    = ^_hDBIObj;      { Statement handle ("new query") }
hDBICur     = ^_hDBIObj;      { Cursor handle }
hDBISes     = ^_hDBIObj;      { Session handle }
hDBIXlt     = ^_hDBIObj;      { Translation handle }
hDBICfg     = ^_hDBIObj;      { Configuration handle }
hDBIXact    = ^_hDBIObj;      { Transaction handle }
hDBIFilter  = ^_hDBIObj;      { Filter handle }
```

Handle Pointers

```
phDBIObj    = ^hDBIObj;       { Pointer to Generic object handle }
phDBIDb     = ^hDBIDb;        { Pointer to Database handle }
phDBIQry    = ^hDBIQry;       { Pointer to Query handle }
phDBIStmt   = ^hDBIStmt;      { Pointer to Statement handle }
phDBICur    = ^hDBICur;       { Pointer to Cursor handle }
phDBISes    = ^hDBISes;       { Pointer to Session handle }
phDBIXlt    = ^hDBIXlt;       { Pointer to Translation handle }
phDBICfg    = ^hDBICfg;       { Pointer to Configuration handle }
phDBIXact   = ^hDBIXact;      { Pointer to Transaction handle }
phDBIFilter = ^hDBIFilter;    { Pointer to Filter handle }
```

Typedefs for Buffers of Various Common Sizes

```
DBIPATH    = Array[0..DBIMAXPATHLEN] of Char;     { Holds a DOS path }
DBINAME    = Array[0..DBIMAXNAMELEN] of Char;     { Holds a name }
DBIEXT     = Array[0..DBIMAXEXTLEN] of Char;      { Holds an extension EXT }
DBIDOTEXT  = Array[0..DBIMAXEXTLEN+1] of Char;    { Holds EXT including '.' }
DBIDRIVE   = Array[0..DBIMAXDRIVELEN] of Char;    { Holds a drive name }
DBITBLNAME = Array[0..DBIMAXTBLNAMELEN] of Char;  { Holds a table name }
```

```
DBISPNAME   = Array[0..DBIMAXSPNAMELEN] of Char; { Holds a stored proc name }
DBIUSERNAME= Array[0..DBIMAXUSERNAMELEN] of Char; { Holds a user name }
DBIKEY      = Array[0..DBIMAXFLDSINKEY-1] of Word; { Holds key fields list }
DBIKEYEXP   = Array[0..DBIMAXKEYEXPLEN] of Char;{ Holds a key expression }
DBIVCHK     = Array[0..DBIMAXVCHKLEN] of Byte;  { Holds a validity check }
DBIPICT     = Array[0..DBIMAXPICTLEN] of Char;  { Holds a picture (Paradox) }
DBIMSG      = Array[0..DBIMAXMSGLEN] of Char;   { Holds an error message }
```

DATA STRUCTURES

BATTblDesc (Batch Table Definition)

The BATTblDesc structure defines a batch table. A batch table is a source or destination table used by DbiBatchMove. The BATTbleDesc structure is defined as follows:

```
pBATTblDesc = ^BATTblDesc;
BATTblDesc = Record
  hDb          : hDBIDb;     { Database handle }
  szTblName    : DBIPATH;    { Table name }
  szTblType    : DBINAME;    { Optional driver type }
  szUserName   : DBINAME;    { Optional user name }
  szPassword   : DBINAME;    { Optional password }
end;
```

CANHdr (Filter Descriptor)

The CANHdr structure is the header for all filter node classes and is defined as follows:

```
pCANHdr = ^CANHdr;
CANHdr = Record
  nodeClass  : NODEClass;   { One of the NODEClass types listed below }
  canOp      : CANOp;       { One of the CANOp types listed below }
end;
```

NODECLASS TYPES

```
NODEClass = (
  nodeNULL,       { Null node }
  nodeUNARY,      { Node is a unary }
  nodeBINARY,     { Node is a binary }
  nodeCOMPARE,    { Node is a compare }
  nodeFIELD,      { Node is a field }
  nodeCONST,      { Node is a constant }
  nodeTUPLE,      { Node is a record }
  nodeCONTINUE,   { Node is a continue node }
  nodeUDF         { Node is a user-defined function (UDF) node }
);
```

CANOp Types

```
pCANOp = ^CANOp;
CANOp = (
  canNOTDEFINED,    { Undefined }
  canISBLANK,       { CANUnary;  is operand blank. }
  canNOTBLANK,      { CANUnary;  is operand not blank. }
  canEQ,            { CANBinary, CANCompare; equal. }
  canNE,            { CANBinary; NOT equal. }
  canGT,            { CANBinary; greater than. }
  canLT,            { CANBinary; less than. }
  canGE,            { CANBinary; greater or equal. }
  canLE,            { CANBinary; less or equal. }
  canNOT,           { CANUnary; NOT }
  canAND,           { CANBinary; AND }
  canOR,            { CANBinary; OR }
  canTUPLE2,        { CANUnary; Entire record is operand. }
  canFIELD2,        { CANUnary; operand is field }
  canCONST2,        { CANUnary; operand is constant }
  canMINUS,         { CANUnary;  minus. }
  canADD,           { CANBinary; addition. }
  canSUB,           { CANBinary; subtraction. }
  canMUL,           { CANBinary; multiplication. }
  canDIV,           { CANBinary; division. }
  canMOD,           { CANBinary; modulo division. }
  canREM,           { CANBinary; remainder of division. }
  canSUM,           { CANBinary, accumulate sum of. }
  canCOUNT,         { CANBinary, accumulate count of. }
  canMIN,           { CANBinary, find minimum of. }
  canMAX,           { CANBinary, find maximum of. }
  canAVG,           { CANBinary, find average of. }
  canCONT,          { CANBinary; provides a link between two. }
  canUDF2,          { CANBinary; invokes a user-defined function. }
  canCONTINUE2,     { CANUnary; stops evaluating records. }
  canLIKE           { CANCompare, extended binary compare }
);
```

CANBinary (Binary Node Descriptor)

```
pCANBinary = ^CANBinary;
CANBinary = Record
  nodeClass      : NODEClass;    { Binary Node }
  canOp          : CANOp;        { Operator }
  iOperand1      : Word;         { Byte offset of Op1 }
  iOperand2      : Word;         { Byte offset of Op2 }
end;
```

CANCompare (Extended Compare Node Descriptor)

```
pCANCompare = ^CANCompare;
CANCompare = Record
```

```
  nodeClass         : NODEClass;    { Extended compare Node (text fields) }
  canOp             : CANOp;        { Operator (canLIKE, canEQ) }
  bCaseInsensitive  : Bool;         { 3 val: UNKNOWN = "fastest", "native" }
  iPartialLen       : Word;         { Partial fieldlength (0 is full length) }
  iOperand1         : Word;         { Byte offset of Op1 }
  iOperand2         : Word;         { Byte offset of Op2 }
end;
     CANConst (Constant Node Descriptor)
pCANConst = ^CANConst;
CANConst = Record
  nodeClass         : NODEClass;    { Constant }
  canOp             : CANOp;        { Operator }
  iType             : Word;         { Constant type }
  iSize             : Word;         { Constant size (in bytes) }
  iOffset           : Word;         { Offset in the literal pool }
end;
```

CANContinue (Break Node Descriptor)

```
pCANContinue = ^CANContinue;
CANContinue = Record
  nodeClass      : NODEClass;  { Break Node }
  canOp          : CANOp;      { Operator }
  iContOperand   : Word;       { Continue if operand is true; Otherwise,
                                 stop evaluating records. }
end;
```

CANExpr (Expression Tree Descriptor)

```
ppCANExpr = ^pCANExpr;
pCANExpr  = ^CANExpr;
CANExpr   = Record
  iVer           : Word;       { Version tag of expression. }
  iTotalSize     : Word;       { Size of this structure }
  iNodes         : Word;       { Number of nodes }
  iNodeStart     : Word;       { Starting offset of Nodes in this }
  iLiteralStart  : Word;       { Starting offset of Literals in this }
end;
```

CANField (Field Node Descriptor)

```
pCANField = ^CANField;
CANField = Record
  nodeClass      : NODEClass;  { Field }
  canOp          : CANOp;      { Operator }
  iFieldNum      : Word;       { Field number }
  iNameOffset    : Word;       { Name offset in Literal pool }
end;
```

CANTuple (Tuple Node Descriptor)

```
pCANTuple = ^CANTuple;
CANTuple = Record
  nodeClass       : NODEClass;    { Tuple (record) }
  canOp           : CANOp;        { Operator }
  iSize           : Word;         { Record size. (in bytes) }
end;
```

CANUdf (User Defined Function Node Descriptor)

```
pCANUdf = ^CANUdf;
CANUdf = Record
  nodeClass       : NODEClass;  { A user-defined function }
  canOp           : CANOp;      { Operator }
  iOffSzFuncName  : Word;       { Offset in literal pool to Function Name
                                  string(0 terminated) }
  iOperands       : Word;       { Byte offset of Operands (concatenated using
                                  canCONT) }
  iDrvDialect     : Word;       { Driver Dialect ID for UDF string supplied }
  iOffSzUDF       : Word;       { Offset in literal pool to UDF string (0
                                  terminated) }
end;
```

CANUnary (Unary Node Descriptor)

```
pCANUnary = ^CANUnary;
CANUnary = Record
  nodeClass       : NODEClass;    { Unary Node }
  canOp           : CANOp;        { Operator }
  iOperand1       : Word;         { Byte offset of Operand node }
end;
```

CBPROGRESSDesc (Progress Callback Descriptor)

The progress callback is used to create progress meters and other visual displays that reflect the progress of potentially long-running operations (such as DbiBatchMove or DbiQExec).

```
pCBPROGRESSDesc = ^CBPROGRESSDesc;
CBPROGRESSDesc = Record
  iPercentDone : Integer;   { This can be any number from -1 to 100. A value
                             between 1 and 100 specifies the percentage
                             done; for example, the value 50 indicates that
                             the execution is half complete. If the value is
                             -1, the progress of execution is indicated via
                             the string szMsg, rather than with a
                             percentage. }
```

```
szMsg          : DBIMSG;       { Specifies a string containing a message. This
                                 message serves as a progress report; for
                                 example, Steps completed: 5. The message is
                                 displayed when iPercentDone is -1. }
end;
```

CFGDesc (Configuration Descriptor)

The CFGDesc structure describes the BDE configuration.

```
pCFGDesc = ^CFGDesc;
CFGDesc = Record
  szNodeName     : DBINAME;                    { Leaf node name }
  szDescription  : Array[0..DBIMAXSCFLDLEN-1] of Char; { Node description }
  iDataType      : Word;                       { Value type (always a string) }
  szValue        : Array[0..DBIMAXSCFLDLEN-1] of Char; { Value }
  bHasSubnodes   : Bool;                        { True, if not leaf node }
end;
```

CLIENTInfo (Client Information)

```
pCLIENTInfo = ^CLIENTInfo;
CLIENTInfo = Record
  szName         : DBINAME;      { Documentary name }
  iSessions      : Word;         { Number of sessions }
  szWorkDir      : DBIPATH;      { Working directory }
  szLang         : DBINAME;      { System language driver (Client supplied) }
end;
```

CRTblDesc (Table Descriptor)

```
pCRTblDesc = ^CRTblDesc;
CRTblDesc = Record
  szTblName      : DBITBLNAME;   { TableName with optional path & extension }
  szTblType      : DBINAME;      { Driver type (optional) }
  szErrTblName   : DBIPATH;      { Error Table name (optional) }
  szUserName     : DBINAME;      { User name (if applicable) }
  szPassword     : DBINAME;      { Password (optional) }
  bProtected     : Bool;         { Master password supplied in szPassword }
  bPack          : Bool;         { Pack table? (restructure only) }
  iFldCount      : Word;         { Number of field defs supplied }
  pecrFldOp      : pCROpType;    { Array of field ops }
  pfldDesc       : pFLDDesc;     { Array of field descriptors }
  iIdxCount      : Word;         { Number of index defs supplied }
  pecrIdxOp      : pCROpType;    { Array of index ops }
  pidxDesc       : PIDXDesc;     { Array of index descriptors }
  iSecRecCount   : Word;         { Number of security defs supplied }
  pecrSecOp      : pCROpType;    { Array of security ops }
```

```
    psecDesc        : pSECDesc;       { Array of security descriptors }
    iValChkCount    : Word;           { Number of val checks }
    pecrValChkOp    : pCROpType;      { Array of val check ops }
    pvchkDesc       : pVCHKDesc;      { Array of val check descs }
    iRintCount      : Word;           { Number of referential integrity specs }
    pecrRintOp      : pCROpType;      { Array of referential integrity ops }
    printDesc       : pRINTDesc;      { Array of referential integrity specs }
    iOptParams      : Word;           { Number of optional parameters }
    pfldOptParams   : pFLDDesc;       { Array of field descriptors }
    pOptData        : Pointer;        { Optional parameters }
end;
```

The CRTblDesc structure is used by both DbiDoRestructure and DbiCreateTable in different ways. Some of the CRTblDesc fields are not used at all with DbiCreateTable; and they are specified only with DbiDoRestructure to modify the table.

CRTblDesc for Creating a Table

The CRTblDesc structure defines the general attributes of the table and supplies pointers to arrays of field, index, and other descriptors.

The optional parameter fields *iOptParams*, *pfldOptParams*, and *pOptData* are used to set other driver-specific attributes of the table. These parameters are used to describe a single record that is constructed by the client and contains the null-terminated ASCII strings that specify the values for these driver-specific attributes.

iOptParams is the number of optional parameters.

pfldOptParams contains a pointer to an array of FLDDesc of *iOptParams* size.

Each of these field descriptors is given a field name equal to the name of the optional parameter (for example, MDXBLOCKSIZE) and has *iLen* and *iOffset* set to the length (including the NULL terminator) and position in the *pOptData* record buffer of the ASCII string containing the value of this parameter (for example, 512).

All other elements of the FLDDesc are ignored.

The *pOptData* record buffer need only be large enough to hold all the null-terminated strings for each optional parameter value. This style of setting optional parameters is also used by DbiOpenDatabase.

The names of the optional parameters can be obtained using DbiOpenCfgInfoList with a configuration path of DRIVERS\DRIVERNAME\TABLECREATE.

The following CRTblDesc structure defines the table structure.

Field	Type	Description
szTblName	DBITBLNAME	The table name, including optional path and extension.
szTblType	DBINAME	The driver type.
szErrTblName	DBIPATH	Error table name (optional).
szUserName	DBINAME	User name (if applicable).
szPassword	DBINAME	The master password (if bProtected is True) (Paradox only).
bProtected	Bool	True if encryption is desired (Paradox only).

bPack	Bool	True if table is to be packed (for restructuring).
iFldCount	Word	The number of field definitions supplied.
percFldOp	pCROpType	The array of field ops.
pfldDesc	pFLDDesc	The array of field descriptors.
iIdxCount	Word	The number of index definitions supplied.
pecrIdxOp	pCROpType	The array of index ops.
pidxDesc	pIDXDesc	The array of index descriptors.
pidxDesc	PIDXDesc	The array of index descriptors.
iSecRecCount	Word	The number of security definitions given (Paradox only).
psecDesc	pSECDesc	The array of security descriptors (Paradox only).
iValChkCount	Word	The number of validity checks (Paradox and SQL only).
pecrValChkOp	pCROpType	The array of validity check ops.
pvchkDesc	pVCHKDesc	The array of validity check descriptors (Paradox and SQL only).
iRintCount	Word	The number of referential integrity specifications (Paradox only).
pecrRintOp	pCROpType	The array of referential integrity ops.
printDesc	pRINTDesc	The array of referential integrity specifications (Paradox only).
iOptParams	Word	The number of optional parameters.
pfldOptParams	pFLDDesc	The array of field descriptors for optional parameters.
pOptData	Pointer	The values of optional parameters.

CRTblDesc for Restructuring a Table

A complete description of CRTblDesc, as used to restructure a table, is described next.

Field	Type	Description
szTblName	DBITBLNAME	The source table name. The table name can contain an extension.
szTblType	DBINAME	If specified, it must match the driver type associated with the source table.
szErrTblName	DBIPATH	Optional. Returns fully qualified table name on error.
szUserName	DBINAME	Optional. Returns the user name.
szPassword	DBINAME	Optional password for the destination table. Only required if bProtected is set to True.
bProtected	Bool	Optional. If True, specifies that a master password is supplied for the destination table. Paradox only.
bPack	Bool	Optional. If True, specifies packing for restructure.

iFldCount, pecrFldOp, and pfldDesc are required to describe the new record structure.

Field	Type	Description
iFldCount	Word	Optional. Used if the record structure is changing. Specifies the number of field operators and field descriptors passed in pecrFldOp and pFldDesc for the new record structure.

continued

FIELD	TYPE	DESCRIPTION
pecrFldOp	pCROpType	Optional. Used if the record structure is changing. Must be crADD if a field is added, crMODIFY if a field is modified, or crCOPY if a field is moved.
pfldDesc	pFLDDesc	Optional. Used if the record structure is changing. Specifies an array of physical field descriptors for the new record structure. ifldNum in each pfldDesc must be 0 if the field is added. Otherwise, it must contain the field position (1 to n) in the old record structures. If a field is dropped, its descriptor is simply left out of the new record structure. Additionally, any changes to dependent objects are made automatically (that is, all single field indexes, validity checks, and auxiliary passwords are dropped).

For all the following objects, only the changes need to be input.

FIELD	TYPE	DESCRIPTION
IdxCount	Word	Optional. Specifies the number of index operators and index descriptors passed in pIdxDesc.
pecrIdxOp	pCROpType	Optional. To change an index, specify crADD, crMODIFY, crREDO, or crDROP.
pidxDesc	pIDXDesc	Optional. Specifies an array of index descriptors.
iSecRecCount	Word	Optional. For Paradox only. Specifies the number of security definitions passed in psecDesc.
pecrSecOp	pCROpType	Optional. To change a security definition, specify crADD, crMODIFY, or crDROP.
psecDesc	pSECDesc	Optional. For Paradox only. Specifies an array of security descriptors.
iValChkCount	Word	Optional. For Paradox only. Specifies the number of validity checks passed in pecrValChkOp and pvchkDesc.
pecrValChkOp	pCROpType	Optional. For Paradox only. To change a validity check, specify crADD, crMODIFY, or crDROP.
pvchkDesc	pVCHKDesc	Optional. For Paradox only. Specifies an array of validity check descriptors.
iRintCount	Word	Optional. For Paradox only. Specifies the number of referential integrity operators passed in printDesc.
pecrRintOp	pCROpType	Optional. For Paradox only. To change a referential integrity operator, specify crADD, crMODIFY, or crDROP. crMODIFY cannot be used to change the name of a referential integrity constraint. To modify the name, use crDROP and crADD.
printDesc	pRINTDesc	Optional. For Paradox only. Specifies an array of referential integrity specifications.
iOptParams	Word	Optional. Specifies the number of optional parameters (for example, language driver information).
pfldOptParams	pFLDDesc	Optional. Specifies an array of field descriptors for optional parameters.
pOptData	Pointer	Optional. Specifies values of optional parameters.

The following operation types are valid only for restructuring the table.

OPERATION TYPE	VALUE	DESCRIPTION
crNOOP	0	Perform no operation
crADD	1	Add a new element
crCOPY	2	Copy an existing element
crMODIFY	3	Modify an element
crDROP	4	Removes an element

CURProps (Cursor Properties)

The cursor properties (CURProps) structure describes the most commonly used cursor properties and is defined as follows.

```
pCURProps = ^CURProps;
CURProps = Record
  szName          : DBITBLNAME;   { Table name (extension not required) }
  iFNameSize      : Word;         { Specifies the size of the buffer needed
                                    to retrieve full table name (including
                                    extension and path, if applicable). }

  szTableType     : DBINAME;      { Driver type }
  iFields         : Word;         { Specifies the number of fields in the
                                    table. The client must allocate a
                                    buffer whose size is: [iFields *
                                    sizeof(FLDDesc)] in order to get the
                                    field descriptors for the table. }

  iRecSize        : Word;         { Specifies the record size, depending on
                                    the xltMODE for the cursor. If the
                                    xltMODE is xltFIELD, iRecSize specifies
                                    the logical record size. In other
                                    words, it is the size of the record if
                                    all fields were represented as BDE
                                    logical types. If the xltMODE is
                                    xltNONE, iRecSize specifies the
                                    physical record size. }

  iRecBufSize     : Word;         { Specifies the record size, depending on
                                    the xltMODE for the cursor. If the
                                    xltMODE is xltFIELD, iRecSize specifies
                                    the logical record size. In other
                                    words, it is the size of the record if
                                    all fields were represented as BDE
                                    logical types. If the xltMODE is
                                    xltNONE, iRecSize specifies the
                                    physical record size. }
```

```
    iKeySize          : Word;          { Specifies the key size of the current
                                         active index (if any). This is the size
                                         of the key buffer that the client must
                                         allocate in order to retrieve a key
                                         using DbiExtractKey. This size changes
                                         if DbiSwitchToIndex is called. }
    iIndexes          : Word;          { Specifies the number of currently open
                                         indexes for this cursor. The client can
                                         call DbiGetIndexDesc with iIndexSeqNo
                                         set from 1 to iIndexes, to have all the
                                         index descriptors returned. The client
                                         could also allocate a buffer whose size
                                         is [iIndexes * sizeof(IDXDesc)] and
                                         have all the index descriptors returned
                                         by calling DbiGetIndexDescs. }
    iValChecks        : Word;          { Number of validity checks for this
                                         table }
    iRefIntChecks     : Word;          { Number of Referential Integrity
                                         constraints for this table }
    iBookMarkSize     : Word;          { Specifies the size of the bookmark.
                                         Bookmarks are always allocated by the
                                         client before DbiGetBookMark is called.
                                         Note that the size of the bookmark
                                         could change if DbiSwitchToIndex is
                                         called. }
    bBookMarkStable   : Bool;          { True, if this cursor supports stable
                                         bookmarks. Stable bookmarks are those
                                         that remain unchanged after another
                                         user has modified the table. For
                                         example, this value is True for Paradox
                                         tables having a primary key, but False
                                         for Paradox heap tables. }
    eOpenMode         : DBIOpenMode;   { Open mode: dbiREADWRITE/dbiREADONLY }
    eShareMode        : DBIShareMode;  { Share mode: dbiOPENSHARED/dbiOPENEXCL }
    bIndexed          : Bool;          { This value is True if there is a
                                         current active index for this cursor.
                                         In other words, it is True if there is
                                         a nondefault order associated with this
                                         cursor. }
    iSeqNums          : Integer;       { 1 = Sequence number concept (Paradox);
                                         0 = Record number concept (dBASE);
                                         <0 = None (SQL) }
    bSoftDeletes      : Bool;          { Supports soft deletes (dBASE only) }
    bDeletedOn        : Bool;          { This value is set to True if the
                                         curSOFTDELETEON property is True. This
                                         field makes sense only if the cursor
                                         supports the soft delete concept. If
                                         True, deleted records can be seen while
                                         using this cursor (dBASE only). }
    iRefRange         : Word;          { Not used }
    exltMode          : XLTMode;       { Value of the translate mode property
                                         for this cursor:
                                          xltNONE = No translations; use
```

```
                                            physical types.
                                   xltFIELD = Field-level translation;
                                            use logical types }
    iRestrVersion   : Word;       { Restructure version number for the
                                     table (Paradox only) }
    bUniDirectional : Bool;       { Set to True if this cursor is
                                     unidirectional (SQL only). }
    eprvRights      : Word;       { Enumerated value that gives the table-
                                     level rights for the user who opened
                                     the table.  Valid values are:
                                     prvNONE = No privileges
                                     prvREADONLY = Read-only table or field
                                     prvMODIFY = Read and modify fields
                                     prvINSERT = Insert + all of above
                                     prvINSDEL = Delete + all of above
                                     prvFULL = Full rights
                                     prvUNKNOWN = Unknown }
    iFmlRights      : Word;       { Family rights }
    iPasswords      : Word;       { Number of auxiliary passwords for this
                                     table (Paradox only).}
    iCodePage       : Word;       { Codepage associated with table. If the
                                     codepage is unknown, the value is 0. }
    bProtected      : Bool;       { This value is set to True if the table
                                     is protected by a password. }
    iTblLevel       : Word;       { Driver-dependent table level }
    szLangDriver    : DBINAME;    { Language driver name }
    bFieldMap       : Bool;       { True if a field map is active for this
                                     table }
    iBlockSize      : Word;       { Physical file blocksize in K }
    bStrictRefInt   : Bool;       { (Paradox only) If True, a referential
                                     integrity check has been specified and
                                     the STRICT bit is set in the header. }
    iFilters        : Word;       { Number of filters currently on the
                                     cursor }
    bTempTable      : Bool;       { True, if the cursor is on a temporary
                                     table. For queries, this means the
                                     result set is canned, rather than live.
                                     This field can be examined to determine
                                     whether the requested preference for
                                     LIVENESS in the DbiSetProp call were
                                     honored. }
    iUnused         : Array[0..15] of Word;  { Not currently used }
end;
```

DBDesc (Database Descriptor)

The DBDesc structure describes a database.

```
pDBDesc = ^DBDesc;
DBDesc = Record
  szName    : DBINAME;    { Logical name (Or alias) }
  szText    : DBINAME;    { Descriptive text }
  szPhyName : DBIPATH;    { Physical name/path }
```

```
  szDbType     : DBINAME;    { Database type }
end;
```

DBIEnv (Environment Information)

The DBIEnv structure defines the BDE environment.

```
pDBIEnv = ^DBIEnv;
DBIEnv = Record
  szWorkDir        : DBIPATH;    { Working directory }
  szIniFile        : DBIPATH;    { Configuration file name }
  bForceLocalInit  : Bool;       { If True, forces local initialization }
  szLang           : DBINAME;    { Language driver of the client }
  szClientName     : DBINAME;    { Client name }
end;
```

DBIErrInfo (Error Information)

The DBIErrInfo structure describes error information.

```
pDBIErrInfo = ^DBIErrInfo;
DBIErrInfo = Record
  iError        : DBIResult;              { Last error code returned }
  szErrCode     : DBIMSG;                 { Error Code }
  szContext     : Array[1..4] of DBIMSG;  { Context info }
end;
```

ELEMENTS OF SZCONTEXT ARRAY

1. Specifies the context-dependent information at the top level of the error stack.
2. Specifies the context-dependent information at the second level of the error stack.
3. Specifies the context-dependent information at the third level of the error stack.
4. Specifies the context-dependent information at the fourth level of the error stack.

DBIQryProgress (Query Progress)

The DBIQryProgress structure describes the status of a query.

```
pDBIQryProgress = ^DBIQryProgress;
DBIQryProgress = Record
  stepsInQry    : Word;    { Total number of steps in query. }
  stepsCompleted: Word;    { Number of steps completed out of total. }
  totElemInStep : Longint; { Total number elements in current step. }
  elemCompleted : Longint; { Number of elements completed in current step. }
end;
```

DRVType (Driver Capabilities)

The DRVType structure describes the driver and its capabilities.

```
pDRVType = ^DRVType;
DRVType = Record              { Driver Description/Capabilities }
  szType         : DBINAME;   { Symbolic name identifying the driver }
  szText         : DBINAME;   { Descriptive text }
  edrvCat        : DRVCat;    { Driver category:
                                drvFILE = File-based (Paradox, dBASE, text}.
                                drvOTHERSERVER = Other kind of server.
                                drvSQLBASEDSERVER = SQL-based server. }
  bTrueDb        : Bool;      { If True, driver supports the true database
                                concept. }
  szDbType       : DBINAME;   { Database type to be used }
  bMultiUser     : Bool;      { If True, the driver supports multiuser
                                access. }
  bReadWrite     : Bool;      { If True, the driver supports read-write
                                access; otherwise, the driver supports
                                read-only access only. }
  bTrans         : Bool;      { If True, the driver supports Transactions. }
  bPassThruSQL   : Bool;      { If True, the driver supports Pass-thru SQL. }
  bLogIn         : Bool;      { If True, the driver requires explicit login. }
  bCreateDb      : Bool;      { If True, the driver can create a database. }
  bDeleteDb      : Bool;      { If True, the driver can drop database. }
  bCreateTable   : Bool;      { If True, the driver can create a table. }
  bDeleteTable   : Bool;      { If True, the driver can delete a table. }
  bMultiplePWs   : Bool;      { If True, the driver can have multiple
                                passwords. }
  iDriverVersion : Word;      { Driver version 1..n }
  bSQLRowid      : Bool;      { If True, the driver supports SQL RowID. }
  iUnused        : Array [0..14] of Word;    {Not currently used }
end;
```

FILEDesc (File Descriptor)

The FILEDesc structure describes a file.

```
pFILEDesc = ^FILEDesc;
FILEDesc = Record             { File description }
  szFileName   : DBIPATH;     { File name (No directory or extension ) }
  szExt        : DBIEXT;      { File extension }
  bDir         : Bool;        { If True, this file is a directory. }
  iSize        : Longint;     { File size in bytes }
  dtDate       : Date;        { Date on the file }
  tmTime       : Time;        { Time on the file }
end;
```

FILTERInfo (Filter Information Descriptor)

The FILTERInfo structure describes a filter.

```
pFILTERInfo = ^FILTERInfo;
FILTERInfo = Record
  iFilterId      : Word;          { ID for the filter }
  hFilter        : hDBIFilter;    { Filter handle }
  iClientData    : Longint;       { Client supplied data }
  iPriority      : Word;          { Priority; 1..N with 1 being highest }
  bCanAbort      : Bool;          { If True, pfFilter can return ABORT }
  pfFilter       : pfGENFilter;   { Client filter function }
  pCanExpr       : Pointer;       { Supplied expression }
  bActive        : Bool;          { If True, the filter is active }
end;
```

FLDDesc (Field Descriptor)

The FLDDesc structure defines a field in a table. This same descriptor structure is both for creating a new table and for retrieving information about the table structure after it has been opened. When the table is created, the last five properties in the field descriptor structure are not used.

```
pFLDDesc = ^FLDDesc;
FLDDesc = Record           { Field Descriptor }
  iFldNum    : Word;       { On input, specifies the field number. This
                             value can be from 1 to curProps.iFields. On
                             output, this is the ordinal number of the field
                             (1 to n). For Paradox, it is the invariant
                             field ID.}
  szName     : DBINAME;     { Name of the field }
  iFldType   : Word;        { Type of the field. In output mode, if translate
                             mode is set to xltNONE, field types represent
                             the physical types of that driver type;
                             otherwise, the types are BDE logical types.}
  iSubType   : Word;        { Subtype of the field. This could be a BDE
                             logical subtype or a driver physical subtype
                             depending on the translate mode setting.}
  iUnits1    : Integer;     { Specifies the number of characters, digits, and
                             so on. The interpretation of this field can
                             depend on the driver and also on the specific
                             field type. For most drivers, if the field is
                             of the numeric type, iUnits1 is the precision
                             and iUnits2 is the scale. }
  iUnits2    : Integer;     { Specifies the number of decimal places and so
                             on. The interpretation of this field can depend
                             on the driver and also on the specific field
                             type. For most drivers, if the field is of the
                             numeric type, iUnits1 is the precision and
                             iUnits2 the scale. }
  iOffset    : Word;        { Reports the computed offset of this field in
                             the record buffer. This offset depends on the
                             translation mode; it could be the offset in the
                             physical or logical representation of the
                             record. This field applies only to existing
                             tables; it is not applicable when a table is
                             created. }
```

```
iLen        : Word;        { Reports the computed length in bytes of this
                             field. The length depends on the translation
                             mode; that is, it could be the length of the
                             logical or physical representation of the
                             field. The application developer uses this
                             value to allocate a buffer in which to retrieve
                             the field value. This field applies only to
                             existing tables; it is not applicable when a
                             table is created. }

iNullOffset : Word;        { Reports the computed offset of the NULL
                             indicator for this field in the record buffer.
                             If zero, there is no NULL indicator. Otherwise,
                             iNullOffset is the offset to an Integer value,
                             which is 1 if the field is NULL. This field
                             applies only to existing tables; it is not
                             specified when a table is created.  }

efldvVchk   : FLDVchk;     { Reports the types of validity checks associated
                             with this field (this field applies only to
                             existing tables; it is not specified when a
                             table is created). The following validity check
                             types can be reported: fldvNOCHECKS,
                             fldvHASCHECKS, or fldvUNKNOWN. }

efldrRights : FLDRights;   { Reports the computed field level rights for
                             this user (this field applies only to existing
                             tables; it is not specified when a table is
                             created). Field rights can be one of the
                             following values: fldrREADWRITE, fldrREADONLY,
                             fldrNONE, or fldrUNKNOWN. }
end;
```

FLDType (Field Types)

The FLDType structure describes a field type.

```
pFLDType = ^FLDType;
FLDType = Record
  iId               : Word;     { ID of the Field Type }
  szName            : DBINAME;  { Symbolic name of the field type }
  szText            : DBINAME;  { Descriptive text }
  iPhyType          : Word;     { Physical/Native type }
  iXltType          : Word;     { Default translated type }
  iXltSubType       : Word;     { Default translated subtype }
  iMaxUnits1        : Word;     { Maximum units allowed (1) }
  iMaxUnits2        : Word;     { Maximum units allowed (2) }
  iPhySize          : Word;     { Physical size in bytes (per unit) }
  bRequired         : Bool;     { If True, supports 'required' option }
  bDefaultVal       : Bool;     { If True, supports user-specified default }
  bMinVal           : Bool;     { If True, the field supports minimum
                                  validity constraint }
  bMaxVal           : Bool;     { If True, the field supports maximum
                                  validity constraint }
  bRefIntegrity     : Bool;     { If True, the field can participate in
                                  referential integrity }
```

```
  bOtherChecks        : Bool;            { If True, the field supports other kinds of
                                          checks }
  bKeyed              : Bool;            { If True, the field type can be keyed }
  bMultiplePerTable   : Bool;            { If True, the table can have more than one
                                          of this type }
  iMinUnits1          : Word;            { Minimum units required (1) }
  iMinUnits2          : Word;            { Minimum units required (2) }
  bCreateable         : Bool;            { If True, the field type can be created }
  iUnUsed             : Array[0..15] of Word;    { Not currently used }
end;
```

FMTBcd (Binary Coded Decimal Format)

The FMTBcd structure describes the format for binary coded decimal.

```
pFMTBcd                  = ^FMTBcd;
FMTBcd = Record
  iPrecision            : Byte;    { 1..64 considered valid }
  iSignSpecialPlaces: Byte;        { Specifies the following values:
                                     Sign bit on = Negative number.
                                     Special bit on = Number is blank.
                                     Places = Number of decimals (0 to
                                              iPrecision). }
  iFraction             : Array[0..31] of Byte; { Array of BCD nibbles, 00..99
                                                  per byte, high nibble first }
end;
```

FMTDate (Date Format)

The FMTDate structure describes the date format for the session.

```
pFMTDate = ^FMTDate;
FMTDate = Record
  szDateSeparator : Array[0..3] of Char; { Date separator character.
                                           Default is '/' }
  iDateMode          : Byte;             { Date format. 0 = MDY (Default), 1 = DMY,
                                           2 = YMD }
  bFourDigitYear   : Boolean;            { If True, writes year as 4 digits. }
  bYearBiased      : Boolean;            { If True, on input add 1900 to year. }
  bMonthLeadingZero : Boolean;           { If True, the month is displayed with a
                                           leading zero. }
  bDayLeadingZero : Boolean;             { If True, the day is displayed with a
                                           leading zero. }
end;
```

FMTNumber (Number Format)

The FMTNumber structure describes the number format for the current session.

```
pFMTNumber = ^FMTNumber;
FMTNumber = Record
```

```
  cDecimalSeparator  : Char;       { Character to be used as the decimal
                                     separator. Default '.' }
  cThousandSeparator : Char;       { Character to be used as the thousands
                                     separator. Default ',' }
  iDecimalDigits     : Byte;       { Number of decimal places. Default is 2. }
  bLeadingZero       : Boolean;    { If True, use leading zeros.  Default
                                     is True. }
end;
```

FMTTime (Time Format)

The FMTTime structure describes the time format for the current session.

```
pFMTTime = ^FMTTime;
FMTTime = Record
  cTimeSeparator  : Char;          { Character to be used as the time
                                     separator. Default ':' }
  bTwelveHour     : Boolean;       { If True, represent as 12-hour time. }
  szAmString      : Array[0..5] of Char; { String to be used to designate
                                     a.m. time. (Only for 12 Hr)
                                     Default is NULL. }
  szPmString      : Array[0..5] of Char; { String to be used to designate
                                     p.m. time. (Only for 12 Hr)
                                     Default is NULL. }
  bSeconds        : Boolean;       { If True, show seconds. Default is True. }
  bMilSeconds     : Boolean;       { If True, show milliseconds. Default is
                                     False }
end;
```

IDXDesc (Index Descriptor)

The IDXDesc structure describes each index in a table. This information is used both when creating a new index and when inquiring about the index after it has been opened.

The fields required in this structure vary by driver type and index type. The first three fields—*szName*, *iIndexId*, and *szTagName* are used to identify the index. A different combination of these three fields is used, depending on the driver type and on the specific index type, as shown here.

DRIVER TYPE	INDEX TYPE
dBASE (ttDbase)	.NDX style: *szName* alone identifies the index. .MDX style: *szName* and *szTagName* together identify the index.
Paradox (ttParadox)	Either *iIndexId* or *szName* identifies the index.
Text driver (ttASCII)	Indexing not supported.
All SQL drivers	*szName* alone identifies the index.

```
pIDXDesc = ^IDXDesc;
IDXDesc = Record
  szName          : DBITBLNAME;    { Index name }
```

```
    iIndexId            : Word;             { Index number }
    szTagName           : DBINAME;          { Index Tag name (dBASE only) }
    szFormat            : DBINAME;          { Optional format (BTREE, HASH etc) }
    bPrimary            : Bool;             { If True, this is the primary index. }
    bUnique             : Bool;             { If True, index contains unique keys. }
    bDescending         : Bool;             { If True, this is a descending index. }
    bMaintained         : Bool;             { If True, this is a maintained index. }
    bSubset             : Bool;             { If True, this is a subset index (dBASE
                                             only). }
    bExpIdx             : Bool;             { If True, this is an expression index
                                             (dBASE only). }
    iCost               : Word;             { Not currently used }
    iFldsInKey          : Word;             { Specifies the number of key fields in a
                                             composite index. If the index is an
                                             expression, set to 0. }
    iKeyLen             : Word;             { Not specified while index is created.
                                             Specifies the physical length of the
                                             key in bytes. The application developer
                                             needs to allocate a buffer of iKeyLen
                                             bytes to use as a key buffer. A key
                                             buffer is used with functions such as
                                             DbiExtractKey and DbiSetToKey. }
    bOutofDate          : Bool;             { If True, the index is out of date. Not
                                             used for index creation. }
    iKeyExpType         : Word;             { Specifies the type of the key
                                             expression (dBASE only). This value can
                                             be one of the following: fldDBCHAR,
                                             fldDBKEYNUM, or fldDBKEYBCD. }
    aiKeyFld            : DBIKEY;           { Array of field numbers in key }
    szKeyExp            : DBIKEYEXP;        { Specifies the key expression for an
                                             expression index (dBASE only). This
                                             field is used only if bExpIdx = True.
                                             The expression is stated as a dBASE
                                             expression. }
    szKeyCond           : DBIKEYEXP;        { Specifies the expression that defines
                                             the subset condition (dBASE only). This
                                             field is used only if bSubset = True.
                                             The expression is stated as a dBASE
                                             expression. }
    bCaseInsensitive : Bool;                { If True, index is case-insensitive. }
    iBlockSize          : Word;             { Block size, in bytes, for this index }
    iRestrNum           : Word;             { Not specified while index is created.
                                             Specifies the internal restructure
                                             number for this index. This number is
                                             set when the index descriptor is
                                             retrieved and should not be changed
                                             when passing the descriptor back to
                                             DbiDoRestructure. }
    iUnUsed             : Array[0..15] of Word;    { Not currently used }
end;
```

IDXType (Index Types)

The IDXType structure describes an index type.

```
pIDXType = ^IDXType;
IDXType = Record
  iId             : Word;            { ID of the index type }
  szName          : DBINAME;         { Symbolic name of the index type }
  szText          : DBINAME;         { Descriptive text }
  szFormat        : DBINAME;         { Optional format (BTREE, HASH etc) }
  bComposite      : Bool;            { If True, composite keys are supported }
  bPrimary        : Bool;            { If True, this index type supports a
                                       primary index }
  bUnique         : Bool;            { If True, this index type supports unique
                                       indexes }
  bKeyDescending  : Bool;            { If True, the key can be descending }
  bFldDescending  : Bool;            { If True, the key can be descending at
                                       the field level }
  bMaintained     : Bool;            { If True, this index type supports the
                                       maintained option }
  bSubset         : Bool;            { If True, this index type supports the
                                       subset expression }
  bKeyExpr        : Bool;            { If True, the key can be an expression
                                       (dBASE only) }
  bCaseInsensitive : Bool;           { If True, this index type supports case-
                                       insensitive keys }
  iUnUsed         : Array[0..15] of Word;   { Not currently used }
end;
```

LDDesc (Language Driver Descriptor)

The LDDesc structure describes a language driver.

```
pLDDesc = ^LDDesc;
LDDesc = Record
  szName             : DBINAME;      { Symbolic name of driver }
  szDesc             : DBINAME;      { Driver description }
  iCodePage          : Word;         { Code page number }
  PrimaryCpPlatform  : Word;         { Platform type to which the drivers
                                       character set corresponds. 1 = DOS
                                       (OEM); 2 = Windows (ANSI); 6 = HP UNIX
                                       (ROMAN8) }
  AlternateCpPlatform : Word;        { Alternate platform type (For internal
                                       use only) }
end;
```

LOCKDesc (Lock Descriptor)

The LOCKDesc structure describes a lock.

```
pLOCKDesc = ^LOCKDesc;
```

```
LOCKDesc = Record
  iType           : Word;          { Lock type (0 for rec lock) }
  szUserName      : DBIUSERNAME;   { Lock owner (User name) }
  iNetSession     : Word;          { Net level session number }
  iSession        : Word;          { BDE session number, if BDE lock }
  iRecNum         : Longint;       { Record number, if a record lock }
  iInfo           : Word;          { Info for table locks (Paradox only) }
end;
```

Lock Types in LOCKDesc

```
lckRECLOCK    = 0;   { Normal Record lock (Write) }
lckRRECLOCK   = 1;   { Special Paradox Record lock (Read) }
lckGROUPLOCK  = 2;   { Paradox Group lock }
lckIMGAREA    = 3;   { Paradox Image area }
lckTABLEREG   = 4;   { Table registration/Open (No lock) }
lckTABLEREAD  = 5;   { Table Read lock }
lckTABLEWRITE = 6;   { Table Write lock }
lckTABLEEXCL  = 7;   { Table Exclusive lock }
lckUNKNOWN    = 9;   { Unknown lock }
```

RECProps (Record Properties)

The RECProps structure describes the record properties.

```
pRECProps = ^RECProps;
RECProps = Record
  iSeqNum        : Longint;  { Specifies the sequence number of the record.
                               Applicable if the cursor supports sequence
                               numbers (Paradox only).   }
  iPhyRecNum     : Longint;  { Specifies the record number of the record.
                               Applicable only when physical record numbers
                               are supported (dBASE only). }
  bRecChanged    : Bool;     { Indicates if the record pointer has changed
                               (dBASE only). }
  bSeqNumChanged : Bool;     { Indicates if the sequence number has changed
                               (Paradox only). }
  bDeleteFlag    : Bool;     { Specifies if the record is deleted.
                               Applicable only when soft delete is supported
                               (dBASE only). }
end;
```

RESTCbDesc (Restructure Callback Descriptor)

The RESTCbDesc structure contains restructure callback information.

```
RESTCbDesc = Record
  iErrCode       : DBIResult;   { Error code number }
  iTblNum        : Word;        { Table number }
```

```
   iObjNum           : Word;              { Sequence or field number for old
                                            objects. Order in CRTbleDesc for
                                            new objects. }
   eRestrObjType     : RESTErrObjType;   { Specifies the object type. }
   uObjDesc          : TuObjDesc;        { Specifies the object descriptor. }
end;
```

Object Types

```
TuObjDesc = Record
  case Integer of
    1: (fldDesc:   FLDDesc);
    2: (idxDesc:   IDXDesc);
    3: (vchkDesc:  VCHKDesc);
    4: (rintDesc:  RINTDesc);
    5: (secDesc:   SECDesc);
end;
```

RINTDesc (Referential Integrity)

The RINTDesc structure describes the referential integrity options for a table (Paradox only).

```
pRINTDesc = ^RINTDesc;
RINTDesc = Record
  iRintNum      : Word;       { Referential integrity number }
  szRintName    : DBINAME;    { A name to tag this integegrity constraint }
  eType         : RINTType;   { The type (rintMASTER or rintDEPENDANT) }
  szTblName     : DBIPATH;    { Other table name }
  eModOp        : RINTQual;   { Modify qualifier (rintRESTRICT or
                                rintCASCADE) }
  eDelOp        : RINTQual;   { Delete qualifier (rintRESTRICT or
                                rintCASCADE) }
  iFldCount     : Word;       { Number of field in the linking key }
  aiThisTabFld  : DBIKEY;     { Fields in this table that make up this
                                referential integrity constraint in this
                                table }
  aiOthTabFld   : DBIKEY;     { Number of fields in the other table }
end;
```

SECDesc (Security Descriptor)

The SECDesc structure describes each security descriptor in the table (Paradox only).

```
pSECDesc = ^SECDesc;
SECDesc = Record
  iSecNum    : Word;    { Number identifying the descriptor }
  eprvTable  : Word;    { Table privileges: prvNONE, prvREADONLY,
                          prvMODIFY, prvINSERT, prvINSDEL, prvFULL,
                          prvUNKNOWN. }
```

```
      iFamRights : Word;        { Family rights: NOFAMRIGHTS, FORMRIGHTS,
                                  RPTRIGHTS, VALRIGHTS, SETRIGHTS, ALLFAMRIGHTS. }
      szPassword : DBINAME;   { NULL-terminated string used as the password }
      aprvFld    : Array[0..DBIMAXFLDSINSEC-1] of Word;
                                { Field level privileges: prvNONE, prvREADONLY,
                                  prvFULL}}
    end;
```

SESInfo (Session Information)

The SESInfo structure provides information about a session.

```
pSESInfo = ^SESInfo;
SESInfo = Record
  iSession   : Word;      { Session ID (1..n) }
  szName     : DBINAME;   { Documentary name of the session }
  iDatabases : Word;      { Number of open databases }
  iCursors   : Word;      { Number of open cursors }
  iLockWait  : Integer;   { Lock wait time (in seconds) }
  szNetDir   : DBIPATH;   { Directory location for the network control file }
  szPrivDir  : DBIPATH;   { Current Private directory }
end;
```

SYSConfig (System Configuration)

The SYSConfig structure provides basic system configuration information.

```
pSYSConfig = ^SYSConfig;
SYSConfig = Record
  bLocalShare   : Bool;         { True, if local files will be shared with
                                  non-BDE applications. }
  iNetProtocol  : Word;         { Network Protocol (35, 40 etc.) }
  bNetShare     : Bool;         { True, if connected to a network. }
  szNetType     : DBINAME;      { Network type }
  szUserName    : DBIUSERNAME;  { Network user name }
  szIniFile     : DBIPATH;      { Fully qualified configuration file name }
  szLangDriver  : DBINAME;      { System language driver }
end;
```

SYSInfo (System Status and Information)

The SYSInfo structure provides BDE system status and information.

```
pSYSInfo = ^SYSInfo;
SYSInfo = Record
  iBufferSpace : Word;   { Size of the buffer space in kilobytes }
  iHeapSpace   : Word;   { Size of the heap space in kilobytes }
  iDrivers     : Word;   { Number of currently loaded drivers }
  iClients     : Word;   { Number of active clients }
  iSessions    : Word;   { Number of sessions (For all clients) }
```

```
  iDatabases     : Word;    { Number of open databases (For all clients) }
  iCursors       : Word;    { Number of cursors (For all clients) }
end;
```

SYSVersion (System Version Information)

The SYSVersion structure provides the BDE system version information.

```
pSYSVersion = ^SYSVersion;
SYSVersion = record
  iVersion       : Word;    { Engine version }
  iIntfLevel     : Word;    { Client interface level }
  dateVer        : Date;    { Version date (Compile/Release) }
  timeVer        : Time;    { Version time (Compile/Release) }
end;
```

TBLBaseDesc (Base Table Descriptor)

The TBLBaseDesc structure provides basic information about a table.

```
pTBLBaseDesc = ^TBLBaseDesc;
TBLBaseDesc = Record
  szName         : DBITBLNAME;  { Table name (no extension or directory) }
  szFileName     : DBITBLNAME;  { File name }
  szExt          : DBIEXT;      { File extension }
  szType         : DBINAME;     { Driver type }
  dtDate         : Date;        { Date on the table }
  tmTime         : Time;        { Time on the table }
  iSize          : Longint;     { Size in bytes }
  bView          : Bool;        { True, if this a view (SQL only). }
end;
```

TBLExtDesc (Extended Table Descriptor)

The TBLExtDesc structure provides additional information about a table.

```
pTBLExtDesc = ^TBLExtDesc;
TBLExtDesc = Record
  szStruct       : DBINAME;  { Physical structure }
  iRestrVersion  : Word;     { Version number }
  iRecSize       : Word;     { Physical record size }
  iFields        : Word;     { Number of fields }
  iIndexes       : Word;     { Number of indexes }
  iValChecks     : Word;     { Number of field validity checks }
  iRintChecks    : Word;     { Number of referential integrity checks }
  iRecords       : Longint;  { Number of records in the table }
  bProtected     : Bool;     { True, if the table is protected. }
  bValidInfo     : Bool;     { If False, all or some of the extended data are
                               not available for this table. }
end;
```

TBLFullDesc (Full Table Descriptor)

The TBLFullDesc structure provides a complete description of the table (base + extended).

```
pTBLFullDesc = ^TBLFullDesc;
TBLFullDesc = Record
  tblBase          : TBLBaseDesc;   { Base description }
  tblExt           : TBLExtDesc;    { Extended description }
end;
```

TBLType (Table Capabilities)

The TBLType structure describes the tables capabilities.

```
pTBLType = ^TBLType;
TBLType = Record
  iId              : Word;     { ID of the table type }
  szName           : DBINAME;  { Symbolic name of the table type }
  szText           : DBINAME;  { Descriptive text }
  szFormat         : DBINAME;  { Format; eg 'HEAP' }
  bReadWrite       : Bool;     { If True, the user can read and write. }
  bCreate          : Bool;     { If True, the user can create new tables. }
  bRestructure     : Bool;     { If True, BDE can restructure this table type. }
  bValChecks       : Bool;     { If True, the user can specify validity checks
                                 for this table type. }
  bSecurity        : Bool;     { If True, this table type can be protected. }
  bRefIntegrity    : Bool;     { If True, this table type can participate
                                 in referential integrity. }
  bPrimaryKey      : Bool;     { If True, this table type supports the
                                 primary key concept. }
  bIndexing        : Bool;     { If True, this table type can have indexes. }
  iFldTypes        : Word;     { Number of physical field types supported }
  iMaxRecSize      : Word;     { Maximum record size }
  iMaxFldsInTable: Word;       { Maximum fields in a table }
  iMaxFldNameLen : Word;       { Maximum field name length }
  iTblLevel        : Word;     { Driver-dependent table level (version) }
  iUnUsed          : Array[0..15] of Word;   { Not currently used }
end;
```

USERDesc (User Information Descriptor)

The USERDesc structure describes a user.

```
pUSERDesc = ^USERDesc;
USERDesc = Record
  szUserName       : DBIUSERNAME; { The user name }
  iNetSession      : Word;        { Net level session number }
  iProductClass    : Word;        { Product class of the user (Paradox only) }
  szSerialNum      : Array[0..21] of Char;   { Serial number (Paradox only) }
end;
```

VCHKDesc (Validity Check)

The VCHKDesc structure provides information about validity checking constraints on a field (Paradox and SQL tables only).

```
pVCHKDesc = ^VCHKDesc;
VCHKDesc = Record
  iFldNum         : Word;       { Field number (1-n) }
  bRequired       : Bool;       { If True, field value is required. }
  bHasMinVal      : Bool;       { If True, has minimum value. }
  bHasMaxVal      : Bool;       { If True, has maximum value. }
  bHasDefVal      : Bool;       { If True, has default value. }
  aMinVal         : DBIVCHK;    { Minimum Value }
  aMaxVal         : DBIVCHK;    { Maximum Value }
  aDefVal         : DBIVCHK;    { Default value }
  szPict          : DBIPICT;    { Picture string }
  elkupType       : LKUPType;   { Lookup/Fill type (Paradox only, see below) }
  szLkupTblName   : DBIPATH;    { Lookup Table name; for information only }
end;
```

Valid LKUPType Values (Paradox Only)

```
lkupNONE            = The table has no lookup.
lkupPRIVATE         = Only current field + private.
lkupALLCORRESP      = All corresponding + no help.
lkupHELP            = Only current field + help and fill.
lkupALLCORRESPHELP  = All corresponding + help.
```

XInfo (Transactions)

The XInfo structure describes a transaction.

```
pXInfo = ^XInfo;
XInfo = Record
  exState  : exState;    { Transaction state: xsACTIVE or xsINACTIVE }
  eXIL     : eXILType;   { Transaction isolation level }
  uNests   : Word;       { Transaction children }
end;
```

Valid eXILType Values

```
xilDIRTYREAD       = Uncommitted changes; no phantoms
xilREADCOMMITTED   = Committed changes; no phantoms
xilREPEATABLEREAD  = Full read repeatability
```

BDE Categorical Reference

Each of the BDE API functions documented in this reference fall into one of the following major categories.

Batch Operation—Handles batch operation tasks.

Callback—Returns information about or registers a callback function.

Capability—Returns information on available databases, tables, indexes, etc.

Configuration File—Return information about (or performs actions upon) configuration files.

Cursor Maintenance—Return information about (or affects) cursors and bookmarks.

Data Access—Performs specific data access operations.

Database—Returns information about (or performs) database-related tasks.

Date/Time/Number Format—Handles formats for the current session.

Environment—Returns information about (or affects) the client application environment.

Error Handling—Returns information about (or performs) related tasks.

Index—Returns information about (or affects) indexes.

Locking—Returns information about (or affects) locks.

Query—Performs query tasks.

Session—Returns information about (or affects) a session.

Table—Returns information about (or performs) tablewide operations.

Transaction—Returns information about (or performs) related tasks.

BATCH OPERATION FUNCTIONS

Each of the following BDE functions handles batch operations such as appending, deleting, or copying records; rebuilding all open indexes; sorting, packing, or emptying tables.

FUNCTION	DESCRIPTION
DbiBatchMove	Appends, updates, deletes, and copies records or fields from a source table to a destination table.
DbiBeginBatch	Applies a Critical Section Lock (CSL).
DbiCopyTable	Copies all or part of the specified source table to a destination table.

continued

FUNCTION	DESCRIPTION
DbiEmptyTable	Deletes all records from the table.
DbiEndBatch Table	Removes a Critical Section Lock.
DbiPackTable	Physically removes from a dBASE table all records that have been marked for deletion.
DbiRegenIndexes	Regenerates all indexes for the specified cursor.
DbiSortTable	Sorts an opened or closed table, either into itself or into a destination table. Options are available to remove duplicates, to enable case-insensitive sorts and special sort functions, and to control the number of records sorted.

CALLBACK FUNCTIONS

Each of the following BDE functions provides support for using callback functions in the client application.

FUNCTION	DESCRIPTION
DbiGetCallBack	Returns a pointer to the function previously registered by the client for the given callback type.
DbiRegisterCallBack	Registers a callback function for the client application.

CAPABILITY FUNCTIONS

Each of the following BDE functions returns information about various capabilities. These include information about available databases, tables, table types, index types, and so on.

FUNCTION	DESCRIPTION
DbiOpenCfgInfoList	Returns a handle to an in-memory table listing all the nodes in the configuration file accessible by the specified path.
DbiOpenDatabaseList	Creates an in-memory table containing a list of accessible databases and their descriptions.
DbiOpenDriverList	Creates an in-memory table containing a list of driver names available to the client application.
DbiOpenFamilyList	Creates an in-memory table listing the family members associated with a specified table.
DbiOpenFieldList	Creates an in-memory table listing the fields in a specified table and their descriptions.
DbiOpenFieldTypesList	Creates an in-memory table containing a list of field types supported by the driver type.
DbiOpenIndexList	Opens a cursor on an in-memory table listing the indexes on a specified table, along with their descriptions.
DbiOpenIndexTypesList	Creates an in-memory table containing a list of all supported index types for the driver type.
DbiOpenLockList	Creates an in-memory table containing a list of locks acquired on the table.

DbiOpenRintList	Creates an in-memory table listing the referential integrity links for a specified table, along with their descriptions.
DbiOpenSecurityList	Creates an in-memory table listing record-level security information about a specified table.
DbiOpenTableList	Creates an in-memory table with information about all the tables accessible to the client application.
DbiOpenTableTypesList	Creates an in-memory table listing table type names for the given driver.
DbiOpenVchkList	Creates an in-memory table containing records with information about validity checks for fields within the specified table.

Configuration File Functions

Each of the following BDE functions is used to create, update, retrieve information from, or delete a BDE configuration file.

Function	Description
DbiAddAlias	Adds a new alias to a configuration file.
DbiCfgAddRecord	Adds configuration file record.
DbiCfgBuildPath	Builds a path for accessing a configuration file.
DbiCfgDropRecord	Deletes a configuration file record.
DbiCfgGetHelp	Gets a help message for a configuration file.
DbiCfgGetNextNode	Gets the next defined node from a configuration file.
DbiCfgGetRecord	Gets a configuration file record.
DbiCfgMerge	Merges two configuration files.
DbiCfgModifyRecord	Modifies a configuration file record.
DbiCfgPosition	Positions the configuration file path.
DbiCfgSave	Saves current configuration to a file.
DbiCfgTranslate	Translates a configuration string.
DbiCloseConfigFile	Closes the configuration file.
DbiDeleteAlias	Removes an alias from a configuration file.
DbiOpenCfgInfoList	Opens a cursor on "Config."
DbiOpenConfigFile	Opens/creates a configuration file.

Cursor Maintenance Functions

Each of the following BDE functions returns information about a cursor or performs cursor-related task including such as positioning a cursor, linking cursors, creating and closing cursors, counting records associated with a cursor, refreshing all buffers associated with a cursor, and filtering, setting, and comparing bookmarks.

Function	Description
DbiActivateFilter	Activates a filter.
DbiAddFilter	Adds a filter to a table but does not activate the filter (i.e., the record set is not yet altered).
DbiBeginLinkMode	Converts a cursor to a link cursor. Given an open cursor, prepares for linked access. Returns a new cursor.
DbiCloneCursor	Creates a new cursor (clone cursor), which has the same result set as the given cursor (source cursor).
DbiCloseCursor	Closes a previously opened cursor.
DbiCompareBookMarks	Compares the relative positions of two bookmarks in the result set associated with the cursor.
DbiDeactivateFilter	Temporarily stops the specified filter from affecting the record set by turning the filter off.
DbiDropFilter	Deactivates and removes a filter from memory and frees all resources.
DbiEndLinkMode	Ends linked cursor mode and returns the original cursor.
DbiExtractKey	Retrieves the key value for the current record of the given cursor or from the supplied record buffer.
DbiForceReread	Refreshes all buffers associated with the cursor, if necessary.
DbiFormFullName	Returns the fully qualified table name.
DbiGetBookMark	Saves the current position of a cursor to the client-supplied buffer called a bookmark.
DbiGetCursorForTable	Finds the cursor for the given table.
DbiGetCursorProps	Returns the properties of the cursor.
DbiGetFieldDescs	Retrieves a list of descriptors for all the fields in the table associated with the cursor.
DbiGetLinkStatus	Returns the link status of the cursor.
DbiGetNextRecord	Retrieves the next record in the table associated with the cursor.
DbiGetPriorRecord	Retrieves the previous record in the table associated with the cursor.
DbiGetProp	Returns a property of an object.
DbiGetRecord	Retrieves the current record, if any, in the table associated with the cursor.
DbiGetRecordCount	Retrieves the current number of records associated with the cursor.
DbiGetExactRecordCount	Retrieves the current number of records associated with the cursor, taking into account any active filter condition.
DbiGetRecordForKey	Finds and retrieves a record matching a key and positions the cursor on that record.
DbiGetRelativeRecord	Positions the cursor on a record in the table relative to the current position of the cursor.
DbiGetSeqNo	Retrieves the sequence number of the current record in the table associated with the cursor.
DbiLinkDetail	Establishes a link between two tables such that the detail table has its record set limited to the set of records matching the linking key values of the master table cursor.
DbiLinkDetailToExp	Links the detail cursor to the master cursor via an expression.
DbiMakePermanent	Changes a temporary table created by DbiCreateTempTable into a permanent table.
DbiOpenTable	Opens the given table for access and associates a cursor handle with the opened table.
DbiResetRange	Removes the specified tables limited range previously established by the function DbiSetRange.
DbiSaveChanges	Forces all updated records associated with the cursor to disk.

DbiSetFieldMap	Sets a field map of the table associated with the given cursor.
DbiSetProp	Sets the specified property of an object to a given value.
DbiSetRange	Sets a range on the result set associated with the cursor.
DbiSetToBegin	Positions the cursor to BOF (i.e., just prior to the first record).
DbiSetToBookMark	Positions the cursor to the location saved in the specified bookmark.
DbiSetToCursor	Sets the position of one cursor (the destination cursor) to that of another (the source cursor).
DbiSetToEnd	Positions the cursor to EOF (i.e., just after the last record).
DbiSetToKey	Positions an index based cursor on a key value.
DbiSetToRecordNo	Positions the cursor of a dBASE table to the given physical record number.
DbiSetToSeqNo	Positions the cursor to the specified sequence number of a Paradox table.
DbiUnlinkDetail	Removes a link between two cursors.

DATA ACCESS FUNCTIONS

Each of the following BDE functions accesses data in a table.

FUNCTION	DESCRIPTION
DbiAppendRecord	Appends a record to the end of the table associated with the given cursor.
DbiDeleteRecord	Deletes the current record of the given cursor.
DbiFreeBlob	Closes the BLOB handle located within the specified record buffer.
DbiGetBlob	Retrieves data from the specified BLOB field.
DbiGetBlobHeading	Retrieves information about a BLOB field from the BLOB heading (tuple) in the record buffer.
DbiGetBlobSize	Retrieves the size of the specified BLOB field in bytes.
DbiGetField	Retrieves the data contents of the requested field from the record buffer.
DbiGetFieldDescs	Retrieves a list of descriptors for all the fields in the table associated with the cursor.
DbiGetFieldTypeDesc	Retrieves a description of the specified field type.
DbiInitRecord	Initializes the record buffer to a blank record, based upon the data types of the fields in that record.
DbiInsertRecord	Inserts a new record into the table associated with the given cursor.
DbiModifyRecord	Modifies the current record of table associated with the cursor with the data supplied.
DbiOpenBlob	Prepares the cursors record buffer to access a BLOB field.
DbiPutBlob	Writes data into an open BLOB field.
DbiPutField	Writes field value to the correct location in the supplied record buffer.
DbiReadBlock	Reads a specified number of records (starting from the next position of the cursor) into a buffer.
DbiSaveChanges	Forces all updated records associated with the cursor to disk.
DbiSetFieldMap	Sets a field map of the table associated with the given cursor.
DbiTruncateBlob	Shortens the size of the contents of a BLOB field, or deletes the contents of a BLOB field from the record, by shortening it to zero.

continued

FUNCTION	DESCRIPTION
DbiUndeleteRecord	Undeletes, or recalls, a dBASE record that has been marked for deletion (i.e., a soft delete).
DbiVerifyField	Verifies that the information specified is a valid data type for the field specified and that all validity checks in place for the field are satisfied. This can also be used to check if a field is blank.
DbiWriteBlock	Writes a block of records to the table associated with the cursor.

DATABASE FUNCTIONS

Each of the following BDE functions returns information about a specific database or available databases or performs a database-related task.

FUNCTION	DESCRIPTION
DbiCloseDatabase	Closes a database and all tables associated with this database handle.
DbiGetDatabaseDesc	Retrieves the description of the specified database from the configuration file.
DbiGetDirectory	Retrieves the current working directory or the default directory.
DbiOpenDatabase	Opens a database in the current session and returns a database handle.
DbiOpenDatabaseList	Creates an in-memory table containing a list of accessible databases and their descriptions.
DbiOpenFileList	Opens a cursor on the virtual table containing all the tables accessible by the client application and their descriptions.
DbiOpenIndexList	Opens a cursor on an in-memory table listing the indexes on a specified table, along with their descriptions.
DbiOpenTableList	Creates an in-memory table with information about all the tables accessible to the client application.
DbiSetDirectory	Sets the current directory for a standard database.

DATE/TIME/NUMBER FORMAT FUNCTIONS

Each of the following BDE functions sets or retrieves date, time, or number formats for the current session or decodes or encodes date and time into or from a TimeStamp record type.

FUNCTION	DESCRIPTION
DbiBcdFromFloat	Converts FLOAT data to binary coded decimal (BCD) format.
DbiBcdToFloat	Converts binary coded decimal data to FLOAT format.
DbiDateDecode	Decodes DATE into separate month, day, and year components.
DbiDateEncode	Encodes separate date components into date for use by DbiPutField and other functions.
DbiGetDateFormat	Gets the date format for the current session.
DbiGetNumberFormat	Gets the number format for the current session.
DbiGetTimeFormat	Gets the time format for the current session.

DbiSetDateFormat	Sets the date format for the current session.
DbiSetNumberFormat	Sets the number format for the current session.
DbiSetTimeFormat	Sets the time format for the current session.
DbiTimeDecode	Decodes time into separate components (hours, minutes, seconds).
DbiTimeEncode	Encodes separate time components into time for use by DbiPutField and other functions.
DbiTimeStampDecode	Extracts separate encoded date and time components from the TimeStamp.
DbiTimeStampEncode	Encodes the encoded date and encoded time into a TimeStamp.

Environment Functions

Each of the following BDE functions returns information about or performs an operation that affects the client application environment.

Function	Description
DbiAnsiToNative	Multipurpose translation function.
DbiDebugLayerOptions	Activates, deactivates, or sets options for the BDE debug layer.
DbiExit	Disconnects the client application from the BDE.
DbiGetClientInfo	Retrieves system-level information about the client application environment.
DbiGetDriverDesc	Retrieves a description of a driver.
DbiGetLdName	Retrieves the name of the language driver associated with the specified object name (table name).
DbiGetLdObj	Retrieves the language driver object associated with the given cursor.
DbiGetNetUserName	Retrieves the users network log-in name. User names should be available for all networks supported by Microsoft Windows.
DbiGetProp	Returns a property of an object.
DbiGetSysConfig	Retrieves BDE system configuration information.
DbiGetSysInfo	Retrieves system status and information.
DbiGetSysVersion	Retrieves the system version information, including the engine version number, date, and time, and the client interface version number.
DbiInit	Initializes the BDE environment.
DbiInitFn	Initializes the BDE environment. (Should not call directly. Use DBiInit.)
DbiLoadDriver	Loads a specified driver.
DbiNativeToAnsi	Translates an OEM string to an ANSI string.
DbiOpenCfgInfoList	Returns a handle to an in-memory table listing all the nodes in the configuration file accessible by the specified path.
DbiOpenDriverList	Creates an in-memory table containing a list of driver names available to the client application.
DbiOpenFieldTypesList	Creates an in-memory table containing a list of field types supported by the table type for the driver type.

continued

FUNCTION	DESCRIPTION
DbiOpenIndexTypesList	Creates an in-memory table containing a list of all supported index types for the driver type.
DbiOpenLdList	Creates an in-memory table containing a list of available language drivers.
DbiOpenTableList	Creates an in-memory table with information about all the tables accessible to the client application.
DbiOpenTableTypesList	Creates an in-memory table listing table type names for the given driver.
DbiOpenUserList	Creates an in-memory table containing a list of users sharing the same network file.
DbiSetProp	Sets the specified property of an object to a given value.
DbiUseIdleTime	Allows the BDE to accomplish background tasks during times when the client application is idle.

ERROR-HANDLING FUNCTIONS

Each of the following BDE functions returns error-handling information or performs an operation that relates to error handling.

FUNCTION	DESCRIPTION
DbiGetErrorContext	After receiving an error code back from a call, enables the client to probe the BDE for more specific error information.
DbiGetErrorEntry	Returns the error description of a specified error stack entry.
DbiGetErrorInfo	Provides descriptive information about the last error that occurred.
DbiGetErrorString	Returns the message associated with a given error code.

INDEX FUNCTIONS

Each of the following BDE functions returns information about an index or indexes or performs an operation that affect an index.

FUNCTION	DESCRIPTION
DbiAddIndex	Creates an index on an existing table.
DbiCloseIndex	Closes the specified index on a cursor.
DbiCompareKeys	Compares two key values based on the current index of the cursor.
DbiDeleteIndex	Removes an index from a table.
DbiExtractKey	Retrieves the key value for the current record of the given cursor or from the supplied record buffer.
DbiGetIndexDesc	Retrieves the properties of the given index associated with the cursor.
DbiGetIndexDescs	Retrieves index properties.
DbiGetIndexForField	Returns the description of any useful index on the specified field.
DbiGetIndexSeqNo	Retrieves the ordinal number of the index in the index list of the specified cursor.
DbiGetIndexTypeDesc	Retrieves a description of the index type.

DbiOpenIndex	Opens the index for the table associated with the cursor.
DbiRegenIndex	Regenerates an index to make sure that it is up-to-date (all records currently in the table are included in the index and are in the index order).
DbiSwitchToIndex	Allows the user to change the active index order of the given cursor.

LOCKING FUNCTIONS

Each of the following BDE functions returns lock status information or acquires or releases a table or record-level lock.

FUNCTION	DESCRIPTION
DbiAcqPersistTableLock	Acquires an exclusive persistent lock on the table, preventing other users from using the table or creating a table of the same name.
DbiAcqTableLock	Acquires a table-level lock on the table associated with the given cursor.
DbiGetRecord	Record-positioning functions have an optional lock parameter.
DbiIsRecordLocked	Checks the lock status of the current record.
DbiIsTableLocked	Returns the number of locks of a specified type acquired on the table associated with the given session.
DbiIsTableShared	Determines whether or not the table is physically shared.
DbiOpenLockList	Creates an in-memory table containing a list of locks acquired on the table.
DbiOpenUserList	Creates an in-memory table containing a list of users sharing the same network file.
DbiRelPersistTableLock	Releases the persistent table lock on the specified table.
DbiRelRecordLock	Releases the record lock on either the current record of the cursor or only the locks acquired in the current session.
DbiRelTableLock	Releases table locks of the specified type associated with the current session (i.e., the session in which the cursor was created).
DbiSetLockRetry	Sets the table and record lock retry time for the current session.

QUERY FUNCTIONS

Each of the following BDE functions performs a Query tasks

FUNCTION	DESCRIPTION
DbiGetProp	Returns a property of an object.
DbiQExec	Executes the previously prepared query identified by the supplied statement handle and returns a cursor to the result set, if one is generated.
DbiQExecDirect	Executes a SQL or QBE query and returns a cursor to the result set, if one is generated.
DbiQExecProcDirect	Directs the execution of a stored procedure.
DbiQFree	Frees the resources associated with a previously prepared query identified by the supplied statement handle.
DbiQInstantiateAnswer	Creates an answer table.

continued

FUNCTION	DESCRIPTION
DbiQPrepare	Prepares a SQL or QBE query for execution and returns a handle to a statement containing the prepared query.
DbiQPrepareProc	Prepares a stored procedure.
DbiQSetParams	Associates data with parameter markers embedded within a prepared query.
DbiQSetProcParams	Sets procedure parameters.
DbiSetProp	Sets the specified property of an object to a given value.

SESSION FUNCTIONS

Each of the following BDE functions returns information about or performs operations that affects the session.

FUNCTION	DESCRIPTION
DbiAddPassword	Adds a password to the current session.
DbiCheckRefresh	Checks for remote updates to tables for all cursors in the current session, and refreshes the cursors if changed.
DbiCloseSession	Closes the session associated with the given session handle.
DbiDropPassword	Removes a password from the current session.
DbiGetCurrSession	Returns the handle associated with the current session.
DbiGetDateFormat	Gets the date format for the current session.
DbiGetNumberFormat	Gets the number format for the current session.
DbiGetSesInfo	Retrieves the environment settings for the current session.
DbiGetTimeFormat	Gets the time format for the current session.
DbiSetCurrSession	Sets the current session of the client application to the specified session.
DbiSetDateFormat	Sets the date format for the current session.
DbiSetNumberFormat	Sets the number format for the current session.
DbiSetPrivateDir	Sets the private directory for the current session.
DbiSetTimeFormat	Sets the time format for the current session.
DbiStartSession	Starts a new session for the client application.

TABLE FUNCTIONS

Each of the following BDE functions returns information about or performs actions on a specific table.

FUNCTION	DESCRIPTION
DbiCreateInMemTable	Creates a temporary in-memory table.
DbiCreateTable	Creates a table.
DbiCreateTempTable	Creates a temporary table that is deleted when the cursor is closed, unless the call is followed by a call to DbiMakePermanent.
DbiDeleteTable	Deletes a table.

DbiDoRestructure	Changes the properties of a table.
DbiGetTableOpenCount	Returns the total number of cursors that are open on the specified table.
DbiGetTableTypeDesc	Returns a description of the capabilities of the table type for the driver type.
DbiIsTableShared	Determines whether the table is physically shared or not.
DbiMakePermanent	Changes a temporary table created by DbiCreateTempTable into a permanent table.
DbiOpenFamilyList	Creates an in-memory table listing the family members associated with a specified table.
DbiOpenFieldList	Creates an in-memory table listing the fields in a specified table and their descriptions.
DbiOpenIndexList	Opens a cursor on an in-memory table listing the indexes on a specified table, along with their descriptions.
DbiOpenLockList	Creates an in-memory table containing a list of locks acquired on the table associated with the cursor.
DbiOpenRintList	Creates an in-memory table listing the referential integrity links for a specified table, along with their descriptions.
DbiOpenSecurityList	Creates an in-memory table listing record-level security information about a specified table.
DbiOpenTable	Opens the given table for access and associates a cursor handle with the opened table.
DbiRenameTable	Renames the table and all of its resources to the specified name.
DbiSaveChanges	Forces all updated records associated with the table to disk.

Transaction Functions

Each of the following BDE functions begins, ends, or returns information about a transaction.

Function	Description
DbiBeginTran	Begins a transaction.
DbiEndTran	Ends a transaction.
DbiGetTranInfo	Retrieves the transaction state.

Xbase to Borland Delphi Conversion Notes

LANGUAGE FEATURES

If you write code directly in Delphi (as opposed to using the interactive design environment), you will notice many features of the language that are similar to Xbase or CA-Clipper. You will also notice several important differences beyond simple syntax conversion. Some things are easier to do with Delphi than they were with Xbase or CA-Clipper, and some things are much harder. Because of the dynamic nature of Xbase (particularly automatic garbage collection), there are several features of the language that are very difficult to replicate by making a generic conversion to a strongly typed language like Delphi.

Documentation Conventions

This section focuses primarily on converting CA-Clipper code to Delphi. However, most of the features of CA-Clipper discussed here are common to all Xbase dialects. If you prefer to read about converting some other dialect of Xbase (like dBASE or FoxPro), simply pretend that you are reading about that dialect whenever you see CA-Clipper mentioned, and in most cases you will still be reading correct information!

Some notational standards have been implemented to make this document readable and brief. These conventions include syntax specifications and variable names.

MODIFIED HUNGARIAN NOTATION

A modified Hungarian Notation familiar to most CA-Clipper developers is used for variable names to indicate type references. (While some might argue that type notation in a dynamically typed language like Xbase is silly, we suggest that it's far sillier *not* to use it when the compiler doesn't do type checking for you, so you can rely only on your own eyes.) Where the type designator is used in Delphi, that is also listed in the data type description in the following table:

Prefix	Example	Data type
a	`aVals := { 1, 2, 3 }`	Xbase and Delphi arrays.
b	`bBlock := {|| .T. }`	In CA-Clipper, code blocks. In Delphi, a logical (Boolean) value.
c	`cValue := Time()`	Xbase character values (could also be a character-based memo field). In Delphi, a single-byte character.
d	`dNow := Date()`	Xbase date values and Delphi TDateTime values.
i	`iNum := 0;`	Delphi Integer or ShortInt.
l	`lValue := .T.`	Xbase logical values.
n	`nVal := 2`	Xbase numeric values (both integer and real) and Delphi LongInts.
r	`rVal := 111.234;`	Delphi real numbers.
s	`sProd := 'Xphiles';`	Delphi string type.

This notation is also used to indicate result values. For example <lExpression> indicates an expression that returns a logical value, like 1 < 2. The typeface used in the second column of the preceding table is used for all source code references in this document.

SYNTAX SPECIFICATIONS

Text that is not enclosed in angle brackets <> indicates keywords. Brackets [] indicate optional text or statements. Ellipses (...) indicate one or more repetitions of the previously mentioned entity. For example, the syntax specification

```
IF <lCondition1>
    <statements>...
[ELSEIF <lCondition2>
    <statements>...
ELSEIF <lConditionN>
    <statements>...]
[ELSE
    <statements>...]
END[IF]
```

indicates that one or more statements must follow the IF <lCondition1> line due to the <statements>... line. The brackets around the ELSEIF ... lines indicate that this part of the syntax expression is optional, as are the ELSE lines, and the IF at the end of the ENDIF keyword.

Statements

(For the discussion of language features, you may wish to open your Delphi Help file, click on the **Object Pascal Language** icon, click on **Language Definition**, and then click on **Statements** and refer to the similar statements while reading this document.)

All Delphi statements end with a semicolon (;), and line breaks are not significant (other than for visual layout of source code). Xbase is a line-oriented language, where the normal statement terminator is the end of line character sequence (carriage return and line feed pair). In Xbase, semicolons may be used to:

- continue a statement to the next line by ending the current line with a single semi-colon or ;
- separate multiple statements on the same line (a comma may also be used as an expression separator in CA-Clipper).

Simple Statements

Both Delphi and Xbase have simple and structured statements. First, we'll discuss the simple statements of both languages. In Delphi, multiple statements can be treated as one statement by enclosing them within a begin and end. Therefore, wherever you see <statement> listed for a Delphi syntax, you can include multiple statements.

Assignment Statements

Assignment statements place the value of an expression into a variable. A *variable* is a named placeholder for a memory location that contains a value. The *expression* is the value or repre-sentation of the value that can be calculated. The assignment operator in both CA-Clipper and Delphi is ":=". Because the variable appears on the left of the operator, it is also called the left-hand side (lhs) value (or l-value). The expression appears to the right of the assignment operator, so it is also called the right-hand side (rhs) value (or r-value).

An assignment statement in CA-Clipper is:

```
nVar := 1 (nVar = 1 is also valid, but not recommended because of ambiguity)
```

An equivalent statement in Delphi would be:

```
nVar := 1;
```

Assignment statements are used to assign the value that will be returned from a function. Either the name of the function or the keyword *Result* can be used to assign this return value. The following listing:

```
function one : string;
begin
   Result := 'One';
end;
```

is functionally equivalent to:

```
function one : string;
begin
   One := 'One';
end;
```

Additional Assignment Operators

CA-Clipper also has assignment operators that can *modify* the value of a variable, by performing a calculation based on the current value of the variable. These shorthand operators can be very convenient to use, and will be missed in Delphi. The remaining CA-Clipper assignment operators are as follows.

OPERATOR	CA-CLIPPER	DELPHI	EXPLANATION
+=	a += 1	a := a + 1;	Addition to numeric, character, or date types
-=	b -= 1	b := b - 1;	Subtraction from numeric, character, or date types.
*=	c *= 2	c := c * 2;	Multiplication of numeric types.
/=	d /= 3	d := d / 3;	Division of numeric types.
%=	e %= 4	e := e mod 4;	Modulus of numeric types.
**=	f **= 5	f := exp(f, 5);	Exponentiation of numeric types.
^=	f ^= 5	f := exp(f, 5);	Exponentiation of numeric types.
++	g++	g := g + 1;	Postincrement operator for numeric and date types. May also be of the form ++g, as a pre-increment operator.
—	h—	h := h - 1;	Postdecrement operator for numeric and date types. May also be of the form —h, as a pre-decrement operator.

By-Reference Operator

The at-sign (@) is used as the unary prefix by-reference operator in both Delphi and CA-Clipper. However, there are some minor differences. In Delphi, variable, procedure, function, and method addresses may all be passed by reference. Addresses for procedures and methods are only used when calling assembly routines or in-line statements.

Use of the @ operator in Xbase is permitted only when passing the address of a variable to another function or procedure. (If you want to reference a procedure, function, or method in CA-Clipper and pass it as a variable, you must reference it in a code block or by name with the macro engine.)

Alias (Datafile Work Area) Operator

The feature you will probably miss most from Xbase is its automatic management of work areas and the automatic resolution of fields referenced by name The alias operator (->) requires an alias (work area) reference on the left-hand side, and a field or variable on the right hand side, as in:

```
alias->identifier
```

You may also alias an expression by enclosing it in parentheses:

```
alias->( expression )
```

This syntax is also referred to as an extended expression. If the alias is M or MEMVAR, the identifier is considered to be a PUBLIC or PRIVATE memory variable. If an expression is aliased (or extended into an alias), the alias specifies the work area in which to evaluate the expression.

Xbase automatically creates a work area for a data file when you open it with the USE ... command or with the dbUseArea() function. When you open a data file, Xbase automatically assigns an alias name to it (which you can override when opening the file). A work area number (from 1 to 250) may also be used to reference the data file. Valid examples are:

```
3->field
table->field
(nTable)->field
( cTable )->field
```

This makes data file manipulation a breeze. Delphi is more complicated, but not unbearably so. First, consider the Xbase example that steps through the file, printing the field called FIRST:

```
USE Example
WHILE ! EOF()
   ? Example->First    // You could also use Field->First
   SKIP
ENDDO
```

Here's a Delphi equivalent done the hard way:

```
var
    Example: TTable;
begin
    Example := TTable.Create(nil);
    Example.DataBaseName := 'c:\example';
    Example.TableName    := 'example.dbf';
    Example.Open;
    while not Example.Eof do begin
       WriteLn( Example FieldByName( 'First' ).AsString );
       Next;
    end;
       Example.Close;
       Example.Free;
end;
```

Here's a slightly easier version, using the WITH statement:

```
var
    Example: TTable;
begin
    Example := TTable.Create(nil);
    with Example do
       begin
       DataBaseName := 'c:\example';
       TableName    := 'example.dbf';
       Open;
       while not Eof do begin
          WriteLn( FieldByName( 'First' ).AsString );
          Next;
       Close;
       Free;
    end;
end;
```

As you can readily see, this aspect of converting Xbase code to Delphi is a somewhat arduous task. Supporting routines can ease the process, but there is no guarantee that conversions will be 100% accurate without manually reviewing and testing the code. See the section on Database Programming for further information.

GOTO Statement

Xbase has no equivalent to the Delphi GOTO statement. It could be faked, but that is poor programming practice.

Procedure Statements

Procedure statements invoke a procedure and do not have a return value. Parameter values may be passed to a procedure if it has been declared to accept parameters. Passing incorrectly typed variables or too many variables will result in a compilation error. Unlike most Xbase dialects, you cannot assign a variable to a procedure call in Delphi. However, Delphi does have an extended syntax compiler directive that can relax some of the compilation restrictions Pascal traditionally imposes on writing code, so you can reference functions without assigning a return value to them. The extended compiler syntax is also very useful for operating on null-terminated strings. See the "$X" topic in the Delphi Help file for details.

STRUCTURED STATEMENTS

Structured statements are constructs comprised of one or more simple statements that are to be executed either sequentially (one after another with no interruption), conditionally (either/or statements), or repeatedly (in some type of loop).

Compound Statements/List Operators

A compound statement in Delphi is a list of one or more statements that is intended to be executed in sequence. When Delphi compiles a compound statement, it is treated as a single statement, which is sometimes important in places where Delphi requires a single statement (like in the conditional construct explained later). The statement block (compound statement list) is indicated with the reserved words **begin** and **end**:

```
begin
    Statement1;
    Statement2;
    .
    .
    .
    StatementN;
end;
```

The closest equivalent CA-Clipper has to compound statements is the list operator. The comma is the binary list operator and is used to group multiple expressions when only one value is expected. The result returned from the list operator is the result of the rightmost expression in the list. For example:

```
? ( 1, 2, 3 )  // Prints: 3
```

CA-Clipper's list operator may also be used inside a code block.

Conditional Statements

Both Delphi and Xbase have two conditional statement constructs: the IF statement and the CASE statement. However, there are differences in the operation of both constructs in the two languages.

IF Statements

The Xbase IF construct has a slightly richer syntax than that of Delphi, but it can be very nearly approximated in Delphi. The syntax for the Xbase statement is:

```
IF <lCondition1>
    <statements>...
[ELSEIF <lCondition2>
    <statements>...
ELSEIF <lConditionN>
    <statements>...]
[ELSE
    <statements>...]
END[IF]
```

The brackets ([]) indicate optional components of the construct.

The Delphi syntax is:

```
if ( <lCondition> ) then <statement>
[else <statement> ];
```

As you may notice from the Xbase syntax, Delphi does not have an ELSEIF keyword. This is not the end of the world, however, because it can be replicated by simply reformatting Delphi source code to be similar in layout to the original Xbase statements. For example:

```
IF nVal == 1
    ? 'One'
ELSEIF nVal == 2
    ? 'Two'
ELSEIF nVal == 3
    ? 'Three'
ELSE
    ? "I can't count that high!"
ENDIF
```

Can be duplicated in Delphi as follows:

```
if ( nVal = 1 ) then
    WriteLn( 'One' )
else if ( nVal = 2 ) then
    WriteLn( 'Two' )
else if ( nVal = 3 ) then
    WriteLn( 'Three' )
else
    WriteLn( 'I can't count that high!' );
```

CASE Statements

The Xbase CASE statement is compiled almost identically to its IF construct. Every CASE clause has its own logical expression to evaluate, and a sequence of statements it may perform. The syntax is:

```
DO CASE
CASE <lCondition1>
   <statements>
[CASE <lCondition2>
   <statements>]
   .
   .
   .
CASE <lConditionN>
   <statements>]
[OTHERWISE
   <statements>]
ENDCASE
```

Delphi's CASE statement is quite different. It is analogous to the switch construct found in C and C++, where a single expression is tested for a result of multiple values. While this is not as flexible as the Xbase CASE statement, it allows the optimizing compiler to greatly improve the execution speed of the conditional construct. Its syntax is:

```
case <Expression> of
   <value1>[..<high value>] : <statement>;
   [<value2>[..<high value2>]: <statement>;
   .
   .
   .
   <valueN>[..<high valueN>]: <statementN>;]
   [else <statement>;]
end;
```

Delphi also imposes some limits on the value types that may be the result of the expression. The expression must return a value that is a byte-sized or a word-sized ordinal type. This means that you can not have <Expression> return a string or long integer. What this means to the Xbase developer is that, when converting Xbase CASE statements to Delphi, use the IF construct unless the test you are performing is easily translatable with the foregoing restrictions.

The following Xbase code shows an example that translates quickly and elegantly to Delphi:

```
DO CASE
CASE cVal >= '0' .AND. cVal <= '9'
   ? vDigit'
CASE cVal >= 'A' .AND. cVal <= 'Z'
   ? 'Uppercase A..Z'
CASE cVal >= 'a' .AND. cVal <= 'z'
   ? 'Lowercase a..z'
OTHERWISE
   ? 'Some other character'
ENDCASE
```

Here is the Delphi equivalent:

```
case ( cVal ) of
   '0'..'9': WriteLn( 'Digit' );
   'A'..'Z': WriteLn( 'Uppercase A..Z' );
   'a'..'z': WriteLn( 'Lowercase a..z' );
   else WriteLn( 'Some other character' );
end;
```

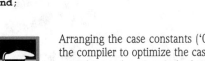

Arranging the case constants ('0'..'9', 'A'..'Z', and 'a'..'z') in ascending order allows the compiler to optimize the case into jumps for the different values. This is definitely something to bear in mind when moving your code from Xbase to Delphi, so that you can squeeze every additional ounce of performance out of the code.

T I P

Loop Statements

Xbase has two loop statements: FOR .. NEXT and WHILE. Delphi has both of these, along with another loop statement, the REPEAT .. UNTIL, which can be replicated in CA-Clipper with two preprocessor directives. Since this document focuses on converting from Xbase to Delphi, the discussion of CA-Clipper's pseudo REPEAT .. UNTIL loop will be mercifully brief.

The FOR Loop

The FOR loop is best used when a block of statements are to be executed a specific number of times or for a specific range of values. The Xbase syntax specification is:

```
FOR <nCounter> := <nStart> TO <nEnd> STEP <nIncrement>]
   <statements>...
   [LOOP]
   <statements>...
   [EXIT]
NEXT
```

The STEP specifier in Xbase allows the loop counter to move either up or down, depending on whether the <nIncrement> value is negative or positive. The Delphi syntax for the loop is:

```
for <oValue> := <oStart> to|downto <oStop> do
   <statement>;
```

The following code example shows an Xbase iterative loop:

```
FOR nCount := 1 TO 100
   nTotal += nCount
NEXT
```

And here is the remarkably similar Delphi iterative loop:

```
for nCount := 1 to 100 do
   nTotal := nTotal + nCount;
```

The WHILE Loop

The WHILE loop is used when you want to test a condition before executing the statements inside the loop even once. Statements inside the loop may execute zero (0) or more times. Here is the syntax for the Xbase version of the WHILE loop:

```
[DO] WHILE <lCondition>
   <statements>...
   [LOOP]
   <statements>...
   [EXIT]
   <statements>...
END[DO]
```

And here is the Delphi WHILE loop:

```
while <lCondition> do
   <statement>;
```

Here is an Xbase example that displays the current time until the time is exactly noon. (This code will work only in the morning, by the way):

```
LOCAL cTime := Left( Time(), 5 )
WHILE cTime < "12:00"
  @ 0, 0 SAY cTime
  cTime := Left( Time(), 5 )
ENDDO
```

Here is the Delphi equivalent (or, at least, close enough):

```
var
    timeExit, timeNow : TDateTime;
begin
   timeNow := Time;
   timeExit := StrToTime( '12:00' );
   while timeNow < timeExit do
   begin
      CursorTo( 0, 0 );
      WriteLn( TimeToStr( timeNow ));
   end;
end;
```

The REPEAT .. UNTIL Loop

As mentioned previously, CA-Clipper does not really have this type of loop, although it can be replicated with the following code:

```
#trans REPEAT => WHILE .T.
#trans UNTIL <lCond> => IF <lCond>; EXIT; END; END
```

In the CA-Clipper translation of the UNTIL directive shown above, the first END terminates the IF statement, and the second END terminates the WHILE loop.

The syntax for Delphi is:

```
repeat
    <statements>...;
until <lCondition>;
```

Declarations

Historically, Pascal has been a strongly typed language, and Xbase has always been a dynamically (some call it weakly) typed language. *Dynamic typing* means that an Xbase variable could have the type of data it represents changed by simply assigning it a new value of a different data type. For example, the following code is 100% acceptable (and frequently written) for Xbase-style code:

```
var := Date()
? var   // date type
var := Time()
? var   // string type
```

No Xbase language flavor would complain about this code, but it would not get past the Delphi compiler. As with all choices, there are good and bad sides to both language implementations: with Xbase, you get a very flexible variable referencing system that performs (comparatively) slowly. With Delphi, you get an extremely fast variable referencing implementation that compiles to machine code, thus allowing maximum run-time performance.

DELPHI'S STRONGLY TYPED VARIABLES

Even though Xbase variables can be changed to a different type at any time, the same is not true of Xbase data fields. At run-time, assigning a character value to a numeric field will cause a run-time error. With Delphi, the likelihood of this happening is infinitesimal, because the compiler would complain long before the code ever got to the point of being executed.

The following table lists the equivalent strong types of Delphi for the standard Xbase data types.

CODE	TYPE	LENGTH	DELPHI TYPE(S)	LENGTH(S)	COMMENTS
B	Code block pointers	N/A	function & procedure	N/A	See dbEval() for code samples.
C	Character	about 65000	char, string & PChar	1, 255 & 65535	PChar requires MemGrab() and Free().
D	Date	8	TDateTime	N/A	A float with special encoding.
F	Float	varies	Real, Single, Double, Extended, Comp	6, 4, 8, 10, 8	
L	Logical	1	Boolean	1	
M	Memo	>= 10	char, string &PChar	1, 255 & 65535	Xbase variables usually return 'C' unless they reference data fields.

continued

Code	Type	Length	Delphi Type(s)	Length(s)	Comments
N	Numeric	varies	Real, Single, Double, Extended, Comp, Integer, ShortInt, Word	varies	Xbase numerics are indiscriminately integers or real numbers.

While this table may initially seem overwhelming, the primary reason it looks so complicated is because Delphi has many standard variable types that fall into the broad Xbase type categories.

Delphi's Character String Types

Because of the way Pascal strings have been historically encoded, the standard string type has always been limited to 255 characters. If you are accustomed to the flexibility of Xbase strings growing to almost 64K or shrinking down to none, this may result in some support problems when converting code to Delphi.

The default string support does not require grabbing and freeing memory, so it is more convenient to use than the longer strings of type PChar, which require allocating and freeing memory. If you have a routine that requires a longer string to be used, you will need to allocate a pointer for the character string, and then deallocate it when you are done. GetMem() and FreeMem() may be used to allocate the string buffer, but a better choice would be to use StrAlloc() and StrDispose(), because the first two bytes of the buffer are used for a 16-bit number that indicates the size of the allocation. In this fashion, you do not have to keep a variable indicating the size of the buffer to pass to FreeMem().

If you do need to work with a longer string, you may want to use the following code sample as a guideline:

```
var
    szText        : PChar;
    wSize         : LongInt;
begin
    .
    .     { Do something to determine the value for wSize here}
    .
      try
      szText      := StrAlloc( wSize ); { Allocate buffer size, up to 65,526
                                          bytes }
    .
    .     { Manipulate, display, or whatever szText }
    .
    finally
    StrDispose( szText );              { Release the allocated buffer — don't
                                        need size }
    end;
end;
```

If you want to work with a copy of a null-terminated string to leave the original string alone, you can do something like the following:

```
try
    szNew         := StrNew( szOriginal ); { Make same-size copy of szOriginal }
```

```
.  { do stuff to szNew }
.
.
finally
   StrDispose( szNew );
end;
```

All other standard data types in Delphi are stack based and will automatically have their memory space freed when the routine they are declared in is exited. As mentioned previously, the majority of your Xbase code will probably work fine with the standard Pascal string variable, but in those situations where more than 255 characters in a string must be manipulated at one time, the previous code examples should provide you the information you need to do it. If you want to see how to work directly with a PChar pointer, consider the routine StrProper(), which converts the entire string to a "Proper Cased" string:

```
function StrProper( szInput : PChar ) : PChar;
var
   wPos,
   wLen     : Word;
   bDoItUp  : Boolean;

begin
   wLen       := StrLen( szInput ) - 1;
   bDoItUp    := True;
   Result     := szInput; { Points to same string! }
   for wPos := 0 to wLen do begin
      if not ( Result[ wPos ] in [ #1..'/', ':'..'@', #91..#96, #123..#127 ] )
      then begin
         bDoItUp := True;
         if ( Result[ wPos ] = #39 ) and ( wPos > 0 ) then
            Result[ wPos - 1 ] := LoCase( Result[ wPos - 1 ] );
      end
      else if bDoItUp then begin
         Result[ wPos ] := UpCase( Result[ wPos ] );
         bDoItUp        := False;
      end
      else
         Result[ wPos ] := LoCase( Result[ wPos ] );
   end; { for }
end; { StrProper() }
```

DELPHI'S DYNAMICALLY TYPED VARIABLES

If you blanched at the type comparison table, do not get too worried! Delphi has several types that are functionally very similar to the dynamically typed variables you are familiar with in Xbase. While changing the type of the value contained in these variables is not always as syntactically convenient as it is in Xbase, it is still rather easy to do. In fact, since Delphi can automatically convert a value to a requested type simply by assigning it, it is sometimes preferable to the easy Xbase syntax.

Dynamic Variable Type: TVarRec

The most basic of these is the type TVarRec, which is actually a conditional record structure that indicates type information inside the record. Here is the declaration of this structure:

```
const
  vtInteger  = 0;
  vtBoolean  = 1;
  vtChar     = 2;
  vtExtended = 3;
  vtString   = 4;
  vtPointer  = 5;
  vtPChar    = 6;
  vtObject   = 7;
  vtClass    = 8;

type
  TVarRec = record
    case Integer of
      vtInteger:  (VInteger: Longint; VType: Byte);
      vtBoolean:  (VBoolean: Boolean);
      vtChar:     (VChar: Char);
      vtExtended: (VExtended: PExtended);
      vtString:   (VString: PString);
      vtPointer:  (VPointer: Pointer);
      vtPChar:    (VPChar: PChar);
      vtObject:   (VObject: TObject);
      vtClass:    (VClass: TClass);
  end;
```

The variable VType indicates the type of the value contained in the structure. See the provided file XBASE.PAS for many examples of TVarRec usage.

Optional Parameters: array of const

One of the handiest features of Xbase is default values for parameters passed to routines, or parameters that may be skipped. We were pleasantly surprised to find that Delphi provides a convenient syntax for the same type of capability by employing a type specifier called array of const. Bracket characters are used to delimit the parameter list. Every element in the array is a TVarRec variable, which allows you to handle variables of any type in your receiving routine.

Here are two functions: the first (Var2String) will convert any TVarRec value into its string equivalent, and the second (VarList2String) will take any number of values, and then convert them to a single string with a space between each value:

```
function Var2String( xVar : TVarRec ) : string;
begin
  case xVar.VType of
    vtInteger  : Result := IntToStr( xVar.VInteger );
    vtBoolean  :
```

```
        if xVar.VBoolean then
            Result := '.T.'
        else
            Result := '.F.';
    vtChar       : Result := xVar.VChar;
    vtExtended   : Result := FloatToStr( xVar.VExtended^ );
    vtString     : Result := xVar.VString^;
    vtPChar      : Result := StrPas( xVar.VPChar );
    vtObject     : Result := 'object:' + xVar.VObject.ClassName;
    vtClass      : Result := 'class:' + xVar.VClass.ClassName;
    else Result := '';
    end;
end; { Var2String() }

function VarList2String( xVars : array of const ) : string;
var
    iVar,
    iVars : Integer;
begin
    if SizeOf( xVars ) > 0 then begin
        Result   := Var2String( xVars[ 0 ] );
        iVars    := High( xVars );
        for iVar := 1 to iVars do
            Result := Result + ' ' + Var2String( xVars[ iVar ] );
    end
    else
        Result := '';
end; { VarList2String() }
```

With the preceding code, it is easy to provide output routines that will support any type of variable. Note that because these routines are intended to be Xbase-compatible, Boolean values return '.T.' and '.F.' rather than 'Y' and 'N'. If you do not like that implementation, simply change the code—it will not break any of the supplied routines because none of them rely on the contents of that return value.

In VarList2String(), you should also notice the type declaration array of const. This type declaration makes it possible to pass a list of parameters to a routine that vary in both type and length, as demonstrated in the following code:

```
sDesc := VarList2String( [ '2 * 4 =', 2 * 4 ] ); { Result is '2 * 4 = 8' }
sDesc := VarList2String( [ 'Delphi','is','cool?', 10 = 2 * 5 ] );
                { Result is 'Delphi is cool? .T.' }
```

DATABASE FIELDS: TFIELD

With the Borland Database Engine (BDE), and also under SuccessWare's Apollo, every field in a data file is represented by a TField object. It is similar to the TVarRec structure, but includes some very convenient properties and methods for automatic type conversion when assigning or retrieving a value:

TFIELD PROPERTY/METHOD	DESCRIPTION
asDate [:=<dValue>]	Gets or sets the value of the field with a date type.
asString [:= <sValue>]	Gets or sets the value of the field with a string type. asString returns 'Y' for Boolean values that are True, and 'N' for Boolean values that are False.
asInteger[:=<iValue>]	Gets or sets the value of the field with an integer type. Converts Boolean values to 0 or 1, rounds up floats, and attempts to determine the numeric value of strings.
asFloat [:= <fValue>]	Gets or sets the value of the field with a real number type.
asBoolean[:=<bValue>]	Gets or sets the value of the field as a Boolean value.
AssignValue(<xValue>)	Assigns the value of the field using one of the already mentioned methods depending on the type of <xValue>. <Value> is a TVarRec.
SetData(<pValue>)	Sets raw data to the field without performing any type conversions. The buffer must have enough room for the data. Use TField.DataSize to determine the proper size for the buffer. Pass nil to set the data to a NULL field.
GetData(<pValue>)	Gets raw data from the field. Again, use TField.DataSize to determine the proper size for the buffer. If the data is NULL, no data are returned, and GetData() returns False. Otherwise, it sets data and returns True.

TField has other properties and methods, and you should familiarize yourself with them. They are documented in the Delphi Help file. Just search for "TField" and go to the "TField Component" entry.

EVENLY DIMENSIONED ARRAYS

Delphi can easily support single- or multidimensional arrays with array dimension declarations. The only difference between Delphi and Xbase arrays is that Delphi arrays must be homogenous (i.e., every element of the array must contain the same data type). This is a trivial limitation, however, because Delphi supports declaring arrays of structures, which can contain various elements of mixed type. In fact, if you deem it necessary, you can even create an array of TVarRec types so you could store mixed types in any element of the array. Here are some examples of array declarations in Delphi code:

```
type
   IntList  = Array[1..100]     of Integer;
   CharData = Array['A'..'Z']   of Byte;
   Matrix   = Array[0..9, 0..9] of Real;

var
   aNames   : Array[ 1..10 ] of String;
   aAmounts : Array[ 0..500 ] of Real;
   aAnyType : Array[ 1..10, 1..5 ] of TVarRec;
```

As you may have noticed, you can declare the dimensions of the array to be any ordinal type. This provides for some tremendous capability when performing some calculations. Suppose that you want to traverse a data file and sum amounts for the range of years 1950 to 2000. The following code will correctly accumulate the amounts for those years falling in that range. (Only the accumulation code is shown, and this routine uses the Year() function from the Xbase compatibility unit.)

```
var
   aYears   : Array[ 1950 .. 2000 ] of Extended;
```

```
   dEntry    : TDateTime;
   eCurrent  : Extended;
begin
   .
   .
   .
   try
      aYears[ Year( dEntry ) ] := eValue;
   except
      { Don't need to do anything here — just to prevent array access errors }
   end;
end;
```

To perform a similar routine in Xbase, you would need to declare the array starting at one (1), which would result in a tremendous amount of wasted space.

There are many cases where an evenly dimensioned array of mixed type is used because Xbase does not support structures (and only recently started supporting objects). For example, CA-Clipper has a Directory() function that returns a two-dimensional (2D) array where each "row" of the array contains the name, date, time, size, and attributes of a given file. As you would guess from the information represented for the file, there are three different data types being used in the secondary array, which at first glance would appear to be difficult to implement in Delphi as a 2D array. However, by employing a simple record structure, the Delphi version of the code is not only just as easy to use, but it is also much more readable. By having a record structure that names each element of the file description, our code becomes quite readable. (Admittedly, CA-Clipper also has a #define manifest constant that references the elements of the subarray, but in this case the notational syntax is just as easy in Delphi.)

Here is the record structure used for Delphi's FindFirst() and FindNext() functions that will list the files in a given directory:

```
TSearchRec = record
   Fill: Array[1..21] of Byte;
   Attr: Byte;
   Time: Longint;
   Size: Longint;
   Name: String[12];
end;
```

The Time value can be converted to Delphi's standard TDateTime type with FileDateToDateTime(), so both the file date and time can be extracted from this one field. The following code creates an equivalent to the CA-Clipper Directory() function that inherits from the TList component for the dynamic array sizing capability.

```
function Directory(           { Get a list of files matching directory spec }
   sMask     : string;        { Directory specification }
   sAttr     : string         { Attributes to find.  '' = any file }
   )         : TDirectory;    { Must use TDirectory.Free when done! }
var
   rFile     : TSearchRec;
begin
   Result := TDirectory.Create;
   if FindFirst( sMask, StrToFileAttr( sAttr ), rFile ) = 0 then begin
```

```
        Result.Add( TFileEntry.Create( rFile ));
        while FindNext( rFile ) = 0 do
          Result.Add( TFileEntry.Create( rFile ))
    end; { if FindFirst() }
end; { Directory() }
```

Dynamic and Ragged Arrays: TList

The Directory() function leads into this topic, because the TDirectory class inherits from the TList class. The line of code calling Result.Add() automatically "grows" the array if necessary. Refer to the TList component documentation for some very important hints for implementing your own dynamic arrays and structures.

The TList class provides very similar functionality to the dynamic and ragged arrays available in several Xbase flavors. Access to them is not quite as convenient, but it is a very powerful capability that provides all the functionality of ragged arrays. Instead of variable types, you must pass a pointer to be added to the list, and pointers are also returned from the list.

Because the TList class has a default property, it is possible to omit the reference to this default property when accessing the list of items contained in the component. This allows you to write code that is syntactically very similar to Xbase array access.

In situations where an array is hard-coded, it may be more desirable to use an array of const type of notation instead of creating a TList object and adding values to it. See the above section on TVarRec for a Delphi source code example.

Code Blocks

An Xbase code block is very similar to a function (or procedure) pointer in other languages. However, there are two primary differences between a code block and a routine pointer:

- A code block does not have to be declared as a separate routine (so it does not require a name to be referenced).
- A code block can refer to variables in the expressions it contains, so variables may be directly accessed and manipulated from within it.

To mimic the action of a code block in Delphi, a function or procedure must be declared, and any variables that are changed inside the code block need to be passed by reference (using the var declaration in the formal parameter list) so they may be changed. To make this process as convenient as possible, the types xbBlockFunc and xbBlockProc have been declared in **XBCOMPAT.PAS** on the CD-ROM. xbBlockFunc is prototyped to return a TVarRec value, and xbBlockProc does not have a return value:

```
type
    xbBlockProc = procedure( xVars : Array of const );
    xbBlockFunc = function( xVars : Array of const ): TVarRec;
```

As you can see, it is assumed that any number of variables may be passed in these routines, which makes modifying the code as flexible as possible. The procedure block type is used in the following routine to accept all the standard entries that are expected for a file entry in a directory list. In this code, every file entry in the directory list is processed by whatever routine cbProc references.

```
procedure TDirectory.Eval(        { Do something to every file entry }
   cbProc       : xbBlockProc     { Procedure "code block" type }
   );
var
   iFile : Integer;
   oFile : TFileEntry;
begin
   for iFile := 1 to Count do begin
      oFile := Get( iFile );
      cbProc( [ oFile.Name, oFile.Size, dToC( oFile.Date ), oFile.Time,
         oFile.Attr ] );
   end;
end; { TDirectory.Eval }
```

The following makes it a trivial matter to list all the files in a directory:

```
oDir := Directory( sDirSpec, '' );
oDir.Eval( QOut );   { List every file in the directory }
```

Xbase Command Compatibility List

This table lists many of the Xbase commands you are familiar with, and the closest (or implemented) Xphiles and Delphi equivalents, along with whatever other information is relevant.

XBASE COMMAND	DELPHI	COMMENTS
ACCEPT		
APPEND BLANK	TTable.Append	Also see TTable.AppendRecord.
APPEND FROM	TBatchMove	
AVERAGE	TQuery.SQLExec()	See TQuery's AVG() function.
CALL		N/A
CANCEL		
CLEAR ALL	ClrScr	Only the screen clearing applies.
CLEAR GETS		N/A
CLEAR MEMORY		N/A
CLEAR SCREEN	ClrScr	Uses WinCrt
CLEAR TYPEAHEAD		N/A
CLOSE	TTable.Close TTable.Active := False	
COMMIT	TTable.Post	
CONTINUE	TQuery SELECT	Closest equivalent, better solutions
COPY FILE	TBatchMove	
COPY STRUCTURE	TTable.FieldDefs	Assign TTable.FieldDefs to a new table object to create a file of the duplicate structure.

continued

XBASE COMMAND	DELPHI	COMMENTS
COPY STRUCTURE EXTENDED		N/A
COPY TO	TBatchMove	
COUNT	TQuery.SQLExec	See SQL's SELECT COUNT().
CREATE	TTable.CreateTable TQuery CREATE TABLE	dbCreate() is easier
CREATE FROM	TTable.CreateTable	Not an exact correlation, but as close as you're going to get.
DELETE	TTable.Delete SQL DELETE	
DELETE FILE	DeleteFile()	
DELETE TAG	TTable.DeleteIndex SQL DROP INDEX	
DIR	TFileListBox TDirectoryListBox	
DISPLAY	TDBGrid	
EJECT	TForm.Print TReport.Print	
ERASE		
FIND	TTable.FindKey()	
GO	TTable.GotoBookmark TTable.GotoCurrent TTable.GotoKey TTable.GotoNearest	
INDEX	TTable.AddIndex() SQL CREATE INDEX	
INPUT	TForm	Create dialogs in the IDE for input.
JOIN	TBatchMove, SQL INSERT	
KEYBOARD		
LABEL FORM		See ReportSmith documentation.
LIST	TDBGrid	
LOCATE		
MENU TO		
NOTE		Use {} or (* *) comment blocks.
PACK	DBIPackTable()	
QUIT	Halt TForm.Close	
READ	TForm.SetFocus	
RECALL	DbiUndeleteRecord() SQL ROLLBACK	
REINDEX	TTable.Reindex	
RELEASE		N/A
RENAME	RenameFile()	

REPLACE	TField.asString TField.asInteger TField.asBoolean TField.asFloat	There are additional TField values to examine.
REPORT FORM	ReportSmith	
RESTORE		N/A
RESTORE SCREEN		N/A
RUN	WinExec()	Windows API function
SAVE		
SAVE SCREEN		N/A
SEEK	TTable.FindKey TTable.FindNearest SQL SELECT	
SELECT		
SET ALTERNATE		
SET BELL		N/A
SET CENTURY		
SET COLOR		
SET CONFIRM		N/A
SET CONSOLE		
SET CURSOR		N/A
SET DATE		
SET DECIMALS		
SET DEFAULT		
SET DELETED		
SET DELIMITERS		N/A
SET DESCENDING		
SET DEVICE		
SET EPOCH		N/A because TDateTime encodes date and time in Delphi.
SET ESCAPE		N/A
SET EVENTMASK		N/A
SET EXACT		
SET EXCLUSIVE		
SET FILTER	TTable.ApplyRange SQL SELECT	
SET FIXED		
SET FORMAT		N/A
SET FUNCTION		N/A
SET INDEX	DBIAddIndex()	
SET INTENSITY		N/A
SET KEY		

continued

XBASE COMMAND	DELPHI	COMMENTS
SET MARGIN		
SET MEMOBLOCK		N/A
SET MESSAGE		N/A
SET OPTIMIZE		N/A
SET ORDER	TTable.IndexName SQL SELECT ... GROUP BY	
SET PATH		
SET PRINTER		
SET PROCEDURE		See Units and Uses keyword.
SET RELATION	TTable.MasterFields TTable.MasterSource	
SET SCOPE	TTable.ApplyRange	
SET SCOPEBOTTOM	TTable.ApplyRange	
SET SCOPETOP	TTable.ApplyRange	
SET SCOREBOARD		N/A
SET SOFTSEEK	TTable.FindNearest	
SET TYPEAHEAD		N/A
SET UNIQUE	TTable.AddIndex	
SET VIDEOMODE		N/A
SET WRAP		N/A
SKIP	TTable.MoveBy() TTable.Next TTable.Prior	
SORT	DbiSortTable()	Use an index instead!
STORE		Direct variable assignments to the same value. The code converter processes this command.
SUM	SQL SUM()	
TEXT		N/A
TOTAL	SQL SUM()	
TYPE		N/A
UNLOCK	TTable.Post	
UPDATE	TBatchMove, SQL UPDATE	
USE	TTable.Open TTable.Active	
WAIT	ShowMessage()	
ZAP	TTable.EmptyTable	

Xbase Function Compatibility List

XBASE FUNCTION	DELPHI	COMMENTS
AADD()	TList.Add() TStringList.Add()	Add a new element to the end of an array.
ABS()	Abs()	Return the absolute value of a numeric expression.
ACHOICE()	TMenu	Execute a pop-up menu.
ACLONE()		Duplicate a nested or multidimensional array.
ACOPY()		Copy elements from one array to another.
ADEL()	TList.Remove	Delete an array element.
ADIR()		Fill a series of arrays with directory information.
AEVAL()		Execute a code block for each element in an array.
AFIELDS()	TTable.FieldDefs	Fill an array with Field definitions.
AFILL()		Fill an array with a specified value.
AINS()	TList.Insert	Insert a NIL element into an array.
ALERT()	MessageDlg()	Display a simple modal dialog box.
ALIAS()		Return a specified work area alias.
ALLTRIM()		Remove leading and trailing spaces from a character string.
ALTD()	N/A	
ARRAY()	TList.Create	
TList.Capacity		Make sure to AFree() the return value when done!
ASC()	Ord()	Convert a character to its ASCII value.
ASCAN()	TList.IndexOf	Scan an array for a value or until a block returns true (.T.).
ASIZE()	TList.Capacity	Grow or shrink an array.
ASORT()		Sort an array.
AT()	Pos()	Return the position of a substring within a character string.
ATAIL()		Return the highest numbered element of an array.
BIN2I()		Convert a 16-bit signed integer to a numeric value.
BIN2L()		Convert a 32-bit signed integer to a numeric value.

continued

851

Xbase Function	Delphi	Comments
BIN2W()		Convert a 16-bit unsigned integer to a numeric value.
BLOBDIRECTEXP()		Export the contents of a BLOB pointer to a file.
BLOBDIRECTGET()		Retrieve data from a BLOB file without referencing a field.
BLOBDIRECTIMP()		Import a file into a BLOB file and return pointer to the data.
BLOBDIRECTPUT()		Put data in a BLOB file without referencing a specific field.
BLOBEXPORT()		Copy the contents of a memo field number to a BLOB file.
BLOBGET()		Get the contents of a BLOB identified by a memo field number.
BLOBIMPORT()		Read the contents of a BLOB file into a memo field.
BLOBROOTGET()		Retrieve the data from the root area of a BLOB file.
BLOBROOTLOCK()		Obtain a lock on the root area of a BLOB file.
BLOBROOTPUT()		Store data in the root area of a BLOB file.
BLOBROOTUNLOC()		Release the lock on a BLOB file's root area.
BOF()	TTable.Bof	Determine when beginning of file is encountered.
BREAK()	Raise	Branch out of a BEGIN SEQUENCE...END construct.
BROWSE()	TDBGrid	Browse records within a window.
CDOW()	DayOfWeek()	Convert a date value to a character day of the week.
CHR()	Chr()	Convert an ASCII code to a character value.
CMONTH()		Convert a date to a character month name.
COL()	Cursor	Return the screen cursor column position.
COLORSELECT()		Activate attribute in current color settings.
CTOD()	StrToDate()	Convert a date string to a date value.
CURDIR()		Return the current DOS directory.
DATE()	Date	Return the system date as a date value.
DAY()	DecodeDate()	Return the day of the month as a numeric value.
DBAPPEND()	TTable.Append	Append a new record to the database in the current work area.
DBCLEARFIL()	TQuery.SQL.Clear	Clear a filter condition.
DBCLEARIND()		Close all indexes for the current work area.
DBCLEARREL()	TTable.MasterFields TTable.MasterSource	Clear active relations.

DBCLOSEALL()	TTable.Close	Close all occupied work areas.
DBCLOSEAREA()	TTable.Close TTable.Active	Close a work area.
DBCOMMIT()	TTable.Post	Flush pending updates.
DBCOMMITALL()	TTable.Post	Flush pending updates in all work areas.
DBCREATE()	TTable.Create	Create a database file from a database structure array.
DBCREATEIND()	TTable.AddIndex	Create an index file.
DBDELETE()	TTable.Delete	Mark a record for deletion.
DBEDIT()	TDBGrid	Browse records in a table layout.
DBEVAL()		Evaluate code block for each record-matching scope/condition.
DBF()	TTable.TableName	Return current alias name.
DBFIELDINFO()	TTable.FieldDefs	Return and optionally change information about a field.
DBFILEGET()		Insert the contents of a field into a file.
DBFILEPUT()		Insert the contents of a file into a field.
DBFILTER()	TTable.ApplyRange TQuery SELECT	Return the current filter expression as a character string.
DBGOBOTTOM()	TTable.Last	Move to the last logical record.
DBGOTO()	TTable.GotoCurrent TTable.GotoBookmark	Position record pointer to a specific identity.
DBGOTOP()		Move to the first logical record.
DBINFO()		Return and optionally change database file information.
DBORDERINFO()	TTable.IndexDefs TTable.IndexName TTable.IndexFields	Return and optionally change order and index file information.
DBRECALL()		Reinstate a record marked for deletion.
DBRECORDINFO()		Return and optionally change information about a record.
DBREINDEX()	TTable.Reindex	Recreate all active indexes for the current work area.
DBRELATION()	TTable.MasterSource TTable.MasterFields	Return the linking expression of a specified relation.
DBRLOCK()	TTable.Edit	Lock the record at the current or specified identity.
DBRLOCKLIST()		Xphiles version returns a cursor that may be used for traversing the list of records rather than an array.
DBRSELECT()		Return the target work area number of a relation.
DBRUNLOCK()		Release all or specified record locks.
DBSEEK()	TTable.FindKey	Move to the record having the specified key value.

continued

XBASE FUNCTION	DELPHI	COMMENTS
DBSELECTAR()		Change the current work area.
DBSETDRIVER()	TTable.TableType	Return the database driver and optionally set a new driver.
DBSETFILTER()	TQuery.SQL TTable.SetRange	Set a filter condition.
DBSETINDEX()		Activate an index file.
DBSETORDER()	TTable.IndexName TTable.IndexFields	Set the controlling order.
DBSETRELAT()	TTable.MasterFields TTable.MasterSource	Relate two work areas.
DBSKIP()	TTable.MovBy() TTable.Next TTable.Prior	Move relative to the current record.
DBSTRUCT()	TTable.FieldDefs	Create an array containing the structure of a database file.
DBUNLOCK()	TTable.Post TTable.Cancel	Release all locks for the current work area.
DBUNLOCKALL()		Release all locks for all work areas.
DBUSEAREA()	TTable.Open TTable.Active	Use a database file in a work area.
DELETED()		Return the deleted status of the current record.
DESCEND()		Create a descending index key value.
DEVOUT()		Write a value to the current device.
DEVOUTPICT()		Write a value to the current device using a picture clause.
DEVPOS()		Move the cursor or printhead to a new position.
DIRCHANGE()	SelectDirectory()	Change the current DOS directory.
DIRECTORY()	TFileListBox	Be sure to use TDirectory.Free when done with access to Directory()'s return value.
DIRMAKE()	SelectDirectory()	Create a directory.
DIRREMOVE()	RmDir()	Remove a directory.
DISKCHANGE()	SelectDirectory()	Change the current DOS disk drive.
DISKNAME()		Return the current DOS drive.
DISKSPACE()	DiskFree()	Return the space available on a specified disk.
DISPBEGIN()		N/A
DISPBOX()		Display a box on the screen.
DISPCOUNT()		N/A
DISPEND()		Display buffered screen updates.
DISPOUT()	WriteLn()	Write a value to the display.
DOSERROR()		Return the last DOS error number.
DOW()	DayOfWeek()	Convert a date value to a numeric day of the week.

DTOC()	DateToStr()	Convert a date value to a character string.
DTOS()	DateToStr()	Convert a date value to a string formatted as yyyymmdd.
EMPTY()		Determine if the result of an expression is empty.
EOF()	TTable.EOF	Determine when end of file is encountered.
ERRORBLOCK()		See try ... except and try ... finally statements.
ERRORLEVEL()		Set the CA-Clipper return code.
EVAL()		See function and procedure pointers in Delphi Help.
EXP()	Exp()	Calculate e**x.
FCLOSE()	FileClose()	Direct compatibility.
FCOUNT()	TTable.Fields.Count	Return the number of fields in the current **.DBF** file.
FCREATE()	FileCreate()	Direct compatibility.
FERASE()	DeleteFile()	Direct compatibility.
FERROR()		Test for errors after a binary file operation.
FIELDBLOCK()		N/A
FIELDGET()		Retrieve the value of a field using the field position.
FIELDNAME()		Return a field name from the current database (**.DBF**) file.
FIELDPOS()		Return the position of a field in a work area.
FIELDPUT()		Set the value of a field variable using the field position.
FIELDWBLOCK()		N/A
FILE()	FileExists()	Direct compatibility.
FKLABEL()		N/A
FKMAX()		N/A
FLOCK()	TTable.Exclusive DbiTableLock()	Direct compatibility.
FOPEN()	FileOpen()	Direct compatibility.
FOUND()		Determine if the previous search operation succeeded.
FREAD()	FileRead()	Direct compatibility.
FREADSTR()		Read characters from a binary file.
FRENAME()	RenameFile()	Direct compatibility.
FSEEK()	FileSeek()	Direct compatibility.
FWRITE()	FileWrite()	Direct compatibility.
GETACTIVE()		Return the currently active Get object.
GETAPPLYKEY()		Apply a key to a Get object from within a reader.
GETDOSETKEY()		Process SET KEY during GET editing.

continued

XBASE FUNCTION	DELPHI	COMMENTS
GETENV()		Retrieve the contents of a DOS environment variable.
GETPOSTVALID()		Postvalidate the current Get object.
GETPREVALID()		Prevalidate a Get object.
GETREADER()		Execute standard READ behavior for a Get object.
HARDCR()		Replace all soft carriage returns with hard carriage returns.
HEADER()		Return the current database file header length.
I2BIN()		Convert a CA-Clipper numeric to a 16-bit binary integer.
IIF()		Return the result of an expression based on a condition.
INDEXEXT()		Return index extension defined by the current database driver.
INDEXKEY()		Return the key expression of a specified index.
INDEXORD()		Return the order position of the controlling index.
INKEY()		Extract a character from the keyboard buffer or a mouse event.
INT()	Int()	Convert a numeric value to an integer.
ISALPHA()	in ['A'.'Z', 'a'..z']	Determine if the leftmost character in a string is alphabetic.
ISCOLOR()		Determine if the current computer has color capability.
ISDIGIT()	in ['0'..'9']	Determine if the leftmost character in a string is a digit.
ISLOWER()	in ['a'..'z']	Determine if the leftmost character is a lowercase letter.
ISPRINTER()	TPrinter	Test to see if a printer driver is available.
ISUPPER()	in ['A'..'Z']	Determine if the leftmost character in a string is uppercase.
L2BIN()		Convert a CA-Clipper numeric value to a 32-bit binary integer.
LASTKEY()		Return INKEY(), the value of the last key extracted from the keyboard.
LASTREC()	TTable.RecordCount	Determine the number of records in the current .DBF file.
LEFT()	Copy()	Extract substring beginning with first character in a string.
LEN()	Length()	Return the length of a string or number of array elements.
LOG()	Ln()	Calculate the natural logarithm of a numeric value.

LOWER()	LowerCase()	Convert uppercase characters to lowercase.
LTRIM()	TrimLeft()[1]	Remove leading spaces from a character string.
LUPDATE()		Return the last modification date of a database (**.DBF**) file.
MAX()		Return the larger of two numeric or date values.
MAXCOL()		Determine the maximum visible screen column.
MAXROW()		Determine the maximum visible screen row.
MCOL()		Determine the mouse cursor's screen column position.
MDBLCLK()		Determine the double-click speed threshold of the mouse.
MEMOEDIT()	TMemo class TMemoField class	Display or edit character strings and memo fields.
MEMOLINE()	TMemo.Lines	Extract a line of text from a character string or memo field.
MEMOREAD()	TMemo.GetSelTxtBuf() TMemoField.AssignValue()	Return the contents of a disk file as a character string.
MEMORY()		Determine the amount of available free pool memory.
MEMOSETSUPER()		N/A
MEMOTRAN()		Replace carriage return/linefeeds in character strings.
MEMOWRIT()		Write a character string or memo field to a disk file.
MEMVARBLOCK()		N/A
MENUMODAL()		N/A
MIN()		Return the smaller of two numeric or date values.
MLCOUNT()		Count the number of lines in a character string or memo field.
MLCTOPOS()		Return position of a string based on line and column position.
MOD()	mod	Return the dBASE III PLUS modulus of two numbers.
MONTH()	DecodeDate()	Convert a date value to the number of the month.
MPOSTOLC()		Return line/ column position of a string based on a position.
NETERR()		Determine if a network command has failed.

continued

---

[1]Available in Delphi 2.0 only.

XBASE FUNCTION	DELPHI	COMMENTS
NETNAME()		Return the current workstation identification.
NEXTKEY()		N/A
NOSNOW()		N/A
ORDBAGEXT()		Return the default order bag **RDD** extension.
ORDBAGNAME()		Return the order bag name of a specific order.
ORDCOND()	TIndexOptions	Options on indexes.
ORDCONDSET()	TIndexOptions	Set the condition and scope for an order.
ORDCREATE()	TTable.AddIndex	Create an order in an order bag.
ORDDESCEND()	TIndexOptions	Return and optionally change the descending flag of an order.
ORDDESTROY()		Remove a specified order from an order bag.
ORDFOR()		Return the FOR expression of an order.
ORDISUNIQUE()	TIndexOptions	Return the status of the unique flag for a given order.
ORDKEY()		Return the key expression of an order.
ORDKEYADD()		Add a key to a custom-built order.
ORDKEYCOUNT()		Return the number of keys in an order.
ORDKEYDEL()		Delete a key from a custom-built order.
ORDKEYGOTO()		Move to a record specified by its logical record number.
ORDKEYNO()		Get the logical record number of the current record.
ORDKEYVAL()		Get key value of the current record from controlling order.
ORDLISTADD()	TTable.AddIndex	Add orders to the order list.
ORDLISTCLEAR()		Clear the current order list.
ORDLISTREBUI()		Rebuild all orders in the order list of the current work area.
ORDNAME()	TTable.IndexName	Return the name of an order in the order list.
ORDNUMBER()		Return the position of an order in the current order list.
ORDSCOPE()	TTable.SetRange	Set or clear the boundaries for scoping key values.
ORDSETFOCUS()	TTable.IndexName	Set focus to an order in an order list.
ORDSETRELAT()	TTable.MasterFields TTable.MasterSource	Relate a specified work area.
ORDSKIPUNIQUE()		Move record pointer to the next or previous unique key.
OS()		Return the operating system name.
OUTERR()		Write a list of values to the standard error device.
OUTSTD()		Write a list of values to the standard output device.

PAD()		Pad character, date, and numeric values with a fill character.
PCOL()		Return the current column position of the printhead.
PCOUNT()		Determine the position of the last actual parameter passed.
PROCLINE()		Return source line number of current or previous activation.
PROCNAME()		Return name of the current or previous procedure or function.
PROW()		Return the current row position of the printhead.
QOUT()	WriteLn()	Display a list of expressions to the console.
RAT()		Return the position of the last occurrence of a substring.
RDDLIST()		Return an array of the RDDs.
RDDNAME()	TTable.TableType	Return name of RDD active in current or specified work area.
RDDSETDEFAULT()	TTable.TableType	Set or return the default RDD for the application.
READEXIT()		Toggle up arrow and down arrow as READ exit keys.
READFORMAT()		N/A
READINSERT()		Toggle the current insert mode for READ and MEMOEDIT().
READKEY()		Determine what key terminated a READ.
READKILL()		N/A
READMODAL()		Activate a full-screen editing mode for a GetList.
READUPDATED()		N/A
READVAR()		N/A
RECCOUNT()	TTable.RecordCount	Determine the number of records in the current database file.
RECNO()	TTable.GetBookMark	Return the identity at the position of the record pointer.
RECSIZE()	TTable.FieldDefs	Determine the record length of a **DBF** file.
REPLICATE()		Replicate() is limited to a 255 character string.
RESTSCREEN()		N/A
RIGHT()		Return a substring beginning with the rightmost character.
RLOCK()	TTable.Edit	
ROUND()	Round()	Return a numeric value rounded to a specified number of digits.
ROW()	Cursor CursorTo()	See WinCRT unit.

continued

Xbase Function	Delphi	Comments
RTRIM()	TrimRight()[2]	Xphiles' RTrim() is limited to 255 characters.
SAVESCREEN()		N/A
SCROLL()	ScrollTo()	See WinCRT unit.
SECONDS()	Now	Return the number of seconds elapsed since midnight.
SELECT()		Determine the work area number of a specified alias.
SET()		Only a subset of Xbase settings is supported. See the source code for further information. You are automatically informed as to which settings are not supported when running the application.
SETBLINK()		N/A
SETCANCEL()		N/A
SETCOLOR()	TForm.Color	Return the current colors and optionally set new colors.
SETCURSOR()		See "hot spots" in Delphi Help.
SETKEY()		Use Event tab in Delphi forms.
SETMODE()		Change display mode to a specified number of rows and columns.
SETPOS()		Move the cursor to a new position.
SETPRC()		Set PROW() and PCOL() values.
SOUNDEX()		The soundex algorithm varies slightly and is more accurate than the CA-Clipper version. It returns up to 10 characters, rather than 4, which makes it more accurate for longer names.
SPACE()		Return a string of spaces.
SQRT()		Return the square root of a positive number.
STR()	IntToStr()	
FloatToStr()		Str() is an existing procedure in Delphi.
STRTRAN()		Search and replace characters within a string or memo field.
STUFF()	Copy()	Delete and insert characters in a string.
SUBSTR()	Copy()	Extract a substring from a character string.
TIME()	Time	Return the system time.
TONE()	MessageBeep()	Sound a speaker tone for a specified frequency and duration.
TRANSFORM()		Convert any value into a formatted character string.
TRIM()	Trim()[3]	Remove trailing spaces from a character string.

[2] Available in Delphi 2.0 only.
[3] Available in Delphi 2.0 only.

TYPE()	TVarRec.VType	Determine the type of an expression.
UPDATED()		Determine whether a GET changed during a READ.
UPPER()	UpperCase() trUpper() AnsiUpperCase()	Convert all alphabetic characters to uppercase. See AnsiUpperCase() for international support.
USED()		Determine whether a database file is in USE.
VAL()	Val()	Convert a character number to numeric type.
VALTYPE()	TVarRec.VType	Determine the data type returned by an expression.
VERSION()	TReport.VersionMajor TReport.VersionMinor	
WORD()	Word()	See "typecasting" in Delphi Help.
YEAR()	DecodeDate()	Convert a date value to the year as a numeric value.

Interbase Structured Query Language (ISQL)

SQL is a query language commonly used on Client/Server database systems to perform queries against existing databases. The SQL language is actually divided into two components, the Data Manipulation Language (DML) and the Data Definition Language (DDL). The DML is used for queries, and the DDL is used for creating and restructuring tables, databases, and indexes.

In Delphi, SQL is implemented as a subset of Interbase SQL and is referred to as ISQL. The following sections describe the statements, functions, data types, and error messages used in the ISQL set. In general, Delphi will support any standard SQL statements that the underlying data server supports, as Delphi has the ability to pass the SQL statement directly to the server for processing.

Note that SQL statements performed against various database servers may have different results, depending on the capabilities of that server. The set of SQL statements that you can use are directly dependent on the capabilities of the data server that you are connected to.

NOTE

A complete discussion of SQL is beyond the scope of this book. The material summarized here is for your convenience. For further information, see the Local Interbase Server SQL Reference help file,[1] the Local Interbase Server SQL Overview help file,[2] and the Windows ISQL help file. Additional information can be found in the Borland Local Interbase Server for Windows User's Guide included with Delphi.

ISQL Statements

Interbase SQL supports the standard SQL command set, as summarized in Table E.1.

---

[1] This help file is not shown in your Delphi program group by default. The help file is called LOCALSQL.HLP and is stored in the \DELPHI\BIN directory in a standard installation.

[2] This help file is not shown in your Delphi program group by default. This help file is called SQLREF.HLP and is stored in the \IBLOCAL\BIN directory in a standard installation.

TABLE E.1 ISQL STATEMENTS

COMMAND	DESCRIPTION
ALTER DATABASE	Adds supplemental files to a database.
ALTER DOMAIN	Modifies most characteristics of an existing domain.
ALTER EXCEPTION	Modifies exception messages.
ALTER INDEX	Enables or disables use of an existing index.
ALTER PROCEDURE	Changes a stored procedure's input, output, or body.
ALTER TABLE	Modifies the structure of a table.
ALTER TRIGGER	Modifies the definition of a trigger.
COMMIT	Ends a transaction, writes pending changes to tables.
CONNECT	Connects to (opens) a database.
CREATE DATABASE	Creates a database and sets its attributes.
CREATE DOMAIN	Defines a set of characteristics for columns created with the CREATE TABLE or ALTER TABLE statements.
CREATE EXCEPTION	Creates a user-defined exception.
CREATE GENERATOR	Defines a generator with a starting value of zero.
CREATE INDEX	Creates an index for a column in a table.
CREATE PROCEDURE	Defines a stored procedure for a database.
CREATE SHADOW	Creates a mirror of a database on a secondary storage device.
CREATE TABLE	Creates a new table, establishes columns and integrity constraints.
CREATE TRIGGER	Defines a new database trigger.
CREATE VIEW	Defines a data view of one or more tables in a database.
DECLARE EXTERNAL FUNCTION	Declares a UDF to a database.
DECLARE FILTER	Declares an existing BLOB filter to the database.
DELETE	Deletes one or more rows from a table or view.
DROP DATABASE	Deletes a database and its data.
DROP DOMAIN	Removes a domain definition from a database.
DROP EXCEPTION	Removes a user-defined exception from a database.
DROP EXTERNAL FUNCTION	Removes a UDF declaration from a database.
DROP FILTER	Removes a BLOB filter declaration from a database.
DROP INDEX	Removes an index from a database.
DROP PROCEDURE	Removes a stored procedure from a database.
DROP SHADOW	Removes a shadow set and terminates the shadowing process.
DROP TABLE	Removes a table and its data, metadata, indexes and triggers.
DROP TRIGGER	Removes a trigger from a database.
DROP VIEW	Removes a view from a database.
EXECUTE PROCEDURE	Executes a stored procedure.
GRANT	Assigns database privileges to users or other database objects.
INSERT	Adds one or more rows to a table or view.
REVOKE	Removes database privileges from a user or database object.
ROLLBACK	Rolls back all DML statements executed since the last COMMIT.

SELECT	Fetches data from tables and views.
SET GENERATOR	Resets starting value for a generator.
SET NAMES	Allows selection of character set.
SET STATISTICS	Recalculates an index's cached retrieval setting.
SET TRANSACTION	Specifies settings for the default transaction.
UPDATE	Modifies one or more rows in a table or view.

ISQL STATEMENT REFERENCE

ALTER DATABASE

Allows the creation of secondary files which are used as alternative storage for a database. On Netware servers only, allows modification of write-ahead log (WAL) protocol.

SYNTAX

```
ALTER { DATABASE | SCHEMA } ADD <add_clause>;
<add_clause> = FILE "<filespec>" [ <fileinfo>] [<add_clause>]
<fileinfo> = LENGTH [=] <int> [PAGE[S]] | STARTING [AT [PAGE]] <int>
[<fileinfo>]
```

ARGUMENTS

FILE	FILE SPECIFICATION
filespec	Quoted string list of one or more secondary files that will receive database pages.
int	Integer value
LENGTH	Specifies length of file in pages.
SCHEMA	Synonym for DATABASE.

SEE ALSO

CREATE DATABASE, DROP DATABASE

ALTER DOMAIN

Modifies attributes of a domain, except for a domain's NOT NULL setting and its data type.

SYNTAX

```
ALTER DOMAIN <domain> {
        [ADD [CONSTRAINT] CHECK (<search_cond>)]
        | [DROP CONSTRAINT]
```

```
      |  [DROP DEFAULT]
      |  [SET DEFAULT { <literal> | NULL | USER }]  };
```

ARGUMENTS

ADD [CONSTRAINT] CHECK	Adds a CHECK constraint to the domain. There can be only one CHECK constraint for a domain.
domain	Domain name
DROP CONSTRAINT	Removes any CHECK constraint from the domain.
DROP DEFAULT	Removes an existing default.
literal	Inserts a string, numeric, or date value.
SET DEFAULT	Specifies the default value for the column.
search_cond	Standard domain search condition expression.

SEE ALSO

CREATE DOMAIN, CREATE TABLE, DROP DOMAIN

ALTER EXCEPTION

Modifies the message associated with an exception.

SYNTAX

```
ALTER EXCEPTION <name> "<message>";
```

ARGUMENTS

message	New message string
name	Exception name

SEE ALSO

ALTER PROCEDURE, ALTER TRIGGER CREATE EXCEPTION, CREATE PROCEDURE, CREATE TRIGGER, DROP EXCEPTION

ALTER INDEX

Allows disabling and enabling of an already created index. The action of disabling and enabling an index rebuilds that index.

SYNTAX

```
ALTER INDEX <name> { ACTIVE | INACTIVE };
```

ARGUMENTS

ACTIVE	Enables index
INACTIVE	Disables index
name	Index name

SEE ALSO

ALTER TABLE, CREATE INDEX, DROP INDEX, SET STATISTICS

ALTER PROCEDURE

Allows you to modify an existing stored procedure, including its input and output parameters, and its body. The syntax is identical to the CREATE PROCEDURE command, except that the keyword CREATE is replaced with ALTER.

SYNTAX

```
ALTER PROCEDURE name
[ ( PARAM <datatype> [, PARAM <datatype> ...]  ) ]
[RETURNS (PARAM <datatype> [, PARAM <datatype> ...])]
AS <procedure_body> [<terminator>];
```

ARGUMENTS

name	*Procedure name*
PARAM	Specifies input parameters for the procedure.
procedure_body	Procedure body, including variable declarations and statements.
RETURNS PARAM	Specifies output parameters for the procedure.
terminator	Marks the end of the procedure.

SEE ALSO

CREATE PROCEDURE, DROP PROCEDURE, EXECUTE PROCEDURE, SET TERM

ALTER TABLE

Allows modification of table structures.

SYNTAX

```
ALTER TABLE table <operation> [, <operation> ...];
<operation> = {ADD <col_def> | ADD <table_constraint> |
      DROP <col >| DROP CONSTRAINT <constraint>}
```

```
<col_def> = <col >{<datatype> | [COMPUTED [BY] (<expr>) | <domain>}
        [DEFAULT {<literal> | NULL | USER}]
        [NOT NULL]
        [<col_constraint>]
        [COLLATE <collation>]
<col_constraint> = [CONSTRAINT <constraint>] <constraint_def> [<col_constraint>]
<constraint_def> = {
        PRIMARY KEY
        | UNIQUE
        | CHECK (<search_condition>)
        | REFERENCES <other_table> [(<other_col >[, <other_col >...])] }
```

ARGUMENTS

col	Unique name of column
col_def	Column definition, including name and data type
COLLATE collation	Adds a collation order to the table.
COMPUTED [BY]	Specifies an expression for a calculated column.
CONSTRAINT	Adds a specified constraint to a column.
constraint	Constraint to add or drop
constraint_def	Column constraint definition
datatype	Column data type
DEFAULT	Specifies a default value for a column.
domain	Domain name
DROP CONSTRAINT	Drops a specified contstraint from the table.
expr	Any expression valid for the column's data type
NOT NULL	Creates a column that cannot contain NULL values.
operation	Operation to perform on the table (i.e, ADD or DROP a column or a constraint)
table	Table name
table_constraint	Table constraint to add

SEE ALSO

ALTER DOMAIN, CREATE DOMAIN, CREATE TABLE

ALTER TRIGGER

Modifies an existing trigger. Omitted arguments default to their current values.

SYNTAX

```
ALTER TRIGGER <name>
        [ACTIVE | INACTIVE]
        [AS <trigger_body>]
```

```
[{BEFORE | AFTER} {DELETE | INSERT | UPDATE}]
[POSITION <number>]
[<terminator>]
```

ARGUMENTS

ACTIVE	Enables the trigger.
AFTER	Sets trigger to execute after the data operation takes place.
BEFORE	Sets trigger to execute before the data operation takes place.
DELETE	Specifies that DELETE operations will cause the trigger to execute.
INACTIVE	Disables the trigger.
INSERT	Specifies that INSERT operations will cause the trigger to execute.
name	Trigger name
number	POSITION (execution order) number (0..32,767)
POSITION	Specifies execution order for multiple triggers.
terminator	Signifies the end of the trigger body (see SET TERM).
trigger_body	Statements in procedure and trigger language
UPDATE	Specifies that UPDATE operations will cause the trigger to execute.

SEE ALSO

CREATE TRIGGER, DROP TRIGGER, SET TERM

COMMIT

Writes all pending updates, thereby culminating the current transaction.

SYNTAX

```
COMMIT
        [WORK]
        [TRANSACTION <name>]
        [RELEASE]
        [RETAIN [SNAPSHOT]];
```

ARGUMENTS

name	Transaction name
RELEASE	Compatibility keyword for older versions of InterBase
RETAIN SNAPSHOT	Returns transaction context after committing changes.
TRANSACTION	Commits pending transaction name. Omitting the transaction name commits the default transaction.
WORK	Keyword required by some databases

SEE ALSO

ROLLBACK

CONNECT

Connects to and initializes database data structures.

SYNTAX

```
CONNECT ["]<filespec>["]
        [USER "<username>" [PASSWORD "<password>"]];
```

ARGUMENTS

filespec	Database file name (quotes are optional)
PASSWORD	Specifies password.
password	Password required to access database
USER	Specifies user name to use for database connection.
username	User name (case-insensitive)

SEE ALSO

SETNAMES

CREATE DATABASE

Creates a database and sets its attributes.

SYNTAX

```
CREATE {DATABASE | SCHEMA} "<filespec>"
        [DEFAULT CHARACTER SET <charset>]
        [LENGTH [=] <int> [PAGE[S]]]
        [PAGE_SIZE [=] <int>]
        [<secondary_file>]
        [USER "<username>" [PASSWORD "<password>"]];
<secondary_file> = FILE "<filespec>" [<fileinfo>] [<secondary_file>]
<fileinfo> = LENGTH [=] <int> [PAGE[S]] | STARTING [AT [PAGE]] <int>
[<fileinfo>]
```

ARGUMENTS

charset	Name of character set as a quoted string
DEFAULT CHARACTER SET	Specifies which character set to use (defaults to NONE).

FILE *filespec*	Specifies one or more database page overflow (secondary) files.
filespec	Database file specification
int	Integer value
LENGTH = *int* PAGES	Specifies file length for primary or secondary database file.
PAGE_SIZE = *int*	Database page size in bytes (defaults to 1024)
PASSWORD	Specifies password to use.
password	Password to use for creating database
STARTING AT PAGE int	Specifies starting page number for an overflow (secondary) file.
USER	Specifies user name to use when creating database.
username	User name

SEE ALSO

ALTER DATABASE, DROP DATABASE

CREATE DOMAIN

Creates a column definition for use by CREATE TABLE and ALTER TABLE statements.

SYNTAX

```
CREATE DOMAIN <domain> [AS] <datatype>
        [DEFAULT {<literal> | NULL | USER}]
        [CHECK (<search_cond>)]
        [COLLATE <collation>]
        [NOT NULL] ;
```

ARGUMENTS

CHECK	Creates a CHECK constraint for the domain.
COLLATE	Sets the domain's collation order.
collation	Collation order
datatype	Data type
DEFAULT	Sets default column value
domain	Domain name
literal	Literal value
NULL	NULL value
search_condition	Valid domain search condition
USER	User defined value

SEE ALSO

ALTER DOMAIN, ALTER TABLE, CREATE TABLE, DROP DOMAIN

CREATE EXCEPTION

Creates a user-defined exception with an associated error message.

SYNTAX

```
CREATE EXCEPTION <name> "<message>";
```

ARGUMENTS

message	Quoted string containing exception message
name	Exception name

SEE ALSO

ALTER EXCEPTION, ALTER PROCEDURE, ALTER TRIGGER, CREATE PROCEDURE, CREATE TRIGGER, DROP EXCEPTION

CREATE GENERATOR

Creates a sequential number generator with a starting value of zero.

SYNTAX

```
CREATE GENERATOR <name>;
```

ARGUMENTS

name	Name for the generator.

SEE ALSO

GEN ID(), SET GENERATOR

CREATE INDEX

Creates an index on a specified column. Indexes may be used to improve performance in WHERE clauses of a SELECT statement.

SYNTAX

```
CREATE
        [ASC[ENDING] | DESC[ENDING]]
        [UNIQUE]
        INDEX <index> ON <table> (<col >[, <col> ...]);
```

ARGUMENTS

ASCENDING	Creates an ascending order index.
col	Column name
DESCENDING	Creates a descending order index.
index	Index name
table	Table name
UNIQUE	Only unique values are added to index keys

SEE ALSO

ALTER INDEX, DROP INDEX, SELECT INDEX, SET STATISTICS

CREATE PROCEDURE

Creates a procedure that is to be stored at the server.

SYNTAX

```
CREATE PROCEDURE <name>
        [(<param> <datatype> [, <param> <datatype> ...])]
        [RETURNS <datatype> [, <param> <datatype> ...])]
        AS <procedure_body>
        [<terminator>]
```

ARGUMENTS

AS	Start of procedure body
datatype	Data type of parameter
DECLARE VARIABLE	Declares local variables used within the procedure.
name	Unique procedure name
param	Input parameters for the procedure
RETURNS param	Output parameters for the procedure
statement	Interbase procedure or trigger language statement
terminator	Signifies end of procedure (see also SET TERM).
var	Variable name

SEE ALSO

SET TERM

CREATE SHADOW

Establishes one or more copies of the database on secondary storage devices for safety.

SYNTAX

```
CREATE SHADOW <set_num>
        [AUTO | MANUAL]
        [CONDITIONAL]
        "<filespec>" [LENGTH [=] <int> [PAGE[S]]]
        [<secondary_file>];
```

ARGUMENTS

AUTO	Sets that attachments and accesses succeed for the database in case the shadow files are not available.
CONDITIONAL	Specifies that a new shadow will be created if the primary shadow is unavailable.
filespec	File specification for the shadow file
LENGTH = int PAGES	Specifies the length (in pages) of an additional shadow file.
MANUAL	Sets that attachments and accesses fail for the database in case the shadow files are not available.
secondary_file	Specifies the shadow file length.
set_num	Indicates to which shadow set to which the specified files belong.

SEE ALSO

DROP SHADOW

CREATE TABLE

Creates a new table and sets its attributes.

SYNTAX

```
CREATE TABLE <table>
        [EXTERNAL [FILE] "<filespec>"]
(<col_def> [, <col_def> | <constraint> ...]);
<col_def> = <col> {<datatype> | COMPUTED [BY] (<expr>) | <domain>}
[<col_constraint>]
[COLLATE <collation>]
[DEFAULT {<literal> | NULL | USER}]
[NOT NULL]
```

ARGUMENTS

col	Column name
col_def	Column definition
COLLATE	Specifies the collation order for the column.
collation	Collation order
COMPUTED BY	Creates a calculated column based on expr.

CONSTRAINT	Specifies constraint to place on a table or column.
constraint	Rule applied to a tables structure or contents
datatype	Column data type
DEFAULT	Sets a default value for a column value.
domain	Domain name
expr	Expression used for calculated column
EXTERNAL FILE	Specifies that the data exists in a file outside of the database.
filespec	Table filename specification
table	Table name

See Also

CREATE DOMAIN, GRANT, REVOKE

CREATE TRIGGER

Defines a trigger that can be executed when a specified data operation occurs.

Syntax

```
CREATE TRIGGER <name> FOR <table >
      [ACTIVE | INACTIVE]
      {BEFORE | AFTER}
      {DELETE | INSERT | UPDATE}
      [POSITION <number>]
      AS <trigger_body>
      <terminator>
```

Arguments

ACTIVE	Enables trigger.
AFTER	Sets trigger to execute after the data operation takes place.
BEFORE	Sets trigger to execute before the data operation takes place.
DELETE	Specifies that DELETE operations will cause the trigger to execute.
INACTIVE	Disables trigger.
INSERT	Specifies that INSERT operations will cause the trigger to execute.
name	Trigger name
number	POSITION (execution order) number (0..32,767)
POSITION	Specifies execution order for multiple triggers.
table	Table name
terminator	Signifies the end of the trigger body (see SET TERM).
trigger_body	Statements in procedure and trigger language
UPDATE	Specifies that UPDATE operations will cause the trigger to execute.

SEE ALSO

ALTER EXCEPTION, ALTER TRIGGER, CREATE EXCEPTION, CREATE TRIGGER, DROP
EXCEPTION, DROP TRIGGER, EXECUTE PROCEDURE

CREATE VIEW

Defines a view of the data in one or more tables.

SYNTAX

```
CREATE VIEW <name>
        [(<view_col> [, <view_col>...])]
        AS <select>
        [WITH CHECK OPTION];
```

ARGUMENTS

name	View name
view_col	View column name(s)
AS	Specifies which rows will be included in the view.
select	Selection criteria for inclusion of rows
WITH CHECK OPTION	Ensures that INSERT or UPDATE operations that affect rows that fall outside of the view are not allowed.

SEE ALSO

CREATE TABLE, DROP VIEW, GRANT, INSERT, REVOKE, SELECT, UPDATE

DECLARE EXTERNAL FUNCTION

Declares a user-defined function (UDF) that exists outside of the database. It is not permitted
on Netware servers.

SYNTAX

```
DECLARE EXTERNAL FUNCTION <name>
        [<datatype> | CSTRING (<int>) [, <datatype> | CSTRING (<int>) ...]]
        ENTRY_POINT "<entryname>"
        MODULE_NAME "<modulename>"
        RETURNS {<datatype> [BY VALUE] | CSTRING (<int>)};
```

ARGUMENTS

BY VALUE	Specifies that the return value of the UDF is by value, rather than by reference.
CSTRING (int)	Specifies a UDF that returns a C-style null-terminated string int bytes in length.

datatype	Parameter data type
entryname	UDF library name
int	Integer value
modulename	UDF object module name
name	UDF name
RETURNS	Specifies UDF return value.

SEE ALSO

DROP EXTERNAL FUNCTION

DECLARE FILTER

Defines a BLOB filter for a database.

SYNTAX

```
DECLARE FILTER <filter>
      INPUT_TYPE <type>
      OUTPUT_TYPE <type>
      ENTRY_POINT "<entryname>"
      MODULE_NAME "<modulename>";
```

ARGUMENTS

entryname	BLOB filter name in library
filter	Filter name
INPUT_TYPE	BLOB subtype to convert data from
modulename	BLOB filter object module name
OUTPUT_TYPE	BLOB subtype to convert data to

SEE ALSO

DROP FILTER

DELETE

Allows deletion of one or more rows from a table or view.

SYNTAX

```
DELETE FROM <table>
      [WHERE <search_cond>];
```

ARGUMENTS

search_cond	Valid search condition
table	Table name
WHERE	Specifies which rows to delete. If omitted, deletes all rows in table.

SEE ALSO

GRANT, REVOKE, SELECT

DROP DATABASE

Deletes the current database.

SYNTAX

```
DROP DATABASE;
```

SEE ALSO

ALTER DATABASE, CREATE DATABASE

DROP DOMAIN

Removes a domain definition from a table.

SYNTAX

```
DROP DOMAIN <name>;
```

ARGUMENTS

name	Domain name

SEE ALSO

ALTER DOMAIN, ALTER TABLE, CREATE DOMAIN

DROP EXCEPTION

Removes a user-defined exception from a database.

SYNTAX

```
DROP EXCEPTION <name>;
```

ARGUMENTS

name	Exception name

SEE ALSO

ALTER EXCEPTION, ALTER PROCEDURE, ALTER TRIGGER, CREATE EXCEPTION, CREATE PROCEDURE, CREATE TRIGGER

DROP EXTERNAL FUNCTION

Removes a user defined function from a database.

SYNTAX

```
DROP EXTERNAL FUNCTION <name>;
```

ARGUMENTS

name	UDF name

SEE ALSO

DECLARE EXTERNAL FUNCTION

DROP FILTER

Removes a BLOB filter declaration from a database.

SYNTAX

```
DROP FILTER <name>;
```

ARGUMENTS

name	BLOB filter name

SEE ALSO

DECLARE FILTER

DROP INDEX

Removes an index from a database.

SYNTAX

```
DROP INDEX <name>;
```

ARGUMENTS

name	Index name

SEE ALSO

ALTER INDEX, CREATE INDEX

DROP PROCEDURE

Removes a stored procedure from a database

SYNTAX

```
DROP PROCEDURE <name>
```

ARGUMENTS

name	Name of an existing stored procedure

See Also

ALTER PROCEDURE , CREATE PROCEDURE, EXECUTE PROCEDURE

DROP SHADOW

Removes a shadow set and terminates the shadowing process.

SYNTAX

```
DROP SHADOW <set_num>;
```

ARGUMENTS

set_num	Shadow set identifier

SEE ALSO

CREATE SHADOW

DROP TABLE

Removes a table from a database.

SYNTAX

```
DROP TABLE <name>;
```

ARGUMENTS

name	Table name

SEE ALSO

ALTER TABLE, CREATE TABLE

DROP TRIGGER

Removes a trigger from a database.

SYNTAX

```
DROP TRIGGER <name>;
```

ARGUMENTS

name	Trigger name

SEE ALSO

ALTER TRIGGER, CREATE TRIGGER

DROP VIEW

Removes a view from a database.

SYNTAX

```
DROP VIEW <name>;
```

ARGUMENTS

name	View name

SEE ALSO

CREATE VIEW

EXECUTE PROCEDURE

Executes a specified stored procedure.

SYNTAX

```
EXECUTE PROCEDURE <name> [<param> [, <param> ...]];
```

ARGUMENTS

name	Procedure name
param	Input parameter for the procedure

SEE ALSO

ALTER PROCEDURE, CREATE PROCEDURE, DROP PROCEDURE

GRANT

Assigns privileges for database objects.

SYNTAX

```
GRANT {
        {ALL [PRIVILEGES] | SELECT | DELETE | INSERT | UPDATE [(<col> [,
        <col> ...])]}
        ON [TABLE] {<tablename> | <viewname>}
        TO {<object> | <userlist>}
        | EXECUTE ON PROCEDURE <procname> TO {<object> | <userlist>}
        };
<object> = PROCEDURE <procname>
```

```
        | TRIGGER <trigname>
        | VIEW <viewname>
        | [USER] <username>
        | PUBLIC [, <object>]
<userlist> = [USER] <username> [, [USER] <username> ...]
        [WITH GRANT OPTION]
```

ARGUMENTS

col	Column name
tablename	Table name
userlist	List of users to grant privileges to
username	User name
viewname	View name
WITH GRANT OPTION	Enables users in *userlist* to grant privileges.

SEE ALSO

REVOKE

INSERT

Inserts one or more new rows into a table or view.

SYNTAX

```
INSERT INTO <tablename> | <viewname>
        [(<col> [, <col> ...])]
        {VALUES (<val> [, <val> ...]) | <select_expr>};
```

ARGUMENTS

tablename	Table name
viewname	View name
INTO	Specifies a table or view to insert data into.
col	Column name
val	Value
VALUES	List of values to insert
select_expr	Select expression that returns values to insert into columns

SEE ALSO

GRANT, REVOKE, SET TRANSACTION, UPDATE

REVOKE

Removes privileges to a database object.

SYNTAX

```
REVOKE [GRANT OPTION FOR]
       { {ALL [PRIVILEGES] | SELECT | DELETE | INSERT |  UPDATE [(<col>
       [, <col> ...])]}
       FROM {<object> | <userlist>}
       | EXECUTE ON PROCEDURE <procname> FROM {<object> | <userlist>} }
       ON [TABLE] {<tablename> | <viewname>} ;
```

ARGUMENTS

col	Columns to revoke privileges from
GRANT OPTION FOR	Revokes authority to grant privileges
object	User or database object name
tablename	Table name
userlist	List of users for whom to revoke privileges
viewname	View name

SEE ALSO

GRANT

ROLLBACK

Rolls back all pending DML statements since last COMMIT.

SYNTAX

```
ROLLBACK [WORK];
```

Arguments

WORK	Keyword for compatibility

SEE ALSO

COMMIT

SELECT

Retrieves data from tables.

SYNTAX

```
SELECT [DISTINCT | ALL] {* | <val> [, <val> ...]}
       FROM <tableref> [, <tableref> ...]
       [GROUP BY <col> [COLLATE <collation>] [, <col> [COLLATE <collation>]
       ...]
       [HAVING <search_condition>]
       [ORDER BY <order_list>]
       [PLAN <plan_expr>]
       [UNION <select_expr>]
       [WHERE <search_condition>];
```

ARGUMENTS

*	Specifies that all columns are to be returned.
alias	Synonym for table or view
ALL	Returns all values (this is the default).
col	Columns for grouping
COLLATE	Specifies the order in which returned data will be collated.
collation	Collation order
DISTINCT	Insures only unique values are returned.
FROM	Specifies data source.
GROUP BY	Specifies sub-groups for the retrieved data based on a list of columns.
HAVING	Search condition for use with GROUP BY
join_type	Specifies which type of JOIN to perform (INNER, OUTER).
joined_table	Refers to a joined table.
order_list	List of columns that specify how returned rows are ordered
ORDER BY	Specifies the columns to order returned values by.
PLAN	Specifies the plan_expr.
plan_expr	Access plan that the InterBase optimizer will use for data retrieval
plan_item	Specifies a table and index method for a plan.
procedure	Stored procedure that returns values like a SELECT statement
search_cond	Valid SQL search condition
SELECT	Specifies what data to return.
table	Table name
tableref	Source from which to retrieve data.
UNION	Creates a table with common columns from other tables.
val	Specifies which columns to return.
view	View name
WHERE	Specifies a search condition.

SEE ALSO

DELETE, INSERT, UPDATE

SET GENERATOR

Sets a generator to a specific value.

SYNTAX

```
SET GENERATOR <name> TO <int>;
```

ARGUMENTS

int	Generator value to set to (-231..230)
name	Generator name

SEE ALSO

CREATE GENERATOR, CREATE PROCEDURE, CREATE TRIGGER, GEN_ID()

SET NAMES

Allows overriding of the default character set for a database.

SYNTAX

```
SET NAMES [<charset>];
```

ARGUMENTS

charset	Specifies the character set to use for a given process (defaults to NONE)

SEE ALSO

CONNECT

SET STATISTICS

Recalculates the selectivity value of an index.

Syntax

```
SET STATISTICS INDEX <name>;
```

Arguments

name	Index name to recalculate selectivity for

See Also

ALTER INDEX, CREATE INDEX, DROP INDEX

SET TRANSACTION

Sets attributes and behavior for the default transaction.

Syntax

```
SET TRANSACTION
        [READ WRITE | READ ONLY]
        [RESERVING <reserving_clause>]
        [WAIT | NO WAIT]
        [[ISOLATION LEVEL]
        {SNAPSHOT [TABLE STABILITY]
        | READ COMMITTED [[NO] RECORD_VERSION]}];
<reserving_clause> = table [, table ...]
        [FOR [SHARED | PROTECTED]
          {READ | WRITE}]
        [, <reserving_clause>]]
```

Arguments

ISOLATION LEVEL	Sets the transaction isolation level (defaults to SNAPSHOT).
NO WAIT	Forces an error in the case of a record lock conflict.
READ ONLY	Enables only read operations on tables.
READ WRITE	Enables both read and write to tables.
RESERVING *<reserving_clause>*	Specifies reserved locks for tables at the start of the transaction.
WAIT	Forces the transaction to wait in the case of a record lock conflict (this is the default value).

UPDATE

Allows modification of one or more rows in a table.

SYNTAX

```
UPDATE {<table> | <view>}
       SET <col >= <val> [, <col >= <val> ...]
       WHERE <search_cond>;
```

ARGUMENTS

col	Column(s) to update
search_cond	Valid SQL search condition
SET	Specifies columns and values.
table	Table name to update
view	View name to update
val	Values to assign to specified columns.
WHERE	Search condition specification

ISQL FUNCTIONS

ISQL includes a series of functions designed to perform calculations and convert values. Functions that perform calculations for a series of values are called *Aggregate functions*. Aggregate functions perform such tasks as calculating all the values for columns returned in a SELECT statement.

Functions that convert from one data type to another are called Conversion functions. These functions either convert data from one type to another or convert CHARACTER data types to uppercase.

The GEN_ID() function (classified as a numeric function) produces a system-generated number that can be used just as a NUMBER variable.

Table E.2 summarizes the functions available in ISQL.

TABLE E.2 ISQL FUNCTIONS

FUNCTION	TYPE	DESCRIPTION
AVG()	Aggregate	Calculates the average of a set of values.
CAST()	Conversion	Converts a column (field) from one data type to another.
COUNT()	Aggregate	Returns the number of rows that satisfy a search condition.
GEN_ID()	Numeric	Returns a system-generated value.
MAX()	Aggregate	Returns the maximum value from a set of values.
MIN()	Aggregate	Returns the minimum value from a set of values.
SUM()	Aggregate	Totals a set of numeric values.
UPPER()	Conversion	Converts a string to uppercase.

AVG()

Calculates the average of a set of values, where <value> is either a numeric column or a numeric expression passed as a parameter.

TYPE

Aggregate

SYNTAX

AVG ([ALL] <nValue> | DISTINCT <nValue>)

ARGUMENTS

ALL	Return value will be an average of all of the values
DISTINCT	Uses duplicate suppression prior to averaging.
nValue	Numeric expression or column

SEE ALSO

COUNT(), MAX(), MIN(), SUM()

CAST()

Converts a value from a character data type to another data type.

TYPE

Conversion

SYNTAX

CAST (<cValue> AS <data_type>)

ARGUMENTS

cValue	Character expression or column
data_type	A valid ISQL data type to convert <value> to

SEE ALSO

UPPER()

COUNT()

Used in conjunction with a SELECT statement to count all rows in a table or column that match a specified condition (i.e., that are including or excluding NULL values, or that contain unique values).

TYPE

Aggregate

SYNTAX

```
COUNT ( * | [ALL] <value> | DISTINCT <value> )
```

ARGUMENTS

*	Counts all rows in the table, including NULL values.
ALL	Counts only non-NULL values in the *value* column.
DISTINCT	Counts all unique, non-NULL values in the *value* column.
value	Numeric column or expression

SEE ALSO

AVG(), MAX(), MIN(), SUM()

GEN_ID()

Returns the current value of *generator,* after incrementing *generator* by *step.*

TYPE

Numeric

SYNTAX

```
GEN_ID ( <generator>, <step> )
```

ARGUMENTS

generator	Generator name
step	Positive or negative increment value for generator (-231..230)

SEE ALSO

CREATE GENERATOR, SET GENERATOR

MAX()

Returns the largest non-NULL value for a given column. Returns a NULL if there are no rows that match the query condition.

TYPE

Aggregate

SYNTAX

```
MAX  ( [ALL] <nValue> | DISTINCT <nValue> )
```

ARGUMENTS

DISTINCT	Returns maximum of only unique values in a column.
ALL	Returns maximum value of all values in a column.
<nValue>	Numeric column or expression

SEE ALSO

AVG(), COUNT(), MIN(), SUM()

MIN()

Returns the smallest non-NULL value for a given column. Returns a NULL if there are no rows that match the query condition.

TYPE

Aggregate

SYNTAX

```
MIN  ( [ALL] <nValue> | DISTINCT <nValue> )
```

ARGUMENTS

ALL	Returns minimum value of all values in a column.
nValue	Numeric column or expression
DISTINCT	Returns minimum of only unique values in a column.

SEE ALSO

AVG(), COUNT(), MAX(), SUM()

SUM()

Calculates the total of all values in a given column.

TYPE

Aggregate

SYNTAX

```
SUM  ( [ALL] <nValue> | DISTINCT <nValue> )
```

ARGUMENTS

ALL	Returns minimum value of all values in a column.
DISTINCT	Returns minimum of only unique values in a column.
nValue	Numeric column or expression

SEE ALSO

AVG(), COUNT(), MAX(), MIN()

UPPER()Function

Converts <cValue> to uppercase

TYPE

Conversion

SYNTAX

```
UPPER ( <cValue> )
```

ARGUMENTS

<cValue>	Character column or expression

SEE ALSO

CAST()

DATA TYPES

ISQL supports most SQL data types except for the SQL DATE, TIME, and TIMESTAMP data types. In addition to standard SQL data types, ISQL also supports binary large object (BLOB) data types and arrays of data types (except for arrays of BLOB data). Table E.3 summarizes the data types available in ISQL statements.

TABLE E.3 ISQL DATA TYPES

NAME	SIZE	RANGE/PRECISION	DESCRIPTION	ALTERNATE KEYWORDS
BLOB	Variable	None	Binary large object.	
CHAR(n)	*n* chars	1 to 32767 bytes	Fixed length CHAR or text string. Maximum number of characters determined by size of each character.	CHARACTER
DATE	64 bits	1 Jan 100 to11 Jan 5941	Includes both date and time time information.	
DECIMAL (*precision, scale*)	variable	*precision*: 1 to 15 *scale*: 1 to 15	Number with a decimal point *scale* digits from the right. *Scale* must be less than *precision*.	
DOUBLE PRECISION	64 bits	1.7 * 10-308 to 1.7 * 10308	Scientific: 15 digits of precision	
FLOAT	32 bits	3.4 X 10-38 to 3.4 X 1038	Single: 7 digits of precision.	
INTEGER	32 bits	-2,147,483,648 to 2,147,483,648	Signed long (longword).	
NUMERIC	variable	*precision*: 1 to 15 *scale*: 1 to 15	Number with a decimal point *scale* digits from the right. *Scale* must be less than *precision*.	
SMALLINT	16 bits	-32768 to 32767	Signed short (word).	
VARCHAR (*n*)	n chars	1 to 32767 bytes	Variable length CHAR or text string type. Maximum number of characters determined by size of each character.	VARYING CHAR, VARYING CHARACTER

ERROR HANDLING

When an SQL statement is executed, a variable called SQLCODE is set to indicate its success or failure. The possible values of the SQLCODE variable are listed in the following table.

SQLCODE	Message	Meaning
< 0	SQL ERROR	Error occurred. Statement did not execute.
0	SUCCESS	Successful execution
+1..99	SQL WARNING	System warning or informational message
+100	NOT FOUND	No qualifying rows found, or end of current active set of rows reached

Both an error number and a message are displayed when an error occurs in ISQL.

File Formats

This appendix provides information on many of the popular data file formats you may use with Delphi.

Rather than listing the structures as only as tables, the file formats are also declared in Delphi code. Additional code is provided at the end of this appendix demonstrating how to read several of the file headers.

BTRIEVE

```
unit BTrieveStats;

uses WinTypes;

type
    BtrieveFileStats = Record        { Btrieve data file stats }
        RecordLength  : Word;        { Length of a single record }
        PageSize      : Word;        { Size of an index page }
        IndexCount    : Word;        { # of index orders in the file }
        RecordCount   : LongInt;     { # of records in the file }
        FileFlags     : Word;        { Various file flags }
        Reserved      : Word;        { 2 Unused bytes }
        UnusedPages   : Word;        { # of index pages unused }
    end;

    BtrieveKeyStats = Record         { Btrieve index key stats }
        KeyPosition   : Word;        { Key position }
        KeyLength     : Word;        { Key length }
        KeyFlags      : Word;        { Key flags }
        KeyCount      : LongInt;     { # of entries in this index }
        KeyType       : Byte;        { Indicator for the key type }
        NullValue     : Byte;        { Null value }
        Reserved      : LongInt;     { 4 unused bytes }
    end;

    BtrieveACS = Array[ 1..265 ] of Byte;

    BtrieveStats = Record            { Record status of a Btrieve file }
        FileStats : BtrieveFileStats; { Btrieve data file statistics }
                                     { Index key statistics }
        KeyStats  : Array[ 1..24 ] of BtrieveKeyStats;
        ACS       : BtrieveACS;      { ACS }
    end;
```

```
const
    { Constants for the FileFlags bits }
    FF_VARILEN      = $0001;
    FF_TRUNCATE     = $0002;
    FF_PREALLOCATE  = $0004;
    FF_COMPRESS     = $0008;
    FF_KEYONLY      = $0010;
    FF_THRESHOLD10  = $0040;
    FF_THRESHOLD20  = $0080;
    FF_THRESHOLD30  = FF_THRESHOLD10 or FF_THRESHOLD20;

    { Constants for the KeyFlags bits }
    KF_ALLOWDUPES   = $0001;
    KF_ALLOWMODS    = $0002;
    KF_KEYTYPE      = $0004;
    KF_HASNULL      = $0008;
    KF_ANOTHERSEG   = $0010;
    KF_HASACS       = $0020;
    KF_DESCENDING   = $0040;
    KF_SUPPLEMENTAL = $0080;
    KF_EXTENDED     = $0100;
    KF_MANUAL       = $0200;

function Btrieve( OpCode        : Word;
                  PositionBlock : Pointer;
                  DataBuffer    : Pointer;
                  DataLength    : PWord;
                  KeyBuffer     : Pointer;
                  KeyLength     : Byte;
                  KeyNumber     : Byte ) : Word; far; external 'WBTRCALL'
                                                        index 1;

var
    StatBuffer : BtrieveStats;
    PosBlock   : Array[ 1..128 ] of Byte;
    DataLen    : Word;
    KeyBuffer  : Array[ 1..64 ] of Byte;

begin
    { Open the file }
    DataLen := 0;
    Btrieve( 0, @PosBlock, NIL, @DataLen, PChar( 'FILENAME.EXT' ), 12,0);

    { Get the stats.  After this call, the StatBuffer will contain the
        file and key specs.  Note that you should pay attention to
        IndexCount and KF_ANOTHERSEG to determine the number of key specs
        actually in used.  Also use KF_HASACS to determine if ACS contains
        valid data.
```

```
    }
    DataLen := SizeOf( BtrieveStats );
    Btrieve( 15, @PosBlock, @StatBuffer, @DataLen, @KeyBuffer, 64, 0 );
    { Close the file }
    DataLen := 0;
    Btrieve( 1, @PosBlock, NIL, @DataLen, NIL, 0, 0 );
end.
```

XBASE FILES

All the Xbase language products have many features in common, including some of the data file formats. The basic data format for Xbase is the (**.DBF**) file, and any Xbase language product (and Delphi) can read any Xbase .DBF file as long as it does not use a memo file. Most Xbase language products can also read report form (**.FRM**), label (**.LBL**), and memory variable (**.MEM**) files, so these are all documented in this section.

Data Tables (.DBF)

The structure of an Xbase data base file (**.DBF**) appears at the beginning of the data file and is at least 66 bytes long. See Table F.1.

TABLE F.1 .DBF TABLE HEADER RECORD

BYTES	DESCRIPTION
00	Type of memo file used (see the signature byte constants below)
01–03	Last update (YYMMDD)
04–07	Number of records in the file (Least significant byte first)
08–09	Data offset (Least significant byte first)
10–11	Length of a record (Least significant byte first)
12–31	Reserved
32–n	Field subrecords (See Table F.2)
n + 1	Header record terminator

The first byte of a **.DBF** file and many of the other Xbase data files is known as a signature byte. Because the standard File Allocation Table in PC operating systems does not support ID bytes for file types, this first byte was used instead. In dBASE III+, the signature byte was either $03 (hexadecimal notation, same as C's 0x03) or $83, indicating a file without or with a memo file, respectively.

Bits of the Signature Byte

As new features were added to the **.DBF** file, additional information was encoded in the bits of the signature byte. In Visual dBASE, every bit of the signature byte is used.

BITS	DESCRIPTION
0–2	Version number
3	If on, a dBASE IV, dBASE for Windows, or Visual dBASE memo file is present
4–6	Indicate the presence of a dBASE IV SQL table
7	On if any memo file is used

Signature Byte Constants

In most cases it will not be necessary to decode a **.DBF** file to this level. To make it easier to recognize the varied **DBF** types, we have declared some constants that recognize .DBF files including Borland's Visual dBASE and Microsoft's Visual FoxPro:

```
{ DBF signature bytes }
_DBF_FOXBASE      = $02;      { FoxBase, no memo }
_DBF_NO_MEMO      = $03;      { dBASE III+ }
_DBF_ENCRYPT      = $06;      { Apollo encrypted, no memo }
_DBF_VFP          = $30;      { Visual FoxPro }
_DBF_DB4_SQL      = $43;      { dBASE IV SQL table, no memo }
_DBF_DB4_SQLSYS   = $63;      { dBASE IV SQL system file, no memo }
_DBF_DBT_MEMO     = $83;      { CA-Clipper/dBASE III+ .DBT memo }
_DBF_DBT_ENCRYPT  = $86;      { Apollo encrypted, no memo }
_DBF_DB4_MEMO     = $8B;      { dBASE IV .DBT memo }
_DBF_DB4_SQLMEMO  = $CB;      { dBASE IV SQL table, memo }
_DBF_SMT_MEMO     = $E5;      { HiPer SIx with memo }
_DBF_SMT_ENCRYPT  = $E6;      { HiPer SIx with memo, encrypted }
_DBF_FPT_MEMO     = $F5;      { FoxPro .FPT memo }
_DBF_FPT_ENCRYPT  = $F6;      { Apollo encrypted, FoxPro memo }
_DBF_FOX_MEMO     = $FB;      { FoxBASE memo }
```

.DBF Header Record

The **.DBF** Header is actually composed of two different structures: a data file header and a data field header. The data file header and each data field header use 32 bytes (to keep the structure size to a convenient base 2 multiple). The **.DBF** Header record comes first:

```
DBFHeaderRec = Record          { .DBF File header record, 32 bytes}
        iSignature  : Byte;    { Type of memo file used (see
                                 constants) }
        iYear       : Byte     { Last update (YMD), Year part }
        iMonth      : Byte;    { Last update (YMD), Month part }
        iDay        : Byte;    { Last update (YMD), Day part }
```

```
    lRecords      : Longint;      { # of records in the file }
    wDataOffset : Word;           { Data offset }
    wRecLen       : Word;         { Length of a record }
    wFiller       : Word;         { 2 unused bytes (should be 0s) }
    bIncomplete : Boolean;        { Incomplete dBASE IV Transaction? }
    bEncrypted    : Boolean;      { dBASE IV Encryption flag }
    sMultiuser    : String[11];   { 12 bytes for multi-user processing }
    iFlags        : Boolean;      { Table flags:
                                    $01 = file has production .MDX / .CDX
                                    $02 = file has memos (VFP)
                                    $04 = file is a Database (.DBC)(VFP) }
    iLanguage     : Byte;         { Language driver ID }
    wFiller2      : Word;         { 2 unused bytes (should be 0s) }
end; { DBFHeaderRec }
```

When you look at the foregoing structure, you will notice that we have employed the Hungarian notation we described in the introductory chapter. Because the signature byte is most conveniently manipulated as a numeric value, I have named it as an integer. The same is true for the year, month, and day the file was last updated. The DBFHeaderRec.sMultiUser field is declared to only 11 characters although the comment states that 12 bytes are reserved because the first byte of a Delphi string is used to indicate the length of the string.

DBF Field Header Record

Immediately following the data file header, the fields begin. The end of the field structures is indicated by one or two bytes (depending on which Xbase product created the file) set to $0D. The structure of the standard DBF field is shown in Table F.2.

TABLE F.2 .DBF FIELD SUBRECORD

BYTES	DESCRIPTION
00–10	Field name, padded with 00h
11	Field type (see DBFieldRec for a complete list of all field types)
	C—Character
	D—Date
	F—Float
	G—General
	L—Logical
	M—Memo
	N—Numeric
12–15	Reserved
16	Length of field (in bytes)
17	Number of decimal places
18–31	Reserved

Because dBASE for Windows and Visual FoxPro have extended the field structure beyond the other DBF formats, We've created an additional structure that includes the additional breakdown of the field extensions. This is primarily because the conditional format of the field becomes highly redundant to type. The following example illustrates our point.

```
DBFieldEnd = Record               { dBASE IV, FoxPro field modifications }
        iFlags       : Byte;      { VFP Field Flags:
                                    $01 System Column (not visible to user)
                                    $02 Column can store null values
                                    $04 Binary column (Char or Memo only) }
        cFiller1     : Byte;      { 2 unused bytes }
        iWorkArea    : Byte;      { Work area }
        sFiller2     : String[9]; { 10 unused bytes }
        bProduction  : Boolean;   { Production .MDX field flag }
end; { DBFieldEnd }

DBFieldRec = Record    { DBF File field header record, 32 bytes }
        szName : Array[ 0..10 ] of Char;       { Field name }
        case cFieldType : Char of              { Field Type }
        'C' :
        ( lPlacement            : Longint;     { Field placement (VFP) }
               wCharLen         : Word;        { Length of character field }
               recInfo          : DBFieldEnd );{ For Visual dBASE, VFP }
        'B', 'D', 'T', 'F', 'G', 'L', 'M', 'N', 'Y', 'I', 'G', 'P':
        ( lPlacement2   : Longint;             { Field placement (VFP) }
               iLength          : Byte;        { Length of field }
               iDecimal         : Byte;        { Decimals of field }
               recInfo1         : DBFieldEnd );{ For Visual dBASE, VFP }
end; { DBFieldRec }
```

Depending on the type of the field, the next two characters after the filler character are either a word containing the length of a character field or the length and decimal precision (if applicable) of the other types of fields. Date fields are always eight characters long, Logicals are one character, and Memo fields are ten characters long.

Although there is a byte in the file immediately after the last field header set to $0D that indicates no more fields, the number of fields can be determined simply be looking at the value of DBFHeaderRec.wDataOffset and doing a simple calculation. The following function accepts a .DBF header (the first 32 bytes in the file) and returns the number of fields the header contains, based on the data offset to the first record in the data file.

```
function DBFieldCount(          { # of fields in data file }
    recDBF   : DBFHeaderRec     { Database file header }
    )          : Integer;
begin
    Result := ( recDBF.wDataOffset - SizeOf( DBFHeaderRec ) - 1 )
        div SizeOf( DBFieldRec ); { Calculate the # of fields }
end; { DBFieldCount() }
```

The following example illustrates how to analyze a **.DBF** file. It uses a dBASE III+/CA-Clipper DBF file.

```
000000  83 5E 03 17 0A 00 00 00-82 01 8C 00 00 00 00 00   .^..............
000010  00 00 00 00 00 00 00 00-00 00 00 00 00 00 00 00   ................
000020  46 49 52 53 54 00 00 00-00 00 00 43 00 00 00 00   FIRST......C....
000030  14 00 00 00 00 00 00 00-00 00 00 00 00 00 00 00   ................
000040  4C 41 53 54 00 00 00 00-00 00 00 43 00 00 00 00   LAST.......C....
000050  14 00 00 00 00 00 00 00-00 00 00 00 00 00 00 00   ................
000060  53 54 52 45 45 54 00 00-00 00 00 43 00 00 00 00   STREET.....C....
000070  1E 00 00 00 00 00 00 00-00 00 00 00 00 00 00 00   ................
000080  43 49 54 59 00 00 00 00-00 00 00 43 00 00 00 00   CITY.......C....
000090  1E 00 00 00 00 00 00 00-00 00 00 00 00 00 00 00   ................
0000A0  53 54 41 54 45 00 00 00-00 00 00 43 00 00 00 00   STATE......C....
0000B0  02 00 00 00 00 00 00 00-00 00 00 00 00 00 00 00   ................
0000C0  5A 49 50 00 00 00 00 00-00 00 00 43 00 00 00 00   ZIP........C....
0000D0  0A 00 00 00 00 00 00 00-00 00 00 00 00 00 00 00   ................
0000E0  48 49 52 45 44 41 54 45-00 00 00 44 00 00 00 00   HIREDATE...D....
0000F0  08 00 00 00 00 00 00 00-00 00 00 00 00 00 00 00   ................
000100  4D 41 52 52 49 45 44 00-00 00 00 4C 00 00 00 00   MARRIED....L....
000110  01 00 00 00 00 00 00 00-00 00 00 00 00 00 00 00   ................
000120  41 47 45 00 00 00 00 00-00 00 00 4E 00 00 00 00   AGE........N....
000130  02 00 00 00 00 00 00 00-00 00 00 00 00 00 00 00   ................
000140  53 41 4C 41 52 59 00 00-00 00 00 4E 00 00 00 00   SALARY.....N....
000150  06 00 00 00 00 00 00 00-00 00 00 00 00 00 00 00   ................
000160  4E 4F 54 45 53 00 00 00-00 00 00 4D 00 00 00 00   NOTES......M....
000170  0A 00 00 00 00 00 00 00-00 00 00 00 00 00 00 00   ................
000180  0D 00 20 48 6F 6D 65 72-20 20 20 20 20 20 20 20   .. Homer
```

901

FIGURE F.1 DBASE III+/CA-CLIPPER .DBF FILE WITH .DBT MEMO.

Figure F.1 shows what a typical database header might look like in a hex editor. Using this information, along with DBFHeaderRec and DBFFieldRec, we can determine the following about this table:

- It has an associated CA-Clipper or dBASE III+ .DBT memo file (83h).
- It was last updated on March 23, 1994 (5E0317h).
- It has ten records in it (0A000000h).
- The first record begins at offset 386 (8201h).
- Each record is 140 bytes long (8C00h).
- The database contains the following field definitions:

NAME	TYPE	LENGTH	DECIMAL
FIRST	C	20	0
LAST	C	20	0
STREET	C	30	0
CITY	C	30	0
STATE	C	2	0
ZIP	C	10	0

continued

NAME	TYPE	LENGTH	DECIMAL
HIREDATE	D	8	0
MARRIED	L	1	0
AGE	N	2	0
SALARY	N	6	0
NOTES	M	10	0

Memo Files (.DBT)

CA-Clipper and dBASE III+ share the same **.DBT** file format, which is quite simple. See Table F.3.

TABLE F.3 CA-CLIPPER .DBT MEMO FILE HEADER

BYTES	DESCRIPTION
00–03	Number of blocks used in the .DBT, including the header
04–511	Unused

You will notice that it is a very inefficient structure that wastes 508 bytes of the file.

```
DBT3HeaderRec = Record                    { dBASE III+/CA-Clipper memo
                                            file header }

     lBlocks  : Longint;                  { # of blocks used, including
                                            header }

     szFiller : Array[ 0..507 ] of Char;  { 508 unused characters }
end; { DBT3HeaderRec }
```

However, these wasted bytes are irrelevant, because every block in this type of **.DBT** file is 512 bytes. This means that even if you store a character string that is 2 characters long, it consumes 512 bytes to be stored (plus the 10 characters used to point to it in the **.DBF** file). If you were to write a 514 byte character string to this **.DBT** file, it would use 2 blocks and consume 1024 characters.

Even worse, blocks in a dBASE III+ compatible **.DBT** file are not reused. To illustrate, imagine the following scenario describing saving a memo field for the same record in a data file. The Blocks column indicates the blocks of the **.DBT** file used for the action. Block 0 is used as the DBT header block.

ACTION	RESULT	BLOCKS
Save 5 characters to memo	Write a 512 byte block to DBT	1
Save 500 characters to memo	Uses the same block from step 1	1
Save 520 characters to memo	Uses the same block, and adds another one	1 + 2
Save 5 characters to memo	Writes new values to first block. Second is unused.	1 – 2
Switch records, save 10 characters to memo	Uses a new block	3

If this isn't enough to convince you to use a different memo file format, you also need to consider that binary strings cannot be stored to this type of **.DBT** file, because the end of a memo file string is indicated with $1A—a byte that could be easily used in a binary string. This header structure does not support encoding the length of the string into the header, so by convention $1A is used to end the string.

Report Forms (.FRM)

Xbase report form files are an interesting mixture of elegance and inconvenience. A fair amount of information can be put into an Xbase report form file, given its finite size. Every column in a report is indexed into a specific region of the report form structure. To make processing a report form easier, we have declared some constants for various report form values:

```
{ FRM file constants }
_FRM_EXP_COUNT   = 55;            { Max # of expressions }
_FRM_MAX_EXPR    = 1440;          { Total bytes for form expressions }
_FRM_MAX_FIELDS  = 25;            { Max # of columns in a form }
```

These constants declarations are used to help define the structure of a report form file. Two different structures are used inside a report form file. The report form field record is the definition of a single column.

```
FRMFieldRec = Record             { FRM field header }
      iWidth        : Shortint;    { Print width of field }
      sFiller1      : String[ 2 ]; { 3 bytes of filler }
      cTotal        : Char;        { Should numbers be totaled? }
      iDec          : Shortint;    { # of Decimal places }
      iExpContents  : shortint;    { Exp # for field's contents }
      iExpHeader    : Shortint;    { Exp # for field's header }
end; { FRMFieldRec }
```

The primary structure of a report form file contains all report form definitions.

```
FRMHeaderRec = Record            { FRM file header }
      iSign1        : Shortint;    { value 02 indicates a FRM file }
      iExpEnd       : Shortint;    { Next free char in ExpArea }
                                   { Array of exp lengths }
      aiExpLength   : Array [ 1.._FRM_EXP_COUNT ] of Shortint;
                                   { Indices ExpArea for start of exp }
      aiExpIndex    : Array [ 1.._FRM_EXP_COUNT] of Shortint;
                                   { Container for expressions indexed
                                     by above arrays }
      pExpArea      : Array [ 0.._FRM_MAX_EXPR - 1 ] of Char;
                                   ( Array of FRMFields. First unused. }
      aFields       : Array [ 1.._FRM_MAX_FIELDS ] of FRMFieldRec;
      iTitle        : Shortint;    { Exp number of title string }
      iGrpOn        : Shortint;    { GROUP ON exp number }
      iSubOn        : Shortint;    { SUB GROUP ON exp number }
      iGrpHead      : Shortint;    { Exp # of GROUP ON heading }
      iSubHead      : Shortint;    { Exp # of SUB GROUP ON heading }
```

```
        iPageWidth      : Shortint;    { Width of page }
        iLinesPerPage   : Shortint;    { # of lines per page }
        iLeftMargin     : Shortint;    { Left margin }
        iRightMargin    : Shortint;    { Right margin }
        iColCount       : Shortint;    { # of columns }
        cDoubleSpace    : char;        { Y if doublespaced, N if not }
        cSummary        : Char;        { Y if summary, N if not }
        cEject          : Char;        { Y if eject page after group,or N }
        iPlusBytes      : Byte;        { bit 0=1: EJECT BEFORE PRINT }
                                       { bit 1=1: EJECT AFTER PRINT }
                                       { bit 2=1: PLAIN report }
        iSign2          : Shortint;    { value 02 }
end; { FRMHeaderRec }
```

Labels (.LBL)

Xbase label files are also a finite size and have specific limitations. Two constants are used for defining the structure.

```
{ LBL file constants }
_LBL_COUNT       = 15;          { 0 .. 15, label line entries }
_LBL_SIZE        = 59;          { 0 .. 59, 60 chars for contents }
```

The expressions that make up the lines of the label are null-terminated character strings.

```
LBLFieldRec = Array[ 0.._LBL_SIZE ] of Char;
```

Here is the structure of the entire label file.

```
LBLHeaderRec = Record              { Label file header }
        iSignature      : Byte;        { Signature byte - should be 1 }
                                       { Description of label file }
        szRemarks       : Array [ 0..59 ] of Char;
        iHeight         : Shortint;    { Height of label }
        iWidth          : Shortint;    { Width of label }
        iLeftMargin     : Shortint;    { Left margin }
        iLabelLine      : Shortint;    { Length of label line }
        iLabelSpace     : Shortint;    { Space between labels }
        iLabelsAcross   : Shortint;    { # of labels across }
        aInfo           : Array [ 0.._LBL_COUNT ] of LBLFieldRec;
        iSignature2     : Byte;        { Same as iSignature }
end; { LBLHeaderRec }
```

The contents of each label row are contained in the array of label field records LBLHeaderRec.aInfo.

Memory Variables (.MEM)

Memory variable files contain the names and contents of dynamic Xbase variables (PUBLIC and PRIVATE) that were saved to a file with the Xbase SAVE ... TO command.

```
MEMVarRec = Record                         { Memory variable file structure }
        szVarName               : Array [ 0..10 ] of Char;{ Variable name }
        cType            : Char;            { Type of variable }
        lFiller1         : Longint;         { 4 unused bytes }
        iLen             : Byte;            { Length of data for variable }
        iDec             : Byte;            { Decimal precision }
                                            { Data values for all but characters
                                              & memos }
        Data             : Array[ 0..13 ] of Char;
end; { MEMVarRec }
```

The field *szVarName* is a null-terminated string containing the name of the saved dynamic variable. The variable type is the same code as a field in a **.DBF**. The data field is used to store the actual values of all fields except for character and memo fields. Character and memo field values follow immediately after the end of the structure, and their length is indicated by interpreting MEMVarRec.iLen and MEMVarRec.iDec as a word.

CA-CLIPPER FILES

Because CA-Clipper originally began as a dBASE III compiler, it is compatible with dBASE III+ data files. It does support dBASE III+ index files (**.NDX**), but it has its own index format as well, which is slightly different so it can support multiuser operations on the file.

Index (.NTX)

The CA-Clipper "standard" index format is an **.NTX** file. Now that CA-Clipper 5.x has Replaceable Database Drivers (RDDs), most CA-Clipper developers are using either the FoxPro or dBASE IV compatible data drivers that are supplied with CA-Clipper. The maximum length of an index expression is 256 characters (255 with a null-terminator) as indicated by the following constant:

```
_NTX_MAX_KEY       = 255;       { Maximum length of NTX key expression }
```

The header structure is very similar to the dBASE III+ NDX file:

```
NTXHeaderRec = Record              { NTX File header, 278 bytes }
        wSign            : Word;    { Value 03 for Clipper file }
        wVersion         : Word;    { Version of Clipper indexing system }
        lRootPage        : Longint; { Offset to the first index page }
        lNextPage        : Longint; { Offset to first unused page }
        wItemSize        : Word;    { Size of the index key + two longs }
        wKeySize         : Word;    { Size of the index key value }
        wKeyDec          : Word;    { Decimal places for numeric index }
        wMaxItem         : Word;    { Maximum # of keys per page }
        wHalfPage        : Word;    { Half of MaxItem }
                                    { Index key expression }
        szExpression     : Array[ 0.._NTX_MAX_KEY ] of Char;
        wUnique          : Word;    { Unique ON=1 OFF=0 }

end; { NTXHeaderRec }
```

dBASE III+ Files

Most of the other Xbase products have direct support for dBASE III+ header files, but they may transparently change the structures after the file has been opened without warning you about it. Because of this, you should be careful to open dBASE III+ specific data files in read-only mode unless you no longer intend to access them with dBASE III+.

Index (.NDX)

As mentioned previously, the **.NDX** file format is very similar to the **.NTX**. The main difference is the size limit of the key expression. It is 488 characters (null-terminated) long, hence the following constant declaration:

```
NDX_MAX_KEY    = 487;  { Maximum length of NDX key expression }
```

The header structure follows:

```
NDXHeaderRec = Record                   { NDX File header, 512 bytes }
      lStartKeyPage  : Longint;         { Record # of root page }
      lTotalPages    : Longint;         { # of 512 byte pages in file }
      lFiller1       : Longint;         { Four unused bytes }
      wKeySize       : Word;            { Size of the index key }
      wMaxItem       : Word;            { Maximum # of keys per page }W
      wKeyType       : Word;            { 01 = Numeric, 00 = char }
      wSizeKeyRec    : Word;            { Size of an NDX_KEY_REC }
      cFiller2       : Char;            { one byte of unused space }
      bUnique        : Boolean;         { Unique ON=1, OFF=0 }
                                        { Index key expression }
      szExpression   : Array[ 0.._NDX_MAX_KEY ] of Char;
end; { NTXHeaderRec }
```

dBASE IV/V, dBASE for Windows, Visual dBASE Files

dBASE IV and above further modified the database file header and would transparently and automatically restructure dBASE III+ **.DBF** and **.DBT** files. dBASE IV also added a multiple-order index file, with an extension of **.MDX**. **.MDX** files are very similar in functionality to FoxPro's compound index file structure, **.CDX**.

Index Files (.MDX)

To facilitate any code you may choose to write for analyzing **.MDX** files, we have included some useful constants:

```
{ MDX File constants }
MDX_SIGNATURE       = 2;         { Type code for .mdx file }
MDX_DESCENDING      = $08;       { Index is descending }
MDX_TAGFIELD        = $10;       { Shows tag is a field in file }
MDX_UNIQUE          = $40;       { Index excludes duplicate keys }
```

```
MDX_FLAG_DESCENDING   = $0008;        { AND with MDXTagHeader.iFlags }
MDX_FLAG_FIELDTAG     = $0010;        { AND with MDXTagHeader.iFlags }
MDX_FLAG_UNIQUE       = $0040;        { AND with MDXTagHeader.iFlags }
```

Multiple dates are stored in the **.MDX** header, so we have a structure for these date stamps:

```
{ dBASE MDX date stamp }
MDXDate = Record
   iYear    : Byte;                { Year is iYear - 1900 }
   iMonth   : Byte;
   iDay     : Byte;
end; { MDXDate }
```

The index file header structure records the date of the last index update and the date the index file was created.

```
{ first 48 bytes of an .MDX file  }
MDXHeader = Record
   iFileType      : Byte;         { Error if not MDXTYPE }
   LastIndex      : MDXDate;      { Last reindex date }
                                  { Root name of associated .dbf }
   szRootDBF      : Array [0..15 ] of Char;
   iBlockSize     : Integer;      { SET BLOCKSIZE value, minimum = 2 }
   iBlockBytes    : Integer;      { Block size in bytes }
   bProduction    : Boolean;      { True if production .mdx, else False }
   sFiller        : String[2];    { 3 unused bytes }
   iIndexCount    : Integer;      { Number of indexes in the file }
   iFiller        : Integer;      { 2 unused bytes }
   lEndFilePage   : Longint;      { Unsigned: page # end of file }
   lNextFreePage  : Longint;      { Unsigned: page # of next free block }
   lFreePages     : Longint;      { Unsigned: pages in next free block }
   Created        : MDXDate;      { File creation date }
   cFiller        : Byte;         { 1 unused byte }
end; { MDXHeader }
```

Note that MDXHeader.szRootDBF contains the name of the **.DBF** file used for the **.MDX** file.

There is one **.MDX** tag descriptor for every index order in the **.MDX** file.

```
{ An .MDX index tag description }
MDXTagDesc = Record
   lIndHeaderPage : Longint;      { page number of index header }
                                  { MDX tag name, null-terminated }
   szTagName      : Array[ 0..10 ] of Char;
   iTagIsField    : Byte;         { 10 if the tag is a field, else 0 }
   aCounters      : Array[ 0..3 ] of Byte;    { usage counters }
   iFiller        : Byte;         { 1 unused byte filler, always 02 }
   cKeyType       : Char;         { C, D, or N for key type }
   sFiller        : String[11];{ 12 unused bytes }
end; { MDXTagDesc }
```

There is one **.MDX** tag header for every index order in the **.MDX** file.

```
{ Header of an index tag }
MDXTagHeader = Record
```

```
    lRootPage    : Longint;   { Unsigned: page number of index root }
    lPagesUsed   : Longint;   { Unsigned: pages used by the index }
    iFlags       : Byte;      { Index status flags: see MDX_FLAG constants }
    cKeyType     : Char;      { C, D or N for key type }
    bSQL         : Boolean;   { True if optimized for SQL, else False }
    cFiller      : Byte;      { 1 unused character }
    wKeyLength   : Word;      { Length of key in bytes }
    lMaxNodes    : Longint;   { Unsigned: maximum nodes in a block }
    wRecLen      : Word;      { Length of an index record in bytes     }
    wChanges     : Word;      { Change counter for optimization }
    cFiller2     : Byte;      { 1 unused character }
    iUniqueFlag  : Integer;   { $40 if UNIQUE, else 0 }
                              { The index key expression }
    szKeyExp     : Array[ 0..100 ] of Char;
end; { MDXTagHeader }
```

MDXTagHeader.szKeyExp is the actual index expression.

Memo Files (.DBT)

This **.DBT** memo file format is more robust than the dBASE III+ **.DBT** file, as shown in Table F.4.

TABLE F.4 DBASE IV/V .DBT MEMO FILE HEADER

BYTES	DESCRIPTION
00–03	Next free block to be used
04–07	Reserved
08–16	Associated .DBF file name
17	Reserved
18–19	Version
20–21	Block size being used, in bytes
22	Encrypted
23	Reserved

The memo file supports a specified block size (the default is 1024 bytes) and may be used to store binary strings.

```
DBT4HeaderRec = Record           { dBASE IV and up header }
        lNextBlock  : Longint; { Next free block to be used }
        lCurBlockSz : Longint; { Size of current block (0 in v1.0 - 1.5 )}
        szDBFName   : Array[ 0..8 ] of Char; { Associated .DBF file name }
        cFiller1    : Byte;    { 1 Reserved byte }
        wVersion    : Word;    { $102 in v1.0 - 1.5 }
        wBlockSize  : Word;    { Block size being used, in K }
        bEncrypted  : Boolean; { Is file encrypted? }
        cFiller2    : Char;    { 1 unused char }
end; { DBT4HeaderRec }
```

dBASE IV-format .DBT files support storage of record data in both dBASE III+ format or dBASE IV format. The first 2 bytes of the memo entry indicate which method was used to store the data. If these first 2 bytes are FFFFh, the dBASE IV-style was used. In this case, the header information listed in Table F.7 applies.

If anything other than FFFFh is stored in the first 2 bytes, it's assumed to be the first 2 bytes of the actual memo text of a dBASE III+ style memo entry. In this case, the memo entry is terminated by 1Ah (ASCII 26), just like in CA-Clipper and dBASE III+ .DBT memo file entries. See Table F.5.

TABLE F.5 dBASE IV .DBT RECORD HEADER (DBFMDX)

BYTES	DESCRIPTION
00–01	Memo record type (See text for explanation.)
02–03	Number of bytes in .DBT group header (Always 0800h)
04–07	Total number of bytes in the memo text
08–n	Memo text (or data), where n equals the length of the memo entry plus the 8 byte record header

FOXPRO FILES

FoxPro has its own index and memo file formats. The index file is more efficient and flexible than the dBASE III+ standard, and the memo file can store binary information, making it a significant improvement over the standard **.DB**T file format.

Index Files (.CDX/.IDX)

```
_CDX_BLK_SIZE   = 512;                    { Size of CDX blocks }
CDXNodeHeadRec = Record                   { CDX file node header }
      iNodeAttribute : Shortint;          { 0: Index, 1: Root, 2: Leaf }
      iNKeys         : Shortint;          { Number of keys in node }
      lLeftNode      : Longint;           { Offset of left sibling (-1 = none) }
      lRightNode     : Longint;           { Offset of right sibling (-1 = none) }
end; { CDXNodeHeadRec }

CDXNodeInfoRec = Record                   { CDX file node information }
      iFreeSpace     : Shortint;          { # of bytes available in node }
      lRecNumMask    : Word;              { Record number mask }
      iDupByteCnt    : Byte;              { Duplicate byte mask count }
      iTrailByteCnt  : Byte;              { Trailing byte mask count }
      iRecNumLen     : Byte;              { # of bits for record number }
      iDupCntLen     : Byte;              { # of bits for duplicate count }
      iTrailCntLen   : Byte;              { # of bits for trailing blank
count }
      iInfoLen       : Byte;              { # of bytes for record number }
end; { CDXNodeInfoRec }

      CDXTagHeadRec = Record              { CDX Tag header }
      lRoot          : Longint;           { Offset of root block }
      lFree_list     : Longint;           { Start of the free list (-1 if none) }
      lLength        : Longint;           { Length of file (non-compact only)
```

```
       iKeyLen          : Shortint;          { Key Length }
       ucTypeCode       : Byte;              { 0x01: Unique; 0x02, 0x04: RYO;
                                               0x08:
                                               Conditional 0x20: Compact; 0x60:
                                               Compound }
```

```
end; { CDXTagHeadRec }
CDXTagRec = Record                           { CDX Tag entry }
       iKeyOn           : Shortint;          { Current key # (0 - based) }
                                             { Current key data (10 bytes for
                                               tag name + null) }
       szKey            : Array[ 0..10 ] of Char;
       pCurPos          : Pointer;           { Pointer to current position
                                               in data }
       iKeyLen          : Shortint;          { Key length }
       sHeader          : CDXNodeHeadRec;    { Node header }
       sNodeInfo        : CDXNodeInfoRec;    { Node info }
       caData           : Array[ 0.._CDX_BLK_SIZE - ( SizeOf( CDXNodeHeadRec)
                        + SizeOf( CDXNodeInfoRec )) ] of Char;{ Data }
end; { CDXTagRec }
```

Memo Files (.FPT)

The header of a FoxPro **.FPT** memo file is similar to that of a **.DBT** memo file, with a few exceptions. The first 4 bytes of an **.FPT** represent the number of the next block to be used. Also, these 4 bytes are stored in most significant byte order, opposite from the **.DBT**.

Of the next 4 bytes, the first two aren't really used at all. The next two (an unsigned integer), also stored in most significant byte order, hold the block size being used by the **.FPT** memo file. This value is adjustable, so the value stored in this position may vary. The default value is 64.

The remainder of the **.FPT** header is unused. See Table F.6.

TABLE F.6 FoxPro .FPT Memo File Header

Bytes	Description
00–03	Next free block to be used
04–05	Unused
06–07	Block size being used, in bytes
08–511	Unused

In CA-Clipper and dBASE III+ **.DBT** memo files, the first 8 bytes of each memo entry actually hold the first 8 bytes of the memo text. However, in FoxPro **.FPT** memo files, these first 8 bytes hold information about the type and length of the data stored in the memo entry. This is immediately followed by the actual memo text or data itself. Since the length of the entry is stored up front, the memo entry is not terminated with any special ASCII value, as is the case for standard **.DBT** memo files. See Table F.7.

TABLE F.7 FOXPRO .FPT RECORD HEADER

BYTES	DESCRIPTION
00–03	Type of data in block
04–07	Length of memo entry, in bytes
08–n	Memo text (or data), where n equals the length of the memo entry plus the 8 byte record header

FoxPro memo files can store binary information in the memo file, because the FPT block record includes the length of the data stored in the block.

```
FPTHeaderRec = Record              { FoxPro memo file header }
     lNextBlock  : Longint;         { Next free block to use, byte
                                      reversed }
     lBlockSize  : Longint;         { Block size being used, byte
                                      reversed }
     sWasted     : Array[ 0..503 ] of Char;   { 504 Unused characters }
end; { FPTHeaderRec }

FPTBlockRec = Record               { FoxPro memo file block }
     lDataType   : Longint;         { Type of data in block }
     lLength     : Longint;         { Length of memo entry, in bytes }
     pBuffer     : Pointer;
     { Memo text (or data), where n equals the length of the memo entry
       plus the 8 byte record header.  The pointer is not really part
       of the structure—it has to be allocated and assigned to the data
       immediately following lLength }
end; { FPTBlockRec }
```

Database/Data Dictionary Files (.DBC)

FoxPro data dictionary files are special-case FoxPro **.DBF** files where each record in the data dictionary covers a specific type of data: the database itself, the database's stored procedures and connections, tables, fields, index tags, relations, and views. Every record contains fields that enable the **.DBC** to relate those records with the appropriate level, showing which fields belong to which table, and so on. There is also a field called USER, which is not natively used by FoxPro and is intended to be used for extending the dictionary.

The primary structural difference between a **.DBC** file and a **.DBF** file is the extra 263 bytes that may occur in the FoxPro **.DBF** file that point back to the parent **.DBC** file. These bytes (if they occur) appear immediately after the header record terminator.

Project Files (.PJT/.PJX)

A FoxPro **.PJX** file is actually a **.DBF** file with the extension renamed. The **.DBF** has a memo file as well—with its extension renamed from **.FPT** to **.PJT**. If you wish to read a FoxPro project file in something other than FoxPro, simply rename the **.PJT** file to **.FPT** (temporarily, of course!) and open the **.PJX** file. You can then traverse all the records and follow the many fields in the project file. Some of the more interesting fields follow:

FIELD NAME	DESCRIPTION
NAME	The name of the source code file
OUTFILE	If defined, the output name of the source code file
HOMEDIR	The starting directory for the named file, if the NAME doesn't have a path
MAINPROG	If True, this source file is the entry point for the project's application (the main routine)

LOCAL INTERBASE SERVER

The Borland Database Engine includes SQL (ISQL) support that can be used locally on any type of data table supported by the Borland Database Engine.

Database Files (.GDB)

Every table created with ISQL is contained in a **.GDB** file. Multiple data tables can be and are contained in a single **.GDB** file. All index orders are contained internally.

PARADOX

Borland does not release the information on the Paradox file formats, so we will simply explain the intended use of the various Paradox file formats here.

Data Tables (.DB)

Paradox data tables have a **.DB** extension. Each data table has an associated .DB file. Paradox data tables have a richer set of data types (such as AutoInc and Time fields), and Delphi is better suited for Paradox table access than dBASE-like data file access, with engine-level data validation features like ValChecks and referential integrity. It is currently missing descending index support. Paradox uses a network control file to do record locking, which can cause deployment issues (see discussion of Lock Files (**.LCK**) for further information). Field naming in Paradox files is more flexible than dBASE files.

PRIMARY INDEXES

All Paradox tables have a primary key, and the primary index is used for reading and updating those values. Primary keys are unique for that entire data table. One or more fields can be used as the primary key, but only one key is the primary key for a file (hence the name). If you wish to change the primary key for a file, you must use the Create Table or Restructure Table dialog boxes in the Database Desktop.

SECONDARY INDEXES

Paradox uses a separate file for every index on a data table. Every index other than the primary index is a secondary index file.

Lock Files (.LCK)

For multiuser access, the Borland Database Engine maintains lock files for every user accessing the data tables. The lock file directory should be contained on a network drive. If a Windows for Workgroups peer-to-peer network is being used, the drive and directory must be the same for all users. For example, if **F:\TABLES** is the shared directory, then all machines (including the host machine) should have a drive F: mapped that accesses the appropriate drive on the host machine. If the actual physical directory on the host machine is **C:\TABLES**, simply use the DOS SUBST command to create a drive F:.

FILE FORMAT UTILITY CODE

Based on the preceding code, here are some utility routines to display structural information from various files. The function dbHeaderRead() will fill any structure you pass it with the raw data in the file starting at position zero. Because it is designed to accept any type of record structure, you must also pass the length of the header to the function. The various Show*() procedures will display the structural information for the files of the format for which they are named.

```
function dbHeaderRead(           { Read in a header from a file }
   sFile        : String;        { Name of file to read }
   var Header;                    { Header structure to read }
   iSize        : Integer;       { Size of header structure }
   )            : Boolean;       { True if read successfully }
var
   iHandle   : Integer;
begin
   Result := False;
   try
      iHandle := fOpen( sFile, FO_READ );
      if iHandle > -1 then
         if FileRead( iHandle, Header, iSize ) = iSize then
            Result := True;
   finally
      FileClose( iHandle );
   end; { try .. finally }
end; { dbHeaderRead() }
```

This routine gives a textual description of the type of the .**DBF** file based on the signature byte.

```
function DBFileType(             { DBF File Type }
   iSignature  : Byte;           { Signature byte }
   )            : String;
begin
```

```
        case iSignature of
        _DBF_FOXBASE              : Result := 'FoxBase, no memo';
        _DBF_NO_MEMO              : Result := 'dBASE III+';
        _DBF_ENCRYPT              : Result := 'Apollo encrypted, no memo';
        _DBF_VFP                  : Result := 'Visual FoxPro';
        _DBF_DB4_SQL              : Result := 'dBASE IV SQL table, no memo';
        _DBF_DB4_SQLSYS           : Result := 'dBASE IV SQL system file, no memo';
        _DBF_DBT_MEMO   : Result := 'CA-Clipper/dBASE III+ .DBT memo';
        _DBF_DBT_ENCRYPT          : Result := 'Apollo encrypted, no memo';
        _DBF_DB4_MEMO   : Result := 'dBASE IV .DBT memo';
        _DBF_DB4_SQLMEMO          : Result := 'dBASE IV SQL table, memo';
        _DBF_SMT_MEMO   : Result := 'HiPer SIx with memo';
        _DBF_SMT_ENCRYPT          : Result := 'HiPer SIx with memo, encrypted';
        _DBF_FPT_MEMO   : Result := 'FoxPro .FPT memo';
        _DBF_FPT_ENCRYPT          : Result := 'Apollo encrypted, FoxPro memo';
        _DBF_FOX_MEMO   : Result := 'FoxBASE memo';
        else                        Result := 'Unrecognized DBF file type';
        end; { case }
end; { DBFileType() }
```

This routine displays the structural information for any **.DBF** file.

```
procedure ShowDBF(                      { Show structure of a .DBF file }
   sFile : String );                    { Name of .DBF file }
var
   recHeader : DBFHeaderRec;
begin
   if dbHeaderRead( sFile, recHeader, SizeOf( recHeader ) ) then
      with recHeader do begin
         WriteLn( 'iSignature  :', iSignature,
            ' (', DBFileType( iSignature ), ')' );
         WriteLn( 'iYear          :', iYear );
         WriteLn( 'iMonth         :', iMonth );
         WriteLn( 'iDay           :', iDay );
         WriteLn( 'lRecords       :', lRecords );
         WriteLn( 'wDataOffset :', wDataOffset );
         WriteLn( 'wRecLen        :', wRecLen );
         WriteLn( 'bIncomplete :', bIncomplete );
         WriteLn( 'bEncrypted  :', bEncrypted );
         WriteLn( 'sMultiuser  :', sMultiuser );
         WriteLn( 'iFlags         :', iFlags );
         WriteLn( 'iLanguage   :', iLanguage );
      end; { with }

end; { ShowDBF() }
```

This routine shows the number of blocks in a dBASE III+ compatible memo file.

```
procedure ShowDBT3(                     { Show structure of a DBT3 file }
   sFile : String );                    { Name of DBT file }
var
   recHeader : DBT3HeaderRec;
begin
```

```
   if dbHeaderRead( sFile, recHeader, SizeOf( recHeader )) then
      WriteLn( 'lBlocks     :', recHeader.lBlocks );
end; { ShowDBT3() }
```

This routine shows the structure of a dBASE IV or preceding memo file.

```
procedure ShowDBT4(              { Show structure of a DBT4 file }
   sFile : String );             { Name of DBT file }
var
   recHeader : DBT4HeaderRec;
begin
   if dbHeaderRead( sFile, recHeader, SizeOf( recHeader )) then
      with recHeader do begin
         WriteLn( 'lNextBlock  :', lNextBlock );
         WriteLn( 'lCurBlockSz :', lCurBlockSz );
         WriteLn( 'szDBFName   :', szDBFName );
         WriteLn( 'wVersion    :', wVersion );
         WriteLn( 'wBlockSize  :', wBlockSize );
         WriteLn( 'bEncrypted  :', bEncrypted );
      end; { with }
end; { ShowDBT4() }
```

This routine displays the structure of a SuccessWare Data Engine native memo file.

```
procedure ShowSMT(               { Show structure of an SMT file }
   sFile : String );             { Name of SMT file }
var
   recHeader : SMTHeaderRec;
begin
   if dbHeaderRead( sFile, recHeader, SizeOf( recHeader )) then
      with recHeader do begin
         WriteLn( 'lNextBlock  :', lNextBlock );
         WriteLn( 'lBlockSize  :', lBlockSize );
      end; { with }
end; { ShowSMT() }
```

Because FoxPro (for some strange reason) uses byte-reversed long integer values, we have a routine for swapping the byte order in Delphi 1.0. Under Delphi 2.0, the new Swap () Function can be used instead.

```
function ReverseBytes(           { FoxPro byte-reversed longints }
      lVal   : longint           { Value to swap }
      )       : longint;
var
      pVal   : Array[ 0..3 ] of byte;
      iTemp  : byte;
begin

   Move( lVal, pVal, SizeOf( lVal ) );

   iTemp      := pVal[ 0 ];
   pVal[ 0 ]  := pVal[ 3 ];
   pVal[ 3 ]  := iTemp;
```

```
    iTemp        := pVal[ 1 ];
    pVal[ 1 ]    := pVal[ 2 ];
    pVal[ 2 ]    := iTemp;

    Move( pVal, lVal, SizeOf( lVal ) );
    Result       := lVal;
end; { ReverseBytes() }
```

This routine shows the structure of a FoxPro memo file, by using the ReverseBytes() function.

```
procedure ShowFPT(                      { Show structure of an FPT file }
    sFile : String );                   { Name of FPT file }
var
    recHeader : FPTHeaderRec;
begin
    if dbHeaderRead( sFile, recHeader, SizeOf( recHeader )) then
        with recHeader do begin
            WriteLn( 'lNextBlock  :', ReverseBytes( lNextBlock ));
            WriteLn( 'lBlockSize  :', ReverseBytes( lBlockSize ));
        end; { with }
end; { ShowFPT() }
```

All the preceding Xbase file structure definitions are contained in the file XBFORMAT.PAS, found on the included CD-ROM.

CREATING .DBF FILES

Because Delphi does not include a convenient way to create a .DBF file that includes numeric fields with a specific decimal precision (the only way to do this is by using SQL's CREATE TABLE with a TQuery), a routine called dbCreate() is provided. It will create any kind of Xbase **.DBF** file—without the use of anything other than native Delphi source code and the preceding structural declarations.

For convenience, we have written a class for data fields and a class for DBF structures to encapsulate all the needed functionality. Here is the code for the DBF field class, TDBField:

```
TDBField = class
    private
    protected
        sName      : String;
        cType      : Char;
        iLength    : Integer;
        iDecimal   : Integer;
        function GetName : String;
        procedure SetName( sNew : String );
        function GetType : Char;
        procedure SetType( cNew : Char );
        function GetLength : Integer;
        procedure SetLength( iNew : Integer );
        function GetDecimal : Integer;
        procedure SetDecimal( iNew : Integer );
    public
        property FieldName : String read GetName write SetName;
```

```
      property FieldType : Char read GetType write SetType;
      property FieldLength : Integer read GetLength write SetLength;
      property FieldDecimal : Integer read GetDecimal write SetDecimal;
      function TypeWord : String;
      constructor Create(                { Create the field entry }
          sFieldName     : String;       { Name of the field }
          cFieldType     : Char;         { Character type code for the field}
          iFieldLength   : Integer;      { Length of the field }
          iFieldDecimal  : Integer       { Decimal precision 4 number fields}
          );
          function IsMemo : Boolean;     { Is field stored in memo file? }
      function Header      : DBFieldRec;
   end; { TDBField }
```

The TDBField class provides all necessary control for the fields in a **.DBF** file. Here are all the routines for the TDBField class:

```
function TDBField.GetName : String;
begin
   Result := sName;
end; { TDBField.GetName }

procedure TDBField.SetName( sNew : String );
begin
   sNew := UpperCase( AllTrim( sNew ));
   if IsSymbol( sNew ) then
      sName := sNew
   else
      Raise EXbFormatError.Create( 'Bad field name: "' + sNew + '"' );
end; { TDBField.SetName() }

function TDBField.GetType : Char;
begin
   Result := cType;
end; { TDBField.GetType }

procedure TDBField.SetType( cNew : Char );
begin
   cNew := UpCase( cNew );
   if cNew in DBFFieldTypes then begin
      cType := cNew;
      if not ( cType in [ 'F', 'N' ] ) then
         iDecimal := 0;
      case cNew of
      'D'    : iLength := 8;
      'L'    : iLength := 1;
      'B',
      'G',
      'M'    : iLength := 10;
      end; { case }
   end { valid type designator }
   else
      Raise EXbFormatError.Create( 'Bad field type: "' + cNew + '"' );
end; { TDBField.SetType() }
```

```
function TDBField.GetLength : Integer;
begin
   Result := iLength;
end; { TDBField.GetLength }

procedure TDBField.SetLength( iNew : Integer );
var
   iLow,
   iHigh : Integer;
begin
   iLow := 1;
   case cType of
   'C' : iHigh := 32733;
   'D' :
      begin
         iLow := 8;
         iHigh := 8;
      end;
   'F' : iHigh := 20;
   'L' : iHigh := 1;
   'B',
   'G',
   'P',
   'M' :
      begin
         iLow := 10;
         iHigh := 10;
      end;
   'N' : iHigh := 19;
   'I' : iHigh := 4;
   end; { case }
   if ( iLow <= iNew ) and ( iNew <= iHigh ) then
      iLength := iNew
   else
      Raise EXbFormatError.Create( LTrim( XbStr( [ iNew ], 5, 0 ) ) +
            ' is a bad field length for a ' + TypeWord + ' field' );
end; { TDBField.SetLength() }

function TDBField.GetDecimal : Integer;
begin
   Result := iDecimal;
end; { TDBField.GetDecimal }

procedure TDBField.SetDecimal( iNew : Integer );
begin
   if ( iNew = 0 ) or ( ( cType in [ 'N', 'F' ] ) and ( iNew > 0 ) and
   ( iNew < iLength - 2 )) then
      iDecimal := iNew
   else
      Raise EXbFormatError.Create(
         'Bad decimal length:  Not numeric field, or too long' );
end; { TDBField.SetDecimal() }

function TDBField.TypeWord : String;
```

```
begin
   case cType of
   'B'   : Result := 'Binary (or FoxPro Double)';
   'C'   : Result := 'Character';
   'D'   : Result := 'Date';
   'F'   : Result := 'Floating point';
   'G'   : Result := 'General or OLE';
   'I'   : Result := 'Integer';
   'L'   : Result := 'Logical';
   'M'   : Result := 'Memo';
   'N'   : Result := 'Numeric';
   'P'   : Result := 'Picture';
   'T'   : Result := 'DateTime';
   'V'   : Result := 'VariField';
   'Y'   : Result := 'Currency';
   else
      Result := 'Unknown';
   end; { case }
end; { TDBField.TypeWord }

function TDBField.IsMemo : Boolean;
begin
   Result := ( cType in [ 'B', 'G', 'M' ] );
end; { TDBField.IsMemo }

function TDBField.Header : DBFieldRec;
begin
   with Result do begin
      FillChar( Result, SizeOf( Result ), 0 );
      StrPCopy( szName, FieldName );
      cFieldType := cType;
      if cType = 'C' then
         wCharLen := FieldLength
      else begin
         iLength  := FieldLength;
         iDecimal := FieldDecimal;
      end; { not character type }
   end; { with Result }
end; { TDBField.Header }

constructor TDBField.Create(          { Create the field entry }
   sFieldName    : String;            { Name of the field }
   cFieldType    : Char;              { Character type code for the field }
   iFieldLength  : Integer;           { Length of the field }
   iFieldDecimal : Integer            { Decimal precision for numeric fields }
   );
begin
   inherited Create;
   try
      FieldName    := sFieldName;
      FieldType    := cFieldType;
      FieldLength  := iFieldLength;
      FieldDecimal := iFieldDecimal;
   except
```

```
        on E : EXbFormatError do
          ShowMessage( E.Message );
    end; { try .. except }
end; { TDBField.Create() }
```

The TDBStruct class is the .**DBF** file structure reader and writer. It contains multiple TDBFields.

```
TDBStruct = Class( TList )
   protected
      iBlockSize  : Integer;          ( Memo file block size }
      function GetField(
         Index    : Integer          { Index of entry to get }
         )        : TDBField;         { Returns the relevant TDBField }
      procedure PutField(
         Index    : Integer;         { Index of entry to put }
         oField   : TDBField );       { TDBField object to put }
      function MakeMemoHeader(        { Write a memo header structure }
         sFile    : String;          ( Name of memo file }
         const Header;                { Header structure to write }
         iSize    : Longint          { Size of header structure }
         )        : Boolean;         { True if successful }
      function MakeDBT3(              { Create dBASE III+/CA-Clipper memo}
         sFile    : String           { Name of .DBF file }
         )        : Boolean;
      function MakeDBT4(              { Create dBASE IV and up memo file }
         sFile    : String           { Name of .DBF file }
         )         :Boolean;
      function MakeSMT(               { Create a HiPer SIx memo file }
         sFile    : String           { Name of .DBF file }
         )        : Boolean;
      function MakeFPT(               { Create a FoxPro memo file }
         sFile    : String           { Name of .DBF file }
         )         :Boolean;
      function MakeMemo(              { Create the memo file for the DBF }
         sFile    : String           { Name of .DBF file }
         )        : Boolean;
      function GetBlockSize : integer;
      procedure SetBlockSize(         { Set the block size }
         iNew : Integer );
   public
      bEncrypt    : Boolean;          { Encrypt the file? }
      sDriver     : String;           { Name of the driver to use }
      procedure Free;
      procedure Eval(                 { Iterate through structure }
         cbProc   : xbBlockProc       { Data type for "code block" }
         );
      function Make(                  { Create the .DBF file }
         sFile    : String            { .DBF file name }
         )        : Boolean;          { True if successful }
      property BlockSize : Integer read GetBlockSize write SetBlockSize;
      function TableType : xbMemoType; { Type of Driver for Table }
      function Signature : Byte;       { Signature byte for DBF }
      function HasMemo :Boolean;       { Is a memo field in the DBF? }
```

```
    function DataOffset : Integer;   { Position of 1st record in file }
    function RecordLength : Integer; { # of bytes per record }
    property Fields[ Index : Integer ] : TDBField read GetField
        write PutField;
    constructor Create;
  end;  { TDBStruct class }
```

The routines for TDBStruct are naturally more complicated than those for the DBF fields, mainly because we have to juggle the logic for creating multiple .**DBF** file types. Fortunately, you don't need to type all this code in, as we originally did!

```
function TDBStruct.GetBlockSize : Integer;
begin
  if iBlockSize = 0 then
    case TableType of
    xbDB3 : Result := 512;
    xbDB4 : Result := 1024;
    xbFPT : Result := 32;
    xbSMT : Result := 1;
    end { case }
  else
    Result := iBlockSize;
end; { TDBStruct.GetBlockSize }

procedure TDBStruct.SetBlockSize(        { Set the block size }
    iNew : Integer );
var
  iLow,
  iHigh : Integer;
begin
  case TableType of
  xbDB3 :
    begin
      iLow := 512;
      iHigh := 512;
    end;
  xbDB4 :
    begin
      iLow := 512;
      iHigh := 1024;
    end;
  else
    begin
      iLow := 1;
      iHigh := 32000;
    end; { else }
  end; { case }
  if ( iNew > 0 ) and ( iNew < 32000 ) then
    iBlockSize := iNew
  else
    Raise EXbFormatError.Create( 'Acceptable BlockSize range is ' +
        IntToStr( iLow ) + '..' + IntToStr( iHigh ) );
end;
```

The routines TDBStruct.GetBlockSize() and TDBStruct.SetBlockSize() configure the size of the memo file blocks.

```
constructor TDBStruct.Create;
begin
   inherited Create;
   bEncrypt    := False;
   iBlockSize  := 0;
end; { TDBStruct.Create }

procedure TDBStruct.Free; { Free all objects created }
var
   iField   : Integer;
begin
   for iField := 1 to Count do
      Fields[ iField ].Free;
   inherited Free;
end; { TDBStruct.Free }

function TDBStruct.GetField( Index: Integer ): TDBField;
begin
   Result := TDBField( inherited Get( Index - 1 ) ); { Convert to 0-based }
end; { TDBStruct.GetField() }

procedure TDBStruct.PutField( Index : Integer; oField : TDBField );
begin
   inherited Put( Index - 1, @oField );
end; { TDBStruct.PutField() }
```

The routines TDBStruct.GetField() and TDBStruct.PutField() allow for easy access to the list of fields in the **.DBF** file. Since Xbase arrays are historically one-based rather than zero-based as most Delphi arrays are, you will notice that these routines convert a one-based ordinal position to a zero-based one (since we are using a TList to contain the DBF fields).

```
procedure TDBStruct.Eval(              { Do something to every field entry }
   cbProc       : xbBlockProc         { Procedure "code block" type }
   );
var
   iField : Integer;
begin
   for iField := 1 to Count do
      with Fields[ iField ] do
         cbProc( [ FieldName, FieldType, FieldLength, FieldDecimal ] );
end; { TDBStruct.Eval }
```

The declaration for xbBlockProc is

```
xbBlockProc = procedure( xVars : Array of const );
```

The following routine converts the *name* of the table type to the appropriate table type enumerated type.

```
function TDBStruct.TableType : xbMemoType;
begin
```

```
      sDriver := UpperCase( sDriver );
      if ( Length( sDriver ) = 0 ) or ( sDriver = 'DEFAULT' )
         or ( sDriver = 'SIXNTX' ) or ( sDriver = 'DBFNTX' ) then
         Result := xbDB3    { Clipper DBF is encoded the same }
      else if ( sDriver = 'DBASE' ) or ( sDriver = 'DBFMDX' ) then
         Result := xbDB4
      else if ( sDriver = 'SIXCDX' ) or ( sDriver = 'SIXFOX' )
         or ( sDriver = 'DBFCDX' ) then
         Result := xbFPT
      else if ( sDriver = 'SIXNSX' ) or ( sDriver = 'DBFNSX' ) then
         Result := xbSMT;
end; { TDBStruct.TableType() }

function TDBStruct.Signature : Byte;
type
   xbMatrixType   = Array[ xbDB3..xbSMT, False..True ] of Byte;
const
   xbMatrix : xbMatrixType = (
      ( _DBF_DBT_MEMO, _DBF_DBT_ENCRYPT ),
      ( _DBF_DB4_MEMO, _DBF_DB4_MEMO ),
      ( _DBF_FPT_MEMO, _DBF_FPT_ENCRYPT ),
      ( _DBF_SMT_MEMO, _DBF_SMT_ENCRYPT ));

var
   xbDriver : xbMemoType;
begin
   Result := _DBF_NO_MEMO;
   try
      xbDriver := TableType;
      if HasMemo then
         Result := xbMatrix[ xbDriver, bEncrypt ]
      else if bEncrypt then
         Result := _DBF_ENCRYPT;
   except
      Result := _DBF_NO_MEMO;
   end;
end; { TDBStruct.Signature }

function TDBStruct.HasMemo : Boolean;    { Is a memo field in the DBF? }
var
   iField   : Integer;
begin
   Result := False;
   for iField := 1 to Count do
      if Fields[ iField ].IsMemo then begin
         Result := True;
         break;
      end;
end; { TDBStruct.HasMemo }

function TDBStruct.DataOffset : Integer; { File position of 1st record }
begin
   Result := SizeOf( DBFHeaderRec ) + Count * SizeOf( DBFieldRec ) + 1;
end; { TDBStruct.DataOffset }
```

```
function TDBStruct.RecordLength : Integer; { # of bytes per record }
var
   iField   : Integer;
begin
   Result := 1;
   for iField := 1 to Count do
      Result := Result + Fields[ iField ].FieldLength;
end; { TDBStruct.RecordLength }
```

TDBStruct.MakeMemoHeader() accepts any one of the memo header structures and creates the specified file, writing out its header.

```
function TDBStruct.MakeMemoHeader(   { Write a memo header structure }
   sFile    : String;                { Name of memo file }
   const Header;                     { Header structure to write }
   iSize    : Longint                { Size of header structure }
   )        : Boolean;               { True if successful }
var
   iPadSize,
   iHandle  : Integer;
   cWipe    : Char;
begin
   Result := False;
   try
      iHandle := FileCreate( sFile );
      if iHandle > -1 then begin
         Result   := FileWrite( iHandle, Header, iSize ) = iSize;
         cWipe    := #0;
         iPadSize := BlockSize;
         while ( iSize < iPadSize ) and ( Result ) do begin
            Result := FileWrite( iHandle, cWipe, 1 ) = 1;
            Inc( iSize, 1 );
         end; { while }
      end; { file created }
      if not Result then
         Raise EXbFormatError.Create( 'Could not create memo file ' +
                                  sFile );
   finally
      FileClose( iHandle );
   end; { try .. finally }
end; { TDBStruct.MakeMemoHeader() }

function TDBStruct.MakeDBT3(   { Create dBASE III+/CA-Clipper memo file }
   sFile    : String           { Name of DBF file }
   )        : Boolean;
var
   recMemo  : DBT3HeaderRec;
   iSize    : Integer;
begin
   try
      iSize := SizeOf( recMemo );
      FillChar( recMemo, iSize, 0 );
      recMemo.lBlocks := 1;
```

```
      Result := MakeMemoHeader( ChangeFileExt( sFile, '.DBT' ), recMemo,
         iSize );
   except
      Result := False;
   end;
end; { TDBStruct.MakeDBT3() }

function TDBStruct.MakeDBT4(          { Create dBASE IV and up memo file }
   sFile     : String                { Name of .DBF file }
   )         : Boolean;
var
   recMemo   : DBT4HeaderRec;
   iSize     : integer;
begin
   try
      iSize := SizeOf( recMemo );
      FillChar( recMemo, iSize, 0 );
      with recMemo do begin
         lNextBlock  := 1;          { Next free block to be used }
         lCurBlockSz := 0;
         StrPCopy( szDBFName, UpperCase( ExtractFileFirst( sFile ) ) );
         wVersion    := _DBT4_VERSION;
         wBlockSize  := BlockSize; { Block size being used, in bytes }
         bEncrypted  := bEncrypt;   { Is file encrypted? }
      end; { with RecMemo }

      Result := MakeMemoHeader( ChangeFileExt( sFile, '.DBT' ), recMemo,
         iSize );
   except
      Result := False;
   end;
end; { TDBStruct.MakeDBT4() }

function TDBStruct.MakeSMT(          { Create a HiPer SIx memo file }
   sFile     : String                { Name of DBF file }
   )         : Boolean;
var
   recMemo   : SMTHeaderRec;
   iSize     : Integer;
begin
   try
      iSize := SizeOf( recMemo );
      FillChar( recMemo, iSize, 0 );
      with recMemo do begin
         lBlockSize := BlockSize; { Block size being used, in bytes }
         if lBlockSize > 512 then
            lNextBlock := 1  { Next free block to be used }
         else
            lNextBlock := 512 div lBlockSize;
      end; { with recMemo }
      Result := MakeMemoHeader( ChangeFileExt( sFile, '.SMT' ), recMemo,
         iSize );
   except
```

```
        Result := False;
      end;
  end; { TDBStruct.MakeSMT() }

  function TDBStruct.MakeFPT(        { Create a FoxPro memo file }
    sFile    : String               { Name of DBF file }
    )        : Boolean;
  var
    recMemo  : FPTHeaderRec;
    iSize    : Integer;
  begin
    try
        iSize := SizeOf( recMemo );
        FillChar( recMemo, iSize, 0 );
        with recMemo do begin
            lBlockSize := BlockSize; { Block size being used, in bytes }
            if lBlockSize > 512 then
                lNextBlock := 1  { Next free block to be used }
            else
                lNextBlock := 512 div lBlockSize;
            lNextBlock    := ReverseBytes( lNextBlock );
            lBlockSize    := ReverseBytes( lBlockSize );
        end; { with recMemo }
        Result := MakeMemoHeader( ChangeFileExt( sFile, '.FPT' ), recMemo,
            iSize );
    except
        Result := False;
    end;
  end; { TDBStruct.MakeFPT() }
```

TDBStruct.MakeMemo() examines the signature byte of the **.DBF** file to determine what type of memo file to create.

```
  function TDBStruct.MakeMemo(      { Create memo file if necessary }
    sFile    : String               { DBF file name }
    )        : Boolean;             { True if successful }
  begin
    try
        case Signature of
          _DBF_DBT_MEMO     : Result := MakeDBT3( sFile );
          _DBF_DB4_MEMO     : Result := MakeDBT4( sFile );
          _DBF_SMT_MEMO,
          _DBF_SMT_ENCRYPT  : Result := MakeSMT( sFile );
          _DBF_FPT_MEMO,
          _DBF_FPT_ENCRYPT  : Result := MakeFPT( sFile );
        else                  Result := True;
        end; { case }
    except
        Result := False;
    end; { try .. except }
  end; { TDBStruct.MakeMemo() }
```

TBStruct.Make() is the main routine that creates a **.DBF** file.

```
function TDBStruct.Make(          { Create the DBF file }
   sFile      : String            { DBF file name }
   )          : Boolean;          { True if successful }
const
   DBF_END_FIELDS : Array[ 0..1 ] of Char = #13+#26;
var
   recDBF     : DBFHeaderRec;
   recField   : DBFieldRec;
   wYear,
   wMonth,
   wDay       : Word;
   iField,
   iHandle    : Integer;
   dNow       : TDateTime;
begin
   Result := False;
   try
      iHandle  := fCreate( sFile, FC_NORMAL );
      if iHandle > -1 then begin
         dNow        := Date;
         DecodeDate( dNow, wYear, wMonth, wDay );
                     FillChar( recDBF, SizeOf( recDBF ), 0 );
         with recDBF do begin
            iSignature  := Signature;
            iYear       := wYear - 1900;
            iMonth      := wMonth;
            iDay        := wDay;
            lRecords    := 0;
            wDataOffset := DataOffset;
            wRecLen     := RecordLength;
            iLanguage   := 27;
         end; { with recDBF }
         if FileWrite( iHandle, recDBF, SizeOf( recDBF )) =
            SizeOf( recDBF ) then
            begin
            for iField := 1 to Count do begin
               recField := Fields[ iField ].Header;
               FileWrite( iHandle, recField, SizeOf( recField ));
            end;
            FileWrite( iHandle, DBF_END_FIELDS, 2 );
            MakeMemo( sFile );
            Result := True;
         end
         else
            Raise EXbFormatError.Create( 'Could not create header for '
               + sFile );
      end; { File created }
   finally
      FileClose( iHandle );
```

```
    end;
end; { TDBStruct.Make() }
```

With the preceding code, it is now easy to create some handy utility routines.

```
function DBFieldCount(              { # of fields in data file }
    recDBF   : DBFHeaderRec         { Database file header }
    )        : Integer;
begin
    Result := ( recDBF.wDataOffset - SizeOf( DBFHeaderRec ) - 1 )
        div SizeOf( DBFieldRec );   { Calc the # of fields }
end; { DBFieldCount() }

function DBStructRead(              { Read the structure from a .DBF file }
    sFile    : String
    )        : TDBStruct;
var
    recHeader   : DBFHeaderRec;
    recField    : DBFieldRec;
    iField,
    iHandle     : Integer;
    oField      : TDBField;
begin
    Result := nil;
    try
        iHandle  := fOpen( sFile, FO_READ );
        if iHandle > -1 then begin
            Result := TDBStruct.Create;
            FileRead( iHandle, recHeader, Sizeof( recHeader ) );
            Result.Capacity := DBFieldCount( recHeader );
            for iField := 0 to Result.Capacity - 1 do begin
                FileRead( iHandle, recField, sizeof( recField ));
                with recField do
                    if cFieldType = 'C' then
                        oField   := TDBField.Create( StrPas( szName ),
                            cFieldType, wCharLen, 0 )
                    else
                        oField   := TDBField.Create( StrPas( szName ),
                            cFieldType, iLength, iDecimal );
                Result.Add( oField );
            end; { for iField }
        end; { File Opened successfully }
    finally
        FileClose( iHandle );
    end; { try .. finally }
end; { DBStructRead() }

function dbCreateStruct(            { Convert array of const to DBStruct }
    aStruct  : Array of const       { Field structure information:
                                        4 array elements per field:
                                        1. Field name (string)
                                        2. Field type (char)
                                        3. Field length (integer)
                                        4. Field decimal (integer) }
```

```
   ) : TDBStruct;                    { Use TDBStruct.Free when done! }
var
   iAdded,
   iField,
   iFields : Integer;
begin
   iFields  := High( aStruct ) div 4;
   try
      Result := TDBStruct.Create;
      Result.Capacity := iFields;
      for iField := 0 to iFields do
         iAdded := Result.Add( TDBField.Create(
            aStruct[ iField * 4 ].VString^,
            aStruct[ iField * 4 + 1 ].VChar,
            aStruct[ iField * 4 + 2 ].VInteger,
            aStruct[ iField * 4 + 3 ].VInteger ) );
   except
      on E : EXbFormatError do
         ShowMessage( E.Message );
   end; { try .. except }
end; { dbCreateStruct() }
```

Perhaps dbCreateStruct() needs a little additional explanation. This routine was designed for people who are used to being able to create a data file structure from CA-Clipper source code, using its dbCreate() routine. Because it is not convenient to create nested arrays of multiple types in Delphi code, we take advantage of its **Array of const** declaration to pass any number of elements to the routine. Every four elements of the array are used as a field designator, so code like the following will work splendidly:

```
var
   aStruct : TDBStruct;
begin
   aStruct             := dbCreateStruct( [
   'FIRST', 'C', 20, 0,           { First name }
   'LAST', 'C', 25, 0,            { Last name }
   'ONBBS', 'L', 1, 0,            { On the BBS? }
   'CISID', 'C', 15, 0,           { CompuServe ID }
   'INTERNET', 'C', 60, 0,        { Internet Address }
   'MESSAGES', 'N', 5, 0,         { # of messages received from them }
   'CONTACTED', 'D', 8, 0,        { Date of last contact }
   'NOTES', 'M', 10, 0 ] );       { Additional notes about person }
   dbCreate( 'TESTMDX.DBF', aStruct, 'DBFMDX', False );
   aStruct.Free;
end;
```

And finally, we have the deceptively simple, most important routine.

```
function dbCreate(                 { Create a data file }
   sDataFile         : String;     { Name of data file to create }
   oStruct           : TDBStruct;  { Database structure object }
   sDriver           : String;     { Name of data driver to use }
   bEncrypt          : Boolean     { Encrypt the file? }
   ) : Boolean;
```

```
begin
   try
      if Length( sDriver ) > 0 then
         oStruct.sDriver := sDriver;
      oStruct.bEncrypt := bEncrypt;
      Result := oStruct.Make( sDataFile );
   except
      Result := False;
   end; { try .. except }
end; { dbCreate() }
```

Delphi Component Heirarchy

1

2

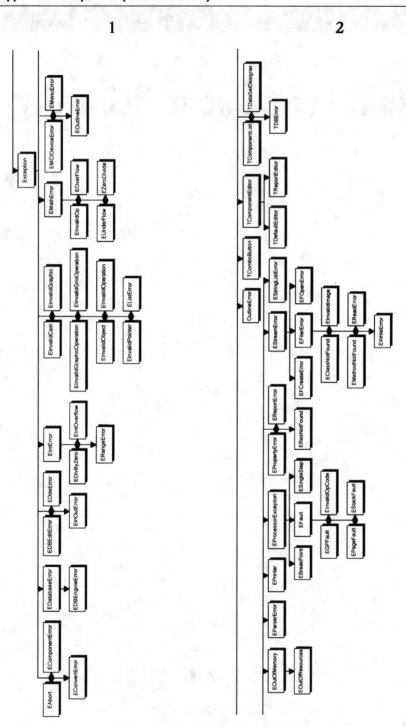

3   4

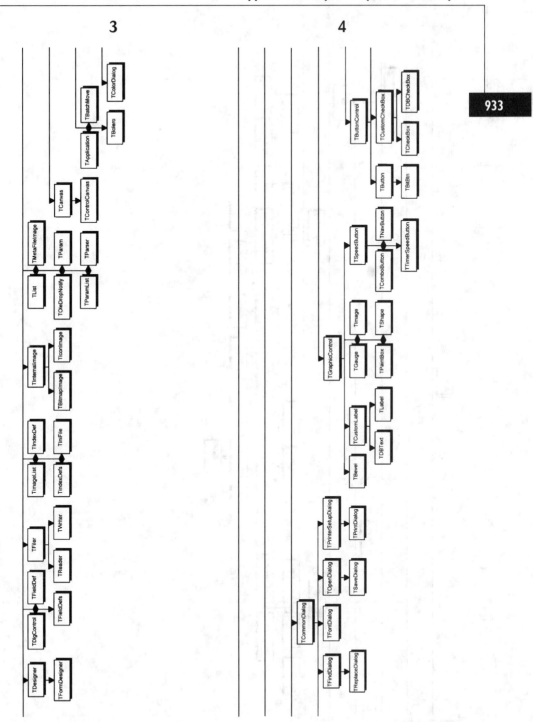

continued

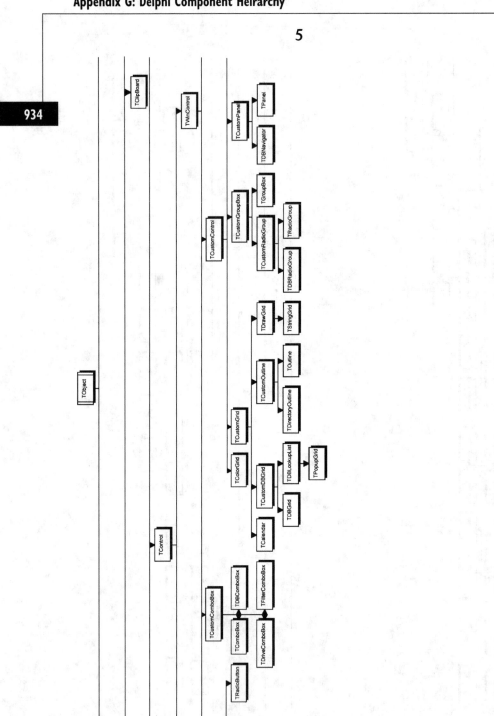

6

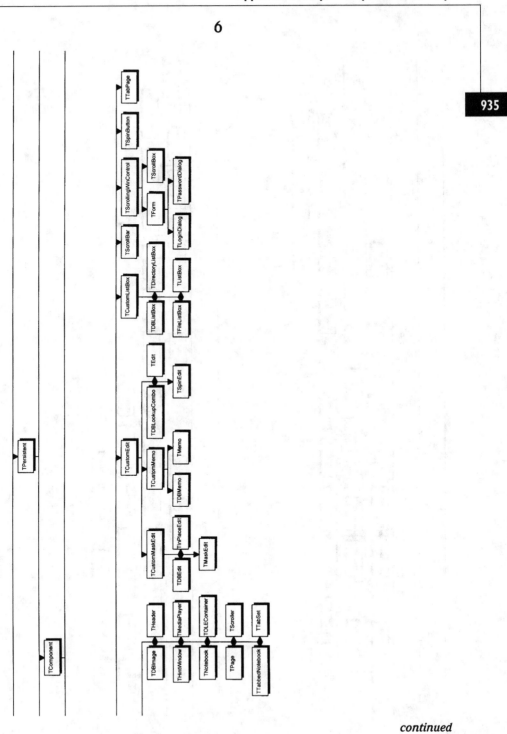

continued

7 8

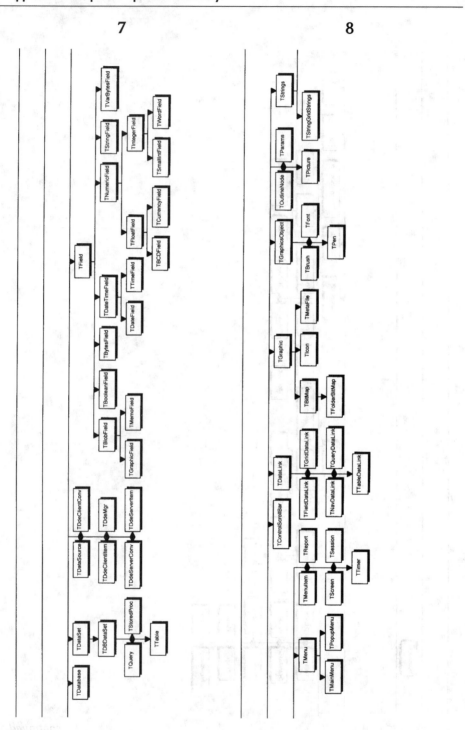

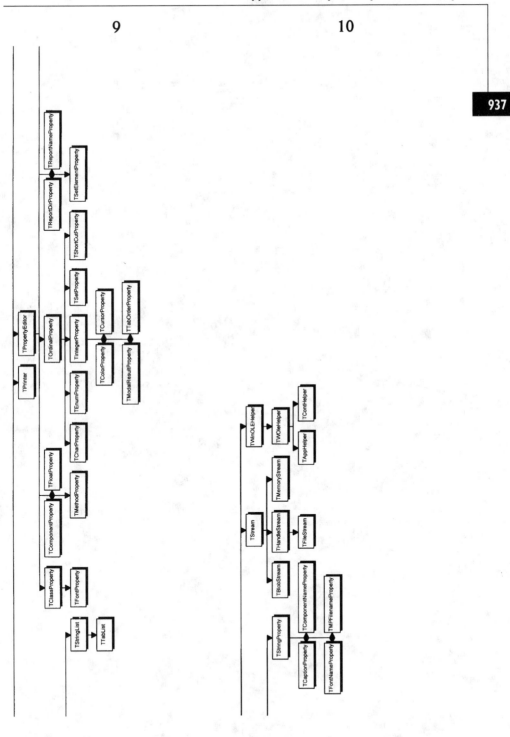

Alternative Database Engines

A database engine is not unlike the engine in your car. You don't see the engine while you're driving. Instead, you manipulate the user interface: the steering wheel, pedals, and other dashboard gadgets. Even though you don't deal directly with the engine, you'll appreciate the difference in engines when a high performance car, such as an Acura NSX, roars past you.

Although the Borland Database Engine is included with Delphi, it is not the only database engine that can be used to drive your Delphi data-base applications. Fortunately, Delphi includes an open architecture, which allows a wide range of different database engines to be connected to Delphi applications.

The following sections cover some of the alternative database engines that can be used with Borland Delphi. This information includes the main features and benefits of each engine and where to get them.

APOLLO

APOLLO is a Delphi-specific incarnation of the SuccessWare Database Engine 2.0 (or SDE2), the latest generation of SuccessWare International's ROCK-solid Engine Technology.

APOLLO provides Delphi database application developers with high-speed, multiuser access to the data and index files used by FoxPro (**.DBF/.FPT/.IDX/.CDX**), CA-Clipper (**.DBF/.DBT/.NTX**), and SuccessWare's own HiPer-SIx (**.DBF/.SMT/.NSX**) data and index file formats.

FIGURE H.1 THE TTABLE OBJECT USING APOLLO.

APOLLO is a 300 KB native VCL replacement for the Borland Database Engine, and hooks into Delphi's VCL at the same layer as the BDE. Because of this, developers still use TTable, TDataSource, TDBGrid, and so on. The only difference is that, after rebuilding Delphi's VCL to include APOLLO, the developer now has five additional options on TTable's TableType list: ttAXFOX, ttAXNTX, ttSXFOX, ttSXNSX, and ttSXNTX. These are visible from the Object Inspector, as shown in Figure H.1.

The ttAXFOX and ttAXNTX table types are for use with Extended System's Advantage Database Server NLM and provide FoxPro and Clipper support respectively. The other three—ttSXFOX, ttSXNSX, and ttSXNTX—provide standard (nonserver) support for FoxPro, HiPer-SIx, and Clipper, respectively.

APOLLO does not duplicate the support for dBASE and Paradox that are already provided by the BDE.

Other APOLLO features include:

- Fast Text Search (FTS) component
- Custom Light Lib image component
- Custom ReportPrinter components
- VariField data storage

- Built-in Mach SIx query optimizer
- Roll-Your-Own (RYO) indexes
- Index scoping
- Conditional indexing
- Subindexing
- Record-level data encryption

Run-Time License/Royalty Requirements

APOLLO has no run-time license or royalty requirements. You are free to distribute APOLLO's .DLL files with your applications.

Client/Server Scalability

As part of a technology-sharing agreement with Extended Systems, Inc., SuccessWare's SDE2 is also available in a client/server version. SDE2/Client-Server Edition is 100% code-compatible with SDE2 and APOLLO and can simply be "plugged-in" to make your existing SDE2/APOLLO applications use the enhanced integrity and speed of the client/server engine.

Vendor Contact Information

SuccessWare International

27349 Jefferson Avenue, Suite 110
Temecula, CA 92590

Voice: 800-683-1657 (Within the U.S. or Canada)
909-699-9657 (Outside the U.S. and Canada)
Fax: 909-695-5679
CIS: Team SuccessWare [74774,2240] or GO SWARE (Section #3)
Web: www.GoSware.com

LOCAL INTERBASE SERVER (LIBS)

The Local InterBase Server (LIBS) is included with Delphi and provides all the features of a SQL server for local, single-user operation. It is a special subset version of the Borland InterBase Workgroup Server.

The Local InterBase Server can be used as a local environment to assist Delphi developers in creating and testing client/server applications, without requiring the specific server that will ultimately be used with the application.

For additional information on LIBS, see the Local InterBase Server User's Guide, included with Delphi. Delphi Client/Server owners can find information on the Borland InterBase Workgroup Server in the Data Definition Guide and Language Reference manuals included with Delphi.

OPEN DATABASE CONNECTIVITY (ODBC)

Open database connectivity (ODBC) allows Windows developers to use a common code interface to a wide range of database engines available through various vendors. An ODBC connection requires:

- A vendor-supplied ODBC driver. Delphi does not include any ODBC drivers.
- The Microsoft ODBC Driver Manager.
- A BDE alias—This can be created with the BDE Configuration Utility or by using the direct BDE API function, DbiAddAlias.

Using the BDE Configuration Utility, an ODBC driver connection can be established allowing a Delphi application to use a variety of different ODBC data sources, including Btrieve, DB2, or Microsoft Access.

By setting the AUTO ODBC option to TRUE, as shown in Figure H.2, a BDE alias can be automatically configured for use with an ODBC driver. With this option set to TRUE, DataSource and driver information will be automatically imported from the **ODBC.INI** file. This file is generally located in the **\WINDOWS** directory.

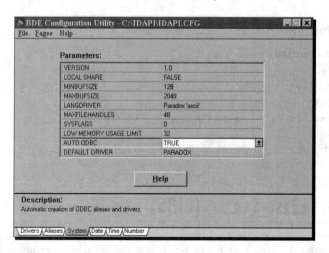

FIGURE H.2 THE SYSTEM PAGE OF THE **BDE** CONFIGURATION UTILITY.

INTERSOLV DataDirect ODBC Pack

INTERSOLV DataDirect is a component of the INTERSOLV Development Suite, a family of tools that can be used individually for tactical advantage or in combination to form a complete client/server development environment.

INTERSOLV DataDirect ODBC Pack provides the industry's most comprehensive set of ODBC drivers, letting you access information in ten operating systems and over 35 databases and formats including:

- Allbase
- DB2
- DB2/6000
- dBASE
- Excel
- FoxPro
- Informix
- Ingres
- Oracle
- Paradox
- Progress
- SQL Server
- SQL/400
- SQL/DS
- Sybase System 10
- Teradata

Vendor Contact Information

INTERSOLV

9420 Key West Avenue
Rockville, MD 20850

Voice: 301-838-5000
Fax: 301-838-5432

Microsoft Jet

Microsoft Jet is the database engine at the core of the popular Microsoft Access database system and also provides powerful capabilities to many other applications. The new 3.0 version of Microsoft Jet has new features and has been enhanced to provide greater performance under Windows 95.

Microsoft Jet ships with Microsoft Access, Microsoft Visual Basic, Microsoft Excel, and Microsoft Visual C++. It cannot be purchased as a stand-alone product.

Microsoft Jet stores data in Microsoft database (.MDB) files. All tables and indexes are stored in this file, as are any forms, reports, macros, and modules used by Microsoft Access. It also supports dBASE, Paradox, and the Microsoft FoxPro database file formats as well as many popular spreadsheet and text formats.

Microsoft Jet can use open database connectivity to connect to external client/server database sources that have ODBC drivers. The ODBC driver for Microsoft SQL Server ships with Jet, and other drivers are readily available for databases from Sybase, Oracle, and other vendors.

Besides the basic features that users have come to expect from any database engine, Microsoft Jet adds advanced capabilities that were previously unavailable on desktop databases. These include:

- **Access to heterogeneous data sources.** Microsoft Jet provides transparent access, via industry-standard ODBC drivers, to over 170 different data formats, including dBASE, Paradox, Oracle, Microsoft SQL Server, and IBM DB2. Developers can build applications in which users read and update data simultaneously in virtually any data format; they can also replace a back-end data store with minimal programming should application requirements change.

- **Engine-level referential integrity and data validation.** Microsoft Jet has built-in support for primary and foreign keys, database-specific rules, and cascading updates and deletes. This means that a developer is freed from having to create rules using procedural code to implement data integrity. Also, these rules are consistently enforced by the engine itself, so they are available to all application programs.

- **Advanced workgroup security features.** Microsoft Jet stores User and Group accounts in a separate database, typically located on the network. Object permissions for database objects (such as tables and queries) are stored in each database. By separating account information from permission information, Jet makes it much easier for system administrators to manage one set of accounts for all databases on a network.

- **Updatable dynasets.** As opposed to most database engines, which return query results in temporary views or snapshots, Microsoft Jet returns a dynaset that automatically propagates any changes users make back to the original tables. This means that the results of a query, even those based on multiple tables, can be treated as tables themselves. You can even base queries on other queries.

- **Query optimization using Rushmore technology.** Microsoft Jet has incorporated this innovative technology from Microsoft FoxPro to enhance query performance.

- **Multiuser features.** Microsoft Jet supports multiple users in all products. You don't have to do anything to enable multiuser access. Microsoft Jet supports both optimistic and pessimistic locking. It also supports transaction processing, with implicit transactions as a new feature in version 3.0.

Vendor Contact Information

Microsoft, Inc.

One Microsoft Way
Redmond, WA 98052-6399

Voice: 800-426-9400
Fax: 206-936-7329
Web: www.microsoft.com

PFX C-LIB FOR WINDOWS

PFX C-Lib for Windows is a full-functioning Windows .DLL that can be called from Delphi. This combination allows for the development of powerful and fast database management systems of enormous size, with access to data in POWERflex or Dataflex data file format.

Vendor Contact Information

PFX USA, Inc.

13200 SW 128th Street, Suite F3
Miami, FL 33186

Voice: 305-255-5501
Fax: 305-255-5508

Powerflex Corporation

695 Burke Road, Camberwell, Suite 2, Level 1
Victoria, 3124, Australia

Voice: 011-61-3-882-7599
Fax: 011-61-3-882-5788

STRUCTURED QUERY LANGUAGE (SQL)

SQL (pronounced **See-Quill**) is a descendant of SEQUEL, short for Structured English QUEry Language, which was designed by IBM in the 1970s. SQL is the language used to construct Relational Database Management Systems (RDBMS) on any hardware platform. Since the first commercial RDBMS using SQL appeared in 1981, SQL has evolved into an industry standard language for network queries across different hardware and software platforms.

The Client/Server edition of Delphi includes Borland SQL Links, which is can be used by Delphi application developers whose users require access to local BDE (dBASE and/or Paradox) databases as well as SQL databases. After installing the SQL Link driver and creating a SQL driver alias, your Delphi application can access data in the exact same way it would access a local dBASE or Paradox table.

Borland SQL Links includes drivers to support the following SQL databases:

- InterBase
- Informix
- Oracle
- Sybase and Microsoft SQL Server

Microsoft SQL Server

Microsoft SQL Server is a scalable high-performance database management system designed for distributed client-server computing. Its powerful management tools, built-in data replication, and open system architecture provide a superior platform for delivering cost-effective information solutions for organizations of all sizes.

Microsoft SQL Server offers the following features/benefits:

- Built-in data replication simplifies complex distributed client-server applications and lets developers put information close to the people who need it.
- A powerful distributed management framework allows developers to centrally manage distributed databases to help systems always perform at their best.
- A true multithreaded parallel design offers scalable high performance on cost-effective, standard hardware to meet your needs today and in the future.
- Engineered for demanding production requirements for reliability, data integrity, and security, it helps keep your vital business data secure from loss or theft.
- Rich integration with desktop technologies such as OLE, ODBC, and electronic mail provides users with unparalleled data access.
- An open architecture based on industry standards helps ensure interoperability with the broadest range of applications, tools, and host gateways.

As a member of the Microsoft Back Office family, SQL Server takes full advantage of Windows NT Server and works with other BackOffice products to create powerful client-server solutions.

Microsoft SQL Server can be used from Delphi through an ODBC connection. Borland SQL Links, included as part of Delphi Client/Server, includes a driver to support Microsoft SQL Server.

Vendor Contact Information

Microsoft, Inc.

One Microsoft Way
Redmond, WA 98052-6399

Voice: 800-426-9400
Fax: 206-936-7329
Web: www.microsoft.com

Oracle7 from Oracle Corporation

Oracle7 enables true enterprise data management from desktop to data center. Oracle7's scalable, reliable, integrated server architecture dynamically adapts to exploit uniprocessor and parallel hardware and to deliver unprecedented performance, scalability, and availability on low-cost open systems platforms. Flexible, integrated, manageable distributed database facilities let you deploy practical distributed solutions that meet your specific business needs. Oracle7 includes all the facilities necessary to construct enterprise-class applications, ensure end-to-end user and data security, and comprehensively manage the Oracle environment.

According to the Oracle Corporation's product information, Oracle7 is the only product in the industry that supports the full range of enterprise data management requirements for on-line transaction processing systems, data warehouses, and client/server and distributed database applications. Oracle7 leverages your investment in development, deployment, and maintenance to deliver the maximum benefits of open, relational systems across your enterprise, while minimizing the risks, complexity, and costs of moving to open systems.

Oracle7 offers the following features/benefits:

- Enterprise-class transaction processing and decision support
- Parallel transaction processing
- Parallel transaction processing on clustered and MPP computers
- Integrated SQL optimizer
- Transactional data access
- High-performance concurrency control
- Reliable query results
- Scalable, parallel decision support
- High availability operations
- High availability applications
- Enterprise-wide distributed solutions
- Transparent distributed query
- Transparent distributed transactions
- Integrating non-Oracle systems
- Data replication
- Global naming
- Enterprise applications development
- Powerful, flexible SQL language
- Declarative integrity constraints

- Powerful, flexible stored procedures and triggers
- Productive application development
- Productive 3GL programmatic interfaces
- Comprehensive national language support
- Enterprise data security
- User authentication
- Network security
- Fine-grained database privileges
- Hierarchical security roles
- Auditing
- Enterprise systems management
- Comprehensive server management
- Data dictionary and dynamic performance tables
- Flexible application identification
- Resource limiter
- Job scheduling
- Open server monitoring
- Transaction processing and decision support

Vendor Contact Information

Oracle Corporation

500 Oracle Parkway
Direct Marketing Department

Voice: (800) 672-2537
            (415) 506-7000 (Outside the U.S. or Canada)

TITAN

Titan is a drop-in VCL-level replacement for the Borland Database Engine that allows Delphi developers to access Btrieve data files without having to use the ODBC layer provided through the BDE.

Titan offers the following features/benefits:

- Allows high-performance access to Btrieve data files without the need for ODBC.
- Supports the use of the standard Delphi data-aware controls like TDBGrid and TDBedit.
- Supports live data in data-aware controls at design-time, as the BDE does.

- Does not require any BDE Dynamic Link Library (.DLL) files to be installed or configured on the target system, a significant savings in installation space. The Titan Engine links right into your .EXE, and only the Btrieve support .DLL files are needed.

- Supports multiple databases through the use of Btrieve standard Data Definition Files (.DDF).

- Supports all the Delphi Visual development tools such as the Database Form Expert, Field Editor, and Master/Detail relationships between tables.

- Supports Btrieve versions 5.1x through 6.1x, including the Btrieve Requestor.

- Fully supports the InfoPower Database Controls, including record filtering with user-defined events and memo field editing.

- Supports the Smithware Extended Data types allowing use of non-standard data files.

Vendor Contact Information

AmiSys Incorporated

1390 Willow Pass Road, Suite 930
Concord, CA 94520-5253

Voice: (510) 671-2103
Fax: (510) 671-2104
CIS: 70441,3250

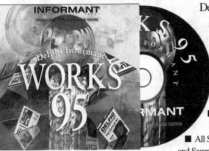

Index

Index

Index

Index

Index

Index

Index

968

ABOUT THE CD-ROM

The enclosed CD-ROM includes the following folders (directories):

- AMAZOAPP—Project files for a simple Delphi database application (Amazo-App) referenced in Chapter 1 (Introduction).

- APOLLO—Demo edition and additional information for SuccessWare's APOLLO 2.0 replaceable database engine for Delphi.

- AQUARIUM—Sample issues of the *Delphi Aquarium*, a monthly electronic magazine and think-tank for Delphi developers.

- BDE_API—Sample code and project files that accompany Chapter 5 (BDE Function Reference). This folder also includes another folder called MORE_BDE which includes some very cool sample projects that use the BDE API functions, generously provided by Reinhard Kalinke.

- BDE_ERRS—Sample code and project files that accompany Appendix A (BDE Error Return Codes).

- DTOPICS—Mike Orriss' excellent database of Delphi tips, tricks, and caveats.

- INFOPOWER—Demo edition of Woll2Woll Software's popular InfoPower components for Delphi.

- INFORMANT—Sample issues of *Delphi Informant* magazine in electronic, Acrobat reader format.

- XPHILES—Information on Xphiles, an Xbase for Delphi add-on by Interface Technologies that includes a code converter and Xbase-compatible library for Delphi.